Using *Write Source*

Your **Write Source** book is loaded with information to help you learn about writing. One section that will be especially helpful is the "Proofreader's Guide" at the back of the book. This section covers the rules for language and grammar.

The book also includes four main units covering the types of writing that you may have to complete on district or state writing tests. In addition, a special section provides samples and tips for writing in science, social studies, math, the applied sciences, and the arts.

Write Source will help you with other learning skills, too—test taking, note taking, and making oral presentations. This makes *Write Source* a valuable writing and learning guide in all of your classes. (The **Quick Tour** on pages **iv–v** highlights many of the key features in the book.)

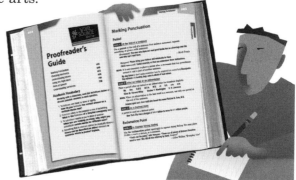

Your *Write Source* guides . . .

With practice, you will be able to find information in this book quickly using the guides explained below.

- The **Table of Contents** (starting on page **vi**) lists the six major sections in the book and the chapters found in each section.
- The **Index** (starting on page **765**) lists the topics covered in the book in alphabetical order. Use the index when you are interested in a specific topic.
- The **Color Coding** used for "A Writer's Resource" (green), and the "Proofreader's Guide" (yellow) make these important sections easy to find. Colorful side tabs also provide a handy reference.
- **Page References** in the book tell you where to turn for additional information about a specific topic. *Example:* (See page **74**.)

> If, at first, you're not sure how to find something in *Write Source*, ask your teacher for help. With a little practice, you will find everything quickly and easily.

HOUGHTON MIFFLIN HARCOURT

WRITE SOURCE

Authors
Dave Kemper, Patrick Sebranek, and Verne Meyer

Illustrator
Chris Krenzke

GREAT
SOURCE®

 HOUGHTON MIFFLIN HARCOURT

23000

WRITE SOURCE Online
www.hmheducation.com/writesource

Quick Guide

Why Write?   1

The Writing Process

The Writing Process   7
One Writer's Process   13
Writing with a Computer   33
Traits of Writing   39
Peer Responding   55
Using a Rubric   61
Publishing Your Writing   73
Creating a Portfolio   83

The Forms of Writing

Narrative Writing
Writing a Phase Autobiography   89
Narrative Paragraph   90
Historical Narrative   129
Writing for Assessment   137

Expository Writing
Writing a Cause-Effect Essay   145
Expository Paragraph   146
Defining a Concept   185
Writing for Assessment   193

Persuasive Writing
Writing a Problem-Solution Essay   201
Persuasive Paragraph   202
Writing an Editorial   239
Writing for Assessment   247

Response to Literature
Analyzing a Theme   255
Analysis Paragraph   256
Writing for Assessment   295

Creative Writing
Writing Stories   313
Writing Plays   323
Writing Poetry   333

Research Writing
Building Research Skills   343
Writing a Research Report   355
Making Oral Presentations   393

Writing Across the Curriculum
Writing in Science   405
Writing in Social Studies   417
Writing in Math   431
Writing in the Applied Sciences   443
Writing in the Arts   453

Tools of Learning

Listening and Speaking   463
Taking Notes   467
Critical Reading   473
Summarizing and Paraphrasing   483
Understanding Assignments   491
Improving Your Vocabulary   501
Writing Business Letters   513
Taking Tests   521

Basic Grammar and Writing

Using Words Effectively   533
Understanding Sentence Style   549
Writing Effective Paragraphs   561

A Writer's Resource

Finding a Topic   582
Knowing the Different Forms   586
Collecting and Organizing Details   588
Creating an Outline   590
Using Transitions   592
Writing Thesis Statements   594
Writing Great Beginnings   595
Developing Great Endings   596
Integrating Quotations   597
Learning Key Writing Terms   598
Using Writing Techniques   600
Adding Graphics to Your Writing   602
Using Proofreading Marks   603

Proofreader's Guide

Punctuation   605
Mechanics   648
Spelling   664
Idioms   672
Using the Right Word   678
Parts of Speech   700
Sentences   738

A Quick Tour of *Write Source*

Write Source contains many key features that will help you improve your writing and language skills. Once you become familiar with this book, you will begin to understand how helpful these features can be.

Checklists serve as effective revising and editing guides within the writing units.

Writing guidelines help you, step by step, to complete different forms of writing.

Rubrics help you evaluate your finished pieces of writing. They also help to keep you on track during your writing.

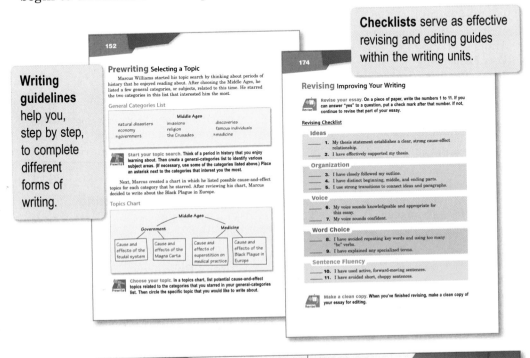

The **writing samples** will stimulate you to write your own effective essays.

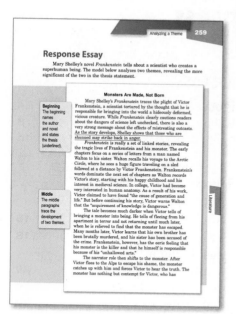

Graphic organizers show you how to organize your ideas for writing.

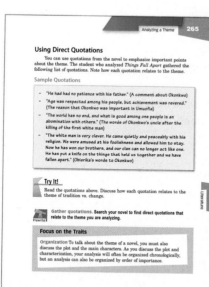

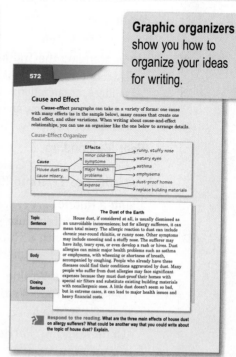

Links to the traits help you appreciate the importance of different traits at different points in the writing process.

contents

The Writing Process

Why Write?... 1

USING THE WRITING PROCESS

Understanding the Writing Process 7
Building Good Writing Habits   8
The Process in Action   10

One Writer's Process 13
STUDENT MODEL "Save Our Murals from Sandblasting"
Prewriting: Selecting a Topic, Gathering Details,
    and Forming a Thesis Statement   15
Writing: Developing Your First Draft   18
Revising: Focusing on Ideas, Using a Peer
    Response Sheet, and Focusing on Style   20
Editing: Checking for Conventions   26
Publishing: Sharing Your Writing   28
Assessing the Final Copy   31
Reflecting on Your Writing   32

Writing with a Computer............................ 33
Understanding the Basics   34

Understanding the Traits of Writing 39
Introducing the Traits   40
  • Ideas, organization, voice, word choice,
    sentence fluency, and conventions   42
Guide for Effective Writing   54

Peer Responding 55
Peer-Responding Guidelines   56
Using the Traits to Respond   58

Using a Rubric 61
Understanding Rubrics   62
Assessing with a Rubric   68
Assessing a Persuasive Essay   72

Publishing Your Writing 73
Designing Your Writing   76

Creating a Portfolio................................ 83
Understanding Portfolios   84
Completing an Evaluation Checklist   87

The Forms of Writing

NARRATIVE WRITING

Writing a Phase Autobiography **89**
Narrative Writing Warm-Up and Paragraph   **90**

STUDENT MODEL "Ready to Go Again"   **91**

Understanding Your Goal   **92**

STUDENT MODEL "Everybody Has a Story"   **93**

Prewriting   **95**

Writing   **101**

Revising   **107**
- **Ideas:** Include necessary events and sensory details.   **108**
- **Organization:** Use effective transition words and phrases.   **110**
- **Voice:** Use appropriate voice.   **112**
- **Word Choice:** Use figures of speech and specific nouns.   **114**
- **Sentence Fluency:** Use long and short sentences.   **116**

Editing   **119**
- **Conventions:** Punctuate introductory phrases and clauses and use adjective forms correctly.   **120**

Publishing: Sharing Your Writing   **123**

Rubric for Narrative Writing   **124**

Evaluating a Personal Narrative   **126**

STUDENT MODEL "Get Rich Quick?"   **126**

Reflecting on Your Writing   **128**

Historical Narrative **129**
STUDENT MODEL "Lurking in the Shadows"   **130**

Writing Guidelines   **132**

Writing for Assessment **137**
Responding to Narrative Prompts   **137**

STUDENT MODEL "Eleanor Roosevelt Teaches Me to Knit"   **140**

Narrative Writing on Tests   **143**

contents

EXPOSITORY WRITING

Writing a Cause-Effect Essay **145**

Expository Writing Warm-Up and Paragraph   **146**

STUDENT MODEL "Houston, We Have a Problem"   **147**

Understanding Your Goal   **148**

STUDENT MODEL "Charlemagne"   **149**

Prewriting   **151**

Writing   **157**

Revising   **163**

- **Ideas:** Provide the proper focus and include enough detail.   **164**
- **Organization:** Develop effective endings.   **166**
- **Voice:** Use a knowledgeable, confident voice.   **168**
- **Word Choice:** Use precise words.   **170**
- **Sentence Fluency:** Use active, forward-moving sentences.   **172**

Editing   **175**

- **Conventions:** Punctuate quoted material correctly and cite your sources.   **176**

Publishing: Sharing Your Essay   **179**

Rubric for Expository Writing   **180**

Evaluating an Expository Essay   **182**

STUDENT MODEL "A Famine That Crushed a Nation"   **182**

Reflecting on Your Writing   **184**

Defining a Concept **185**

STUDENT MODEL "Compromise: Let's Meet in the Middle"   **186**

Writing Guidelines   **188**

Writing for Assessment **193**

Responding to Expository Prompts   **193**

STUDENT MODEL "Words Sing. They Hurt. They Teach."   **196**

Expository Writing on Tests   **199**

PERSUASIVE WRITING

Writing a Problem-Solution Essay **201**

Persuasive Writing Warm-Up and Paragraph   **202**

STUDENT MODEL "Certain Inalienable Rights"   **203**

Understanding Your Goal   **204**

STUDENT MODEL "Conservation Can Prevent an Oil Crisis"   **205**

Prewriting   **207**

Writing   **211**

Revising   **217**

• **Ideas:** Explain the problem and present a solution.   **218**

• **Organization:** Grab attention and provide information.   **220**

• **Voice:** Use an authoritative voice and treat the reader with respect.   **222**

• **Word Choice:** Use direct, active verbs.   **224**

• **Sentence Fluency:** Vary sentence types.   **226**

Editing   **229**

• **Conventions:** Use correct pronoun-antecedent agreement and eliminate double subjects.   **230**

Publishing: Sharing Your Essay   **233**

Rubric for Persuasive Writing   **234**

Evaluating a Persuasive Essay   **236**

STUDENT MODEL "Put a Stop to Sweatshops"   **236**

Reflecting on Your Writing   **238**

Writing an Editorial **239**

STUDENT MODEL "Let Love Rule"   **240**

Writing Guidelines   **242**

Writing for Assessment **247**

Responding to Persuasive Prompts   **247**

STUDENT MODEL "Dear Editor"   **250**

Persuasive Writing on Tests   **253**

RESPONSE TO LITERATURE

Analyzing a Theme **255**

Writing Warm-Up and Paragraph   **256**

STUDENT MODEL "Scrooge's Awakening"   **257**

Understanding Your Goal   **258**

STUDENT MODEL "Monsters Are Made, Not Born"   **259**

Prewriting   **261**

Writing   **267**

Revising   **273**

- **Ideas:** Write a clear, complete thesis statement.   **274**
- **Organization:** Write coherent paragraphs that flow smoothly from one to the next.   **276**
- **Voice:** Maintain a point of view throughout.   **278**
- **Word Choice:** Use literary terms and words with the correct connotation.   **280**
- **Sentence Fluency:** Use short and balanced sentences effectively. Avoid commonly confused words.   **282**

Editing   **285**

- **Conventions:** Punctuate interrupting words and phrases correctly.   **286**

Publishing: Sharing Your Essay   **289**

Rubric for a Response to Literature   **290**

Evaluating a Response to Literature   **292**

STUDENT MODEL "Land Values"   **292**

Reflecting on Your Writing   **294**

Writing for Assessment **295**

Responding to a Fiction Prompt   **298**

STUDENT MODEL "Ethan Sees Red"   **300**

Respond to a Nonfiction Prompt   **304**

STUDENT MODEL "An Accursed Vice"   **306**

Responding to Literature on Tests   **311**

CREATIVE WRITING

Writing Stories **313**
The Shape of Stories **314**
STUDENT MODEL "Building Foundations" **316**
Prewriting: Planning Your Writing **318**
Writing: Creating the First Draft **319**
Revising: Improving Your Story **320**
Editing: Checking for Style and Accuracy **320**
Story Patterns **321**
Elements of Fiction **322**

Writing Plays **323**
STUDENT MODEL "Suiting Up" **324**
Prewriting: Deciding on a Character and a Desire,
Selecting a Conflict, Planning the Starting Point,
and Thinking About Stage Directions **327**
Writing: Creating Your First Draft and Developing
Your Characters **330**
Revising: Improving Your Writing **331**
Editing: Checking for Conventions **331**
Sample Radio Script **332**
STUDENT MODEL "Life in the Express Lane"

Writing Poetry **333**
Sample Free-Verse Poem **334**
STUDENT MODEL "Perfection" **334**
Prewriting: Choosing a Focus and Gathering Details **335**
Writing: Developing Your First Draft and Using
Poetic Techniques **336**
Revising: Focusing on the Traits **337**
Editing: Checking for Errors **337**
Publishing: Sharing Your Poem **337**
Sample Skeltonic Verse **338**
STUDENT MODEL "Fashion Statement" **338**
Sample Lunes **339**
Using Special Poetry Techniques **340**

contents

RESEARCH WRITING

Research Skills **343**
Primary vs. Secondary Sources **344**
Evaluating Sources of Information **345**
Using the Internet **346**
Using the Library **347**
Using Reference Books **350**

Research Report **355**
Title Page and Outline **356**
STUDENT MODEL "The Aswan High Dam" **357**
Prewriting: Selecting a Topic, Gathering Questions
and Ideas, Creating Note Cards, Avoiding
Plagiarism, Keeping Track of Your Sources,
Writing Your Thesis Statement, and Outlining
Your Ideas **364**
Writing: Starting Your Research Report, Developing
the Middle Part, Ending Your Research Report,
and Creating Your Works-Cited Page **373**
Revising: Improving Your Writing and
Using a Traits Checklist **385**
Editing: Checking for Conventions and Adding
a Title **389**
Publishing: Sharing Your Report **392**

Making Oral Presentations **393**
Planning Your Presentation **394**
Creating Note Cards **396**
Considering Visual Aids **398**
Practicing Your Speech **399**
Delivering Your Presentation **400**
Evaluating a Presentation **401**
Preparing a Multimedia Report **402**

WRITING ACROSS THE CURRICULUM

Writing in Science **405**

Taking Classroom Notes **406**

Taking Reading Notes **407**

Keeping a Learning Log **408**

Writing Guidelines: Lab Report **410**

Writing Guidelines: Problem-Solution Essay **412**

Writing Guidelines: Science-Article Summary **414**

Other Forms of Writing in Science **416**

Writing in Social Studies **417**

Taking Notes **418**

Keeping a Learning Log **419**

Writing Guidelines: Descriptive Report **420**

Writing Guidelines: Editorial-Cartoon Response **422**

Writing Guidelines: Document-Based Essay **424**

Writing in Math **431**

Taking Notes **432**

Keeping a Learning Log **433**

Writing Guidelines: Article Summary **434**

Writing Guidelines: Written Estimate **436**

Writing Guidelines: Statistical Argument **438**

Writing Guidelines: Response to a Math Prompt **440**

Other Forms of Writing in Math **442**

Writing in the Applied Sciences **443**

Taking Notes **444**

Keeping a Learning Log **445**

Writing Guidelines: Descriptive Essay **446**

Writing Guidelines: Comparison-Contrast Essay **448**

Writing Guidelines: Essay of Analysis **450**

Other Forms of Practical Writing **452**

Writing in the Arts **453**

Taking Classroom Notes **454**

Keeping a Learning Log **455**

Writing Guidelines: Response to an Art Prompt **456**

Writing Guidelines: Research Report **458**

Other Forms of Writing in the Arts **461**

The Tools of Learning

Listening and Speaking **463**
Listening in Class **464**
Speaking in Class **465**
A Closer Look at Listening and Speaking **466**

Taking Notes **467**
Taking Classroom Notes **468**
Taking Reading Notes **471**
Taking Meeting Minutes **472**

Critical Reading **473**
Critical Reading: SQ3R **474**
Before You Read **475**
As You Read **477**
After You Read **478**
Reading Fiction **479**
Reading Poetry **481**

Summarizing and Paraphrasing **483**
Sample Article **484**
STUDENT MODEL "Global Positioning System?" **485**
Guidelines for Summarizing **486**
Summarizing an Article **487**
Strategies for Paraphrasing **488**
Sample Paragraphs and Paraphrases **489**
Paraphrasing a Paragraph **490**

Understanding Writing Assignments **491**
Types of Assignments **492**
Levels of Thinking **493**
• Recall **494**
• Understand **495**
• Apply **496**
• Analyze **497**
• Synthesize **498**
• Evaluate **499**
Planning Your Writing Time **500**

Improving Your Vocabulary 501

Understanding Word Parts   502

Prefixes   503

Suffixes   505

Roots   506

Writing Business Letters 513

Writing a Business Letter   514

Tips for Writing Letters of Request   515

Parts of a Business Letter   516

Creating an E-Mail Message   518

Tips for Writing E-Mail Messages   519

Sending a Letter   520

Taking Tests 521

Preparing for a Test   522

Test-Taking Tips   523

Taking Objective Tests   524

Taking Essay Tests   526

STUDENT MODEL "NATO's Role in the War on Terrorism"   529

Taking Standardized Tests   530

Tips for Standardized Tests   531

contents

Basic Grammar and Writing

Using Words Effectively **533**

Nouns: Using General and Specific Nouns, and
Creating Metaphors **534**

Pronouns: Engaging and Persuading Your Readers **536**

Verbs: Establishing Time and Creating
Verbal Metaphors **538**

Adjectives: Making a Precise Point and Emphasizing
the Quality of a Noun **540**

Adverbs: Writing Strong Beginnings and Avoiding
Adverb Props and Adverb Redundancy **542**

Prepositions: Creating Similes and Using
Prepositional Phrases as Adjectives **544**

Conjunctions: Creating Tension and Pivot Points **546**

Understanding Sentence Style **549**

Sentence Patterns **550**

Sentence Length **551**

Sentence Variety **552**

Sentence Combining **554**

Sentence Problems **556**

Sentence Agreement **559**

Sentence Modeling **560**

Writing Effective Paragraphs **561**

The Parts of a Paragraph   "Power and Glory" **562**

Types of Paragraphs **564**

• **Narrative** "My First Driving Lesson" **564**

• **Descriptive** "The Northside Youth Center" **565**

• **Expository** "Step, Toe, Heel" **566**

• **Persuasive** "Helping One Child Helps the World" **567**

Writing Guidelines **568**

Types of Details **569**

Patterns of Organization **571**

• **Chronological Order** **571**

• **Cause and Effect** **572**

• **Classification** **573**

• **Comparison and Contrast** **574**

Modeling Paragraphs **575**

Connecting Paragraphs in Essays **577**

Paragraph Traits Checklist **579**

A Writer's Resource

A Writer's Resource **581**

Getting Started
Finding a Topic **582**
Writing Prompts **584**
Sample Topics **585**

Finding the Right Form
Knowing the Different Forms **586**

Using Graphic Organizers
Collecting and Organizing Details **588**
Creating an Outline **590**

Connecting Sentences
Using Transitions **592**

Strengthening Your Essay
Writing Thesis Statements **594**
Writing Great Beginnings **595**
Developing Great Endings **596**
Integrating Quotations **597**

Learning the Vocabulary of Writing
Learning Key Writing Terms **598**
Using Writing Techniques **600**

Using Graphics
Adding Graphics to Your Writing **602**

Marking Corrections to Writing
Using Editing and Proofreading Marks **603**

contents

Proofreader's Guide

Marking Punctuation 605
   Period and Exclamation Point   **605**
   Question Mark   **606**
   Comma   **608**
   Semicolon   **618**
   Colon   **620**
   Hyphen   **624**
   Apostrophe   **628**
   Quotation Marks   **632**
   Italics (Underlining)   **636**
   Parentheses and Diagonal   **638**
   Dash   **640**
   Ellipsis   **642**
   Brackets   **644**

Checking Mechanics 648
   Capitalization   **648**
   Plurals   **654**
   Numbers   **658**
   Abbreviations   **660**
   Spelling   **664**

Understanding Idioms 672

Using the Right Word 678

Parts of Speech 700
   Noun   **701**
   Pronoun   **704**
   Verb   **714**
   Adjective   **728**
   Adverb   **730**
   Preposition   **732**
   Conjunction   **734**
   Interjection   **734**

Understanding Sentences 738
   Constructing Sentences   **738**
   Using Sentence Variety   **746**
   Getting Sentence Parts to Agree   **752**
   Diagramming Sentences   **760**

Credits 764

Test Prep!
  A review test in standardized-test format follows each of the six sections in the Proofreader's Guide.

Why Write?

Wouldn't it be nice if each of your writing assignments meant something to you personally . . . if each one helped you make sense of your life? Unfortunately, that is not the case. You are often asked to summarize facts, recall and interpret information, and explore topics in research papers. These assignments are important for academic reasons. Yet they seldom get at your heartbeat—what makes you who you are.

But there is a type of writing that you can control, a type of personal writing that will help you explore your cares and concerns. This chapter will help you learn more about this valuable form of writing.

- **Reasons to Write**
- **Getting Started**
- **Using a Writer's Notebook**

"All glory comes from daring to begin."

—Eugene F. Ware

Reasons to Write

Experienced writers have their own reasons for writing. Some people write in order to sort out their thoughts, while others write simply because it makes them happy. Whatever the reason, writing has a special meaning to them. The following thoughts may help you more fully appreciate the value of personal writing.

Writing helps you . . .

Learn more about yourself.

Writing lets you look deep within yourself, sometimes with surprising results. When you keep a writer's notebook of your thoughts and feelings, you may, as you read your entries later, see yourself in a whole new light.

Learn more about your world.

By recording observations of the world around you (what you hear and see and sense), you can learn from the events that shape you. Your observations also serve as a fascinating record of your time in history. Finally, writing about your classes helps you remember and make sense of what you are learning.

Share your ideas and insights.

Sometimes writing is the best way to share your thoughts with others. Unlike conversation, writing gives you time to decide exactly what you want to say before anyone else "hears" it.

Express what you know.

Writing actually helps you become a better thinker. It lets you review what you already know, reflect on it, and add new thoughts. Think of writing as exercise for your mind.

Tip

Remember, writing is a skill. As with all other skills, the more you practice, the better you will become.

Learn to observe. Take a minute to look around you. Write freely for 5 minutes about your surroundings, recording details about the sights and sounds in this setting. Try this activity in a variety of places, such as a park, coffee shop, or bus stop. Did you make any surprising observations?

Getting Started

Think of writing as a skill. Just as you set aside time to improve your musical or athletic skills, do the same with writing. Exercise your mind as well as your body. Your writing will improve if you make an honest effort.

Where should I write?

Write in school. Here are ways you can write throughout your day:

- Take classroom notes.
- Keep a learning log in each of your classes.
- Complete writing assignments and papers.

Write at home. Writing in your spare time can help you gain fluency—the ability to write quickly and easily. Here are ways to write at home:

- Write e-mail messages and letters.
- Keep a writer's notebook. (See pages **4–5**.)
- Create short stories and poems.

Write wherever you are. Write in a car, on the bus, or on the subway. In her book *Writing Down the Bones,* Natalie Goldberg suggests that you write wherever you feel comfortable.

What should I write about?

You can write about anything and everything. The more you write, the more you learn. Here are just a few things you can write about:

- **Observations:** What is happening around you right now? What do you think about what is happening?
- **Memories:** What was the best moment of your day? Your week? Your year? What was the worst moment?
- **Hopes and dreams:** What do you want in life? What do you wish for your future?
- **People:** What person means the most to you? What person do you admire? What sort of person do you not understand?
- **Places:** Where are you right now? Where do you wish you were? Where do you never want to be again?
- **Things:** What is your favorite possession? Your least favorite? What one invention would you like to outlaw, and why?

 Find inspiration. Write freely for 5 to 10 minutes about your favorite place. What surprising things did you discover in this writing? Underline at least two ideas.

Using a Writer's Notebook

Your most powerful writing tool can be a notebook reserved exclusively for daily writing. A **writer's notebook** (also called a *journal*) is a place to record your thoughts on any topic. As you write regularly in your notebook, you will make countless discoveries about your world.

In his book *Breathing In, Breathing Out: Keeping a Writer's Notebook,* Ralph Fletcher compares a writer's notebook to a compost heap. Over time, all the cuttings and leftovers that a gardener composts turn into rich fertilizer. In the same way, all the thoughts and feelings that you record can turn into useful starting points for your future writing.

Ensuring Success

To make sure that your writer's notebook is a success, consider the quantity, quality, and variety of your entries. Also follow the rules at the bottom of this page.

- **Quantity:** Teachers often require a certain number of pages or entries per grading period. Know your teacher's requirements for your notebook.
- **Quality:** Approach each entry with a high level of enthusiasm and interest. Develop your ideas fully with sensory, memory, and reflective details.
- **Variety:** Write some of your entries from different points of view. For example, after an argument with a friend, write about it from your friend's point of view, or from the perspective of someone who overheard the argument.

Rules for a Writer's Notebook

- **Date each entry.** The date on an entry helps you find it later and puts those thoughts into perspective with other entries.
- **Write freely.** Don't worry about producing perfect copy. Just get your ideas on paper.
- **Write regularly.** Develop the habit of writing daily.
- **Reflect on your work.** Reread your entries to consider the discoveries you have made and to look for writing ideas.

Taking It Personally

Here is a page from a student writer's notebook. This entry focuses on an old lunch box.

Sample Notebook Entry

April 9, 2011
     Last week, Dad announced that it was time for spring-cleaning. As I dug through the garage, I found my old lunch box. Most kids had lunch boxes featuring the latest toys, cartoon characters, or comic-book heroes. My lunch box was different.

     My lunch box looked like a pirate's chest. Bright splatters covered the surface because my grandpa used the lunch box when he was a painter. I would look at the paint, trying to imagine each color on an entire house. Mint green was the worst, I thought.

     Even though I secretly loved that lunch box, it was so embarrassing to see kids pointing at me and laughing. I remember being relieved when everyone started using brown bags for lunch. Grandpa's lunch box was put on a shelf where it gathered dust.

     After wiping the dirt and cobwebs off the lunch box, I realized that it would make a perfect container for my art supplies at school. The funny thing is, now my friends think Grandpa's lunch box is cool.

This notebook entry captures a time in the writer's life. It . . .
- starts with a "seed idea" (an old lunch box),
- describes the object's appearance and uses, and
- reflects on its importance.

Remember: Keeping a writer's notebook lets you look at ordinary things in new ways, describe your feelings, choose good descriptive words, and practice writing until you feel confident.

Write a quick reflection. Think about an object that was once very important to you. Write freely for 5 to 10 minutes about that object. Share what it meant and still means to you.

www.hmheducation.com/writesource

Using the Writing Process

Writing Focus

Understanding the Writing Process   **7**
One Writer's Process   **13**
Writing with a Computer   **33**
Understanding the Traits of Writing   **39**
Peer Responding   **55**
Using a Rubric   **61**
Publishing Your Writing   **73**
Creating a Portfolio   **83**

Academic Vocabulary

Working with a classmate, read the definitions below and discuss your answers to each question.

1. When you revise something, you make changes in order to improve it.
   Why is it helpful to get feedback from a classmate or teacher before you revise a piece of writing?

2. Something makes an impact if it has a strong effect or leaves a lasting impression.
   What important experiences in your life have left an impact on you?

3. To maximize is to increase something as much as possible or to make the most of it.
   How can you maximize the benefits of a study session?

4. An element is a feature or characteristic.
   What are some key elements of books or movies that you enjoy?

Understanding the Writing Process

The writing process begins before you put pen to paper. In fact, the writing process begins the day you think your first thoughts, and it never really stops. You are subconsciously involved in the writing process every day of your life. Each of your experiences becomes part of what you know, what you think, and what you have to say. Writing is the process of getting those thoughts and experiences on paper.

The steps in the writing process discussed in this book include *prewriting, writing* or *drafting, revising, editing*, and *publishing*. All of these steps are equally important. If you follow the process for each writing project, you (and your readers) will be pleased with the results.

- **Building Good Writing Habits**
- **Understanding the Writing Process**
- **The Process in Action**
- **Focusing on the Traits**

"Don't think and then write it down. Think on paper."

—Harry Kemelman

Building Good Writing Habits

Writing success begins with good writing habits. Follow the tips below and you will see real improvement in your writing.

When to Write

Set aside time each day to write. Regular writing will help you develop fluency—the ability to write quickly and easily.

"Write about it by day, and dream about it by night."
—E. B. White

Where to Write

Write in school and at home. Write on the bus or in a coffee shop. Just keep writing wherever you can.

"I write anywhere, but I still like cafes."
—J. K. Rowling

"Write in a place that you feel safe."
—George Heard

What to Write

Write about anything and everything that interests you—personal experiences, current events, music, books, or sports.

"If a story is in you, it has got to come out."
—William Faulkner

How to Write

Relax and let the words flow. Share your true feelings and, before long, your distinctive writing voice will develop.

"The beautiful part of writing is that you don't have to get it right the first time, unlike, say, a brain surgeon."
—Robert Cormier

"There are a thousand ways to write, and each is as good as the other if it fits you."
—Lillian Hellman

Write about a quotation. Read through the quotations above and pick one that stands out. Write freely for 5 to 10 minutes about what this quote means to you. Afterward, share your thoughts with a classmate.

Understanding the Writing Process

Before a piece of writing is ready to share, it should have gone through a series of steps called the *writing process*. This page contains brief descriptions of these steps.

The Steps in the Writing Process

Prewriting

The first step in the writing process involves selecting a specific topic, gathering details about it, and organizing those details into a writing plan.

Writing

During this step, the writer completes the first draft using the prewriting plan as a guide. This draft is a writer's *first* chance to get everything on paper.

Revising

During revising, the writer reviews the draft for five key traits: *ideas, organization, voice, word choice,* and *sentence fluency.* After deciding what changes to make, the writer deletes, moves, adds to, and rewrites parts of the text.

Editing

Editing the revised draft involves checking it for *conventions*—punctuation, capitalization, spelling, and grammar. A writer should also proofread the final copy before sharing it.

Publishing

The final step in the writing process is publishing. It is the writer's opportunity to share his or her work with others.

Analyze your process. Are all of the steps in the writing process of equal importance? Why or why not? Would you follow all of these steps for every type of writing? Explain.

The Process in Action

The next two pages give a detailed description of each step in the writing process. The graphic below reminds you that, at any time, you can move back and forth between the steps in the writing process. Be aware that if you put more effort and care into the early stages of the process, you'll move through the later stages more easily.

Prewriting Selecting a Topic

- Search for topics that meet the requirements of the assignment.
- Select a specific topic that appeals to you.

Gathering and Organizing Details

- Gather as many ideas and details as you can about the topic.
- With the purpose of the assignment in mind, find one point to emphasize about the topic—either an interesting part or your personal feeling about it. This will be the focus, or thesis, of your writing.
- Decide which details to include in your writing.
- Organize your details into a writing plan, perhaps using an outline or a chart.

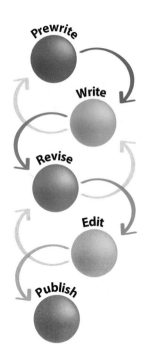

Writing Developing the First Draft

- When writing the first draft, concentrate on getting your ideas on paper. Don't try to produce a perfect piece of writing.
- Use the details you collected and your prewriting plan as a guide, but feel free to add new ideas and details as you go along.
- Make sure your writing has a beginning, a middle, and an ending.

Tip

Write on every *other* line and on only *one* side of the paper when using pen or pencil and paper. Double-space on a computer. This will give you room for revising, the next step in the process.

Revising Improving Your Writing

- Set aside your first draft for a while so you can return to it with a fresh perspective.
- Read your first draft slowly and critically.
- Use these questions as a revising guide:
  - Is my topic interesting for the reader?
  - Does the beginning catch the reader's attention?
  - Are the ideas in order and easy to understand?
  - Have I included enough details to support my central idea?
  - Does the ending leave the reader with something to think about?
  - Do I sound interested in and knowledgeable about the topic?
  - Are the nouns specific and the verbs active?
  - Are the modifiers (adjectives and adverbs) clear and descriptive?
  - Does the whole piece read smoothly?
- Ask at least one other person to review your writing and give suggestions.
- Make as many changes as necessary to improve your writing.

Editing Checking for Conventions

- Check for errors in punctuation, capitalization, spelling, and grammar.
- Have at least one other person check your writing for errors.
- Prepare a neat final copy.
- Proofread the final copy before publishing it.

Publishing Sharing Your Writing

- Share your writing with friends, classmates, and family.
- Consider submitting your writing to a newspaper or other publication.
- Also consider including the writing in your portfolio.

Tip

For assignments, save all your work. Refer to your original writing and to the teacher's comments on the graded piece for ideas and inspiration for future writing projects.

 Consider the process. Think about a recent writing assignment. Did you go through a process similar to the one explained here? List at least three steps that will help you improve your next writing assignment.

Focusing on the Traits

Writing is complicated, so don't try to focus on everything at once. For example, don't check your punctuation while considering the effectiveness of your beginning and ending paragraphs. Using the writing process will help you to focus on each trait of good writing at the appropriate times. (See pages 39–54.)

Connecting the Traits to the Writing Process

Prewrite

Ideas — What topic should I write about? What part of the topic should I focus on? What details should I include?

Organization — How should I organize my details? Which graphic organizer should I use for my planning?

Voice — What is my attitude about the topic?

Write

Ideas — What do I want to say?

Organization — How do I want to arrange my ideas?

Voice — How do I want to sound?

Revise

Ideas — Are my ideas clear and complete?

Organization — Do my beginning, middle, and ending work well?

Voice — Have I created an appropriate tone?

Word Choice — Have I chosen specific nouns and active verbs?

Sentence Fluency — Are my sentences varied? Do they read smoothly?

Edit

Conventions — Have I used correct punctuation, capitalization, spelling, and grammar?

Publish

All Traits — What do you think of my work?

Try It!

Reflect on the traits. When you develop a piece of writing, do you consider all of the traits listed above? Explain. Are some traits more important than other ones? Explain.

One Writer's Process

Although every individual snowflake is different, all snowflakes are formed by the same natural process. In the same way, although every writer has a unique style, the best writers approach writing with the same writing process. Moving through the process, step by step and often back and forth, allows writers to express their ideas clearly, meaningfully, and accurately.

This chapter shows how student writer Nakeisha Williams used the writing process to develop a persuasive essay about saving murals in her community. As you follow her work, you'll see how she shaped her initial ideas into a convincing essay.

- Previewing the Goals
- Prewriting
- Writing
- Revising
- Editing
- Publishing
- Assessing the Final Copy
- Reflecting on Your Writing

"Write, write, and write some more. Think of writing as a muscle that needs lots of exercise."

—Jane Yolen

Previewing the Goals

The goal of persuasive writing is to defend a position in a well-organized way. Before Nakeisha began writing, she looked over the goals shown below. Nakeisha also looked over the rubric for persuasive writing on pages **234–235**. Considering these points and reminders helped her get started.

Traits of Persuasive Writing

■ **Ideas**
Select a timely topic that you care about, one that you agree with or oppose. Use specific reasons and details to defend your position.

■ **Organization**
Create a beginning that states your opinion, a middle that uses facts and examples to support your opinion, and an ending that makes a call for action.

■ **Voice**
Use a confident voice that balances facts and feelings and a tone that is appropriate for your topic and audience.

■ **Word Choice**
Choose fair and precise words to state and defend your position. Explain important terms that may be unfamiliar to your audience.

■ **Sentence Fluency**
Write clear, complete sentences with varied beginnings. Sentences should flow together so the reader can follow your argument.

■ **Conventions**
Follow rules of punctuation, capitalization, spelling, and grammar.

Try It!

Answer the following questions about the goals of Nakeisha's assignment:

1. What must Nakeisha remember when selecting a topic?
2. What should Nakeisha remember about organization?
3. How should she sound (voice) in her essay?

Prewriting Selecting a Topic

Nakeisha's teacher wrote this persuasive writing prompt on the board.

> Write a persuasive essay about a controversy at school or in our community. Choose a current, important issue that you feel strongly about. Your topic should be specific enough to cover in a few paragraphs.

Nakeisha used sentence starters to help her think of controversies in her school and community. She put an asterisk next to her chosen issue.

Sentence Starters

People at my school disagree about . . .
- banning food and drinks in study hall.
- renovating the school theater.

People in my community disagree about . . .
- more lighting in the skate park.
- eliminating the downtown murals.*

Reflecting on the Topic

Nakeisha did some freewriting to explore her ideas on the topic.

Freewriting

Mom said that the city council is discussing removing the murals because they are chipped and faded. I think the murals should be repaired, maintained, and saved. Hawkins students are proud of the work they did to create those murals. The unity, diversity, and creativity themes are still important today. Too much time and effort were put into this project . . .

▶ Try It!

On your own paper, complete the two sentence starters above. Write at least two or three endings for each sentence. Choose one issue from your list that you feel strongly about.

Prewriting Gathering Details

It's important to gather details that support your position. Nakeisha went to the library to find information about the downtown murals. She looked through newspapers, magazines, and Internet sources.

Sources of Information

To keep track of her research, Nakeisha recorded complete source information on note cards.

Sample Source Notes

Stellpflug, Olivia. "Mural Masterpiece." Hawkins City Herald 3 May 2008: A1.

Edmund Burke School. "Community Service Program Overview." Our Programs. Edmund Burke School, n.d. Web. 10 Apr. 2011.

Corporation for National & Community Service. "Benefits of Volunteering." About Us and Our Programs. Corporation for Natl. & Community Service, 8 Apr. 2011. Web. 9 Apr. 2011.

Quotations

During her research, Nakeisha recorded quotations from interviews. Nakeisha's teacher asked students to use quotations from at least two sources.

Sample Quotations

Interview with a Hawkins student:
"Even though I was only a freshman, I made many friends as we all worked together."
"I thought, wow, these themes are real!"
"It was fun, not work."
Source: Keri Ellings

Interview with a Hawkins teacher:
"The after-school art club could take on the responsibility of restoring and preserving the downtown murals. The city would not have to pay anything."
Source: Ms. Larson, art teacher

Try It!

Look for information about the issue you chose. Find one informative newspaper article and list two people that you could interview.

Forming a Thesis Statement

Once Nakeisha had enough information, she was ready to write a thesis statement for her essay. In persuasive writing, the thesis statement expresses an opinion. It consists of two parts: a specific topic and a particular feeling or an opinion about it.

A specific topic **+** a particular feeling **= an effective opinion statement.**

Nakeisha's Opinion Statement

> The Hawkins High murals (specific topic) should be saved because they showcase important themes and quality work by students in their own community (particular feeling).

Organizing the Essay

Next, Nakeisha organized her information (main points and supporting details) in a modified outline.

Nakeisha's Modified Outline

Thesis statement: The Hawkins High murals should be saved because they showcase important themes and quality work by students in their own community.

Pride students have about murals
- Quotation from Corporation for National & Community Service
- Entire student body involvement (planning, designing, painting)
- Student interview, Keri Ellings

Sense of importance in community that murals give students
- Teenagers feeling unheard and unseen
- Murals as a positive form of expression
- Destroying murals upsetting to students

Important themes of the murals
- Unity
- Diversity
- Creativity

City's concern about expense of maintaining murals
- Teacher interview, Ms. Larson
- Art Club plan

Writing Developing Your First Draft

Nakeisha referred to her outline as she wrote her first draft. At this point, she wanted to get all her ideas on paper and not worry about getting everything just right.

Nakeisha's First Draft

The first paragraph states the issue and ends with the opinion statement.

Each middle paragraph covers one part of the issue.

Save Our Murals from Sandblasting

Its been nearly three years since students painted the downtown murals. In a suprising move, the city council recently proposed removing the art. The murals have begun to fade and peel The Hawkins High murals should be saved because they showcase important themes and quality work by students in their own community.

The students are proud of the murals. "Pride, satisfaction, and a sense of accomplishment" are valuable benefits of volunteerism, according to the Corporation for National & Community Service. Everybody in the school had a chance to submit possible themes for the murals. Then the art teachers chose twenty of the best ideas for a schoolwide vote. The entire student body voted to choose the themes of unity, diversity and creativity. Three art classes made designs that the school then approved. For an entire month, students volunteered after school to complete the murals. Teachers and parents were impresed by how well students pull together. A student who work on the murals said that she really enjoyed painting.

Allowing the murals to remain would give students a sense of importance in their community. All too often, adults don't realize that teenagers can feel unheard and unseen. If noticed by an adult, some teenagers feel that anything they do or say is negatively viewed. Their music is too loud or their hair is a weird color. The mural project allowed students to express themselves in a positive way. Many schools across the country agree that getting involved gives "student volunteers a sense of community" along with "increased self-esteem and a clearer sense of

A source of information is given in parentheses.

identity" (Edmund Burke School). If the city sandblasts the murals, students at Hawkins could think that their voice doesn't matter.

A reason to save the murals is the message each one conveys. Every day thousands of people drive through downtown. Before the murals, commuters and shoppers had nothing to look at but brick walls and billboards. Now people can find inspiration in the themes expressed in the murals. Unified Universe shows teenagers. Divine Diversity presents costumed children. Creative Culture features young people. If the city removes the murals, it's saying that these issues aren't important.

An opposing argument is addressed.

The city says the reason for removing the murals is the estimated expense of maintenance. Art club students have already planned a yearly schedule for fund-raising and maintenance. Since painting will be done after school, any interested students will be encouraged to join in. In response, one of the Hawkins High art teachers, Ms. Larson, said, "The after-school art club will take on the responsibility of restoring and preserving the downtown murals. The city won't have to pay anything." With that kind of support from the school, the city shouldn't remove the one piece of public art created by the students of Hawkins High.

The ending paragraph sums up the issue and closes on a strong note.

The murals give teenagers a sense of pride and belonging, while also sharing a good message with all who pass. In addition, maintaining the murals wouldn't cost the city a single penny, since students would do all of the work. Last weekend, students took petitions to downtown businesses and residential neighborhoods. The 500 signatures prove that the community has united with students at Hawkins.

Try It!

Look through Nakeisha's first draft. Then answer these questions: Does Nakeisha's first draft contain all the information that she outlined (page 17)? Does she add any new details? If so, what are they? What else might she have included? Try to name at least one idea.

Revising Focusing on Ideas

After Nakeisha completed her first draft, she set aside her essay for a day. Then she rechecked the goals on page 14 and reviewed her first draft. Nakeisha's thoughts below reveal the changes she planned to make.

Ideas

Select a timely topic that you care about and agree with or oppose. Use specific reasons and details to defend your position.

"Some of my details don't fit my opinion statement. I need to add more information from the student interview."

Organization

Create a beginning that states your opinion, a middle that uses facts and examples to support your opinion, and an ending that calls for action.

"I need smoother transitions between sentences and paragraphs."

Voice

Use a confident voice that balances facts and feelings and a tone that is appropriate for your topic and audience.

"I need an opening that sets the right tone (the need for action) for my essay."

Try It!

Choose a classmate to be your partner. Together, review the changes in Nakeisha's first revision on page 21. What other changes in ideas, organization, or voice would you make to Nakeisha's essay? Name two.

Nakeisha's First Revision

Here are the revisions that Nakeisha made in the first part of her essay.

Using a quotation strengthens the voice in the opening.

"Powerful murals painted by students of Hawkins High School have brought new life to downtown," stated the Hawkins City Herald in a front-page article (Stellpflug A1).

Its been nearly three years since ~~students painted~~ that article praised the ~~the downtown~~ murals. In a suprising move, the city council recently proposed removing the art. The murals have begun to fade and peel The Hawkins High murals should be saved because they showcase important themes and quality work by students in their own community.

A transition helps link two paragraphs.

First of all, ~~The~~ students are proud of the murals. "Pride, satisfaction, and a sense of accomplishment" are valuable benefits of volunteerism, according to the Corporation for National & Community Service. Everybody in the school had a chance to submit possible themes for the murals. Then the art teachers chose twenty of the best ideas for a school-wide vote. The entire student body voted to choose the themes of unity, diversity and creativity. Three art classes made designs that the school then approved. For an entire month, students volunteered after school to complete the murals. Teachers and parents were impresed by how well students pull together. A ~~student~~ Keri Ellings, who worked on the murals said ~~that she really enjoyed painting~~. "Even though I was only a freshman, I made many friends as we all worked together. I thought, wow, these themes are real!"

The specific words from a student worker are added.

Peer Response Sheet

Writer: <u>Nakeisha Williams</u> Responder: <u>Carter Cole</u>

Title: <u>Save Our Murals from Sandblasting</u>

What I liked about your writing:

- <u>I can tell you care about your topic.</u>
- <u>You include personal interviews.</u>
- <u>You gave background information.</u>

Changes I would suggest:

- <u>Wouldn't a transition make the beginning of the fourth paragraph stronger?</u>
- <u>Could you provide more details about the murals?</u>
- <u>Could you use Ms. Larson's quotation earlier in the essay?</u>
- <u>Could you sound more direct at the end of the fifth paragraph?</u>

Try It!

Review Carter's suggestions for improvement. Which suggestion seems to be most important? Explain why. Add at least one new suggestion to improve Nakeisha's writing. Look at the explanation of ideas, organization, and voice on page **20** to help you make a suggestion.

Nakeisha's Revision Using a Peer Response

Using Carter's comments, Nakeisha revised her essay again. The changes she made in two middle paragraphs are shown here.

A topic sentence is strengthened.	*Perhaps the most important* ∧A reason to save the murals is the message each one conveys. Every day thousands of people drive through downtown. Before the murals, commuters and shoppers had nothing to look at but brick walls and billboards. Now people can find inspiration in the themes expressed in the murals. Unified Universe shows teenagers *supporting the earth*, Divine Diversity *from around the world* ∧ presents costumed children. Creative Culture features *artists, musicians, and dancers* young ~~people~~. If the city removes the murals, it's saying that these issues aren't important.
Specific details are added.	
A quotation is moved for greater impact.	The city says the reason for removing the murals is the estimated expense of maintenance. Art club students have already planned a yearly schedule for fund-raising and maintenance. Since painting will be done after school, any interested students will be encouraged to join in. In response, one of the Hawkins High art teachers, Ms. Larson, said, "The after-school art club will take on the responsibility of restoring and preserving the downtown murals. The city won't have to pay anything." With that kind of support from the school, the city ~~shouldn't remove~~ *has no excuse to remove the one work* ~~the one piece~~ of public art created by the students of Hawkins High.
Voice is made clearer and stronger.	

Revising Focusing on Style

Nakeisha also reviewed her writing for its flow and style. Her thoughts below tell you what changes she planned to make.

Word Choice

Choose fair and precise words to state and defend your position. Explain important terms that may be unfamiliar to your audience.

"I should find appropriate replacements for overused words (mural). I also want to add more exciting verbs and modifiers."

Sentence Fluency

Write clear, complete sentences with varied beginnings. Sentences should flow together so the reader can follow your argument.

"I should combine some of my short sentences to create a better flow in the text."

Try It!

Review Nakeisha's improved essay on page 25. What other changes in word choice could she make? Name one or two. What other improvements in sentence fluency could she make? Name one.

Nakeisha's Improvements in Style

Here are the changes in word choice and sentence structure Nakeisha made in the first part of her essay.

> **Sentences are combined to improve sentence fluency.**

"Powerful murals painted by the students of Hawkins High School have brought new life to downtown," ~~stated~~ proclaimed the Hawkins City Herald in a front-page article (Stellpflug A1). Its been nearly three years since that article praised the murals. In a suprising move, the city council recently proposed removing the art, ~~The murals have~~ which has begun to fade and peel The Hawkins High murals should be saved because they showcase important themes and quality work by students in their own community.

First of all, students are proud of ~~the murals~~ their efforts. "Pride, satisfaction, and a sense of accomplishment" are valuable benefits of volunteerism, according to the Corporation for National & Community Service. Everybody in the school had ~~a chance~~ an opportunity to submit possible themes for the murals,

> **Word choice is improved.**

before ~~Then~~ the art teachers ~~chose~~ selected twenty of the best ideas for a schoolwide vote. The entire student body voted to choose the themes of unity, diversity and creativity. Three art classes ~~made~~ created lively designs that the school then approved. For an entire month, students volunteered after school to complete the ~~murals~~ work. Teachers and parents were impresed by how well students of all ages and abilities pull together. Keri Ellings, who ~~worked~~ assisted on the murals said, "Even though I was only a freshman, I made many friends as we all worked together. . . .

Editing Checking for Conventions

Finally, Nakeisha was ready to edit her essay. She checked her work for punctuation, capitalization, spelling, and grammar errors.

Conventions

Follow rules of punctuation, capitalization, spelling, and grammar.

"I'll check my essay and correct any errors in punctuation, capitalization, spelling, or grammar."

For help with conventions, Nakeisha used the "Proofreader's Guide" in the back of her *Write Source* textbook and the checklist below.

PUNCTUATION

_____ **1.** Do I use end punctuation correctly?

_____ **2.** Do I use commas correctly?

_____ **3.** Do I correctly italicize or use quotation marks for titles?

_____ **4.** Do I use apostrophes correctly?

MECHANICS (Capitalization and Spelling)

_____ **5.** Have I capitalized all the proper nouns and adjectives?

_____ **6.** Have I spelled words correctly?

_____ **7.** Have I used the spell-checker on my computer?

_____ **8.** Have I double-checked words my spell-checker may have missed?

GRAMMAR

_____ **9.** Do I use the proper tense and voice for my verbs?

_____ **10.** Do my subjects and verbs agree in number?

_____ **11.** Do my pronouns clearly agree with their antecedents?

DOCUMENTATION

_____ **12.** Are sources of information properly presented and documented?

Try It!

Find four or five errors in Nakeisha's revised draft on page 25. Did you find the same errors as Nakeisha found on page 27?

Nakeisha's Editing for Conventions

Here are Nakeisha's corrections in the first part of her essay. See the inside back cover of this textbook for common editing and proofreading marks.

The title of the newspaper is marked for italics.

Punctuation, spelling, and number errors are corrected.

A verb-tense error is corrected.

"Powerful murals painted by the students of Hawkins High School have brought new life to downtown," proclaimed the Hawkins City Herald in a front-page article (Stellpflug A1). It's been nearly three years since that article praised the murals. In a *surprising* (suprising) move, the city council recently proposed removing the art, which has begun to fade and peel. The Hawkins High murals should be saved because they showcase important themes and quality work by students in their own community.

First of all, the students are proud of their efforts. "Pride, satisfaction, and a sense of accomplishment" are valuable benefits of volunteerism, according to the Corporation for National & Community Service. Everybody in the school had an opportunity to submit possible themes for the murals before the art teachers selected *20* twenty of the best ideas for a schoolwide vote. The entire student body voted to choose the themes of unity, diversity, and creativity. Three art classes created lively designs that the school then approved. For an entire month, students volunteered after school to complete the project. Teachers and parents were *impressed* (impresed) by how well students of all ages and abilities pull *ed* together. Keri Ellings, who assisted . . .

Publishing Sharing Your Writing

Nakeisha used the information below to produce a clean final copy of her essay.

Tips for Handwritten Copies

- Use blue or black ink and write clearly.
- Write your name according to your teacher's instructions.
- Skip a line and center your title on the first page; skip another line and begin your essay.
- Indent each paragraph and leave a one-inch margin on all four sides.
- Place your last name and the page number in the upper right-hand corner of each page.

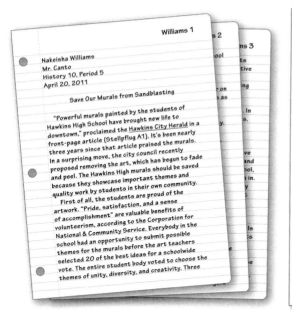

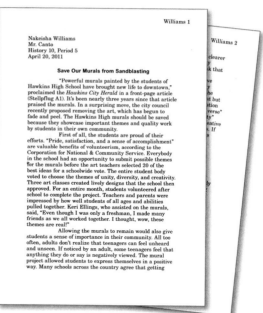

Tips for Computer Copies

- Use an easy-to-read font set at 12-point type size.
- Double-space the text and set your margins so that you have a one-inch space around the outside of each page.
- For more tips on using a computer, see pages 33–38.

Nakeisha's Final Copy

Nakeisha proudly presented a printed copy of her essay to Mr. Canto and volunteered to share her writing about the downtown murals with the class.

Williams 1

Nakeisha Williams
Mr. Canto
History 10, Period 5
April 20, 2011

Save Our Murals from Sandblasting

"Powerful murals painted by the students of Hawkins High School have brought new life to downtown," proclaimed the *Hawkins City Herald* in a front-page article (Stellpflug A1). It's been nearly three years since that article praised the murals. In a surprising move, the city council recently proposed removing the art, which has begun to fade and peel. The Hawkins High murals should be saved because they showcase important themes and quality work by students in their own community.

First of all, the students are proud of their efforts. "Pride, satisfaction, and a sense of accomplishment" are valuable benefits of volunteerism, according to the Corporation for National & Community Service. Everybody in the school had an opportunity to submit possible themes for the murals before the art teachers selected 20 of the best ideas for a schoolwide vote. The entire student body voted to choose the themes of unity, diversity, and creativity. Three art classes created lively designs that the school then approved. For an entire month, students volunteered after school to complete the project. Teachers and parents were impressed by how well students of all ages and abilities pulled together. Keri Ellings, who assisted on the murals, said, "Even though I was only a freshman, I made many friends as we all worked together. I thought, wow, these themes are real!"

Allowing the murals to remain would also give students a sense of importance in their community. All too often, adults don't realize that teenagers can feel unheard and unseen. If noticed by an adult, some teenagers feel that anything they do or say is negatively viewed. The mural project allowed students to express themselves in a positive way. Many schools across the country agree that getting involved gives "student volunteers a sense of community" along with "increased self-esteem and a clearer sense of identity" (Edmund Burke School). If the city sandblasts the murals, students at Hawkins could think that their voice doesn't matter.

Perhaps the most important reason to save the murals is the message each one conveys. Every day thousands of people drive through downtown. Before the murals, commuters and shoppers had nothing to look at but brick walls and billboards. Now people can find inspiration in the themes expressed in the paintings. *Unified Universe* shows teenagers supporting the earth. *Divine Diversity* presents costumed children from around the world. *Creative Culture* features young artists, musicians, and dancers. If the city removes the murals, it's saying that these issues aren't important.

The city says the reason for removing the murals is the estimated expense of maintenance. In response, one of the Hawkins High art teachers, Ms. Larson, said, "The after-school art club will take on the responsibility of restoring and preserving the downtown murals. The city won't have to pay anything." Art club students have already planned a yearly schedule for fund-raising and maintenance. Since painting will be done after school, any interested students will be encouraged to join in. With that kind of support from the school, the city has no excuse to remove the one work of public art created by the students of Hawkins High.

The murals give teenagers a sense of pride and belonging, while also sharing a powerful message with all who pass. In addition, maintaining the murals wouldn't cost the city a single penny, since students would do all the work. Last weekend, students took petitions to downtown businesses and residential neighborhoods. The 500 signatures prove that the community has united with students at Hawkins to voice their opinion loud and clear: "Save the murals!" Because the experience of the students working together on the original mural project was so positive, maybe Hawkins High should replace one of the three murals every four years so that more students have a chance to create a mural sometime during their high school years.

Assessing the Final Copy

The teacher used a rubric like the one found on pages **234–235** to assess Nakeisha's final copy. A **6** is the very best score that a writer can receive for each trait. Nakeisha's teacher included comments under each trait.

6   Ideas

You chose an interesting and timely topic. I understand how students feel about the murals. Your choice of details makes your argument very convincing.

5   Organization

You clearly state your position in the beginning, you offer strong support for your opinion in each middle paragraph, and you make a final call for support in the ending.

5   Voice

You obviously care about this issue. Your voice conveys a sense of concern and urgency that fits the topic.

4   Word Choice

Although you made some substitutions, the word choice could be stronger.

5   Sentence Fluency

You use a wide variety of sentences. Your sentences read smoothly from one idea to another.

6   Conventions

Your writing follows the rules of writing and is free of careless errors.

Review the assessment. Do you agree with the scores and comments made by Nakeisha's teacher? Why or why not? In a brief paragraph, discuss your own reaction to Nakeisha's essay and how you would assess it.

Reflecting on Your Writing

After completing her essay, Nakeisha filled out a reflection sheet. This helped her think about the assignment and plan for future writing.

Nakeisha Williams
Mr. Canto
History 10, Period 5
April 20, 2011

Persuasive Essay: Save Our Murals from Sandblasting

1. The best part of my essay is . . .
   my introduction. It uses a powerful quotation to support a solid opinion statement.

2. The part that still needs work is . . .
   my word choice. I should avoid overusing certain words.

3. The most important part of my prewriting and planning was . . .
   exploring the history of the murals and interviewing people who were involved in creating them. That gave me the details I needed to support my position.

4. During revising, I spent a lot of time . . .
   developing better transitions between sentences and between paragraphs.

5. The thing I've learned about this type of essay is . . .
   that it's very important to choose a topic that I care about. If I don't care, it will be difficult to convince others to support my opinion.

6. Here is one question I still have about direct quotations . . .
   How do I handle them if the person I'm quoting wants to remain anonymous?

Writing with a Computer

Writer William Zinsser calls the computer his "perfect new writing toy" because it allows him to write, and rewrite, more easily. When you write with a computer, it's likely that you'll stay at a piece of writing longer, take more risks, and get more feedback from your writing peers.

The computer can be helpful during each step of the writing process, but it is especially useful when revising and editing. You can easily rewrite, rearrange, or cut parts of your first draft right on the screen—or input the changes you've made on a printed copy. You can also use the spell-checker and a grammar checker to help you edit your revised writing for errors.

- **Understanding the Basics**
- **Prewriting**
- **Writing**
- **Revising**
- **Editing and Proofreading**
- **Publishing**

"I prefer the printout method [of revision]. . . . I find it very satisfying to be scribbling, slashing, and marking up on paper."

—David Michael Kaplan

Understanding the Basics

Basically, a computer is a machine that receives information *(input)*, *processes* it, and *outputs* the results. Here is a quick overview of how a computer works as a writing tool.

Input: You'll most often provide input by using a keyboard or mouse. Tablet and pocket computers may have a touch screen, on which a stylus is sometimes used.

- **Keyboard:** A keyboard contains letters, numbers, and other characters. It allows users to type faster than they can write longhand.
- **Mouse:** The mouse allows users to select items with an arrow, position the cursor, or highlight areas of text.
- **Stylus:** A stylus is like a pencil for writing on an electronic drawing pad or a touch-sensitive computer screen. It can also point and select like a mouse.

Process: Input is processed by a program loaded into the computer's memory from storage. Knowing the difference between memory and storage can save you a lot of trouble.

- **Program:** Often called software, programs are instructions a computer uses to recognize input, process it, store it, and output it.
- **Memory:** Often called RAM (random-access memory), computer memory operates only when the power is on. If you shut down your computer before you save your work, that work is lost—so save often.
- **Storage:** Most computers have a built-in hard drive for permanent storage. Data saved on the hard drive is kept when the computer shuts down. Removable storage includes CD's, DVD's, and flash memory devices. (Pocket computers use internal flash memory instead of a hard drive.)

Output: After information has been processed, the computer must output it to the user.

- **Monitor:** Often referred to as a computer screen, a monitor shows the user immediate results of his or her input.
- **Printer:** A printer allows a computer to output text and graphics on paper. This printout is commonly called hard copy.

Tip

Most computer programs have built-in help files. Look for "Help" in the program's menu. You can browse those files to learn more about the program.

Prewriting

For some prewriting strategies, pencil and paper may work well. For others, a computer can speed up the process. This page discusses ways a computer can help during prewriting.

Selecting a Topic

- **Journaling:** Use a computer to keep a personal journal or learning log. Review your journal entries to find ideas for essays or stories. Then copy and paste material into a new file, and start writing!
- **Freewriting:** Use a computer to write freely to discover possible writing ideas. Simply let your thoughts flow. It's helpful to begin with a focus in mind—one that is related to your assignment.

Gathering and Organizing Details

- **Creating Graphic Organizers:** Use the table function on your word processor to create T-charts, sensory charts, 5 W's charts, time lines, and gathering grids. The table automatically expands to include as much information as you add.

T-Chart

Cause	Effect

Sensory Chart

See	Hear	Smell	Taste	Touch

Time Line

First	
Next	
Then	
After	

- **Researching:** Use your computer and its Internet connection to conduct research. Search for relevant Web sites and print out pages that seem to be helpful. Be sure to keep track of useful Web sites as *favorites* or *bookmarks*.
- **Listing and Outlining:** Use the computer to list main points and details. Then rearrange the details in logical outline order. Activate the outline function of your computer so that it automatically labels each new line of your outline with the correct letter or number.

Try It!

Create graphic organizers. Use your word processor's table function to create a T-chart, a sensory chart, or a time line.

Writing

Once you know how to type or keyboard, writing a first draft on a computer is much easier than writing a draft longhand. Here are some helpful writing tips.

Getting Started

- **Start a new document.** Always begin a new document for each project. Keep your organizer or outline and all drafts in the same folder.
- **Let your ideas flow.** Refer to your outline as you write, but feel free to include new ideas as they come to mind. For now, don't worry about getting every word or sentence just right.

Tip

If you can't resist the temptation to make a lot of changes during first drafts, turn off your monitor. This should help you maintain a free flow of ideas because you won't see what you're writing.

Keeping It Going

- **Stay with your writing.** Using a computer will help you to thoroughly develop a piece of writing. If you are having trouble with one part, fill it in with placeholder text, or just write a note to yourself.
- **Save often.** Many word-processing programs have an "auto-save" feature. You can set this to save your files automatically every few minutes. By saving often, you will avoid unexpectedly losing your work to a cranky computer or a power outage.
- **Share your work.** Writing on a computer makes it easier for you to share early drafts. You can simply print out a copy for others to read. By sharing your work, you become more aware of a real audience.

Try It!

Drafting on a computer in a writing lab or writing center enhances a sharing of ideas since your work is more public and you can easily print multiple copies. The next time you write with a group of classmates in the lab, share different parts of your draft, especially those parts that don't seem to be working well.

Process

Revising

On handwritten copy, making revisions can be messy. There will be crossed-out sentences, words written in the margins, and circled ideas. When writing on a computer, the text automatically adjusts with every change, so there's no mess. The tips below can help you get the most out of revising on a computer.

Managing Your Document

- **Start with a printout.** Begin by reading a printed copy of your first draft. Then make changes on this copy before you make changes on the computer. (It's easier to make quick notes and experiment on a printed copy of your work.)
- **Save each round of revisions.** Save a printed copy of each set of revisions; also save each set separately on the computer (*revision 1, revision 2,* and so on), using your word processor's Save As . . . command. If you work in this way, you will have an accurate history of the changes you have made.
- **Save major deletions.** Dump large chunks of deleted text into a separate file so that you can easily review them if necessary.
- **Use multiple windows.** For example, you can keep two files open when you need to move text from one file to another.

FYI

Using a computer during revising makes it easier to conduct group-advising sessions because everyone can have a clean printout to read and respond to.

Employing the Features

- **Use "Cut," "Copy," and "Paste."** Use these features to delete, add, or rearrange words, phrases, sentences, and paragraphs.
- **Learn to drag text.** To move text, highlight it; click on it again, holding down the button; and drag it to a new spot.
- **Try out "Track Changes."** Your software may allow you to keep track of the changes you make. (See your help file.)
- **Learn about other revising features.** Look for features such as *search and replace, word count,* and *dictionary functions*.

Try It!

Take a toolbar tour. Click on each item on your main toolbar and check each drop-down menu. Explore some of these features.

Editing and Proofreading

Most word-processing programs offer two main tools to help with editing and proofreading: the grammar checker and the spell-checker.

Understanding Your Grammar Checker

- **Watch for agreement errors.** Pay attention to underlined subject-predicate pairs. The underlining often means that the grammar checker has identified an agreement problem. Select the best change suggested by the checker.
- **Watch for passive sentences.** Note when a whole sentence is underlined in green. Typically this means it is passive in construction. Consider reworking the sentence in the active voice. (See page **722.2**.)
- **Keep a critical eye.** Be aware that grammar checkers can be wrong in what they flag as a problem. When in doubt, check the "Proofreader's Guide" in this book before following a suggestion.

Using Your Spell-Checker

- **Set the spell-check option to "Auto-Correct."** This feature corrects misspellings when they are first typed in.
- **Watch for words underlined in red as you type.** Correct errors yourself or let the checker suggest replacements.
- **Spell-check the final document.** When you finish editing, run the spell-checker on the whole document. The checker flags any word that isn't in its database. Carefully monitor the changes your checker makes. Always proofread a printout of the final copy. A spell-checker won't catch a homophone *(their, there, they're)* or a word that is spelled correctly but may not be the word you want.

Try It!

Explore the options available on your grammar and spell-checkers. Enable and disable different features by clicking on them. Decide which settings work best for you.

Publishing

Before you share your final copy, be sure that the document itself is well designed. See pages **76–78** for information about designing your writing with a computer.

Understanding the Traits of Writing

An effective piece of writing is like a good stew. Many ingredients combine to create something nourishing and tasty. The ingredients in a piece of writing are known as **traits**, and they include *ideas, organization, voice, word choice, sentence fluency,* and *conventions.* Only with a proper balance or combination of these traits will you create a piece of writing worth sharing.

The next page in this chapter introduces you to the traits of writing. The pages that follow give writing samples that show the traits in action. Learning about the traits of writing—and putting them into practice—will help you write better in all your classes, whether you are writing a personal narrative, a book review, or a persuasive essay. Think of this chapter as your guide to good writing.

- **Introducing the Traits**
- **The Traits in Action**
- **Understanding the Traits**
- **Guide for Effective Writing**

"When I write . . . it's like driving a team of horses and giving them the lead but not letting them run away in a totally different direction."

—Monica Hughes

Introducing the Traits

The following chart identifies the important traits of effective writing. Write with these traits in mind, and you will be pleased with the results.

Traits of Writing

- **Ideas**

  Strong writing presents a clear focus, or message. The writing contains specific ideas and details that support the focus.

- **Organization**

  Effective writing creates a meaningful whole—with interesting and distinct beginning, middle, and ending parts. The supporting details are arranged in the best order.

- **Voice**

  Writing that has voice reflects the writer's personality. It is engaging and appropriate for the audience.

- **Word Choice**

  Good writing contains specific nouns, verbs, and modifiers. The word choice helps deliver a clear message.

- **Sentence Fluency**

  Effective writing flows smoothly from sentence to sentence. None of the sentences cause the reader to stumble or become confused. Sentence structures and lengths vary.

- **Conventions**

  Strong writing follows the rules for punctuation, capitalization, spelling, and grammar. It is carefully edited to be as error free as possible.

FYI

Also consider the trait of *presentation*. An effective final copy follows the accepted guidelines for margins, indenting, spacing, and so on. The writing's appearance affects the reader's overall impression. (See pages **76–78**.)

The Traits in Action

The following excerpt from an essay by Kendall McGinn displays an effective use of the traits of writing.

Buffalo Nation

Specific details engage the reader.

Before the Europeans came to North America, the native people of the plains and the buffalo were one *Pte Oyate*, or Buffalo Nation. The big bull *tatanka* was life itself. The Native Americans followed the herds and used the buffalo for food, clothing, shelter, and medicine. A Lakota leader summed up this unity between human and animal: "When the Creator made the buffalo, he put power in them. When you eat the meat, that power goes into you, heals the body and spirit" (qtd. in Hodgson 69).

The passage is arranged chronologically.

During the expansion of the United States, however, Europeans nearly eliminated the North American buffalo through a senseless slaughter of the animal. The population of 100 million buffalo in 1700 had, in fact, been reduced to 1,000 by 1889. But surprisingly, the buffalo has made a comeback (Allen 100).

The writer sounds knowledgeable and interested.

In recent years, the number of buffalo has increased to nearly 400,000. Cable Network News owner Ted Turner raises almost 10,000 buffalo on his Montana and New Mexico ranches. "I guess I've gone buffalo batty," Turner says. He supports the raising of buffalo as an excellent source of low-fat meat (Hodgson 75).

Specific nouns and verbs create clear images.

Buffalo ranchers are learning that raising buffalo is more cost-effective and more environmentally safe than raising cattle. Here are four reasons why:

- Buffalo don't overeat.
- Their sharp hooves loosen hard soil.
- Buffalo improve grass crops.
- They adapt to any climate.

Varied sentences create a flow of ideas.

Buffalo living in Florida seem just as happy as those living in Alaska. In Hawaii, they even survived a hurricane. Hawaiian rancher Bill Mowry recalls how the buffalo "loved every minute of it" (qtd. in Allen 105).

Understanding Ideas

Strong essays, research papers, and stories engage the reader with quality ideas. An interesting topic hooks the reader, and effective supporting details (*facts, examples, quotations,* and so on) hold the reader's attention. Writer Lancelot Law Whyte understands the importance of quality ideas when he says, "There are few experiences quite as satisfactory as getting a good idea."

Establishing a Focus

Your writing would go on and on if you tried to say everything about a topic. That is why it is so important to establish a focus for your writing. Your focus may be based on your main feelings about a topic or on a special part of the topic you wish to emphasize. An effective focus gives you a starting point and directs your writing.

Sample Paragraph

Carefully read the following paragraph, paying close attention to the topic, the focus, and the specific details.

Not to Be Denied

Jackie Robinson's personal attributes allowed him to break major league baseball's color barrier in 1947. When Brooklyn Dodgers president Branch Rickey brought him up to play for the major league club, Robinson courageously faced racism and verbal abuse. Determined and proud, he had the discipline to play through these challenges. Tremendously fast on the base paths, Robinson stole 29 bases his first year. Over his career, he stole home no fewer than 19 times! His excellent defensive skills made him a stellar infielder, playing three different positions during his career. An intelligent and disciplined hitter, he batted .311 for his career.
In 1947 he was named Rookie of the Year, and in 1949 won the Most Valuable Player award. His competitive nature helped his team win the pennant in both seasons. His legacy lives on today, as he is the only player to have his number retired by all major league baseball franchises.

 Respond to the reading. What is the focus of the paragraph? What details support this focus? Name two.

Supporting the Focus

Below is a list of four types of details you can use to support the focus of your writing.

Types of Details

- **Facts** are details that can be proven.
- **Statistics** present numerical information.
- **Examples** illustrate a main point.
- **Quotations** are direct statements from other people.

Sample Paragraph

Read the following paragraph, paying close attention to the types of details that it includes.

Hypersonic Travel

The X-15 rocket plane was the most successful and innovative experimental aircraft ever to take to the skies. A total of three X-15's flew 199 missions between 1959 and 1968. The plane looked futuristic with its black color, long, sleek fuselage, and stubby wings and tail. It didn't take off from the ground. Instead, the X-15 was dropped at high altitude from the wing of a B-52 bomber, gliding until the pilot fired a rocket engine that could be throttled up and down like a jet. This was the first rocket with so much pilot control. Unlike any other aircraft, the X-15 was steered by rockets in the plane's nose! According to an expert at the Smithsonian, the X-15 flew "so high that it functioned more as a spacecraft than an airplane." Over its years of service, the X-15 blew away all existing speed and altitude records and pioneered hypersonic technology that aided NASA's Gemini, Apollo, and space shuttle programs. Now retired, the two surviving X-15's are preserved in museums in Washington, D.C., and Dayton, Ohio.

Respond to the reading. Name one fact and one statistic in the paragraph. What does the quotation add to the writing?

Try It!

Write a paragraph about a topic of your choice. Do some research and use at least three of the four types of details listed above.

Understanding Organization

Writer Donald Murray says that strong writing stems from "the solid construction of thoughts." A clear plan of organization gives writing unity, which makes it easy to follow from one point to the next. When you're planning the structure of a piece of writing, think in terms of the three main parts—the beginning, the middle, and the ending.

Connecting the Ending to the Beginning

To close a piece of writing in an efficient way, simply remind the reader about the topic or focus that was introduced in the beginning. Making this connection brings the writing full circle and helps put everything in perspective.

Sample Paragraph

Read the following paragraph, paying close attention to the first and last sentences.

Long-Distance Swimmer

A few years ago, a group of scientists hoped to gain insight into the roaming patterns of sharks. To conduct their study, they attached a satellite tracking device to the tail of Nicole, a female great white shark they had located in the Indian Ocean. The tag started recording data in November 2003. It was set to break off, float to the surface, and transmit its recorded information to a satellite in February 2004. Shark experts expected Nicole to migrate a thousand miles or so up the coast of Africa. When the device broke loose and beamed up its report, the marine biologists couldn't believe what they discovered. Nicole had made her way some 7,000 miles (9,800 kilometers) across the Indian Ocean, all the way to Australia! With the device gone, researchers could no longer track Nicole. However, a zoologist in South Africa had collected photo records of the dorsal fin markings of Nicole and many other sharks. Six months later, the zoologist recognized Nicole off the Cape of Good Hope, right back where she had started. This shark had traveled a total of 12,400 miles (20,000 kilometers)! That a marine animal had such an expansive roaming pattern took the scientists completely by surprise.

 Respond to the reading. What is the topic of this paragraph? How does the closing sentence connect with the beginning?

Process

> "If I can write everything out plainly, perhaps I will myself understand better what has happened."
>
> —Sherwood Anderson

Connecting the Supporting Ideas

Transitions can be used to connect one sentence to another sentence or one paragraph to another paragraph. The type of transitions you use depends on the organization of your writing. Some transitions show time, others compare, still others add information, and so on.

Sample Paragraph

In the following paragraph the transitions (highlighted) help organize the writing chronologically.

Technical Precision

Every time a driver turns the ignition key of a car, he or she puts into action an amazing mechanical sequence. First, the starter motor spins the engine's crankshaft. Immediately, valves open in one cylinder, allowing the perfect mixture of gasoline and air to enter the combustion chamber above the piston. Then that piston rises, compressing the combustible mixture. Next, the car's electrical system discharges power to the spark plug at exactly the right time, and the spark triggers a very powerful explosion in the air-fuel combination. The resulting force drives the piston down. Meanwhile, the process of injection and spark is repeated for the next piston in the firing order, and as that one is propelled downward, the reaction brings the first one up. The rising piston forces the fumes left from the explosion into the exhaust system. Quickly, all of the pistons undergo this four-step action. The process is repeated over and over, many times per second, and when it works well, the engine runs so smoothly that the driver doesn't even have to think about what is occurring under the hood.

 Respond to the reading. What is the topic of this paragraph? How do the transitions help organize the details?

 Try It!

Write a paragraph that describes a process that you understand well. Use transitions as needed. (See pages **592–593** for a list of transitions.)

Understanding Voice

Voice is that special quality that makes writing your own. Novelist John Jakes emphasizes the importance of voice when he says, "Be yourself. Above all, let who you are, what you are, what you believe shine through every sentence you write, every piece you finish."

Knowing Your Purpose and Your Audience

Always know why you are writing—your *purpose*. Are you sharing information, arguing for or against something, or explaining a process? Also consider your reader—your *audience*. How much do they know about your subject? How can you gain and hold their attention? When you understand your purpose and audience, it's much easier to know how you should sound.

- For example, if you're writing a personal narrative, you probably want to sound friendly and personable.
- Or, if you're writing a persuasive letter to your school board, you will want to sound respectful, sincere, and concerned.

Sample Paragraph

The writer of the following example sounds very serious and sincere in an attempt to get his audience to act.

Save a Life!

Last June, while driving her son home from a baseball game, Pam Withers lost control of her car on wet pavement and skidded into a tree. Her son was unhurt, but Mrs. Withers was rushed to the hospital, bleeding from several deep cuts. Her condition was listed as critical as her family gathered at the hospital. Doctors stitched her wounds, and after a number of transfusions, she finally stabilized. The fully recovered Mrs. Withers is my mother. She is very thankful for the many generous blood donors. Without them, my mother may not have lived. Next week, there will be a blood drive at Northside High School. Please make time to stop in the gymnasium between 8:00 a.m. and 3:00 p.m. and give blood. Your donation could help save a life.

 Respond to the reading. Does the voice seem appropriate for the purpose and intended audience of the writing? Explain.

Process

> "You have to write a million words before you find your voice as a writer."
>
> —Henry Miller

Knowing Your Topic

Your writing voice will hold the reader's attention if you are interested in and knowledgeable about your topic. To sound interested, be sure to choose a topic that you have strong feelings about. To sound knowledgeable, be sure to learn as much as you can about the topic before you start writing.

Sample Paragraph

In this sample, the writer shares her knowledge about a topic that clearly interests her.

Perfect Pitch

Backpacking into a remote area can be both thrilling and rewarding. However, a trip can be marred for a backpacker who ignores certain important considerations. When pitching a tent, always place it in a spot clear of looming rotten limbs or loose rocks that could be knocked down by wind or rain and crush your shelter. In avalanche country, beware of snowfields or cornices on higher terrain and keep your tent out of any prospective slide paths. The ground under the tent should be dry, of course, but it should also be a little higher than the surrounding area. Otherwise, a sudden rainstorm could leave you sleeping in a puddle. Also, be sure that you securely stake out the corners of your tent and attach a good rain fly. Finally, do not camp on or near an animal trail. Hang food from a tree and always keep food out of your tent. With a little attention to these details, you will minimize any potential risks and maximize your enjoyment of the wilderness experience.

 Respond to the reading. What details reveal the writer's knowledge of the topic? Name three. How does she communicate her interest?

Try It!

Write freely for 10 minutes about a topic that truly interests you. When you finish, underline at least four or five ideas that demonstrate your interest in and knowledge about the topic.

Understanding Word Choice

French writer Guy de Maupassant had this to say about word choice: "Whatever you want to say, there is only one word to express it, only one verb to give it movement, only one adjective to qualify it." His thoughts stress the importance of choosing your words very carefully when you write.

Starting with Strong Verbs

Writer William Sloane feels that strong verbs are especially critical: "Verbs are the action words of the language, and most important."

Sample Paragraph

Note the effective action verbs used in the following paragraph.

Categorical Fury

Tropical cyclones regularly carve destructive paths across our planet. Called hurricanes when they strike the Americas, these massive storms are rated from category one (weakest) to five (strongest) on the Saffir-Simpson Scale. Category-five hurricanes unleash more energy than the combined blast of hundreds of nuclear weapons. The distinctive "eye" of the storm is an area of very low barometric pressure. The winds surrounding this eye can reach speeds greater than 155 mph. Should a category-five hurricane hit land, it can hurl a surge of water 18 to 20 feet high, devastating low-lying areas far inland. Howling winds rip the roofs from buildings, wipe out neighborhoods, and level huge trees. In addition, torrential rains flood vast regions of land. These mighty storms terrify us as few other natural occurrences can.

Respond to the reading. What is the topic of this paragraph? What verbs seem especially strong? Name three. Why did the writer use these verbs? Explain.

Try It!

Write freely for 8 to 10 minutes about something powerful and dramatic that you have witnessed. It could be an accident, a storm, a sporting event, or something else. Afterward, circle at least three verbs that seem especially strong, and underline two or three verbs that could be stronger.

"The best metaphors are spontaneous, arising naturally out of the writer's imagination. Some metaphors, though, have become clichés and lost whatever power they once had."

—Scott Rice

Using Metaphors

A metaphor compares an idea or an image in your writing to something new and brings the idea to life for your reader.

- **To Create a Picture** In the example that follows, note how the basic idea becomes a powerful picture when it is stated metaphorically.

  Basic Idea: My presentation was a real disappointment.

  Metaphor: My presentation was a real choke sandwich, all peanut butter and no jelly.

Tip

Avoid overused words or phrases and metaphors such as "The sun was a ball of fire." They have become clichés.

- **To Expand an Idea** An extended metaphor can unify ideas in a series of sentences. Note how the metaphor (comparing family relationships to fabric) is extended in the following passage.

  Metaphor: My family is a rich tapestry of personalities.

  Extended: My family is a rich tapestry of personalities. We were at loose ends last summer, at least until the reunion in August. Whatever feelings had been torn over my brother's divorce and whatever emotions had frayed over my grandmother's illness were mended at the county park.

 Respond to the reading. How is the idea of rich tapestry expanded in the example above? Identify specific metaphoric words and phrases used.

Try It!

Write a basic metaphor about someone or something that you know well. Then try to extend that metaphor in a short passage. Use the examples above as a guide.

Understanding Sentence Fluency

Writer Gloria Naylor pays careful attention to each and every sentence in her work. She states, "The bottom line for me is the sentence in front of my face. If nine out of ten of them hit the mark, then I'm satisfied."

Checking for Variety

Use the following strategy to ensure sentence variety in your writing.

- **Vary sentence beginnings.** In one column on a piece of paper, list the opening words of each sentence in a piece of writing. (Do you need to vary some of your sentence beginnings?)
- **Vary sentence lengths.** In another column, write the number of words in each sentence. (Do you need to change the length of some sentences?)

Sample Paragraph

Read the following paragraph, paying attention to the sentence structure.

Rite of Passage

The vast marsh seethed with movement, as if a living carpet covered the ground. Wings rustling, heads bobbing, and feathers extended, thousands of Canada geese claimed this wetland for the night. With the new day, they will continue on their journey north, a flight repeated year after year after year. As the sun crests the horizon, several geese will honk. Here and there, a few will take to the air, powerful wing strokes thrashing the waters. More geese will join the chorus in a growing crescendo. Suddenly, hundreds of the big birds will take wing pulling the rest of the flock with them, as all the birds explode into the spring sky.

 Respond to the reading. On a piece of paper, analyze the sample paragraph for sentence fluency using the strategy above as a guide.

Try It!

Write freely for 10 minutes about animals (wild or domestic) in action. Check your sentence fluency using the strategy above.

Process

Adding Style to Your Sentences

You'll find many excellent examples of sentence style in various essays, articles, and books. Experienced writers use a variety of sentences, including balanced sentences and periodic sentences.

- A **balanced sentence** emphasizes a similarity or contrast between two or more equal parts (words, phrases, or clauses).

  "Ask not what your country can do for you; ask what you can do for your country."

  —1961 Inaugural Address, President John F. Kennedy

  Note: One way to recognize a balanced sentence is to remove transition words (*but, also, since, now, then,* and so on) and break the sentence into its parts. The parts should be equal.

- A **periodic sentence** is a longer sentence that postpones the main idea (in blue) till the end.

  "Whether I shall turn out to be the hero of my own life, or whether that station will be held by anybody else, these pages must show."

  —*David Copperfield,* Charles Dickens

Try It!

Write sentences modeled after the balanced and periodic sentences below. The first sentence has been modeled for you.

"In a hole in the ground, there lived a hobbit."

—*The Hobbit,* J. R. R. Tolkien

Student Version: In the back of the bus, there sat my little brother.

1. "The law is equal before all of us; but we are not all equal before the law."

   —Preface to *The Millionairess,* George Bernard Shaw

2. "In the chair which stood before the writing-table in the middle of the room sat the figure of Lord Clarenceux."

   —"The Ghost of Lord Clarenceux," Arnold Bennett

3. "It was the best of times, it was the worst of times, it was the age of wisdom, it was the age of foolishness."

   —*A Tale of Two Cities,* Charles Dickens

4. "From a private hospital for the insane near Providence, Rhode Island, there recently disappeared an exceedingly singular person."

   —*The Case of Charles Dexter Ward,* H. P. Lovecraft

Understanding Conventions

Effective writing is easy to follow because, among other things, it adheres to the conventions for punctuation, capitalization, spelling, and grammar. Writer and editor Patricia T. O'Conner summarizes the importance of punctuation in this way: "When you write, punctuation marks are the road signs that guide the reader, and you wouldn't be understood without them."

Knowing the Basic Rules

The English language is always growing; it includes more words than any other "living" language. It stands to reason then that there are a lot of rules for using English. The checklist below can guide you as you check your writing for conventions. Also see the "Proofreader's Guide" (pages **604–763**).

Conventions

PUNCTUATION

_____ **1.** Do I use end punctuation after all my sentences?

_____ **2.** Do I use commas and semicolons correctly?

_____ **3.** Do I use apostrophes to show possession (*that girl's keys* and *those girls' keys*)?

_____ **4.** Do I use quotation marks and italics correctly?

CAPITALIZATION

_____ **5.** Do I start each sentence with a capital letter?

_____ **6.** Do I capitalize the proper names of people and places?

_____ **7.** Do I avoid improper capitalization (*my mom,* not *my Mom*)?

SPELLING

_____ **8.** Have I checked my spelling using a spell-checker?

_____ **9.** Have I also checked my spelling with a dictionary?

GRAMMAR

_____ **10.** Do I use correct forms of verbs (*had eaten,* not *had ate*)?

_____ **11.** Do I use the correct word (*their, there, they're*)?

_____ **12.** Do my subjects and verbs agree in number (*the car races* and *the cars race*)?

The Responder's Role

Respond honestly, but be careful of the author's feelings. Be sure that your comments are constructive, not destructive. Follow these tips.

- **Listen (or read) carefully.** Peer responding only works if you pay close attention to the writing.

- **Take notes.** Write comments directly on your copy of the writing to show the author exactly where revisions are needed.

- **Start with positive feedback.** Find something good in the writing and make specific comments about what you liked.

- **Ask questions.** Don't hesitate to ask the author about parts that need clarification. Be specific and polite.

- **Avoid "piling on."** Allow one responder to finish before commenting.

- **Make suggestions.** When you point out a problem, try to include a possible solution. (See the chart below.)

Giving Constructive Criticism	
Don't give commands . . . "You should make the beginning grab my attention."	**DO give suggestions . . .** "Wouldn't the beginning be stronger with a different hook?"
Don't focus on the writer . . . "You don't follow any logical order."	**DO focus on the writing . . .** "Is the order of your ideas clear?"
Don't focus on the problem . . . "There aren't enough details to make your main point."	**DO focus on the solution . . .** "More details would help me understand your main point."
Don't give general comments . . . "I thought it was boring."	**DO give specific advice . . .** "Could you use a personal story to support your main point?"

Try It!

Rewrite the unhelpful comments below to make them more constructive.

1. You don't sound like you really believe in your opinion.
2. Your closing sentence doesn't work.
3. I don't understand your solution.

Using the Traits to Respond

When you respond, you are trying to help the author improve his or her writing by rethinking, refocusing, or revising. It can be useful to consider the traits of writing as you respond. Start by thinking about *ideas, organization,* and *voice.*

Addressing Ideas, Organization, and Voice

Ideas: Help the author focus on the ideas.

- How would you state the main idea of your writing?
- I think you're trying to say . . . . Is that right?
- Is . . . the main idea in your writing?
- The most important details, to me, are . . .
- Could you give a few more details about . . . ?
- I got the impression you want the reader to feel . . . . Is that right?

Organization: Help the author focus on organization.

- I liked the way you got my attention by . . .
- Which sentence is your topic sentence (or focus statement)?
- Did you organize your paragraphs by . . . ?
- What main point do these details support?
- Could you make a smoother transition between these two paragraphs?
- What are you trying to say with this ending?

Voice: Help the author focus on voice.

- I can see your personality in this sentence: . . . .
- You really reveal how you feel about the topic when you . . .
- What audience are you trying to reach with the writing?
- Do you think you might sound too formal (or informal) in this paragraph?
- The writing makes me feel . . . about the topic.
- Are you being fair to both sides in this paragraph?

Try It!

Read one of the essays in this book. Write down one or two responses to the essay for each of these traits: *ideas, organization,* and *voice.*

Addressing Word Choice and Sentence Fluency

Later in the responding process, try to address the author's *word choice* and *sentence fluency*. Here are some suggestions for doing this.

Word Choice: **Help the author focus on nouns, verbs, and modifiers.**

- I think . . . are especially strong verbs.
- Can you use more specific nouns for . . . ?
- Have you used too many modifiers in this paragraph? Would it convey the same meaning if you took out . . . ?
- Could you give a definition or an explanation of . . . ?
- I wonder if you really mean . . . ? Is there a better word for that?
- I noticed you used the word . . . three times. Maybe you can find a synonym.

Sentence Fluency: **Help the author focus on sentences.**

- I like the sentences that emphasize the different parts of your topic in the beginning.
- Do you have too many sentences beginning with . . . ?
- In the middle paragraphs, could you combine some short sentences into longer sentences for variety?
- Transition sentences effectively connect your paragraphs.
- I like the variety of sentences in your ending.

Try It!

Using the same essay you reviewed on page **58**, write down one response for *word choice* and one for *sentence fluency*.

Tip

Listen carefully to your peers' comments, but remember that you don't have to make every change that they suggest. You should weigh the value of each comment and proceed accordingly. The following tips can help you use peer responses effectively.

- Trust your own judgment about your writing.
- Think about which issues are most important to you.
- Pay special attention to comments made by more than one responder.
- Seek another opinion if you are not sure about something.
- Ask questions if you are not sure what a responder means.
- Be patient. Focus on one problem area at a time.

Sample Peer Response Sheet

Use a response sheet like the one below to make comments about one of your classmate's essays. (The example includes sample responses.)

Peer Response Sheet

Writer: _Veronica Gomez_   Responder: _David James_

Title: _Compromise: Let's Meet in the Middle_

What I liked about your writing:

- I liked how you related the topic to history and to everyday life.
- The questions in the first paragraph really got me thinking about your topic.
- The folk saying was kind of funny.
- I'm glad you showed that compromises don't always work.

Changes I would suggest:

- Could you give a specific example about compromising between students and teachers?
- Do you really need to mention that compromise can be a noun and a verb? Does that fact give any insight about your topic?
- "Human social interaction" seems like a complicated phrase. Can you say that another way?

Try It!

Exchange a recent piece of your writing for a classmate's work.

1. Read the paper once to get an overall feel for it.
2. Read the paper again, paying careful attention to its strengths and weaknesses.
3. Fill out a response sheet like the one above.

Using a Rubric

Learning how to assess writing is one of the best ways to become a stronger writer. Assessing writing helps you think like a professional writer and take on the responsibility of making meaningful changes in your work. You learn to assess using a writing rubric, a scoring guide that lists the main traits for a specific form of writing. As you gain more experience with rubrics, you will come to better understand and appreciate the qualities inherent in effective writing.

Rubrics aren't just for final assessment. They can also guide your early writing and provide specific suggestions for making improvements. By using a rubric throughout the writing process, you can expect to produce a quality piece of writing. In this chapter, you will learn all about rubrics—from reading a rubric to using one to assess a persuasive essay.

- **Understanding Rubrics**
- **Reading a Rubric**
- **Getting Started with a Rubric**
- **Revising and Editing with a Rubric**
- **Assessing with a Rubric**
- **Assessing in Action**
- **Assessing a Persuasive Essay**

"Rubrics help students and
teachers define quality."
—Heidi Goodrich

Understanding Rubrics

A **rubric** is simply a rating scale. Have you ever rated the quality of something on a scale of 1 (terrible) to 10 (fantastic)? With rubrics, you can rate your writing—in this case on a scale of 6 (amazing) to 1 (incomplete).

| 6 | 5 | 4 | 3 | 2 | 1 |
| Amazing | Strong | Good | Okay | Poor | Incomplete |

The quality of any piece of writing can be rated on the basis of six traits: *ideas, organization, voice, word choice, sentence fluency,* and *conventions.* (For an introduction to these traits, see pages **39–54**.) A single essay might be well organized (score of 5) but have repetitive, general word choice (score of 3).

Rating Guide

Here's a brief description of the rating scale.

A **6** means that the writing is **amazing**.
It far exceeds expectations for a certain trait.

A **5** means that the writing is very **strong**.
It clearly meets the requirements for a trait.

A **4** means that the writing is **good**.
It meets most of the requirements for a trait.

A **3** means that the writing is **okay**.
It needs work to meet the main requirements for a trait.

A **2** means that the writing is **poor**.
It needs a lot of work to meet the requirements of a trait.

A **1** means that the writing is **incomplete**.
The writing is not yet ready to be assessed for a trait.

Reading a Rubric

Rubrics in this book are color coded according to the trait. *Ideas* appear in a green strip, *organization* in a pink strip, and so forth. There is a description for each rating to help you assess your writing for a particular trait.

Rubric for Persuasive Writing

6 Ideas	**5**	**4**
The thesis is clearly presented and well defended by reasons that challenge the reader to act.	The thesis is clear. All reasons effectively support the argument and call to action.	The problem and solution are clear. Most reasons support the solution.
Organization		
All parts of the essay work to introduce and convincingly support the writer's opinion.	The opening outlines the argument (opinion). The middle provides clear support. The ending reinforces the opinion.	The opening outlines the argument (opinion). The middle provides support, but the ending needs work.
Voice		
The writer's voice is confident, positive, and convincing.	The writer's voice is confident and persuasive.	The writer's voice is confident, but it may not be persuasive enough.

Guiding Your Writing

A rubric helps you . . .
- **plan your work**—knowing what is expected;
- **create a strong first draft**—focusing on *ideas, organization,* and *voice;*
- **revise and edit your work**—considering each trait; and
- **assess your final draft**—rating the traits throughout the whole piece of writing.

Think about the rubric. Read the level-5 descriptions above. How do ideas, organization, and voice differ from level 5 to level 4? What does it take to achieve a 6 for each trait?

Getting Started with a Rubric

Each of the writing units in this book includes a page like the one below. This page, which is arranged according to the traits of writing, explains the main requirements for developing the essay in the unit. Studying the "goals" page will help you get started with your planning.

204

Understanding Your Goal

Your goal in this chapter is to write a well-organized persuasive essay that explains a problem and convinces the reader to accept your solution. The traits listed in the chart below will help you plan and write your essay. The rubric for persuasive writing on pages 234–235 will also guide you.

Traits of Persuasive Writing

- **Ideas**
  Use facts and reasoning to explain a problem and defend a solution.

- **Organization**
  Create a beginning that introduces the problem and states your solution, a middle that provides support and answers an objection, and an ending that restates your solution.

- **Voice**
  Use a persuasive voice that is appropriate for your topic and audience.

- **Word Choice**
  Choose the most effective words to construct a convincing argument.

- **Sentence Fluency**
  Write clear, complete sentences with varied beginnings.

- **Conventions**
  Check your writing for errors in capitalization, punctuation, spelling, and grammar.

Literature Connections: In his essay "Tolerance," E. M. Forster argues that tolerance, not love, is the solution to big problems faced by post–World War II society.

"Opinions are made to be changed or how is truth to be got at?"

—Lord Byron

A Closer Look at Understanding Your Goal

The following steps will help you get an overview of the assignment in each writing unit.

1. **Read through the traits chart** to familiarize yourself with the unit's goals.

2. **Focus on *ideas, organization,* and *voice*** at the start of the project, when you are prewriting and writing. These traits form the foundation of good writing.

3. **Identify specific requirements** for each trait (such as "supporting your opinion with logical reasons" and "sounding persuasive and respectful").

4. **Ask questions** if you aren't sure about any part of the assignment.

A Special Note About the Traits

Different traits are important at different stages of the writing process. The following chart shows when the specific traits are important.

During **prewriting** and **writing**, focus on the *ideas, organization,* and *voice* in your work.

During **revising**, focus on *ideas, organization, voice, word choice,* and *sentence fluency.* (For some assignments, your teacher may ask you to pay particular attention to one or two of these traits.)

During **editing** and proofreading, concentrate on *conventions*— spelling, punctuation, capitalization, and grammar.

When you are **assessing** your final copy, consider all six traits. (For some assignments, your teacher may ask you to assess the writing for just a few of the traits.)

Exercise

Write a paragraph. Review the goals on page **64**. Then write a persuasive paragraph defending your solution for a school-related problem. Keep the traits in mind as you write.

Revising and Editing with a Rubric

6 My position is well defended with persuasive reasons. Thoughtful ideas call for action.

5 My position is clear and supported with persuasive reasons. I respond to an important objection.

4 My position statement is clear and I could make my reasons more specific. I respond to an objection.

In this book, the pages that deal with revising and editing begin with a rubric strip. Each strip focuses on one trait of writing and will help you improve your first draft. The strip on these two pages focuses on the *ideas* for a persuasive problem-solution essay.

How can rubric strips help me assess my writing?

A rubric strip can help you look objectively at your writing. Follow these steps as you use the rubric strip to consider each trait:

1. Begin by reading over the number 5 description (a rating of strong).
2. Decide if your writing rates a 5 for that trait.
3. If not, check the 6 or 4 descriptions.
4. Continue until you find the rating that most closely matches your writing.
5. Notice that levels 4, 3, 2, and 1 indicate how you can improve your writing.

In education today, students are talented and willing to work, and they should be given opportunities to make a difference in society. Through community service, students learn values and become more caring individuals. If community service became a requirement for graduation, some would complain at first. Yet teens enjoy working together. Some may argue that such a requirement would strain the teachers, but other adults could get involved. Through this experience, students would learn how to become good citizens. In a self-centered society, community service teaches an important lesson.

Try It!

Review the persuasive paragraph above. Then rate it for ideas using the rubric strip at the top of these two pages as a guide. Explain your rating.

3 I need a more convincing response to an objection and more reasons to support my position.

2 My position statement is unclear. I need to rethink my position from start to finish.

1 I need to choose a position and learn how to defend it with reasons.

How can rubric strips help me revise and edit?

Once you have rated your writing for a given trait, you will see ways to improve your score. The writer of the paragraph on page **66** gave his ideas a score of 4. The score description indicates the main thing he could do to improve his work: make the supporting reasons more specific.

In the main writing units, each rubric strip is followed by brief lessons that will help you revise or edit to improve your writing for each trait: ideas, organization, voice, word choice, sentence fluency, and conventions.

Making Changes

The writer decided to add specific reasons to make his case stronger. He added a thought-provoking idea to his closing sentence to call the reader to action. He made the following changes.

Ideas More specific details are added.	. . . If community service became a requirement for graduation, some would complain at first. Yet, *most* teens enjoy working together. *and changing the lives of those in need.* Some may argue that such
Qualifiers make the case more convincing.	a requirement would strain the teachers, but other adults could get involved. *That would encourage a sense of community.* Through this experience,
The closing sentence is made more compelling.	students would learn *the importance of citizenship and teamwork.* how to become good citizens. In a self-centered society, community service teaches an ~~important~~ *a* lesson *that could change the world.*

Revise your paragraph for ideas. Revise the paragraph you wrote on page **65**, using the strip on these two pages as a guide.

Assessing with a Rubric

Follow these four steps when you use a rubric (see pages **70–71**) to assess a piece of writing.

1. **Create a response sheet.** On your own paper, write each of the key traits from the rubric, preceded by a short line. Under each trait, leave two or three lines to allow for comments.

2. **Read the final copy.** First, get an overall feeling for the writing. Then read more carefully, paying attention to each trait.

3. **Assess the writing.** Use the rubric to rate each trait. First, check the level-5 rubric description and then go up or down the scale until you find the correct rating. Write the score next to the trait on your assessment sheet.

4. **Provide comments.** Under each trait, make helpful comments for improving the writing.

Response Sheet   Title: _____

_____   Ideas

_____   Organization

_____   Voice

_____   Word Choice

_____   Sentence Fluency

_____   Conventions

Evaluator: _____

Exercise

Assess your persuasive paragraph. Make a response sheet like the one above. Evaluate your paragraph using the rubric on pages **234–235**. For each trait, write a comment about something you did well and something you'd like to improve. (See the sample on page **71**.)

234

Rubric for Persuasive Writing

The following rubric will help guide and assess your persuasive writing. Use it to improve your writing using the six traits.

Each rubric addresses all six traits of writing.

6 Ideas	5	4
The thesis is clearly presented and well defended by reasons that challenge the reader to act.	The thesis is clear. All reasons effectively support the argument and call to action.	The problem and solution are clear. Most reasons support the solution.
Organization		
All parts of the essay work to introduce and convincingly support the writer's opinion.	The opening outlines the argument (opinion). The middle provides clear support. The ending reinforces the opinion.	The opening outlines the argument (opinion). The middle provides support, but the ending needs work.
Voice		
The writer's voice is confident, positive, and convincing.	The writer's voice is confident and persuasive.	The writer's voice is confident, but it may not be persuasive enough.
Word Choice		
The writer chooses words that are powerful, precise, engaging, and persuasive.	The writer chooses words that effectively persuade the reader.	The writer's word choice should be more persuasive.
Sentence Fluency		
The sentences are clear, concise, varied, and engaging.	The sentences are clear and varied in type and beginnings.	More variety in sentence beginnings is needed. There is good sentence variety.
Conventions		
The essay is free of writing errors.	Errors in conventions are few. The reader is not distracted by these errors.	There are a few errors in conventions, and they are distracting.

235 lem-Solution Essay

3	2	1
		A new focus and reasons are needed.
		The organization is unclear and incomplete.
		The writer has not considered voice.
Precise and persuasive words are needed.	The words chosen do not create a clear message.	Word choice has not been addressed.
More variety in sentence beginnings and types is needed.	Most sentences begin the same way and are simple sentences.	There is little sentence variety. Ideas do not flow smoothly.
There are a number of errors that may confuse the reader.	Frequent errors make the essay difficult to read.	Nearly every sentence contains errors.

Process

Persuasive

The rubrics provide a scale in which 6 is the highest rating. A 1 is the lowest.

Assessing In Action

In the following essay, the writer tries to convince you that fuel conservation is essential. Read the essay, paying attention to its strengths and weaknesses. Then read the student self-assessment on the following page. **(The essay contains some errors.)**

Approaching Empty

No one knows how long the world's oil supply will last, but experts agree that eventually the supply will not be able to meet the world's demands. Energy conservation and the development of new technology is essential now, not later (Yaffe). For the sake of future generations, people shouldn't use as much energy as they want to, just because they can afford it.

The United States is a wealthy nation, and low energy costs of the past made inefficiency affordable. This nation lags far behind other developed nations in energy-saving technology. It has 2 percent of the world's known oil supply, makes up 5 percent of the world's population, and consumes 25 percent of the world's oil (Yaffe).

The oil crisis of the 1970s taught people a lesson in conservation. This lead to advances in technology so that today people use 40 percent less energy than they would have without more energy-efficient cars, appliances, and so on. However, once fuel became inexpensive again, consumerism reached an all-time high (Mezger). Without major changes people will face fuel shortages, blackouts, recessions, and war.

Before another crisis arises, people must learn to conserve energy and support energy-efficient technology (ASE). Tax incentives should be given for buying hybrid vehicles and ENERGY STAR rated homes and appliances. Higher demand will encourage technology development.

Some people say that it's not necessary to do anything! They predict that some new technology will save the day. It is true that this nation's most valuable resource is its ingenuity, but renewable resources only supply 2.5 percent of the world's energy today (Sykes). Didn't people learn anything from the 2005 tragedy of failed levees in New Orleans? It's better to spend millions of dollars now to fix a problem, than billions of dollars after the "impossible" happens.

Sample Self-Assessment

The student who wrote "Approaching Empty" created the following assessment sheet to evaluate his essay. He used the persuasive rubric on pages 234–235 as his assessment guide. Under each trait, he wrote comments about the strengths and weaknesses of his writing.

Response Sheet   Title: _Approaching Empty_

4 Ideas
I've included telling statistics. But overall more detail is needed.

4 Organization
My essay follows my outline. The ending could be split in two—one paragraph to answer objections and one for final thoughts.

5 Voice
I am confident and sound persuasive.

4 Word Choice
I should have explained a technical term, ENERGY STAR.

4 Sentence Fluency
I begin my sentences in a variety of ways. Most of my sentences are long, but some shorter ones would add power.

5 Conventions
The few errors I found weren't distracting.

Evaluator: _Allan_

Exercise

Review the assessment. On your own paper, explain why you do or do not agree with the ratings and comments above. Consider each trait carefully.

Assessing a Persuasive Essay

Read the essay below, focusing on its strengths and weaknesses. Then follow the directions at the bottom of the page. **(The essay contains errors.)**

Music and the Arts Make Education Complete

Funding for music and art programs in schools across the country have been cut or greatly reduced (VH1). This is an unfortunate trend. Music and the arts should be supported because they are critical for a well-rounded education.

Studies have proven the positive affect of music and the arts in school. Students who participate in music and arts programs are four times more likely to be recognized for academic achievement. ("Americans"). Other studies reveal that music and the arts help develop critical thinking, cognitive development, and a positive self-esteem.

For most students school is the only place they can get instruction in music and the arts because private lessons are very expensive ("Americans"). Students should not miss out on the benefits of music and the arts just because of their economic status.

Schools support sports programs because sports encourage teamwork. Studies also show that students in sports get better grades. Both of these things are true for music and arts students though, too (Blair and Bruhn). Besides, not everyone can shoot hoops well enough to make the basketball team. At the same time, not everyone can play an instrument well enough to be first chair in a jazz band, or sketch a life-like drawing, but anyone with the desire can still participate.

Music and the arts require discipline, practice, and studying just like any other subject. They also develop creativity, encourage self-expression, and teach students how to work in a group. A program that can do all of those things should be part of every student's education.

Exercise

Assess the persuasive essay you have just read, using the rubric on pages **234–235** as your guide. To get started, create an assessment sheet like the one on page **68**. Remember: After rating each trait, write at least one comment about a strength and one about a weakness.

Publishing Your Writing

You've written many essays, articles, and reports since you've started high school. Many of these pieces were probably read by an audience of one, the teacher who made the assignment. But what if the size of your audience was greatly expanded, and included all of your classmates? How would that affect your feelings about writing? More than anything else, it would help you feel part of a writing community, which makes the process of writing a very meaningful and satisfying experience.

Of course, not everything you write is meant to be shared with an audience. You may not want to open up your journal to the world, but you could take a story idea from your journal, develop it, and then post it on your Web page or submit it to a magazine. Or you could finish a poem you started in your personal writing and recite it at an open-mike night.

This chapter will help you with all of your publishing needs—from preparing a piece for publication to launching your own Web site.

- Preparing to Publish
- Publishing Ideas
- Designing Your Writing
- Publishing Online
- Creating Your Own Web Site
- Finding Places to Publish

"No piece of writing, regardless of how much you polish and fuss with it, comes out exactly as you want it to."

—Tom Liner

Preparing to Publish

Your writing is not ready to share until you have taken it through all the steps in the writing process. The tips below will help you prepare your writing for publication.

Publishing Tips

- **Take advantage of peer response sessions.**
  Make sure that you have addressed the important concerns identified by your classmates.
- **Check for the traits of writing.**
  The ideas, organization, voice, word choice, sentence fluency, and conventions in your writing are all important. (See pages **39–54**.)
- **Put forth your best effort.**
  Continue working until you feel good about your writing from start to finish.
- **Save all drafts for each writing project.**
  Then you will be able to double-check the changes you have made.
- **Seek editing help.**
  Ask at least one trusted editor to check your work for conventions. Another person may spot errors that you miss.
- **Prepare a neat final copy.**
  Use a pen (blue or black ink) and one side of the paper if you are writing by hand. Select a typestyle that is easy to read if you are using a computer. (Always use a computer when you submit your writing to outside publishers.)
- **Consider different publishing options.**
  There are many ways to publish writing. (See page **75**.)
- **Follow all publishing guidelines.**
  Each publisher has certain requirements for publishing. Be sure to follow the publisher's guidelines exactly.

Try It!

Prepare to publish. Follow the tips above to get your next piece of writing ready to publish. Before submitting your work, have a friend read your writing out loud. Listen carefully. Does your writing say everything you'd like it to say? Does your personal voice come through in your writing?

> "I see self-editing as crucial to the process as the initial writing."
>
> —Peter Straub

Publishing Ideas

The simplest way to publish your writing is to share it with a friend or classmate. Other publishing ideas, such as entering a writing contest, take more time and effort. Try a number of these publishing ideas during the school year. All of them will help you grow as a writer.

Self-Publishing

- Newsletter
- Greeting Cards
- Personal Book
- Web Site
- Web Log

Performing

- Sharing with Classmates
- Reading to Other Audiences
- Multimedia Presentation
- Open-Mike Night

Sending It Out

- Local Newspaper
- Magazines
- Web Sites or E-zines
- Writing Contests
- Young Writers' Conferences

Sharing in School

- Literary Magazine
- Writing Portfolio
- Classroom Collection
- School Newspaper/Yearbook

Posting

- Bulletin Boards
- Display Cases
- Business Windows
- Literary/Art Fairs

Think about publishing. How many of these publishing ideas have you tried since you've been in high school? Which other ones would you like to try? Why? Which ones would you not like to try? Why?

Designing Your Writing

Always focus first on the content of your writing. Then consider its design, or appearance. For most types of publishing, you'll want to use a computer for your final copy. These guidelines will help you to design your writing.

Selecting an Appropriate Font

- **Choose an easy-to-read font.** In most cases, a serif typestyle is best for the text, and a sans serif style works for headings.

  The letters of **serif** fonts have "tails"—as in this sentence.

  The letters of **sans serif** fonts are plain, without tails—as in this sentence.

- **Include a title and headings.** Use the title to introduce your paper and use headings to guide the reader through the text. Headings break a long report into readable parts.

Using Consistent Spacing and Margins

- **Set clear margins.** Use a one-inch margin (top, bottom, left, and right).
- **Indent paragraphs.** Use a half-inch indent.
- **Use one space after every period.** This will improve the readability of your paper.
- **Avoid awkward breaks.** Don't leave a heading or the first line of a paragraph at the bottom of a page or a column. Never split a hyphenated word between pages or columns.

Including Graphic Elements

- **Use lists if appropriate.** Use numbered lists if your points have a clear number order. Otherwise, use bulleted lists (like the ones on this page).
- **Include graphics.** Use tables, charts, or illustrations to help make a point. Keep graphics small within the text. If a graphic needs to be large, display it on its own page.

Try It!

Working with a partner, compare the design features of chapters from two textbooks. How are the design features the same? How are they different? Decide which design is the most effective, based on the text's audience and purpose.

Effective Design in Action

The following two pages show a well-designed student essay. The side notes explain the design features.

James Castillo
Mr. Rodriquez
Computer Technology
Nov. 18, 2011

The title is 16-point sans serif type, centered.

Warning for Computers: It's Flu Season

How can a computer act "sick"? Maybe its applications aren't working correctly, or it's crashing and restarting every few minutes. If so, a computer might be infected with a virus. Unfortunately, chicken soup and a lot of rest won't do any good. To ensure that a computer remains up and running, users should understand computer viruses so they can protect their computers in the future.

Centered subheadings (14-point sans serif type) identify main sections.

The Culprits

The Internet is an amazing but dangerous tool. With the click of a mouse, a user can communicate with people all over the world. That's also what makes it so dangerous for a computer. On the Internet, everyone is a neighbor, even the computer hacker with criminal intentions. These harmful hackers design destructive software programs called viruses.

The Viruses

Like human viruses, a computer virus can make a copy of itself. Then it spreads from one host to another. Since computer viruses are programs, they have the ability to delete files, format hard drives, or change home pages.

The body text is 12-point serif type, double-spaced.

Computer viruses can be spread through floppy discs, CD's, e-mail attachments, and downloads. However, most viruses are spread through e-mail attachments. Once the attachment is opened, the virus activates, and infects a computer. Then the virus can send a copy of itself to everyone in a user's e-mail address book. Since a familiar e-mail address is the sender, friends open the attachment, and the whole process repeats itself. So how can an individual avoid these hidden dangers?

Protect Your Computer

Just like human viruses, there's no 100-percent-sure way to protect a computer. Following the steps below improve the odds.

1. **Install an anti-virus program from a trusted source.**
   New viruses are discovered every day, so it is important to stay current with all the updates.

2. **Also install firewall software.**
   Without a firewall, hackers can find a way to take control of a computer. Then they rent a "zombie" computer to criminals who want to send spam or attack other computers without having it traced back to them.

3. **Never open spam or unexpected e-mail attachments.**
   Suspicious files should be deleted. Files from a trusted friend can be saved and then opened.

4. **Keep software updated.**
   Over time, "holes" may be discovered in software programs. Download update "patches" from the program's Web site.

Remove a Virus

If a computer does become infected, it should be disconnected from the Internet to keep from infecting others. It's like staying home from school when having the flu. Then run a virus scan and use the removal tool to get rid of the virus. If that doesn't work, get help from a "doctor"—your program's software support.

Don't let the threat of computer viruses keep you from enjoying the World Wide Web. Install anti-virus programs, stay updated, and use caution. A little effort can help keep a computer healthy all year long.

A numbered list helps the reader digest related information.

Publishing Online

The Internet offers many publishing opportunities, including online magazines and writing contests. The information below will help you submit your writing for publication on the Net. (At home, always get a parent's approval first. In school, follow all guidelines established by the administration.)

Checking Local Sites

Ask your teacher whether your school has a Web site where students can post work. Also check with local student organizations to see if any of them have Web sites that accept submissions.

Finding Other Sites

Use a search engine to find sites that publish student work. Pay special attention to online magazines for young adults. If you don't have any luck with getting published, consider creating your own Web site. (See pages 80–81.)

Submitting Your Work

Once you find online sites where you would like to submit your work, carefully follow these tips.

- **Understand the publishing guidelines for each site.** Be sure to share this information with your teacher and your parents.
- **Send your writing in the correct form.** Some sites have online forms. Others will ask you to send your writing by mail or e-mail. Always explain why you are sending your writing.
- **Provide contact information.** Don't give your home address or any other personal information unless your parents approve.
- **Be patient.** Within a week or so of your submission, you should receive a note from the publisher verifying that your work has been received. However, it may take many weeks for the publisher to make a decision about publishing it.

Try It!

Select a piece of writing that you would like to publish online. Find at least two Web sites that publish this type of student writing. Follow the guidelines and submit your writing to each site.

Creating Your Own Web Site

To create a Web site on your home computer, check with your Internet service provider to find out how to get started. If you are using a school computer, ask your teacher for help. Then follow these steps.

Planning Your Site

Begin by answering the following questions:
- What will be the purpose of this Web site?
- How are my favorite sites set up?
- How many pages will I include?
- How will my pages be linked together?

Creating the Pages

First plan your pages by sketching them out. Then create each page as a text file. Most word-processing programs let you save a file as a Web page. If yours doesn't, you will have to add hypertext markup language (HTML) codes to format the text and make links to graphics and other pages. You can find instructions about HTML on the Net.

Testing Your Pages

Use your browser to open your first page. Then follow any links to make sure they work correctly. Finally, check the content and the look of all pages.

Uploading the Site

Ask your Internet provider how to upload your finished pages. (If you're working at home, make sure to get your parents' approval first. If you're using school equipment, work with a teacher.) When you complete this step, visit your site to make sure it still works.

Publicizing the Site

Once your site is up, e-mail your friends and tell them to visit it. Ask visitors to your site to spread the word to other people they know.

Try It!

If you're interested in creating a personal Web site, start your planning. Then sketch out your pages.

Sample Home Page

This home page includes links to the student's selected photos, songs, and other writing. It also gives information about her favorite musicians and her first shows.

Acoustic Soul Sista'

Home

Pics of Me and My Friends

My Songs

My Other Writing

Links

Acoustic Soul Sista' Sierra Warren

My guitar and I are inseparable. Over the summer, I took lessons from Ms. Shai. She taught me some challenging chords. I also recorded some tracks in her basement studio. One of her other students, Jamel, played on the percussion tracks for me. We finished three songs that I wrote myself. Click on the song title below to listen.

Seasons of Me

Inseparable

Dreamin' in Color

My favorite artists: India Arie, Alicia Keys, Etta James, Stevie Wonder

****My First Shows****

08	October 2010	8:00 pm	Open Mike at the Coffee Bean
15	October 2010	7:00 pm	10th Annual Music Showcase at Lakewood High
23	October 2010	7:00 pm	Ms. Shai Presents at the Workplay Theater
30	October 2010	10:00 am	Lakewood High's Radio Show "Local Flava'" on 92.7 AM

Finding Places to Publish

The suggestions below will help you research places you can publish your writing. Before you submit writing anywhere, however, be sure you understand the conditions of the publication and share this information with your parents.

School Days

If you have written about a topic that interests or affects others in your age group, school publications provide some good publishing options. Your school's newspaper is a good choice for expository or persuasive writing about school-related topics. A student literary magazine or journal offers publishing opportunities for a variety of writing forms, but especially for narrative writing, literary criticism, and poetry. There may even be a page for student writing on your school's Web site. If there isn't, perhaps you should be the one to start it!

Your Own Backyard

The people in a community generally share some interests or background—that's what brought them together as a community in the first place. As a result, ideas that draw your attention may also appeal to your community as a whole. You may find that local publications, such as a local newspaper or neighborhood newsletter, are interested in publishing your writing.

Explore the Possibilities

If you have a favorite national or regional magazine, it may accept writing from outside writers on certain topics. There are also writing contests that accept submissions; many of these contests are even geared toward young writers. A librarian can help you research the possibilities. You can also look in *Writer's Market*—available in most libraries—for more places to publish. Thanks to modern technology, there are publishing options such as blogs that were not available in the past. By posting comments, readers can interact with other writers on a blog. Additionally, authors—including best-selling authors—have self-published their work for many years, but advances in technology have opened up many new possibilities. Enter "self publishing" into a search engine to investigate whether it has potential for you as a writer.

Tip

Before submitting your work to a publication, check the submission guidelines to be sure your writing is in an acceptable form and style. Include a self-addressed stamped envelope when submitting your work to help ensure that you receive a response, as well as your returned work if it is not published.

Creating a Portfolio

A **writing portfolio** is a collection of your work that shows your skill as a writer. It is different from a writing folder that contains writing in various stages of completion. In most cases, you will be asked to compile a showcase portfolio, a collection of your best writing, at the end of a quarter or a semester. By reviewing your portfolio, a teacher can assess your growth as a writer.

Developing a portfolio gives you ownership of your writing in three important ways: (1) You decide, for the most part, what writing to include. (2) You evaluate your strengths and weaknesses. (3) You make certain that your collection shows you at your best. You are, after all, presenting yourself in your portfolio. It says, "This is who I am; this is what I can do."

- **Understanding Portfolios**
- **Parts of a Portfolio**
- **Creating a Cover Sheet**
- **Completing an Evaluation Checklist**

"Learn to evaluate your own work with a dispassionate eye."

—Sue Grafton

Understanding Portfolios

There are four basic types of writing portfolios: a *showcase portfolio*, a *growth portfolio*, a *personal portfolio*, and an *electronic portfolio*.

A **showcase portfolio** presents the best writing you have done during a term. This type of portfolio is used for evaluation.

A **growth portfolio** shows your progress as a writer. It contains writing assignments that show how your skills are developing.

A **personal portfolio** contains writing you want to keep and share with others. Many writers and artists keep personal portfolios arranged according to themes, styles of writing, and so on.

An **electronic portfolio** is any type of portfolio available online or on a disc. It often includes writing, graphics, video, and sound.

Creating a Portfolio

Use these tips as a guide when you develop a writing portfolio. Also make sure to follow your teacher's instructions.

Tip

- **Know what is expected of you.** Make sure that you understand all of the requirements for your portfolio.

- **Keep track of all your work.** Save all your prewriting notes, rough drafts, and revisions for each writing project. Then you will have everything you need when compiling your portfolio.

- **Store your papers in a safe place.** Reserve a special folder to keep all of your work.

- **Set a reasonable schedule for creating your portfolio.** You can't put together an effective portfolio by waiting until the last minute.

- **Take pride in your work.** Make sure that your portfolio shows you at your best.

Parts of a Portfolio

Most showcase portfolios contain the following parts. (Check with your teacher for specific requirements.)

- A **table of contents** lists the material included in your portfolio.
- A **brief essay** or **letter** introduces your portfolio, telling how you put it together, how you feel about it, and what it means to you.
- A **collection of writing samples** presents your best work. (Your teacher may require that you include all of your planning, drafting, and revising for one or more of your writings.)
- A **cover sheet** for each sample explains why you selected it.
- **Evaluations, reflections,** or **checklists** identify the skills you have mastered, as well as the skills that you still need to work on.

Writing Your Opening Pages

The first two pages of a showcase portfolio are shown here.

Table of Contents

Showcase Portfolio
Amanda Knight

Table of Contents

Letter from Amanda Knight 1

Personal Narrative
"Back to My Roots"
 Inspiration List 2
 Research Family Tree 3
 Rough Draft 4
 First Revision 7
 Final Draft 11

Persuasive Essay
"Don't Take My Wheels Away" 15

Expository Essay
"Wolves at the Dinner Table" 18

Opening Letter

Dear Mr. Burke,

I feel like my writing has improved this semester, and that I accomplished my goal to follow each step in the writing process. The one thing that I learned (and will never forget) is that a first draft can always be improved. This showcase portfolio includes my three best pieces for the semester.

My first piece is a personal narrative, "Back to My Roots," which describes how the movie *Roots* inspired me to research our family history. This was my last piece for the semester, so I felt very confident using the writing process. I've included all of my work for this paper. During my research, I discovered that my great-great-great-grandfather was a runaway slave who escaped to the North and fought in the Civil War! As I revised my story, I tried to use a more personal voice to show the pride I have in my heritage.

I've also included my persuasive essay, "Don't Take My Wheels Away." I did a lot of research about the move to raise the driver's license age to 18. I feel like I made a solid case for my opinion against this move. My strong feeling about this issue definitely comes through in this piece as well. I was very careful to refer to reliable and authoritative sources in this paper.

My final piece is an expository essay, "Wolves at the Dinner Table." It explains the history of the domestic dog. I'd like to be a teacher someday, so I used this opportunity to explain history in an interesting, entertaining, and informative way.

Sometimes I hold back when I write, so my true voice doesn't come through. I'll continue to work on voice next semester. Also, I may sign up to be a history tutor so I can work with others on writing about history.

Enjoy the holidays. I'm looking forward to next semester!

Sincerely,
Amanda Knight

Try It!

Imagine that you are putting together a showcase portfolio. Think of two pieces of writing that you would include in it. In a brief paragraph, explain the reasons for your choices.

Creating a Cover Sheet

It is common to attach a cover sheet to each writing project in a showcase portfolio. Your cover sheet should do one or more of the following things:

- Tell why you chose the piece for your portfolio.
- Explain the process of writing you used and any problems that you experienced.
- Describe the strong points and the weak points in the writing.
- Reflect on the writing's importance to you.

Sample Cover Sheet

Our assignment was to explain how species change over time. Looking at the floppy ears and stumpy legs of my basset hound, Coda, I couldn't imagine why an animal would evolve like that on its own. I'd heard that dogs came from wolves, but Coda seemed a far cry, or "howl," from the long-legged predators of the wild. I was curious to see if what I had heard was true.

I began my research by visiting animal Web sites like NOVA and Animal Planet. I learned that wolves were the first animals to be successfully domesticated by humans, but I found several theories about how this happened and when.

I checked for theories and facts that most experts agreed on, and I covered differing theories in separate paragraphs. After my first draft, I felt like my essay was informative but uninteresting. I decided to include Coda as a specific example. I researched breeding and found that hunters wanted a dog that they could follow on foot. Short legs keep bassets from moving too fast, and long ears stir up the scent of a rabbit trail. Adding a specific example made my essay more interesting and easier to remember.

Before this assignment, I never realized that I had a descendent of the wolf begging at my dinner table! I assumed that things had always been the way they were. But now I realize just how much things change, and I'd like to learn more about the history of different people and cultures. This essay reveals my genuine interest in writing about history.

Try It!

Write a sample cover sheet for a piece you'd like to include in a portfolio.

Completing an Evaluation Checklist

It is also common to include a final evaluation checklist in a portfolio. The form should review your writing strengths, weaknesses, and progress.

Sample Evaluation Checklist

Evaluation Form

Writer: <u>Amanda Knight</u>   Class & Term: <u>English/3</u>

Skills Mastered:

1. I follow the steps in the writing process.
2. I now organize my prewriting notes before I begin writing.
3. I participate in peer-responding sessions.
4. If my writing is missing something, I'm pretty good at figuring out what it needs.

Skills to Work On:

1. I get distracted by other interesting topics when I do research, and I forget to focus on my assignment.
2. I need to review grammar rules, especially using commas correctly.
3. My writing voice needs more personality.
4. I need to choose words that "show" instead of "tell."

Goals:

1. I want my writing voice to sound more like me.
2. I want to read more to learn how other writers capture their audience.

Final Thoughts:

1. I have become a much better writer this semester thanks to following the writing process.
2. I organize my notes so that my first drafts are better. Now it's easier to revise my writing into a solid final draft.

Try It!

Create a form like the one above on your own paper. Then fill it in to evaluate your own progress as a writer.

www.hmheducation.com/writesource

Narrative Writing

Writing Focus

Writing a Phase Autobiography — 89
Historical Narrative — 129
Responding to Narrative Prompts — 137

Grammar Focus

Adjective Forms — 120
Punctuating Introductory Phrases and Clauses — 121

Academic Vocabulary

Working with a classmate, read the definitions below and discuss possible answers to each question.

1. A narrative tells a story. It can be fiction or nonfiction. **What nonfiction narratives have you read recently?**

2. A phase is a particular period or stage of development. **What phase of the writing process (prewriting, writing, revising, editing, or publishing) do you find most difficult? Why?**

3. An aspect is a quality or part of something, especially as considered from a certain point of view. **Why might certain aspects of an experience seem more important or less important over time?**

4. Something that is relevant has a connection to the matter at hand. **What relevant information could you add to a discussion about your favorite game or pastime?**

Narrative Writing
Writing a Phase Autobiography

A phase autobiography re-creates an extended period in your life that changed you. This type of narrative writing invites the reader to experience what you experienced, and it illustrates the lessons you learned from it. If a reader says, "That was an inspiring story. I know just what you went through," the writer should know that he or she has succeeded.

For this chapter, you will share an extended life-changing experience, such as caring for a sick relative, campaigning for student council president, or surviving summer camp. Your phase autobiography will hold the reader's interest if it includes four key elements: action, sensory details, dialogue, and personal reflection.

Writing Guidelines

Subject: A period that changed you
Form: Phase autobiography
Purpose: To share a life-changing time in your life
Audience: Classmates

"We all have big changes in our lives that are more or less a second chance."

—Harrison Ford

Narrative Writing Warm-Up: Being Selective

When you write a phase autobiography, it's important to include specific details. However, you don't want to overwhelm the reader with too much information—after all, your life-changing experience could extend over several months. You need to be selective. Choose specific details that share the main focus of your experience.

A writer compiled the list of details below for a narrative paragraph. After reading through his list, he crossed out the ideas that weren't important enough to include.

Sample Details List

> **Waterskiing**
> - A friend asked me to go waterskiing with him.
> - ~~It was Memorial Day weekend.~~
> - I was hoping my parents would say no.
> - I didn't want to look silly.
> - ~~Even my friend's kid sister can ski.~~
> - The boat had 150 hp motor.
> - ~~The skis were huge.~~
> - ~~My friend's cousins showed up.~~
> - My first attempt left me with a mouth full of water.
> - I finally got up on the skis and sailed across the lake.
> - There was no wind and the water was like glass.
> - I even crossed the wake without falling.
> - ~~I pulled and leaned so that I was running parallel to the boat.~~
> - ~~I waved to people on the shore.~~
> - I was so pleased, and my friend celebrated with me.
> - After a rest, I was ready to go again.

Note: This final list of details guided the writer as he wrote a paragraph about the experience that changed him. (See the next page.)

Try It!

Think of an experience that changed you. List the details related to the experience. Then review your list and cross out any unimportant ideas. Remember, you don't need to share every detail, just a good story.

Writing a Narrative Paragraph

A narrative paragraph shares an important experience. Remember that a paragraph has three main parts:

- The **topic sentence** introduces the experience.
- The **body sentences** share details that re-create the experience.
- The **closing sentence** reflects on the experience and how it changed the writer.

Sample Narrative Paragraph

In the following narrative paragraph, the writer shares an experience that changed him—water-skiing for the first time.

Narrative

The **topic sentence** introduces the experience.

The **body sentences** share the important details.

The **closing sentence** reflects on the experience.

Ready to Go Again

I was always a bit nervous about my athletic ability until a friend asked me to go water-skiing with him. At first, I hoped my parents would say no because I was afraid of looking silly, but they thought it was a great idea. I got more worried when I saw the massive 150 hp motor on the back of the boat waiting next to the dock. Bill went first to show me what to do. He sliced through the water, leaped over the wake, and sailed off the ski jump, landing perfectly. All too soon, it was my turn. I jumped in the water, pulled on the skis, and signaled I was ready. The boat surged forward, catching me off guard; I swallowed half the lake. Bill's dad stopped the boat. Patiently, Bill and his dad showed me once more how to use my arms and legs. This time I was ready, and I suddenly found myself standing on skis zipping over the water. The water looked like glass because there were no waves or wind that day. I yelled, "Yahoo!" Carefully, I made my way across the wake, and I didn't fall! When we returned to the dock, I laughed and celebrated. Bill and his relatives shouted, "You were great!" After others had their turns, I was ready to go again. **I suddenly realized that I didn't have to be an expert to enjoy a sport.**

Write your narrative paragraph. Review the three parts of a paragraph (top of page) and what they do. Then use your details list from page 90 to write a narrative paragraph about an experience that changed you.

Understanding Your Goal

Your goal in this chapter is to write about a period in your life that changed you. The traits in the following chart can help you plan and write your phase autobiography. The rubric for narrative writing on pages 124–125 will also guide you.

Traits of Narrative Writing

- **Ideas**
  Share an important extended time in your life, making sure that each specific event adds to the overall story. Support your focus with a variety of details (sensory, memory, dialogue).

- **Organization**
  Develop a clear beginning, middle, and ending that together form a meaningful whole.

- **Voice**
  Use a personal, interested voice appropriate for your topic.

- **Word Choice**
  Choose words that fit the tone (serious, comic, uplifting) of your story. Use figures of speech to add interest to your narrative.

- **Sentence Fluency**
  Write sentences of varied length and structure. Occasionally, use them for special effect.

- **Conventions**
  Check your writing for errors in punctuation, capitalization, spelling, and grammar.

Literature Connections: "Typhoid Fever," an excerpt from Frank McCourt's autobiography *Angela's Ashes,* is about the author's stay in a hospital—a memorable but sad period during his childhood.

Phase Autobiography

In this phase autobiography, the student writer tells about cooking meals at a shelter for homeless men. The side notes explain key parts of the essay.

Beginning
The writer starts in the middle of the action and introduces the situation.

Middle
Descriptive details pull the reader into the experience.

Everybody Has a Story

"The Star Center for homeless men needs volunteers to cook dinner," my pastor announced from the pulpit.

I shot a fearful glance at my mom. Already, her eyes were lit up, so I knew I was doomed. "It'll be fun," she said, gripping my leg. "You and me, every other Sunday."

A week later, Mom and I pulled up in front of a large, gray building at about 4:30 p.m. The sidewalk was filled with litter, and about 30 guys, a lot of them unshaven, were standing around. "The shelter doesn't open until 6:00 p.m.," explained Pat, the director, as she opened the door. "And the men have to be out by 8:00 a.m. The idea is that during the day, they should be looking for work or in training."

I kept my head down as I followed my mom into the dining area and kitchen. Everything I saw depressed me: the stained cinder-block walls, the smudged windows, the beat-up metal chairs and tables, and the tiny kitchen with the huge old-fashioned stove. The shelter smelled funny, too, like dirty socks mixed with floor cleaner. Numbly, I bumped along doing whatever Mom or Pat asked me to do: filling pots, cutting bread, tearing lettuce, washing dishes. By the end of the evening, my sweaty skin itched beneath my shirt, but I'd somehow managed to avoid making eye contact with any of the men.

"Well, what did you learn?" Mom asked on the ride home.

"That I never want to work in food service."

My remark wasn't enough of a hint because two weeks later, we were back. I started by peeling potatoes and heating up green beans and planned to switch to washing dishes afterward, but Mom moved me up front to serve. My hot sweat turned cold. Up they came, a line of men shuffling, bent over, with plates in their hands. Some had watery, bloodshot eyes; most were missing teeth. What was I supposed to say to them? When I put mashed potatoes on the plate of the first one, he looked me right in the eye and said, "Thank you." So I said, "You're welcome."

After everybody had been served, the director, Pat, put a candle into a piece of cake, lit it, and presented it to a man with a Santa Claus-like, long white beard. Everyone sang "Happy Birthday," and the man grinned.

"That's Jimmy," Pat told me later. "He's 50 today, and, thanks to AA, it's his first sober birthday in 25 years."

Middle
Dialogue moves the story along.

Two weeks later, Mom sent me up to serve again, but it wasn't so bad this time. I recognized Jimmy and most of the other guys, and I remembered some of their names. For instance, there was Bob, who always brought homework from his adult literacy class. I also met Darrell, who actually had a college degree but had lost his home and family because he kept having episodes of mental illness. Now, he insisted, he was taking his medication and looking for a job. Over the next few months, I found out they all had stories. The other crazy thing I discovered was that I wanted to hear their stories.

Over time, the guys at the Star Center stopped being bums and became just guys with stories. Actually, they didn't change at all. I was the one who changed. Mom even stopped asking what I'd learned because she could just tell.

Ending
The writer reflects on how the experience has changed him.

At school, I've started organizing the other kids to donate stuff that the guys need—deodorant, foot powder, socks—and I can usually convince a friend or two to come along on Sunday afternoons to cook with us. Cooking for 30 grown men is a lot of work! Who knows, maybe I'll even go into social work. I seem to have a knack for helping people who are down on their luck.

Respond to the reading. Answer the following questions.

Ideas (1) Which phase does the writer focus on? (2) Which sensory details help make the phase come alive? Name two or three.

Organization (3) How does the writer start his phase autobiography? (4) How does he organize the middle part?

Voice & Word Choice (5) Does this writer sound interested? Explain. (6) Which words or phrases are most appealing to you? Why?

Narrative

> "Of all the subjects available to you as a writer, the one you know best is yourself."
>
> —William Zinsser

Adding Dialogue

Dialogue enriches a phase autobiography by moving the action along, by revealing aspects of the speakers' personalities, and by simply adding information. The chart below shows how Sarah can present the same information without and with dialogue. (The dialogue examples are taken from the model on pages **103–106**.)

	Without Dialogue	**With Dialogue**
Show a speaker's personality	As the jagged piece of metal scratched my arm, I began to question why I had joined the tech theater crew.	"Ouch!" I yelped as the jagged piece of metal scratched my arm, making marks like animal tracks. "Are we having fun yet?"
Keep the action moving	We decided to ask for more help.	"Please give us more help," we begged Mr. Peterson.
Add information	My grandpa told me to always do my best work.	I could hear my grandpa's voice in my head: "You don't want your name on anything you're not proud of."

Prewrite

Consider dialogue for your phase autobiography. For practice, write some dialogue that would be appropriate near the beginning of your story. (See page **616** for information about punctuating dialogue.)

Prewriting Reviewing Features of a Narrative

Read the following excerpt from a phase autobiography, watching for action details, sensory details, personal thoughts, and dialogue.

From "Charting a New Course"

The sixth day dawned with a golden orange sky, flecked with purple clouds. The sea was calm, and a brisk wind filled the sails.

We had been onboard the *John Gray Williamson*, a 64-foot sailing yacht, for nearly a week. Our crew of 12—four adult leaders and eight boys aged 14 to 17—were part of a Boy Scout expedition to the Bahamas. I imagined myself living in a time when sailors relied on wind rather than oil for power. I loved rubbing my fingers along the polished oak decks, which smelled of salt and varnish.

Then I noticed the leaders gazing off the starboard side at a massive cloud formation. Its base melted into the sea in dark columns.

The captain began barking orders: "Break down the sails!" he yelled to three of us standing near him. We had just barely untied the last knot to bring the sail down when the wind began roaring, and we got pelted with rain. I couldn't see my friend. I cried out, "Where are you, Pete?" Then I saw him struggling toward me. The boat rocked back and forth, making it hard to keep firm footing, and the boom swung around wildly. Just before the boom grazed over our heads, I screamed, "Watch out!" and tackled Peter.

Then a tremendous gust of wind struck the starboard side of the ship, tipping it dramatically. "I'm going over!" I shouted. Two scouts called out, "Hold on!" and grabbed my arm to keep me from sliding into the waves. I flopped down on the deck and grabbed a mast, frightened but relieved.

Thirty-five minutes later, we emerged from the storm into bright, blue sky and afternoon sunshine. The captain said that the storm was classified as a "white squall" because of the blinding torrent of rain it produces. It was odd to look back and see the black sky with occasional flickers of lightning. We'd made it!

 On your own paper, identify at least one example of each narrative feature—*action details, sensory details, personal thoughts,* or *dialogue*—in the sample above. Be sure to use similar elements in your phase autobiography.

Writing

With your planning in place, you're ready to write your first draft. This is your first opportunity to put the key elements in place: the beginning, middle, and ending of your story.

Keys to Effective Writing

1. Use the details you gathered and organized as a general guide.

2. Do not tell every detail about this phase in your life. Include just the details that allow the reader to appreciate the essence of this time; otherwise, your writing will go on and on.

3. Avoid getting "stuck" as you write the first draft by not fretting over each word.

4. Build suspense in the middle part of your story to keep the reader interested.

5. Use sensory details and dialogue to help the reader experience the events.

Writing Getting the Big Picture

The chart below shows how the parts of a phase autobiography work together. (The examples are from Sarah's essay on pages **103–106**.)

Beginning

The **beginning** gets the reader's attention and identifies the topic of the writing—in this case, a phase.

Opening Paragraphs

"Ouch!" I yelped to my best friend, Hannah, as the jagged piece of metal scratched my arm, making marks like animal tracks. "Are we having fun yet?"

This was my first musical as part of the Riverside High School tech crew. And I was determined, and excited, to help with the backdrops.

Middle

The **middle, or body,** paragraphs use details, description, and dialogue to develop the phase.

At first, I had been disappointed not to be assigned to the carpentry crew.

But Mr. Peterson, who taught our sixth-hour stagecraft class, had his rules for technical crews.

So for three weeks, day after day, we cut the chain link and attached it, cut and attached. . . .

Ending

The **ending** explains the importance of this time in the writer's life.

Closing Sentences

Working with more than 100 people with different skills and personalities taught me how to get along with others, even some people I didn't especially like. And I had high hopes for being on the carpentry crew for the next show.

Starting Your Phase Autobiography

Once you've planned the main parts of your phase autobiography, you're ready to write your first draft. An effective opening should do these things:

- Grab the attention of the reader.
- Include relevant background information.
- State the topic, or phase, that you will write about.

Beginning Part

The writer grabs the reader's attention.	"Ouch!" I yelped to my best friend, Hannah, as the jagged piece of metal scratched my arm, making marks like animal tracks. "Are we having fun yet?"
	"Well, you could wear long sleeves," she said smugly, looking down at her own protected, sweat-shirted arms.
	"Nah," I said. "It's too hot in here." Then I picked up the bolt cutter and went back to work.
Background information is given.	Hannah and I were working side by side with two other kids, building the chain-link fence that would be the backdrop for one of the scenes in our high school musical, <u>West Side Story</u>. Our tech director, Mr. Peterson, had welded the frame for the fence out of 1 1/2-inch pipe. It was our job to cut the chain link—the kind you see in people's yards—with a bolt cutter and attach it to the frame with cable ties.
The phase is identified.	This was my first musical as part of the Riverside High School tech crew. And I was determined, and excited, to help with the backdrops.

Write your beginning. On your own paper, write the beginning part of your phase autobiography. Use transitions to connect your ideas.

Transition Words and Phrases
To shift time: **later, before, then**
To shift location: **between, across, at the edge**
To create a contrast: **however, on the other hand, even so**
To show cause and effect: **because, as a result, due to**
To add information: **in addition, in fact, also**

Writing Developing the Middle Part

Beginning

Middle

Ending

The middle part, or body, of your phase autobiography shares the important information about your experience. *Remember:* Your goal is to tell a good story and hold the reader's interest. Use the tips below as a guide to your writing.

- **Include the key actions,** showing how you tackled your challenge. (See pages **97–98** for help.)
- **Add sensory details** to create vivid pictures in the reader's mind.
- **Share your personal thoughts** and feelings as needed; use dialogue as appropriate.
- **Maintain suspense!** (See page **98.**)

Middle Paragraphs

The writer includes her personal thoughts and feelings.

The writer shows her personality through dialogue.

Sensory details create effective images.

At first, I had been disappointed not to be assigned to the carpentry crew. I love working with wood, ever since I was ten and my grandpa helped me build a small chair.

But Mr. Peterson, who taught our sixth-hour stagecraft class, had his rules for the technical crews. "You have to work your way up to certain jobs," he told us. "But don't worry—by the end of high school, you'll have done a little of everything."

So for three weeks, day after day, we cut the chain link and attached it, cut and attached. Though my hands and arms ached, I could hear my grandpa's voice in my head: "You don't want your name on anything you're not proud of." As a result, I tried to measure and cut the pieces carefully. Hannah and I usually worked silently—that's the kind of friends we are—just wanting to get the job done.

At first, it made me mad when other kids goofed off, like when the boys started shooting staples at each other with the staple gun. Turning to them with a scowl, I yelled, "Cut it out, you guys!" They just laughed and kept shooting. Since they ignored me, I just ignored them, too.

Although it took about three weeks, we could finally step back and look at the finished fence. It was huge—almost 35 feet wide and 15 feet tall!—so it would look real to the audience. Someone else painted signs like graffiti to hang on it. Then the big moment: five or six of us lifted the fence on a pipe, called a fly rail, so it could be moved around. Then Jon, our "fly man," moved it slowly on stage. It really looked like a fence!

But there was still more to be done. Our next assignment was to paint a fake brick wall made out of three large wooden flats covered in muslin. If I thought building the chain-link fence had been tedious, that was nothing compared to painting the wall. We spent days drawing chalk lines to look like bricks, then painting them red and adding gray edges for mortar. If we made a mistake, we'd have to whitewash it and start over. "I guess we're learning patience," I sighed.

And as we added more "layers" of brick, the bottom chalk line slipped on the diagonal, making it look like the building was leaning. So we'd erase it and start over, trying to make everything look straight. But time was running out. Opening night was only a week away, and we still had half of the wall to finish. "Please give us more help," we begged. Mr. Peterson assigned two of the Staple Gun Boys—not the most diligent workers. Then we persuaded the janitor to let us stay late, and we asked our teachers for extensions on our homework.

By opening night, the wall was upright and in place, and it looked, well, almost straight. Hannah and I were exhausted. At the end of the opening night show, the audience applauded the cast and musicians long and hard. Backstage, the rest of us who made the show happen—the painters, prop people, electricians, sound people, stage managers, costumers, and, of course, we scenery builders—high-fived each other.

> Each new action builds suspense.

> Other key actions build to the climax.

> The writer describes how the situation turned out.

 Write **Write your middle paragraphs.** Use your prewriting notes to guide your writing. Keep the following drafting tips in mind.

Tip

- Remember that your purpose is to tell about a period that changed you.
- Don't worry about having everything correct in the first draft. Relax and let your ideas flow. If necessary, leave blank spaces and fill them in later.
- Add important ideas that occur to you as you're writing.

Writing Ending Your Phase Autobiography

The ending is your opportunity to reflect on the experience and summarize for the reader what you learned about yourself. Be truthful and sincere. Coming full circle is one idea for an effective ending. You can "come full circle" if you connect the ending with the beginning.

- **Key idea in the beginning**

  "Ouch!" I yelped to my best friend, Hannah, as the jagged piece of metal scratched my arm, making marks like animal tracks. "Are we having fun yet?"

- **Key idea in the ending**

  I'd put blood, sweat, and tears into building those sets, but I got even more out of the experience.

Ending Paragraph

In the conclusion, the writer reflects on how she has grown.

> I'd put blood, sweat, and tears into building those sets, but I got even more out of the experience. I learned how to stick with a job until it's finished, and I learned about teamwork. Working with more than 100 people with different skills and personalities taught me how to get along with others, even some people I didn't especially like. And I had high hopes for being on the carpentry crew for the next show.

Write your ending and form a complete first draft. Complete your phase autobiography by telling what you learned during that period of your life. Put together a complete copy of your story, double-spacing on the computer or writing on every other line so you have room to revise.

Tip

If you have trouble with the ending, put your writing aside for a while. This will give you time to reflect on the importance of the experience. Or ask friends or family members how they saw you change as a result of your experience.

Revising

Your first draft gets the basic story of your phase onto the page. During the revising step, you improve your first draft by reorganizing, rewriting, adding to, or deleting different parts as needed. Focus on *ideas, organization, voice, word choice,* and *sentence fluency.*

Narrative

Keys to Effective Revising

1. Set your first draft aside for a day or two, if possible, before you begin revising.

2. Be sure each main part—the beginning, the middle (or body), and the ending—works well.

3. Revise any parts that seem confusing. Add more details to any parts that seem incomplete.

4. Pay special attention to your writing voice. Do you sound interested and sincere?

5. Be sure you have chosen the right words to describe your experience.

6. Be sure your sentences read smoothly.

Revising **for** Ideas

6 My writing tells about a phase, and my ideas and details are totally engaging.

5 My narrative includes the necessary events and sensory details.

4 My narrative includes the necessary events, but I could use more sensory details.

When you revise your phase autobiography for *ideas*, you want to be sure you have covered only the necessary events and included plenty of sensory details. The rubric above will guide you.

Have I included only necessary events?

You have included only necessary events if each event covers a critical experience during the phase. As you read each event, ask yourself, "What's the point?" If you can't think of the point, cut the event from your narrative.

Exercise

Read through the following time line to get a sense of the total phase. Then reread each event and ask yourself, "What's the point?" Decide which events do not move the narrative along.

Week 1	Aunt Shaelee lost her job.
Week 2	My cousin Shayna moved in to share my tiny bedroom.
Week 3	Shayna and her boyfriend broke up.
Week 4	I caught Shayna wearing my favorite sweater.
Week 5	I put a tape line across our bedroom.
Week 6	My favorite sweater was missing, and I accused Shayna.
Week 7	Shayna and her boyfriend got back together.
Week 8	I found my sweater in the bottom of my locker and apologized.
Week 9	Shayna and I made up. We had a good week.
Week 10	Shayna's mom got a new job, and Shayna moved out.
Week 11	Shayna and I get together on weekends.

Revise

Review the events in your phase autobiography. Ask yourself, "What's the point?" for each event. Remove events that do not move the narrative along.

Narrative

3 I include some unnecessary events, and I need more sensory details.

2 Many events are unnecessary, and I need sensory details.

1 I need to learn more about the events and details in a phase autobiography.

Have I included enough sensory details?

You have included enough sensory details if the reader can truly experience the sights, sounds, and smells associated with the phase. (Depending on your topic, you may or may not cover all of the senses.)

Exercise

Read the following paragraph from a phase autobiography. Then, on your own paper, list one or two sights, sounds, and smells.

> There I was in chemistry class at the end of the year. Our teacher, Mr. Wilm, said we should get rid of our chemicals. Without thinking I dumped several test tubes together into the waste sink, which smelled of bleach. Splashing together, the chemicals puffed into a white cloud and a foul odor quickly spread. Yelling my name, Mr. Wilm rushed my way, his feet pounding the floor. Suddenly, the safety fan roared to life and the alarm blared, forcing us to cover our ears. I didn't understand what I had done wrong. Mr. Wilm slammed the button to stop the alarm and exclaimed that I may have created a poisonous gas. Fortunately, it wasn't, but I collapsed into a chair suddenly drenched in a cold sweat.

Revise

Check your details. Review your narrative to be sure that you have included sensory details. If not, add some.

Ideas
Sensory details make the experience vivid.

But there was still more to be done. Our next

made out of three large wooden flats covered in muslin
assignment was to paint a fake brick wall. If I thought

building the chain-link fence had been boring, . . .

Revising for Organization

6 The organization makes my phase autobiography very enjoyable to read.

5 My beginning and ending connect, and I use a variety of effective transitions.

4 My beginning and ending connect, but I need more variety in my transitions.

When you revise for *organization,* be sure that your writing has a clear beginning, middle, and ending. It is also important to use a variety of transitions. The rubric above will guide your revision.

Does the ending connect with the beginning?

The ending of your phase autobiography connects with the beginning if the two parts work together to show how the phase changed you. Here are three strategies for connecting the ending with the beginning.

- Use a question and answer.

  Beginning: When Mom asked me to walk the Appalachian Trail with her, I thought, "Do I really want to do this?"

  Ending: Mom and I looked back over the 400 miles we'd hiked together, and I knew that it was the best thing I'd ever done.

- Use a challenge and an outcome.

  Beginning: I sat shivering, staring at the high school pool, and thought I'd never be strong enough to become a lifeguard.

  Ending: All the chlorine and swallowed water was worth it when I got my lifesaving certificate.

- Use foreshadowing.

  Beginning: When I showed up at my best friend's house on the first day of summer, I should have noticed how pale he looked.

  Ending: We were just kids when that horrible summer began, but as John fought—and beat—cancer, we both grew up.

Revise

Reread your beginning and your ending. If they do not clearly connect, use one of the strategies above to make them work together.

Narrative

3 My beginning and ending need to connect, and I need variety in my transitions.

2 I need a clear beginning, middle, and ending, and I need transitions.

1 My narrative is very confusing. I need to start over.

Have I used effective transition words and phrases?

Your transitions will be most effective if you use a variety of them. Using only transitions that indicate time can become tedious. *First* one thing happened, *then* another thing happened, *next* a third thing happened, . . . A variety of transitions will help you indicate not just the order of events but also their *meaning*.

> Most of the people taking the lifesaving course were members of the swim team. I wasn't on the team, though, and I'd actually taught myself to swim. In the pool, my inexperience showed. As a result, I struggled to swim 12 feet down, put on a mask, and fill it with air. I also gasped as I towed classmates using the cross-chest carry. Because I was the slowest swimmer, I often was still swimming laps after the other students were gone. Usually, my goggles leaked, so my eyes burned with chlorine. Everybody told me I should give up, but I didn't.

Exercise

For each blue transition above, write whether it indicates time, location, contrast, cause and effect, or added information.

Check your transitions. Review your phase autobiography, underlining transition words or phrases. Decide whether they add meaning to your writing. Revise as necessary.

Revise

Organization
The writer uses a variety of transitions.

So for three weeks, day after day,
We cut the chain link and attached it, cut and
           Though
attached. My hands and arms ached, I could hear my
grandpa's voice in my head: "You don't want your name on
                          As a result,
anything you're not proud of." I tried to measure and cut
the pieces carefully. Hannah and I usually worked . . .

Revising **for** Voice

6 My writer's voice captures the experience perfectly.

5 My voice is appropriate to my topic, and I sound interested.

4 My voice is appropriate to my topic, but it sounds flat in a few spots.

When you revise for *voice,* be sure that your voice matches your feeling about the topic and shows your interest. The rubric above can guide you.

Is my voice appropriate for the topic?

Your voice is appropriate for the topic if it matches your attitude or feeling about the phase in your life. Here are adjectives that can describe attitude.

friendly	smart	silly	enthusiastic	bitter	sarcastic
know-it-all	timid	humorous	anxious	sad	flip

Here are some examples of voice:

Sarcastic: Sure, I can wash the dishes. I've got nothing to do tonight except practice the piano, clean my room, and do three hours of homework.

Sad: I wailed, as any seven-year-old would, after finding our cat poisoned.

Enthusiastic: Our student trip to Belize includes a fantastic trek through the rain forest. I can hardly wait!

Exercise

For each sentence, write an adjective that describes the attitude.

1. When we moved to our new neighborhood last summer, I sat on the porch a lot, hoping new friends would simply appear.
2. You are so kind to take time to visit me in the hospital.
3. After rolling down the hill, flattening a marker flag or two, I stood up quickly, like a feline who's fallen from the back of a chair, stretched, and assumed a nonchalant pose.
4. I stepped weakly onto the tattered rope bridge, shaky, eyeing the swollen creek below.

Check your voice. Read your narrative out loud and think of an adjective to describe your voice. Is that adjective appropriate for the phase?

Revise

3 My voice sometimes is not appropriate, and I need to sound more interested.

2 My voice sounds inappropriate and uninterested.

1 I need to learn how to create voice.

Do I sound interested in my topic?

You sound interested if you share personal thoughts and feelings with the reader. Don't simply report facts, but share how you felt about those facts.

DON'T Write

The Grand Canyon is a mile deep, you know.

DO Write

I felt dizzy standing on the rim of the Grand Canyon, my shadow swallowed up as I looked thousands of feet straight down.

Exercise

Rewrite each factual sentence below, using your imagination to place yourself in the scene. Report your thoughts and feelings.

1. The Grand Canyon is, on average, 10 miles wide.
2. The Colorado River winds 277 miles through the canyon.
3. People who hike to the bottom must each carry one gallon of water.
4. The temperature at the base of the canyon wall is often 110° F.
5. Trails within the canyon often run along cliff edges.

Revise

Check your interest level. Read your narrative and place an asterisk (*) next to personal thoughts and feelings. If necessary, add more of these personal elements to improve your voice.

Voice
The writer adds personal thoughts and feelings.

But time was running out. Opening night was only a
          "Please give us more help," we begged.
week away, and we still had half of the wall to finish. Mr.
                    —not the most diligent workers.
Peterson assigned two of the Staple Gun Boys.

Revising for Word Choice

6 My word choice captures the experience and relates it vividly.

5 My nouns are specific, and I have used effective figures of speech.

4 Most of my nouns are specific, and I have used some figures of speech.

When you revise for *word choice,* be sure that you have incorporated a few figures of speech and have used specific nouns. Use the rubric strip above as a guide.

How can figures of speech add to my writing?

Figures of speech can make your narrative writing more engaging.

A **simile** is a comparison using the words *like* or *as: Her hair swished like a velvet curtain.*

A **metaphor** is a comparison of two things in which no word of comparison (*as* or *like*) is used: *He's a bolt of lightning.*

Personification is a literary device in which the author speaks of or describes an animal, object, or idea as if it were a person: *My bicycle was happy to be washed.*

Onomatopoeia is the use of a word whose sound suggests its meaning, as in *clang, buzz,* and *twang: The whirring of the buzz saw surprised us.*

Caution: Be as original as you can. Avoid cliches such as *busy as a bee, on his merry way, the spitting image of his father,* and *right off the bat.*

◤ Exercise

On your own paper, write an example for each figure of speech. Be original!

1. Simile:

2. Metaphor:

3. Personification:

4. Onomatopoeia:

Check your writing for figures of speech. Read through your phase autobiography and look for places where you can use figures of speech.

Revise

3 I need to use more specific nouns and better figures of speech.

2 My nouns are all general, and I need to experiment with figures of speech.

1 I need help finding the right words for my narrative.

Have I used specific nouns?

You have used specific nouns if your writing gives the reader a very clear picture of what is happening. General nouns produce a vague impression, but specific nouns provide a sharp focus.

General	More Specific	Most Specific
woman	zookeeper	Zookeeper Sandra Davis
animal	great ape	bonobo chimpanzee
holiday	the Fourth of July	July 4, 2009

Exercise

Replace the general nouns in the following sentences with specific nouns. Use a dictionary, a thesaurus, and your imagination.

1. When I worked at the <u>lumberyard</u>, a <u>man</u> trained me.
2. I had to clean <u>tools</u> and help <u>people</u> with <u>merchandise</u>.
3. Sometimes I used a <u>saw</u> to cut <u>wood</u>.
4. I loaded <u>vehicles</u> and lifted heavy <u>objects</u>.

Revise

Make your nouns more specific. Make a chart with three columns labeled "General," "More Specific," and "Most Specific." Read through your phase autobiography, watching for general nouns. When you find one, write it down; then write a synonym that is more specific and one that is most specific. Consider replacing general nouns with more specific synonyms.

Word Choice
A specific noun and a figure of speech improve word choice.

"Ouch!" I yelped to my best friend, ~~as~~ the jagged piece
Hannah,
making marks like animal tracks ∧
of metal scratched my arm. "Are we having fun yet?"

Revising for Sentence Fluency

6 My sentences are skillfully written and hold the reader's interest throughout.

5 I have varied the lengths and beginnings of my sentences.

4 My sentences have different beginnings, but I should vary their lengths.

When you revise for *sentence fluency,* be sure that you have a variety of sentence beginnings and lengths. Use the rubric strip above as a guide.

Have I varied my sentence beginnings?

You have varied your sentence beginnings if some sentences begin with the subject, some with a phrase, and some with a clause. Also, avoid starting too many sentences with "I." Note how repetitive this paragraph sounds.

> I stepped out of my grandfather's car and looked at the farm fields. I saw unending shafts of golden wheat extending to the edge of the world. I could see grain silos standing on the horizon ten miles away. I was used to living in canyons of glass and steel. I wondered if I'd be able to survive out here on the wide-open plains.

Here are the same ideas with varied beginnings.

> I stepped out of my grandfather's car and looked at the farm fields. Unending shafts of golden wheat extended to the edge of the world. On the horizon, I could see grain silos. Used to living in canyons of glass and steel, I wondered if I would I be able to survive out here on the wide-open plains.

Exercise

Rewrite the following paragraph to vary the sentence beginnings.

> I turned to see the 100-year-old farmhouse with its wooden clapboards and wraparound porch. I could see Grandma sitting on the rocker there, watching the wheat wave. I noticed her cat, weaving through the spindles of the rail. I thought that life here would be tough during the windy hot summers and the stinging cold winters. I would probably go stir-crazy.

Revise

Check your sentence beginnings. Begin some sentences with phrases and clauses, and avoid repetitive "I" sentences.

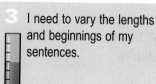

3 I need to vary the lengths and beginnings of my sentences.

2 My sentences sound choppy, and some are incomplete.

1 I need help to improve my sentence style.

Have I used long and short sentences effectively?

You have used long and short sentences effectively if they enhance the meaning and impact of your story. Long sentences can carry multiple details and show relationships between the ideas. Very short sentences, because they stand out, can be used for dramatic impact and emphasis. The following passage starts with two long sentences, carrying a lot of meaning, and ends with a short sentence for dramatic effect.

> **My grandparents' farm was cluttered with buildings, including two greenhouses, an old chicken coop, and a massive stone barn that stayed cool even on the hottest days. As I looked out into one garden, I saw some workers planting delicate green shoots from the greenhouse, while other workers were spreading compost.** For a city girl, this was another world.

Revise

Check your sentence style. Watch for places in your narrative where a long sentence could be used to elaborate on an idea or a description and where a short sentence could be used for dramatic effect.

Sentence Fluency
Ideas are connected in longer sentences.

Hannah and I were working side by side with two other kids. We were building the chain-link fence that would be the backdrop for one of the scenes in our high school musical, <u>West Side Story</u>. Our tech director, Mr. Peterson, had welded the frame for the fence out of 1 1/2-inch pipe. It —the kind you see in people's yards— was our job to cut the chain link with a bolt cutter and attach it to the frame with cable ties. ~~It's the kind of chain link you see in people's yards.~~

Revising Using a Checklist

Check your revising. On your own paper, write the numbers 1 to 12. Put a check by the number if you can answer "yes" to that question. If not, continue revising that part of your phase autobiography.

Revising Checklist

Ideas

_____ **1.** Have I focused on an extended period of time that changed me?
_____ **2.** Does each action or event add to the phase autobiography?
_____ **3.** Have I used sensory details and dialogue?

Organization

_____ **4.** Do I have a clear beginning, middle, and ending?
_____ **5.** Does the ending connect with the beginning?
_____ **6.** Do I use a variety of transition words and phrases?

Voice

_____ **7.** Is my voice appropriate for the topic?
_____ **8.** Do I sound interested in my topic?

Word Choice

_____ **9.** Have I used any figures of speech?
_____ **10.** Have I used specific nouns whenever possible?

Sentence Fluency

_____ **11.** Have I varied my sentence beginnings?
_____ **12.** Have I used long and short sentences for special effect?

Make a clean copy. When you've finished revising your story, make a clean copy to edit.

Editing

Once you've made your revisions, you should edit your writing for conventions: punctuation, capitalization, spelling, and grammar.

Keys to Effective Editing

1. To guide your corrections, refer to a dictionary, a thesaurus, and the "Proofreader's Guide" in the back of this book.

2. Watch for any words or phrases that may be confusing to the reader.

3. Check your phase autobiography for the correct use of punctuation, capitalization, spelling, and grammar.

4. Use the editing and proofreading marks inside the back cover of this book.

5. Edit on a computer printout and then enter your changes into the computer.

Narrative

Editing for Conventions

6 My grammar and punctuation are correct, and the copy is free of spelling errors.

5 I have a few minor errors in grammar, spelling, or punctuation, but they won't confuse the reader.

4 I must correct a number of errors in punctuation, spelling, or grammar that may distract the reader.

When you edit for *conventions,* you check punctuation, capitalization, spelling, and grammar. Use the rubric strip above to guide your editing.

Have I used adjective forms correctly?

You have used adjective forms correctly if you have used the positive form to describe a single noun or pronoun, the comparative form to compare two nouns or pronouns, and the superlative form to rank three or more.

Positive	Comparative	Superlative
hard	harder	hardest
difficult	more difficult	most difficult
good	better	best

For many short adjectives, the comparative form is created by adding *-er,* and the superlative form by adding *-est.* For longer adjectives, the comparative form is created by using the word *more* or *less,* and the superlative form by using *most* or *least.* Some adjectives have irregular forms: *bad, worse, worst.*

Grammar Exercise

Find the adjective-form errors and indicate how each should be corrected.

My desire to get a job was badder than ever. I checked the most late classified ads, I made phone calls, and I set up interviews. But I couldn't land a job, and I was more frustrated than ever. Then I heard about the perfectest job, working as an assistant to the athletic director at the local community center. Believe it or not, the athletic director hired me right after my interview! I couldn't have been happier.

Edit for adjective forms. Check the adjectives in your narrative and be sure to use the adjective forms correctly.

Edit

3 I need to correct some errors that will confuse my reader.

2 I need to fix many errors that make my writing hard to read and understand.

1 I need help finding errors and making corrections.

How should I punctuate introductory phrases and clauses?

Place a comma after longer introductory phrases and all introductory clauses.

No comma: Soon I decided I couldn't live someone else's life.

Longer introductory phrase: During the summer before my junior year, my weird haircut grew out.

Introductory clause: When stores would take back the clothes or music, I returned them.

Grammar Exercise

Indicate where commas should be placed in the following paragraph.

No matter what my friends thought Mr. Foyle was not a control freak. As a matter of fact he gave me a lot of responsibilities right away. I started by setting up the teams for the spring youth basketball league. Then I had to plan a practice schedule for all of the teams. When I finished the scheduling my next task was to help Mr. Foyle set up the league games. After my first weekend on the job I knew I was going to like this job.

> **Conventions**
> Longer introductory phrases and introductory clauses are followed by a comma.

Turning to them with a scowl, I yelled, "Cut it out, you guys!" They just laughed and kept shooting. Since they ignored me, I just ignored them, too.

Although it took about three weeks, we could finally step back and look at the finished fence. It was huge . . .

Editing Using a Checklist

Edit

Check your editing. On a piece of paper, write the numbers 1 to 12. Put a check by the number if you can answer "yes" to that question. If not, continue to edit your narrative for that convention.

Editing Checklist

Conventions

PUNCTUATION

_____ **1.** Do I use end punctuation after all my sentences?

_____ **2.** Do I use commas after longer introductory word groups?

_____ **3.** Do I use commas correctly in compound and complex sentences?

_____ **4.** Do I punctuate my dialogue correctly?

_____ **5.** Do I use apostrophes to show possession *(a girl's book)*?

CAPITALIZATION

_____ **6.** Do I start all my sentences with capital letters?

_____ **7.** Do I capitalize all proper nouns?

SPELLING

_____ **8.** Have I spelled all my words correctly?

_____ **9.** Have I double-checked the words my spell-checker may have missed?

GRAMMAR

_____ **10.** Do I use correct forms of verbs *(had gone,* not *had went)*?

_____ **11.** Do my pronouns agree with their antecedents?

_____ **12.** Do I use the right words *(to, too, two; their, there, they're)*?

Creating a Title

- Focus on the tone of your narrative: **Behind the Scenes**
- Give the words rhythm: **Cut and Attach, Draw and Paint**
- Play with words: **Go Along to Get Along**

Publishing Sharing Your Phase Autobiography

After you have completed revising and editing, you can make a neat final copy of your story to share. Other publishing ideas include recording your narrative, presenting it on a class Web site, or simply sharing it with a group of your peers. (See the suggestions below.)

Publish

Make a final copy. When you write your final copy, follow your teacher's instructions or use the guidelines below. (If you use a computer, see pages 76–78 for formatting tips.) Create a clean copy of your phase autobiography and carefully proofread it.

Focusing on Presentation

- Use blue or black ink and write neatly.
- Write your name in the upper left-hand corner of page 1.
- Skip a line and center your title; skip another line and begin your essay.
- Double-space your narrative.
- Indent every paragraph and leave a one-inch margin on all four sides.
- Write your last name and the page number in the upper right-hand corner of every page after the first one.

Make a recording

Record your phase autobiography. Be sure to use an expressive voice. Give the recording and a printed copy of it to someone as a gift.

Share with a younger audience

Ask if you and several classmates could read your phase autobiographies to younger students. When each author is finished, ask the students what they liked about the story, and why. And if you're feeling brave, ask what they didn't like, and why.

E-mail your story

E-mail your phase autobiography to a small group of friends and relatives not associated with your school. Ask for feedback. Also ask them to share a few details about a period of time that changed them.

Narrative

Rubric for Narrative Writing

Use the following rubric as a guide for assessing your narrative writing. Refer to it whenever you want to improve your writing.

6	**5**	**4**
Ideas		
The narrative shares a significant event. Details make the essay memorable.	The writer shares an interesting experience. Specific details help maintain interest.	The writer tells about an interesting experience. Details need to show, not tell.
Organization		
The structure of the narrative makes it enjoyable and easy to read.	The narrative has a clear beginning, middle, and ending. Transitions are helpful.	For the most part, the narrative is organized. Most of the transitions are helpful.
Voice		
The writer's voice effectively captures the experience for the reader.	The writer's voice sounds natural. Dialogue helps hold the reader's interest.	The writer's voice creates interest in the essay, but dialogue needs to sound more natural.
Word Choice		
The writer's excellent word choice creates a vivid picture of the event.	Specific nouns, verbs, and modifiers create clear images and feelings.	Specific nouns are used, but stronger verbs and modifiers would create a clearer picture.
Sentence Fluency		
The sentences are skillfully written to hold the reader's interest.	The sentences show variety and are easy to understand.	The sentences are varied, but some should flow more smoothly.
Conventions		
The narrative has no errors in spelling, grammar, or punctuation.	The narrative has a few minor errors in punctuation, grammar, or spelling.	The narrative has some errors that may distract the reader.

3   **2**   **1**

The writer should focus on one event. Some details do not relate to the essay.

The writer should focus on one experience. More details are needed.

The writer should select an experience and provide details.

The order of events must be corrected. More transitions are needed.

The beginning, middle, and ending all run together. The order is unclear.

The narrative must be organized.

The writer's voice can usually be heard. More dialogue is needed.

The voice is weak. Dialogue is needed.

The writer sounds uninvolved or disinterested in the essay.

More specific nouns, verbs, and modifiers would paint a clearer picture of the event.

Better words are needed. Words are overused or too general to paint a clear picture.

The writer has not considered word choice or has used words incorrectly.

A better variety of sentences is needed. Sentences do not flow smoothly.

Many incomplete or short sentences make the writing choppy.

Few sentences are written well. Help is needed.

The narrative has several errors.

Numerous errors make the narrative confusing.

Help is needed to find errors and make corrections.

Evaluating a Phase Autobiography

As you read the narrative below, focus on the writer's strengths and weaknesses. Then read the student self-assessment on page 127. (**The essay contains a few errors.**)

Get Rich Quick?

For my buddy Chris and me, the beginning of tenth grade was the worst. We were too young to get a work permit or to drive. And we NEVER had enough money to buy the stuff we wanted. Over the summer, we had thought about starting a lawn mowing service, but our parents were too busy to drive us to the jobs, and our neighborhood was spread out, so it wasn't practical to wheel the mowers around.

Then, in late September, we hit on the idea of a raking and snow shoveling service. We could easily walk or bicycle around town with the equipment.

"Get rich quick!" said Chris.

"Video games, here we come!" I said

So C&C Raking & Snow Shoveling Services was born.

On the flyer we put in people's mailboxes, we listed our rates. By the end of the week, we had six jobs scheduled.

The first one, on Monday, was for Mrs. Sims, a nice, retired school teacher who even brought out cookies while we worked. "I have a bad back, or I'd do this myself," she said. "I'm so happy you boys are here." She had a big lawn, with several trees on the side. It took about three hours, and we split the $20.

Monday night, there was a big storm, and lots of leaves blew to the ground. The phone started ringing, and I said yes to five more jobs.

Tuesday, it rained hard all day, so we had to postpone our next job. But Mr. Edgars didn't understand. He called Tuesday night. "I'm disappointed you boys didn't show up," he yelled. "Better be here tomorrow."

So we had to do two jobs on Wednesday and didn't get home until after dark. We got only $12 from Mr. Edgars, even though he made us drag brush to the street in addition to the raking. He also walked around the yard, pointing to the few leaves that were left. "There's a leaf, there's a leaf," he cried, while Chris and I took turns picking them up. I hoped he wouldn't call back.

Then it rained both Thursday and Friday, so on Saturday we had to rush around doing three jobs. The leaves were soggy and our arms ached. And the five people who called on Monday night all called back, demanding to know when we would be there. I started dreading the sound of the phone. I asked my dad to help us on Saturday. "Sure, just this once," he growled. "But this business was your idea—you've got to figure out how to mange it."

It was only mid-November. I wanted to quit, but my dad said I couldn't until all the raking jobs were handled. "You can eliminate the snow shoveling," he said, "but you've got to follow through on what you promised people."

So even though Chris and I were exhausted, behind in our homework, and tired of being "the boss," we stuck with it. By the time all of the trees were bare, Chris and I had made $250 each.

Once the pressure was off, I realized that I liked advertising the business and negotiating with customers. Maybe I would take econ courses in high school . . . and maybe major in business at college. I was starting to see a future for myself.

Student Self-Assessment

Narrative Rubric Checklist

Title: Get Rich Quick?

Writer: Charles Roland

__5__ **Ideas**
- Does each event add to the phase autobiography?
- Have I used a variety of details?

__4__ **Organization**
- Does the ending connect with the beginning?
- Are my transition words and phrases effective?

__5__ **Voice**
- Is my voice appropriate for the topic?
- Do I sound interested in my topic?

__4__ **Word Choice**
- Have I used any figures of speech?
- Have I used specific nouns?

__5__ **Sentence Fluency**
- Have I varied my sentence beginnings?
- Have I used long and short sentences well?
- Have I used any sentences for special effect?

__4__ **Conventions**
- Have I used adjectives correctly?
- Have I correctly punctuated introductory phrases and clauses?

OVERALL COMMENTS:

Each event adds to the story.

My ending doesn't connect as well as it could to the beginning.

My voice sounds natural.

I didn't use any figures of speech.

My sentences flow together.

I think I used too many commas after introductory phrases.

Reflecting on Your Writing

You've worked hard to write a phase autobiography that your classmates will enjoy. Now take some time to think about your writing experience. Finish each of the sentence starters below on your own paper. This kind of reflection will help you see how you are growing as a writer.

My Phase Autobiography

1. The strongest part of my writing is . . .

2. The part that still needs work is . . .

3. The main thing I learned about writing a phase autobiography is . . .

4. In my next personal writing, I would like to . . .

5. One question I still have about narrative writing is . . .

Narrative Writing
Historical Narrative

Writer Grace Paley advises that "you write from what you know, but you write in what you don't know." This advice is especially helpful when it comes to writing a historical narrative, which re-creates a significant event or experience from the past. While it's important to share accurate details about the event, you were not an eyewitness and so cannot know everything. That's when you need to "expand" the narrative with details that make sense within the context of the story.

This chapter begins with a sample historical narrative based on an event involving Louis Pasteur and one of his patients. The rest of the chapter provides guidelines that will help you write your own historical narrative.

Writing Guidelines

Subject: An important historical moment
Form: Historical narrative
Purpose: To share a significant event from the past
Audience: Classmates

"Tell me facts and figures and you touch my mind, but tell me a story and you touch my soul."

—Anne McCaffrey

Sample Historical Narrative

A historical narrative shares a significant experience from the past. In the following sample, DaShawn Mathews shares a lifesaving experience in the life of Joseph Meister, who received the first rabies vaccine from Louis Pasteur. The narrative is told from the point of view of Joseph as a 16-year-old.

Beginning
The first paragraph sets the scene.

Middle
The second paragraph jumps right into the action.

Descriptive words bring the story to life.

Lurking in the Shadows

In the summer of 1885, I was nine years old, living with my family in the Alsace region of Germany. On the morning of July 4, I was walking alone on the road that led to school. I never even saw the dog lurking in the shadows of the butcher shop.

The snarling beast leapt from nowhere, slamming me to the ground. Pain seared through my body as the huge dog ripped at my arms and legs. "Help! Help!" I shouted. Foam and saliva from the dog's mouth splattered onto me, and blood stained my clothes.

Suddenly, I heard a voice yell, "Someone save little Joseph from that rabid dog!" The vicious attack finally ended when strong hands pulled me to safety. That evening, I screamed in agony as Dr. Weber poured carbolic acid on my wounds to stop the bleeding.

Two days later, after traveling nearly 300 miles, my mother and I arrived at the Paris office of Louis Pasteur, who was working on a rabies vaccination. Mother knew that rabies causes seizures, paralysis, and eventually death, so she pleaded with Pasteur to save me. I struggled to stand, because the deep bites on my legs were incredibly painful. Pasteur seemed hesitant, but Mother convinced him to examine me.

Several men in white coats peered down at me as I lay on a cold table. "Due to the severity and number of bites, it's almost inevitable that this boy will come down with rabies and die," whispered a gruff voice.

Pasteur looked uneasy and concerned. He ushered the men over to his desk and explained that he would try a rabies vaccine treatment, even though it hadn't been tried on humans. I heard Pasteur say, "Joseph will be given a series of shots for at least 10 days."

Terrified, I screamed and tried to sit up.

Narrative

Dialogue adds realism.

Pasteur quickly came to my side and gently explained that the shots wouldn't hurt much. "Just a tiny sting," he promised. Pasteur's eyes were warm and friendly. His whiskery beard reminded me of my grandfather's beard. I decided that I could trust this man.

For the next 10 days, I received shots of the rabies vaccine. Pasteur grabbed my skin just below my rib cage and pinched it into a fold. I didn't watch as he pushed the needle into my skin. Thankfully, the injections weren't very painful. I didn't understand how the vaccination worked, but I did know that I wasn't getting sick.

My mother was so excited to see me every morning. Pasteur's face drooped with concern because he was so afraid that I would get sick with rabies and die.

Ending
The final paragraph explains the significance of the story.

Pasteur shouldn't have worried because I never developed rabies. Less than a month after I was attacked, Pasteur decided that I was healthy enough to go home. Newspapers declared that my amazing recovery was the result of Pasteur's miraculous rabies vaccination. In the months and years ahead, rabies vaccinations were used to treat thousands of people around the world. I was the first of many.

 Respond to the reading. Answer the following questions about the historical narrative you have just read.

Ideas (1) What specific facts about this experience does the writer share? Name at least three.

Organization (2) What transitions does the writer use to help organize the narrative?

Voice & Word Choice (3) Does the writer create a believable firsthand experience? Why or why not? (4) Which descriptive words seem especially strong? Name two.

 Literature Connections: *The Johnstown Flood* by David McCullough is a historical narrative about a terrible nineteenth-century natural disaster.

Prewriting Selecting a Topic

After paging through his history book, DaShawn created a chart of possible topics (events) for his historical narrative. He listed only topics that were brief and specific. With each topic, DaShawn chose a specific narrator.

Topics Chart

TOPIC (Specific Events)	NARRATOR
Signing the Declaration of Independence	Thomas Jefferson
Louis Pasteur's first human trial with his rabies vaccine*	Joseph Meister, first person treated with the vaccine
A day in an 1800s tenement sweatshop	Girl working in garment sweatshop

Choose your topic. Create a chart, listing historical events and possible narrators. Put an asterisk next to the event that you would like to write about.

Prewrite

Gathering Details

The next step is to research your topic and take careful notes. Remember that you are writing from the perspective of someone who personally experienced this moment in time. DaShawn used note cards to organize his research notes.

Sample Notes

Pasteur, Louis
- says that germs affect fermentation
- proves his theory
- says that germs cause diseases
- develops anti-rabies vaccine
- treats Joseph Meister with vaccine in 1885
- story of Louis Pasteur pages 8–10

Meister, Joseph
- lives in Meissengott in Alsace
- attacked by a rabid dog while walking to school
- bitten badly, rescued by a local bricklayer
- first person treated for rabies with vaccine
www.founderofscience.net/Rabies.htm

Gather details. Research your topic, using a variety of sources to find information for your narrative. Take careful notes.

Prewrite

Organizing Your Details

Historical narratives are usually written in chronological order. DaShawn used a time line to organize the information he had gathered. Above the line, he listed specific dates from the story; below the line, he listed the details.

Sample Time Line

July 4, 1885	July 6, 1885	July 16, 1885	End of July 1885
– Joseph is bitten. – The wounds are treated with carbolic acid that evening.	– Joseph is taken to Paris by mother. – Pasteur and colleagues discuss the options. – Joseph gets first shot that morning.	– Joseph receives last shot in a series of rabies vaccinations. – Pasteur is very nervous about Joseph's health.	– Joseph does not get rabies. – Joseph is sent home healthy.

Prewrite

Organize your details. Create a time line, listing dates or specific times above the line and details below it. The following types of details will make your story engaging.

- **Historic details:** facts about *Who? What? When? Where?* and *Why?*
- **Sensory details:** what your character may have seen, heard, smelled, tasted, or touched
- **Reflective details:** what your character may have thought or felt
- **Actions:** what your character may have done or experienced
- **Dialogue:** what your character may have said or heard

Focus on the Traits

Voice The narrative on pages **130–131** is written from the firsthand perspective of a character remembering the experience. This personal voice pulls the reader into the action.

Writing Creating Your First Draft

After gathering and organizing your details, read the following tips. They will guide you as you write your first draft.

Writing Your Beginning Paragraph

Introduce the main character and the setting. Provide details to capture the reader's interest and keep him or her reading.

> In the summer of 1885, I was nine years old, living with my family in the Alsace region of Germany. On the morning of July 4, I was walking alone on the road that led to school. I never even saw the dog lurking in the shadows of the butcher shop.

Creating Your Middle Paragraphs

- Jump into the action of the moment.
  > The snarling beast leapt from nowhere, slamming me to the ground.
- Provide descriptive details.
  > Foam and saliva from the dog's mouth splattered onto me.
- Include natural-sounding dialogue.
  > "Due to the severity and number of bites, it's almost inevitable . . . "
- Add thoughts, feelings, and explanations as needed.
  > Pasteur's face drooped with concern because he was so afraid that I would get sick with rabies and die.

Developing a Strong Ending Paragraph

Share the results of the event or why it was significant.

> Pasteur shouldn't have worried because I never developed rabies. Less than a month after I was attacked, Pasteur decided that I was healthy enough to go home. Newspapers declared that my amazing recovery was the result of Pasteur's miraculous rabies vaccination. In the months and years ahead, rabies vaccinations were used to treat thousands of people around the world. I was the first of many.

Write your first draft. Use your time line (page 133) and the tips above to guide your writing. Get all of your ideas on paper and don't worry yet about mistakes.

Revising Improving Your Writing

Use the following checklist to improve your writing.

Revising Checklist

Ideas

___ **1.** Are my facts, such as names and dates, accurate?

___ **2.** Do I use details, thoughts, and feelings to engage the reader?

Organization

___ **3.** Does my beginning introduce the main character?

___ **4.** Do the middle paragraphs convincingly re-create the event?

___ **5.** Does the ending explain the significance of the event?

Voice

___ **6.** Does the story sound like a realistic firsthand experience?

___ **7.** Do I use dialogue effectively?

Word Choice

___ **8.** Have I used specific nouns and vivid verbs?

___ **9.** Do I use the senses (sight, sound, smell, taste, touch)?

Sentence Fluency

___ **10.** Are my sentences smooth and logical?

___ **11.** Have I used a variety of short and long sentences?

Creating a Title

- Be clever or humorous: **Vaccine Vanquishes Villain**
- Use an expression or common saying: **A Shot in the Dark**
- Use a line from the narrative: **Lurking in the Shadows**

Revise

Revise your first draft. Use the checklist above to review and make changes to your first draft. Then add a title.

Editing Checking for Conventions

After making revisions, you're ready to edit your writing for punctuation, capitalization, spelling, and grammar errors. The following checklist can help you with this step. (See the "Proofreader's Guide" for more about writing rules.)

Editing Checklist

Conventions

PUNCTUATION

_____ **1.** Do I use end punctuation correctly after all sentences?

_____ **2.** Do I use apostrophes to show possession (*Pasteur's beard*)?

_____ **3.** Do I use commas correctly?

CAPITALIZATION

_____ **4.** Do I capitalize all proper nouns?

_____ **5.** Do I capitalize the speakers' first words in portions of dialogue?

SPELLING

_____ **6.** Have I checked for spelling errors?

GRAMMAR

_____ **7.** Do I use the correct forms of verbs (*had gone*, not *had went*)?

_____ **8.** Do my subjects and verbs agree in number (*She was running*, not *She were running*)?

_____ **9.** Do I use the right words (*too, to, two*)? Remember, a computer grammar checker does not catch all usage errors.

Correct your narrative. Use the checklist above to find and correct any errors. Also ask a classmate, friend, or family member to check your work. Then create a neat final copy and proofread it again.

Edit

Publishing Sharing Your Writing

Take time to share your work with classmates and family members.

Share your historical narrative. If you read your narrative to the class, practice first. Then read it clearly and with feeling. Consider using a prop or costume appropriate for the story.

Publish

Writing for Assessment
Responding to Narrative Prompts

In one section of his autobiography *Good Old Boy,* Willie Morris states, "Almost every afternoon when the heat was not too bad my father and I would go out to the old baseball field behind the armory to hit flies." Morris's father would hit ball after ball into the outfield, and the author, then a young boy, would try to catch them. Because of all this practice, Morris became a skilled center fielder.

You, too, have learned many skills during your lifetime. You may, for example, have learned how to ride a bike or swim or knit or play the guitar. Narrative writing prompts on assessment tests often ask you to recall such a learning experience. To respond effectively, you must share the key details related to the experience and tell why it was (or is) important to you. This chapter will guide you through the process of responding to narrative writing prompts.

Writing Guidelines

Subject: Narrative prompt
Form: Response to a prompt
Purpose: To demonstrate competence
Audience: Instructor

"Pain is temporary. It may last a minute, or an hour, or a day, or a year, but eventually it will subside and something else will take its place. If I quit, however, it lasts forever."

—Lance Armstrong

Prewriting Analyzing a Narrative Prompt

A prompt is a set of directions that tells you what to write. For example, a narrative prompt tells you to write about a significant personal experience. To effectively respond to the prompt, you must first understand it. The **STRAP questions** below will help you to analyze a narrative prompt.

Using the STRAP Questions

Subject: What specific experience (memorable, life changing, challenging, inspiring) should I write about?

Type: What type of writing (personal narrative, personal essay, autobiographical article) should I create?

Role: What role (student, son or daughter, friend, community member) should I assume as the writer?

Audience: Who (principal, parent, city official, classmates) is the intended reader?

Purpose: What is the goal (share, re-create, entertain, illustrate, inspire) of my writing?

Try It!

Analyze these prompts, answering the STRAP questions for each one.

1. Your local paper is promoting healthful living. Write an article for this promotion in which you share an experience you had on your personal quest for health or fitness.

2. Think about a time when you wanted something very badly and were not able to obtain or achieve it. What did you learn from the experience? Write a narrative that will appear in a booklet for younger students in your school district.

3. "The only way to help yourself is to help others." Share a personal experience that reveals the truth of these words.

Tip

Some prompts do not contain key words for every STRAP question. Use your best judgment to find answers for all the questions.

Planning Your Response

Once you understand a prompt thoroughly, you can plan your response. The following graphic organizers can help you complete your planning.

Narrative Graphic Organizers

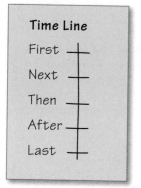

Time Line

First
Next
Then
After
Last

5 W's Chart

Who?	
What?	
When?	
Where?	
Why?	

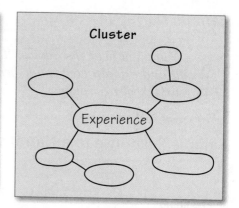

Cluster

Experience

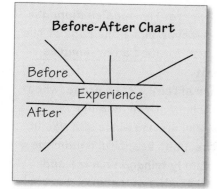

Before-After Chart

Before
Experience
After

Specific Details Chart

Key Actions	Details	Feelings

Prewrite

Reread the narrative prompts on page 138. **Choose one prompt to respond to and create a graphic organizer like one of those above to plan your response.**

Tip

Be sure to use your time wisely. For example, if you have 45 minutes to respond to a prompt, consider using the first 5 to 10 minutes to analyze the prompt and plan your response, and the last 5 minutes to revise and edit it. That leaves 30 to 35 minutes for writing your response.

Writing Responding to a Prompt

After planning your response, it's time to begin writing. Be sure to keep your audience in mind as you write. Consider the following narrative prompt and response.

Sample Narrative Prompt

You often hear the advice, "Learn by doing." Recall how you learned a skill and explain how it has benefited you. Write a narrative to appear in your school newspaper.

Sample Response to a Narrative Prompt

The **beginning** introduces the writer's focus (underlined).

Each **middle** paragraph presents details about the experience.

Eleanor Roosevelt Teaches Me to Knit

"Knit one, purl two," I whispered to myself as I rubbed the textured yarn between my fingers. The needles dipped in and out, forming a neat row of stitches along the edge of the scarf. <u>The process of knitting, even for just a few minutes, made me feel happy and confident.</u>

I learned to knit the summer after seventh grade, when I begged my grandmother to teach me. Gran (and she is a very hip gran, by the way) had been knitting since she was in college, and she always wears the most beautiful handmade things. She is known for her elegantly fringed scarves and boldly patterned sweaters. And she always looks content when she knits. "It's the world's greatest relaxer," she says.

At first, I thought I'd never get the hang of it. I fumbled with the needles. I tangled up the yarn. I kept "dropping a stitch" by letting the yarn slip off the needle by mistake. Then, five or six rows later, I would notice a hole, and I'd have to ask Gran to fix it. Every time, she patiently used a crochet hook to work the dropped stitch back up and onto the needle.

Even when I finally mastered the stitches, my first projects weren't always successful. One sweater was too

Narrative

short. The vest I made for my dad was uneven on the bottom. He wore it anyway, mostly when he walked the dog.

The following summer I almost gave up knitting for good. I wanted to knit something spectacular, so I saved my allowance and bought some expensive wool to make a poncho. I used small needles to work the intricate design. When it was time for school to start again, I was really discouraged because I had only finished a piece about 14 inches square!

But Gran's encouragement kept me knitting. She quoted her idol, former First Lady Eleanor Roosevelt. "Eleanor said, 'You must do the things you think you cannot do,'" Gran said. "I think that applies to knitting as well as to anything else."

I took Gran's advice and continued to knit. But I decided to wait with the poncho. Instead, I perfected my skills on easier patterns that used large needles. Two of my favorite pieces included a silky choker and a backpack made out of a multicolored rayon and cotton. A lot of my friends really liked my backpack. Some people even asked me where I bought it!

| The **ending** tells what the writer learned from the experience. |

Any frustrations I may have had with learning how to knit were well worth it. Knitting helped me become even closer to Gran. It also helped me learn more about fabrics, colors, and design. Most importantly, it built up my self-confidence and taught me not to be afraid to try new things, even if that meant "dropping a stitch" every now and then.

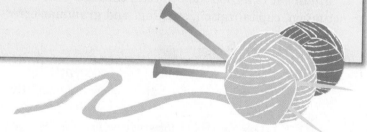

Write

Practice responding to a narrative prompt. Review the prompt you chose on page 138, your answers to the STRAP questions, and your graphic organizer. Then write a response in the amount of time provided by your teacher.

Revising Improving Your Response

Most writing tests allow you to make changes to your response, but be sure you know the number and kinds of changes that are allowed.

Using the STRAP Questions

Return to the STRAP questions to guide your revisions.

> **Subject:** Does my response focus on a specific experience related to the prompt?
>
> **Type:** Have I written in the form requested by the prompt (personal narrative, essay, article)?
>
> **Role:** Have I assumed the role indicated in the prompt (student, friend, son or daughter, community member)?
>
> **Audience:** Have I kept my intended audience in mind and used language appropriate for that audience?
>
> **Purpose:** Does my response accomplish the goal called for by the prompt (share, re-create, entertain, illustrate, inspire)?

Improve your work. Review your response, using the STRAP questions as a guide. Make any changes neatly in the time allowed.

Editing Checking for Conventions

Finally, it is a good idea to read through your draft again to check for punctuation, capitalization, spelling, and grammar errors.

Conventions

_____ 1. Have I used commas and end punctuation correctly?
_____ 2. Have I capitalized all proper nouns and the first word of every sentence?
_____ 3. Have I checked for spelling errors?
_____ 4. Do my subjects and verbs agree (*he was*, not *he were*)?
_____ 5. Have I used the right words (*there, they're*, or *their*)?

Check for conventions. Review your response for punctuation, capitalization, spelling, and grammar errors. Neatly correct any errors.

Narrative Writing on Tests

The following tips will guide you whenever you are asked to write a response to a narrative prompt.

Before you write . . .

- **Understand the prompt.**
  Use the STRAP questions and remember that a narrative prompt asks you to share or re-create an experience.
- **Plan your response.**
  Spend several minutes planning your response. Use an appropriate graphic organizer to help you. (See page **139**.)

As you write . . .

- **State the focus of your response in the beginning.**
  Keep your purpose *(to share, to illustrate)* in mind as you write.
- **Be selective.**
  Include specific details that effectively re-create your experience.
- **End in a meaningful way.**
  Tell why the experience has been important to you.

After you've written your first draft . . .

- **Check for completeness and correctness.**
  Use the STRAP questions on page **142** to revise your work. Then check for errors in punctuation, capitalization, spelling, and grammar.

Plan and write a response. Analyze one of the prompts below, using the STRAP questions. Then plan and write your response. Complete your work within the time allotted by your teacher.

Narrative Prompts

- A Chinese proverb says, "Give a man a fish and you feed him for a day. Teach a man to fish and you feed him for a lifetime." In a personal narrative, share a time in your life when you really learned to do something for yourself. Your audience is your classmates.
- In an article for your school newspaper, describe an accomplishment that made you really proud. Make the experience come alive with vivid details and dialogue.

www.hmheducation.com/writesource

Expository Writing

Writing Focus

Cause-Effect Essay 145
Defining a Concept 185
Responding to Expository Prompts 187

Grammar Focus

Active and Passive Voice 172
Punctuating Quotations 176

Academic Vocabulary

Working with a classmate, read the definitions below and discuss possible answers to each question.

1. Expository writing explains and informs.
   What are some types of expository writing that you read every day?

2. A category is a class or division.
   Into what categories can you divide popular music?

3. A scenario is a general outline or model of events.
   What is the basic scenario of the last movie you watched?

4. Evidence is the proof that something occurred or is factual.
   What kinds of details would provide strong evidence about a particular event?

Expository Writing
Cause-Effect Essay

You studied thoroughly for your geometry test, so you feel confident that you will do well. You ran hard at track practice, so you know that you'll be sore tomorrow. Life is a series of actions and reactions, causes and effects. When you reflect upon these actions, you gain a better understanding of your life, and the bigger world around you. That is why keeping a writer's notebook or personal journal can be so enlightening.

In the same way, you can better understand history if you reflect upon the circumstances surrounding important events. What caused the Black Plague to spread across Europe? What effect did Gutenberg's printing press have on literacy and learning? In this chapter you will write a cause-effect essay about an important historical event or time. As you think and write about your topic, you will see how it connects with other times and events.

Writing Guidelines

Subject: A historical event
Form: Cause-effect essay
Purpose: To make connections
Audience: Classmates

"The cause is hidden, but the result is known."

—Ovid

Expository Writing Warm-Up: Focusing on a Specific Topic

Teachers usually base their writing assignments on a general subject that you are studying. For example, your science teacher could ask you to write about the space program in the United States. Before doing any writing, you would have to narrow or limit the subject to a specific topic suitable for the assignment.

Here's how one student narrowed the general subject—the United States space program—to a specific topic suitable for an expository paragraph.

Narrowing a Subject

- U.S. space program (general subject)
  - Manned missions
    - Apollo missions
      - Apollo 13 (specific topic)

Try It!

Narrow one of the general subjects listed below until you identify a specific topic suitable for an expository paragraph. (Afterward, research the topic if you don't know a lot about it.)

General subjects: **community life, current medicine, high school athletics, weather, movie industry, automobiles, security issues**

Writing Your Topic Sentence

Think of the topic sentence as the engine that powers the rest of a paragraph. A topic sentence should identify the specific topic and identify a particular feeling or feature about it that you want to emphasize.

The Apollo 13 spaceflight (specific topic) **nearly ended in disaster** (a particular feature).

Try It!

Write a topic sentence about your specific topic using the sample above as a guide. (Refer to page **563** for more information.)

Writing an Expository Paragraph

An expository paragraph shares information about a specific topic. The paragraph may present facts, give directions, define terms, explain a process, or so on. The following paragraph explains the causes of the *Apollo 13* disaster. Remember that a paragraph has three main parts:

- The **topic sentence** identifies what the paragraph is about.
- The **body sentences** support the idea expressed in the topic sentence.
- The **closing sentence** reminds the reader of the topic or summarizes the paragraph.

Expository

"Houston, We Have a Problem"

Topic Sentence

The *Apollo 13* spaceflight on April 17, 1970, nearly ended in disaster. The problem—an oxygen leak and loss of electricity—was first noted by astronaut Jack Swigert. He calmly informed the mission control center in Houston of the situation. A NASA investigation later determined that the cause of the problem stemmed from inadequate thermostatic switches that somehow were not noticed during the safety inspections. The switches malfunctioned when they overheated, igniting the insulation surrounding the oxygen tank and causing an explosion. The crew had to move from the command module into the smaller lunar module, which was not designed to hold three people. There was limited water and heat in this module, and condensation on the walls created the fear of short circuits. Four tense days passed before the crew landed safely in the Pacific Ocean. As a result of the mission, safety checks of space modules have become more rigorous. In addition, NASA discovered that astronauts were very well prepared to handle such emergencies. More importantly, they learned that respect and teamwork between astronauts and ground control were invaluable.

Body

Closing Sentence

Write your own expository paragraph. Use your planning from page 146 and the paragraph above as a guide for your writing.

Understanding Your Goal

Your goal in this chapter is to write a well-organized expository essay about a historical event that has a clear cause-and-effect relationship. The traits listed in the chart below will help you plan and write your essay. The rubric on pages **180–181** will also guide you.

Traits of a Cause–Effect Essay

■ **Ideas**

Select an interesting historical event. Develop your essay by establishing the cause-effect relationship related to the event.

■ **Organization**

Include a strong beginning that creates interest and states your thesis. In the middle, support your thesis with reliable, well-researched information. Tie all of your main points together in the ending.

■ **Voice**

Sound knowledgeable about and interested in your topic. Voice is your individual "fingerprint" and distinguishes your writing from another's.

■ **Word Choice**

Select words and phrases that express *exactly* what you want to say. If necessary, check a thesaurus for more precise words.

■ **Sentence Fluency**

Write sentences that flow smoothly from one idea to the next.

■ **Conventions**

Use correct punctuation, grammar, capitalization, and spelling.

Literature Connections: For a longer account of the *Apollo 13* spaceflight, read "The Race to Save *Apollo 13*" by Michael Useem. It explains how the efforts of NASA employees led to the safe return of the astronauts.

Expository

Cause-Effect Essay

In the following expository essay, the writer identifies the effects of Charlemagne's unification of Europe. The notes in the left margin explain the key parts of the essay.

Beginning
The first paragraph introduces the topic and gives the thesis statement (underlined).

Middle
The middle paragraphs provide background information and discuss three effects.

Charlemagne

"By the sword or the cross," proclaimed Charles the Great, one of the most fearless and colorful leaders of the Middle Ages. Better known as Charlemagne, this leader utilized both the sword and the cross to become the first crowned emperor of the Holy Roman Empire, a political area including most of Western and Central Europe. During his 32-year rise to power, he was able to unify the nations of that area into a strong, single entity. Charlemagne's unification of Europe brought peace to all the people, stabilized the European economy, and promoted education.

Charles was the son of Pippin, king of the Franks, whose title he inherited in 768. With this responsibility, Charles developed the leadership and management skills he eventually used to rule much of Europe. He gained control of European lands by political maneuvering and by waging war, also spreading Christianity to unite the people under a common religion. Charles earned the reputation of being a fair-minded, diplomatic leader (Judd). In the year 800, Pope Leo III crowned Charles as Emperor *Carolus Magnus*. That Latin name translates to *Charlemagne* in Old French. Charlemagne brought about solidarity among kingdoms and unified continental Europe.

One of Charlemagne's greatest gifts was his skillful peacemaking ability. Prior to his reign, civil uprisings erupted continually as peasants grew weary of funding military campaigns by paying heavy taxes or forfeiting their land. Charlemagne organized the resources of each region to avoid heavy taxing. He started by collecting tolls, custom duties, and tributes from conquered peoples and distributing the funds to the regions where they were most needed (Judd). Charlemagne endeared himself to his subjects when he showed mercy to captured invading troops. When peasant and nobleman alike realized that they were being treated fairly, a feeling of trust and peace spread throughout Europe.

The writer uses facts, quotations, and paraphrases to develop his thesis.

In order to maintain peace, Charlemagne soon realized that he needed to stabilize the economy in the entire region. He divided larger parcels of land into more manageable estates that were self-contained and administered by a steward or caretaker. Each estate had a bustling center of commerce surrounded by a market, church, guilds, and public buildings. The remaining land was rented to the farmers who produced the crops that fed the people living on the estate. In return, the stewards provided protection and administered justice. The changes instituted by Charlemagne created an intricately balanced system of commerce and trade and stabilized the European economy (Axelrod).

With peace and a more stable economy in place, Charlemagne was then able to concentrate his efforts on education. He assembled the greatest minds of the entire region into an "academy" whose members traveled with and advised Charlemagne. Artists, scientists, and teachers, who were educated at the monasteries, were sent to other regions to share their knowledge. Due to Charlemagne's efforts, education was promoted and learning flourished throughout his empire.

Charlemagne died in 814 at the age of 72. During his reign as king of the Franks and as emperor, he succeeded in unifying Europe, leaving behind a legacy of peace, economic stability, and an appreciation for the value of education. He cherished the written word and preserved the rich culture of his era. Although historians may judge Charlemagne as a foreign invader rather than a hero, it is difficult to imagine how Europe would have developed without the influence of this dynamic leader who lived "by the sword or the cross."

Ending
The final paragraph ties all the key points together and connects with the thesis statement.

Respond to the reading. Answer the following questions.

Ideas (1) What is the primary focus of this essay?

Organization (2) How does the thesis statement help structure this cause-effect essay?

Voice & Word Choice (3) How would you rate the writer's level of interest in the topic? Very interested? Somewhat interested? Not interested? Explain your choice.

Prewriting

During the initial step in the writing process, you will select a specific topic, gather details, establish a thesis statement, and create a basic structure for your writing.

Keys to Effective Prewriting

1. Choose a specific historical event to write about.

2. Refer to a variety of sources and gather information about your topic. Consider quotations, explanations, and facts.

3. Write a thesis statement that identifies a specific cause-effect relationship related to the topic.

4. Identify the key points that support the thesis statement.

5. Organize your details using an outline or another graphic organizer.

Prewriting Selecting a Topic

Marcus Williams started his topic search by thinking about periods of history that he enjoyed reading about. After choosing the Middle Ages, he listed a few general categories, or subjects, related to this time. He starred the two categories in this list that interested him the most.

General Categories List

Middle Ages

natural disasters   invasions   discoveries

economy   religion   famous individuals

*government   the Crusades   *medicine

Start your topic search. Think of a period in history that you enjoy learning about. Then create a general-categories list to identify various subject areas. (If necessary, use some of the categories listed above.) Place an asterisk next to the categories that interest you the most.

Next, Marcus created a chart in which he listed possible cause-and-effect topics for each category that he starred. After reviewing his chart, Marcus decided to write about the Black Plague in Europe.

Topics Chart

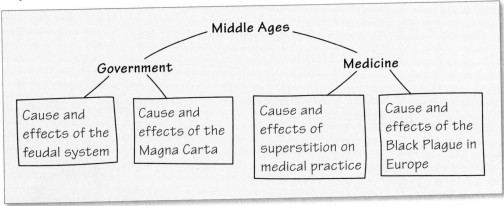

Choose your topic. In a topics chart, list potential cause-and-effect topics related to the categories that you starred in your general-categories list. Then circle the specific topic that you would like to write about.

Gathering Your First Thoughts

To gather his initial thoughts about the Black Plague, Marcus did the following freewriting. He recorded what he knew about the topic and asked some interesting questions.

Freewriting

The Black Plague pretty much devastated Europe during the 1300s. I read that about a third of the population died. Anyone infected died a horrible, painful death, usually within three days. I know it was spread by fleas on ship rats. That means port cities were probably hardest hit. What about the countryside? Did the farmers get the plague? That must have affected how much food there was. What about the clergy? What happened to religion and education back then? What about the culture of the time? What kinds of treatments were available? Did any of them work, or did the doctors die? Is it still possible to catch the plague today? I think there is an inoculation and a cure.

Freewrite on your topic. To get started, write down everything you already know about your topic. Write for 5 to 10 minutes.

Prewrite

Listing Your Sources

As you gather your information, keep track of the sources you use so that you can correctly cite them in your essay. You'll need the following information.

- **Book:** Author's name. Title. Publisher and city. Copyright date.
- **Magazine:** Author's name. Article title. Magazine title. Date published. Page numbers.
- **Newspaper:** Author's name. Article title. Newspaper title. City. Edition (if listed). Date published. Section. Page numbers.
- **Internet:** Author's name (if listed). Page title. Site title. Date posted or copyright date (if listed). Site publisher or sponsor. Date visited.
- **Video:** Title. Director. Distributor. Release date.

List your sources. Keep a list of your sources and include the information shown above. Whenever you find a new source,

Prewrite

Expository

Prewriting Collecting and Organizing the Details

A gathering grid (see page **367**) is an effective way to collect and organize details for an essay. However, sometimes you need more space to record a quotation, to paraphrase important information, or to list important details. In these cases, you should use note cards.

Number each new card and identify the question or main point that the card covers. Then write your notes. If you used a source, identify it at the bottom of the note card.

Sample Note Cards

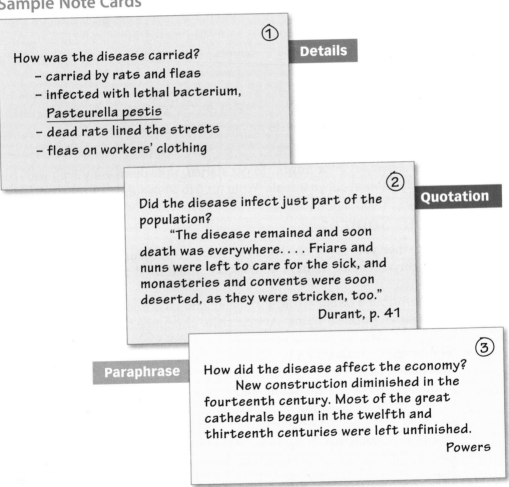

①　**Details**

How was the disease carried?
- carried by rats and fleas
- infected with lethal bacterium, <u>Pasteurella pestis</u>
- dead rats lined the streets
- fleas on workers' clothing

②　**Quotation**

Did the disease infect just part of the population?
　"The disease remained and soon death was everywhere. . . . Friars and nuns were left to care for the sick, and monasteries and convents were soon deserted, as they were stricken, too."
　　　　　　Durant, p. 41

Paraphrase　③

How did the disease affect the economy?
　New construction diminished in the fourteenth century. Most of the great cathedrals begun in the twelfth and thirteenth centuries were left unfinished.
　　　　　　Powers

Prewrite

Collect and organize your information. Use a gathering grid and note cards to collect information for your essay.

Expository

Focusing on Causes and Effects

Once you complete your research, find the cause-and-effect relationship in your topic. A cause-effect organizer can help you complete this step. The three essays in this chapter put forth one main cause (stated in the thesis) and follow with its effects. However, this is not the only way to develop a cause-effect essay. You can also start with one main effect and follow with its causes.

Cause-Effect Organizer

Focus your efforts. Use the graphic organizer above (or on page 588) to identify the cause-effect relationship related to your historical event.

Prewrite

Writing a Thesis Statement

The thesis statement of your essay should establish the focus or direction of your writing. Marcus's thesis statement covers the main points included in his cause-effect organizer.

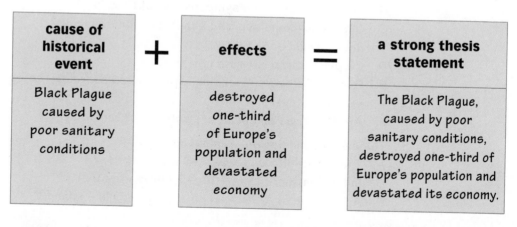

cause of historical event		effects		a strong thesis statement
Black Plague caused by poor sanitary conditions	**+**	destroyed one-third of Europe's population and devastated economy	**=**	The Black Plague, caused by poor sanitary conditions, destroyed one-third of Europe's population and devastated its economy.

Write your thesis statement. Use the model above to create a thesis statement for your essay. Try different versions until you are satisfied.

Prewrite

Prewriting Outlining Your Essay

Before you write your first draft, you should outline the main information you will use to develop your thesis. (Not all of the specific details need to be included in your outline.) Below is the first page of Marcus's sentence outline. (See pages **590–591** for more about outlining.)

Thesis Statement: The Black Plague, caused by poor sanitary conditions, destroyed one-third of Europe's population and devastated its economy.

Background information about the cause.

I. Poor sanitation fostered conditions that were perfect for the spread of the disease.
  A. Rats and fleas carried the microbe called <u>Pasteurella pestis</u>.
  B. Dead rats lined the streets where children played.
  C. The fleas from rats got on the clothing of workers.
  D. Touching the dead bodies of plague victims was common.
  E. The disease infected multiple family members.

The first effect is explored.

II. Once the outbreak took hold, the disease spread uncontrollably.
  A. The first symptoms of the plague were similar to those of a common cold.
  B. Then more-extreme symptoms would set in.
  C. Once individuals started shaking uncontrollably, death would soon follow.
  D. Proper medical care did not exist.
  E. Some resorted to bleeding; others used astrology to prescribe "cures."
  F. Apothecaries and peddlers sold quack remedies.

III. The disease did not discriminate.
  A. The loss of life was greatest in big cities.
  B. In London, more than 100,000 lives were lost.
  C. An average of 1,000 people died weekly in England.

Prepare a sentence outline. Begin with your thesis statement. Then include the main points (I., II., III.) and supporting details (A., B., C.). You do not need to include every detail in your outline.

Prewrite

Writing

Now that you have completed your prewriting, you are ready to compose your first draft. As you write, refer to your outline and your research notes.

Keys to Effective Writing

1. Get all of your ideas down on paper in your first draft.

2. In the first paragraph, state your thesis, identifying a significant cause and its major effects. The middle paragraphs should clarify the cause and discuss the key effects.

3. Include well-reasoned supporting details in each paragraph.

4. Use smooth transitions to connect your ideas.

5. Write on every other line or double-space to leave room for notes and changes.

Writing Getting the Big Picture

The graphic that follows shows how the parts of your essay should fit together. (The examples come from the student essay on pages **159–162**.)

Beginning

The **beginning** introduces both the topic and the thesis.

Thesis Statement
The Black Plague, caused by poor sanitary conditions, destroyed one-third of Europe's population and devastated its economy.

Middle

The **middle** paragraphs provide background information about the cause and explore its effects.

Topic Sentences
Poor sanitation fostered conditions that were perfect for the spread of the disease. **(Background about cause)**

Once the outbreak took hold, the disease spread uncontrollably, killing millions. **(Effect)**

The disease did not discriminate. **(Effect)**

The plague had a devastating impact on the European economy. **(Effect)**

Ending

The **ending** paragraph ties all the information together and concludes with a memorable final sentence.

Closing Sentences
Today, medicines are available to combat most infectious diseases. Still, the specter of diseases like the Black Plague continues to motivate researchers striving to avert other plagues.

"Write freely and as rapidly as possible and throw the whole thing on paper."

—John Steinbeck

Starting Your Essay

The beginning of your essay should capture the reader's interest, introduce your topic, and state your thesis. Here are some ways to start your essay.

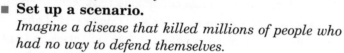

- **Set up a scenario.**
  Imagine a disease that killed millions of people who had no way to defend themselves.
- **Ask a question.**
  What was it really like during the Black Plague?
- **Use a quotation.**
  "Black Plague brought death and devastation," wrote Boccaccio, "and nary a whimper could be heard."
- **Present unusual or surprising information.**
  During the Middle Ages, the Black Plague descended, and, after only five years, one-third of Europe's people had died.

Beginning Paragraph

Marcus starts his beginning paragraph with a *scenario*. He follows the first sentence with information that leads to his thesis statement, the final sentence of the paragraph.

> The writer captures the reader's interest and leads up to the thesis statement (underlined).

Imagine a disease that killed millions of people who had no way to defend themselves. At its height, from 1348 to 1351, the bubonic plague, better known as the "Black Plague" because of the black spots it caused on the skin, brought Europe to its knees. In <u>The Decameron</u>, Giovanni Boccaccio observed, "Almost everyone expected death. . . . And people said, 'This is the end of the world.'" <u>The Black Plague, caused by poor sanitation, destroyed one-third of Europe's population and devastated its economy.</u>

Write

Write your beginning. Try one of the suggestions above to capture your reader's attention. Then add information that leads to your thesis statement.

Expository

Writing Developing the Middle Paragraphs

Beginning

Middle

Ending

Refer to your outline as you write the middle section of your essay. Be sure to expand on the key ideas with specific details (*facts, quotations, paraphrases,* and so on).

Middle Paragraphs

Background information makes the cause clearer.

Poor sanitation fostered conditions that were perfect for the spread of the disease. Rats and fleas carried the microbe called <u>Pasteurella pestis</u>, the lethal bacterium that spread the disease. Dead, infected rats lined the streets, lying within inches of places where little children played. The fleas got on the clothing of workers who brought the plague into their homes, and the fleas spread easily, infecting people through their bites. Since few people understood the nature of diseases, touching the dead bodies of plague victims was a common practice; unfortunately, it was not common practice to wash one's hands afterward. After one family member became infected, it wasn't long before other family members would become sick, too. Cleanup crews often found houses containing several dead—a husband and wife, two or three brothers, a father and a son, and the like (Powers).

A paraphrase puts information in the writer's own words.

The first effect is discussed.

Once the outbreak took hold, the disease spread uncontrollably, killing millions. The first symptoms of the plague were similar to those of a common cold, and most people ignored the chills, fever, and coughs. Tragically, this was the period when the disease was most contagious. Then more-extreme symptoms would set in. Victims' bodies would become mottled with blackish spots and swelling boils. Once individuals started shaking uncontrollably, death would soon follow. No one had ever encountered an epidemic as destructive as the Black Plague; as a result, proper medical care did not exist. The most common treatment was bleeding, and many doctors used astrology to prescribe "cures" based on the position of the planets (Powers). Pope Clement VI sat between two fires, which probably saved him, as heat could kill the germs (Knox), but this was not understood at the time. Apothecaries and peddlers sold quack remedies, and desperation created a market for anything that offered hope. However, nothing worked, and the death rate soared.

> A quotation is included.

The disease did not discriminate. An unknown author stated, "The disease remained and soon death was everywhere. . . . Friars and nuns were left to care for the sick, and monasteries and convents were soon deserted, as they were stricken, too" (qtd. in Durant 41). The loss of life was greatest in the big cities where overcrowding allowed the disease to spread more quickly. John Kelly explains that in London alone, more than 100,000 lives were lost. Of 28 monks in Westminster Abbey, 27 died of the plague. An average of 1,000 people died weekly in England, and survivors buried bodies by the hundreds in mass graves (215–216).

> The second effect is explored.

The plague had a devastating impact on the European economy. By 1363, the plague had affected nearly all business and commerce in Europe. Building came to a halt as workers died or fled. New construction diminished in the fourteenth century, and most of the great cathedrals begun in the twelfth and thirteenth centuries were left unfinished (Powers). Without a source of labor, business people tried to import workers from other countries by offering them financial incentives. The remaining healthy workers were too fearful to accept the offers. With fewer workers available, wages became inflated and most business owners could not afford to keep their workers on the job. As wages rose, the

> Informative details explain the effect.

cost of goods rose, too. Farmers died because of the plague as well, decreasing the amount of food available, which, in turn, forced food prices to skyrocket. It was not until the late Renaissance, a period of intellectual and artistic revival ending in the 1600s, that most countries began to recover some of the population and economic ground that was lost because of the plague.

Expository

Write your middle paragraphs. Follow your outline and use transitions to connect your thoughts and paragraphs. Ideas should flow in a logical order and relate to one another.

Write

Writing Ending Your Essay

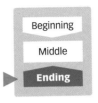

Your ending should contain important last thoughts for the reader. Here are some ways to create a strong ending.

■ **Reflect on the importance of your topic.**
Still, the specter of diseases like the Black Plague continues to motivate researchers striving to avert other plagues.

■ **Include additional information of interest.**
Tragically, people had little knowledge of how germs, or "wee-beasties," as they were called at the time, were transferred between humans. That critical information would come later.

■ **Provide an effective quotation.**
"How many valiant men, how many fair ladies, breakfasted with their kinfolk and the same night supped with their ancestors."

Ending Paragraph

The writer refers to the thesis and includes additional information of interest.

> Unsanitary conditions made the Black Plague one of the worst natural disasters ever to affect Europe. The effects were felt in cities and rural areas alike. Families in both areas were torn apart. The loss of a third of the population had a devastating impact on the European economy, and it took many years to recover. The plague eventually ceased, after having lingered on for almost 300 years. No doubt improved sanitation and an emphasis on personal hygiene helped, but no one knows for sure why the plague ended. Today, medicines are available to combat most infectious diseases. Still, the specter of diseases like the Black Plague continues to motivate researchers striving to avert other plagues.

Write your ending. Write the final paragraph of your essay, using one or more of the strategies above.

"The writing itself has been as important to me as the product. I have always been somewhat indifferent as to whether I have been working on a solemn novel or an impertinent paragraph."
—Sinclair Lewis

Revising

When you revise, you improve your writing. You add details, cross out unnecessary ideas, rewrite unclear parts, and reorder passages as needed.

Keys to Effective Revising

1. If possible, set your first draft aside for a day or two before you do any revising.

2. Check your opening paragraph. Have you effectively introduced your topic and clearly stated your thesis?

3. Review your middle paragraphs to be sure that they explore the causes and effects related to the topic.

4. Check your ending paragraph. Have you effectively connected with your thesis and provided a memorable final idea?

5. Be sure that you have developed and maintained a knowledgeable, interested voice.

6. Review your writing for precise words and a variety of sentences.

Expository

Revising for Ideas

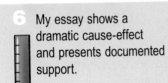

6 My essay shows a dramatic cause-effect and presents documented support.

5 My essay shows effective cause-effect relationships, and my support is strong.

4 My essay lists adequate cause-effect relationships, but I could use more support.

When you revise for *ideas*, check your thesis statement to see if it shows a clear cause-effect relationship. Also be sure that the effects carry equal weight, meaning that they are of equal importance. In addition, be sure that each paragraph contains enough supporting detail. The rubric strip above will help you revise for ideas.

Does my thesis statement provide the proper focus?

Your thesis statement provides the proper focus if it clearly establishes a cause-effect relationship. In the sample essays in this chapter, the thesis identifies one main cause plus two or three resulting effects. (Each effect carries equal weight.)

Charlemagne's unification of Europe *(cause)* **brought peace to all the people** *(effect)*, **stabilized the European economy** *(effect)*, **and promoted education** *(effect)*.

The Black Plague, caused by poor sanitary conditions *(cause)*, **destroyed one-third of Europe's population** *(effect)* **and devastated its economy** *(effect)*.

Revise

Review your thesis statement. Answer these questions to check the effectiveness of your thesis statement. Revise your thesis as needed.

1. Does the first part of my thesis statement identify the historical event? If so, what is it?

2. Does the second part of my thesis identify the main effects? If so, what are they?

3. Do the resulting effects carry equal weight, meaning that they are of equal importance? Explain.

4. Could I state my thesis more effectively? Write another version to find out.

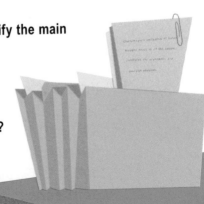

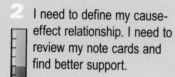

3 My essay shows a basic cause-effect relationship. It needs stronger support.

2 I need to define my cause-effect relationship. I need to review my note cards and find better support.

1 I need to understand the cause-effect relationship and how to use support.

Have I included enough detail?

You have included enough detail if the body sentences in each paragraph clearly and completely support the topic sentence. A well-written paragraph often contains three levels of detail.

Level 1: Topic sentence: In order to maintain peace, Charlemagne soon realized that he needed to stabilize the economy in the entire region.

Level 2: Clarifying sentence: He divided larger parcels of land into more manageable estates that were self-contained and . . .

Level 3: Completing sentence (an explanation, a quotation, or a paraphrase): Each estate had a bustling center of commerce surrounded by a market, church, guilds, and public buildings.

Note: Most paragraphs include at least two clarifying sentences, each one usually followed by one or two completing sentences.

Revise

Check for levels of detail. As you read through your essay, try putting a 1 next to each topic sentence, a 2 next to each clarifying sentence, and a 3 next to each completing sentence. Then decide if you have included enough detail.

Ideas
A completing detail is added.

. . . The first symptoms of the plague were similar to those of a common cold, and most people ignored the chills, fever, and coughs. Then more-extreme symptoms would set in.
Tragically, this was the period when the disease was most contagious.

Victims' bodies would become mottled with blackish spots . . .

Revising for Organization

6 My essay shows an exceptional cause-effect organizational pattern. My transitions work well.

5 My essay shows an effective cause-effect organizational pattern. My transitions fit.

4 My essay shows an adequate organizational pattern, but my transitions could be stronger.

To revise for *organization*, be sure that the beginning, middle, and ending parts work well together. Also make sure that you have used transition words and phrases to connect the paragraphs in your essay. The rubric strip above can guide your revision.

Does my ending paragraph work well?

Your ending paragraph works well if it helps the reader understand the importance or value of the information presented in the main part of your essay. An effective ending may often do these three things:

- remind the reader of your thesis,
- summarize the important points that you covered, and
- leave the reader with a final thought about the topic.

> **The thesis is restated.**
>
> **Main points are highlighted.**
>
> **The closing adds a final thought.**
>
> Unsanitary conditions made the Black Plague one of the worst natural disasters ever to affect Europe. The effects were felt in cities and rural areas alike. Families in both areas were torn apart. The loss of a third of the population had a devastating impact on the European economy, and it took many years to recover. The plague eventually ceased, after having lingered on for almost 300 years. No doubt improved sanitation and an emphasis on personal hygiene helped, but no one knows for sure why the plague ended. Today, medicines are available to combat most infectious diseases. Still, the specter of diseases like the Black Plague continues to motivate researchers striving to avert other plagues.

Revise

Evaluate your ending. As you review your final paragraph, label the different parts, using the information above as a guide. Did you restate your thesis, summarize the main points, and leave the reader with a final thought? Revise as needed.

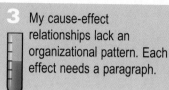

3 My cause-effect relationships lack an organizational pattern. Each effect needs a paragraph.

2 It is not clear which paragraphs belong in the beginning, middle, or ending. I need stronger transitions.

1 I need to check my outline and organizational pattern and reorganize my essay.

Are the paragraphs of my essay clearly connected?

The paragraphs of your essay will be clearly connected if you have effectively used either or both of these linking strategies:

- Choose a key word or phrase from one paragraph and repeat it in the next.
- Start a new paragraph with a transition word or phrase such as *in addition, more importantly,* and so on.

In the sample below, a key word (shown in red) from one paragraph is repeated in the next.

> . . . When peasant and nobleman alike realized that they were being treated fairly, a feeling of trust and peace spread throughout Europe.
>
> In order to maintain peace, Charlemagne soon realized that he needed to stabilize the economy in the entire region.

Revise

Check the flow of your essay. Review your writing to make sure that you have effectively linked your paragraphs. Make changes as needed.

Organization
A key phrase is repeated to connect the paragraphs.

> . . . The Black Plague, caused by poor sanitation, destroyed one-third of Europe's population and devastated its economy.
>
> Poor sanitation
> ∧ ~~The way of life~~ fostered conditions that were perfect for the spread of the disease. Rats and fleas carried the microbe called <u>Pasteurella pestis</u>, the lethal bacterium . . .

Revising **for** Voice

6 My voice sounds perfect for the topic, purpose, and audience. The writing is engaging.

5 My voice is effective for the topic, purpose, and audience. The writing is engaging.

4 My voice is adequately knowledgeable. The writing is somewhat interesting.

When you revise for *voice*, be sure that you use the proper informational voice and that you sound knowledgeable and confident. The rubric strip above can help you.

Have I used the proper voice in my essay?

If you've "kept your distance," then you've probably used the proper voice. The purpose of a cause-effect essay is to inform the reader, not to get too close and personal with the reader. You'll be right on track if your essay engages the reader with a lot of interesting information.

Too close and personal: I've learned about the early battles during the Civil War. Now I know about the Battle of Gettysburg, especially when Pickett's men made their final charge. It was unbelievable.

Proper distance: The Union troops on Cemetery Ridge destroyed the ranks of Pickett's men, which meant not only the end of the battle, but also the eventual collapse of the Confederate army.

Exercise

Read the following statements; then label each one TCP (too close and personal) or PD (proper distance).

1. If you'd been a passenger on that voyage across the Atlantic, you'd have been blown away by the ship's incredible speed.

2. On April 14, 1912, the largest ship ever built, the *Titanic*, collided with an iceberg just before midnight.

3. If I had been scrambling around the deck of the *Titanic*, I would have been scared to death.

Revise for voice. Carefully review your essay for voice, making sure that you have kept the proper distance. Revise as needed.

Revise

3 My support is basic. To make my voice more knowledgeable, I need to include more information.

2 My support is weak. My voice sounds as if I do not understand the subject.

1 I need to research my topic further to establish a knowledgeable voice.

Do I sound confident in my essay?

You'll sound confident in your essay if you have a clear and thorough understanding of your topic. Simply put, there is a direct link between your knowledge of a topic and the level of confidence in your voice. In the following samples, it's clear which writer is confident and which is not.

Not confident: When the *Hindenburg* crashed in 1937, many people died. The great airship caught fire, which probably caused the explosion.

Confident: When the German zeppelin *Hindenburg* caught fire and crashed on May 6, 1937, 36 people lost their lives. Some people thought the crash occurred on the zeppelin's maiden voyage, but the *Hindenburg* had already made 17 round-trip excursions across the ocean, including 10 trips to the United States and 7 to Brazil.

Revise

Check for the confidence in your voice. Carefully review your essay, looking for parts where you don't speak with the proper level of authority. Research and revise as needed.

Voice
An idea is changed because it is "too close and personal."

Imagine a disease that killed millions of people who had
∧ ~~I've had pneumonia and bronchitis, but I've never had to~~
no way to defend themselves.
~~deal with an incurable disease like the bubonic plague~~ At its

height, from 1348 to 1351, the bubonic plague, better known

as the "Black Plague" because of the black spots it caused

on the skin, brought Europe to its knees. In The Decameron,

Giovanni Boccaccio observed, "Almost everyone expected . . . "

Expository

Revising for Word Choice

6 My word choice is superb. My words are vivid and precise. I explain or define unusual terms.

5 My word choice is effective. I do not repeat words and have eliminated unnecessary words.

4 My word choice is adequate, but I need to eliminate a few unnecessary words.

Revising for *word choice* involves, among other things, checking for unnecessary repetition of key words. Also be sure that you have explained any specialized or technical terms. The rubric strip above will help you revise.

How should I check my essay for word choice?

When you check for word choice, be sure that you look for the unnecessary repetition of key words.

Unnecessary repetition: In the 1800s, some men preferred wandering the mountains, away from civilization. These fiercely independent mountain men hunted and trapped in the mountains, earning enough to be able to return to the mountains each year.

Revised passage: In the 1800s, some men preferred wandering the mountains, away from civilization. These fiercely independent men hunted and trapped in the mountains, earning enough to be able to return to them each year.

Exercise

Revise the following passage by addressing the unnecessary repetition of key words and by using action verbs in place of some "be" verbs. (Reword as needed.)

Although Morgan horses are small in size, these horses soon proved to be valuable workhorses, racehorses, and riding horses. People were fascinated by Morgan horses, spirited yet gentle horses that they are.

 Revise for variety in your word choice. Check the effectiveness of your word choice using the information above as a guide. Rewrite sentences as needed.

Revise

3 My word choice needs
work. I have to replace
some unnecessary words
and clarify a few terms.

2 I have to address a number
of word choice problems,
including unnecessary
words and unfamiliar terms.

1 I need special help with my
word choice.

Do I need to explain or clarify any words?

You need to explain or clarify any specialized terms that may be unfamiliar to the reader. Notice the explanation (shown in blue) in the following sentence.

> **Better known as Charlemagne, this leader utilized both the sword and the cross to become the first crowned emperor of the Holy Roman Empire,** a political area including most of Western and Central Europe.

Expository

Exercise

For each sentence that follows, choose the ending that best explains the word without interrupting the flow.

1. In the early 1800s, photography was made possible because of the invention of emulsion,
   a. a liquid sprinkled with silver crystals that coats the film.
   b. the chemical covering the surface of film.

2. German-born Johannes Gutenberg spent his mid-adult years in exile,
   a. which had to do with leaving his country to live elsewhere.
   b. a self-imposed relocation to France.

Revise

Check for specialized words. Make sure that you have explained any technical or unfamiliar words that you have used. Revise as needed.

Word Choice
An explanation is added.

Rats and fleas carried the microbe called Pasteurella
the lethal bacterium that spread the disease
pestis. Dead infected rats lined the streets, lying within
inches of places where little children played. . . .

Revising **for** Sentence Fluency

6 My sentences are masterful. They flow naturally and are varied in type and length.

5 My sentences are effective and flow well. Most are varied in type and length.

4 My sentences are adequate, but I could use even more variety in length and type.

To revise your *sentence fluency*, be sure that your sentences are active and forward moving. Also be sure that you avoid series of short, choppy sentences. The rubric strip above will help you revise.

Have I used active, forward-moving sentences?

You have used forward-moving sentences if they use the active voice. In passive sentences, the action is done by someone or something other than the subject. Such sentences can disrupt the flow of your writing. (See **722.2** for more information.)

Active: The plague devastated entire villages.

Passive: Entire villages were devastated by the plague.

Grammar Exercise

Identify each sentence as being either active or passive. Change each passive sentence into an active sentence.

1. In the 1200s, nearly all of early Russia, the Ukraine, and Siberia were ruled by the Tatars.
2. A potent fighting force was created by the Turkic Tatars combining with the Mongol forces.
3. The Jamaican Arawaks were kept as slaves by the Spaniards.
4. The English invaded Jamaica and conquered the Spanish in 1655.
5. Iran was once referred to as Persia by the Western world.
6. The Persian Empire was conquered by Alexander the Great around 330 B.C.E.
7. Some ancient people of Asia crossed a land bridge between Siberia and Alaska seeking food.
8. In the 1800s, British criminals were sent to Australia by the courts.

Revise

Check for active sentences. Carefully review your first draft for active and passive sentences. Rewrite any passive sentences that clearly disrupt the flow of your essay.

3 My sentences are basic. I need more variety in sentence type and length.

2 I have too many simple sentences that begin the same way.

1 I need help to understand how to vary my sentences.

Do I need to combine or expand any of my sentences?

You may need to combine or expand series of short sentences that sound short and choppy. You can use the 5 W's and H—*Who? What? Where? When? Why?* or *How?*—to help you expand short sentences.

Passage #1 *(Short, choppy sentences)*

The Vikings were accomplished sailors. They plundered the coasts of Europe. They made raids starting in the eighth century. The Viking horde attacked England, and then they continued south to Africa. The Vikings believed that it was good to die in battle. The Vikings were fierce warriors.

Passage #2 *(Sentences combined and expanded)*

The Vikings were accomplished sailors and adventurers who plundered the coasts of Europe from the ninth through the eleventh centuries. The Viking horde made their first attack on England in C.E. 793 and continued as far south as the northern coast of Africa. Because they believed that the gods favored heroes who died in battle, Vikings were fierce warriors.

Revise

Check for short, choppy sentences. Review your first draft for series of short, choppy sentences. Rewrite these sentences as needed.

Sentence Fluency

Short, choppy sentences are combined and expanded.

With
∧Fewer workers were available, Wages became inflated, Most
                                                    on the job
business owners could not afford to keep their workers.
As   the cost of goods rose, too.
∧Wages rose. Farmers died because of the plague as well,

decreasing the amount of food and increasing prices.

Revising Improving Your Writing

Revise your essay. On a piece of paper, write the numbers 1 to 11. If you can answer "yes" to a question, put a check mark after that number. If not, continue to revise that part of your essay.

Revising Checklist

Ideas

_____ **1.** My thesis statement establishes a clear, strong cause-effect relationship.

_____ **2.** I have effectively supported my thesis.

Organization

_____ **3.** I have closely followed my outline.

_____ **4.** I have distinct beginning, middle, and ending parts.

_____ **5.** I use strong transitions to connect ideas and paragraphs.

Voice

_____ **6.** My voice sounds knowledgeable and appropriate for this essay.

_____ **7.** My voice sounds confident.

Word Choice

_____ **8.** I have avoided repeating key words and using too many "be" verbs.

_____ **9.** I have explained any specialized terms.

Sentence Fluency

_____ **10.** I have used active, forward-moving sentences.

_____ **11.** I have avoided short, choppy sentences.

Make a clean copy. When you've finished revising, make a clean copy of your essay for editing.

Editing

Once you have completed your revisions, you are ready to edit your essay for punctuation, capitalization, spelling, and grammar. These rules of English are called *conventions*.

Keys to Effective Editing

1. Edit your essay using a dictionary, a thesaurus, and the "Proofreader's Guide." (See pages 604–763.)

2. Check your writing for punctuation, capitalization, spelling, and grammar errors.

3. Also have a trusted classmate check your writing for errors. (Writers usually work with an editor.)

4. If you're using a computer, edit on a printout of your essay. Then enter your changes on the computer.

5. Use the proofreading marks located inside the back cover of this book.

Editing for Conventions

6 My editing shows total mastery of conventions. My essay is error free.

5 My editing shows effective control of conventions. My essay has a few minor errors.

4 My editing is adequate, but I need to avoid grammar, spelling, and punctuation errors that may distract the reader.

Editing for *conventions* involves checking the punctuation, capitalization, spelling, and grammar of your writing. These two pages will help you correctly punctuate quotations and credit sources. The rubric strip above can guide you.

Is quoted material in my essay punctuated correctly?

You have this material punctuated correctly if you have placed quotation marks before and after the exact words of any person or material you may have quoted. (See pages **632–634** for more information.)

■ Place quotation marks before and after words in direct quotations.
Alexander Graham Bell said, "Mr. Watson, come here. I want to see you."

■ Place periods and commas inside quotation marks. However, if you are citing a source at the end of a sentence, place the period after the citation—as in the example below.
An unknown author stated, "The disease remained and soon death was everywhere. . . . Friars and nuns were left to care for the sick, and monasteries and convents were soon deserted, as they were stricken, too" (qtd. in Durant 41).

■ Use single quotation marks to punctuate a quotation within a quotation.
Obviously heartbroken, the magistrate explained, "As I rode through the famine-blighted countryside, I heard someone cry out, 'Please, sir, a bit of bread for my family,' and I wept in pity."

Edit

Check quotations. Review your essay to be sure you have correctly punctuated quoted material. Use the information above to help you.

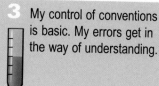

3 My control of conventions is basic. My errors get in the way of understanding.

2 I have to make many corrections because my errors make my essay confusing to read.

1 I need help with correcting conventions.

Have I credited my sources correctly?

You have credited your sources correctly if you have cited them either in the text of your paper or in parenthetical citations and created a works-cited page. Use the guidelines below and pages **374** and **381–384** to cite sources.

- Cite the author and the title in your text when possible.
  In Marchione di Coppo Stefani's book *The Florentine Chronicle*, we learn that the Black Plague killed most of the domesticated animals.

- Use the author's last name. If the author is unknown, use the first significant word from the title in the parenthetical reference.
  The changes instituted by Charlemagne created a balanced system of commerce and trade and stabilized the European economy (Axelrod).

- Give the page number if you are citing only part of a work.
  Author John Kelly writes that the port of Calais was probably the main source of the plague in England (188).

- Place the period after a parenthetical reference.
  Charles earned the reputation of being a fair-minded, diplomatic leader (Judd).

Edit

Credit sources. Review your essay to be sure that you have correctly credited your sources. Create a works-cited page.

Conventions
A quotation within a quotation is punctuated correctly.

In <u>The Decameron</u>, Giovanni Boccaccio observed,
"Almost everyone expected death. . . . And people said, "This
is the end of the world."" The Black Plague, caused by . . .

Editing Using a Checklist

Edit

Check your editing. On a piece of paper, write the numbers 1 to 10. If you can answer "yes" to a question, put a check mark after that number. Continue editing until you can answer "yes" to all the questions.

Editing Checklist

Conventions

PUNCTUATION

_____ **1.** Do I punctuate all my sentences correctly?

_____ **2.** Have I correctly punctuated direct quotations?

_____ **3.** Have I correctly cited my sources? (See pages **374** and **381–384.**)

CAPITALIZATION

_____ **4.** Do I begin every sentence with a capital letter?

_____ **5.** Have I capitalized proper nouns and adjectives?

SPELLING

_____ **6.** Have I spelled all my words correctly?

_____ **7.** Have I double-checked the words my spell-checker may have missed?

GRAMMAR

_____ **8.** Do I use the correct forms of verbs *(we were*, not *we was)*?

_____ **9.** Do subjects and verbs agree in number?

_____ **10.** Have I used the right words *(there, their, they're)*?

Creating a Title

When you write informational essays and reports, it's important to engage your reader with an attention-getting title. Here are some ideas:

- Establish the proper tone: **A Plague for the Ages**
- Catch the reader's attention: **The "Wee-Beasties" of Death**
- Use an idea from the essay: **One of Europe's Worst Disasters**

Publishing Sharing Your Essay

About editing your essay, make a neat final copy, proofread it, and then share it. You could post it on a Web site, read your writing to your classmates, or turn your writing into a multimedia presentation. (See the suggestions below.)

 Make a final copy. Follow your teacher's instructions or use the guidelines below to format your essay. (If you are using a computer, see pages 76–78.) Create a clean final copy of your essay and carefully proofread it.

Focusing on Presentation

- Use blue or black ink and write neatly.
- Write your name in the upper left corner of page 1.
- Skip a line and center your title; skip another line and start your writing.
- Indent every paragraph and leave a one-inch margin on all four sides.
- Write your last name and the page number in the upper right corner of every page after page 1.

Ideas for Publishing

Post Your Essay on a Web Site

Upload your paper to a school or personal Web site. Add graphic elements to enhance the key cause-effect relationships in your essay.

Submit Your Essay

Submit your essay to a school publication or create a classroom anthology of essays.

Present Your Essay to Your Class

Create an oral presentation for your classmates. Use visual aids to enhance your presentation.

Expository

Rubric for Expository Writing

Use the following rubric as a guide for assessing your expository writing. Refer to it whenever you want to improve your writing.

6	**5**	**4**
Ideas		
The ideas in the essay are compelling from start to finish.	The essay shows a clear relationship between thesis and supporting evidence.	The essay presents a clear topic and thesis. More support is needed.
Organization		
The essay shows thoughtful use of an organizational pattern. Transitions are strong.	The essay shows an effective use of an organizational pattern. Transitions are appropriate.	The essay follows an organizational pattern. Transitions could be stronger.
Voice		
The writing voice is lively, engaging, and memorable.	Voice is appropriate for the topic, purpose, and audience and sounds knowledgeable.	Voice fits the audience and sounds knowledgeable in most places.
Word Choice		
Word choice is vivid and precise. Special terms are defined or explained.	Word choice is effective. Words are not repeated and special terms are defined.	Word choice is adequate. Some common words could be replaced.
Sentence Fluency		
Sentences are carefully crafted. Sentences flow naturally and vary in type and length.	Sentences flow well and are varied in type and length.	Sentences could use more variety in type and length.
Conventions		
Editing shows mastery of conventions. Essay is error free.	Editing is effective, but a few errors in grammar, spelling, or punctuation remain.	A few too many errors remain.

3

The essay shows an understanding of the topic and thesis. More support is needed.

The essay does not follow an organizational pattern. Key points need separate paragraphs and transitions.

Voice sounds uneven. It should match topic, purpose, and audience.

Word choice needs to be more precise, and common words need to be replaced.

Sentences are basic. More variety is needed in sentence type and length.

Control of conventions is basic. Errors sometimes get in the way of understanding.

2

The topic and thesis should be more focused. The essay needs specific support that relates to the topic.

The beginning, middle, and ending parts need to be made clear.

Voice sounds as if the writer does not have a good understanding of the subject.

A thesaurus is needed to find more-expressive words in many places.

Too many sentences are simple and begin the same way.

Many corrections are needed to make the essay less confusing.

1

The topic should be reworked and a new thesis formed.

The essay should be organized.

Voice does not show confidence.

The writer needs help choosing stronger words throughout.

Most sentences need to be rewritten.

The writer needs help in understanding editing conventions.

Evaluating a Cause-Effect Essay

Read the cause-effect essay below. Decide which elements of the essay are strong and which could be stronger. Then read the student self-assessment on the next page. **(This student essay contains some errors.)**

A Famine That Crushed a Nation

Ever since 1600 when the potato was successfully introduced in Ireland, the Irish had depended upon it for food. In September 1845, an airborne fungus found in the holds of ships travelling from North America to England struck the potato crop hard. From 1845 to 1850, the Great Irish Potato Famine ravaged Ireland, leading to massive crop failures and starvation, evictions on a large scale, and wholesale emigrations to the United States and Canada.

This terrible crop failure meant low food supplies, which drove prices beyond the reach of the poor. Crop failures during the following years added to the devastation, the situation of the Irish grew desperate. One man told the British House of Commons in 1847. . . "a quarter of her [Ireland's] population will perish unless you come to her relief." With the widespread starvation diseases such as typhus, dysentary, and scurvy began to weaken and kill people of all ages. The magistrate of Cork said, "Their demoniac yells are still ringing in my ears, and their horrible images are fixed upon my brain." (Nicholas Cummins)

Great Britain, which governed Ireland at the time, did not fully understand the scope of the disaster, and placed the responsibility for the poor on the shoulders of the English landlords. Some landlords attempted to do their part, but many did not care about their Irish renters. Landlords had tenants arrested and their families thrown out of their homes. Other tenants gathered their families and roamed the countryside often having only grass and weeds to eat. Hundreds of families were crammed onto ships (called coffin ships because so many died on board) and sent to Canada. Landlords emptied thousands of small farms.

Ireland could not handle all of the unemployed poor. The famine had ravaged the economy. The potato blight continued. Left without choices, thousands began to emigrate to England, but most went to Canada or the United States. More than one million people left their homeland, and about one million died of starvation.

The potato famine of 1845 to 1850, turned a precarious balance of governmental policys, economic conditions, and single-crop dependency into a devastating crisis. First, people experienced crop loss and starvation. Then, the government failed to grasp the scope of the disaster. Next, self-serving landlords evicted their tenants. Finally, all of the deaths and massive emigration crippled the nation. Many years passed before Ireland was able to recover from the damaged done to its government, its economy, its food supply, and its people.

Student Self-Assessment

Expository Rubric Checklist

Title: A Famine That Crushed a Nation
Writer: Mira Chang

5 **Ideas**
- Are my ideas original and well researched?
- Is my thesis statement clear?
- Do the details support the key points?

4 **Organization**
- Does the writing follow my outline and organizational plan?
- Are my beginning, middle, and ending strong?
- Do I use logical transitions?

5 **Voice**
- Does my voice fit the audience?
- Does it sound knowledgeable?
- Does it sound like my writing?

4 **Word Choice**
- Are my words precise and lively?
- Do I define special terms?
- Have I used a thesaurus?

4 **Sentence Fluency**
- Are my sentences varied in type and length?
- Do they begin differently?

3 **Conventions**
- Is my essay free from errors in grammar, punctuation, and spelling?
- Do I cite my sources correctly?

OVERALL COMMENTS:
My topic is unusual. I use some anecdotes and quotations. Paragraph 2 has especially strong support.

My organization is good, but I need to explain the relationships between government, landlords, and the people in paragraph 3.

My voice sounds knowledgeable and fits my audience.

I need to define some terms.

My sentences need to be more varied in paragraph 4.

I have some grammatical and spelling errors, and I need to cite a few sources.

Review your essay.
Rate your essay and write comments that explain why you gave yourself the scores you did.

Reflecting on Your Writing

After you have completed your cause-effect essay, take a few moments to reflect on your writing experience. On a separate piece of paper, finish each sentence starter below. Reflecting helps you to learn more about writing and to apply what you've learned to future assignments.

My Cause-Effect Essay

1. The strongest part of my essay is . . .

2. The part that still needs work is . . .

3. The prewriting activity that worked best for me was . . .

4. The main thing I learned about writing a cause-effect essay is . . .

5. In my next cause-effect essay, I would like to . . .

6. One question I still have about writing a cause-effect essay is . . .

Expository Writing
Defining a Concept

What is the real meaning of freedom? How do you explain love, health, or strength? What does it mean to compromise, enjoy, communicate, or celebrate? While you can look up these words in a dictionary, each of them represents a concept that extends far beyond any single definition.

In this chapter, you'll read a sample expository essay that presents a detailed definition of compromise, going well beyond the basic definition of the term. After that, you'll be asked to choose another interesting term and write your own expository essay of definition—one that shows your understanding of the concept and its importance.

Writing Guidelines

Subject: A complex term
Form: Essay of definition
Purpose: To define the concept
Audience: Classmates

"A concept is stronger than a fact."
—Charlotte P. Gillman

Essay of Definition

In the following essay, Veronica Baban explains a concept that is valuable in all aspects of life.

Beginning
The beginning introduces the topic and presents the thesis statement (underlined).

Middle
Each middle paragraph expands on a specific aspect of the definition.

Compromise: Let's Meet in the Middle

Do people have to work hard in order to reach an agreement? Do the parties involved often give up something to arrive at common ground? If so, they know what it means to compromise. They understand that they can't always get everything they want in every situation, that life often involves as much "giving" as it does "taking." In fact, the concept of the compromise lies at the very heart of social interaction.

The dictionary defines compromise as "a settlement of differences in which each side makes concessions." In terms of usage, compromise is used as a verb or a noun: When someone compromises (*a verb*), he or she reaches an agreement or a compromise (*a noun*). The modern word compromise comes from the Latin word *compromissum*, meaning "mutual promise." Common synonyms for compromise include "settlement," "agreement," "bring to terms," "strike a balance," and "resolve." The opposite of compromising is to act unilaterally, without thinking about the other side.

There is an old saying, "A compromise is an agreement where nobody's happy." As in all sayings, this one has a grain of truth. In a compromise both sides must give up something. Of course, a compromise can be influenced by the relative power of the two sides. For example, an employer or a teacher has more power than an employee or a student, which may affect the eventual agreement. Still, working out compromises is essential in both work- and school-related situations.

Compromise has played a key role throughout history. The Magna Carta, signed in England in 1215 by King John and his chief nobles, may be the most famous historical compromise. The king had to renounce certain royal powers, respect key legal procedures, and accept that the will of the king could be bound by law. The U.S. Constitution, framed in the 1700s, is another masterpiece of compromise. It established the balance of power between the executive, legislative, and judicial branches of government, a compromise that remains the foundation in American life today.

Expository

Middle
The essay expands the definition from historical to personal terms.

Most agreements between countries or regions represent compromise. Because of deception or different values, these agreements may not always succeed. The Missouri Compromise is a famous agreement in U.S. history. The northern states allowed the new state of Missouri to be a slave state with the understanding that no other slave states would be admitted to the union. The compromise lasted for more than 30 years, but slavery was such a polarizing issue that the agreement eventually fell apart. The Civil War was the result.

The ability to compromise is critical in all aspects of life—from maintaining friendships to conducting business. It is especially useful within a family. A husband may enjoy professional sports, while his wife may enjoy attending concerts. In a strong marriage there would be a compromise, each partner occasionally sharing in the other partner's interest. Or a teenage son may want more use of the family car. His parents suggest that he work a little harder around the house; in return they will free up the car more often. The son agrees with the compromise, and everyone is satisfied.

Ending
The ending puts the concept in perspective.

In many ways, compromise makes free societies work. Whatever the situation, the two sides must determine what is most important to them and what they will be willing to give up. Then, and only then, the give and take of ideas can take place until a compromise is reached. British statesman Edmund Burke identified the value of compromise best when he stated: "All government—indeed, every human benefit and enjoyment, every virtue and every prudent act—is founded on compromise and barter."

 Respond to the reading. Answer the following questions in response to the essay.

Ideas **(1) What parts of the definition really stand out? Name two and explain you answer.**

Organization **(2) How does the ending connect with the thesis?**

Voice & Word Choice **(3) How would you describe the writer's voice (comical, personal, interested, informative)? Explain your choice.**

 Literature Connections: In *Cesar's Way,* Cesar Millan provides an extended definition of the pack concept and explains how it applies to domestic dogs.

Prewriting Selecting a Topic

In your expository essay, you will be defining a complex, abstract term. (An *abstract term* is one you can think about but not see or touch.) Before writing her essay, Veronica brainstormed possible topics. She started with one word, *freedom*, and added others as quickly as they came to mind. Here is her list.

Concepts List

freedom	compromise	love	humor	enemy
conflict	anger	sadness	friendship	failure
disappointment	happiness	disagreement	weakness	success
liberty	confusion	strength	tragedy	satisfaction

Focusing Your Topic

The topic should be broad enough to discuss in a multiparagraph essay—examining what the term means, how it is important historically, how it relates to real life, and so on. After brainstorming, Veronica looked over her list. She crossed out topics that were either too broad or too narrow. From the remaining words, she chose the one that she wanted to write about and put an asterisk next to it.

~~freedom~~	*compromise	~~love~~	~~humor~~	enemy
conflict	~~anger~~	~~sadness~~	friendship	failure
~~disappointment~~	~~happiness~~	~~disagreement~~	weakness	success
~~liberty~~	~~confusion~~	strength	tragedy	~~satisfaction~~

Prewrite

Create your own concepts list. Brainstorm a list of possible topics to define. Begin with a term that interests you and quickly write down other concepts that come to mind after that. Then look over your list, crossing out concepts that you feel will not give you the right amount of material for an essay. Finally, put an asterisk next to the topic that interests you the most. You may also want to consider the terms in Veronica's list.

Gathering and Organizing Details

After choosing your topic, consider what the term means, how it is important in history and in everyday life, how it is used in sayings or quotations, and so on. As Veronica researched her term, she took notes.

Notes

Dictionary definition: a settlement of differences in which each side makes a concession

Parts of speech: noun and verb

Word history: comes from <u>compromissum</u>, meaning "mutual promise"

Synonyms: settlement, agreement, bring to terms, strike a balance, resolve

Saying: "A compromise is an agreement where nobody's happy."

Historical importance: Magna Carta, Constitution, Missouri Compromise

Quotation: "All government—indeed, every human benefit and enjoyment, every virtue and every prudent act—is founded on compromise and barter."
—Edmund Burke

Note: Even though you may not use the exact dictionary definition in your essay, it is important to your understanding of the concept.

Prewrite

Gather and organize your details. Research your term, taking notes as you go along. Begin with a dictionary definition; then include your own ideas about the term as well as examples of its historical and everyday importance. Use the information above as a guide.

Writing a Thesis Statement

Your thesis statement should introduce the topic and explain its importance. Veronica used this formula to write her thesis statement.

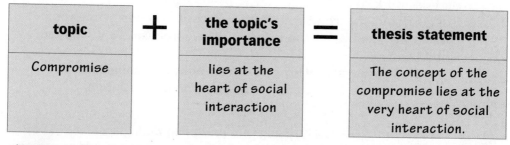

topic	**+**	the topic's importance	**=**	thesis statement
Compromise		lies at the heart of social interaction		The concept of the compromise lies at the very heart of social interaction.

Prewrite

Write a thesis statement. Use the formula above to shape your thesis statement for your essay.

Writing Creating Your First Draft

The tips below can guide your writing of each part of the essay.

Beginning Paragraph

The **beginning** should get the reader's attention, give some background, and include the thesis statement. Here are strategies for starting out.

- **Provide a personal story.** My mom and I reached a compromise about the weekend, with me agreeing to babysit on Friday night and Sunday, and her letting me go out on Saturday night.
- **Ask a challenging question.** Do people have to work hard in order to reach an agreement?
- **Refer to a well-known issue.** Many teenagers in Burlington wanted a skate park, but the city officials planned for a picnic area. They compromised by putting some skateboard ramps in one corner.

Middle Paragraphs

The **middle** paragraphs should explain the concept. Consider these directions as you write.

- Develop a paragraph for each part of your definition.
- Write a topic sentence for each paragraph.
- Include plenty of details to explain each part.
- Use transition words and phrases to link your ideas.

Ending Paragraph

The **ending** wraps up the definition and reminds readers of the concept's importance. Use these strategies.

- **Write a summary.** In many ways, compromise makes free societies work.
- **Suggest that the reader use the concept.** The next time your parents say "No!" ask them if they will compromise. That way you will all win.
- **Give the reader something to think about.** If things aren't going your way, a little compromise may provide a solution.

Write

Write your first draft. Using your prewriting work (pages 188–189) and the suggestions above, put your ideas down on paper. Add any interesting details and examples that occur to you while you are writing.

Revising Improving Your Writing

The checklist below will help you to improve your essay.

Revising Checklist

Ideas

_____ **1.** Have I chosen an interesting concept and defined it clearly?
_____ **2.** Have I included interesting examples and details?

Organization

_____ **3.** Do I include a strong beginning, middle, and ending?
_____ **4.** Are my details in a logical order?
_____ **5.** Does each paragraph have a topic sentence?
_____ **6.** Have I used transitions to connect my ideas?

Voice

_____ **7.** Does my voice fit the topic and the audience?
_____ **8.** Do I show enthusiasm for the topic?

Word Choice

_____ **9.** Have I used specific nouns, verbs, and modifiers?
_____ **10.** Do I explain any technical terms?

Sentence Fluency

_____ **11.** Do my sentences flow smoothly?
_____ **12.** Have I used a variety of sentence types?

Revise

Improve your first draft. Use the checklist above as you review your first draft and make changes. If possible, ask a classmate to review your work.

Creating a Title

- **Use a humorous phrase:** Compromising Situations
- **Use a brief, descriptive phrase:** Let's Meet in the Middle
- **Be straightforward:** What It Means to Compromise

Editing Checking for Conventions

When you have completed your revising, it's time to edit your paper for punctuation, capitalization, spelling, and grammar.

Editing Checklist

Conventions

PUNCTUATION

_____ 1. Have I used end punctuation correctly?

_____ 2. Have I used commas correctly in compound and complex sentences?

CAPITALIZATION

_____ 3. Did I capitalize all proper nouns and proper adjectives?

_____ 4. Did I capitalize the first word in each sentence?

SPELLING

_____ 5. Did I double-check my spelling and look for errors my spell-checker might miss?

_____ 6. Did I double-check the spelling of any special terms?

GRAMMAR

_____ 7. Have I used the correct forms of verbs (_I did_, not _I done_)?

_____ 8. Do my verbs and subjects agree in number (_they were_, not _they was_)?

Edit your essay of definition. Use the checklist above as you review your work for errors. Ask a partner to check your work, too. Then write a neat final copy and proofread it.

Publishing Sharing Your Writing

After completing your essay, be sure to share it with a number of different audiences. You can also post your work on a personal Web site.

Publish your essay. Share your writing with classmates and family members. Afterward, ask for their reactions.

Writing for Assessment
Responding to Expository Prompts

When you explain or inform in a longer piece of writing, you're developing an expository essay. Effective expository writing begins with your complete understanding of a topic, and it ends with a written piece that shows your ability to share this knowledge clearly with your reader. What happens in between is all of the planning, drafting, and revising you do to produce your essay.

On assessment tests, you may be asked to write explanations in response to expository prompts. Of course, your time is limited for this type of expository writing, so you must make the best use of every available minute. This chapter will show you how to complete such a response, adapting the writing process as you work against the clock.

Writing Guidelines

Subject: Expository prompt
Form: Response essay
Purpose: To demonstrate competence
Audience: Instructor

"Good writers are those who keep the
language efficient. That is to say,
keep it accurate, keep it clear."

—Ezra Pound

Prewriting Analyzing an Expository Prompt

Most writing tests ask you to respond to a prompt. A prompt is a set of directions that tells you what to write. It's crucial for you to analyze the prompt carefully so that you write a response that fits the requirements of the test. When you analyze a prompt, answer the following **STRAP questions:**

Su̲bject: What subject (school, schedule, homework policy, healthy living, friendships) should I write about?

T̲ype: What form (essay, letter, announcement, report, article) of writing should I create?

R̲ole: What position (student, community member, son or daughter, friend) should I assume as the writer?

A̲udience: Who (classmates, teacher, principal, parents, city council) is the intended reader?

P̲urpose: What is the goal (inform, explain, evaluate) of my writing?

These key words are often found in **expository** prompts: *explain, analyze, compare and contrast, outline,* and *define.*

Try It!

Analyze these prompts by answering the five STRAP questions above.

1. Aristotle once said, "Happiness depends upon ourselves." Everyone knows the word "happiness," but most of us have a different idea of what it means to be happy. Define the word "happiness" and include two or three clear examples.

2. Many high school students have part-time jobs. Students often choose jobs that are based on economical factors and personal preferences. Identify a part-time job that you would like to have, analyze the duties involved, and explain why you believe the job would suit you.

3. In a letter to a friend, compare and contrast two classes that you are currently taking. In your letter, explain the positive and negative aspects of each class.

Tip

Some prompts do not contain key words for every STRAP question. You will have to use your best judgment to answer these questions.

Planning Your Response

Once you have answered the STRAP questions, you should quickly plan your response. The following graphic organizers can help.

Graphic Organizers

Quick List (Any Essay)
1. First Point
   —Detail 1
   —Detail 2
2. Second Point
   —Detail 1
   —Detail 2
3. Third Point
   —Detail 1
   —Detail 2

Time Line (How-To/Process)
First
Next
Then
After
Last

T-Chart (Two-Part Essay)
Topic:

Part A	Part B
*	*
*	*
*	*
*	*

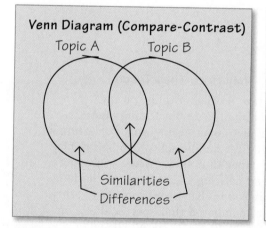

Venn Diagram (Compare-Contrast)
Topic A   Topic B
Similarities
Differences

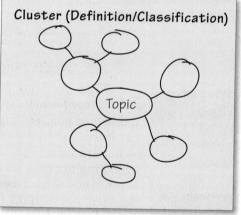

Cluster (Definition/Classification)
Topic

Prewrite

Reread the expository prompts on page 194. Choose one prompt and use one of the graphic organizers above to quickly organize a response to the prompt.

Tip

Manage your time wisely. Allow enough time for prewriting, revising, and editing. For example, if you have 45 minutes to respond, use 5 to 10 minutes to analyze the prompt and plan your response, 30 to 35 minutes for writing, and the last 5 minutes for revising and editing.

Writing Responding to a Prompt

After answering the STRAP questions and using a graphic organizer to plan your response, it's time to begin writing. Make sure to use a tone and level of language appropriate to your topic and to your audience. Review the sample prompt and response that follow.

Sample Expository Prompt

Life is full of new and challenging experiences. Think about a challenge you have faced (an illness, the need to acquire a new skill, dealing with a difficult person). Write an essay about the challenge. Describe it, explain how you dealt with it, and tell how it changed you.

Try It!

Answer the STRAP questions for this prompt. Remember that answering these questions will help you understand the prompt and form your response. (See page **194**.)

Sample Response

> **Words Sing. They Hurt. They Teach.**
>
> Whenever I had to face a crisis, I relied on my grandfather for help. Grandpa liked memorizing quotations, and he had one ready for just about everything. For example, just before I played in my first middle school football game, he handed me a piece of paper that said, "When you've got something to prove, there's nothing greater than a challenge." Another one of his favorites was "Kites rise highest against the wind, not with it." I remembered that specific quote on the night I sat with my family in the hospital. Grandpa was awake, but he couldn't move his left side, and he couldn't speak. As he tried to form words, there was a fear in his eyes that I had never seen before. I'm sure he had seen it in mine with each childhood challenge that I'd met. Now the roles were turned. <u>That night, I faced the greatest challenge of my life: helping my grandfather recover from his stroke.</u>
>
> The first thing I did was collect quotations that I thought Grandpa would like. I found dozens of them about challenge, adversity, health, and any other topics that I thought would encourage him. Then I printed out each

The **beginning** paragraph describes the challenge and states the thesis (underlined).

Each **middle** paragraph explains the steps the writer took to meet the challenge.

quotation on a card until I had a stack of them. I planned to use those cards to encourage my grandfather to fight against his illness.

I read the quotations to him and reminded him of how he'd always used quotations to encourage me. Then I got the bright idea that I'd try to get Grandpa to read them aloud as a part of his speech therapy. We worked together. I made a game out of it, and because Grandpa loved a good challenge, he worked hard. Slowly, his speech improved.

The most important thing that I did to face this challenge was to face it with strength. There were days when I was frustrated that Grandpa wasn't the way that he used to be. At times, I was angry with him because I thought that he wasn't working hard enough. Some of the time, I wanted to give up. I hung in there, though, and it took a lot of patience. I grew stronger with each small bit of progress, as well as each setback.

The **final** paragraph explains how the writer was changed by the challenge.

Due to determination and a lot of hard work on both our parts, Grandpa got better. As he did, our relationship changed. The challenge of facing my grandfather's illness and helping him learn to speak again was a rite of passage for me. I had done a lot of growing up. I was no longer a boy relying on my grandfather for help whenever I faced an unfamiliar or unpleasant experience. Grandpa and I were equals now. We had become two men helping each other through the rough spots of life.

Expository

Write

Practice responding to an expository prompt. Review the prompt you chose from page 194, reminding yourself of the STRAP questions and the graphic organizer you have created. Then write a response to the prompt in the amount of time your teacher gives you.

Revising Improving Your Response

Most writing tests allow you to make corrections to improve your work, though you should find out ahead of time how many are allowed. Always make changes and corrections as neatly as possible. If the test allows revising and editing, use the STRAP questions to guide your changes.

Subject: Does my response focus on the topic in the prompt? Do my main points support my thesis?

Type: Have I followed the correct form (essay, letter, article)?

Role: Have I assumed the position indicated in the prompt?

Audience: Have I used the right level of language for my audience?

Purpose: Does my writing accomplish the goal set forth in the prompt?

Improve your work. Reread your response, asking yourself the STRAP questions above. Make neat changes in the time your teacher allows.

Editing Checking Your Response

Check your response for punctuation, capitalization, spelling, and grammar errors. Careless errors can confuse the reader.

Conventions

_____ **1.** Have I used end punctuation for every sentence?

_____ **2.** Have I capitalized all proper nouns and the first word of each sentence?

_____ **3.** Have I checked my spelling?

_____ **4.** Do my subjects and verbs agree (*it does,* not *it do*)?

_____ **5.** Have I used the right word (*there, they're, their*)?

Check your conventions. Review your response for punctuation, capitalization, spelling, and grammar errors. Make neat corrections in the time your teacher allows.

> "If you can read your writing to yourself without wincing, you have probably gotten it right."
>
> —George V. Higgins

Expository Writing on Tests

Use the following tips as a guide whenever you respond to an expository writing prompt.

Before you write . . .

- **Understand the prompt.**
  Review the STRAP questions listed on page **194**.
  Remember that an expository prompt asks you to *explain*.
- **Plan your time wisely.**
  Spend several minutes making notes and planning before starting to write. Use a graphic organizer. (See page **195**.)

As you write . . .

- **Decide on a focus or thesis for your response.**
  Keep your main idea or purpose in mind as you write.
- **Be selective.**
  Use examples and explanations that directly support your focus.
- **End in a meaningful way.**
  Remind the reader about the importance of the topic.

After you've written a first draft . . .

- **Check for completeness.**
  Use the STRAP questions on page **198** to revise your work.
- **Check for correctness.**
  Check your punctuation, capitalization, spelling, and grammar.

 Plan and write a response. Analyze one of the prompts below, using the STRAP questions. Then plan and write a response. Complete your work in the time your teacher gives you.

Expository Prompts

- Good parents or guardians demonstrate many valuable qualities. Choose three qualities of a good parent or guardian and write an essay that includes examples to support your choices.
- The German poet Johann Wolfgang von Goethe said, "There is nothing insignificant in the world. It all depends on the point of view." Explain why it is important to see a situation from another person's point of view.

Expository

www.hmheducation.com/writesource

Persuasive Writing

Writing Focus

Problem-Solution Essay **201**

Writing an Editorial **239**

Responding to Persuasive Prompts **247**

Grammar Focus

Pronoun-Antecedent Agreement **230**

Avoiding Double Subjects **231**

Academic Vocabulary

Working with a classmate, read the definitions below and discuss possible answers to each question.

1. When you convince people of something, you lead them to agree with your or believe you.
   How could you convince your parents that you've finished your homework?

2. An argument is a course of reasoning for or against something.
   Has a persuasive argument ever changed your mind about something? Explain.

3. Insight is the ability to understand something or the outcome of understanding it.
   How can you gain insight into cultures different from your own?

4. Something that is precise is exact and clearly expressed.
   Why do you need to be precise when you give directions to a particular location?

Persuasive Writing
Problem-Solution Essay

The world is full of problems, from big ones like global warming to smaller ones like giving skateboarders a safe place to practice their sport. The world is also full of potential solutions. People everywhere have opinions about solving the world's problems. You probably do, too. But convincing people to accept your solutions can be a challenge.

One way to persuade people to accept your solution is to write a problem-solution essay. To write an effective problem-solution essay, you must accomplish two goals. First, explain the problem clearly so that your audience understands it. Second, use facts and reasoning to convince the audience that your solution is the best one.

In this chapter, you'll write a problem-solution essay that tackles a social, political, or environmental problem.

Writing Guidelines

Subject: A social, political, or environmental problem
Form: Problem-solution essay
Purpose: To convince people to accept your solution
Audience: Classmates and community members

"A problem is a chance for you to do your best."
—Duke Ellington

Persuasive Writing Warm-Up: Finding Problems

People often say "The problem with the world today is . . ." but rarely say "The solution is . . ." When you write a problem-solution paragraph, you have to complete both sentences. Jules brainstormed paragraph topics by completing these sentences four times.

Sentence Completion

The **problem** with the world today is . . .	extremists.
The **solution** is . . .	moderate people should stand up and take charge.
The **problem** with the world today is . . .	too much testing in schools.
The **solution** is . . .	teachers should find other ways to measure progress.
The **problem** with the world today is . . .	third-world countries can't compete.
The **solution** is . . .	third-world debt relief.
The **problem** with the world today is . . .	globalization causes child labor.
The **solution** is . . .	enforce the UN rules on the rights of the child.

Try It!

Complete the sentence starters above three or four times. Then select one problem and solution that you would like to write a paragraph about. Conduct some research to help you explain the problem and promote your solution.

Writing a Problem-Solution Paragraph

A problem-solution paragraph explains a current problem and promotes a specific way to solve the problem. It includes effective details to support the solution. A problem-solution paragraph has three parts:

- The **topic sentence** states the problem and proposes the solution.
- The **body sentences** promote the solution.
- The **closing sentence** calls to implement the solution.

Sample Persuasive Paragraph

Jules wrote the following paragraph about the United Nations Conventions on the Rights of the Child.

The **topic sentence** names the problem and solution.

The **body sentences** promote the solution.

The **closing sentence** calls to implement the solution.

Certain Inalienable Rights

As globalization sends more children into sweatshops and the flesh trade, it's time for the United States to ratify the United Nations Conventions on the Rights of the Child (CRC). This piece of legislation was created in 1989 to protect those under the age of 18 against bonded labor (slavery) and labor that is dangerous or that interferes with education. The CRC also protects children from being tried as adults or executed. Most of the United Nations member countries have ratified these conventions, but the United States has not. The reasons relate to conflicts with some state laws and a concern that the United States not be beholden to foreign powers. However, in this time of globalization, the United States buys huge quantities of goods from third-world nations in which child labor is rampant. The best way to stop this practice is for the United States to ratify the CRC and enforce it not only within its own shores, but also in its selection of trade partners.

Persuasive

Write a problem-solution paragraph. Review the sample paragraph above and then write your own problem-solution paragraph on the topic you selected on page 202.

Understanding Your Goal

Your goal in this chapter is to write a well-organized persuasive essay that explains a problem and convinces the reader to accept your solution. The traits listed in the chart below will help you plan and write your essay. The rubric for persuasive writing on pages 234–235 will also guide you.

Traits of Persuasive Writing

- **Ideas**
  Use facts and reasoning to explain a problem and defend a solution.

- **Organization**
  Create a beginning that introduces the problem and states your solution, a middle that provides support and answers an objection, and an ending that restates your solution.

- **Voice**
  Use a persuasive voice that is appropriate for your topic and audience.

- **Word Choice**
  Choose the most effective words to construct a convincing argument.

- **Sentence Fluency**
  Write clear, complete sentences with varied beginnings.

- **Conventions**
  Check your writing for errors in capitalization, punctuation, spelling, and grammar.

Literature Connections: In his essay "Tolerance," E. M. Forster argues that tolerance, not love, is the solution to big problems faced by post–World War II society.

"Opinions are made to be changed or how is truth to be got at?"

—Lord Byron

Problem-Solution Essay

A problem-solution essay clearly explains a problem and then proposes a solution. In this sample essay, the student writer defends his solution to the problem of the world's dwindling oil supply.

Conservation Can Prevent an Oil Crisis

Beginning
The beginning introduces the problem and proposes a solution (underlined).

Gasoline continues to become more and more expensive. The reason is simple—the world's oil supply is slowly being used up. People are using more oil than ever. In fact, many economists are worried that an oil crisis might happen. If it did, prices of gasoline, home heating oil, and many other products would rise quickly. People would struggle to heat their homes and buy gas for their cars. Businesses would slow production—or even close down. And the world might even experience an economic depression. <u>However, there is a way to prevent an oil crisis—conserve oil.</u>

Middle
The first middle paragraph uses facts to explain the problem.

The world's appetite for oil is huge. In 2005, people in the United States used more than 20 million barrels of oil per day to fuel cars, heat homes, and make plastics, clothing, and paint ("International"). The United States government estimates current trends show world wide energy usage will go from 80 million barrels a day in 2003 to 98 million barrels a day by 2015. Unless people learn how to conserve, the demand for oil will soon exceed the supply. To avoid a crisis, we must all do our best to conserve oil.

The second, third, and fourth middle paragraphs add reasons in support of the solution.

Oil conservation makes sense for many reasons. First of all, oil conservation will help to preserve a valuable resource. In 2003, the average passenger vehicle in the United States got about 22 miles per gallon ("Motor"). Today's fuel-efficient vehicles can get more than 30 miles per gallon (Stanton). If everyone chose a higher-mileage vehicle, cut out unnecessary car trips, and took public transportation whenever possible, the United States would save millions of barrels of oil every day. That, in turn, would help the nation's oil supply last longer.

Conserving oil also helps to protect the environment. Automobiles, home oil burners, and other oil-consuming technologies contribute to air pollution and global warming. When oil and gasoline are burned, polluting gases are released into the atmosphere. One of these gases, carbon dioxide, may cause global warming. Using less oil for transportation and home heating will reduce air pollution and the effects of global warming.

Finally, conserving oil can save consumers money. Conservation decreases demand for oil, which causes prices of gasoline, heating oil, and other petroleum-based products to drop, or at least to increase at a slower rate. Conservation also saves consumers money directly. At $3 per gallon, using 10 fewer gallons would save $30. Decreased usage increases savings.

Some people say that the best way to prevent an oil crisis is to drill more oil wells (Parrish 86). That might help, but it's a short-term solution. No one knows how much oil is left. However, it is a fact that the supply is limited. Drilling might increase supplies for a while, but conservation is smarter. It makes the most of the available oil supply.

Gasoline is expensive now, but in the future it could cost $5 per gallon or more. If people don't act now to conserve oil, these prices could come soon. Conserving oil not only stretches oil supplies and saves consumers money but also cuts pollution. Everyone can help. Drivers can avoid gas-guzzling SUV's and opt for more fuel-efficient cars. Homeowners can insulate their homes and turn down their thermostats in the winter. Everyone can play a part in preventing an oil crisis.

> The last middle paragraph addresses an objection.

> **Ending**
> The ending restates the solution and gives the reader something to think about.

Respond to the reading. Answer the following questions.

Ideas (1) What are three reasons the writer gives for conserving oil?

Organization (2) Which paragraph explains the problem in detail? (3) Which paragraph begins to explain the proposed solution?

Voice & Word Choice (4) Does the writer sound knowledgeable and persuasive? Explain.

Prewriting

In prewriting, you will select a social, political, or environmental problem that affects people, gather reasons and details to support a solution, and organize your ideas. Careful prewriting makes persuasive writing easier and more effective.

Keys to Effective Prewriting

1. Choose a problem that affects people. Decide on a solution to the problem.

2. Gather the best reasons and details to support your solution.

3. Address an important objection.

4. Write a clear position statement to guide your writing.

5. Create a list or an outline as a planning guide.

Persuasive

Prewriting Selecting a Problem

Problems are a part of life. To find a writing topic, student writer Guerdy Regis answered two key questions about problems that affect the people in her town and in other communities. After reviewing her answers, she marked the problem that she would like to write about with an asterisk. Then she stated her solution to the problem.

List of Problems

What problems have been covered in the news?
- global warming and its damage to the environment
- the increasing cost of health care
- the growth of hunger in the United States*
- a decline in the number of people who vote

What social, environmental, or political problems have we discussed in class?
- increased crime in our state
- the reemergence and spread of tuberculosis
- a lack of good jobs for factory workers

Solution to hunger in the United States: *The best way to solve the hunger crisis in the United States is to support local food banks.*

Prewrite

Choose a topic. On your own paper, answer each of the questions above in two or three different ways. Then put an asterisk next to the problem that you feel most strongly about. Also write a sentence that summarizes your solution to the problem.

Focus on the Traits

Ideas Choose a solution that you can defend with several clear, convincing reasons. You may have to do some research before you can identify a strong solution. The more knowledge you have about your topic, the easier it will be to defend your solution.

Gathering Reasons to Support Your Solution

After you have chosen a problem and stated your solution, you need to gather reasons to support the solution. Guerdy used a chart to gather reasons that support her solution.

Reasons Chart

Solution: The best way to solve this country's hunger crisis is to support local food banks.

Reasons	Supporting Details
Food banks do a great job of getting food to the people who need it.	– 23 million served in 2001 – food banks know local situation – many people work with food banks – food banks deliver food
Food banks help businesses and the environment.	– accept food from restaurants and other businesses – save businesses money – keep food out of waste stream
Food banks are economically efficient.	– use volunteers – don't require fancy offices or tons of paperwork

Prewrite

Create a reasons chart. Create your own reasons chart, identifying at least three reasons to support your solution. Also include details that support each reason.

Focus on the Traits

Organization Persuasive essays are often organized by order of importance. After you have finished your chart, consider ranking your reasons from least important to most important. This ranking will help you do some early planning for your essay.

Persuasive

Prewriting Gathering Objections

When you present your solution to a problem, it is wise to defend it against at least one strong objection. Such a strategy can make your position even more convincing. How can you anticipate the objections? Start with a little research.

- Read local newspapers and monitor local television and radio news reports to find arguments that both support and oppose your solution.
- Think of class discussions. Recall any objections classmates had to your solution.
- Ask the opinions of your friends and family. See if you can identify their objections and work to overcome them.

While researching her topic, Guerdy found the following three objections to her solution. She put an asterisk next to the strongest objection.

> – Food banks already have plenty of support.
> – Government programs like food stamps provide all the help people need.*
> – Not many people in the United States use food banks.

Gather objections. Use the strategies above to gather and list three objections to your solution. Put an asterisk next to the strongest objection.

Countering an Objection

Countering an objection simply means arguing against it. Guerdy listed three reasons for disagreeing with the objection she chose to address.

> **Objection:** Government programs like food stamps provide all the help people need.*
>
> 1. Even with food stamps, the hunger problem has grown.
> 2. Despite government help, millions of people still visit food banks.
> 3. Applying for food stamps takes time. Some people need food right away.

Counter an important objection. Write down the strongest objection to your argument. List several reasons why you disagree with it.

Writing

You have chosen a problem, proposed a solution, developed support for it, and identified an objection to address. Now you are ready to write.

Keys to Effective Writing

1. Write on every other line or double-space on the computer to make room for changes later on.

2. Introduce the problem and state your solution in the beginning.

3. Provide background information about the problem and the reasons for your solution in the middle paragraphs.

4. Include specific details to support your reasons.

5. Address an important objection.

6. Reemphasize your solution in the ending part.

Persuasive

Writing Getting the Big Picture

The graphic below shows how the elements of a problem-solution essay should fit together. Use this graphic and your prewriting plan to guide the writing of your first draft. (The examples are from the student essay on pages 213–216.)

Beginning

The **beginning** introduces the problem and proposes a solution.

Thesis Statement
People can help end hunger in this country by supporting local food banks.

Middle

The **middle** paragraphs explain the problem and supply reasons for supporting the solution.

Topic Sentences
Hunger affects people in the United States, and the problem is worsening.

First and foremost, food banks deserve support because they know how to put food in the hands of the people who need it.

In addition, food banks operate in a very efficient way.

Lastly, food banks serve the environment well.

Some people argue that food banks are not necessary.

Ending

The **ending** restates the solution to the problem, sums up the supporting reasons, and offers a final important thought.

Closing Sentence
After all, everyone deserves at least one good meal a day.

Starting Your Essay

The beginning paragraph of your problem-solution essay should capture the reader's attention, outline the problem, and propose a solution. Here is a three-step process that will help you write your beginning paragraph.

- **Begin with a powerful opening sentence.**
  Capture the reader's attention with a dramatic idea.
  Every day, needless hunger devastates families in the United States.

- **Lead up to your thesis statement.**
  Add a few ideas that help the reader appreciate the problem.
  What is it like to be hungry? How does it feel? Initially, . . .

- **State your thesis.**
  Your thesis statement proposes your solution to the problem.
  People can help end hunger in this country by supporting local food banks.

Beginning Paragraph

> The problem is introduced.

> The writer proposes a solution (underlined).

Every day, needless hunger devastates families in the United States. What is it like to be hungry? How does it feel? Initially, the stomach starts to rumble, and the mouth waters. Then thoughts of food fill the mind. It becomes hard to concentrate. Most people head for the kitchen or the cafeteria, find some food, and the hunger is history. Now what if there is no food in sight? Sadly, millions of men, women, and children in this country face hunger every day. <u>People can help end hunger in this country by supporting local food banks.</u>

Write a beginning paragraph for your essay. Use dramatic, engaging language to introduce the problem and propose a solution (in your opinion statement).

"Write visually, write clearly, and make every word count."

—Gloria D. Miklowitz

Writing Developing the Middle Part

The middle part of your essay defines the problem in detail and provides the main reasons that support your solution. Begin each paragraph with a topic sentence, and then add details that support it. Also address an objection in the last middle paragraph.

Beginning

Middle

Ending

Using Transitions

Transitions move your essay smoothly from one paragraph to the next. They can also show the order of importance of your ideas. The following chart includes transitions that could connect your middle paragraphs.

Paragraph 1	Paragraph 2	Paragraph 3
First of all ———→	Also ——————————→	The best reason
One reason ———→	Another reason ——→	Most importantly
First and foremost ——→	In addition ———→	Lastly

Middle Paragraphs

> **Facts and statistics define the problem.**
>
> **A topic sentence introduces each middle paragraph (underlined).**

<u>Hunger affects people in the United States, and the problem is worsening.</u> In 2000, about 33 million Americans did not know how or where they would get the food they needed to stay healthy ("Current"). By 2007, that number had grown to 38 million. Hunger affects people in many ways. Children who are hungry have a harder time learning, and they may experience delays in physical development. Hunger affects the health of grown-ups, too, and makes it harder for them to work and care for their families (Wiseman).

<u>First and foremost, food banks deserve support because they know how to put food in the hands of the people who need it.</u> In 2006, one network of food banks across the United States collected, stored, and distributed enough food to feed 25 million hungry people ("2nd Harvest"). It's a massive effort that has been going on for years. Because food banks are local, they often know where

to locate and how to reach out to people who need food. People often feel more comfortable visiting a local food bank than they do applying for assistance from a government agency.

In addition, food banks operate in a very efficient way. Because they rely largely on donations and the work of volunteers, food banks keep their costs low. That means money donated to a food bank isn't wasted. For example, the Davis City Food Bank uses 90 cents of every dollar donated to buy food for hungry men, women, and children.

Lastly, food banks serve the environment well. Every day, grocery stores, restaurants, and other businesses throw out tons of unneeded food or food beyond its expiration date. This food is safe and edible but often ends up in landfills. Many food banks now work to collect this food and redistribute it to hungry people. The process also keeps food from being wasted and filling landfills. Businesses can save money, too. Instead of paying a trash hauler to take away the food they don't need, businesses can have the food bank pick up the food for free.

Some people argue that food banks are not necessary. They think that government programs such as food stamps are enough to ease the hunger problem. However, not all the people who need food qualify for government programs, and applying for government help can take time. Hungry people need to be fed when they are hungry, and food banks do just that. Also, even with government programs, the hunger problem has escalated. Without food banks, the problem will only keep getting worse.

> **Each middle paragraph explores a reason that supports the solution.**

> **The fifth middle paragraph counters an objection.**

Persuasive

Write

Write your middle paragraphs. Create middle paragraphs that define the problem and give the reasons that support your solution. Start each paragraph with a topic sentence and follow with details that support it. Your final middle paragraph should respond to a significant objection.

Writing Ending Your Essay

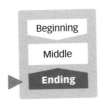

Beginning

Middle

Ending

The main part of your essay should define the problem, propose a solution, and defend the solution using solid reasons. When all of that information is in place, you are ready to write your ending. Your ending paragraph should do all of the following things:

- Restate your solution to the problem.
- Summarize the main reasons that support your solution.
- Make a call to action and/or give the reader an important final insight.

Ending Paragraph

The solution is restated.

A call to action is made.

A final insight is provided.

> Supporting local food banks is the best way to help ease the hunger problem. Individuals can provide support by volunteering their services or by donating money or food. In either case, hungry people get the food they need, and surplus food gets used. Concerned citizens should contact their local food banks today and offer their help because government programs can't do enough. By backing food banks, people can help to alleviate hunger in this country. After all, everyone deserves at least one good meal a day.

Write

Write your ending paragraph and prepare a complete first draft. Use the ideas listed above as a guide to develop your final paragraph. Then prepare a copy of your entire essay. Write on every other line or double-space on the computer. This will give you room for revising.

Try It!

If you have followed the traditional persuasive essay structure, your first draft should have turned out well. That structure includes four parts:

1. Introduce the problem and state your opinion (solution).
2. Support your opinion.
3. Answer an objection.
4. Wrap up your argument.

To make sure that your essay is complete, mark each paragraph with the correct number—a 1 next to your opening paragraph, a 2 next to each supporting paragraph, and so on.

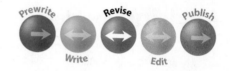

Revising

Revising is the process of improving a first draft. When you revise, you add or delete details, rearrange parts of your writing, and work on developing a more convincing, persuasive voice. You also check your word choice and sentence fluency.

Keys to Effective Revising

1. After setting your first draft aside for a day or two, read it through to get a feeling for how well your essay works.

2. Be sure you have clearly stated the problem and your solution.

3. Check your paragraphs. They should have topic sentences followed by supporting details in logical order.

4. Be sure you've used an authoritative, respectful voice.

5. Check your writing for precise nouns and direct, active verbs.

6. Be sure you have used different kinds of sentences with varied beginnings.

Persuasive

Revising for Ideas

6 My problem is presented effectively and compelling reasons support my solution.

5 I explain an important problem, and my solution is supported with logical reasons.

4 I state a problem, and most of my reasons support my solution.

When you revise for *ideas*, be sure you have clearly explained the problem and convincingly argued for your solution. Use the rubric strip above to guide your revision.

Have I effectively explained the problem?

You have effectively explained the problem if the reader understands its importance. Make sure to use revealing facts and details in your explanation.

- **Use facts and statistics to make the problem clear and show its significance.**

    In 2000, about 33 million Americans did not know how or where they would get all the food they needed to stay healthy.

- **Explain how the problem affects people.**

    Children who are hungry have a harder time learning, and they may experience delays in physical development.

Try It!

Read the paragraph below. How would you revise the paragraph to more effectively explain the problem of soda consumption?

1   Increased consumption of soda is causing problems for students at
2   Centerville High. More and more kids are drinking soda. Not many kids
3   are drinking water, juice, and milk. While milk and juice have important
4   nutrients, soda does not. According to Ms. Barton, our school nurse, that
5   is bad news for kids' health.

Make the problem clear. Read your essay. If necessary, add facts and statistics that help to explain your problem and reveal its effects on people.

Revise

"I've noticed those with the most opinions often have the fewest facts."

—Bethania McKenstry

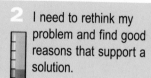

3 I need a more important problem and more convincing reasons to support my solution.

2 I need to rethink my problem and find good reasons that support a solution.

1 I need to learn how to present a problem and support a solution.

Have I convincingly argued for my solution?

You have convincingly argued for your solution if you have included compelling reasons supported by provable facts. The following exercise can help you decide how well you have supported your solution.

Use the following checklist to review the quality of your argument.

_____ **1.** Do I still believe in the solution I propose? Explain.

_____ **2.** Do I have three compelling reasons to support my solution? Underline each one.

_____ **3.** Do I have provable facts to support each reason? Check the accuracy of each fact.

_____ **4.** Do I effectively counter a main objection? Circle that part.

Check your essay. If you answered "no" to any of the statements above, revise your essay as necessary to strengthen your argument.

Revise

Persuasive

Ideas Adding provable facts makes the solution more convincing.

In addition, food banks operate in a very efficient way. Because they rely largely on donations and the work of volunteers, food banks keep their costs low. That means money donated to a food bank isn't wasted~~on paying large~~ ~~salaries to employees, or furnishing fancy offices. Instead,~~ ~~money provides food~~ for hungry men, women, and children.

For example, the Davis City Food Bank uses 90 cents of every dollar donated to buy food

Revising for Organization

6 All of the parts of my essay work together to build to a thoughtful, convincing solution.

5 My overall organization is clear, and my reasons lead effectively to the solution.

4 Most parts of my essay are organized well except for one part.

When you revise for *organization*, you check the structure of your essay. You make sure that the beginning, middle, and ending parts form a meaningful whole. Use the rubric strip above as a guide in your revising.

Do I have an effective beginning paragraph?

You have an effective beginning paragraph if you grab the reader's attention, provide information that identifies the topic (the problem), and state your opinion.

Flowchart

The Elements of a Beginning		
Capture the reader's attention. →	Identify the topic (problem). →	State your opinion (a solution).

Try It!

Rewrite the paragraph below, improving its organization. Use the flowchart above as your guide to complete your work.

> During rush hour, more than 4,000 cars travel down Elm Street. The best solution to the traffic problem is to widen the Elm Street Bridge so that additional lanes can be added. The bridge is only one lane wide with stoplights at either end. Last Thursday, a huge traffic jam on the Elm Street Bridge tied up traffic for four hours! Even on the best day, traffic rolls over the bridge very slowly.

Revise

Check the beginning of your essay. If the beginning of your essay is missing any elements, add them. If any elements seem out of place, put them in the correct order.

3 I need to reorganize the middle part of my essay to build to the ending.

2 I need to include a beginning, a middle, and an ending in my essay.

1 I need to learn how to organize a problem-solution essay.

Does my ending accomplish its purpose?

The ending part of your essay accomplishes its purpose if you sum up your position, review the supporting reasons, and give the reader a final insight. To build a strong ending, use the following strategy.

- First, restate your solution to the problem.
- Next, summarize the reasons that support your solution.
- If necessary, briefly restate your answer to an objection.
- Finally, leave the reader with something to think about.

Check the organization of your ending. Make sure all of the elements are present and in the correct order. Revise your ending to add or rearrange elements.

Revise

Persuasive

Organization
A summarizing detail is added.

A final sentence gives the reader something to think about.

    Supporting local food banks is the best way to help

ease the hunger problem. Individuals can provide support
                or by donating money or food
by volunteering their services. In either case, hungry

people get the food they need, and surplus food gets used.

Concerned citizens should contact their local food banks

today and offer their help because government programs

can't do enough. By backing food banks, people can help to
            After all, everyone deserves at least one good meal a day.
alleviate hunger in this country.

Revising for Voice

6 My knowledgeable voice creates total confidence in my solution.

5 My voice respects my audience, and my use of facts gives my voice authority.

4 My voice respects my audience, but I need to use more facts to sound knowledgeable.

In order to convince people to support your solution, you need to use an authoritative, reasonable *voice*. Use the rubric strip above as your guide.

Have I used an authoritative voice?

You have used an authoritative voice if you sound knowledgeable and sincere rather than too emotional. Your voice is not authoritative if you use weak, general statements. One way to improve your voice is to include plenty of specific facts in your essay.

Less Authoritative Voice

When a supertanker spills oil, it damages the ocean. It damages beaches, too. The damage caused by an oil spill can last a long time. And it can cost a lot to clean up.

More Authoritative Voice

A supertanker accident can spill as much as 2 million barrels of oil into the ocean. Oil spills cause incredible damage. In 1989, the supertanker *Exxon Valdez* spilled 527,000 barrels of oil. The oil killed thousands of sea birds, hundreds of sea otters, and contaminated 1,300 miles of shoreline. Nine years later, much of that shoreline was still contaminated with oil. Exxon spent $2.1 billion on its cleanup efforts.

Revise

For more authority, add facts. Review your essay. Does your voice sound authoritative? If it doesn't, replace weak, general statements with reliable, specific facts.

"When your writing is filled with details, it has a lot more impact."

—Ivan Levison

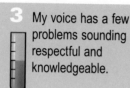

3 My voice has a few problems sounding respectful and knowledgeable.

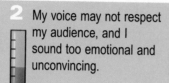

2 My voice may not respect my audience, and I sound too emotional and unconvincing.

1 I need to learn how to create a respectful, knowledgeable voice.

Do I treat my reader with respect?

You have treated your reader with respect if you don't use overly emotional or aggressive language. Using such language may make the reader feel as if he or she were being attacked. In addition, ridiculing people who oppose your solution is one way to lose an argument.

In the following paragraph, a writer uses an unreasonable, overly aggressive voice to propose a solution.

> **Some people think the Elm Street Bridge doesn't need to be widened to four lanes. They must have rocks in their heads. Get a clue! If the bridge isn't widened, people will continue to sit in traffic forever. Widening the bridge is the only solution.**

Try It!

Rewrite the paragraph above so that it sounds respectful and reasonable. Trade papers with a classmate. Discuss each other's changes.

Revise

Check your voice for respect. Review your essay, making sure that you don't sound too emotional or aggressive in parts. Revise as needed.

Voice
An aggressive sentence is deleted and an overemotional one is revised.

Some people argue that food banks are not necessary. They think that government programs such as food stamps are enough to ease the hunger problem. ~~That's completely ridiculous.~~ However, not all the people who need food qualify for government programs, and applying for government help can take time. ~~takes forever!~~

Revising for Word Choice

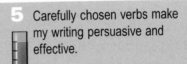
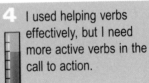

6 My words make a powerful case as I present my problem and solution.

5 Carefully chosen verbs make my writing persuasive and effective.

4 I used helping verbs effectively, but I need more active verbs in the call to action.

Checking for word choice means making sure you have chosen the most effective words to make your argument. For example, carefully chosen helping verbs can express opinions and even encourage people to act. The rubric strip above can help you check *word choice*.

Have I expressed my opinion using helping verbs?

You have used helping verbs effectively if your opinion statements include words like *should* and *would*.

Making a Recommendation

People who want lower taxes should vote **for the new town budget.**
(*Should* is often used to recommend action or to appeal to a sense of duty.)

Looking Toward the Future

If people would eat better and exercise more**, health-care costs** would not be **so high.**
(*Would* is often used to express what the future might be like if people take action.)

Exercise

Read the paragraph below. Add the helping verbs *should* and *would* to help the writer express an opinion.

1 Students who want better-tasting, more-nutritious food served in
2 the cafeteria _____ participate in Tuesday's Food Forum. If everyone _____
3 share their ideas about better food choices, the school nutritionists _____
4 be able to create new menu options that everyone can enjoy.

Revise

Use helping verbs to express an opinion. Review your essay carefully. Where possible, use helping verbs such as *should* and *would* to express your opinion.

3 I need to add some helping verbs and use more direct verbs.

 2 I need to use helping verbs and direct verbs.

1 I need to learn how to use verbs to state an opinion and make a call to action.

Have I used direct, active verbs to get the reader to act?

You have used direct, active verbs if they clearly state the action you want people to take. The verbs in the following statement clearly tell the reader what actions to take: *Meet* with your counselor today and *plan* your schedule.

 Try It!

Read the paragraph below. Rewrite it using active verbs that clearly tell the reader what actions to take.

Anyone who wants to help can come to the senior citizens center on Saturday morning. You can help paint the recreation room. You can work on repairing the front steps. Or you can even plant some shrubs in the front yard. The people who use the center will be glad you did.

Revise

Review your call to action. Be sure you have used direct, active verbs to make your call to action. Revise as needed.

Persuasive

Word Choice
Direct, active verbs make the position stronger.

A helping verb is added to a statement of opinion.

In either case, hungry people get the food they need, and surplus food gets used. Concerned citizens ∧should contact their ~~your~~ local food banks today and offer∧their ~~your~~ help because government programs can't do enough. By backing food banks, people can help to alleviate∧ ~~stop~~ hunger in this country. After all, everyone deserves∧ ~~should get~~ at least one good meal a day.

Revising for Sentence Fluency

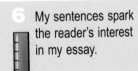
6 My sentences spark the reader's interest in my essay.

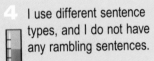
5 I have skillfully used a variety of sentence types.

4 I use different sentence types, and I do not have any rambling sentences.

When you revise for *sentence fluency*, you check to see that you have used different kinds of sentences and that they flow smoothly. You also fix any rambling sentences. The rubric strip above can help you revise.

Have I written any rambling sentences?

You have written rambling sentences if you have used too many *and*'s to connect ideas. To fix a rambling sentence, take out some of the conjunctions to form separate, shorter sentences as needed.

Rambling Sentence

We will begin the Children's Education Project next month and we will make our schools stronger and the children will benefit right away and if we delay accepting the project, we could lose funding and we would have to rewrite the entire grant next year.

Corrected Sentences

We will begin the Children's Education Project next month. Doing so will make our schools stronger, and the children will benefit right away. If we delay accepting the project, we could lose funding, which would require rewriting the entire grant next year.

Try It!

Rewrite the following rambling sentence.

Creating a new park in Brandon will offer more recreation opportunities and it will give kids safe options for having fun and these benefits can only happen if you vote yes and so you should go to the polls this Tuesday and vote for the new park.

Revise

Eliminate rambling sentences. Read your essay carefully and revise any rambling sentences.

3 I use different types of sentences, but I need to eliminate rambling sentences.

 2 Most of my sentences are the same type and some sentences ramble on and on.

 1 I need to use different types of sentences and learn to correct rambling sentences.

Have I used different kinds of sentences?

You have used different kinds of sentences if your essay contains a mix of declarative, imperative, and interrogative sentences.

- Declarative sentences make a statement. The problem is worsening.
- Imperative sentences make commands. Imagine that you are hungry.
- Interrogative sentences ask questions. What is it like to be hungry?

 ## Exercise

In the following paragraph, identify each kind of sentence. Explain how sentence variety makes the paragraph more effective.

1 Supporting the clean-water initiative will stop the spread of cholera.
2 What is cholera? It's an intestinal disease that is caused by bacteria in
3 contaminated water. And how dangerous is it? If left untreated, cholera is
4 deadly. So support the clean-water initiative. For people in many parts of
5 the world, clean water often means the difference between life and death.

 Revise for sentence variety. Review your essay, checking to see if you have used different kinds of sentences.

Revise

Persuasive

Sentence Fluency
Three sentences are reworked as questions.

Every day, needless hunger devastates families in the
    What is it like to be hungry?
United States. ∧ ~~You probably have never been really hungry.~~

How does it feel? Initially, the stomach starts to rumble . . .
    Now what if there is no food in sight?
∧ ~~Some people don't have that ability.~~

Revising Improving Your Writing

Revise

Check your revising. On a piece of paper, write the numbers 1 to 10. If you answer "yes" to a question, put a check mark next to that number. If not, continue to work on that part of your essay.

Revising Checklist

Ideas

_____ **1.** Do I clearly explain a significant problem?

_____ **2.** Do I use solid reasons to argue for the solution?

Organization

_____ **3.** Does my beginning cover the necessary elements?

_____ **4.** Does my ending bring my essay to an effective close?

Voice

_____ **5.** Do I use an authoritative voice?

_____ **6.** Do I treat the reader with respect?

Word Choice

_____ **7.** Do I use helping verbs to express opinions?

_____ **8.** Do I use direct, active verbs to make calls to action?

Sentence Fluency

_____ **9.** Have I fixed any rambling sentences?

_____ **10.** Do I use different kinds of sentences?

Revise

Make a clean copy. When you are finished revising, make a clean copy of your essay to edit for conventions.

Editing

When you have finished revising your problem-solution essay, it is time to edit for conventions: punctuation, capitalization, spelling, and grammar.

Keys to Effective Editing

1. Use a dictionary, a thesaurus, and the "Proofreader's Guide" in the back of this book to check your writing.

2. Check your writing for correct punctuation, capitalization, spelling, and grammar.

3. Have a classmate edit your writing. You are too close to your writing to catch everything.

4. If you are using a computer, edit your essay on a printed copy and then key in the changes. Otherwise, write a new, final handwritten copy that includes the changes.

5. Use the editing and proofreading marks inside the back cover of this book.

Editing for Conventions

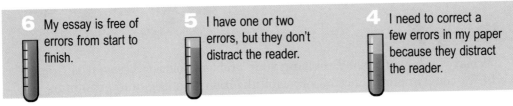

6 My essay is free of errors from start to finish.

5 I have one or two errors, but they don't distract the reader.

4 I need to correct a few errors in my paper because they distract the reader.

Editing for *conventions* means checking punctuation, capitalization, spelling, and grammar. The rubric strip above can help guide your editing.

How can I check for pronoun-antecedent agreement?

You can check for pronoun-antecedent agreement if you remember that a pronoun and its antecedent must agree in three ways. (See pages **704–705** for more information.)

Agreement in Person

If people **want transportation to improve,** they **should start taking the subway.**
(The third-person pronoun *they* agrees with the antecedent *people.*)

Agreement in Number

Before a person **votes,** he or she **should consider the consequences.**
(The singular pronoun *he* or *she* agrees with the antecedent *person.*)

Agreement in Gender

Susan Wells **helped raise money for the hospital, and** she **is glad** she **did.**
(The feminine pronoun *she* agrees with the antecedent *Susan Wells.*)

Grammar Exercise

Read the following sentences. If necessary, correct the pronouns so that they agree with their antecedents in person, number, and gender. (You may need to change a verb, too.)

1. The members of the school board announced his decision.
2. If people want to help, you should donate usable clothing.
3. Every person can come to the meeting if they so choose.
4. When a person volunteers, they feel good.
5. The woman went to the debate so they could register voters.

Edit

Check for pronoun-antecedent agreement. Read your essay carefully. Correct any pronoun that does not agree with its antecedent in person, number, and gender.

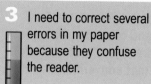

3 I need to correct several errors in my paper because they confuse the reader.

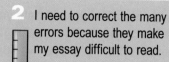

2 I need to correct the many errors because they make my essay difficult to read.

1 I need help finding errors and making corrections.

How can I check for double subjects?

You can check for double subjects by making sure that you have not included any unnecessary pronouns right after a subject noun. Double subjects are incorrect.

Double Subject

Wanda she **thinks it is a good idea to stop the importation of exotic pets.**

Corrected Subject

Wanda **thinks it is a good idea to stop the importation of exotic pets.**

Grammar Exercise

Rewrite any sentence below that contains a double subject.

1. After leaving the factory, the pollutants they flow into the river.
2. Mr. Erickson and Mr. Stein approve of the new water system.
3. Mr. Stein he will vote in favor of funding the new water system.
4. Last year, the extensive cleanup it was costly.

Edit

Check for double subjects. To make your essay clearer, locate and eliminate any double subjects.

Persuasive

Conventions
A pronoun-antecedent agreement error is corrected.

Two double subjects are eliminated.

However, not all the people who need food qualify for government programs, and applying for government help can take time. Hungry people ~~they~~ need to be fed when ~~we~~ *they* are hungry, and food banks ~~they~~ do just that. Also, even with government programs, the hunger problem has escalated.

Editing Checking for Conventions

Edit

Check your editing. This checklist will help you edit your essay for conventions: punctuation, capitalization, spelling, and grammar. On a piece of paper, write the numbers 1 to 10. If you can answer "yes," put a check after that number. If you can't, continue to edit for that convention.

Editing Checklist

Conventions

PUNCTUATION

_____ **1.** Do I use end punctuation after all my sentences?

_____ **2.** Do I use commas after long introductory phrases and after clauses?

_____ **3.** Do I use commas to separate equal adjectives?

CAPITALIZATION

_____ **4.** Do I start all my sentences with capital letters?

_____ **5.** Do I capitalize all proper nouns and adjectives?

SPELLING

_____ **6.** Have I spelled all words correctly?

_____ **7.** Have I checked the words my spell-checker may have missed?

GRAMMAR

_____ **8.** Do my subjects and verbs agree in number?

_____ **9.** Do my pronouns agree with their antecedents?

_____ **10.** Have I avoided double subjects?

Creating a Title

After your editing is complete, add a title that describes your essay and catches your reader's attention. Here are several ways to approach this task.

- Summarize the issue: **Food Banks Ease Hunger Pangs**
- Call to action: **Back Food Banks and Reduce Hunger**
- Hook the reader: **Help Put an End to Hunger**

Publishing Sharing Your Essay

The purpose of a problem-solution essay is to convince others to help solve a problem. So after you've finished editing your essay for conventions, it's time to share your paper with your classmates, present your essay in a debate, publish it in a newspaper, or send it to an official who can help.

Publish | **Format your final copy.** To format a handwritten essay, use the guidelines below or follow your teacher's instructions. (If you are using a computer, see pages 76–78.) Make a clean copy and carefully proofread it.

Focusing on Presentation

- Write neatly using blue or black ink.
- Write your name in the upper left corner of page 1.
- Skip a line and center your title; skip another line and start your essay.
- Indent every paragraph and leave a one-inch margin on all four sides.
- Write your last name and the page number in the upper right corner of every page after page 1.

Persuasive

Stage a Debate

Invite a group of friends or family to debate different solutions to the problem. Invite audience members who have not decided on a solution. Present and defend your idea. Then allow others to present and defend their ideas. After the debate, ask the audience to choose a solution based on the debate.

Contact an Official

Identify an official who might be able to help solve your problem. Send your essay to that person along with a cover letter briefly outlining the problem and your proposed solution. Remember to use a respectful tone in your letter, and to encourage the official to take action.

Publish a Letter

Reformat your essay as a letter to the editor of a local newspaper. Make sure your letter conforms to the newspaper's submission guidelines. Then e-mail your letter or send it through the postal service.

Rubric for Persuasive Writing

The following rubric will help guide and assess your persuasive writing. Use it to improve your writing using the six traits.

6	**5**	**4**
Ideas		
The thesis is clearly presented and well defended by reasons that challenge the reader to act.	The thesis is clear. All reasons effectively support the argument and call to action.	The problem and solution are clear. Most reasons support the solution.
Organization		
All parts of the essay work to introduce and convincingly support the writer's opinion.	The opening outlines the argument (opinion). The middle provides clear support. The ending reinforces the opinion.	The opening outlines the argument (opinion). The middle provides support, but the ending needs work.
Voice		
The writer's voice is confident, positive, and convincing.	The writer's voice is confident and persuasive.	The writer's voice is confident, but it may not be persuasive enough.
Word Choice		
The writer chooses words that are powerful, precise, engaging, and persuasive.	The writer chooses words that effectively persuade the reader.	The writer's word choice should be more persuasive.
Sentence Fluency		
The sentences are clear, concise, varied, and engaging.	The sentences are clear and varied in type and beginnings.	More variety in sentence beginnings is needed. There is good sentence variety.
Conventions		
The essay is free of writing errors.	Errors in conventions are few. The reader is not distracted by these errors.	There are a few errors in conventions, and they are distracting.

3

The thesis could be clearer. More supporting reasons are needed.

The opening outlines the argument. The middle and ending need work.

The writer's voice needs to be more confident and persuasive.

Precise and persuasive words are needed.

More variety in sentence beginnings and types is needed.

There are a number of errors that may confuse the reader.

2

The thesis is unclear. Reasons to support the argument are needed.

The beginning, middle, and ending run together.

The writer's voice rambles on without any confidence.

The words chosen do not create a clear message.

Most sentences begin the same way and are simple sentences.

Frequent errors make the essay difficult to read.

1

A new focus and reasons are needed.

The organization is unclear and incomplete.

The writer has not considered voice.

Word choice has not been addressed.

There is little sentence variety. Ideas do not flow smoothly.

Nearly every sentence contains errors.

Evaluating a Persuasive Essay

Read the student writer's persuasive essay below. Focus on its strengths and its weaknesses. Then read the student self-assessment on the next page. **(This essay contains some errors.)**

Put a Stop to Sweatshops

Most people spend a lot of time choosing the clothes they wear, but little time worrying about where those clothes come from? Many clothes are manufactured in sweatshops, which are factories where the owners treat workers unfairly. Sweatshops pay extremly low wages and demand long hours in conditions that are often unsafe and workers who complain can be fired, threatened, or even beaten (Harris). However, it's possible to put a stop to sweatshops by boycotting the clothing made in them.

Owners of sweat shops often treat workers badly. At one sweatshop, workers made sneakers for 16 cents an hour. They worked more than 70 hours a week. They were fined if they refused to work extra hours even though they weren't paid for the time. At another factory, workers were paid 1.3 cents for every baseball cap they sewed. The caps sold for more than $15 each in the United States (Lee, 45). That's outragous! But you can help.

Boycotting sweatshop clothes and the stores that sell them is a great way to help eliminate sweatshops. A boycott can work since it directly affects the profits of clothing manufacturers and retailers. When a manufacturer relies on low-paid workers, it can produce huge profits ("Why" 36). If people refuse to buy clothing made in sweatshops, the manufacturer will lose money instead. So write to or call the headquarters of your favorite stores, and ask if all the workers who make their garments are treated fairly. Do some Web research. A number of organizations are dedicated to opposing sweatshops. Many of them offer online resources.

Another reason to boycott sweatshops is that it rewards clothing manufacturers and retailers who sell "sweat-free" apparel. Sweat free means that the people who make the garments are paid a fair wage and are treated well. Take a look on the Internet, and you can find retailers and clothing manufacturers who sell sweat-free clothes ("Shop" 59). Give them your business, and your purchases will send a clear message It pays to treat workers fairly.

When people boycott sweatshop clothes, that's news. Boycotting stores that sell sweatshop goods, and asking others to do the same, focuses media attention on the issue. Coverage in the media will help spread the word that sweatshops abuse their workers.

Some people insist that sweatshops provides necessary jobs to workers who otherwise wouldn't have jobs at all. Still most sweatshop jobs aren't good enough to help workers build better lives. Many clothing companies and retailer make huge profits from sweatshop labor. They could offer higher pay and safer working conditions and still produce a good profit.

Taking actions against sweatshops isn't difficult and it can make a big difference. So boycott clothing made in sweatshops and choose sweat-free clothing and stores that sell it. Help clothing workers everywhere lead better lives.

Student Self-Assessment

Persuasive Rubric Checklist

Title: Put a Stop to Sweatshops
Writer: Kara Stively

5 **Ideas**
- Do I clearly explain the problem and the solution?
- Do I defend my solution with clear, compelling reasons?

4 **Organization**
- Does the beginning introduce the problem and my solution?
- Does the middle offer solid reasons that support the solution?
- Does my ending sum up my solution and leave the reader with something to think about?

5 **Voice**
- Is my voice authoritative, backed by facts?
- Is the tone of my voice reasonable?

4 **Word Choice**
- Do I use words that are powerful and precise?
- Do I use commands to encourage action?

5 **Sentence Fluency**
- Do I use different kinds of sentences?
- Do I vary my sentence beginnings?

3 **Conventions**
- Does my essay avoid most errors in punctuation, spelling, and grammar?

OVERALL COMMENTS

I define the problem and offer good reasons to support my solution. A few of my paragraphs could use more details.

My ending does not leave the reader with something to think about.

My voice sounds authoritative without being emotional.

More precise word choice would make my essay stronger.

My sentences flow smoothly.

I need to check more carefully for errors!

Persuasive

Use the rubric.
Rate your essay using the rubric on pages 234–235. Write comments that explain why you gave yourself the scores you did.

Reflecting on Your Writing

After you finish your problem-solution essay, take some time to reflect on your essay and your writing experience. On a separate sheet of paper, complete each sentence below. This writing will help reinforce what you've learned about writing a persuasive essay and help you to apply that learning to future assignments.

My Problem-Solution Essay

1. The strongest part of my essay is . . .

2. The part that still needs work is . . .

3. The prewriting activity that worked best for me was . . .

4. The main thing I learned about writing a problem-solution essay is . . .

5. In my next problem-solution essay, I would like to . . .

6. One question I still have about writing a problem-solution essay is . . .

Persuasive Writing
Writing an Editorial

In six weeks, your city will vote on whether or not to change the zoning regulations for schools. The new zoning would force you to go to a different high school. Do you think you could convince people to vote "no" to the zoning change? You could try—in an editorial for your city's newspaper. An editorial is a persuasive essay that presents your opinion about an important, timely topic and often includes a call for action.

In this chapter, you'll read a sample editorial about the writer's desire to see Valentine's Day celebrated differently at her school. Then you'll write your own editorial to express your opinion about a recent issue or event. Choose a topic that you feel strongly about. Your confidence and conviction will prompt the reader to agree with your point of view.

Writing Guidelines

Subject: Opinion about a school-related issue
Form: Editorial
Purpose: To present an opinion about a timely and important topic
Audience: Classmates

"Sentences are sharp nails, which force truth upon our memories."
—Denis Diderot

Editorial

In the following editorial, Hannah presents her opinion that Valentine's Day should be celebrated differently at her school. Her editorial was printed in the school's February newsletter.

Beginning
The beginning introduces the topic and presents the opinion statement (underlined).

Middle
Each paragraph supports Hannah's opinion.

Let Love Rule

Valentine's Day. Does any other holiday tap into the deepest emotions, bitter or sweet? During the season of chocolates, roses, cards, and stuffed animals, someone always gets left out. Nowhere is the sting more humiliating and unnecessary than at school. <u>At Benchfield High, students should be more sensitive about how they celebrate Valentine's Day.</u>

The first taste of Valentine's Day comes as soon as children can scribble their friends' names. They stuff valentines into decorated shoe boxes. The rules are simple: Students give a valentine to everyone in class. Of course, a student can always add a carefully chosen candy heart, or save the biggest card of the bunch for that special someone. It's impossible to make life completely fair, but at least teachers and parents try to make this situation as fair as possible.

Middle school students have the carnation fund-raiser: white for "friends," pink for "like," and red for "love." The rule, "all or none," no longer applies. Girls with armfuls of floral trophies giggle with valentine glee. Meanwhile, others can only hope that their lack of colorful carnations will just help them fade into the background.

In high school, the carnation parade is bigger than ever, but carnations alone just don't cut it. Now, on Valentine's Day, the pressure is on to do something extraordinary.

During class, the names of the lucky few are called over the intercom. They go to the office to pick up towering arrangements of flowers and balloons. Even if an individual can ignore these huge displays, they probably find themselves wondering, "Will someone special remember me? Will I be the only one without a valentine?" Talk about distracting, and depressing.

Persuasive

Hannah considers an opposing viewpoint and provides a solution.

A student's love/hate relationship with Valentine's Day can easily change depending on whether or not he or she has a sweetie. Certainly students should show their special someone that they care. But when at school, can't students celebrate Valentine's Day in a way that doesn't flaunt popularity and make others feel excluded?

Introducing a Valentine's Day fund-raiser might be the answer. Instead of carnations, students could buy "Hearts of Hope." Each dollar gets a buyer a paper heart to post on the wall. Each wall represents a different charity. On Valentine's Day, the money would be split between the charities based on the number of hearts on each wall. The money could provide toys for needy children, help for the senior citizen center, and so on. Maybe people can't make life fair, but they can make it a little better?

Ending
The ending leaves the reader with strong, final thoughts.

At its heart, Valentine's Day is about love; it's not a popularity contest. It's time for Benchfield High to put popularity on the bench and let love rule.

Respond to the reading. Answer the following questions.

Ideas (1) What is the main point of Hannah's editorial? (2) How does she inspire the reader to take action?

Organization (3) How does Hannah organize the middle part of her editorial?

Voice & Word Choice (4) What words or phrases convey her feelings about the topic? Name three.

Literature Connections: Many newspapers and magazines print editorials on controversial topics. The *Weekly Reader* editorial "Harmless Fun?"—about video game violence—is an example of a magazine editorial written for a teenage audience.

Prewriting Selecting a Topic

The purpose of your editorial is to express your opinion about a timely and important topic. To find a topic for her editorial, Hannah completed a sentence starter about several important issues at her school. After looking over her possible topics, she realized she didn't have enough information about some of the issues, and another matter wasn't up for vote for six months. She chose the Valentine's Day issue, which seemed to be perfect for the school paper.

Sentence Starter

Students at my school are saying that . . .
- the online driver's ed course is a big help.
- Valentine's Day is a popularity contest.*
- we might lose open-campus lunch if students keep skipping class.
- bathroom graffiti is becoming a problem.
- the possible school zoning change for next year is unfair.

Prewrite

Choose your topic. Complete the sentence starter above in three or four different ways. Put an asterisk (*) next to the topic that you would like to write about. Remember that you need a strong opinion in order to present a convincing editorial.

Focus on the Traits

Ideas An editorial is a form of persuasive writing. An effective persuasive essay includes specific examples that support your opinion. Your argument will also be more convincing if you do the following:

- **Address an opposing point of view.** Respectfully address, and counter, the other side of the argument.
  While it's true that plastic bags are convenient for shoppers, they are more than inconvenient for the environment.

- **Make a final call to action.** Encourage the reader to agree with your opinion and take appropriate action as a result.
  Urge friends and family to reuse more durable kinds of shopping bags.

Gathering and Organizing Details

After choosing your topic, you need to gather convincing details to support your opinion. Hannah created a quick list based on her experiences, her personal feelings, and the feelings of others. Here is part of her list.

Quick List

> - People send flowers and gifts to school.
> - In grade school, everyone got a valentine.
> - We should do a fund-raiser for a charity.

Next, Hannah arranged her details chronologically. She also considered the other side of the argument and a possible solution.

Details Chart

early years in school	– stuffed valentines in shoe boxes
middle school	– held carnation fund-raiser
	– popularity contest made some feel left out
high school	– continue carnations
	– give "special someones" bouquets or balloons
other viewpoint	– people with my opinion are just jealous
possible solution	– find another way to celebrate

Persuasive

Writing an Opinion Statement

An editorial needs a strong opinion statement on a timely, important topic.

timely and important topic		your opinion about the topic		a thesis statement
Valentine's Day	**+**	Need to be more sensitive about how students celebrate	**=**	At Benchfield High, students should be more sensitive about how they celebrate Valentine's Day.

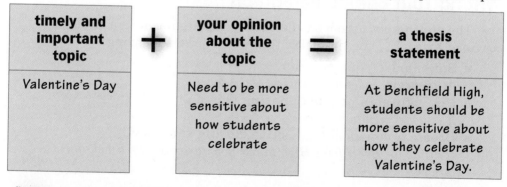

Write an opinion statement. Using the formula above, state the opinion that you will develop in your editorial.

Prewrite

Writing Creating Your First Draft

The following tips will help you write your editorial. Also refer to the planning that you did on the previous page.

Writing Your Beginning Paragraph

The **beginning** paragraph should introduce the topic in an interesting way and present your opinion statement. Here are strategies for capturing your reader's attention.

- **Present a question or interesting details about the topic.**
  Does any other holiday tap into the deepest emotions, bitter or sweet?
- **Explain why the topic is important.**
  During the season of chocolates, roses, cards, and stuffed animals, someone always gets left out.
- **Share a quotation.**
  "To love and be loved is to feel the sun from both sides."

Writing Your Middle Paragraphs

The **middle** paragraphs should build your argument in a logical way, explain the opposing point of view, and offer a possible solution.

- Organize your points in a logical way with examples and illustrations.
- Present the opposing argument accurately, but reveal its weaknesses.
- Avoid attacking others or preaching.
- Be brief and direct.
- Offer a reasonable solution.

Writing Your Ending Paragraph

The **ending** paragraph should sum up the argument in a strong, convincing way. Use the tips below to create a powerful ending.

- **Summarize your opinion.**
  At its heart, Valentine's Day is about love.
- **Put your spin on the opposing viewpoint.**
  It is not a popularity contest.
- **Create a memorable, positive closing sentence.**
  It's time for Benchfield High to put popularity on the bench and let love rule.

Write your first draft. Use your prewriting work and the tips above to develop your editorial.

Write

Revising Improving Your Editorial

Once you complete your first draft, set it aside for a while. Then use the guidelines below to revise your editorial.

Revising Checklist

Ideas

_____ **1.** Do I have a strong opinion statement?
_____ **2.** Do I support my position with examples and reasons?
_____ **3.** Do I address the other side of the argument?
_____ **4.** Have I provided a reasonable call to action?

Organization

_____ **5.** Does my essay have a strong beginning, middle, and ending?
_____ **6.** Have I organized my points in a logical way?

Voice

_____ **7.** Is my voice confident and convincing?
_____ **8.** Does my voice show my interest in the topic?

Word Choice

_____ **9.** Have I used strong words to make a powerful case?

Sentence Fluency

_____ **10.** Do my sentences flow and vary in length?

Revise your first draft. Use the checklist above as you revise your first draft. Ask a partner to read your editorial and make suggestions as well.

Revise

Creating a Title

- Ask a question: **Why Can't We Be Fair?**
- State the topic: **Celebrate Valentine's Day in a New Way**
- Call for action: **Let Love Rule**

Editing Checking for Conventions

After you've revised your editorial, it's important to edit it. The following checklist can help you spot any errors in punctuation, capitalization, spelling, and grammar.

Editing Checklist

Conventions

PUNCTUATION

_____ 1. Have I ended my sentences with the correct punctuation?

_____ 2. Have I used commas correctly?

_____ 3. Have I punctuated quotations correctly?

CAPITALIZATION

_____ 4. Do I capitalize the first word in each sentence?

_____ 5. Do I capitalize all proper nouns and proper adjectives?

SPELLING

_____ 6. Do I spell all my words correctly?

_____ 7. Have I double-checked for spelling errors that my spell-checker might miss?

GRAMMAR

_____ 8. Do I use the correct forms of verbs (*I went,* not *I gone*)?

_____ 9. Do my subjects and verbs agree in number (Everyone *is* going, not Everyone *are* going)?

_____ 10. Have I used the right words (*there, their, they're*)?

Edit your editorial. Use the checklist above to edit for conventions. Have a partner check your work, too. Then prepare a final copy and proofread it.

Edit

Publishing Sharing Your Editorial

Share your timely editorial with friends and family as soon as possible. If appropriate, consider submitting your editorial to your school or city newspaper, a magazine, or a Web page. Let your voice be heard.

Writing for Assessment
Responding to Persuasive Prompts

Developing a well-organized and convincing persuasive argument can take time. Sometimes, however, you don't have much time to convince people to agree with you. Let's say you're trying to get permission from your parents to spend Saturday night at a classmate's house, or you're trying to convince a friend to go to a concert with you. At times like these, you'll need to organize and present your argument quickly and effectively.

Responding to a persuasive prompt on a test presents a similar problem. Within a set time limit, you'll need to choose a position, structure your argument, and present it in a logical, effective manner. This chapter will show you how to use the writing process to create a clear, effective persuasive response in a timed situation.

Writing Guidelines

Subject: Persuasive prompt
Form: Response essay
Purpose: To demonstrate competence
Audience: Instructor

"Good writing is clear thinking made visible."
—Bill Wheeler

Prewriting Analyzing a Persuasive Prompt

In order to respond effectively to a persuasive prompt, you must analyze it carefully, using the following **STRAP questions** as a guide.

> **Subject:** What topic should I write about?
>
> **Type:** What form (essay, letter, editorial, article, report) of writing should I create?
>
> **Role:** What position (student, son or daughter, friend, employee, citizen) should I assume as the writer?
>
> **Audience:** Who (teacher, parents, classmates, employer, official) is the intended reader?
>
> **Purpose:** What is the goal (persuade, respond, evaluate, tell, describe) of my writing?

Sample Analyzed Prompt

Subject
Type
Role
Audience
Purpose

You are a resident of Bradford. **The town's** recreation director **has announced** a plan to close the recreation center **during the summer months because not many kids use it. Write** a letter **to the director** arguing for or against this decision.

Try It!

Analyze these prompts by answering the STRAP questions. (Use your best judgment to form an answer for every question.)

1. Your state plans to double license fees for drivers under age 18. The money will be used to fund driver-education programs. Write an editorial for your student newspaper supporting or opposing this decision.

2. Funds are needed to buy props for your school play. As president of the drama club, write a letter to parents encouraging them to donate money to the prop fund.

Planning Your Response

Once you have answered the STRAP questions, you should quickly plan your persuasive response. The following graphic organizers can help you.

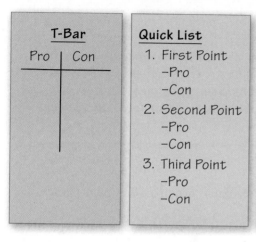

T-Bar

Pro | Con

Quick List

1. First Point
   –Pro
   –Con
2. Second Point
   –Pro
   –Con
3. Third Point
   –Pro
   –Con

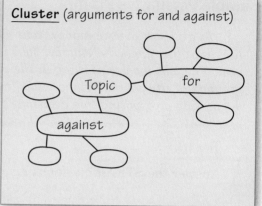

Cluster (arguments for and against)

Topic — for

against

Considering Both Sides

The graphic organizers include space for both pro and con arguments because your response should consider both sides to see where the strongest position lies. In general, facts make the strongest argument, but a reasonable appeal to emotion can also provide strong support.

When planning a persuasive response, you should always present and respond to at least one main objection. By countering the objection, you will strengthen your own position. You will also demonstrate that you have considered both sides of an issue.

Prewrite

Use a graphic organizer to plan a response. Reread the persuasive prompts on page 248. Choose one prompt and use a graphic organizer to plan your response.

Tip

In a timed writing test, plan carefully. Allow yourself time for planning before you write and for revising and editing after you write. For example, if you have 45 minutes to respond to a prompt, use the first 5 minutes to analyze the prompt and plan your response, the last 5 minutes to revise and edit your response, and the time in between to write your response.

Persuasive

Writing Responding to a Prompt

Once you have answered the STRAP questions and planned your response using a graphic organizer, you can begin writing.

Sample Persuasive Prompt

> In an effort to save money, your city council is considering a proposal to reduce the number of summer jobs it gives to high school students each year. The jobs involve working in the recreation department maintaining the grounds of city parks. Write a letter to the editor of your local newspaper, supporting or opposing this decision.

Try It!

Answer the STRAP questions for the above prompt. (See page **248**.)

Sample Response

Beginning
The beginning paragraph leads up to the opinion (underlined).

Dear Editor:

When school lets out every summer, the city's high school students go out to look for jobs. For many students, these jobs are important. Summer jobs allow students to make the extra money they need to save for college, maintain a car, or even save for next year's school clothes. But this summer, students in our city might have a harder time finding work. The city council has decided to cut summer jobs in the recreation department. <u>However, for the good of the city and its young people, these jobs should be restored.</u>

Middle
Each middle paragraph presents a reason that supports the opinion.

One reason to restore the jobs is that they may actually end up helping the city and the recreation department save money. Every summer, student workers mow lawns, clean up litter, and help keep parks neat and clean. But they often get paid much less than full-time workers. So hiring a student is like getting a full-time worker for less than full-time pay. And that's a great deal for the city.

In addition, students who work for the city in the summer are not only earning money, but continuing their education. They learn important job skills such as getting to work on time, following directions, using tools and equipment safely, and working as a team. Learning these skills will help students succeed at college and in their careers. So spending money on summer jobs for students is an investment that will pay off in the future.

Finally, students who work during the summer are less likely to become bored. If kids are busy, they are less likely to get into trouble. Students who work for the city are also more likely to have respect for the city and its property. This respect means that young people will take better care of city facilities.

Objection
The final middle paragraph addresses an objection.

Some people might argue that students hired by the city don't work hard enough for their money. Maybe some students don't work as hard as they could, but this is true for adults, too. The fact remains that most students will work hard and gladly contribute to making city parks better for everyone.

Ending
The ending summarizes the argument and offers a final plea.

Reducing the number of student summer jobs will not only result in bored students, but it may end up costing the city more in the end. The small amount of money the city pays to hire students for the summer is an investment. And that investment pays off not only in better city parks, but also in students having the skills they need to succeed in the years beyond high school. So please encourage the city council to maintain this program. Everyone in town will benefit.

Sincerely,

Angel Hernandez

Persuasive

Write

Respond to a persuasive prompt. Review the prompt you chose on page 248, your answers to the STRAP questions, and your graphic organizer. Then write a response to the prompt in the time your teacher gives you.

Revising Improving Your Response

Before you begin a writing test, find out whether you will be allowed to make changes in your writing. If this is allowed, always make your changes neatly. The STRAP questions below can guide your revisions.

> **Subject:** Does my response focus on the topic of the prompt? Do my main points support the opinion stated in my first paragraph?
>
> **Type:** Have I used the form requested in the prompt (essay, letter, editorial, article, report)?
>
> **Role:** Have I assumed the position called for in the prompt?
>
> **Audience:** Have I used appropriate language for my audience?
>
> **Purpose:** Does my response accomplish the goal of the prompt?

Revise

Improve your work. Reread your response, asking yourself the STRAP questions above. Make necessary changes to your response.

Editing Checking Your Response

After revising, read through your response one final time, checking for errors in punctuation, capitalization, spelling, and grammar.

Editing Checklist

Conventions

_____ 1. Have I used end punctuation for each sentence?

_____ 2. Have I capitalized all proper nouns and the first word of each sentence?

_____ 3. Have I spelled all words correctly?

_____ 4. Have I made sure my subjects and verbs agree?

_____ 5. Have I used the right words (*their, they're, there*)?

Edit

Check your conventions. Read through your response one final time. In the time allowed, neatly correct any errors in punctuation, capitalization, spelling, and grammar.

Persuasive Writing on Tests

Use this guide when preparing to respond to a persuasive writing prompt.

Before you write . . .

■ **Analyze the prompt.**
Use the STRAP questions. Remember that a persuasive prompt asks you to use facts and logical reasons to persuade or convince.
■ **Plan your response.**
Decide how much time you will spend on planning, writing, revising, and checking conventions. Use a graphic organizer to gather details and organize your response.

As you write . . .

■ **Support your argument.**
Keep your main idea or opinion in mind as you write. All your reasons should clearly support your opinion.
■ **Answer an objection.**
Make your argument stronger by answering a likely objection.
■ **Craft a powerful ending.**
In the final paragraph, summarize your opinion and supporting reasons and make a final plea to the reader.

After you've written a first draft . . .

■ **Revise and edit.**
Use the STRAP questions to revise your response. Correct any errors in punctuation, capitalization, spelling, and grammar.

Try It!

Plan and write a response. Choose one of the prompts below, and analyze it with the STRAP questions. Next, use a graphic organizer to gather details and plan your response. Then write, revise, and edit your response.

■ Your school food service wants to buy more produce from local farmers. This food is a bit more expensive, but it is pesticide free. Write a letter to the food service director giving your reasons for supporting or objecting to the plan.
■ One of your friends wants to join either the school band or the school chorus, but can't join both. This person has asked you for help deciding which to choose. Write a letter (or e-mail message) suggesting to your friend the best course of action.

Persuasive

Response to Literature

Writing Focus

Analyzing a Theme   255
Responding to Prompts About Literature   295

Grammar Focus

Parallel Structure   283
Commonly Confused Words   286
Punctuating Interrupting Words and Phrases   287

Academic Vocabulary

Working with a classmate, read the definitions below and discuss possible answers to each question.

1. Theme is the underlying message about life or human nature that a writer wants the reader to understand. **What do you think might be a common theme in adventure stories?**

2. To reveal something is to show it or make it known. **What does the way your bedroom is decorated reveal about you?**

3. When things are unified, they are made into a cohesive unit. **What do you think it means for a paragraph to be unified?**

4. Things that are parallel are alike in some way, such as having the same grammatical form. **In what way are two parallel roads similar?**

Response to Literature
Analyzing a Theme

When you tell someone what happens first, second, and third in a novel, you are describing its *plot*. When you talk about the author's message, you are explaining the *theme*. Although reading a compelling story is one of life's great pleasures, the real reward is the new perspective you gain by figuring out its theme. Quality novels are full of insights into life; they can help you think, act, dream, hope, learn, accept, appreciate, and on and on.

In order to understand the theme of a novel, you must examine the interplay between the characters, the plot, the setting, and the symbols. A novel may have one overall theme, or it may have several, each one a significant message and worthy of discussion.

Writing Guidelines

Subject:	**A novel**
Form:	**Literary analysis**
Purpose:	**To analyze a theme**
Audience:	**Classmates**

"Each novel is a kind of voyage of discovery."

—Margaret Lawrence

Writing Warm-Up: Subject vs. Theme

First, you need to understand the difference between the *subject* of the novel and its theme. The subject describes, in a general way, what the story is about; the theme is the message about life that the story suggests. Study the following chart to discern this difference.

Subject vs. Theme Chart

Novel	Subject	Theme
The Red Badge of Courage	This story is about an inexperienced young man who enlists to fight in the Civil War.	A young soldier learns that courage in war is defined by how a soldier reacts to fear, death, and failure.
A Christmas Carol	An old miserly man is hard-hearted and sees no meaning in Christmas, rejecting any involvement in the holiday.	A bitter old man learns that Christmas is a yearly reminder about the importance of love and the rewards of generosity and kindness toward one's fellow humans.
Fahrenheit 451	This is a story about a society in which free expression is limited by a strong central government.	Government can only control the minds of people who allow themselves to become uninformed and thoughtless.

Try It!

Work with a classmate to create a chart like the one above. Try to list at least three novels that you both have read. For each novel, write a subject statement (what the book is about) and a theme statement (the book's message about life). Remember, a novel may have more than one theme.

> "He conceived persons with torn bodies to be peculiarly happy. He wished that he, too, had a wound, a red badge of courage."
> —Stephen Crane, The Red Badge of Courage

Writing a Paragraph Analysis

You can analyze the theme of a novel in one paragraph by following these guidelines:

- In the **opening sentence**, include the title, author, and subject of the novel.
- In the **body sentences**, briefly describe the elements (character, plot, setting, symbols) of the novel that reveal the theme.
- In the **closing sentence**, state the theme of the novel.

Sample Paragraph Analysis

The **opening sentence** introduces the title, author, and subject of the novel.

The **body sentences** describe the elements of the novel that reveal the theme.

The **closing sentence** states the theme (underlined).

Scrooge's Awakening

In Charles Dickens's *A Christmas Carol*, the main character, Ebenezer Scrooge, is a hard-hearted man who sees no meaning in Christmas. Flashbacks reveal that he has become more and more focused on his business, shunning contact with friends and relatives. Scrooge is a character living in a cocoon of selfishness, blinded to the world beyond his counting house. One Christmas Eve Scrooge follows his usual holiday pattern—refusing requests for charity, berating his employee for wanting to take Christmas Day off, and rejecting the holiday dinner invitation of his only nephew. But as darkness falls, the setting shifts to mysterious images of deceased acquaintances, lost youth, and a prophecy of Scrooge's own cold and lonely death. What he sees horrifies him and brings him to his senses. Scrooge learns that Christmas is a yearly reminder about the importance of love and the rewards of generosity and kindness toward one's fellow humans.

Literature

Write

Write a paragraph analysis. Using one of the novels you identified on the previous page, write a paragraph in which you briefly analyze a major theme of the novel. Be sure to include the three parts explained above.

Understanding Your Goal

Your goal in this chapter is to write an essay that analyzes a main theme in a novel. The chart below lists the key traits of a literary analysis essay, with specific suggestions for this assignment. Consult this chart and the rubric on pages 209–291 for guidance as you write.

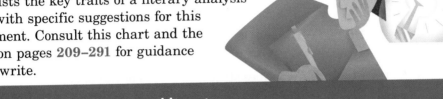

Traits of a Response to Literature

- **Ideas**
  Select a novel you have read. Write a thesis statement that explains your interpretation of the novel's theme. Use specific details and quotations from the text to support the statement.

- **Organization**
  Include clear beginning, middle, and ending parts. Use transitions to effectively connect sentences and paragraphs.

- **Voice**
  Show your interest in the novel and a thorough knowledge of its subject and theme.

- **Word Choice**
  Use literary terms that reveal your understanding of the novel. Choose precise, vivid words to share your ideas.

- **Sentence Fluency**
  Write sentences that read well and flow smoothly.

- **Conventions**
  Correct all punctuation, capitalization, spelling, and grammar errors.

Literature Connections: Some universal themes recur throughout works of literature and beyond. To help you think about theme, consider reading Kevin Young's foreword to the book *Blues Poems*. In it, Young analyzes some common themes in the blues genre of poetry and music.

Response Essay

Mary Shelley's novel *Frankenstein* tells about a scientist who creates a superhuman being. The model below analyzes two themes, revealing the more significant of the two in the thesis statement.

Beginning
The beginning names
the author
and novel
and states
the thesis
(underlined).

Middle
The middle paragraphs
trace the development
of two themes.

Monsters Are Made, Not Born

Mary Shelley's *Frankenstein* traces the plight of Victor Frankenstein, a scientist tortured by the thought that he is responsible for bringing into the world a hideously deformed, vicious creature. While *Frankenstein* clearly cautions readers about the dangers of science left unchecked, there is also a very strong message about the effects of mistreating outcasts. As the story develops, Shelley shows that those who are shunned may strike back in anger.

Frankenstein is really a set of linked stories, revealing the tragic lives of Frankenstein and his monster. The early chapters focus on a series of letters from a man named Walton to his sister. Walton recalls his voyage to the Arctic Circle, where he sees a huge figure traveling on a sled followed at a distance by Victor Frankenstein. Frankenstein's words dominate the next set of chapters as Walton records Victor's story, starting with his happy childhood and his interest in medieval science. In college, Victor had become very interested in human anatomy. As a result of his work, Victor claimed to have found "the cause of generation and life." But before continuing his story, Victor warns Walton that the "acquirement of knowledge is dangerous."

The tale becomes much darker when Victor tells of bringing a monster into being. He tells of fleeing from his apartment in terror and not returning until much later, when he is relieved to find that the monster has escaped. Many months later, Victor learns that his own brother has been brutally murdered, and his sister has been accused of the crime. Frankenstein, however, has the eerie feeling that his monster is the killer and that he himself is responsible because of his "unhallowed arts."

The narrator role then shifts to the monster. After Victor flees to the Alps to escape his shame, the monster catches up with him and forces Victor to hear the truth. The monster has nothing but contempt for Victor, who has doomed him to an unhappy existence. It becomes clear that the monster begins his existence as a gentle creature trapped in a frightening body. After escaping from Victor's apartment, he is ill treated by everyone he meets. He cannot understand why until one day he sees his reflection in a pool of water and realizes why people loathe him. Longing for companionship, he eavesdrops on happy lives and secretly helps others whenever he can. However, in an awful series of events, the monster is attacked by a mob he has tried to befriend and is shot by the companion of a girl he has saved from drowning. At that point, he declares war on all men, killing Victor's brother and framing his sister.

The monster's story makes it obvious that Victor's creation is vicious not because he is created that way, but because Victor abandons him and because others mistreat him. There is one last chance for Victor to ease the monster's loneliness—by creating another monster to keep him company. But Victor fails to take action. Walton encounters Frankenstein in the Arctic because Victor is chasing down his creation, intent on killing him. Finally, Walton's last report tells how Victor gets sick and dies before he can catch his monster, and the giant, satisfied that Frankenstein is dead, wanders off to perish on the ice.

Ending
The ending analyzes the two themes and expresses the importance of the second in quotations from the text.

Through *Frankenstein*, Mary Shelley expresses her fears that science left unchecked could be dangerous. However, in the end, that theme is not nearly as moving as the monster's message—mistreating others is risky. This theme becomes clear when he states, "There was none among the myriads of men that existed who would pity or assist me; and should I feel kindness toward my enemies?" It is the monster's plight that haunts the reader as the monster recalls that he sought shelter from the weather, but "still more from the barbarity of man," and no shelter was given.

Respond to the reading. Answer the following questions.

Ideas (1) What theme becomes the focus of this analysis? (2) Which key quotation from the novel supports this theme?

Organization (3) How is the middle part of the analysis organized?

Voice & Word Choice (4) Does the writer sound knowledgeable about his topic? Explain.

Prewriting

The writing process begins with prewriting—selecting a novel to analyze and planning what you will say about it. Always provide evidence from the novel to support your main ideas.

Keys to Effective Prewriting

1. Select an interesting novel, one that you have recently read and enjoyed.

2. Identify the main theme of the novel.

3. Find the key elements of the novel that reveal the main theme.

4. Write a clear thesis statement that states the theme.

5. Decide how to organize the information in your middle paragraphs.

6. Write a topic sentence for each middle paragraph.

Prewriting Selecting a Topic

Completing a topics chart like the one below allows you to list novels you have read recently, state what the novels are about, and record possible themes.

Topics Chart

Title and author of the novel	What the novel is about	Possible themes
Brave New World by Aldous Huxley	A future government controls life so that everyone is happy.	– government vs. the individual – the "right" to happiness – life's shortcomings
Things Fall Apart* by Chinua Achebe	A man experiences changes in his Nigerian village during the late 1800s.	– native culture – manhood – evangelism – tradition vs. change

Select a topic. Make a topics chart like the one above. List at least two or three novels. Then put an asterisk next to the novel that you will analyze.

Prewrite

Tip

Choose a novel you have read, understand, and enjoy. You will find it much easier to analyze the theme of such a book.

I picked Things Fall Apart mostly because it's an amazing book. I identify with the main character. I have to struggle for everything I get, and things keep changing around me. I like the book because the main character struggles with the same issues that I struggle with.

Reflect on your choice. As in the example above, write a few sentences that explain the reason for your choice.

Prewrite

Identifying a Main Theme

Your next challenge is to identify the theme you will analyze. Choose one of the possible themes you listed in your topics chart (previous page) or look further by using the three strategies that follow:

- **Look for clues in the title.**
  Paper combusts at 451 degrees Fahrenheit.
  —Ray Bradbury, *Fahrenheit 451*

- **Look in the novel for the author's statement about life.**
  "A man can be destroyed but not defeated."
  —Ernest Hemingway, *Old Man and the Sea*

- **Identify a life lesson that emerges in the novel.**
  Wang Lung sees that genuine happiness is living on the land.
  —Pearl S. Buck, *The Good Earth*

Try It!

Search for a theme. Answer the following questions to find a main theme in your novel.

1. What clues does the title offer about a main theme? Explain.

2. What statements about life does the author make?

3. What lessons about life do the main character's actions reveal?

4. Are there any symbols that play a significant role in the novel? How do they relate to the main character's actions?

Identify a main theme. After answering the "Try It!" questions, complete the sentence below to identify a main theme of your novel.

Prewrite

A main theme of my novel is _____

_____

Literature

Focus on the Traits

Ideas Authors sometimes stretch language beyond its literal meaning by using figures of speech such as *simile, metaphor, personification,* or *hyperbole.* Look for these figures of speech as you analyze your novel, since they often contain thematic ideas.

Prewriting Gathering Details

To gather details for your analysis, list the major actions and the significant thoughts and feelings of the main characters in the novel. Focus on examples that reflect the theme. The chart below corresponds with the essay on pages **269–272**. (The side notes reveal the writer's thoughts about various elements in the plot.)

Plot Chart

Novel Title: Things Fall Apart

Theme: Tradition vs. change

The wrestling match is not important to the theme.

- At 18, Okonkwo becomes famous for winning a wrestling match.
- Okonkwo's father, Unoka, is irresponsible and constantly in debt, and Okonkwo is ashamed of him.
- Okonkwo becomes a powerful, prosperous, respected man.

Tradition is a key idea.

- Tradition rules the village of Umuofia, and Okonkwo follows the rules, except when his temper gets him in trouble.
- Okonkwo becomes a member of egwugwu, a powerful, secret cult that dispenses justice in Umuofia.
- At the funeral of the clan's most respected elder, Okonkwo accidentally kills the elder's son and must go into exile for seven years as punishment.

The second part of the story starts when Okonkwo leaves Umuofia.

- Okonkwo goes to a village that his mother came from, and is accepted by her relatives.
- His friend Obierika visits him and tells him about white men who wiped out a neighboring village.
- Later, Obierika returns with stories of white missionaries who have converted many clan members in Umuofia, including Okonkwo's oldest son.

The traditions of the natives and the teachings of the missionaries conflict.

- After seven years, Okonkwo returns to find that life in Umuofia has changed much because of missionaries.
- Europeans have set up a government and courts.
- Mr. Brown, a kind and compassionate missionary, gets sick and is replaced by Rev. Smith, who causes trouble.
- Okonkwo's aggressive ways end in tragedy.

Using Direct Quotations

You can use quotations from the novel to emphasize important points about the theme. The student who analyzed *Things Fall Apart* gathered the following list of quotations. Note how each quotation relates to the theme.

Sample Quotations

- "He had had no patience with his father." (A comment about Okonkwo)

- "Age was respected among his people, but achievement was revered." (The reason that Okonkwo was important in Umuofia)

- "The world has no end, and what is good among one people is an abomination with others." (The words of Okonkwo's uncle after the killing of the first white man)

- "The white man is very clever. He came quietly and peaceably with his religion. We were amused at his foolishness and allowed him to stay. Now he has won our brothers, and our clan can no longer act like one. He has put a knife on the things that held us together and we have fallen apart." (Obierika's words to Okonkwo)

Try It!

Read the quotations above. Discuss how each quotation relates to the theme of tradition vs. change.

Gather quotations. Search your novel to find direct quotations that relate to the theme you are analyzing.

Prewrite

Focus on the Traits

Organization To talk about the theme of a novel, you must also discuss the plot and the main characters. As you discuss the plot and characterization, your analysis will often be organized chronologically, but an analysis can also be organized by order of importance.

Literature

Prewriting Writing a Thesis Statement

Now that you have gathered details, you are ready to write your **thesis statement**. Your thesis statement should connect an element of the novel—usually character, setting, or action—to the theme.

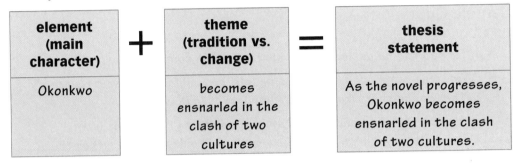

element (main character)		theme (tradition vs. change)		thesis statement
Okonkwo	**+**	becomes ensnarled in the clash of two cultures	**=**	As the novel progresses, Okonkwo becomes ensnarled in the clash of two cultures.

Form a focus. Write a thesis statement for your response essay using the formula above.

Prewrite

Organizing the Middle Paragraphs of Your Essay

Each middle paragraph should address a different stage in the explanation of the theme. The writer of the sample essay on pages 269–272 planned her middle paragraphs by writing a topic sentence for each one.

Topic Sentence 1 (First middle paragraph)

Okonkwo is known far beyond the village of Umuofia for his personal achievements and extraordinary bravery and toughness.

Topic Sentence 2 (Second middle paragraph)

Although Okonkwo feels his exile is the worst thing that could happen to him, the coming of the Europeans proves to be a problem on a much larger scale.

Topic Sentence 3 (Third middle paragraph)

Obierika returns two years later with more stories about missionaries, their churches, their courts, and their converts.

Plan your middle paragraphs. Review your plot chart from page 264. Add any important details you may have left out. Write a topic sentence for each middle paragraph of your essay. Then decide on the best order for your paragraphs.

Prewrite

Writing

Once you have finished your prewriting, you are ready to write the first draft of your analysis. Your thesis statement, plot chart, quotations, and topic sentences will guide your writing.

Keys to Effective Writing

1. Write on every other line so that you have room to make changes later.

2. Use your thesis statement and topic sentences as a guide to organize your writing.

3. Support your topic sentences with specific details from the novel.

4. Refer to your plot chart and sample quotations for details, adding more if needed.

5. Get all of your thoughts on paper.

6. Tie your ideas together with transitions.

Literature

Writing Getting the Big Picture

Remember that an essay includes three main parts—the beginning, the middle, and the ending. You are ready to begin writing your response if you have . . .

- discovered the theme,
- written a clear thesis statement that ties the theme to the novel, and
- planned and organized your paragraphs.

The chart below shows how the three parts of a response-to-literature essay fit together. The examples are from the essay on pages **269–272.**

Beginning

The **beginning** names the novel and the author, summarizes the plot, and states the thesis.

Thesis Statement
As the novel progresses, Okonkwo becomes ensnarled in the clash of two cultures.

Middle

The **middle** paragraphs show different stages in the development of the theme.

Topic Sentences
Okonkwo is known far beyond the village of Umuofia for his personal achievements and extraordinary bravery and toughness.

Although Okonkwo feels his exile is the worst thing that could happen to him, the coming of the Europeans proves to be a problem on a much larger scale.

Obierika returns two years later with more stories about missionaries, their churches, their courts, and their converts.

Ending

The **ending** paragraph analyzes the theme.

Closing Sentences
Okonkwo's plight symbolizes the choice faced by many conquered or controlled peoples—submit to a new way of life or perish. Okonkwo tragically experiences the latter.

Starting Your Analysis

Your opening paragraph should set the scene for the rest of your analysis. It should include the following information:

- **the title and author of your novel,**
- **background information about the plot and characters, and**
- **your thesis statement.**

Beginning Paragraph

> The first paragraph introduces the novel and gives the thesis statement (underlined).

Things Fall Apart by Chinua Achebe focuses on Nigeria in the late 1800s, a time of great change in Africa. Okonkwo, a leader in his village, is a commanding and merciless man deeply involved in the traditional life of his village, Umuofia. The first part of the novel follows Okonkwo's life to the point where an accident threatens to wipe out everything he has worked for. Unknown to Okonkwo, however, something even more disturbing is about to affect his people. White missionaries begin to travel throughout his homeland, bringing their religion. Soon, their laws and their government follow. These missionaries change everything in his village. As the novel progresses, Okonkwo becomes ensnarled in the clash of two cultures.

Write

Write your beginning. As you develop your beginning, include the title of the novel and its author, a brief plot summary, and your thesis statement.

Tip

If you have trouble getting started, try one of these strategies.

- **Talk about your story with a classmate** before you begin to write.
- **Write freely** without trying to produce the perfect analysis right away.
- **Reread the sample on pages 259–260** to see how that writer started his analysis.
- **Think of someone you believe should read this book,** and write with that person in mind.

Writing Developing the Middle Part

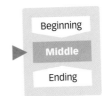

Beginning

Middle

Ending

Each middle paragraph explores a stage in your explanation of the theme and how it is revealed in the novel. Your writing should focus on the elements of the novel and any literary devices that are important to the theme.

Middle Paragraphs

> The first middle paragraph summarizes the first part of the novel dealing with traditional life.

Okonkwo is known far beyond the village of Umuofia for his personal achievements and extraordinary bravery and toughness. The force that drives him is the fact that he "had no patience with his father," who was irresponsible and constantly in debt, preferring to drink and play the flute. Okonkwo thinks of his father as "effeminate" and is determined that no one will think of him in that way. Because "age was respected among his people, but achievement was revered," Okonkwo works harder than anyone to provide food for his family, reveres the words of the mystic oracles, kills without mercy, and obeys the priestess Chielo. As a result, he rises to the highest circle of Umuofia's powerful men. Okonkwo is a spiritual man, like his fellow clansmen, and he believes that the living and their ancestors move back and forth between life and death. Unfortunately, he makes a mistake at the funeral of the clan's elder, accidentally killing the elder's son. Knowing that he has done wrong, he immediately takes the step that tradition dictates, exiling himself from Umuofia for seven years.

> The second middle paragraph explains the changes brought by the missionaries.

Although Okonkwo feels his exile is the worst thing that could happen to him, the coming of the Europeans proves to be a problem on a much larger scale. His friend Obierika visits Okonkwo in his village of exile two years later and brings news that the Abame settlement has been wiped out by white men. This action was done in retaliation for the death of another white man who rode an "iron horse"—a bicycle—through a group of panicked villagers. They apparently attacked him because he did not reply to their questions. Okonkwo's wise uncle Uchendu feels the people of Abame were fools to kill the white man on the bicycle. He says, "Never kill a man who says nothing," for the man's silence holds an ominous secret, whereas "There is nothing to fear from someone who shouts."

<u>Obierika returns two years later with more stories about missionaries, their churches, their courts, and their converts.</u> Okonkwo learns that the Europeans have taken control of Umuofia and that his oldest son, Nwoye, has converted to their religion. Okonkwo feels that this happened because Nwoye is weak willed and worthless. He is angered even more when he learns that Mr. Kiaga, a native interpreter for the white missionaries, has praised natives like Nwoye, saying, "Blessed is he who forsakes his father and his mother for my sake." Though Kiaga finds it "blessed" to forsake the old ways, Okonkwo feels it is cursed.

> Each new paragraph begins with a topic sentence (underlined).

Write

Write your middle paragraphs. Use your topic sentences, plot chart, and sample quotation list to guide your writing. Try to include an example of figurative language or symbolism to enhance the theme for the reader.

Tip

Most literary analyses are organized chronologically, providing events in the order they appear in the novel. Use transition words and phrases that show time to connect your ideas.

Transitions That Show Time

After	Before	In the end	That night
As soon as	During	Later	Then
At the start	Finally	Soon	When

Other types of transitions are also useful for connecting ideas. The sample paper uses time transitions *(the first part of the novel, two years later, eventually)* as well as those that show cause and effect *(as a result, because)* and contrast *(however, though, unfortunately).*

Literature

Writing Ending Your Analysis

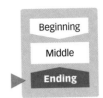

Beginning

Middle

Ending

Your essay starts with a thesis statement that connects the theme to a key element (plot, character, setting) in the novel. In the middle paragraphs, you show how the theme develops during the course of the action. The ending is your final chance to comment on and analyze the theme. Here are some suggestions for this final part of your essay.

- Show how the character has changed because of the theme.
- Use a quotation from the story.
- Predict how the theme might affect the characters in the future.
- State the theme as a basic truth about life.

Ending Paragraph

> Eventually, Okonkwo serves his seven-year exile and returns to Umuofia, inflamed by Obierika's analysis of the situation:
>
> **A quotation sums up the fatal situation.**
>
> The white man came quietly and peaceably with his religion. We were amused at his foolishness and allowed him to stay. Now he has put a knife on the things that held us together, and we have fallen apart.
>
> Okonkwo takes up his role as a warrior against the invaders, and in a disastrous series of events, becomes a kind of disgraced martyr. Okonkwo's traditions have been ridiculed and insulted by some of the missionaries, but the damage goes far beyond religious issues. An entire society has been uprooted. The title of a book the English commissioner writes about his African adventures reveals the European attitude toward the natives: The Pacification of the Primitive Tribes of the Lower Niger. Okonkwo's plight symbolizes the choice faced by many conquered or controlled peoples—submit to a new way of life or perish. Okonkwo tragically experiences the latter.

The final ideas state the thesis as a basic truth.

Write

Write your ending and form a complete first draft. Develop the last paragraph using one or more of the suggestions above. Make a clean copy of your complete essay. Double-space or write on every other line to make room for changes.

Revising

Now that your first draft is complete, you are ready to begin the revision process. Focus on ideas, organization, and other key traits to make changes that will improve your writing.

Keys to Effective Revising

1. Read your essay aloud to see whether it makes sense from start to finish.

2. Check your thesis statement to be sure it includes the theme of the story.

3. Be sure that each middle paragraph supports and explains the thesis statement.

4. Check your ending. Have you given a final analysis of the theme you developed in your essay?

5. Check to see that your voice sounds knowledgeable.

6. Review your writing for precise words and a variety of smooth-flowing sentences.

Revising for Ideas

6 My essay shows an in-depth analysis of the theme.

5 My essay has a clear thesis statement and analyzes the theme of the novel.

4 My essay has a thesis statement, but my analysis of the theme needs to be stronger in a few places.

When you revise for *ideas*, be sure that your thesis statement is clear and complete and that your analysis of the novel clearly develops the theme. Use the rubric strip above to help you revise.

Is my thesis statement clear and complete?

Your thesis statement will be clear and complete if you state the theme and connect it with at least one element (plot, character, setting) of the novel. Here are some guidelines to help you evaluate how theme is revealed.

1. Does the **plot** seem to propel the characters? How do the events work together to create the theme?
2. Do the **characters** create the conflicts, problems, and solutions? Is there one central character?
3. Is the **setting** an important and continuing presence in the novel? How does it impact the characters and their actions?

Try It!

In these thesis statements, identify the theme and the key element.

1. In the end, however, two young sharecroppers demonstrate the hope that happiness can eventually return after terrible loss.
2. The isolated location of the island creates an atmosphere that reveals the fragile nature of society's control over individuals.
3. The moment he discovered the baby on his doorstep, the reclusive Silas Marner began the journey out of isolation and greed, a journey that would reveal the true value of love.

Tip

It's important to be aware of a novel's narrator. Some stories are told by minor characters or bystanders, some by main characters, and some by **omniscient narrators** who are not part of the story. Knowing the narrator's relationship to the story is important to your analysis of the theme.

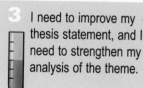 **3** I need to improve my thesis statement, and I need to strengthen my analysis of the theme.

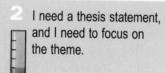 **2** I need a thesis statement, and I need to focus on the theme.

1 I need to learn more about how to identify and analyze a theme.

Does my analysis clearly reveal the theme?

Your analysis will clearly reveal the theme if you support your ideas with details from the book. Focus on details that apply directly to the theme.

- **Choose events related to the theme.**
  Knowing that he has done wrong, he immediately takes the step that tradition dictates, exiling himself from Umuofia for seven years.
      not
  Okonkwo had three wives.

- **Mention secondary characters only as they expand the theme.**
  Obierika returns two years later with more stories about missionaries.
      not

  Mr. Brown is a kind and compassionate missionary.

 ## Exercise

Read the paragraph below. Which detail does not apply to the theme?

1 Word spread that the white men had formed a court in Umuofia to protect
2 followers of their religion. The procedures were different from those used in
3 the natives' system of justice, resulting in anger and misunderstanding when
4 a villager was hanged for killing a missionary. News of the execution was
5 transmitted by *ekwe*, a hollowed-out wooden instrument.

 Review your first draft for ideas. Be sure that you have a clear and complete thesis statement and that your analysis clearly reveals the theme.

Revise

Ideas
The writer deletes a detail not related to the theme.

Things Fall Apart by Chinua Achebe focuses on Nigeria

in the late 1800s, a time of great change in Africa.

Achebe was born in 1930. Okonkwo, a leader . . .

Literature

Revising for Organization

6 All of the parts of my essay work together to create an insightful analysis.

5 The beginning, middle, and ending work well, and my paragraphs are coherent and smooth.

4 I have a beginning, a middle, and an ending, but in a few places my paragraphs aren't smooth or coherent.

Organization is the way ideas are arranged in an essay. Your paragraphs should flow smoothly from one to the next within an essay, and the ideas within each paragraph should also flow smoothly from one sentence to the next. The rubric strip above will help you revise for organization.

Do my paragraphs flow smoothly from one to the next?

Your paragraphs will flow smoothly if each opening sentence includes a key word or idea from the previous paragraph. Study these opening sentences from the middle paragraphs of the sample essay.

Opening Paragraph to First Middle Paragraph

As the novel progresses, <u>Okonkwo</u> becomes ensnarled in the clash of two cultures.

> **<u>Okonkwo</u> is known far beyond the village of Umuofia for his personal achievements and extraordinary bravery and toughness.** (*The main character's name ties the last sentence in the previous paragraph to the first sentence in the next paragraph.*)

First Middle Paragraph to Second Middle Paragraph

Knowing that he has done wrong, he immediately takes the steps that tradition dictates, <u>exiling</u> himself from Umuofia for seven years.

> **Although Okonkwo feels his <u>exile</u> is the worst thing that could happen to him, the coming of the Europeans proves to be a problem on a much larger scale.** (*The key word exile links the last sentence in the previous paragraph to the first sentence in the next paragraph.*)

Review your first draft. Check each opening sentence and decide if your paragraphs flow smoothly. The opening sentence should connect in some way with the previous paragraph. Revise accordingly.

Revise

3 The beginning, middle, or ending is weak, and I need more coherent paragraphs that flow smoothly.

2 My essay runs together, and my paragraphs do not flow well.

1 I need to learn how to organize a response to literature.

Is each paragraph of my analysis coherent?

A paragraph will be coherent if the sentences within it flow smoothly from one to the next. *Unity* is a key characteristic of coherent paragraphs. It is best to delete any phrase or sentence that does not clearly support the topic of the paragraph.

Try It!

Carefully read the following paragraph. Then decide which sentence should be eliminated to make the paragraph more coherent.

1   The novel is a lesson in how to raise a family. Marmee helps three
2   girls overcome teenage anxiety and tragedy by anchoring them in religion,
3   common sense, and love. Nowadays, people turn to counseling or
4   antidepressants. As adults, the girls carry Marmee's teachings into their
5   own productive lives as a pianist, an artist, and a writer.

Revise

Review your first draft for smooth flow and coherence. Be sure that each paragraph is clear and unified. Revise any problems.

Literature

Organization
A sentence is removed to make the paragraph more coherent.

This action was done in retaliation for the death of another white man who rode an "iron horse"—a bicycle—through a group of panicked villagers. ~~Some early bicycles were called velocipedes.~~ They apparently attacked him because he did not reply to their questions. Okonkwo's wise uncle . . .

Revising for Voice

<table>
<tr>
<td>6 My writer's voice sounds distinctive, engaging, and knowledgeable throughout.</td>
<td>5 My voice sounds knowledgeable, and I use a third-person point of view.</td>
<td>4 My voice sounds knowledgeable most of the time, and most of my pronouns are third person.</td>
</tr>
</table>

Voice is the way your writing sounds. In a literary analysis, it's important to sound knowledgeable and to maintain the third-person point of view throughout. The rubric strip above will help you revise for voice.

Do I maintain a third-person point of view throughout?

You have maintained a third-person point of view if you have consistently used third-person pronouns *(he, she, it, they)*. Avoid using first-person pronouns *(I, we)* or the second-person pronoun *(you)*.

Try It!

The paragraph below sometimes drifts away from the third-person point of view. On your own paper, rewrite the paragraph so that the voice is consistently third person. In places, you will need to completely change the sentence structure to correct the point of view.

> In *The Old Man and the Sea*, an old fisherman named Santiago is tested beyond normal human endurance. He goes out in his boat one morning, and you catch sight of a huge swordfish. Santiago hooks it, and I thought he was never going to land it, but next thing you know, it's lashed to the boat. Then you see sharks all around, eating pieces of the fish. Santiago must summon every ounce of strength in his struggle against the sharks, and you realize that courage is not limited to young heroes. Santiago says, "Man is not made for defeat. A man can be destroyed but not defeated." You feel he is courageous because of his actions.

Revise

Check for third-person point of view. Read your analysis to see whether you have maintained a third-person point of view throughout. Make any necessary revisions.

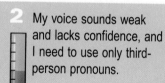

3 Sometimes my voice lacks confidence, and my point of view is inconsistent.

2 My voice sounds weak and lacks confidence, and I need to use only third-person pronouns.

1 I need to learn more about voice.

Do I sound knowledgeable about the book?

Your voice will sound knowledgeable if you show a clear understanding of the theme and write with confidence about it. Keep these tips in mind.

- **Be direct.** Use the fewest words possible to get your point across, and avoid flowery or wordy language.
- **Avoid starting sentences with "It is" or "There is."** These constructions lack energy and direction.
- **Avoid waffle words** such as *kind of, sort of, in a way, maybe, might,* or *seemed like* that overly qualify what you write.

Try It!

Rewrite the following sentence to make it sound more knowledgeable. Use the strategies given above.

It seems like Manolin wants to go along on the fishing trip with Santiago, but there is the problem that his parents think that maybe he shouldn't go because it seems to them that the old man might be bad luck.

Revise

Check your essay for voice. Reread your essay, marking any places that do not sound knowledgeable. Revise as needed.

Voice
Waffle words are deleted.

The force that ~~kind of~~ drives him is ~~probably~~ the fact that he "had no patience with his father," who was ~~sort of~~ irresponsible and constantly in debt, preferring to drink and play the flute. Okonkwo thinks of his father as . . .

Literature

Revising **for** Word Choice

6 My word choice demonstrates my careful analysis of the novel.

5 My word choice exhibits appropriate connotation, and I use literary terms correctly.

4 I use words with correct connotation, but I should use more literary terms.

When you revise for *word choice*, carefully choose words with the correct connotation. Also include literary terms in your analysis. Use the rubric above to help you revise for word choice.

Do I use words with the correct connotation?

Your words will have the correct connotation if they convey the appropriate *feeling*. Here are two ways to improve the connotation of your words.

- **Replace words that have the wrong feeling.**
  Lost in the vast deserts of New Mexico, Father Jean Latour *trotted* along in search of water. (The word *trotted* sounds bouncy and energetic. The word *trudged* has a more appropriate feeling.)
- **Replace bland words with strong words.**
  Dying of thirst, the father *went* to his knees in prayer. (The word *went* is nondescript; *crumpled* is a vivid word.)

Try It!

For each underlined word, suggest another word with a better connotation. Use a dictionary or thesaurus if you need help.

1. When he opened his eyes, Father Latour <u>viewed</u> a juniper tree in the shape of a cross.
2. Afterward, his horse led him to a small pool, and Father Latour <u>sipped</u> the fresh water.
3. A <u>sneer</u> of thankfulness <u>slashed</u> across his face.
4. Renewed and refreshed, Father Latour <u>staggered</u> away, <u>groping</u> for the path to Sante Fe.

Revise

Revise for connotation. Consider the words you have used in your analysis. Replace any words that have the wrong feeling or are too bland for the message you wish to convey.

3 I need to choose words with more-appropriate connotation and include literary terms.

2 Many words have the wrong connotation, and I use no literary terms.

1 I need to learn more about word choice.

Have I effectively used literary terms in my analysis?

You have effectively used literary terms if they reveal your understanding of the novel and help you to express yourself. Like science, history, and mathematics, literature has its own set of specialized terms (*conflict, theme, symbol, metaphor,* and so on).

Try It!

Read the paragraph below and explain how the underlined literary terms add meaning to the analysis.

> In *Fahrenheit 451*, Bradbury's references to the natural world serve as <u>symbols</u> of reality. For example, Montag experiences the sensation of smell for the first time when he tries to escape down the river. The nomadic lifestyle also becomes a <u>metaphor</u> for returning to an unstructured, natural existence. Gradually, artificial, urban <u>settings</u> turn out to be less and less real for Montag.

Revise for literary terminology. Review your analysis to be sure that you have used appropriate literary terms as needed.

Revise

Literature

Word Choice
Words are changed to improve the connotation.

> . . . The first part of the novel follows Okonkwo's life to the point where an accident _∧happens to wipe out everything he
> *threatens*
> has worked for. Unknown to Okonkwo, however, something even more _∧negative is about to affect his people.
> *disturbing*

Revising for Sentence Fluency

| 6 | The sentences in my analysis convey my ideas in a smooth, clear, distinctive way. | 5 | My sentences read smoothly, are balanced, and have a somewhat pleasing rhythm. | 4 | Most of my sentences read smoothly, but I need to balance some of them and use some short sentences. |

To revise for *sentence fluency*, check that you have used short sentences for emphasis and that all of your sentences flow smoothly. The rubric strip above will help you.

Have I effectively used short sentences in my analysis?

You have used short sentences effectively if they make a point. As you know, good writing includes a variety of sentences that create a pleasing rhythm. A well-placed short sentence or two can effectively interrupt that rhythm and call attention to an important idea. In the passages below, notice the effect of the short sentences in bold.

> At the head of a shallow ravine, a mere depression of the ground, lay a small group of bodies. He saw, and, swerving suddenly from his course, walked rapidly toward them. Scanning each one sharply as he passed, he stopped at last above one which lay at a slight remove from the others, near a clump of small trees. **He looked at it narrowly. It seemed to stir.** He stooped and laid his hand upon its face. **It screamed.**
>
> —Ambrose Bierce

> Okonkwo takes up his role as a warrior against the invaders, and in a disastrous series of events, becomes a kind of disgraced martyr. Okonkwo's traditions have been ridiculed and insulted by the missionaries, but the damage goes far beyond religious issues. **An entire society has been uprooted.**
>
> —Student Writer

Review your first draft. Read your essay to see whether you have used short sentences for emphasis. Make any necessary revisions.

Revise

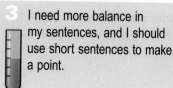

3 I need more balance in my sentences, and I should use short sentences to make a point.

2 My sentences are out of balance and have no real rhythm. I need to use short sentences to make a point.

1 I need to learn more about sentences.

Are my sentences balanced?

Your sentences are balanced if certain elements within each are *parallel*, or stated in the same way. Study the following examples to see the difference that parallel structure can make.

Unparallel: Granny knew that her love could be seen in the food she cooked, her making all the clothes, and the gardens she liked growing.

Parallel: Granny knew that her love could be seen in the food she had cooked, the clothes she had made, and the garden she had grown.

Unparallel: Granny remembered her life and is preparing for dying.

Parallel: Granny remembered her life and prepared for death.

Grammar Exercise

Revise the following unparallel sentences to make them parallel.

1. Thinking about her life made Granny feel like rolling up her sleeves and she could put the whole place right again.

2. She remembered lighting the lamps, the scrubbing of wooden floors, and how she cared for her little children.

Revise

Revise for sentence fluency. Be sure that your sentences are balanced so that they read smoothly.

Literature

Sentence Fluency
A sentence is revised for parallel structure.

. . . Okonkwo works harder than anyone to provide food for his family, reveres the words of the mystic oracles, to kill without mercy, and he obeys the priestess Chielo.

Revising Improving Your Writing

Check your revising. On a piece of paper, write the numbers 1 to 12. If you can answer "yes" to a question, put a check mark after that number. If not, continue to work with that part of your essay.

Revising Checklist

Ideas

_____ **1.** Is my thesis statement clear and complete?

_____ **2.** Do my ideas develop the book's theme?

_____ **3.** Are all my supporting details related to the theme?

Organization

_____ **4.** Have I written a clear beginning, middle, and ending?

_____ **5.** Do my paragraphs flow smoothly from one to the next?

_____ **6.** Is each paragraph coherent and unified?

Voice

_____ **7.** Do I maintain a third-person point of view throughout?

_____ **8.** Do I sound knowledgeable about the novel?

Word Choice

_____ **9.** Do I use words with the correct connotation?

_____ **10.** Have I effectively used literary terms in my analysis?

Sentence Fluency

_____ **11.** Do I use short sentences for emphasis in my analysis?

_____ **12.** Are my sentences balanced (parallel in structure)?

Make a clean copy. When you finish revising your essay, make a clean copy for editing.

Editing

After you've finished revising your essay, it's time to edit for the following conventions: punctuation, capitalization, spelling, and grammar.

Keys to Effective Editing

1. Use a dictionary, a thesaurus, and the "Proofreader's Guide" in the back of this book (pages 604–763).

2. Use quotation marks correctly for direct quotations.

3. Check all of your writing for correct punctuation, capitalization, spelling, and grammar.

4. If you use a computer, edit on a printout and then enter your changes on the computer.

5. Use the editing and proofreading marks inside the back cover of this book.

Literature

Editing for Conventions

6 My grammar and punctuation are correct, and the copy is free of spelling errors.

5 I have one or two errors in grammar, spelling, or punctuation, but they won't distract the reader.

4 I need to correct a few errors in punctuation, spelling, or grammar that may distract the reader.

Conventions are the rules for punctuation, capitalization, grammar, and spelling. To edit for conventions, use the rubric strip above as a guide.

Have I correctly used commonly confused words?

You can avoid misusing similar words by checking your writing carefully. Here are some terms to watch for in a literary analysis.

- An **allusion** is an indirect reference to someone or something.
  An **illusion** is a false picture or appearance.
  A **delusion** is a belief that is out of touch with reality.
- **Cite** means to quote.
  A **site** is a location.
  Sight is the act of seeing.

Grammar Exercise

Choose the correct word in each set of parentheses.

1. The *Fellowship of the Ring* makes continual *(allusions, illusions, delusions)* to an earlier War of the Ring.
2. The ring is altogether evil, so anyone who thinks it can be used for good is suffering from a(n) *(allusion, illusion, delusion)*.
3. The Ring of Power gives its wearer invisibility, creating the *(allusion, illusion, delusion)* that the person is not there.
4. To find out about the ring, Gandalf must ride to Minas Tirith, *(cite, site, sight)* of the greatest human library.
5. When he returns to tell the horrible truth to Frodo, he *(cites, sites, sights)* the old rhyme "One Ring to Rule Them All."
6. When Gandalf places the ring in the fire, he sees a terrible *(cite, site, sight)*—the inscription that showed this was the "one ring."

Edit

Check for misused words. Use the definitions above and those in the "Proofreader's Guide" to be sure that the words in your essay are correct.

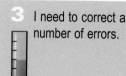 **3** I need to correct a number of errors.

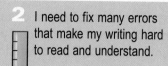 **2** I need to fix many errors that make my writing hard to read and understand.

1 I need help making corrections.

How do I punctuate interrupting words and phrases?

You should place commas before and after any words or phrases that interrupt the flow of your sentences. Common interrupting words and phrases include the following:

however	in fact	by contrast	of course	for example
true	as a rule	as a result	in response	after all

 ### Grammar Exercise

Rewrite the following paragraph, inserting commas as needed for any interrupting words or phrases.

Hobbits are as a rule peaceable people who aren't interested in adventure. When a Black Rider appears in the Shire however Frodo Baggins must journey from his comfortable home. He carries the one ring that can enslave the world. Frodo could use the ring to turn invisible, but doing so would in fact make him easier to detect by the Black Rider. Instead, Frodo and his companions flee across country. At an old watchtower, five Black Riders catch up to them, and Frodo is stabbed by a rider's blade. The tip breaks off in the wound and as a result Frodo becomes ill.

 Edit for conventions. Check your essay for words or phrases that interrupt the flow of your sentences. Make sure to set off these words or phrases with commas.

Edit

Literature

Conventions
An interrupting word is punctuated.

Unknown to Okonkwo‸however‸something even more disturbing is about to affect his people. White missionaries begin to travel throughout his homeland, bringing their . . .

Editing Checking for Conventions

Edit

Check your editing. On a piece of paper, write the numbers 1 to 12. Put a check mark by the number if you can answer "yes" to that question. If not, continue to edit your essay for that convention.

Editing Checklist

Conventions

PUNCTUATION

_____ **1.** Does each sentence have correct end punctuation?

_____ **2.** Have I used quotation marks correctly with direct quotations?

_____ **3.** Do I correctly punctuate compound and complex sentences?

_____ **4.** Have I used commas to set off interrupting words and phrases?

_____ **5.** Do I use apostrophes to show possession *(in Poe's story)*?

CAPITALIZATION

_____ **6.** Do I start all my sentences with capital letters?

_____ **7.** Have I capitalized all proper nouns?

SPELLING

_____ **8.** Have I spelled all my words correctly?

_____ **9.** Have I double-checked the words my spell-checker may have missed?

GRAMMAR

_____ **10.** Have I used correct verb tenses throughout?

_____ **11.** Do my pronouns and antecedents agree?

_____ **12.** Have I used the right words *(its, it's)*?

Creating a Title

- Focus on the theme: **Good Intentions and Bad Results**
- Refer to a character: **The Pacification of Okonkwo**
- Be creative: **When Cultures Clash, *Things Fall Apart***

Publishing Sharing Your Essay

Now that you've finished writing, revising, and editing your essay, it is time to publish it. See the suggestions in the boxes below for a variety of ways to present your essay.

Make a final copy. Follow your teacher's instructions or use the guidelines below to format your paper. (If you are using a computer, see pages 76–78.) Write a final copy of your essay and proofread it for errors.

Focusing on Presentation

- Use blue or black ink and write neatly.
- Write your name in the upper left corner of page 1.
- Skip a line and center your title; skip another line and start your writing.
- Indent every paragraph and leave a one-inch margin on all four sides.
- Write your last name and the page number in the upper right-hand corner of every page after page 1.

Publish in a Class Literary Magazine

Set up your work in a multicolumn format, add headlines, and include photos or paintings of the author and characters. Consider adding "sidebar" graphics or comments.

Make a Recording

Read your analysis and record it on a CD or DVD. Consider including appropriate music, sound effects, and video clips.

Post Your Essay on the Web

Submit your work to a community, school, or class Web site or post it on a family Web site.

Literature

Rubric for a Response to Literature

Use this rubric for guiding and assessing your writing. Refer to it whenever you want to improve your writing using the six traits.

6	**5**	**4**
Ideas		
The ideas show a deep understanding of the reading.	The essay has a clear thesis statement and a variety of necessary supporting details.	The essay has a clear thesis statement. Unnecessary details need to be cut.
Organization		
All the parts work together to create an insightful essay.	The organization pattern fits the topic and purpose. All parts of the essay are well developed.	The organization pattern fits the topic and purpose. A part of the essay needs better development.
Voice		
The voice expresses interest and in-depth understanding. It engages the reader.	The voice expresses interest in and understanding of the topic.	The voice expresses interest but needs to show more understanding.
Word Choice		
The word choice reflects critical thinking about the reading.	The word choice, including the use of literary terms, creates a clear message.	The word choice is clear, but more literary terms would improve the essay.
Sentence Fluency		
The sentences create a clear flow of ideas throughout the essay.	The sentences are skillfully written and keep the reader's interest.	No sentence problems exist. More sentence variety is needed.
Conventions		
Grammar and punctuation are correct, and the copy is free of all errors.	The essay has one or two errors that do not interfere with the reader's understanding.	The essay has a number of careless errors in punctuation and grammar.

3	**2**	**1**
The thesis statement is too broad. A variety of details are needed.	The thesis statement is unclear. More details are needed.	The essay needs a thesis statement and details.
The organization fits the essay's purpose. Some parts need more development.	The organization doesn't fit the purpose.	A plan needs to be developed and followed.
The voice should show more interest in the topic and express more understanding.	The voice does not show interest in or an understanding of the topic.	The writer needs to understand how to create voice.
The word choice is too general, and more literary terms are needed.	Little attention was given to word choice.	The writer needs help with word choice.
A few sentence problems need to be corrected, and much more variety is needed.	The essay has many sentence problems.	The writer needs to learn how to construct sentences.
The errors in the essay confuse the reader.	The number of errors makes the essay hard to read.	Help is needed to make corrections.

Evaluating a Response to Literature

Read the following analysis of a theme. Then read the student's self-evaluation on the next page. **(There may be errors in the essay below.)**

Land Values

The Good Earth, by Pearl S. Buck, is the story of Wang Lung, a simple farmer who becomes a wealthy man by acquiring more and more land. As he does, he loses his traditional way of life and values. In the end, Wang Lung is haunted by the words he spoke as a young man: "Land is one's flesh and blood."

The basic conflict of Wang Lung's life is foreshadowed when his father arranges for him to marry a young woman from the big city. O-lan is a servant girl working for a rich family, the House of Hwang. When Wang Lung goes to get his future bride to take her back to his father's farm, he is shocked by the high prices and the rude ways of the city. The House of Hwang, with its impersonal atmosphere and showy wealth, is a huge contrast to life in the village. When Wang Lung brings O-lan home however, she immediately fits in with the traditional ways of the farm.

Wang Lung's life with O-lan begins happily as they work the land and prosper. They have a son, save their money, and live by the traditional, old-fashioned values that have been in place for centuries. They are so successful, in fact, that Wang Lung buys land from the House of Hwang, although O-lan warns that they already have enough land. Wang Lung does not realize that he has begun to turn away from the traditional values toward something new—ambition.

Ambition is so satisfying to Wang Lung that over the years he buys much more land from the failing House of Hwang. One of the ironies in the novel is that, although land is the source of traditional life, obtaining more land leads him from that life. Wang is gradually overcome by lazy relatives, starving villagers, and spoiled children. Although he continues to gain land and wealth, he seems less and less satisfied with his life. Wang Lung goes to the city, seeking escape, and gets involved in fast living, forgetting the morals that he was raised with. At one point, he agrees to cut off his pigtails, a symbol of his traditional, rural background, because an attractive woman in the city laughs at him for wearing them.

Life back on the farm becomes more and more complicated, with huge tracts of land, numerous buildings, and many workers to manage. Because there is so much to keep track of, Wang Lung hires people to take care of business for him, and Wang Lung ends up with nothing to do all day but deal with his family troubles. In the ultimate irony of the novel, Wang Lung decides to move everyone to the old House of Hwang, which has been abandoned by its bankrupt owners. Wang Lung's family has become like the one he despised when he went to bring O-lan home.

Wang Lung doesn't have much to be happy about, but he does have one remaining comfort—when he picks up a hoe to work in the field, he says, "The land did again its healing work." As an old man, Wang Lung returns to live out his life on the old farm. He still loves the land, thinking, "It is the end of a family—when they begin to sell the land." Wang Lung sees that wealth is not everything; there is more happiness in living on the land—man's true home.

Student Self-Assessment

Response Rubric Checklist

Title: Land Values
Writer: Sarah Gritzmacher

3 Ideas
- Do I have a clear thesis statement?
- Do I use effective details?

5 Organization
- Does the beginning give background information and state the theme?
- Does the middle develop the theme?
- Does the ending analyze the theme?

5 Voice
- Does my voice sound knowledgeable?

5 Word Choice
- Have I used correct literary terminology?

5 Sentence Fluency
- Do my sentences read smoothly?

5 Conventions
- Have I avoided usage and punctuation errors?

OVERALL COMMENTS:

My thesis statement isn't clear. I should have written more about other characters and how they influenced the theme.

I have a strong beginning, middle, and ending.

I show interest in the book.

I use several literary terms.

I begin sentences in several ways.

My paper is almost error free.

Use the rubric. Rate your essay using the rubric on pages 290–291. Write comments about your scores.

Literature

Reflecting on Your Writing

Reflect on your finished analysis of a theme by completing each starter sentence below. These comments will help you check your progress as a writer.

My Response to Literature

1. The strongest part of my essay is . . .

2. The part that still needs work is . . .

3. The main thing I learned about writing an analysis of a theme is . . .

4. In my next response to literature, I would like to . . .

5. One question I still have about writing an analysis of a theme is . . .

6. Right now I would describe my writing ability as . . . (excellent, good, fair, poor)

Writing for Assessment
Responding to Prompts About Literature

Some assessment tests require you to respond to prompts about literature. These prompts may focus on something you have read before the test, to something you read during the test, or to a combination of the two. Your response should show how well you understand the literature and how clearly you can form your thoughts within a limited amount of time. To prepare for this type of writing, carefully read your assignments in English class and pay particular attention to terms related to literature, such as *theme, symbol, character, metaphor,* and *irony.*

This chapter will help you to develop responses to literary prompts. You will learn to analyze various types of prompts, to use the writing process in a test situation, and to respond to fiction and nonfiction.

Writing Guidelines

Subject: **Literature prompt**
Form: **Response to a prompt**
Purpose: **To demonstrate competence**
Audience: **Instructor**

"Literature adds to reality, it does not simply describe it."
—C. S. Lewis

"Literature is news that stays news."
—Ezra Pound

Prewriting Analyzing a Literature Prompt

Prompts about literature ask you to respond to specific characteristics of a story, a poem, a novel, or a nonfiction selection. Look for key words that tell you exactly what the prompt requires. In the sample prompt below, key words and phrases are underlined. The word *analyze* (red) gives the main direction or focus for the response.

Sample Prompt

In Joan Aiken's story "Searching for Summer," the <u>setting</u> and the <u>title are important clues to the theme</u>. <u>When</u> does the story take place? What are the characters <u>really searching for</u>? <u>How</u> does the story suggest a frightening possibility? <u>Analyze how the story serves as a warning about the dangers of present-day technology.</u>

Try It!

Copy the following sample prompts on a sheet of paper. Underline key words and phrases for each prompt and make notes about the kinds of supporting information that you would need for your response.

1. In her essay "Border: A Glare of Truth," Pat Mora discusses her feelings about moving to Ohio from El Paso, the place where she grew up. What is the "truth" that Mora learns about her early life in the border country of the Southwest? Using specific examples from her essay, prove how moving away from the border actually brought her closer to her heritage.

2. The title of D. H. Lawrence's poem "Piano" names an object that takes on a special meaning. Explain the significance of the title and its symbolic importance for Lawrence's narrator. Cite specific examples from the poem to support your thesis.

Planning Your Response

Once you analyze and understand a prompt, you are ready to plan your response. If a reading selection is provided, examine it carefully for information related to the prompt. Then form a topic sentence and organize the details.

Sample Prompt and Selection

In this excerpt from A. Conan Doyle's "A Study in Scarlet," Sherlock Holmes explains the effective use of one's memory. In a paragraph, analyze how he makes his point with comparisons.

"You see," he explained, "I consider that a man's brain originally is like a little empty attic, and you have to stock it with such furniture as you choose. A fool takes in all the lumber of every sort that he comes across, so that the knowledge which might be useful to him gets crowded out, or at best is jumbled up with a lot of other things so that he has a difficulty in laying his hands upon it. Now the skillful workman is very careful indeed as to what he takes into his brain-attic. He will have nothing but the tools which may help him in doing his work, but of these he has a large assortment, and all in the most perfect order.

> Comparisons are underlined.

Writing a Topic Sentence

After reading the prompt and selection, a student wrote this topic sentence.

> **Sherlock Holmes thinks of the brain** (specific topic) **as an empty storage space, where care must be taken to avoid cluttering the memory with useless facts** (particular focus).

Creating a Graphic Organizer

The writer used a T-chart to organize the elements being compared.

Comparisons	
Memory	**Everyday Objects**
– jumbled memory	– "takes in lumber of every sort"
– helpful memory	– "the tools which may help him"

Writing Responding to a Fiction Prompt

The following prompt and fiction selection show how a student underlined words and phrases and added some notes on a copy of the selection to address the focus of the prompt (red).

Sample Prompt and Selection

The following excerpts from the first chapter of Edith Wharton's novel *Ethan Frome* describe the night Ethan walked to town and caught a glimpse of a church dance. Explain how Edith Wharton uses the setting to help you understand Ethan's emotions.

From *Ethan Frome* by Edith Wharton

Stillness, cold, shades of black and white except for yellow light from church basement

The village lay under two feet of snow, with drifts at the windy corners. In a sky of iron the points of the Dipper hung like icicles and Orion flashed his cold fires. The moon had set, but the night was so transparent that the white house-fronts between the elms looked gray against the snow, clumps of bushes made black stains on it, and the basement windows of the church sent shafts of yellow light far across the endless undulations.

Young Ethan Frome walked at a quick pace along the deserted street. . . . [T]he church reared its slim white steeple. . . . As the young man walked toward it the upper windows drew a black arcade along the side wall of the building. . . .

At the end of the village he paused before the darkened front on the church. . . . The hush of midnight lay on the village, and all its waking life was gathered behind the church windows, from which strains of dance-music flowed with the broad bands of yellow light. . . .

Heat, movement inside church contrast with cold outside.

Seen thus, from the pure and frosty darkness in which he stood, it seemed to be seething in a mist of heat. The metal reflectors of the gas-jets sent crude waves of light against the whitewashed walls, and the iron flanks of the stove at the end of the hall looked as though they were heaving with volcanic fires. The floor was thronged with girls and young men. . . .

> A lively young man and a girl with colorful scarf dance.
>
> The guests were preparing to leave, and the tide had already set toward the passage where coats and wraps were hung, when a <u>young man</u> with a sprightly foot and a shock of black hair <u>shot</u> into the middle of the floor and <u>clapped</u> his hands. The signal took instant effect. The musicians hurried to their instruments . . . and the lively young man, after <u>diving</u> about here and there in the throng, drew forth a <u>girl</u> who had already wound a <u>cherry-coloured</u> "fascinator" about her head, and, leading her up to the end of the floor, <u>whirled</u> her down its length to the <u>bounding tune</u> of a Virginia reel.
> <u>Frome's heart was beating fast</u>. . . .

Writing a Thesis Statement

After reading the excerpt and taking notes, the student wrote the following thesis statement for her response essay.

> **Wharton helps the reader understand the feelings of a man** (specific topic) **who sees through a church basement window a scene much different from his colorless world** (particular focus).

Creating a Graphic Organizer

The writer created a T-chart to list important details about the setting.

on the way to the church	in the church basement
"two feet of snow"	"shafts of yellow light"
"hush of midnight"	"strains of dance-music"
"sky of iron," constellations	"broad bands of yellow light"
"hung like icicles"	"seething in a mist of heat"
"flashed his cold fires"	"waves of light," "whitewashed walls"
"black stains"	"stove . . . heaving with volcanic fires"
"white steeple"	"cherry-coloured 'fascinator'"

Student Response

In this student response to the excerpts from *Ethan Frome*, note how the writer used details from the novel to support the thesis statement.

Ethan Sees Red

In this excerpt from *Ethan Frome*, Ethan walks into a village one cold winter night to get a glimpse of a dance in a church basement. He is definitely portrayed as an outsider in this passage. <u>Wharton helps the reader understand the feelings of this man who sees through a church basement window a scene much different from his colorless world.</u>

Ethan was out late at night, as "the hush of midnight lay on the village." Bleak images in shades of black and white mark his journey. He seems to be a part of the quiet landscape as he walks under a "sky of iron" filled with constellations "hung like icicles" or flashing "cold fires." The shadows cast by these night lights are "black stains" on the snow. As he approaches the church, the "white steeple" rises above the black walls of the building. He avoids those walls, attracted by something much different from the night that surrounds him.

In contrast with the stark surroundings, the windows of the church basement send out inviting "shafts of yellow light." As Ethan looks in, "strains of dance-music" flow. Inside is a scene "seething in a mist of heat" with "waves of light" washing the walls and a stove, "heaving with volcanic fires."

Middle
The middle paragraphs include details from the excerpts.

Suddenly, a young man dives into the throng of dancers and pulls out a girl with a "cherry-coloured" scarf on her head. The young man and the girl whirl to the "bounding tune of a Virginia reel."

Wharton shows a man as cold and gray as the snowy winter's night in which he finds himself. Then a warm room, snappy music, lively dancing, and a girl in a red scarf give Ethan an emotional wake-up call. As Wharton relates, "Frome's heart was beating fast." The contrast between the winter night and the party has had a dramatic effect on Ethan—an effect that could be important in the rest of the story.

Ending
The closing summarizes the thesis.

Respond to the reading. Answer the following questions about the student response.

Ideas (1) How does the thesis statement respond to the focus of the prompt? (2) What types of details does the student use to support her thesis?

Organization (3) How does the writer organize the middle two paragraphs in the response?

Voice & Word Choice (4) List two words or phrases quoted from the novel that are particularly effective.

Practice Literature Prompt

Whenever you respond to a writing prompt, especially in a timed situation, begin by studying the prompt. Look for the key word to find out what you are to do: *compare, explain, analyze,* and so on. Consider the questions and specific points of the prompt carefully before you read the selection. Quote examples and specific details from the selection to support your thesis, but share your own insights also—based on the connections you make as you read or recall a selection.

Practice Prompt and Selection

The following excerpt from Edith Wharton's novel *Summer* introduces the reader to the character Charity Royall. Does Wharton tell you what kind of person Charity is, or are you allowed to decide for yourself? Examine how the author develops this character. Support your ideas with examples from the excerpt.

From *Summer* by Edith Wharton

A girl came out of lawyer Royall's house, at the end of the one street of North Dormer, and stood on the doorstep.

The little June wind, frisking down the street, shook the doleful fringes of the Hatchard spruces, caught the straw hat of a young man just passing under them, and spun it clean across the road into the duck-pond.

As he ran to fish it out the girl on lawyer Royall's doorstep noticed that he was a stranger, that he wore city clothes, and that he was laughing with all his teeth, as the young and careless laugh at such mishaps.

Her heart contracted a little, and the shrinking that sometimes came over her when she saw people with holiday faces made her draw back into the house and pretend to look for the key that she knew she had already put into her pocket. A narrow greenish mirror with a gilt eagle over it hung on the passage wall, and she looked critically at her reflection, wished for the thousandth time that she had blue eyes like Annabel Balch, the girl who sometimes came from Springfield to spend a week with old Miss Hatchard, straightened the sunburnt hat over her small swarthy face, and turned out again into the sunshine.

"How I hate everything!" she murmured.

The girl walked along, swinging her key on a finger, and looking about her with the heightened attention produced by the presence of a stranger in a familiar place. What, she wondered, did North Dormer look like to people from other parts of the world? She herself had lived there since the age of five, and had long supposed it to be a place of some importance. But about a year before, Mr. Miles, the new Episcopal clergyman at Hepburn, who drove over every other Sunday—when the roads were not ploughed up by hauling—to hold a service in the North Dormer church, had proposed, in a fit of missionary zeal, to take the young people down to Nettleton to hear an illustrated lecture on the Holy Land; and the dozen girls and boys who represented the future of North Dormer had been piled into a farm-wagon, driven over the hills to Hepburn, put into a way-train and carried to Nettleton.

In the course of that incredible day Charity Royall had, for the first and only time, experienced railway-travel, looked into shops with plate-glass fronts, tasted coconut pie, sat in a theatre, and listened to a gentleman saying unintelligible things before pictures that she would have enjoyed looking at if his explanations had not prevented her from understanding them. This initiation had shown her that North Dormer was a small place, and developed in her a thirst for information that her position as custodian of the village library had previously failed to excite. For a month or two she dipped feverishly and disconnectedly into the dusty volumes of the Hatchard Memorial Library; then the impression of Nettleton began to fade, and she found it easier to take North Dormer as the norm of the universe than to go on reading. . . .

The sight of the young man turning in at Miss Hatchard's gate had brought back the vision of the glittering streets of Nettleton, and she felt ashamed of her old sun-hat, and sick of North Dormer, and jealously aware of Annabel Balch of Springfield, opening her blue eyes somewhere far off on glories greater than the glories of Nettleton.

"How I hate everything!" she said again.

 Respond to a literature prompt. Read the practice prompt again to be sure that you understand its focus. Then carefully reread the excerpt from the Wharton novel. Next, form a thesis statement, quickly arrange your main details in a graphic organizer, and write your essay.

Writing Responding to a Nonfiction Prompt

The following prompt and nonfiction selection show how a student underlined words and phrases and jotted some notes on a copy of the selection to address the focus of the prompt (red).

Sample Prompt and Selection

The following excerpt from Michel de Montaigne's essay "On Liars" examines a common problem in a thoughtful way. Do you agree or disagree with Montaigne's opinions on lying? Is lying as serious a problem as he feels it is? Using examples from your own life and the world in general, express your own feelings about liars and lying and how these feelings relate to Montaigne's.

From "On Liars" by Michel de Montaigne

I know quite well that grammarians make a distinction between telling an untruth and lying. They say that to tell an untruth is to say something that is false, but that we suppose to be true, and that the meaning of lying is to go against one's conscience, and that consequently it applies to those who say the opposite of what they know; it is of them I am speaking. . . .

Difference between untruth and lying

Now liars either invent the whole thing, or they disguise and alter an actual fact. If they disguise and alter, it is hard for them not to get mixed up when they refer to the same story again and again because, the real facts having been the first to lodge in the memory and impress themselves upon it by way of consciousness and knowledge, they will hardly fail to spring into the mind and dislodge the false version, which cannot have as firm or assured a foothold. . . .

Lying is indeed an accursed vice. We are men, and we have relations with one another by speech. If we recognized the horror and gravity of an untruth, we should more justifiably punish it with fire than any other crime. I commonly find people taking the most ill-advised pains to correct their children for their harmless faults and worrying them about heedless acts which leave no trace and have no consequences. Lying—and in a lesser degree

Lying must be corrected, or else.

stubbornness—are, in my opinion, <u>the only faults whose birth and progress we should consistently oppose</u>. They grow with a child's growth, and once the tongue has got the knack of lying, it is difficult to imagine how impossible it is to correct it. Whence it happens that we find <u>some otherwise excellent men subject to this fault and enslaved by it</u>. I have a decent lad as my tailor, whom I have never heard to utter a single truth, even when it would have been to his advantage.

How does lying have so many shapes?

If, like the truth, falsehood had only one face, we should know better where we are, for we should then take the opposite of what a liar said to be the truth. But <u>the opposite of a truth has a hundred thousand shapes and a limitless field</u>.

There are a thousand ways of missing the bull's-eye, only one of hitting it. . . .

Writing a Thesis Statement

After reading the excerpt, the student developed a thesis statement.

Montaigne is right about lying (specific topic) **when he says that it is just the beginning of even worse behavior** (particular focus related to the prompt).

Creating a Graphic Organizer

The student used a simple outline to plan his response.

I. Lying may be the beginning of bigger problems.
II. Dad caught Charlie lying about something he had done wrong and punished him for the lie.
III. Dad was thinking ahead and trying to keep Charlie from getting into the habit of lying.
IV. Continued lying becomes an enslaving habit, hard if not impossible to break.

Literature

Student Response

The following essay is a student response to the prompt and excerpts from Montaigne's essay "On Liars."

"An Accursed Vice"

Beginning
The first paragraph builds up to the thesis statement (underlined).

When I first read "On Liars," Montaigne sounded a little too extreme and impractical. Should liars be punished more severely than other wrongdoers? Is teaching a kid not to lie more important than anything else? Is lying "an accursed vice" when there are so many other awful things going on in the world? But when I thought about the things that seem worse than lying, it occurred to me that they also fit the essayist's definition of lying: going "against one's conscience." Perhaps Montaigne is right when he says that lying is just the beginning of even worse behavior.

Middle
The middle paragraphs develop the writer's argument, using a personal anecdote and a reflection.

The real problem may be that repeated lying changes a person. In the beginning, children sometimes lie because they think it is easier than telling the truth. My six-year-old brother Charlie watched Dad sawing a piece of wood, so when Dad wasn't around, Charlie took the saw and cut through one of the steps on the back deck. Dad asked Charlie if he cut the step, but Charlie blamed it on "someone else." Then Dad did something that I didn't expect. He punished Charlie for lying rather than for ruining the steps. Charlie was a little puzzled by this, but it made a big impression on me.

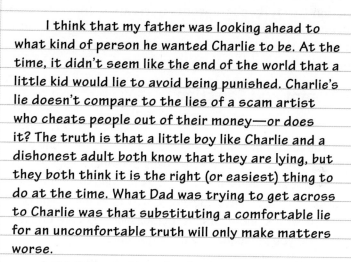

I think that my father was looking ahead to what kind of person he wanted Charlie to be. At the time, it didn't seem like the end of the world that a little kid would lie to avoid being punished. Charlie's lie doesn't compare to the lies of a scam artist who cheats people out of their money—or does it? The truth is that a little boy like Charlie and a dishonest adult both know that they are lying, but they both think it is the right (or easiest) thing to do at the time. What Dad was trying to get across to Charlie was that substituting a comfortable lie for an uncomfortable truth will only make matters worse.

I think Montaigne clearly states that there is no such thing as harmless lying because every lie makes one a little less able to live with the truth. As the liar's conscience gets weaker and weaker, that person's life becomes a lie.

Ending
The ending revisits the thesis and shares a final insight.

Literature

 Respond to the reading. Answer the following questions about the student response.

Ideas (1) What is the main point of the student response? (2) What anecdote does the student use to develop the argument?

Organization (3) How do the two middle paragraphs relate to each other?

Voice & Word Choice (4) What two phrases does the writer use from Montaigne's essay? Why does he use them?

Practice Writing Prompt

When you read and respond to fiction or nonfiction, notice that the writer of the selection carefully chose words to create a character, establish a setting, share information, stir up an emotion, and so on. You should be equally careful to choose the right words for your response to address whatever the prompt requires.

Practice Prompt and Selection

The following student editorial addresses the topic of cyber-bullying. Analyze how the writer uses personal anecdotes, common experience, and national news stories to build the argument. In your analysis, consider these questions: How does each type of evidence make the writing more (or less) persuasive? How are opposing opinions used? Are you persuaded by the argument?

"Rebooting Cyber-Bullies"

Nearly every teenager has been picked on or insulted at some point, but how many have endured insults that the whole world could see? Recently, somebody posted untrue, rude comments about me on my personal Web site. I had been cyber-bullied! Cyber-bullying is similar to regular verbal bullying, except that it is done with the use of technology—the Web, instant messaging, e-mail, cell phone text messages, and so on.

Victims of any kind of bullying suffer negative consequences. What makes cyber-bullies especially dangerous is that technology offers them greater access to their victims. It also allows them to bully anonymously and to humiliate their victims in a very public way. Some people may think that cyber-bullying is not that big a deal because it isn't physical, but anyone who's been the target of electronic threats knows they are not harmless.

Recent news reports about cyber-bullying are waking people up to the dangers of this trend. For one thing, the reports have shown that cyber-bullying can lead to real violence. They've also revealed that an alarming number of teens, up to 60% by some estimates, have been victimized. In response, many schools are now punishing cyber-bullies as severely as they can.

Instituting "zero tolerance" policies for cyber-bullying probably seems like the right thing to do. If students use technology to terrorize their classmates, especially at school, why shouldn't they be punished? Why shouldn't they be suspended or even thrown out of school permanently? The answer is complicated, but I don't think zero tolerance is the solution to cyber-bullying. Severely punishing bullies of any kind can have unintended effects. In fact, it often just leads to even more bullying.

So what can parents and teachers do about cyber-bullying? Studies show that cyber-bullies have often been bullied themselves. Many cyber-bullies are motivated by anger, revenge, or frustration. They may like the security and confidence of hiding behind a fake online personality. Others may just think they're being funny and don't understand how harmful their behavior can be. Whatever the motive, punishment alone won't work. There is no "one size fits all" solution to cyber-bullying, but understanding it is a start.

Schools and parents must create a tolerant environment. Schools should provide ongoing counseling, mentoring, and leadership programs, as well as information about the cyber-bullying epidemic. School officials should reach out to bullies. They should try to understand them and reform them rather than blindly punishing them. It may be surprising that the victim of a cyber-bully does not support harsh punishment, but the cycle of revenge has to stop somewhere.

 Respond to the writing prompt. Reread the practice prompt on page 308 to be sure that you understand its focus. Then reread the selection. Next, form a thesis statement, briefly list your main ideas in a graphic organizer, and write your response essay.

Literature

Revising Improving Your Response

Always review your response at the end of a writing test. Make any changes and corrections as neatly as possible. Use the following questions to help you revise your response.

- **Ideas:** Does my thesis statement address the focus of the prompt? Do the details support the thesis?

- **Organization:** Have I included a beginning, a middle, and an ending? Does each paragraph have a focus? Do I conclude with an insight about the literature selection?

- **Voice:** Do I sound clear in my thinking?

- **Word Choice:** Do the words that I use reflect my clear understanding of the literature selection? Have I avoided any unnecessary repetition?

- **Sentence Fluency:** Are all of my sentences complete? Do my sentences flow smoothly from one to the next?

Improve your work. Reread your practice response, asking yourself the questions above. Make any changes neatly.

Editing Checking Your Response

In your final read-through, check your punctuation, capitalization, spelling, and grammar.

Conventions

- _____ **1.** Have I used end punctuation for every sentence?
- _____ **2.** Have I capitalized all proper nouns and first words of sentences?
- _____ **3.** Have I checked the spelling in my work?
- _____ **4.** Have I made sure my subjects and verbs agree?
- _____ **5.** Have I put quotation marks around the exact words that I quoted from the selection?

Check your response. Read over your work, looking for errors in punctuation, capitalization, spelling, and grammar. Make corrections neatly.

Responding to Literature on Tests

Use the following tips as a guide whenever you respond to a prompt about literature. These tips will help you respond to both fiction and nonfiction selections.

Before you write . . .

- **Be clear about the time limit.**
  Plan enough time for prewriting, writing, and revising.
- **Understand the prompt.**
  Be sure that you know what the prompt requires. Pay special attention to the key word that tells you what you need to do.
- **Read the selection with the focus of the prompt in mind.**
  Take notes that will help you form your thesis. If you're working on a copy of the selection, underline important details.
- **Form your thesis statement.**
  The thesis statement should identify the specific topic plus the particular focus of the prompt.
- **Make a graphic organizer.**
  Jot down main points and possible quotations for your essay.

As you write . . .

- **Maintain the focus of your essay.**
  Keep your thesis in mind as you write.
- **Be selective.**
  Use examples from your graphic organizer and the selection to support your thesis.
- **End in a meaningful way.**
  Start by revisiting the thesis. Then try to share a final insight about the topic with the reader.

After you've written a first draft . . .

- **Check for completeness and correctness.**
  Use the questions on page **310** to revise your essay. Then check for errors in punctuation, capitalization, spelling, and grammar.

Try It!

Plan and write a response. Read a prompt your teacher supplies. Analyze it, read the selection, form a thesis statement, list ideas in a graphic organizer, and write your essay. Then revise and edit your response. Try to complete your work within the time your teacher gives you.

Literature

www.hmheducation.com/writesource

Creative Writing

Writing Focus

Writing Stories   **313**

Writing Plays   **323**

Writing Poetry   **333**

Academic Vocabulary

Working with a classmate, read the definitions below and discuss possible answers to each question.

1. A conflict is a struggle or problem.
   Think of a time you faced a serious conflict. How did you overcome it?

2. The foundation of something is what it is built or based upon.
   How can what you learn in school be the foundation for what you do later in life?

3. A device is something intended to achieve a particular effect.
   What is the effect of the literary device foreshadowing (hinting at what will happen later in a story)?

4. A technique is a special way of doing something.
   What study techniques do you use to help you prepare for a test?

Writing Stories

You are a born storyteller. You may find that talking about your experiences helps you to make sense out of your life. You may also enjoy making up stories, but that might not be as easy for you as it once was. It's no fault of your own. You're simply more focused on real-life experiences at this point in your life.

Here's the best way to feel inventive again: Sit down and start writing. Write simple stories, crazy stories, stories modeled after the ones you read now and the ones you read when you were younger.

This chapter will help you get started. It discusses the basic plot, offers a sample story and story-writing guidelines, and ends with a discussion of story patterns and important terms related to fiction.

Writing Guidelines

Subject: **A conflict within the main character**
Form: **Short story**
Purpose: **To engage and entertain**
Audience: **Classmates**

"The only way to learn to write short stories is to write them, and then try to discover what you have done."

—Flannery O'Connor

The Shape of Stories

Think of special experiences in your life: a key game, a family reunion, starting at a new school, getting your driver's license. These experiences build in excitement to a high point that really makes the event memorable. Fiction works in the same way. The story builds until the action reaches the climax, the most intense part of the plot.

Beginning with the Plot

The plot refers to the events or actions that move a story along from start to finish. A plot has five parts: *exposition, rising action, climax, falling action,* and *resolution.* The plot line below shows how these parts work together.

Plot Line

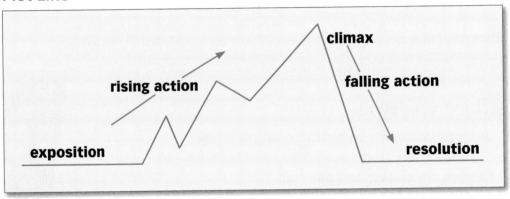

Exposition

The *exposition* is the beginning part of a story. In it, the main character, the conflict, and the setting are introduced. The conflict is the problem that the main character faces. The setting is the place and the time of the action. The following example demonstrates the sort of information that you would share in the exposition.

> Marina is in her room, cuddling her cat, Feather. Feather is very old, has lost his eyesight, and has extreme difficulty moving around. The cat had once belonged to her beloved grandmother, who has since passed away. Marina's parents and the veterinarian have suggested that Feather be put to sleep, but Marina is resisting.

Rising Action

In a short story, the *rising action* usually includes at least two or three important actions involving the main character and his or her problem. This builds suspense into the story.

First Action: Marina talks with her little sister Rosie about their ailing cat, Feather, especially how playful he used to be. Marina tries to play with the cat, but Feather shows no interest.

Second Action: Marina starts to tell Rosie stories about their grandmother. She talks about how much their grandmother had loved Feather.

Third Action: Rosie admits that she doesn't remember much about their grandmother because she was so little when their grandmother died. Marina accuses her sister of forgetting about this special person.

Climax

The *climax* is the moment of truth, or the most exciting part, when the character confronts his or her problem head-on. All the action leads up to the climax. In the best stories, the main character is changed by the climax.

Marina's mother comes in, and Marina confesses that she wants to keep the cat alive because it is her connection with her grandmother. She is afraid that if the cat dies, so will her memories. Her mother assures her she won't forget her grandmother, and that it is cruel to make Feather suffer. Marina decides to let the veterinarian put Feather to sleep.

Falling Action

The *falling action* involves the main character as he or she begins to deal with life after the moment of truth.

Marina declares that she will never forget her grandmother. Marina's mother assures her that anyone who is truly loved is never forgotten.

Resolution

The *resolution* brings the story to a natural, thought-provoking, or surprising conclusion. (In some stories, it's hard to tell the difference between the falling action and the resolution because they are so closely related.)

Marina's mother brings out a photo album. She and Marina sit down with Rosie to tell stories about Grandma.

Creative Writing

Sample Story

Read and enjoy the sample story by Thea Karas. The side notes indicate how the story develops from the exposition to the resolution.

Building Foundations

Alan sniffed the fragrant blend of open earth, fresh cement, and new wood, almost forgetting how miserable he was feeling. The Construction Class students were actually building a house. As the students grouped around the site for Mr. Hanson's instructions, Alan's friend Sara sidled up and nudged him, her soft lily-of-the-valley cologne mingling pleasantly with the construction smells.

"So, what happened? I thought you were taking Tiffany to the dance," she whispered.

His agony returned. "She got a better offer."

Sara didn't say anything more as Mr. Hanson explained the day's activity: creating foundation walls.

Working in teams, the students began building up the short walls of the crawl space that would serve to support the rest of the house. Alan and Sara worked side by side on the prepared footings, Sara slapping down mortar and Alan setting the cinder blocks.

"I'm sorry about Tiffany," Sara said softly as she tapped her trowel against the mortar bucket. "But why did you ask her to begin with?"

Alan thought about Tiffany, her glossy black hair and amber eyes. Even now, her heady jasmine perfume seemed to fill his senses. "She's just so pretty."

"Pretty boring," Sara snorted. "What do you two have to talk about?"

Alan considered. What *did* they talk about? Tiffany was into international affairs. When they'd eaten lunch together on Friday, all she had talked about was how some country he had never even heard of was being repressed by another country he hadn't heard of! He had sat silent the whole time, just looking at those amber eyes.

"Here." Sara shoved the mortar bucket at him. "Let's switch jobs." He began slapping the grainy gray mortar on top of the blocks.

"I love this class," Sara grunted as she hoisted a cinder block into place. "It's great to build something."

"Yeah, I can't wait to get to the real stuff—putting down the floors, putting up the walls, and fitting windows. This is kinda boring."

"It is pretty tedious," Sara admitted, "but think about it. If we don't do a good job on the foundation, the rest of the house could shift and even fall apart!"

Alan grinned at her enthusiasm. "You're not given to hyperbole, are you?"

Sara blushed, a blond wisp escaping from her hat and curling around her face. "I just think foundations are important." Alan tried to imagine Tiffany working next to him, but the picture wouldn't form. He admired how skillfully Sara skimmed her trowel along, cleaning off the excess mortar.

"So how's your biology project coming?" he asked.

Alan almost forgot about Tiffany as they discussed genetics. When it was time to get back on the bus, Sara checked her watch. "Wow, time flies . . . "

" . . . when you're having fun!" Alan finished, and they both laughed.

A wayward curl dipped across Sara's eye, and Alan reached over to brush it away. Her eyes were green with little yellow flecks, and looking at them, Alan suddenly felt his knees go weak.

As they started up the bus steps, he looked back at the wall he and Sara had built together. *It's a good foundation,* he thought to himself. *It will support a good house.* Then he plopped down in the seat next to Sara and caught a delicate whiff of lily-of-the-valley cologne.

"Hey, Sara," he said, "about the dance . . . "

Climax
Alan feels an attraction to Sara.

Falling Action and Resolution
The story comes to a satisfying end.

Respond to the reading. Review the story and answer these questions.

Ideas (1) Who is the main character? (2) What is his or her conflict?

Organization (3) What events are included in the rising action?

Voice & Word Choice (4) How realistic does the dialogue sound? Explain. (5) What specific building terms does the writer use?

Literature Connections: "Everyday Use" by Alice Walker is a short story with a subtle conflict that builds toward a meaningful climax.

Creative Writing

Prewriting Planning Your Writing

Fiction writers plan stories in different ways. For example, C. S. Forester thinks "first of something to be done and then . . . of an interesting character to do it." William Faulkner, on the other hand says he, "begins with a character, usually, and once he stands up on his feet and begins to move, all I do is trot along behind." Another writer may start with a particular setting.

No matter how you start, just remember that most short stories begin with a main character doing some activity, and a conflict occurs. As you plan your story, identify at least the main character and his or her problem.

Creating Characters

Who is the central person in your story? You can base this character on someone you know, but don't embarrass a person by making the main character too much like him or her.

Also decide on one or two supporting characters who will be involved in the action. Including too many characters, however, may make your story unnecessarily complicated.

Considering a Conflict

For this assignment, your main character should be in conflict with him- or herself. Alan, the main character in the sample story on pages **316–317**, has to work out his feelings toward Tiffany. Think about possible conflicts that your main character could deal with: his or her relationship with someone, peer pressure, stage fright, meeting expectations, and so on.

Establishing a Setting

Your setting can be any place that allows your main character to deal with the conflict. Limit yourself, though, to one main location and a brief span of time. The sample story takes place at a construction site during one class.

Thinking about the Action

The conflict requires the main character to act, so list two or three actions that could move your story along. Also consider the climax, or turning point.

Plan your story. Using the guidelines above, choose a main character, a conflict, and a setting. Then list or three two actions that result from the conflict.

Prewrite

Writing Creating Your First Draft

Stories are built with a few interesting characters, realistic dialogue, and believable action. Also consider the following points about story writing.

Starting Your Story

To get the reader's attention, start your story in one of these ways.

- **Start in the middle of the action.**
  Without slowing down, Zack artfully dodged the rock flung at his head.

- **Begin with dialogue.**
  "Never flown before, huh?" the flight attendant asked as I clutched the arms of my seat, preparing for takeoff and the end of my young life.

- **Make an attention-grabbing statement.**
  Everyone always oohs and aahs over my cute little brother, but I know the truth: He was sent from an alien planet to destroy the earth.

In the exposition you should establish the setting, introduce the main character, and identify the conflict. Once you have given your reader this background information, you are ready to write the middle part of your story.

Developing the Action

Place your character in the first challenging action. Then build suspense with each new action or struggle, leading up to the climax.

- Create dialogue that sounds real and natural. Let the words reflect what the characters think and feel.
- Include sensory details. Describe what the characters hear, see, smell, taste, and feel.
- Show instead of tell what is happening. For example, instead of saying "Alan was sad," say "Alan slumped into his seat." Instead of "Sara felt embarrassed," write "Sara blushed."
- Build to a climax, when the main character confronts the problem.

Bringing the Story to a Close

After the climax, end the story quickly. Show how your character has been changed by the climax.

Write

Write your first draft. Use your planning from page 318 plus the information above as a general guide.

Creative Writing

Revising Improving Your Story

Ask yourself the following questions when you review and revise your first draft. (Also see page **322**.)

Story Checklist

_____ Do my characters talk and act like real people?

_____ Is my conflict believable? Does it test my main character?

_____ Do all the actions build toward the climax?

_____ Did I show rather than tell?

_____ Does the main character change after the climax?

Revising in Action
New details show instead of tell.

A wayward curl dipped across Sara's eye, and Alan
reached over to brush it away. Her eyes were green, and
_{with little yellow flecks}
looking at them, Alan suddenly felt ~~like he was starting to~~
_{his knees go weak.}
~~have feelings for Sara.~~

Editing Checking for Style and Accuracy

When you edit your revised story, check capitalization, punctuation, grammar, and spelling.

Editing in Action
A missing word is added, and a verb is corrected.

^{up}
. . . As they started the bus steps, he looked back at the
^{built}
wall he and Sara had ~~builded~~ together. It's a good foundation,
he thought to himself. It will support a good house.

Revise and edit your story. Use the information above to help you revise and edit the first draft of your story.

Revise

Story Patterns

Many short stories follow a basic pattern. Here are brief descriptions of some popular short-story patterns.

The Quest

The main character goes on a journey into the unknown, overcomes a number of obstacles, and returns either victorious or wiser. Heroic myths follow this pattern, but so do many modern stories.

A young woman fights for the right to join an all-male sports team.

The Discovery

The main character follows a trail of clues to discover an amazing secret. Mystery and suspense novels use this pattern.

A curious young man discovers that the bully at school is . . .

The Rite of Passage

A difficult experience changes the main character in a significant and lasting way. These stories are also called *coming of age* stories.

A young soldier learns about responsibility while on the battlefield.

The Choice

The focus in this type of story is a decision the main character must make. Tension builds as the decision approaches.

A young adult must decide to follow the crowd or follow her own conscience.

The Union

Two people fall in love, but they are held apart by a number of obstacles. Their struggle to come together only causes their love to grow stronger. Sometimes they succeed, and sometimes they fail.

A young deaf man falls in love with a gifted violinist and then struggles to understand the music he can't hear.

The Reversal

In this pattern, the main character follows one course of action until something causes him or her to think or act in a different way.

A young woman quits school, but then discovers her true love is painting and enrolls in an art school.

Creative Writing

Elements of Fiction

The following terms describe elements of literature. This information will help you discuss and write about novels, poetry, essays, and other literary works.

Antagonist The person or force that works against the hero of the story (See *protagonist*.)

Character A person or an animal in a story

Conflict A problem or clash between two forces in a story
- **Person vs. person** A problem between characters
- **Person vs. himself or herself** A problem within a character's own mind
- **Person vs. society** A problem between a character and society, the law, or some tradition
- **Person vs. nature** A problem with an element of nature, such as a blizzard or a hurricane
- **Person vs. destiny** A problem or struggle that appears to be beyond a character's control

Mood The feeling a piece of literature creates in a reader

Narrator The person or character who tells the story, gives background information, and fills in details between dialogue

Plot, Plot Line See pages 314–315.

Point of View The angle from which a story is told
- In **first-person point of view,** one character is telling the story.
- In **third-person point of view,** someone outside the story is telling it.
- In **omniscient point of view,** the narrator tells the thoughts and feelings of all the characters.
- In **limited omniscient point of view,** the narrator tells the thoughts of one character at a time.
- In **camera view** (objective), the narrator records the action from his or her own point of view without any other characters' thoughts.

Protagonist The main character or hero in a story (See *antagonist*.)

Setting The place and time period in which a story takes place

Theme The author's message about life or human nature

Tone The writer's attitude toward his or her subject (*angry, humorous,* and so on)

Writing Plays

At one time or another, we have all felt that we were sure about something, only to learn that maybe we didn't know as much as we thought. A play is an excellent literary form for exploring such a feeling and for considering what a character might do when things don't work out in the expected way.

In a play, you develop your story almost exclusively through dialogue. Each new exchange between characters moves the story toward the climax or high point of interest. The only other device that you have to work with is stage direction, which provides explanations about the characters' actions onstage.

In this chapter, you will read a brief play about a student who "thinks" he knows all about the world of work. Then guidelines will help you develop your own play about an individual who learns a lesson about life.

Writing Guidelines

Subject: Learning a lesson about life
Form: Brief play
Purpose: To entertain and enlighten
Audience: Classmates

"Drama is life with the
dull bits cut out."
—Alfred Hitchcock

Sample Play

In the following play by student writer Matt Gertz, the main character thinks he knows what it takes to get a job. The side notes identify key points in the development of the play. (See page **329** for an explanation of the abbreviations used in the stage directions.)

Suiting Up

Characters: **Wesley**, a high school student seeking a job
Luke, his friend
Tori, another friend
Mr. Hayes, a potential employer
Kyle, a student

Scene 1

(The only furniture on the stage is in the UC area—a desk with two chairs, one behind the desk, one in front. At the beginning, Mr. Hayes and Kyle are seated, frozen, in the dark UC area. Tori stands, frozen, in the dark DR area. As the curtain rises, the DL pool of light comes up, where Luke is bouncing a basketball. Wesley enters from DR and comes into the light. He is dressed casually, even a little sloppily, with shirttail untucked and shoelaces untied.)

LUKE: Hey, Wesley, you wanna shoot some hoops?
WESLEY: Can't. I'm heading over to the Food Mart to interview for a job.
LUKE: You joining the ranks of the employed? Cool.
WESLEY: Yeah, I gotta start earning some bucks if I want to get a car.
LUKE: A car? You can't get your license for another six months.
WESLEY: I know, but it'll take me at least that long to get a down payment.
LUKE: What kind of job?
WESLEY: Stocking shelves. I figure a big, strong guy like me . . .
LUKE: You think you look okay for a job interview?
WESLEY: Sure. It's not an executive position, right?
LUKE: Well, good luck, buddy.
WESLEY: Thanks. Catch you later.

Stage Directions
The stage setup and characters are described.

Beginning
The play starts right in the middle of the action.

(The DL light goes down and Luke freezes as Wesley moves toward the DR section. The light comes up on Tori as Wesley crosses into her area.)

TORI:	Hey, Wesley. You seen Luke?
WESLEY:	Hi, Tori. Yeah, he's at the park shooting hoops. See ya.
TORI:	Where are you headed in such a hurry?
WESLEY:	Job interview at Food Mart.
TORI:	Er—shouldn't you go home and change first? You look like you just overhauled an engine or something.
WESLEY:	Heck, it's only a stocking job. They won't care what I look like.
TORI:	Don't you want to make a good impression?
WESLEY:	My shining personality will win them over.
TORI:	Right. Well, good luck!

Middle
Each new interchange adds a complication and builds tension.

(The light goes down and Tori freezes as Wesley moves toward UC. The light comes up on Mr. Hayes and Kyle. Kyle rises, they shake hands, and Kyle turns and leaves.)

MR. HAYES:	Next! *(Wesley peeks in.)* Ah, Wesley Jones, isn't it? Come in, son.
WESLEY:	Thank you, sir. *(Enters and extends his hand for a handshake, politely sits down.)*
MR. HAYES:	*(Eyes Wesley's grungy clothes.)* Well. Let's see here. *(Looks over Wesley's application.)* Hmmm. Ah, you're on the basketball team. Well, we have other students involved in after-school activities. We can always work schedules around.
WESLEY:	*(Politely)* Yes, sir.
MR. HAYES:	Your grades are good, too.
WESLEY:	Yes, sir, I can do that and hold a job.
MR. HAYES:	Yes. Well, Wesley, I'll tell you. You seem like a pleasant young man. But I'm not going to give you the job.
WESLEY:	*(Surprised)* Sir? But why?
MR. HAYES:	There's a lot of competition in this world, Wesley. Did you see that young man who just went out?
WESLEY:	Kyle? My grades are better than his!

Creative Writing

MR. HAYES: Maybe, but did you see the way he was dressed?

WESLEY: Heck, I have a suit, too!

MR. HAYES: But you didn't wear it, did you? He took the trouble to be well groomed. That shows me that he wants this job. Your clothes tell me you don't really care.

WESLEY: But I do care! I'd work really hard for you!

MR. HAYES: Maybe you would, Wesley, but I have to *see* that before I can hire you. I'm sorry, son. First impressions do count.

WESLEY: Yes, sir. (*He rises to leave, then turns.*) Thank you, Mr. Hayes.

MR. HAYES: Try again another time, Wesley. (*Wesley nods and goes right as the light goes down and Mr. Hayes exits left.*)

(*The light goes up DC. Wesley appears from the right wearing a suit and tie. Luke and Tori move to the area and Luke whistles.*)

LUKE: Whoa, who died?

WESLEY: There's another opening at the Food Mart. This time I'm going to get it.

TORI: Ah—

WESLEY: Don't say it, Tori. Okay, so you were right.

TORI: (*Smiling*) I wasn't going to say a thing.

WESLEY: Maybe this time Mr. Hayes'll get the chance to see my shining personality.

TORI: I'm sure of it. After all, you're *suited up* for success! Good luck, Wesley.

Middle
The main character realizes his mistake.

Ending
The main character sets a new course of action.

Respond to the reading. Answer these questions about the play.

Ideas (1) What main point or theme does the play develop?

Organization (2) In what part of the play does the climax occur? What happens after this point?

Voice & Word Choice (3) How does the writer make the dialogue sound natural? Point out examples from the play.

Literature Connections: You have seen how the main character in a play can change after not getting what he wants. Consider reading *The Brute* by Anton Chekhov for another example of this.

Prewriting Choosing Your Main Character

In a play, the main character usually wants something, but faces a problem that keeps him or her from achieving it. As you start your planning, choose a main character and decide on something he or she wants.

The main character of the play is the **protagonist**. This person is changed in some way by the action. Matt decided to write about a teenage boy like himself. He named the character Wesley. Then Matt made a list of things Wesley might want, and starred the one he would write about.

List of Wants

Wesley wants . . .	to have a girlfriend to earn high grades to find a job ∗ to buy a car

Choose your main character. Decide on a main character for your play and make a list of things this person may want to achieve or obtain. Choose one that would make an interesting play.

Selecting a Conflict

The conflict occurs when something stands in the way of the main character. Matt compiled the following list before selecting a conflict. He starred the problem he thought was most interesting.

Potential Conflicts

Things that could keep Wesley from finding a job
- His parents
- His attitude ∗
- His grades
- His after-school activities

List possible conflicts. Be sure these conflicts are believable. Then place an asterisk beside the one that you will use in your play.

Identifying Other Characters

Other characters in your play must serve specific purposes. They may be used to explain important background information or to make things more complicated. In the sample play, we know that Wesley, the main character, wants to get a job. Each of the other characters contributes in some way to the action.

Character List

> Wesley's friend Luke brings up the idea that Wesley may not be suitably dressed for a job interview.
> Wesley's friend Tori reinforces the idea that he is not dressed properly.
> Mr. Hayes also points out Wesley's mistake about his attire.
> Kyle presents a contrast, showing someone properly dressed for an interview.

Prewrite

List additional characters for your play. Explain what the function of each will be. (Limit yourself to a few additional characters.)

Planning the Starting Point

Start your play right in the middle of the action. Work in any necessary background information in interchanges between the characters. Matt decided that the action would begin with a conversation between Luke and Wesley about the interview Wesley was going to. Matt also listed background information that he may need to work in early in the play. (Later, Matt crossed out ideas that were unnecessary.)

Background Information

> **What the audience needs to know:**
> – Wesley is going on a job interview.
> – ~~He has just come from basketball practice.~~
> – He wants to work as a stocker at the Food Mart.
> – He needs to earn money to buy a car.
> – ~~His parents said they would cover his car insurance if he bought a car.~~

Prewrite

Plan how to start your play. Decide which action will begin your play. Also decide what your audience needs to know so they will be able to follow the story line. (Later, you may find that some of these ideas are unnecessary.)

Considering the Stage Directions

Because a play is a visual as well as an oral medium, the writer must plan the characters' movements onstage. **Stage directions** are the nondialogue parts of a play that identify where the characters are and what they are doing in each scene.

In Matt's play, the action moves smoothly from one location to the next. The opening stage descriptions describe the setup for each acting area that will be used.

Stage Directions

> *(The only furniture on the stage is in the UC area—a desk with two chairs, one behind the desk, one in front. At the beginning, Mr. Hayes and Kyle are seated, frozen, in the dark UC area. Tori stands, frozen, in the dark DR area. . . .)*

Prewrite

Plan your opening stage directions. Describe where and how the opening action of your play takes place. Try to keep things simple.

Using Proper Stage Terminology

Below is a diagram of the basic acting areas on a stage and the shorthand used to refer to each area. Use this shorthand in your stage directions.

Stage Diagram

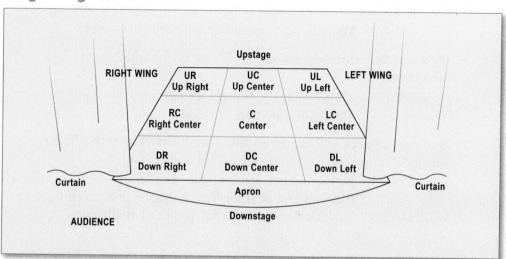

Writing Creating Your First Draft

Remember that the characters tell the story. Imagine what they will say and do in response to the play's conflict. Use the following drafting tips to guide your writing.

Beginning

- **Start right in the middle of the action** and work in the necessary background information. (See page **328**.)

Middle

- **Use dialogue and action to present the play's ideas.** Make sure the dialogue sounds natural.
- **Add complications (problems) to build suspense.** Don't let the character solve the problem too quickly.
- **Build to the climax.** This is the point where the character comes face-to-face with his or her problem and responds to it in some way.

Ending

- **Bring your play to a close.** Show how your character has changed because of what he or she has learned.

Developing Your Characters

You can explain a character to the audience in three ways.

1. **By what the character says.** From Wesley's words, we learn that he doesn't think he needs to dress up for the interview.

   WESLEY: My shining personality will win them over.

2. **By what the character does.** This can be found in stage directions.

   WESLEY: Thank you, sir. *(Enters and extends his hand for a handshake, politely sits down.)*

3. **By what others say to, or about, the main character.** Their thoughts can reveal personality traits of the character.

   TORI: Er—shouldn't you go home and change first? You look like you just overhauled an engine or something. . . .

   MR. HAYES: Your clothes tell me that you don't really care.

Revising Improving Your Writing

Read your play out loud or have someone else read it to you. Change any lines that sound forced or unnatural. Use these questions when revising.

Revising Checklist

Ideas

_____ **1.** Is the main character's conflict believable?
_____ **2.** Does the action include complications (problems)?
_____ **3.** Does each character serve an important role within the play?

Organization

_____ **4.** Does each complication build on the previous one?
_____ **5.** Is the climax easily recognized?
_____ **6.** Do stage directions help move the action along?

Voice

_____ **7.** Does the dialogue sound natural and believable?

Sentence Fluency

_____ **8.** Does the dialogue flow naturally from one speaker to the next?

Editing Checking for Conventions

Use the following checklist as a guide when you check your play for proper formatting and for conventions.

Conventions

_____ **1.** Does the play follow the basic script format?
_____ **2.** Have I checked for capitalization and punctuation errors?
_____ **3.** Have I checked for spelling errors?

Revise and edit your writing. Use the checklists above as a guide when you revise and edit the first draft of your play.

Revise

Creative Writing

Sample Radio Script

In radio drama, your audience can only imagine the action.

LIFE IN THE EXPRESS LANE

(SCENE: A GROCERY STORE CHECKOUT LINE. WE CAN HEAR VOICES, THE DING OF THE SCANNER.)

LOUDSPEAKER: Manager to checkout three, please. Manager to three.

CHECKER: Er—ma'am, this is the express checkout. Eight items or less. You really should go to the regular line.

GLADYS: This one's quicker.

CHECKER: Yes, that's because people only have eight items or less. Usually.

GLADYS: So how many do I have? It's not that much more.

CHECKER: Ma'am, your cart is completely full.

GLADYS: They're big items.

MALE VOICE: Guess she didn't see the sign.

CHECKER: Really, ma'am, it's not fair to the others in line.

GLADYS: Some of my stuff is two-for-one. They should count as one.

FEMALE VOICE: Hey, is this really the express lane?

GLADYS: Next, I suppose you'll want to count each of the bananas in a bunch!

CHECKER: Okay, okay, ma'am. Let's just get going here.

(SOUND OF SCANNER BEGINS.)

GLADYS: I'm a long-time customer. I don't need to be treated so poorly.

CHECKER: I'm very sorry, ma'am. That'll be $63.47, please.

GLADYS: Honestly, I don't need to be lectured about—er— oh, my.

CHECKER: Ma'am? Is there a problem?

GLADYS: Well, I seem to have forgotten my wallet.

MALE VOICE: Oh, man! You've got to be kidding!

CHECKER: (*Sighs.*) I'm sorry, I'll have to close for a few minutes.

VOICES: (*Background grumbling grows loud; then fades out.*)

Try It!

Write a radio script about an interesting scene from your life.

Writing Poetry

Have you ever read a poem and thought, "I know that feeling"? Part of the pleasure of reading poetry is that sense of connection between poet and reader. As Italian poet Salvatore Quasimodo put it, "Poetry is the revelation of a feeling that the poet believes to be interior and personal, which the reader recognizes as his own."

A poem reveals much about a poet's inner feelings, especially when it is an autobiographical poem. In this chapter, you will learn to write an autobiographical free-verse poem. You will also learn about two special forms of poetry: Skeltonic verse and a lune poem. No matter what form you work with, you will learn something new about yourself as you develop your thoughts and feelings.

Writing Guidelines

Subject: Self-portrait
Form: Free-verse poem
Purpose: To entertain
Audience: Friends, family, and classmates

"I should not talk so much about myself if there were anybody else whom I knew as well."

—Henry David Thoreau

Sample Free-Verse Poem

Most traditional poetry follows a specific pattern of rhythm and rhyme. Free-verse poems, on the other hand, develop a structure of their own. This makes free verse ideal for an autobiographical poem. Eli Pulkkinen wrote the following free-verse poem to tell about a moment of self-discovery.

Perfection

His teeth were not perfect,
so only his lips smiled,
until one day,
laughing at a joke, he
glanced up to find a stranger
laughing with him—
a grin so inviting
that for a moment
he did not recognize
the mirror,
his own reflection.

—Eli Pulkkinen

 Respond to the reading. On your own paper, reflect on the ideas, organization, and voice of the free-verse poem above.

Ideas (1) What does this poem reveal about the writer?

Organization (2) If you were to divide this poem into three parts—beginning, middle, and ending—where would you divide it? Why?

Voice & Word Choice (3) This poem is about a moment of self-discovery. Why do you think the poet used third-person pronouns (*his, he*)? (4) How does the title relate to the poem's message?

Tip

Some poems rely on many sensory details to build a mental picture. Others are more sparse, like the one above. In either case, the poet must carefully choose the best words to convey the poem's idea.

 Literature Connections: A former U.S. Poet Laureate, Billy Collins tends to write free verse in a playful, conversational style. His many popular poems include "Today" and "Christmas Sparrow."

Prewriting Choosing a Focus

When writing an autobiographical poem, you should focus on one particular idea, event, or feeling that reveals your personality. To choose that focus, you can use one of the following strategies.

Looking in a Mirror

When artists draw a self-portrait, they use a mirror. Poets can do the same. Take time to examine your own face in a mirror and jot down notes about what you see. How would you describe each of your features? What personality do you see looking back at you? How do your features reveal that personality?

Making a Personality Cluster

Write your name in a circle; then list your personality traits around it. Expand your cluster to include ideas about how you reveal each trait. (See page **582** for more about clustering.)

Reviewing Your Journal or a Photo Album

Browse through your journal to find interesting ideas or events. Or look through a family album for a photo that shows your personality or brings to mind an important memory. Eli chose an entry from his journal.

> Sept. 14, 2011
> Today at my part-time job, I was sweeping the break room when Rhoda said something that made me bust out laughing. When I looked up, I saw this other guy behind her with a big, amazing grin. For a minute, I didn't realize it was my own reflection in the break-room mirror. Seeing that grin, I don't think I'm going to be so self-conscious about my smile anymore.

Eli boiled down this memory to a purpose statement:

> I want to share the surprise of the moment when I realized the laughing stranger with the great smile was me.

Select a focus. Use one of the techniques above to choose a specific feature, idea, or memory that reveals something about your personality. Then write a purpose statement to identify the focus of your poem.

Prewrite

Creative Writing

Prewriting Gathering Details

One of the best ways to gather details for a self-portrait poem is to make a list. Eli made the following list of essential details for his poem:

> 1. Feeling shy about my teeth
> 2. Laughing at Rhoda's joke
> 3. Noticing a stranger laughing
> 4. Being shocked that he was my own reflection

Prewrite

Make a list of details to include in your poem. Put them in the order you want to use in your poem.

Writing Developing Your First Draft

Many poets begin by writing sentences, focusing on ideas and the sound of the words. Then they break those sentences into shorter lines to improve the rhythm and make a poem. Eli started with this first draft:

> I was shy about my teeth. Then one day, while laughing at a joke, I saw this stranger laughing, too. His smile was so surprising that for a moment I didn't realize it was my own reflection.

Using Poetic Techniques

Rhythm is a special sound technique that separates prose from poetry. One way poets create rhythm is by breaking their writing into unique phrasing for a desired effect and meaning.

Line Breaks

Line breaks help to set the pace and rhythm of a poem. They help control the poem and add emphasis to certain words.

> I was shy about my teeth.
> Then one day,
> while laughing at a joke,
> I saw this stranger
> laughing, too.
> His smile was so surprising
> that for a moment
> I didn't realize
> it was my own reflection.

Write

Write your first draft. Start with phrases or sentences that get across the idea. Then add line breaks to control the rhythm and add emphasis.

Revising Focusing on the Traits

The first draft of a poem often comes in a rush of creativity. Revision is your chance to polish and perfect the poem until it moves a reader to feel as you do. In particular, look at the following traits.

- **Ideas** Do I use effective details? Does my poem show my feelings without telling the reader what to think?
- **Organization** Do I use line breaks effectively to control the rhythm of my poem?
- **Voice** Does my poem show inventiveness and personality?
- **Word Choice** Are my words precise and interesting?
- **Sentence Fluency** Do the lines of my poem have an appealing rhythm?

Compare the first draft of Eli's poem on page **336** to his final draft on page **334**. What changes did he make? Which version seems most effective to you?

Revise your poem. Using the questions above as a guide, keep revising until your poem is the best that it can be.

Editing Checking for Errors

Because poems are shorter than most other types of writing, every word and punctuation mark is important. Careful editing is necessary.

- **Conventions** Is my poem free from errors that could distract a reader?

Edit your poem. Poems sometimes break the rules, but never by accident. Edit your poem for careless errors and make a neat final copy.

Publishing Sharing Your Poem

When your poem is finished, share it with other people. Here are three ways to do that.

- **Post it.** Put it on a bulletin board or a Web site.
- **Submit it.** Send your poem to a contest or magazine.
- **Perform it.** Read your poem to friends and family.

Present your poem. Poems are made to be shared, so let other people read or hear what you have created. Ask your teacher to suggest other publishing ideas.

Creative Writing

Sample Skeltonic Verse

While free-verse poetry is a relatively new creation, it isn't the first attempt to approach poetry in a different way. Back in the fifteenth century, a poet named John Skelton (ca. 1460–1529) believed that the forms of the time were making poetry dull.

Skelton invented a new form we now call "skeltonic" or "tumbling" verse. The lines are relatively short—three to six words on average—and they carry an end rhyme for as long as the poet feels it is working. Then the lines shift to a new rhyme.

Lasandra Kersch wrote "Fashion Statement," a Skeltonic-verse poem, as a self-portrait. Kersch's poem is based upon an extended simile, comparing herself to a parrot.

Fashion Statement

I'm like a parrot.
I swear it.
A bright green blouse, I'll wear it
with a pair of jeans orange as a carrot.
My merit
is I don't fear
what I hear
about what not to wear,
or the fashion this year.
Let me elaborate.
It's deliberate.
My style's not moderate.
I've got a doctorate
in "Color it!"
That's my self-portrait,
and I'm proud of it.
You ask me why?
It means I'm fly,
Wise guy.

—Lasandra Kersch

Tip

- **Select a topic.** What are you like? Think of a simile or metaphor that describes you, as Lasandra did.

- **Gather details.** Make a list identifying how your simile or metaphor relates to you.

- **Write your poem.** Use inventive rhymes to make your poem fun. (Check a rhyming dictionary for help.) Work with the rhythm until the poem reads well aloud.

Write

Create a poem. Following the writing tips above, write your own self-portrait Skeltonic-verse poem. Continue writing lines to share your thoughts as long as the verse remains interesting.

Using the Library

The Internet may be a good place to initiate your research, but a library is often a more valuable place to continue it. Most libraries contain a wide range of resources.

Books

- **Reference** books include encyclopedias, almanacs, dictionaries, atlases, and directories, plus resources such as consumer information guides and car-repair manuals. Reference books provide a quick overview of research topics.

- **Nonfiction** texts are a good source of facts that can serve as a foundation for your research. Check the copyright dates to be sure you are reading reasonably up-to-date information. (Some libraries organize nonfiction using the Library of Congress system, but most libraries use the Dewey decimal system as shown on page **349**.)

- **Fiction** can sometimes aid or enhance your research. For example, a historical novel can reveal people's feelings about a particular time in history. (Fiction books are grouped together in alphabetical order by the authors' last names.)

Periodicals

Periodicals (*newspapers* and *magazines*) are grouped together in a library. Use the *Readers' Guide to Periodical Literature* to find articles in periodicals. (See page **354**.) You will have to ask the librarian for older issues.

The Media Section

The media section of your library includes DVD's, CD-ROM's, CD's, cassettes, and videotapes. These resources are valuable, but remember that directors and screenwriters may present events from their personal viewpoints.

Computers

Computers are available in most libraries, and many are connected to the Internet, although there may be restrictions on their use.

Try It!

Visit your school or public library. Which sections would you use if you were researching the origin of the moon's craters? Which sections would help you find material on the history of filmmaking? Are there any sections you would use for both topics? List them.

Research

Using the Computer Catalog

Some libraries still use a card catalog located in a cabinet with drawers. Most libraries, however, have put their entire catalog on computer. Each system varies a bit, so ask for help if you're not sure how the system in your library works. A **computer catalog** lists the books held in your library and affiliated systems. It lets you know if a book is available or if you must wait for it.

Using a Variety of Search Methods

When you are using a computer catalog, you can find information about a book with any of the following methods:

1. If you know it, enter the **title** of the book.
2. If you know the **author** of the book, enter the first and last names.
3. A general search of your **subject** will also help you find books on your topic. Enter either the subject or a related keyword.

Sample Computer Catalog Screen

The key to the right identifies the types of information provided for a particular resource, in this case, a book. Once you locate the book you need, make note of the call number. You will use this to find the book on the shelf.

1. **The Aswan High Dam**
2. Parks, Peggy J.

3. **Publisher:** Blackbirch
Publishing date: 2004
Pages: 289pp.
ISBN: 1-56711-329-X
Copy information: 1 copy at Forest Library Center
2 copies at Newman Library

4. **Call number:**
620.4111
P371p

5. Describes the building of the Aswan High Dam, built on the Nile. Includes techniques and difficulties, as well as the effect on the thousands of Nubians whose lands were flooded.

6. **Subject:** Dams/Egypt/20th Century
Dams/Egypt/Engineering

7. **Availability:** **Return date:** **Reserve:**
Checked out January 12, 2009 Yes _____

8. **Location:** Adult nonfiction

1. Title heading
2. Author's name
3. Publisher, copyright date, and other book information
4. Call number
5. Descriptive info
6. Subject heading(s)
7. Availability status
8. Location information

Try It!

Select a topic that interests you and look it up on a computer catalog. Identify two different works on the topic and locate them in the library.

Understanding Call Numbers

All nonfiction books are arranged in the library according to their **call numbers**. Call numbers are usually based on the **Dewey decimal classification** system, which divides nonfiction books into 10 subject categories:

000–099	**General Works**	500–599	**Sciences**
100–199	**Philosophy**	600–699	**Technology**
200–299	**Religion**	700–799	**Arts and Recreation**
300–399	**Social Sciences**	800–899	**Literature**
400–499	**Languages**	900–999	**History and Geography**

A call number often has a decimal in it, followed by the first letter of an author's name. Note how the following call numbers are ordered.

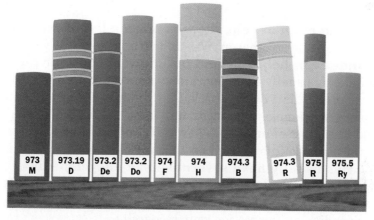

| 973 M | 973.19 D | 973.2 De | 973.2 Do | 974 F | 974 H | 974.3 B | 974.3 R | 975 R | 975.5 Ry |

Identifying the Parts of a Book

Each part of a book provides valuable information. The **title page** includes the title of the book, the author's name, and the publisher's name and city. The **copyright page** follows with the year the book was published. The **preface**, **foreword**, or **introduction** comes before the table of contents and tells why the book was written. The **table of contents** lists the names and page numbers of sections and chapters in the book. At the end of the book, you may find at least one **appendix**, containing various maps, tables, or lists. Finally, the **index** is an alphabetical list of important topics and their page numbers in the book.

Try It!

Select a nonfiction book on a topic that interests you. On a note card, write the book's title and call number, the publisher's name and city, and the year it was published. Then select a term related to your topic and find it in the index. Write down the page numbers given there.

Using Reference Books

A reference book is a special kind of nonfiction book that contains specific facts or background information. The reference section includes encyclopedias, dictionaries, almanacs, and so on. Usually, reference books cannot be checked out, so you must use them in the library.

Referring to Encyclopedias

An encyclopedia is a set of books (or files or Web pages) that contains basic information on topics from A to Z. Topics are arranged alphabetically. Here are some tips for using encyclopedias.

Tips for Using Encyclopedias

- **At the end of an article, there is often a list of related articles.** You can read these other articles to learn more about your topic.
- **The index can help you find out more about your topic.** The index is usually in a separate volume or at the end of the last volume. It lists every article that contains information about a topic. For example, if you look up "dams" in the index, you would find a list of articles—"Aswan Dam," "Hoover Dam," and so on—that include information on that topic. (See below.)
- **Libraries usually have several sets of encyclopedias.** Review each set and decide which one best serves your needs. (Always check with your teacher first to see if you can use an encyclopedia as a source for your research.)

Sample Encyclopedia Index

Encyclopedia volume → **Aswan Dam** A: 852 with pictures
Egypt **E: 118-132**
Dams **D: 15-20**

Page numbers → Lake Nasser **L: 42**
See also the list of related articles in the Egypt *article.*

Related topics → Abu Simbel, Temple of **A: 19**
Ramsas II **R: 135**
Amon-Re **A: 438**
Nubia **N-O: 382**
Delta **D: 147**

Consulting Other Reference Books

Most libraries contain a number of different kinds of reference books in addition to encyclopedias.

Almanacs

Almanacs are books filled with facts and statistics about many different subjects. *The World Almanac and Book of Facts* contains celebrity profiles; statistics about politics, business, and sports; plus consumer information.

Atlases

Atlases contain detailed maps of the world, continents, countries, and so on. They also contain statistics and related information. Specialized atlases cover topics like outer space and the oceans.

Dictionaries

Dictionaries contain definitions of words and their origins. Biographical dictionaries focus on famous people. Specialized dictionaries deal with science, history, medicine, and other subjects.

Directories

Directories list information about groups of people, businesses, and organizations. The most widely used directories are telephone books.

Periodical Indexes

Periodical indexes list articles in magazines and newspapers. These indexes are arranged alphabetically by subject.

- The *Readers' Guide to Periodical Literature* lists articles from many publications. (See page **354**.)
- The *New York Times Index* lists articles from the *New York Times* newspaper.

Other Reference Books

Some reference books do not fit into any one category:

- *Facts on File* includes thousands of short but informative facts about events, discoveries, people, and places.
- *Facts About the Presidents* presents information about all of the presidents of the United States.
- *Bartlett's Familiar Quotations* lists thousands of quotations from famous people.

Research

Checking a Dictionary

A dictionary gives many types of information:

- **Guide words:** These are the first and last words on the page. Guide words show whether the word you are looking for will be found alphabetically on that page.
- **Entry words:** Each word defined in a dictionary is called an entry word. Entry words are listed alphabetically.
- **Etymology:** Many dictionaries give etymologies (word histories) for certain words. An etymology tells what language an English word came from, how the word entered our language, and when it was first used.
- **Syllable divisions:** A dictionary tells where to divide a word.
- **Pronunciation and accent marks:** A dictionary tells you how to pronounce a word and also provides a key to pronunciation symbols, usually at the bottom of each page.
- **Illustrations:** Some entries provide an illustration or a photograph.
- **Parts of speech:** A dictionary tells you what part(s) of speech a word is, using these abbreviations:

n.	**noun**	*intr. v.*	**intransitive verb**	*adj.*	**adjective**
pron.	**pronoun**	*tr. v.*	**transitive verb**	*adv.*	**adverb**
conj.	**conjunction**	*interj.*	**interjection**	*prep.*	**preposition**

- **Spelling and capitalization:** The dictionary shows the acceptable spelling, as well as capitalization, for words. (For some words, more than one spelling is given.)
- **Definitions:** Some dictionaries are large enough to list all of the meanings for a word. Most standard-size dictionaries, however, will list only three or four of the most commonly accepted meanings. Take time to read all of the meanings to be sure that you are using the word correctly.

Try It!

Find an article on a topic that interests you and select three words that are unfamiliar to you. Look them up in the dictionary.

1. Identify the part(s) of speech for each word.
2. Give the first two meanings for the word.
3. Explain the etymology (if given) for each word.

Sample Dictionary Page

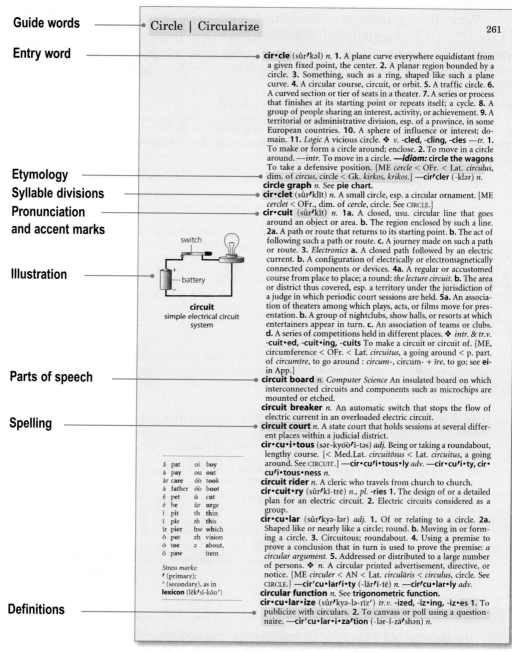

Guide words —

Entry word —

cir•cle (sûr′kəl) *n.* **1.** A plane curve everywhere equidistant from a given fixed point, the center. **2.** A planar region bounded by a circle. **3.** Something, such as a ring, shaped like such a plane curve. **4.** A circular course, circuit, or orbit. **5.** A traffic circle. **6.** A curved section or tier of seats in a theater. **7.** A series or process that finishes at its starting point or repeats itself; a cycle. **8.** A group of people sharing an interest, activity, or achievement. **9.** A territorial or administrative division, esp. of a province, in some European countries. **10.** A sphere of influence or interest; domain. **11.** *Logic* A vicious circle. ❖ *v.* **-cled, -cling, -cles** —*tr.* **1.** To make or form a circle around; enclose. **2.** To move in a circle around. —*intr.* To move in a circle. **—idiom: circle the wagons** To take a defensive position. [ME *cercle* < OFr. < Lat. *circulus,* dim. of *circus,* circle < Gk. *kirkos, krikos.*] **—cir′cler** (-klər) *n.*

Etymology —

Syllable divisions —

circle graph *n.* See **pie chart.**
cir•clet (sûr′klĭt) *n.* A small circle, esp. a circular ornament. [ME *cerclet* < OFr., dim. of *cercle,* circle. See CIRCLE.]

Pronunciation and accent marks —

cir•cuit (sûr′kĭt) *n.* **1a.** A closed, usu. circular line that goes around an object or area. **b.** The region enclosed by such a line. **2a.** A path or route that returns to its starting point. **b.** The act of following such a path or route. **c.** A journey made on such a path or route. **3.** *Electronics* **a.** A closed path followed by an electric current. **b.** A configuration of electrically or electromagnetically connected components or devices. **4a.** A regular or accustomed course from place to place; a round: *the lecture circuit.* **b.** The area or district thus covered, esp. a territory under the jurisdiction of a judge in which periodic court sessions are held. **5a.** An association of theaters among which plays, acts, or films move for presentation. **b.** A group of nightclubs, show halls, or resorts at which entertainers appear in turn. **c.** An association of teams or clubs. **d.** A series of competitions held in different places. ❖ *intr. & tr.v.* **-cuit•ed, -cuit•ing, -cuits** To make a circuit or circuit of. [ME, circumference < OFr. < Lat. *circuitus,* a going around < p. part. of *circumīre,* to go around : *circum-,* circum- + *īre,* to go; see **ei-** in App.]

Illustration —

circuit
simple electrical circuit
system

Parts of speech —

circuit board *n. Computer Science* An insulated board on which interconnected circuits and components such as microchips are mounted or etched.
circuit breaker *n.* An automatic switch that stops the flow of electric current in an overloaded electric circuit.
circuit court *n.* A state court that holds sessions at several different places within a judicial district.
cir•cu•i•tous (sər-kyoō′ĭ-təs) *adj.* Being or taking a roundabout, lengthy course. [< Med.Lat. *circuitōsus* < Lat. *circuitus,* a going around. See CIRCUIT.] **—cir•cu′i•tous•ly** *adv.* **—cir•cu′i•ty, cir•cu′i•tous•ness** *n.*

Spelling —

circuit rider *n.* A cleric who travels from church to church.
cir•cuit•ry (sûr′kĭ-trē) *n., pl.* **-ries 1.** The design of or a detailed plan for an electric circuit. **2.** Electric circuits considered as a group.
cir•cu•lar (sûr′kyə-lər) *adj.* **1.** Of or relating to a circle. **2a.** Shaped like or nearly like a circle; round. **b.** Moving in or forming a circle. **3.** Circuitous; roundabout. **4.** Using a premise to prove a conclusion that in turn is used to prove the premise: *a circular argument.* **5.** Addressed or distributed to a large number of persons. ❖ *n.* A circular printed advertisement, directive, or notice. [ME *circuler* < AN < Lat. *circulāris* < *circulus,* circle. See CIRCLE.] **—cir′cu•lar′i•ty** (-lăr′ĭ-tē) *n.* **—cir′cu•lar•ly** *adv.*
circular function *n.* See **trigonometric function.**

Definitions —

cir•cu•lar•ize (sûr′kyə-lə-rīz′) *tr.v.* **-ized, -iz•ing, -iz•es 1.** To publicize with circulars. **2.** To canvass or poll using a questionnaire. **—cir′cu•lar•i•za′tion** (-lər-ĭ-zā′shən) *n.*

Using Periodical Guides

Periodical guides are located in the reference or periodical section of the library. These guides alphabetically list topics and articles found in magazines, newspapers, and journals. Some guides are printed volumes, some are CD-ROM's, and some are on library Web sites. Ask your librarian for help.

Readers' Guide to Periodical Literature

The *Readers' Guide to Periodical Literature* is a well-known periodical reference source and is found in most libraries. The following tips will help you look up your topic in this resource:

- Articles are always listed alphabetically by author and topic.
- Some topics are subdivided, with each article listed under the appropriate subtopic.
- Cross-references refer to related topic entries where you may find more articles pertinent to your topic.

Sample *Readers' Guide* Format

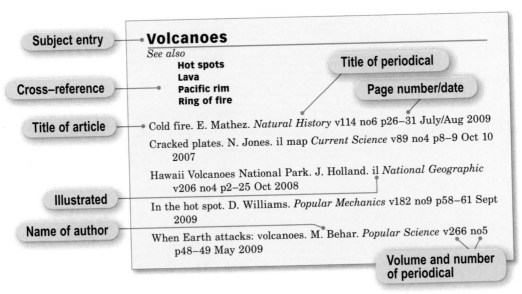

Subject entry — **Volcanoes**

See also

Cross–reference —
    Hot spots
    Lava
    Pacific rim
    Ring of fire

Title of periodical

Page number/date

Title of article — Cold fire. E. Mathez. *Natural History* v114 no6 p26–31 July/Aug 2009

Cracked plates. N. Jones. il map *Current Science* v89 no4 p8–9 Oct 10 2007

Hawaii Volcanoes National Park. J. Holland. il *National Geographic* v206 no4 p2–25 Oct 2008

Illustrated — In the hot spot. D. Williams. *Popular Mechanics* v182 no9 p58–61 Sept 2009

Name of author — When Earth attacks: volcanoes. M. Behar. *Popular Science* v266 no5 p48–49 May 2009

Volume and number of periodical

Tip

The librarian will have a list of magazines in the library's collection. Check it for the magazine you seek. If you need an older issue, it might be in the archives. If so, ask the librarian to get it for you.

Research Writing
MLA Research Report

Thomas Carlyle, the Scottish essayist and historian, once wrote, "Man is a tool-using animal." He went on to explain, "Nowhere do you find him without tools; without tools he is nothing, with tools he is all." In nature, most creatures adapt to their environment. People, on the other hand, tend to use their tools to adapt the environment to meet their needs. Consider, for example, great works of engineering such as the Empire State Building, the Great Wall of China, or the Hoover Dam. Not only were these monuments built with tools, they are—in effect—tools themselves, helping humans change their environment.

This chapter will help you to write an MLA research report about a great work of engineering that interests you. (MLA is the most common documentation style for research writing.) In the process, you will learn why and how the work came to be, and what effect it has had on the world.

Writing Guidelines

Subject: A great work of engineering
Form: MLA research report
Purpose: To research and present accurate information
Audience: Classmates

"It is good to rub and polish our brain against that of others."
—Michel de Montaigne

Title Page and Outline

After watching a PBS special about dams, Olen Juneau became interested in Egypt's Aswan High Dam. He decided to write a research paper about that topic. His paper starts on the next page. Below are the title page and outline of his paper. Some teachers require these additional pages. If your teacher requires them, follow any special instructions he or she may give you.

The Aswan High Dam

Olen Juneau
Ms. Kai
Language Arts
18 May 2009

Title Page
Center the title one-third of the way down the page. Center and double-space the writer information two-thirds of the way down the page.

Outline
Center the title one inch from the top of the page. Double-space throughout.

The Aswan High Dam

i

THESIS STATEMENT: The Aswan High Dam has solved many important problems for Egypt, but it has also created new ones.

I. Before the dam was built, Egyptians had to live with annual floods along the Nile.
   A. Flooding came after the rainy season in the highlands.
   B. This annual flooding helped to fertilize the land, but sometimes this was too much water.
   C. A dam was needed.
II. In years with little rain, Egypt had less flooding, but that also meant less water for irrigation.
   A. Egypt is mainly desert, so crops are watered by irrigation.
   B. Before the dam, Egyptians stored floodwater for irrigation after the flood season.
   C. In dry years, they could not capture enough water and suffered drought and famine.

Sample MLA Research Report

↓1/2"↑

Juneau 1 ←—1"—→

Olen Juneau
Ms. Kai
Language Arts
18 May 2011

The entire report is double-spaced.

The Aswan High Dam

Humans have been building dams for thousands of years. One of the oldest examples is the Saad El Kafara, built in Egypt around 2700 B.C.E. Its main purpose was to stop catastrophic flooding during wet years, but its water storage also allowed for increased irrigation of croplands. While most dams over the ages have been built for these two purposes, huge new dams in the past century have provided the added benefit of hydroelectric power for the world's growing population. However, people are discovering that these large dams also have many detrimental effects on the environment. Egypt's High Dam at Aswan illustrates this critical trade-off. The Aswan High Dam has solved many important problems for Egypt, but it has also created new ones.

Reasons for the Dam

Before the dam was built, Egyptians had to live with annual floods along the Nile. Each year, after the rainy season in the highlands, the river would spill over its banks onto the Egyptian countryside. While this annual flooding helped to fertilize the land, sometimes there was just too much water. For example, "between 1860 and 1880, there were four major floods that forced people to flee to higher ground" (Parks 12). They desperately needed a dam to help prevent this recurring damage.

Beginning
The writer introduces his topic and states his thesis (underlined).

Middle
The first middle section explains the historical background.

Research

In years with little rain, Egypt had less flooding, but that also meant less water for irrigation. Egypt is mainly desert, so crops grown there must be watered by irrigation. Before the dam was built, the Egyptians captured floodwater and stored it in pools for irrigation use during the rest of the year. In dry years, however, they could not capture enough water to last. The result was drought and famine (11).

By building a dam, the people of Egypt hoped to accomplish several things. A dam would help to stop catastrophic floods during wet years. It would also prevent Egypt from running out of water during dry years. In fact, it would store enough water to allow even more land to be irrigated. This was important because Egypt's population started to outgrow its crop production during the twentieth century (*Building*).

Building the Dam

The first Aswan Dam was built between 1898 and 1902, while Egypt was a colony of Great Britain. It was designed by William Willcocks, a British engineer who was very familiar with traditional Egyptian irrigation. Willcocks built a dam that would let the silt-laden water of each year's early rains pass through to fertilize the croplands below. The dam then stored later rainwater to be used for irrigation during the rest of the year (Pearce 50). Unfortunately, Willcock's dam didn't hold enough water to last through dry years, even after being raised twice, once in 1912 and again in 1933. Also, the dam almost overflowed in 1946, which happened to be a very wet year (Parks 14).

A source of information (Parks, page 11) is paraphrased.

Headings help guide the reader from section to section.

The second middle section details how the dam came into existence.

Juneau 3

In 1952, Egypt became independent from Britain, and its new government decided to build a dam that could hold enough water for three years of irrigation. The project quickly became a touchy subject, because Egypt didn't want to hire British engineers to design the dam. As a gesture of friendship, Germany donated plans to the new government. In 1956, the World Bank, Great Britain, and the United States offered to fund the project, but they cancelled those plans when Egypt bought Soviet weapons to fight Israel (17–20). The Soviet Union agreed to fund the dam if Egypt agreed to use only Soviet engineers and equipment. By 1959, plans were complete and the project began ("Aswan Dam" 40).

First, the valley that the dam would flood had to be cleared. This meant moving more than 100,000 Nubian people to new lands. Also, the new lake would cover many ancient temples and other monuments. In 1960, the United Nations Educational, Scientific, and Cultural Organization (UNESCO) asked governments around the world to help move these monuments. In all, 23 were rescued before the reservoir was filled, though many more were lost (*Building*).

Next, preparations had to be made for the dam's actual construction. New roads and railroads had to be built to carry men and equipment to the construction site. In addition, an electrical station had to be built at the old Aswan Dam to supply power for the project. Also, the town of Aswan had to be prepared to host the thousands of workers that would be needed (Parks 27).

Once building began, the construction team faced very harsh conditions. The terrain was extremely rugged,

Page numbers alone (17–20) refer to the last source cited (Parks).

Each paragraph begins with a topic sentence, followed by supporting details.

Research

rapidly wearing out tires on construction equipment. Daytime temperatures reached 135 degrees Fahrenheit in the shade, so most work had to be done at night. Under these conditions, the Soviet equipment broke down five times faster than expected. This caused expensive delays while replacement parts were shipped from the Soviet Union or equipment was sent back there for repair. In 1961, with little progress made, the Egyptian government brought in Egyptian construction experts to replace the Soviet engineers, and it began using equipment from Sweden and Great Britain (28–29).

The dam was finally completed in July 1970, ten years after the project began. It was by far the largest engineering work of its time, costing over $1 billion (*Building*). More than 50,000 people worked on the dam, using 17 times more material than was used to build the Great Pyramid. The finished dam stretches two miles wide and 364 feet high. The reservoir (holding the water) covers an area larger than the state of Delaware (Parks 35).

Effects of the Dam

The Aswan High Dam immediately helped control flooding. Before the Nile was dammed, floods sometimes forced evacuation of the Nile Valley and its delta, with a great loss of life and property. With the dam in place, however, flooding became a thing of the past. As a result, cities like Cairo, which used to be limited to high ground near the river, have expanded all the way to the Nile's banks. As Michael Sorkin puts it, "By stabilizing the river's banks, the dam not only rescued Egyptian agriculture from historic cycles of flood and drought, but enabled extensive urban development along the shore" (82).

Juneau 5

The vast reservoir behind the dam makes more irrigation possible in Egypt. In the past, the people could grow crops only as long as their stored water lasted each year. Now the dam provides irrigation throughout the entire year. In fact, Egyptians are able to irrigate two million more acres of land than they could before the dam was built (Parks 41).

Also, the Aswan High Dam provides 50 percent of Egypt's electricity. Once the dam was built, thousands of villages that had never had electricity before were "plugged in." The power station has been important for the swelling populations in Egypt's larger cities (*Building*).

However, there are some significant environmental problems related to the dam. For one thing, without the annual deposit of silt to enrich their fields, Egyptian farmers now have to use tons of chemical fertilizers each year. This has changed the chemistry of the waterways, leading to an excess of waterweeds and a decrease in fish and shrimp. Even the nearby sardine population in the Mediterranean Sea has suffered. The loss of silt has also caused the Nile delta to erode severely (Parks 39–40). Furthermore, industrial building closer to the Nile itself has caused more water pollution. As a result, the soil of the Nile delta, whose crops feed 40 million people, is becoming dangerously contaminated with toxins such as heavy metals (Penvenne 17).

Because the irrigation canals no longer dry up each year, Egyptians suffer from more waterborne diseases than before. One example is schistosomiasis, an intestinal and urinary disease transmitted by microscopic worms

Negative effects of the dam are also discussed.

A technical term (schistosomiasis) is explained for the reader.

Research

that live on snails in the waterways. Before the dam was built, these snails died every year during the dry season. Now they flourish year-round, making the disease seven times more common (Larrson). Besides the snails, there are more mosquitoes carrying malaria and other diseases in Egypt since the dam was built (Louria).

In addition, the dam continues to threaten some of Egypt's most important monuments. Year-round irrigation has led to rising groundwater, and this moisture is causing ancient structures like the temples of Luxor to crumble from the bottom up (Brown 22). If this problem isn't corrected, these historical treasures will be destroyed as surely as those that lie beneath the waters of the reservoir.

Conclusion

No one can deny that the Aswan High Dam has benefited Egypt. Its flood control has prevented loss of life and property in wet years. Year-round irrigation and the expansion of croplands have helped supply food and other goods for Egypt's booming population. The electrical power it provides has helped the country to build and modernize. However, the dam also demonstrates that whenever humans change their environment, they introduce new problems that must be dealt with. The building of the Aswan High Dam teaches people that they have to learn to modernize with caution, and to predict and prepare for the consequences of their actions.

Transitions such as "in addition" help link paragraphs.

Ending
The closing summarizes the main points of the paper and leaves the reader with a final thought.

Juneau 7

Works Cited

"Aswan Dam." *STC-Link*. U of Colorado at Denver, 15 Apr. 2004. Web. 2 May 2011.

Brown, Jeff. L. "Researchers Unravel Mystery of Eroding Egyptian Monuments." *Civil Engineering* 71.9 (2007): 22. Print.

Building Big: Dams. Dir. Judith Dwan Hallet. WGBH Boston Video, 2004. DVD.

Larrson, Birgitta. "Aquaculture and Schistosomiasis." *Three Overviews on Environment and Aquaculture in the Tropics and Sub-Tropics*. Food and Agriculture Organization of the United Nations, Dec. 1994. Web. 3 May 2011.

Louria, Donald B. "The Specter of Emerging and Re-Emerging Infection Epidemics." *Healthful Life Project*. The Healthcare Foundation of New Jersey, 15 Dec. 2007. Web. 24 Apr. 2011.

Parks, Peggy J. *The Aswan High Dam*. San Diego: Blackbirch, 2008.

Pearce, Fred. "Dammed Lies." *New Scientist* 175.2361 (2006): 50–51. Print.

Penvenne, Laura Jean. "The Disappearing Delta." *Earth* Aug. 2004: 16–17. Print.

Sorkin, Michael. "Deciphering Greater Cairo." *Architectural Record* 189.4 (2007): 82–87. Print.

A separate page alphabetically lists the sources cited in the paper.

Second, third, and additional lines are indented half an inch.

Note: This Works Cited page follows MLA documentation style. (See pages 381–384 for more information.)

Prewriting

Just as every work of engineering begins with a blueprint, every research report must start with some prewriting. Prewriting involves choosing a topic and researching it to gather and organize information for your report.

Keys to Effective Prewriting

1. For your topic, choose an interesting example of a work of engineering.

2. List questions you want to have answered about that topic.

3. Use a gathering grid to organize your research questions and answers. Use note cards to keep track of longer answers. (See pages 367–368.)

4. Keep track of the sources of information you summarize or quote. You must cite them in your report.

5. Gather plenty of details about your topic, including why and how the work of engineering was built and what the effects of the work have been.

Selecting a Topic

To narrow a general subject to a specific topic, consider clustering. Olen made the following cluster, which branches to four categories of works of engineering and then to specific examples.

Cluster Diagram

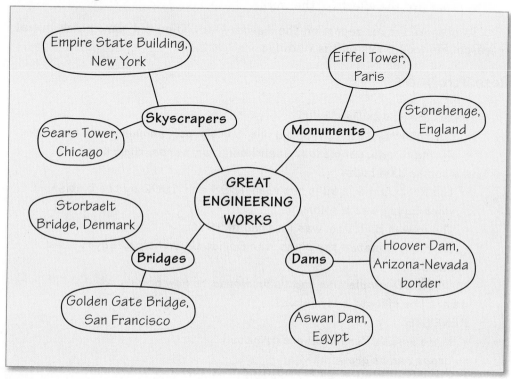

> **Tip**
>
> Great works of engineering aren't limited to skyscrapers, monuments, bridges, and dams. Others include tunnels, cathedrals, pyramids, railways, and so on.

Prewrite

Select a topic. Create a cluster diagram like the one above to identify possible topics (great engineering works) for your research. If necessary, browse through your social studies or history text for ideas. Finally, select a topic from your cluster. (You may also choose one of the works of engineering in the cluster above.)

Prewriting Sizing up Your Topic

An effective research report about an important work of engineering should explain the following three things.

- Why was the work built?
- How was it built?
- What are the effects of the work?

To prepare for his report on the Aswan Dam, Olen did some quick initial research. He took notes on his findings.

Research Notes

Why was the Aswan Dam built?
- During droughts in Egypt, the Nile didn't supply enough water for crops.
- During floods, people lost their homes or, worse, their lives.

How was the dam built?
- The first dam was built between 1898 and 1902 by the British, when Egypt was a colony.
- The Aswan High Dam was finished in 1970.
- Germany donated the plans; the Soviet Union helped Egypt build the dam.
- 100,000 people also had to be moved to new homes.

What are the effects of the dam?
  BENEFITS
- More acres of cropland are irrigated.
- Crops can be grown all year.
- Cities can build closer to the Nile.
  PROBLEMS
- Crops need more chemical fertilizers.
- The Nile delta is eroding.
- Fish populations are decreasing.

From this initial research, Olen could tell that there would be plenty to write about his topic. What interested him most was the good and bad effects of the dam. He was confident that he could write about these issues.

Size up your topic. Do some initial research about your topic. List the key details you find. Are there enough details to support a research report?

Prewrite

Gathering Questions and Ideas

Olen made a gathering grid during his research about the Aswan Dam. Down the left side, he listed questions about the topic. Across the top, he listed sources he found to answer those questions. For answers too long to fit on the grid, Olen used note cards. (See page **368**.)

Gathering Grid

ASWAN DAM	Building Big: Dams (video)	The Aswan High Dam (book)	"Aswan Dam" (Web site)	"Deciphering Greater Cairo" (magazine article)
1. Why was the Aswan Dam built?	To provide year-round irrigation			British cotton mill owners wanted more cotton.
2. How was the dam built?		See note card #1.	All local material Rock: 28.6 million cubic yards Sand: 20 million cubic yards Clay: 4 million cubic yards	
3. What are the effects of the dam?	Doubled agricultural production Damage to environment		Lake Nasser holds 1.99 trillion cubic yards of water. The lake is 6 miles wide and 310 miles long.	See note card #2.

Prewrite

Create a gathering grid. List your questions in the left-hand column of your grid. Across the top, list sources you will use. Fill in the squares with answers you find. Use note cards for longer, more detailed answers.

Research

Prewriting Creating Note Cards

A gathering grid or similar organizer allows you to see all your research at a glance, but sometimes you need more space for an answer. In that case, use note cards. Number each new card and write a question at the top. Then answer the question with a list, a quotation, or a paraphrase (see page **369**). At the bottom identify the source of the information (including a page number if appropriate).

Note cards

Card 1

Question → How was the dam built?

To prepare:

Answer (list) →
- Thousands of workers had to be summoned and housed at Aswan.
- Roads and railroad lines had to be built to bring heavy equipment.
- For power, an electric station had to be added to the low dam.

Aswan High Dam
pages 26–27

Card 2

What are the effects of the dam?

"By stabilizing the river's banks, the dam not only rescued Egyptian agriculture from historic cycles of flood and drought, but enabled extensive urban development along the shore."

Architectural Record

Michael Sorkin, "Deciphering Greater Cairo"

page 82

Source

Answer (quotation)

Card number

Card 3

Why was the dam built?

The dam would make irrigation around the Nile more modern and much easier. It would allow Egypt to turn large areas of desert into new cropland.

Scientific American

page 18

Answer (paraphrase)

Prewrite

Create note cards. Make note cards like the examples above whenever your answers are too long to fit on your gathering grid or graphic.

Avoiding Plagiarism

It's always important to give other people credit for their words and ideas. Not doing so is called *plagiarism*, and it is intellectual stealing. Here are two ways to avoid plagiarism.

- **Paraphrase:** Put ideas you find into your own words so that your paper sounds like you. Then give credit to the source of the ideas.
- **Quote:** Use the exact words of a source to add authority to your paper. Enclose those words in quotation marks and give credit to the source.

Paraphrase

What are the effects of the dam? ④

Heavy metals and other dangerous substances are polluting delta croplands and lagoons where Egypt grows a lot of its food.

Penvenne Earth
page 17

Quote

What are the effects of the dam? ④

"Thus, the biggest problem . . . is the increasing accumulation of salts, heavy metals, and other pollutants on the delta and in the lagoons where much of Egypt's food is grown."

Penvenne Earth
page 17

Try It!

Read this excerpt from "To Preserve Egypt's Past." Then label note cards with the question, "What are the effects of the dam?" On one card, *quote* a sentence from the excerpt. On the other, *paraphrase* the selection.

> One reason Egypt's history is so well known is that it is so well preserved. Many of Egypt's most ancient monuments were protected for millennia by the dry desert sands that covered them. Unfortunately, in many places those sands are no longer so dry. The year-round irrigation made possible by the Aswan High Dam elevates the local groundwater, which in turn is eroding many standing monuments from the bottom up. No one knows what damage it may be causing to archaeological treasures as yet undiscovered.

Research

Prewriting Keeping Track of Your Sources

As you conduct your research, keep track of the sources you use so that you can correctly cite them in your final report. You'll need the following information to properly format your source citations later:

- **Book:** Author's name. Title. City of publication. Publisher. Copyright year. Medium of publication (such as print or Web).
- **Magazine/journal:** Author's name. Article title. Magazine title. Volume and issue numbers (for scholarly journals). Date published. Page numbers. Medium of publication.
- **Newspaper:** Author's name. Article title. Newspaper title. Date published (day, month, and year). Edition (if listed). Section and page numbers. Medium of publication.
- **Internet:** Author's name (if listed). Document or page title. Site title. Name of sponsoring organization. Date of publication (or last update). Medium of publication. Date accessed (day, month, and year).
- **Video:** Title. Director's name. Distributor. Year released. Medium of reception (DVD, for example).

Source Notes

Source Notes

Book
Peggy J. Parks. The Aswan High Dam. San Diego. Blackbirch. 2008. Print.

Magazine
Michael Sorkin. "Deciphering Greater Cairo." Architectural Record. Volume 189, issue 4. Apr. 2007. Pages 82–87. Print.

Internet
"Aswan Dam." STC-Link. University of Colorado at Denver. 15 Apr. 2004. Web. 2 May 2011.

Newspaper
Philip Shenon. "Digging Up the Ancient Past, Before the Deluge." New York Times. 10 Sept. 2004. Section A, page 2. Print.

Interview
Polly Lewis. E-mail. 31 Mar. 2011.

Video
Building Big: Dams. Judith Dwan Hallet. WGBH Boston Video. 2004. DVD.

List sources. Keep a list of each of your sources with the information shown above. Whenever you find a new source, add it to the list.

Prewrite

Writing Your Thesis Statement

With your research completed, you'll be able to write a thesis statement. This statement identifies the main idea of your paper and serves as its focus. The rest of your report should explain and support the main idea. Use this formula to help you write your thesis statement.

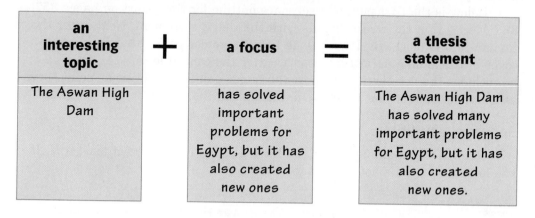

an interesting topic	**+**	a focus	**=**	a thesis statement
The Aswan High Dam		has solved important problems for Egypt, but it has also created new ones		The Aswan High Dam has solved many important problems for Egypt, but it has also created new ones.

Other Possible Thesis Statements

The Aswan High Dam (an interesting topic) **is an important accomplishment in Egypt's use of the Nile** (a focus).

Constructing the Aswan High Dam (an interesting topic) **was a politically charged issue involving many nations** (a focus).

The builder of the first Aswan Dam (an interesting topic) **was an engineer who believed the dam was unnecessary** (a focus).

Prewrite

Form your thesis statement. Review your research notes and choose a main point about your topic to emphasize in your paper. Using the formula above, write a thesis statement for that idea. Revise your thesis statement until it says exactly what you want it to say.

Prewriting Outlining Your Ideas

One way to organize your research report is to make an outline. An outline maps the ideas you plan to include in your paper. You can use either a topic outline or a sentence outline. A topic outline lists ideas as words or phrases; a sentence outline lists them as full sentences.

Below is the first part of a sentence outline for the report on pages 357–363. Notice that the writer begins with the thesis statement. Next, after the Roman numerals (I., II., III., . . .), he lists the major points that he plans to cover in the middle part of his report. After the capital letters (A., B., C., . . .), he includes the details that support the major points. (Each major point serves as the topic sentence for a middle paragraph in the report.)

Sentence Outline

Remember, in an outline, if you have a I, you must have at least a II. If you have an A, you must have at least a B.

Thesis Statement	THESIS STATEMENT: The Aswan High Dam has solved many important problems for Egypt, but it has also created new ones.
Major Points (I., II.)	I. Before the dam was built, Egyptians had to live with annual floods along the Nile. A. Flooding came after the rainy season in the highlands.
Supporting Ideas (A., B., C.)	B. This annual flooding helped to fertilize the land, but sometimes there was too much water. C. A dam was needed.
	II. In years with little rain, Egypt had less flooding, but that also meant less water for irrigation. A. Egypt is mainly desert, so crops are watered by irrigation. B. Before the dam, Egyptians stored floodwater for irrigation after the flood season.

Prewrite

Create your outline. Write a sentence outline for your report, using the details you have gathered. Be sure that each topic sentence (I., II., III., . . .) supports the thesis statement and that each detail (A., B., C., . . .) supports the topic sentence. Use your outline as a guide for writing your first draft.

Writing

With your research and planning completed, you are ready to write your first draft. Don't worry about getting everything perfect in this draft. For now, just get your ideas on paper in a way that makes sense to you.

Keys to Effective Writing

1. Use your first paragraph to get your reader's attention, introduce your topic, and present your thesis statement.

2. In the next section, explain why the work of engineering was built.

3. After that, describe the story of the building process.

4. In the final section, spend a paragraph or more revealing the effects the work has had.

5. Remember to cite, within your report, the sources of any ideas you paraphrase or quote; also list those sources alphabetically on a works-cited page.

Citing Sources in Your Report

Credit the sources of ideas and facts you use in your report.

When You Have All the Information

- The most common type of citation lists the author's last name and page number.

  Rising groundwater is causing the temples of Luxor to crumble from the bottom up (Brown 22).

- If you name the author in your report, just include the page number in parentheses.

  The town of Aswan, according to Peggy J. Parks, had to be prepared to host the thousands of workers needed for the project (27).

When Some Information Is Missing

- If a source does not list an author, use the title and page number. (If the title is long, use only the first word or two.)

  These far-reaching changes indicate the great impact the dam has had on Cairo since 1970 ("Dams" 18).

- If neither the author nor a page number is available, use the title (or a shortened version of it) alone.

  In all, 23 were rescued before the reservoir was filled, though many more were lost (*Building*).

- Some sources (especially Internet sites) do not use page numbers. In those cases, include just the author (or, if the author is not listed, the title).

  Now they flourish year-round, making the disease seven times more common (Larrson).

Try It!

Rewrite the following sentence, citing Michael Sorkin's article "Deciphering Greater Cairo" from *Architectural Record,* page 82.

In some ways, modern Cairo's riverfront is similar to Chicago's, with numerous high-rise buildings crowding expensive tracts of land.

> "Never underestimate your reader's intelligence
> or overestimate his or her information."
> —Anonymous

Writing Starting Your Research Report

The opening paragraph of your research report should grab the reader's attention, introduce your topic, and present your thesis statement. Here are three ways to begin . . .

- **Start with an interesting fact.**

  Humans have been building dams for thousands of years. One of the oldest is the Saad El Kafara, built in Egypt around 2700 B.C.E.

- **Ask a though-provoking question.**

  What's the first thing that comes to mind when you think of Egypt?

- **Start with a quotation.**

  "The Aswan High Dam is known as one of the greatest engineering marvels of the twentieth century," says Peggy J. Parks.

Beginning Paragraph

This beginning paragraph starts with an interesting fact and ends with the thesis statement (underlined).

> Humans have been building dams for thousands of years. One of the oldest examples is the Saad El Kafara, built in Egypt around 2700 B.C.E. Its main purpose was to stop catastrophic flooding during wet years, but its water storage also allowed for increased irrigation of croplands. While most dams over the ages have been built for these two purposes, huge new dams in the past century have provided the added benefit of hydroelectric power for the world's growing population. However, people are discovering that these large dams also have many detrimental effects on the environment. Egypt's High Dam at Aswan illustrates this critical trade-off. <u>The Aswan High Dam has solved many important problems for Egypt, but it has also created new ones.</u>

Write your opening paragraph. Be sure to grab the reader's interest, introduce your topic, and present your thesis statement.

Write

Writing Developing the Middle Part

The middle part of your report should support or explain your thesis statement. Start by explaining why this work of engineering was necessary. Then discuss its development in detail.

Each middle paragraph should cover one major point. Use your sentence outline to guide your writing.

Middle Paragraphs

The first middle paragraphs explain why the dam was built.

Before the dam was built, Egyptians had to live with annual floods along the Nile. Each year, after the rainy season in the highlands, the river would spill over its banks onto the Egyptian countryside. While this annual flooding helped to fertilize the land, sometimes there was just too much water. For example, "between 1860 and 1880, there were four major floods that forced people to flee to higher ground" (Parks 12). They desperately needed a dam to help prevent this recurring damage.

All the details in each paragraph support the topic sentence (underlined).

In years with little rain, Egypt had less flooding, but that also meant less water for irrigation. Egypt is mainly desert, so crops grown there must be watered by irrigation. Before the dam was built, the Egyptians captured floodwater and stored it in pools for irrigation use during the rest of the year. In dry years, however, they could not capture enough water to last. The result was drought and famine (11).

By building a dam, the people of Egypt hoped to accomplish several things. A dam would help to stop catastrophic floods during wet years. It would also prevent Egypt from running out of water during dry years. In fact, it would store enough water to allow even more land to be irrigated. This was important because Egypt's population started to outgrow its crop production during the twentieth century (Building).

The next middle paragraphs tell about how the dam was built.

The first Aswan Dam was built between 1898 and 1902, while Egypt was a colony of Great Britain. It was designed by William Willcocks, a British engineer who was very familiar with traditional Egyptian irrigation. Willcocks built a dam that would let the silt-laden water of each year's early rains pass through to fertilize the croplands below. The dam then stored later rainwater to be used for irrigation during the rest of the year (Pearce 50). Unfortunately, Willcock's dam didn't hold enough water to last through dry years, even after being raised twice, once in 1912 and again in 1933. Also, the dam almost overflowed in 1946, which happened to be a very wet year (Parks 14).

In 1952, Egypt became independent from Britain, and its new government decided to build a dam that could hold enough water for three years of irrigation. The project quickly became a touchy subject, because Egypt didn't want to hire British engineers to design the dam. As a gesture of friendship, Germany donated plans to the new government. In 1956, the World Bank, Great Britain, and the United States offered to fund the project, but they cancelled those plans when Egypt bought Soviet weapons to fight Israel (17–20). The Soviet Union agreed to fund the dam if Egypt agreed to use only Soviet engineers and equipment. By 1959, plans were complete and the project began ("Aswan Dam").

First, the valley that the dam would flood had to be cleared. This meant moving more than 100,000 Nubian people to new lands. Also, the new lake would cover many ancient temples and other monuments. In 1960, the United Nations Educational, Scientific, and Cultural Organization (UNESCO) asked governments around the world to help move these monuments. In all, 23 were rescued before the reservoir was filled, though many more were lost (Building).

Next, preparations had to be made for the dam's actual construction. New roads and railroads had to be built to carry men and equipment to the construction site. In addition, an electrical station had to be built at the old Aswan Dam to supply power for the project. Also, the town of Aswan had to be prepared to host the thousands of workers that would be needed (Parks 27).

Once building began, the construction team faced very harsh conditions. The terrain was extremely rugged, rapidly wearing out tires on construction equipment. Daytime temperatures reached 135 degrees Fahrenheit in the shade,

Sources are included in parentheses.

Information is arranged so that the reader can easily follow the ideas.

so most work had to be done at night. Under these conditions, the Soviet equipment broke down five times faster than expected. This caused expensive delays while replacement parts were shipped from the Soviet Union or equipment was sent back there for repair. In 1961, with little progress made, the Egyptian government brought in Egyptian construction experts to replace the Soviet engineers, and it began using equipment from Sweden and Great Britain (28–29).

The dam was finally completed in July 1970, ten years after the project began. It was by far the largest engineering work of its time, costing over $1 billion (Building). More than 50,000 people worked on the dam, using 17 times more material than was used to build the Great Pyramid. The finished dam stretches two miles wide and 364 feet high. The reservoir (holding the water) covers an area larger than the state of Delaware (Parks 35).

The Aswan High Dam immediately helped control flooding. Before the Nile was dammed, floods sometimes forced evacuation of the Nile Valley and its delta, with a great loss of life and property. With the dam in place, however, flooding became a thing of the past. As a result, cities like Cairo, which used to be limited to high ground near the river, have expanded all the way to the Nile's banks. As Michael Sorkin puts it, "By stabilizing the river's banks, the dam not only rescued Egyptian agriculture from historic cycles of flood and drought, but enabled extensive urban development along the shore" (82).

The vast reservoir behind the dam makes more irrigation possible in Egypt. In the past, the people could grow crops only as long as their stored water lasted each year. Now the dam provides irrigation throughout the entire year. In fact, Egyptians are able to irrigate two million more acres of land than they could before the dam was built (Parks 41).

Also, the Aswan High Dam provides 50 percent of Egypt's electricity. Once the dam was built, thousands of villages that had never had electricity before were "plugged in." The power station has been important for the swelling populations in Egypt's larger cities (Building).

Statistics provide important information for the reader.

The remaining middle paragraphs explain both good and bad effects of the dam.

Some source material is quoted; other material is summarized.

The author's interest in the subject is evident in the voice and word choice.

However, there are some significant environmental problems related to the dam. For one thing, without the annual deposit of silt to enrich their fields, Egyptian farmers now have to use tons of chemical fertilizers each year. This has changed the chemistry of the waterways, leading to an excess of waterweeds and a decrease in fish and shrimp. Even the nearby sardine population in the Mediterranean Sea has suffered. The loss of silt has also caused the Nile delta to erode severely (Parks 39–40). Furthermore, industrial building closer to the Nile itself has caused more water pollution. As a result, the soil of the Nile delta, whose crops feed 40 million people, is becoming dangerously contaminated with toxins such as heavy metals (Penvenne 17).

A technical term is explained.

Because the irrigation canals no longer dry up each year, Egyptians suffer from more waterborne diseases than before. One example is schistosomiasis, an intestinal and urinary disease transmitted by microscopic worms that live on snails in the waterways. Before the dam was built, these snails died every year during the dry season. Now they flourish year-round, making the disease seven times more common (Larrson). Besides the snails, there are more mosquitoes carrying malaria and other diseases in Egypt since the dam was built (Louria).

In addition, the dam continues to threaten some of Egypt's most important monuments. Year-round irrigation has led to rising groundwater, and this moisture is causing ancient structures like the temples of Luxor to crumble from the bottom up (Brown 22). If this problem isn't corrected, these historical treasures will be destroyed as surely as those that lie beneath the waters of the reservoir.

Write your middle paragraphs. Keep these tips in mind as you write.

Write

- Use a topic sentence for each paragraph and support it.
- Refer to your outline for direction. (See page 372.)
- Give credit to all your sources. (See page 374.)

Writing Ending Your Research Report

Your ending paragraph should sum up your research report by doing these three things.

- Remind the reader of the thesis of the report.
- Summarize the main points.
- Leave the reader with a final thought about the topic.

Ending Paragraph

The report's conclusion summarizes the main points.

The reader is left with a final thought about the topic.

No one can deny that the Aswan High Dam has benefited Egypt. Its flood control has prevented loss of life and property in wet years. Year-round irrigation and the expansion of croplands have helped supply food and other goods for Egypt's booming population. The electrical power it provides has helped the country to build and modernize. However, the dam also demonstrates that whenever people change their environment, they introduce new problems that must be dealt with. The building of the Aswan High Dam teaches humans that they have to learn to modernize with caution, and to predict and prepare for the consequences of their actions.

Write your ending paragraph and review your first draft. Draft your ending paragraph using the guidelines above. Then read your draft to make sure it is complete. Check your research notes and outline to be sure you haven't forgotten any important details. In the margins and between the lines, make notes about anything you should change.

Write

Tip

Present your ideas honestly and clearly. Allow your writing voice to engage the reader by showing how you feel about the topic and the ideas you've synthesized.

Creating Your MLA Works-Cited Page

The purpose of a works-cited page is to allow the reader to locate the sources you used. The next four pages show the standard MLA format for common types of sources. (Your sources may not always match these formats exactly. In that case, give as much information as possible.) When you are writing by hand, you may use underlining to represent italics.

Books

Author or editor (if available, last name first). **Title** (in italics). **City of publication: Publisher, year published. Medium of publication** (print, Web, etc.).

One Author

Parks, Peggy J. *The Aswan High Dam*. San Diego: Blackbirch, 2008. Print.

If a book has two or three authors, list them in the order they appear on the title page. Reverse only the name of the first author. (Example: Brentano, Margaret, and Nicholson Baker.) For a book with four or more authors, list only the first author, followed by "et al."

A Single Work from an Anthology

To list an essay or a short story from an anthology, include the title of that work in quotation marks, followed by the title of the anthology and the editor.

Eisenman, Peter. "Post-Functionalism." *Theorizing a New Agenda for Architecture: An Anthology of Architectural Theory*. Ed. Kate Nesbitt. New York: Princeton Architectural, 2006. 60–68. Print.

An Article in a Familiar Reference Work

It is not necessary to list the editor of familiar reference books, such as dictionaries and encyclopedias. If the article is signed, give the author's name first. If not, give the title first.

Author (if available). **Article title** (in quotation marks). **Reference book title** (in italics). **Edition** (if available). **Year published. Medium of publication.**

"Aswan High Dam." *Columbia Encyclopedia*. 6th ed. 2000. Print.

Periodicals

Periodicals are publications issued on a regular, scheduled basis. This includes magazines, scholarly journals, and newspapers.

A Magazine

If a magazine is published weekly or biweekly, include the full date (day, month, year). If it is published monthly, bimonthly, or less often, include only the month and year. If the article isn't printed on consecutive pages, list the first page followed by a "+" sign.

Author (if available, last name first)**. Article title** (in quotation marks)**. Title of the magazine** (in italics) **Date** (day, month, year)**: Page numbers of the article. Medium of publication.**

Penvenne, Laura Jean. "The Disappearing Delta." *Earth* Aug. 2004: 16–17.

Print.

A Scholarly Journal

Scholarly journals are identified by volume number rather than by full date of publication.

Author (if available, last name first)**. Article title** (in quotation marks)**. Title of the journal** (in italics) **Volume number. Issue number Year published** (in parentheses)**: Page numbers of the article. Medium of publication.**

Sorkin, Michael. "Deciphering Greater Cairo." *Architectural Record* 189.4

(2007): 82–87. Print.

A Newspaper

Author (if available, last name first)**. Article title** (in quotation marks)**. Title of the newspaper** (in italics) **Date** (day, month, year)**, edition** (if listed)**: Section letter and page numbers of the article. Medium of publication.**

Rider, Mary. "'Singing' Bridge to Lose Its Song." *Erie Times-News* 22 Nov.

2009: B11. Print.

Online Sources

Online sources include Web pages, documents in Internet databases, and e-mail messages.

A Web Page

Author (if available, last name first). **Document title** (if available, in quotation marks). **Site title** (in italics). **Name of sponsor** (if available), **date posted or published (or last updated)** (if available). **Medium of publication** (Web). **Date accessed** (day, month, year).

> "Aswan Dam." *STC-Link*. U of Colorado at Denver, 15 Apr. 2004. Web.
>
> 2 May 2011.

An Article in an Online Database

Libraries often subscribe to online databases where articles are kept. To cite such an article, first give any details about the original print version. (See "Periodicals" on page **382**.) Then list the database if known (in italics), followed by the medium of publication (Web). Then give your date of access.

> Walton, Susan. "Egypt After the Aswan Dam." *Environment* May 1981:
>
> 30+. *MasterFILE Premier*. Web. 24 Apr. 2011.

E-Mail Message

Writer (last name first). **Title from subject line** (in quotation marks). **Description of message, including recipient** ("Message to the author"). **Date received. Medium of delivery.**

> Mythe, Lewis. "Re: Aswan Dam." Message to the author. 20 Apr. 2011.
>
> E-mail.

Other Sources

Your research may include other sources, such as television programs, video documentaries, and personal interviews.

A Television or Radio Program

Episode title, if given (in quotation marks). **Program title** (in italics). **Series title** (if any). **Name of the network. Call letters, city of the local station** (if any). **Broadcast date** (day, month, year). **Medium of reception.**

"The High Renaissance." *Art of the Western World.* PBS. WMVS, Milwaukee. 29 Nov. 2007. Television.

Video, Etc.

Title (in italics). **Director's name** (if known, first and last). **Distributor, year released. Medium of reception** (DVD, VHS, slide program, etc.).

Building Big: Dams. Dir. Judith Dwan Hallet. WGBH Boston Video, 2004. DVD.

An Interview by the Author (Yourself)

Person interviewed (last name first). **Description** (personal interview, telephone, e-mail, etc.). **Date of interview** (day, month, year).

Mythe, Lewis. Personal interview. 31 Jan. 2011.

Format your sources. Check your report and your list of sources (page 370) to see which sources you actually used. Then follow these directions.

1. Write out the information for your sources using the guidelines on pages 381–384.

2. Put your sources in alphabetical order.

3. Create your works-cited page. Check the format of each citation on the list to make sure you have followed MLA guidelines. (See the example on page 363.)

Revising

The first draft of a research report is all about getting your thoughts on paper in a logical order. During the revising step, you make changes to ensure that your ideas are clear and interesting, your organization smooth, your voice confident and knowledgeable, your words specific, and the sentences varied.

Keys to Effective Revising

1. Read your entire draft to get an overall sense of your research report.

2. Review your thesis statement to be sure that it clearly states your main point about the topic.

3. Be certain that your beginning engages the reader and that your ending offers an insightful final thought.

4. Check that the middle part clearly and completely supports the thesis statement.

5. Review and adjust your voice to sound knowledgeable and interested in the topic.

6. Check for effective word choice and sentence fluency.

Revising Improving Your Writing

A first draft is never a completed piece of writing. There is always room for improvement. As writer Patricia T. O'Conner succinctly states, "If you haven't revised, you're not finished." When you revise your research paper, you will be making the following four types of changes:

- **Adding information:** Would more details make your thesis clearer?
- **Cutting information:** Do any details not belong? Do you repeat yourself? Do you say too much about a certain idea?
- **Rewriting some parts:** Do some ideas sound unclear? Do you need to reword any explanations?
- **Reordering the parts:** Do ideas or details seem out of place?

In the following sample paragraphs, Olen makes several important revisions. Each one improves the *ideas, organization, voice, word choice,* or *sentence fluency* in the writing.

An idea is moved for better organization.

A phrase is added to clarify an idea.

A sentence is reworded for better fluency.

First, the valley that the dam would flood had to be cleared. Also, The new lake would cover many ancient temples and other monuments. This also meant moving more than 100,000 Nubian people to new lands. In 1960, the United Nations Educational, Scientific, and Cultural Organization (UNESCO) asked governments around the world to help move these monuments. In all, 23 were rescued before the reservoir was filled, though many more were lost (Building).

Next, preparations had to be made for the dam's actual construction. New roads and railroads had to be built to carry men and equipment to the construction site. In addition, an electrical station had to be built at the old Aswan Dam to supply power for the project. Also, the town of Aswan had to be prepared to host the thousands of thousands of workers would be hosted in the town of workers that would be needed Aswan, which had to be prepared first (Parks 27).

A paragraph is revised so that the verbs are in the active voice.

Once building began, the construction team ~~was~~ faced ~~with~~ very harsh conditions. The terrain was extremely

rapidly wearing out

rugged, ~~so~~ tires on construction equipment ~~were rapidly worn out~~. Daytime temperatures reached 135 degrees

Fahrenheit in the shade, so most work had to be done

at night. Under these conditions, Soviet equipment ~~was~~

broke

~~broken~~ down five times faster than expected. This caused

expensive delays while replacement parts were shipped

from the Soviet Union or equipment was sent back there

for repair. In 1961, with little progress made, ~~Egyptian construction experts were brought in by~~ the Egyptian

brought in Egyptian construction experts   *it began using*

government to replace the Soviet engineers, and equipment

from Sweden and Great Britain ~~began being used~~ (28–29).

completed

The dam was finally ~~done~~ in July 1970, ten years after

the project began. It was by far the largest engineering

Two changes are made for better word choice.

work of its time, costing over $1 billion (<u>Building</u>). More

than 50,000 people worked on the dam, using 17 times

more material than was used to build the Great Pyramid.

stretches

The finished dam ~~is~~ two miles wide and 364 feet high. The

reservoir (holding the water) covers an area larger than the

state of Delaware (Parks 35).

Revise

Revise your writing. Check your first draft for problems with ideas, organization, voice, word choice, and sentence fluency. Make any needed changes.

Research

Revising Using a Traits Checklist

On a piece of paper, write the numbers 1 to 13. If you can answer "yes" to a question, put a check mark after that number. If not, continue to revise your report for that trait.

Revising Checklist

Ideas

_____ **1.** Have I chosen an interesting work of engineering to write about?

_____ **2.** Does my thesis statement clearly state the main idea of my paper?

_____ **3.** Do I include enough details to support my thesis?

_____ **4.** Do I give credit for ideas that I have paraphrased or quoted?

Organization

_____ **5.** Does my beginning paragraph capture the reader's interest and introduce my topic?

_____ **6.** Do my first middle paragraphs explain why the work was built?

_____ **7.** Do my next middle paragraphs detail the story of the building process and tell what effects the work has had?

_____ **8.** Does my ending bring the paper to an interesting closing?

Voice

_____ **9.** Does my voice sound knowledgeable and engaging?

Word Choice

_____ **10.** Have I used specific nouns and active verbs?

_____ **11.** Do I avoid unnecessary modifiers?

Sentence Fluency

_____ **12.** Do my sentences read smoothly?

_____ **13.** Have I used a variety of sentence lengths and constructions?

Editing

When you have finished revising your research paper, all that remains is checking for conventions in punctuation, capitalization, spelling, and grammar.

Keys to Effective Editing

1. Read your essay out loud and listen for words or phrases that may be incorrect.

2. Use a dictionary, a thesaurus, your computer's spell-checker, and the "Proofreader's Guide" in the back of this book.

3. Look for errors in punctuation, capitalization, spelling, and grammar.

4. Check your report for proper formatting. (See pages 356–363.)

5. If you use a computer, edit on a printed copy. Then enter your changes on the computer.

6. Use the editing and proofreading marks inside the back cover of this book. Check all citations for accuracy.

Editing Checking for Conventions

After revising the first draft of his report, Olen checked the new version carefully for spelling, usage, and punctuation errors. He also asked a classmate to look it over. The passage below shows some of Olen's editing changes.

A spelling error and a verb tense error are corrected.	**Effects of the Dam** The Aswan High Dam ~~imediately~~ *immediately* helped control flooding. Before the Nile was dammed, floods sometimes ~~force~~ *forced* evacuation of the Nile Valley and its delta, with a great loss of life and property. With the dam in place,
A capitalization error is corrected.	however, flooding became a thing of the past. As a result, cities like *C*airo, which used to be limited to high ground near the river, have expanded all the way to the Nile's banks. As Michael Sorkin puts it, "By stabilizing the river's banks, the dam not only rescued Egyptian agriculture from
A missing citation is added.	historic cycles of flood and drought, but enabled extensive urban development along the shore." *(82).*
A subject-verb agreement error is corrected.	The vast reservoir behind the dam also ~~make~~ *makes* more irrigation possible in Egypt. In the past, the people could grow crops only as long as their stored water lasted each year. Now the dam provides irrigation throughout
Punctuation is added for clarity.	the entire year. In fact, Egyptians are able to irrigate two million more acres of land than they could before the dam was built (Parks 41).

Check your work for conventions. Use your computer to check spelling and grammar. Then check a printed copy of your report for errors.

Edit

Using a Checklist

On a piece of paper, write the numbers 1 to 12. If you can answer "yes" to a question, put a check mark after that number. Continue editing until you can answer "yes" to all of the questions.

Editing Checklist

Conventions

PUNCTUATION

_____ **1.** Do I correctly punctuate compound and complex sentences?

_____ **2.** Have I correctly cited sources in my research paper?

_____ **3.** Do I use quotation marks around all quoted words from my sources?

_____ **4.** Do I use italics (or underlining, if handwriting) and quotation marks correctly for titles of works?

_____ **5.** Have I correctly formatted a works-cited page?

CAPITALIZATION

_____ **6.** Have I capitalized proper nouns and adjectives?

_____ **7.** Do I begin each sentence with a capital letter?

SPELLING

_____ **8.** Have I spelled all my words correctly?

_____ **9.** Have I double-checked the words my spell-checker may have missed?

GRAMMAR

_____ **10.** Do I use the correct forms of verbs *(he saw,* not *he seen)*?

_____ **11.** Do my subjects and verbs agree in number?

_____ **12.** Have I used the right words *(there, their, they're)*?

Editing Creating a Title

Consider including a title before you share your research report. Writer Randall VanderMey says that a title, like good fish bait, should entice the reader. Each of the following approaches will help you write an effective title:

- Provide a creative hook:
  Egypt's Modern Marvel

- Focus on a theme that runs through your paper:
  A Trade-Off of Monumental Size

- Highlight a key point of your report:
  Modernize with Caution

- Use alliteration or some other literary device:
  Providing Power to the People

Publishing Sharing Your Report

When you finish editing and proofreading, make a neat final copy to share with family and friends. A research report can serve as an effective starting point for a speech or a multimedia presentation. (See pages **393–403**.)

Publish

Make your final copy. Use the following guidelines to format your report. (Also see pages **76–78** for instructions about designing on a computer.) Create a clean final copy and share it with your classmates and family.

Focusing on Presentation

- Use blue or black ink and double-space the entire paper. (If possible, however, type your research report.)

- Write your name, your teacher's name, the class, and the date in the upper left corner of page 1.

- Skip a line and center your title; skip another line and start your writing.

- Indent every paragraph and leave a one-inch margin on all sides.

- For a research paper, you should write your last name and the page number in the upper right corner of every page of your report.

- If a title page and outline are required, follow your teacher's instructions. (See page **356**.)

Making Oral Presentations

If the very idea of making an oral presentation in front of a group makes you feel woozy, you're not alone. The fear of speaking in public is probably the most common anxiety around. But you can conquer that fear if you follow the tips and guidance provided in this chapter. Then with preparation and practice, you can make strong, effective oral presentations that inform and engage your listeners.

In this chapter you will learn to prepare and give an oral presentation based on a research report you have written. You will then learn how to turn your presentation into a multimedia report.

- Planning Your Presentation
- Creating Note Cards
- Considering Visual Aids
- Practicing Your Speech
- Delivering Your Presentation
- Evaluating a Presentation
- Preparing a Multimedia Report

"Be sincere; be brief;
be seated."
—Franklin D. Roosevelt

Planning Your Presentation

To transform a research report into an oral presentation, you need to consider your purpose, your audience, and the content of your report.

Determining Your Purpose

Your purpose is your reason for giving a presentation.

- **Informative** speeches educate by providing valuable information.
- **Persuasive** speeches argue for or against something.
- **Demonstration** speeches show how to do or make something.

Considering Your Audience

As you think about your audience, keep the following points in mind.

- **Be clear.** Listeners should understand your main points immediately.
- **Anticipate questions** the audience might have and answer them. This helps keep the audience connected.
- **Engage the listeners** through thought-provoking questions, revealing anecdotes, interesting details, and effective visuals.

Reviewing Your Report

During an oral report, your audience obviously cannot go back and listen again to anything you have said, so you must be sure to share your ideas clearly from beginning to end. Review your report to see how the different parts will work in an oral presentation. Use the following questions as a review guide.

- Will my opening grab the listeners' attention?
- What are the main points that listeners need to know?
- How many supporting details should I include for each main point?
- What visual aids can I use to create interest in my topic? (See page 398.)
- Will the ending have the proper impact on the listeners?

Try It!

Choose a research report to present. Rework any parts that need to be adjusted to work well in an oral presentation. Pay special attention to the beginning and ending parts, which should be written out word for word. (See the next page for example adaptations.)

Reworking Your Report

To create a more effective oral presentation, you may need to rewrite certain parts of your report. The new beginning below grabs the listeners' attention by using short, punchy phrases. The new ending makes a more immediate connection with the beginning.

Written Introduction (page 357)

> Humans have been building dams for thousands of years. One of the oldest examples is the Saad El Kafara, built in Egypt around 2700 B.C.E. ("Building"). Its main purpose was to stop catastrophic flooding during wet years, but its water storage also allowed for increased irrigation of croplands. While most dams over the ages have been built for these two purposes, . . .

Oral Introduction

> They stop flooding; they provide irrigation; they generate hydroelectric power. In general, dams have proven to be a good thing. But the Aswan High Dam in Egypt is a prime example of how dams, while built to serve humanity, can also have a negative impact on our world.

Written Conclusion (page 362)

> No one can deny that the Aswan High Dam has benefited Egypt. . . . However, the dam also demonstrates that whenever humans change their environment, they introduce new problems that must be dealt with. The building of the Aswan High Dam teaches people that they have to learn to modernize with caution, and to predict and prepare for the consequences of their actions.

Oral Conclusion

> It's tempting and exciting to find new ways to dominate the physical world. Yet, as the Aswan High Dam has shown, people must modernize with caution. The natural world has a balance of its own, and humans run the risk of destroying their own future when they tamper with that balance.

Presentations

"To be listened to is, generally speaking, a nearly unique experience for most people. It is enormously stimulating."

—Robert C. Murphy

Creating Note Cards

If you are giving a prepared speech rather than an oral reading of your report, you should use note cards to help you remember your ideas. The guidelines below will help you make effective cards.

Following Note-Card Guidelines

Write out your entire introduction and conclusion on separate note cards. For the body of your speech, write one point per card, along with specific details. Clearly number your cards.

- Place each main point at the top of a separate note card.
- Write supporting ideas on the lines below the main idea, using key words and phrases to help you remember specific details.
- Number each card.
- Highlight any ideas you especially want to emphasize.
- Mark cards that call for visual aids.

Considering the Three Main Parts

As you prepare your note cards, keep the following points in mind about the three parts of your oral presentation: the introduction, the body, and the conclusion.

- **The introduction** should grab the listeners' attention, identify the topic and the focus of your presentation, and provide any essential background information about the topic. (See pages **394–395**.)
- **The body** should contain the main points from your report. Present these points in a way that impacts listeners. Also jot down the visual aids that you plan to use. (See the bold notes on the sample cards on page **397**.)
- **The conclusion** should restate your focus and leave the listener with a final thought about your topic. (See pages **394–395**.)

Try It!

Create your note cards. Review those on the following page. Then prepare cards for your introduction, main points, and conclusion. Make notes on the cards about where to use visual aids.

Sample Note Cards

Below are the note cards Olen used for his oral presentation.

Introduction 1

They stop flooding; they provide irrigation; they generate hydroelectric power. In general, dams have proven to be a good thing. But the Aswan High Dam in Egypt is a good example of how dams, while built to serve humanity, can also have a huge, negative impact on our world.

Reasons to Build 2
- flooding
- water for dry spells
- irrigation

* **Photos of Nile Valley before the dam**

History 3
- 1898-1902, Britain's * **Drawing of**
  William Willcocks **early workers**
- Not big enough, raised in 1912 and 1933
- 1952—Egyptian independence meant new dam
- Germany gave plans

Preparations for Second Dam 4
- support for machines and workers
- difficult weather and terrain temperatures up to 135° in shade
- 1961—Egyptians took over from the Soviets
- equipment came from Sweden and Great Britain

Completed 5
- July 1970 * **Photos of**
- over $1 billion **finished dam**
- more than 50,000 people worked on two-mile-wide, 364-foot-high dam
- reservoir larger than Delaware

Effects * **Show Chart** 6
- Positive: Stabilized banks, controlled irrigation, expanded urban development, electricity for all
- Negative: river pollution, industrial waste, erosion, waterborne diseases, ancient statues crumbling

Conclusion 7

It's tempting and exciting to find new ways to control our physical world. Yet, as the Aswan High Dam has shown, people must modernize very carefully. The natural world has a balance of its own, and humans run the risk of destroying their own future if they tamper with that balance.

Considering Visual Aids

Consider using visual aids during your speech. They can make your presentation clearer and more meaningful. Here are some examples.

Posters	include words, pictures, or both.
Photographs	help people see what you are talking about.
Charts	explain points, compare facts, or show statistics.
Maps	identify or locate specific places being discussed.
Objects	show the audience important items related to your topic.
Computer slides	project your photographs, charts, and maps onto a screen and turn your speech into a multimedia presentation. (See pages **402–403**.)

Indicating When to Present Visuals

Write notes in the margins of your note cards to indicate where a visual aid would be helpful. Olen considered the following visuals for his presentation about the Aswan High Dam.

- Photos of Nile Valley before the dam
- A drawing of workers on the first dam
- A photo of the finished dam
- A chart comparing the pros and cons of the dam

Try It!

List possible visual aids. Identify two or three visual aids you could use in your presentation. Explain how and when you would use each one.

Tip

When creating visual aids, keep these points in mind.

- **Make them big.** Your visuals should be large enough for everyone in the audience to see.
- **Keep them simple.** Use labels and short phrases rather than full sentences.
- **Make them eye-catching.** Use color, bold lines, and simple shapes to attract the audience.

Practicing Your Speech

Practice is the key to giving an effective oral presentation. Knowing what to say and how to say it will help eliminate those "butterflies" speakers often feel. Here are some hints for an effective practice session.

- **Arrange your note cards in the proper order.** This will eliminate any confusion as you practice.
- **Practice in front of a mirror.** Check your posture and eye contact and be sure your visual aids are easy to see.
- **Practice in front of others.** Friends and family can help you identify parts that need work.
- **Record or videotape a practice presentation.** Do you sound interested in your topic? Are your voice and message clear?
- **Time yourself.** If your teacher has set a time limit, practice staying within it.
- **Speak clearly.** Do not rush your words, especially later when you are in front of your audience.
- **Work on eye contact.** Look down only to glance at a card.
- **Speak up.** Your voice will sound louder to you than it will to the audience. Rule of thumb: If you sound *too* loud to yourself, you are probably sounding just right to your audience.
- **Look interested and confident.** This will help you engage the listeners.

Practice Checklist

To review each practice session, ask yourself the following questions.

- **1.** Did I appear at ease?
- **2.** Could my voice be heard and my words understood?
- **3.** Did I sound like I enjoyed and understood my topic?
- **4.** Were my visual aids interesting and used effectively?
- **5.** Did I avoid rushing through my speech?
- **6.** Did I include everything I wanted to say?

Try It!

Practice your presentation. Practice your speech in front of family or friends. Also consider videotaping your speech.

Presentations

Delivering Your Presentation

When you deliver a speech, concentrate on your voice and body language. Voice quality and body language communicate as much as your words do.

Controlling Your Voice

Volume, tone, and *pace* are three aspects of your formal speaking voice. If you can control these three aspects of voice, your listeners will be able to follow your ideas.

- **Volume** is the loudness of your voice. Imagine that you are speaking to someone in the back of the room and adjust your volume accordingly.
- **Tone** expresses your feelings. Be enthusiastic about your topic and let your voice show that.
- **Pace** is the speed at which you speak. For the most part, speak at a relaxed pace.

Tip

You can make an important point by slowing down, by pausing, by increasing your volume, or by emphasizing individual words.

Considering Your Body Language

Your body language (*posture, gestures,* and *facial expressions*) plays an important role during a speech. Follow the suggestions given below to communicate effectively.

- **Assume a straight but relaxed posture.** This tells the audience that you are confident and prepared. If you are using a podium, let your hands rest lightly on the surface.
- **Pause before you begin.** Take a deep breath and relax.
- **Look at your audience.** Try to look toward every section of the room at least once during your speech.
- **Think about what you are saying** and let your facial expressions reflect your true feelings.
- **Point to your visual aids** or use natural gestures to make a point.

Try It!

Deliver your presentation. As you deliver your speech, make sure to control your voice and exhibit the proper body language.

Evaluating a Presentation

Evaluate a presentation using the following evaluation sheet. Circle the description that best fits each assessed area. Then offer two comments: one positive comment and one helpful suggestion.

Peer Evaluation Sheet

Speaker _____ Evaluator _____

1. Vocal Presentation

Volume:

Clear and loud   Loud enough   A little soft   Mumbled

Pace:

Relaxed   A little rushed or slow   Rushed or slow   Hard to follow

Comments:

a. _____

b. _____

2. Physical Presentation

Posture:

Relaxed, straight   A bit stiff   Fidgeted a lot   Slumped

Eye contact:

Excellent contact   Made some contact   Quick glances   None

Comments:

a. _____

b. _____

3. Information

Thought provoking   Interesting   A few good points   No ideas

Comments:

a. _____

b. _____

4. Visual Aids

Well used   Easy to follow   Not clear   None used

Comments:

a. _____

b. _____

Preparing a Multimedia Report

You can enhance an oral report using electronic aids such as slides and sound. In order to use these effectively, you must plan exactly where each slide or sound bite will fit into your speech.

Here is a planning script for a multimedia report on the Aswan High Dam. What will be *seen* appears in the "Video" column, and what will be *heard* appears in the "Audio" column. Note that the directions for the speaker are general, not the actual words to be spoken.

Planning Script

Video	Audio
1. **Title Screen:** "The Aswan High Dam"	1. SPEAKER: Introduction SOUND: Music begins
2. **Slide 2:** "Reasons for Building the Dam," various photos of the Nile Valley before the dam	2. SPEAKER: Explain background of drought and flooding. SOUND: Babble of Egyptian voices
3. **Slide 3:** "History of the Dam," photos of the early building of the first dam	3. SPEAKER: Give history of first dam and its problems. SOUND: Construction noises and men's voices
4. **Slide 4:** "Preparation of Second Dam," photos of the ancient statues that are now covered by water	4. SPEAKER: Explain the difficulties of building and the political jockeying. SOUND: Somber music
5. **Slide 5:** "Size of Dam," photos of final dam	5. SPEAKER: Describe the finished dam. SOUND: Dam turbines
6. **Slide 6:** "Positive Effects of Dam," chart of points	6. SPEAKER: Present positive effects of the dam. SOUND: Upbeat music
7. **Slide 7:** "Negative Effects of Dam," chart of points	7. SPEAKER: Present negative effects of the dam. SOUND: Somber music
8. **Slide 8:** Picture of Dam	8. SPEAKER: Conclusion SOUND: Music up and out

Multimedia Report Checklist

Use the following checklist to help you improve your multimedia report. When you can answer "yes" to all of the questions, your report is ready.

Revising Checklist

Ideas

_____ 1. Have I included the main ideas of my written report in my multimedia report?

_____ 2. Have I effectively supported my main ideas?

_____ 3. Does each slide or sound bite suit the audience and the purpose of the report?

Organization

_____ 4. Do I state the topic in my introduction?

_____ 5. Do I include the important main points in the body?

_____ 6. Do I restate my focus in the conclusion?

Voice

_____ 7. Do I sound interested and enthusiastic?

_____ 8. Is my voice clear, relaxed, and expressive?

Word and Multimedia Choices

_____ 9. Are the words and pictures on each slide easy to read and see?

_____ 10. Have I chosen the best audio and video clips?

Presentation Fluency

_____ 11. Does my report flow smoothly from point to point?

Conventions

_____ 12. Is each slide free of grammar, spelling, capitalization, and punctuation errors?

Writing Across the Curriculum

Writing Focus

Writing in Science   **405**

Writing in Social Studies   **417**

Writing in Math   **431**

Writing in the Applied Sciences   **443**

Writing in the Arts   **453**

Academic Vocabulary

Working with a classmate, read the definitions below and discuss possible answers to each question.

1. A lecture is a talk given to an audience or class.
   How do you make sure you understand the important points in a teacher's lecture?

2. A hypothesis is an explanation that accounts for a set of facts and that can be tested.
   Why is it important to test a hypothesis?

3. Data is factual information. (The word *data* is also the plural form of the singular *datum*, so it sometimes takes a plural verb.)
   How can data help you make decisions? Think of a specific example.

4. A supplement is an addition, one that's usually made to complete or improve something.
   How can your class notes act as a supplement to your textbook?

Writing in Science

Writing is central to science. It allows scientists to express their hypotheses, to record their observations, and to communicate their conclusions. In that way, writing gives structure to the scientific method.

Science classes—whether biology, chemistry, physics, geology, astronomy, or life sciences—take you on a journey of discovery into the natural world. Writing lets you chart your course.

This chapter covers the types of writing that will help you in your science classes. Writing about what you learn in lectures and laboratories can deepen your own knowledge of the subject and allow you to share your understanding with others.

- Taking Classroom Notes
- Taking Reading Notes
- Keeping a Learning Log
- Writing Guidelines: Lab Report
- Writing Guidelines: Problem-Solution Essay
- Writing Guidelines: Science-Article Summary
- Other Forms of Writing in Science

"Science is organized knowledge."
—Herbert Spencer

Taking Classroom Notes

Taking good notes helps you focus on a lecture, remember key points, and understand new material. Here are a few tips on taking good notes in class.

Before you take notes . . .

- **Set up your notes.** Use a three-ring binder so you can add handouts to your notes, or use a notebook with a folder in the back.
- **Date each entry** in your notebook and write down the topic.
- **Organize each page.** Consider using the two-column format, with lecture information on the left and questions on the right.

As you take notes . . .

- **Listen for key words.** Pay attention to information that comes after phrases such as *for example, as a result,* or *most importantly.*
- **Write information your teacher puts on the board** or on an overhead. This is often the most important material.
- **Use your own words** as much as possible.
- **Write questions** in the second column of your notebook.
- **Draw pictures.** Use quick sketches to capture complex ideas.

After you've taken notes . . .

- **Reread your notes** after class. Add information to make the notes clear.
- **Research the answers** to any questions you wrote.
- **Review your notes** before the next class to be ready for discussions.
- **Study your notes** to prepare for quizzes and tests.

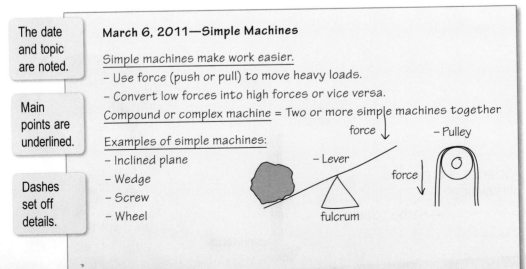

The date and topic are noted.

Main points are underlined.

Dashes set off details.

March 6, 2011—Simple Machines

Simple machines make work easier.
- Use force (push or pull) to move heavy loads.
- Convert low forces into high forces or vice versa.

Compound or complex machine = Two or more simple machines together

Examples of simple machines:
- Inclined plane
- Wedge
- Screw
- Wheel

– Lever

– Pulley

force

force

fulcrum

Taking Reading Notes

Note taking can increase your understanding of reading assignments. Here are some tips on taking reading notes.

Before you take notes . . .

- **Write the date, chapter, book, and topic** before each entry.
- **Organize each page.** Try a two-column format with wide margins. Put your notes on the left and your thoughts and questions on the right.
- **Quickly skim the assigned text.** Read the title, introduction, headings, and summaries. Look at the graphics and charts.

As you take notes . . .

- **Write down headings or subtopics.** Note important details under each. Record any questions or thoughts that you have.
- **Use your own words** to help you understand the material.
- **Summarize graphics.** Make a sketch or note the main ideas.
- **List vocabulary words.** You can look up definitions later.

After you've taken notes . . .

- **Review your notes.** Then write down any other questions you may have. Find answers and add them to your notes.

Sept. 22, 2011: Exploring Chemistry, chapter 2, section 1
Periodic Table of the Elements*

Questions and thoughts are listed in the second column.

*The periodic table is a way of classifying elements: a universal language for chemistry.
Elements
— sorted by rows and columns
— organized by similarities in their properties
— ordered by increasing atomic numbers
— grouped in columns
— are liquid, gas, or solid

Q: How did the periodic table start?

A: Russian professor Dmitry Mendelyev pioneered a chart to organize elements.

Try It!

Take notes on the next reading assignment you do.

Keeping a Learning Log

A **learning log** is a specialized journal that lets you reflect on the material you are learning in class. In a learning log, you write about new concepts by connecting them to previous knowledge or experiences. Here are some tips for keeping a learning log.

Before you make an entry . . .

- **Set up your learning log** in a binder or notebook.
- **Write the topic and date of each entry** so you can find it easily.
- **Leave wide margins** for writing thoughts and questions that occur to you later.

As you make an entry . . .

- **Summarize key concepts** and develop meaningful comparisons.
- **Apply new ideas** to what you already know.
- **Write down any questions** you have about the subject.
- **Predict how the new ideas** may prove helpful in the future.
- **Write about** what the ideas mean to you.

After you've made an entry . . .

- **Review your entries** so you can better understand what you are learning.
- **Research any questions** you have and write down the answers.
- **Continue your reflections** by writing new observations or questions in the margins.

Tip

Most topics are like packed suitcases. You can grab the topic by the handle and carry it around without really understanding what's inside it. Writing helps you "unpack" a complicated topic. What are the main ideas? How do these ideas relate to each other? What do these ideas mean to me? When you write answers to questions such as these, you make learning personal— and you begin to understand what is inside the topic you are carrying around.

Try It!

Follow the guidelines above to set up your own learning log. When you have a few minutes during or after class, write about the day's topic in order to "unpack the ideas."

Learning-Log Entries

Here are sample learning-log entries by a chemistry student. The student thinks about the ideas discussed in class, analyzes them, and tries to apply them to current issues and to his own life.

Sample Learning Log

After recording the date and topic, the student reviews ideas from his class.

He writes questions about the topic in the margin.

He reflects on the complex issues.

He finds answers to his questions.

February 18—Chemical Pollution

The class discussion today was about chemicals in the environment. Mrs. Marshall said that fuels, pesticides, paints, cleaners, and other chemicals can cause a lot of harm.

Sometimes natural disasters are to blame. After Hurricane Katrina, many chemicals mixed with floodwaters. When the water drained away, chemicals got into the soil and air. Chlorine, benzene, and gasoline caused huge problems.

Sometimes ignorance is the problem. People pour oil or chemicals into street drains and pollute the water. They dump paint cans in the woods and burn plastics that pollute the air. These actions are as much a problem as natural disasters.

February 22—Exxon Valdez

Mrs. Marshall showed a documentary about the Exxon Valdez oil spill, which occurred when a tanker ran aground in Alaska. Biologists continue to study the long-term effects on area habitats.

Cleaning up after an accident or a disaster is important, but it's more important to prevent these things from happening. One way is to switch to alternative energy sources like wind power.

Another way is to use "green chemistry" to develop environmentally friendly compounds. For example, in Australia, researchers use the genes of pests to make pesticides that target only one creature. Also, natural, nonpolluting cleansers like lemon juice (citric acid) and vinegar (acetic acid) work as well as chemicals do.

Q: How can polluted soil be cleaned up?

A: The EPA Web site said contaminated soil and sediment would have to be removed, and clean fill would have to be added.

Q: What can the government do about spills?

A: Oil doesn't dissolve in water, allowing some spills to be contained. Police and fire departments have "haz-mat" teams for hazardous material spills.

Writing Guidelines Lab Report

A **lab report** is one of the simplest yet most powerful types of scientific writing you will do. It outlines the scientific method by stating a hypothesis, setting up a method for testing it, recording observations, and offering conclusions.

Prewriting

- **Select a topic.** Follow your science teacher's assignment or (if given a choice) select a topic that interests you.
- **Plan the experiment.** Follow the planning your teacher provides. If you have selected the experiment, plan it, gather materials, and be sure you understand each step.
- **Follow the proper format.** Use the lab-report format provided by your teacher or follow the lab-report model on page **411**.

Writing

- **Lay the groundwork.** State the purpose (what the experiment is designed to prove), list materials, and note variables. Then write your hypothesis—what you expect the experiment will prove.
- **Describe procedures.** Use specific language to make each step clear.
- **Record your observations.** Describe what you see, hear, smell, and so forth, in chronological order exactly as it happens.
- **Write a conclusion.** Tell whether your hypothesis was correct or not. Explain why.

Revising

- **Improve your writing.** Review your first draft for *ideas, organization,* and *voice.* Ask these questions: *Have I clearly stated my hypothesis and conclusion? Have I described the experiment in chronological order and included enough details?*
- **Improve your style.** Check your *word choice* and *sentence fluency.* Ask these questions: *Have I correctly used and explained scientific terms? Do my sentences read smoothly?*

Editing

- **Check for conventions.** Proofread your report for errors in punctuation, capitalization, spelling, and grammar. Fix any errors.
- **Prepare a final copy.** Make a neat final copy of your lab report.

Lab Report

The lab report below describes a simple in-class experiment on suspensions and emulsions.

Sample Lab Report

The beginning states the purpose, the materials, the variables, and the hypothesis.

The middle outlines the procedure and records observations.

The ending tells whether the hypothesis was right or not, and why.

Suspensions and Emulsions

Purpose: To find out which liquids combine and which do not

Materials: 20 ml oil, 20 ml vinegar, egg yolk, two large beakers

Variables: Ingredients

Hypothesis: Oil and vinegar won't mix. When shaken up together, they will form a suspension, but the two parts will separate again. The egg yolk will mix with the vinegar but not with the oil.

Procedure: In the first step, I poured 10 ml of oil into a beaker and added 10 ml of vinegar. Then I shook the liquids and waited for several minutes. I observed the results. In the second step, I combined 10 ml of oil, 10 ml of vinegar, and an egg yolk and shook the liquids. Again, I observed the results.

Observations: When I mixed the oil and vinegar together, the oil and vinegar looked as though they had dissolved. However, minutes later, the oil and vinegar separated. When I combined the oil, vinegar, and egg yolk and shook the beaker, the liquid didn't separate.

Conclusions: My hypothesis that oil and vinegar would not mix was right. They are immiscible. The oil and vinegar made a suspension, but then they separated again.

However, my hypothesis about the egg yolk was wrong. I thought it would mix with the vinegar but not with the oil. The yolk actually mixed with both substances and made them join.

The yolk must be an emulsifier, which allows immiscible substances to blend. The egg yolk, vinegar, and oil form a colloid, which is a stable system of particles dispersed in something else.

Try It!

Perform a science experiment assigned by your teacher or select one that interests you. Describe it completely in a lab report.

Writing Guidelines Problem-Solution Essay

Scientists often research problems and use their knowledge to find solutions. A problem-solution essay explores a problem and possible solutions. Follow these guidelines to write a problem-solution essay.

Prewriting

- **Select a topic.** If your teacher doesn't assign a specific topic, review your class notes, learning log, and textbook for ideas. Think about problems that relate to class topics, such as the hazards of nuclear energy, bird flu, or earth-crossing asteroids.
- **Gather details.** Research your topic so that you understand it thoroughly. Explore the causes of the problem and investigate any solutions that have been suggested.
- **Outline your essay.** Write a thesis statement that names the problem. Next, explain its background, its causes, and why it's serious. Name solutions and indicate which solution you think is best and why.

Writing

- **Connect your ideas.** Create a beginning that introduces the topic and leads to your thesis statement. Write a middle that fully explains the problem and possible solutions. Include the supporting details you gathered. Write an ending that focuses on a particular solution.

Revising

- **Review your writing.** Review your first draft for *ideas, organization,* and *voice.* Ask these questions: *Does my essay clearly explain the problem and explore possible solutions? Does it include plenty of scientifically valid details? Does my voice sound knowledgeable and appropriate?*
- **Improve your style.** Check your *word choice* and *sentence fluency,* asking these questions: *Have I correctly used and defined any scientific terms? Do my ideas flow smoothly?*

Editing

- **Check for conventions.** Proofread your essay for errors in punctuation, capitalization, spelling, and grammar.
- **Prepare a final copy.** Make a neat final copy of your essay.

Problem-Solution Essay

In this essay, a student explains the problem of drug-resistant bacteria.

Sample Essay

The **beginning** introduces the topic and leads to the thesis statement.

The End of the Miracle Drug?

Over the past 75 years, scientists have developed antibiotics to battle illnesses caused by bacteria. These "miracle drugs" were prescribed even for viral infections such as colds and the flu. Now, antibiotic overuse has led to a number of health risks.

The first **middle** paragraphs explain the problem.

The most obvious risk from antibiotic overuse is the evolution of a "super bug," or bacteria resistant to antibiotics. When an antibiotic is improperly prescribed, it kills some bacteria, leaving resistant cells to multiply. The U.S. Centers for Disease Control and Prevention warned in 1995 that patients infected with drug-resistant bacteria are more likely to require lengthy hospitalizations.

A less obvious risk is pollution. European researchers first reported antibiotics in the water supply in the 1990s. The U.S. Environmental Protection Agency also found antibiotics in water and sediment downstream from waste treatment sites. Sadly, unused antibiotics are sometimes flushed down the toilet. The effects of long-term exposure to antibiotics are unknown.

Another paragraph offers solutions.

Medical and government officials are trying to solve the problem. Doctors are educating patients about antibiotic overuse, and government agencies now closely monitor antibiotic use in cattle, pigs, and other food animals. Scientists are working on methods of removing antibiotics from water in treatment plants.

The **ending** restates the thesis and adds a solution.

Though antibiotics have worked "miracles" for 75 years, their overuse has robbed them of effectiveness and caused environmental contamination. Knowing when to ask for an antibiotic—and knowing how to properly dispose of unused antibiotics—will go a long way to solving this problem.

Try It!

Write a problem-solution essay. Select a problem related to your class work and follow the writing guidelines on the previous page.

Writing Guidelines Science-Article Summary

Scientists do a great deal of reading to keep up with new discoveries in their fields. The ability to read and summarize an article helps both scientists and students. Here are some guidelines to help you summarize science articles.

Prewriting

- **Find an article.** Browse through magazines such as *National Geographic* or *Popular Science*, looking for articles that relate to your class work. Page through your science textbook or visit reliable Internet sites such as *www.nasa.gov* or *www.science.gov*.
- **Read the article.** Quickly read the article you select to get its overall message. Then reread it more carefully for details.
- **Focus on the summary.** Write down the main idea of the article.
- **Gather details.** Select only the most important details that support the main idea of the article. Your summary should be no more than one-third the length of the original article.

Writing

- **Connect your ideas.** Write your topic sentence, add details to support it, and create a closing sentence that wraps up your summary.
- **Paraphrase information.** Use your own words for the summary. Avoid plagiarism by not copying exact phrases and sentences from the article itself.

Revising

- **Improve your writing.** Review your first draft for *ideas, organization*, and *voice*. Ask these questions: *Have I identified the main idea of the article? Have I included only important details? Have I used a topic sentence, body sentences, and a closing sentence? Have I put the ideas in my own words?*
- **Improve your style.** Check on your *word choice* and *sentence fluency*, asking these questions: *Have I used specific nouns and active verbs? Does my summary read smoothly?*

Editing

- **Check for conventions.** Proofread your revised writing summary for errors in punctuation, capitalization, spelling, and grammar.
- **Prepare a final copy.** Make a neat final copy of your summary.

Science-Article Summary

The following professional article from a science news magazine is summarized in the student paragraph below.

Tapping the Earth's Heat

Scientists and environmentalists are increasingly concerned about the limited supply of fossil fuels and the impact of fuel emissions on global warming. As a result, scientists and inventors are looking for alternative sources of energy. One such low-cost, renewable resource—geothermal energy—may be right under our feet.

Geothermal energy has a long history. Early Roman builders and engineers tapped into underground hot springs to help heat homes. Pioneers used underground caves, cooler than the outside air in summer, to store ice and perishable products.

Today, geothermal energy can be used even in areas where there are no hot springs or caves. Modern geothermal systems take advantage of the earth's relatively constant temperature a few feet below ground. Depending on latitude, temperatures underground range from 45 to 75 degrees Fahrenheit.

Geothermal heating and cooling systems exchange heat with the earth rather than with outside air and thus require less energy. These systems often pipe air or water underground (or underwater), where a heat exchanger raises or lowers the temperature. Then a pump transfers the heat from the earth into the building in winter and discharges excess heat from the building into the ground in summer. In summer, the excess heat may also be used to heat the water in the water heater.

Geothermal heating systems may initially cost more to install than fossil fuel systems. However, according to the Environmental Protection Agency (EPA), they save money in operating and maintenance costs. They are also environmentally clean and cost effective.

Sample Summary

Topic Sentence	**Geothermal Energy** **Geothermal energy can be a low-cost, renewable energy source to heat or cool homes using the earth's own temperature.** Geothermal energy works by drawing heat from the earth or underground water using underground pipes and a heat pump. Because the earth's underground temperature is pretty constant, the underground air or water doesn't have to be heated or cooled as much. **That's how geothermal systems can save money and conserve energy.**
Body Sentences	
Closing Sentence	

Try It!

Write a summary of an article assigned by your teacher or one of your own choosing. Follow the writing guidelines on the previous page.

Other Forms of Writing in Science

Cause-Effect Essay

Chemistry—Explain the effect of automobile emissions on the atmosphere. Then discuss the effect that hydrogen-powered vehicles would have on the environment.

Classification Essay

Geology, Earth Science, or *Chemistry*—Write a classification essay describing three types of igneous rocks. Describe their appearance, hardness, and composition, and tell how each type of rock is formed.

Definition Essay

Biology or Earth Sciences—Write a definition essay in which you thoroughly explain a concept that you have just learned about. Examine the concept from four or five different points of view.

Process Essay

Chemistry or Geology—Write a process essay describing how scientists create synthetic diamonds. Discuss how synthetic diamonds are used.

Opposing-Views Essay

Physics, Biology, or *Chemistry*—Write an opposing-views essay about a controversial proposal, such as replacing gasoline with ethanol (made from corn). Explain both sides of the argument.

Position Essay

Any Science—Read about controversial new theories in biology, earth-space science, physics, chemistry, or any other area of science that interests you. Choose one theory and write a position essay that provides support for the theory and defends it against opposing viewpoints.

Writing in Social Studies

No two human beings are the same, and no two human societies are either. Social studies focuses on this diversity. As a student of social studies, you may need to survey a variety of documents (speeches, graphs, maps, photos, reports, and so on) and respond to them in writing. You'll need to analyze the documents, summarize and organize the information, and create a response that satisfies the criteria of the assignment.

This chapter models several types of writing you may be asked to do in your social studies classes. It addresses writing a descriptive report, interpreting an editorial cartoon, and responding to a series of documents. You'll also find helpful tips on taking notes, organizing data, and keeping a learning log.

- **Taking Notes**
- **Keeping a Learning Log**
- **Writing Guidelines: Descriptive Report**
- **Writing Guidelines: Editorial Cartoon Response**
- **Writing Guidelines: Document-Based Essay**

"History will be kind to me, for I intend to write it."

—Winston Churchill

Taking Notes

Note taking helps you learn, understand, and remember new material. Effective notes also help you do better on tests and writing assignments.

Before you take notes . . .

- **Write the topic and date** at the top of each page.
- **Do your assigned reading** before you come to class. This will make it easier to follow what is being discussed. (See page **407**.)

As you take notes . . .

- **Listen carefully** and write down the main ideas.
- **Copy what the teacher writes** on the board or on an overhead.
- **Condense information.** Use phrases and lists, not full sentences.
- **Use your own words** for the most part.
- **Note new or unfamiliar terms** and add a definition later.

After you've taken notes . . .

- **Review your notes** as soon as possible.
- **Find answers to any questions** you still have.

Sample Notes

The date and topic are noted.	**November 11, 2011** **Veterans Day** **History of the holiday** – 1st was November 11, 1921—known as Armistice Day – date same as the armistice that ended WWI in 1918 – honored soldiers who died in WWI
Main points are underlined.	**Changes in the holiday** – became a national holiday in 1938 – name changed to Veterans Day in 1954 – today, honors all military veterans
Key words are defined.	**Vocabulary** armistice: an agreement among combatants to stop fighting veteran: a person who has served in the military

Try It!

Follow the tips and sample above the next time you take notes in class.

Keeping a Learning Log

What is a **learning log**? It's a specialized notebook in which you can reflect on the ideas and facts you learn in class. Entries in your learning log can help you clarify your understanding of a topic and connect your learning to the real world.

Before you make an entry . . .

- **Write the date and topic** on the page each time you make an entry.

When you make an entry . . .

- **Summarize key concepts** and compare them to more familiar ideas.
- **Connect to the material** by explaining what it means to you.

After you've made an entry . . .

- **Review your entries** to see how well you understand the class material.

Sample Entry

The date and topic are given.	November 11, 2011 Veterans Day 　　Today we learned the history of Veterans Day. My uncle James is a veteran, but I never gave much thought to the holiday. Today's class changed all that.
New information is reviewed.	The holiday was established to honor soldiers who died in World War I, but later it was changed to honor all soldiers. Talking about the holiday made me think more about the men and women who have made sacrifices to
A personal connection is made.	defend our country. It also made me curious about how my town celebrated the first Veterans Day. I think I'll do some research about that topic and write about it for my descriptive report assignment.

Try It!

Keep a learning log for one of your classes. Summarize material to understand it better and make a personal connection to your learning.

Writing Guidelines Descriptive Report

Often in social studies, you will need to describe an event or a location. Use the following guidelines to create a descriptive report.

Prewriting

- **Select a topic.** A topic may be assigned by your teacher. If not, choose a specific event, time, or place that relates to your course work—something you would like to know more about.
- **Gather details.** Learn all you can about your topic. Read books and Web-site articles. Study maps, graphs, and charts. This information will help you write a clear and interesting essay.
- **Outline your essay.** Organize your notes to put related details together. If you are describing an event, consider organizing your details in chronological order. If you are describing a place, consider organizing your details by order of location or by some other logical order.

Writing

- **Connect your ideas.** Start by introducing your topic. Capture your reader's attention with a few interesting details and then write your thesis statement. In the middle paragraphs, describe your topic, one main point at a time. Write an ending that sums up your thesis.

Revising

- **Improve your writing.** Review your first draft for *ideas, organization,* and *voice.* Make sure that you have included details that help the reader clearly understand what you are describing.
- **Improve your style.** Check for *word choice* and *sentence fluency.* Ask these questions: *Have I correctly used and explained new terms? Do my sentences read smoothly?*

Editing

- **Check for conventions.** Proofread your report and correct any errors in punctuation, capitalization, spelling, and grammar.
- **Prepare a final copy.** Make a neat final copy of your descriptive report. Proofread this copy and make corrections before sharing it.

Descriptive Report

In this essay, a student writer describes the first Veterans Day celebrated in his hometown.

Sample Report

Morrisville's First Veterans Day

On November 11, 1921, ceremonies in Washington, Paris, and London recognized the sacrifice of soldiers killed in World War I. On that same day, residents of Morrisville also honored their fallen soldiers. That was the first Armistice Day, a holiday that later became Veterans Day.

Armistice Day got its name from the treaty that ended World War I. The day honored the veterans who had lost their lives in the First World War. According to the records of the Carle County Clerk's Office, 83 men from Morrisville served in the United States Expeditionary Force during World War I. Of those 83 men, 14 died serving their country. In a town as small as Morrisville, most people knew at least a few if not all of those men, so it's little wonder that the whole town turned out for the memorial.

Photographs in the archives of the Morrisville Historical Society show the buildings on the town's main street draped with red, white, and blue bunting. Similar decorations covered the horse-drawn wagons and the few automobiles present. The people who gathered in Parish Park, 1,200 according to the *Morrisville Daily Examiner*, dressed in their finest clothing.

The focus of the day's ceremonies was the dedication of the sculpture *Fallen Heroes*. The granite carving, created by Morrisville sculptor Henry O'Brien, depicts a World War I soldier carrying a wounded comrade. The names of Morrisville citizens who died in the war are carved in the statue's base.

Morrisville's mayor, a 50-year-old businessman named Andrew Harrington, dedicated the statue with a stirring speech. In his talk, he called for the citizens to remember "those noble men of our town who set aside the cares of farm, home, and family to serve the greater good of their nation and of the world." He then asked the crowd to observe a minute of silence in honor of the fallen.

In 1954, the holiday was changed to Veterans Day, in memory of U.S. soldiers who died in all wars. Even so, reminders of the first Armistice Day remain in Parish Park. Though worn by time and weather, Henry O'Brien's sculpture still stands, as do a row of memorial oak trees planted by the town's children that day. They still provide shade to park visitors, and a place to pause and remember.

Writing Guidelines Editorial-Cartoon Response

Editorial cartoons use images and words to comment on important issues. Usually, a cartoon makes a point with an exaggerated representation called a caricature. A cartoon may also include symbols, labels, and brief captions. When you respond to an editorial cartoon, the following guidelines will help.

Prewriting

- **Analyze the cartoon.** Carefully review both the visual and text elements included in the cartoon. If you are not sure what a particular element means, ask for help.
- **Gather details.** List the different elements of the cartoon on a piece of paper. Write a brief description next to each one.

> **Dripping fire hose:** Instead of shooting water, the hose is just dripping.
> **Monkey wrench:** The wrench is labeled "budget cuts," and the mayor is using it to turn off the fire hydrant.

- **Plan your response.** Identify the main point of the cartoon and write a topic sentence that focuses on that point. Then choose details from the cartoon you will use to support your topic sentence.

Writing

- **Connect your ideas.** Start with your topic sentence and follow with supporting details. End with a sentence that restates the main point of the cartoon.

Revising

- **Improve your writing.** Ask yourself if you have clearly and completely explained the editorial cartoon. Is your paragraph well organized? Does your voice reveal the tone of the cartoon? Revise to make the explanation clearer.
- **Improve your style.** Check for *word choice* and *sentence fluency*.

Editing

- **Check for conventions.** Correct any errors in punctuation, capitalization, spelling, and grammar.
- **Prepare a final copy.** Make a neat final copy and share it.

Editorial Cartoon

Small fires only?

Sample Response

Student writer Brandon Powers developed the following paragraph after analyzing the editorial cartoon above.

Fire Department Budget Squeeze

This editorial cartoon suggests that the mayor (or city) is not providing enough money for the fire department to do its job. In the cartoon, a firefighter holds a hose, but rather than shooting a strong stream of water, the hose only drips. The reason for the problem is depicted to the left. The mayor uses a large wrench, marked "budget cuts," to turn off a fire hydrant. The meaning is clear: the mayor is in control of the flow of money to the fire department, and he isn't giving the department enough. A text caption reads "Small fires only???" Put together, these elements suggest that unless it is given more money, the fire department can't do its job.

◤ Try It!

Choose an editorial cartoon from a local or national newspaper. Use the guidelines on page **422** and the sample above to create a written response to the cartoon.

Writing Guidelines Document-Based Essay

In social studies class, you may be asked to respond to a series of documents. The documents may include excerpts from books, magazines, Web pages, diaries, or other text sources. They may also include visual documents such as photographs, maps, editorial cartoons, tables, graphs, or time lines.

You may be asked to answer a question about each document. Your main job, however, is to write an extended essay using all of the documents.

Prewriting

- **Read all the information thoroughly.** In addition to the documents, review the introduction to the topic and your responses to any questions about each document.
- **Make sure you understand the prompt.** Words such as *compare, explain, define,* and so on, indicate the type of thinking and writing that is expected.
- **Analyze each document.** Consider how it relates to the other documents. Be aware of documents that present opposing views.
- **Organize your facts.** Use a graphic organizer to plan your essay, perhaps an outline. Pull together information from all the documents and from your own prior knowledge.

Writing

- **Write your introductory paragraph.** Develop a thesis statement based on the prompt.
- **Write the body of your essay.** Follow your graphic organizer, using each main point in a topic sentence that explains part of your thesis.
- **Write a concluding paragraph.** Briefly restate your position.

Revising

- **Improve your writing.** Review your essay for *ideas, organization,* and *voice.* Then check for *word choice* and *sentence fluency.*

Editing

- **Check for conventions.** Correct any errors in punctuation, capitalization, spelling, and grammar.
- **Prepare a final copy.** Make a neat final copy of your essay.

Sample Documents

Introduction: More and more consumers have decided to choose organically grown food. Advocates say the food is better for people's health. They also claim organic methods benefit the environment and the small farm.

Document One

What Is Organic Farming?

Today's prevalent farming practices aim to maximize the amount of crops grown and control the quality of the product. These practices, however, often come with unintended consequences. Conventional farming relies on chemical pesticides and fertilizers applied to soil and directly sprayed on crops. Though these chemicals kill bugs and boost yields, they can also can kill wildlife and pollute water sources. Many pesticides are even known to cause cancer and other diseases in humans, the ultimate consumers of the food crops being treated.

Concern over the damaging effects of agricultural chemicals has given rise to the organic-farming movement. Farmers who grow "organic" foods depend on crop rotation, mechanical cultivation, and natural fertilizers like compost to promote growth. To inhibit pests, organic farmers use predatory species such as birds and carnivorous insects. They also plan their growing season with the life cycles of common pests in mind. Additionally, there are many natural pesticides—such as dried pyrethrum flowers, oil from the neem tree, and spinosad bacteria—that meet organic standards.

Only the most important information is included in the summary.

Task: Summarize the main differences between organic and conventional growing practices. Why do some consumers prefer organic foods?

Conventional farmers use chemicals to fertilize their crops and protect the crops from insect pests. Organic farmers rely on natural insect predators, planting crops when insects are not around, and using natural pesticides and fertilizers. People who choose organic foods do so because they fear damage to their health and the environment from conventional farming practices.

Document Two

10 Reasons to Eat Organic Food

1. Protect your health. The food choices you make now may affect your future well-being.
2. Safeguard the water supply. Human populations depend on the availability of clean water.
3. Conserve energy. Many organic farms sell their food locally, so it requires less energy to transport.
4. Reduce soil erosion. Organic practices sustain soil, the foundation of the food chain.
5. Avoid chemicals. According to the EPA, many pesticides and most herbicides and fungicides are carcinogenic.
6. Maintain biodiversity. Organic farming includes crop rotation and intercropping (the planting of more than just one crop in a given space).
7. Protect the health of farm workers. The high risk of pesticide poisoning makes an already difficult job dangerous.
8. Support family farms. Most organic farms are small farms comprising fewer than 100 acres.
9. Encourage fair and transparent economics. The price of conventional food does not include the billions of dollars in subsidies the government pays or the cost of testing and cleaning up chemicals. These costs are passed on to taxpayers.
10. Enjoy what you eat. Testing has proven that certain fruits have higher flavonoid counts when grown organically. Organic foods just taste better.

Task: Make a chart listing the benefits of organic farming for consumers, farmers, and the environment.

Farmers	Consumers	Environment
– less danger from chemicals – more business for small farmers – less energy use – less soil erosion	– protect health – protect water quality – better-tasting food	– protect water quality – lessen erosion – maintain biodiversity

A word or two is all that is needed to list answers in a chart.

Document Three

U.S. certified organic cropland and pasture, 1992–2001

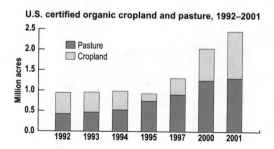

Source:
USDA;
Agrisystems
International

> **Graph data becomes text.**

> **Acreage is stated as a number, as a ratio, and as a percentage.**

Task: Explain the growth in U.S. certified organic farmlands from 1992 to 2001. State at least two of the statistics in a different mathematical form (ratio, fraction, and so on).

> Organic acreage more than doubled from 0.9 million to 2.5 million acres in 10 years. Though the ratio of cropland to pasture began at 50/50, pasture steadily increased. In 1995, pasture was 80% of the total organic acreage. By 2001, organic cropland had rebounded to more than 1 million acres.

Document Four

Organic Farming Revives Family Dairies

Lee King grew up on a small dairy farm and wanted to continue the family business. The industrial scale of big dairy operations, however, made it difficult for him to compete. "Giant farms can offer milk at rock-bottom prices," King says. "I would go out of business if I tried to do the same." King was frustrated until he heard about organic farming. Because consumers are willing to pay a little more for organic goods, farmers like King can recoup the cost of feeding their livestock organic grains. And because most organic dairy farms are smaller, King won't always be undersold by the competition. "Going organic saved my farm," he insists.

> **The response notes a main point from the document.**

Task: How can organic farming practices help dairy farmers compete?

> Organic dairy farmers get more money for their milk than conventional dairy farmers do.

Document Five

Certified Organic Farming Operations

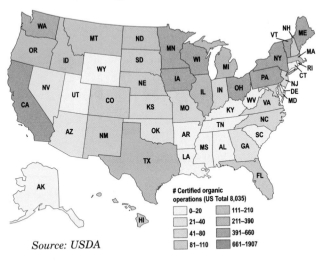

Certified organic
operations (US Total 8,035)

0–20	111–210
21–40	211–390
41–80	391–660
81–110	661–1907

Source: USDA

Task: Based on this map, identify U.S. states and regions in which organic farming is most and least prevalent.

> _Organic farming is most prevalent on the West Coast and in the Northeast and the upper Midwest. California has the most organic farms, while Kentucky, Alabama, and Mississippi are three of the states that have very few organic operations._

Statistics are used to make some generalizations.

Document Six

"A thing is right when it tends to preserve the integrity, stability and beauty of the biotic community. It is wrong when it tends otherwise."

—Aldo Leopold, conservationist

Previous knowledge is used to answer the question.

Task: How does this quotation relate to organic farming?

> _Conventional farming can damage the biotic community, but organic farming does not._

Document-Based Essay

A student writer develops an essay using the original documents.

Task: Extended Essay

Using all six documents and your own knowledge about this topic, write an essay explaining the growth of organic farming in the United States.

Documents 1, 2, 3, and 4
The opening defines organic farming and states the thesis.

Document 1
The writer compares organic and conventional farming.

Document 2
Prior knowledge is also used.

Organic Is Growing

People who have spent any time in a grocery store's produce section have seen some organically grown produce. Organic farms don't use chemical fertilizers or pesticides, and for many reasons, the production of organic foods is growing. In a few years, the amount of organic farmland has more than doubled. Natural-food stores selling organic foods are everywhere. Even regular supermarkets now sell organic food products. Why is the organic boom happening? According to people who grow and buy these foods, it's because organic growing protects the health of people and the environment— and makes business sense, too.

Conventional farms use chemical fertilizers and pesticides to help plants grow and to kill pests. But these chemicals can kill other plants and animals, pollute water supplies, and cause diseases such as cancer. Some chemicals linger on foods that people buy in the store. When farmers use organic practices, they fertilize crops with all-natural manure and compost. Against pests, they use natural pesticides that don't harm other animals or people.

Environmentalists love organic farming because it is safe for the environment. Organic farming keeps chemicals out of the water system, protecting plants and animals in lakes and streams and protecting drinking water for people. Organic techniques prevent soil erosion and keep chemicals out of the soil, the farmer's most valuable asset. Finally, organic farming uses less energy and creates less pollution.

Consumers like organic produce because it minimizes health risks. Eating organic food means less exposure to toxic chemicals, which can harm the health of humans—especially children. Many consumers say organic foods simply taste better. Some chefs use organic foods in their restaurants, saying their customers appreciate the difference.

Consumer demand has helped fuel a boom in organic farming. From 1992 to 2001, the amount of land in the U.S. farmed organically more than doubled, from just under 1 million acres to just under 2.5 million. California leads the way, but organic farms can be found in most states. Why are more farmers choosing to grow organically? For one reason, farmers live in close contact with the land and respect it. They want to preserve their farms for future generations. They also like the idea of providing healthier food. But business reasons play a big role, too. Organic farmers receive a higher price for their products, helping them survive and compete with large corporate farms. For many farmers, growing organically can make the difference between farming and going out of business.

In coming years, organic farms may continue to grow for good reason. Organic farming represents an environmentally safe and profitable alternative to conventional farming. And as conservationist Aldo Leopold put it, "A thing is right when it tends to preserve the integrity, stability and beauty of the biotic community. It is wrong when it tends otherwise." Organic farming recognizes every human being and animal as part of the biotic community.

Documents 3, 4, and 5
Facts from a graph and a map help to tell the story of organic farming's growth.

Document 6
A powerful quotation helps sum up the reasons for the growth of organic farming.

Essay Checklist

_____ 1. Do all the ideas in my essay support my thesis statement?

_____ 2. Do I cover all the requirements outlined in the prompt?

_____ 3. Do I summarize the main points in my conclusion?

_____ 4. Do I refer to information from all the documents?

_____ 5. Do I include some of my own knowledge about this topic?

_____ 6. Have I checked my punctuation, grammar, and spelling?

Writing in Math

Some people think in numbers. They have no trouble solving quadratic equations or figuring out logarithms. Other people think in words. They have no trouble diagramming complex sentences or writing research reports.

Most of us, though, are somewhere in the middle. We need words to help us with our numbers, and we need numbers to help us with our words. When a kindergartner struggles to solve a story problem, words and numbers have to work together. The same is true when Stephen Hawking writes a mathematical description of the universe.

This chapter will help you understand the different ways writing can help you in math class.

- **Taking Notes**
- **Keeping a Learning Log**
- **Writing Guidelines: Article Summary**
- **Writing Guidelines: Written Estimate**
- **Writing Guidelines: Statistical Argument**
- **Writing Guidelines: Response to a Math Prompt**
- **Other Forms of Writing in Math**

"Nature's great book is written in mathematics."

—Galileo

Taking Notes

Here are some note-taking tips for math classes.

Before you take notes . . .

- **Use a three-ring binder** to store your notes so that you can add handouts, worksheets, tests, and so on.
- **Write the date and topic** at the beginning of each entry.

As you take notes . . .

- **Write procedures** on the left and examples on the right.
- **Write what your teacher puts on the board** or overhead. This information often contains concepts, terms, and examples.
- **Use your own words** and write down questions.
- **Draw pictures.** Use diagrams to help you visualize the concept.

After you've taken notes . . .

- **Find answers** to your questions.
- **Study your notes** before the next class and again before exams.

Sample Notes

November 3, 2011
Geometric Applications

To solve a geometry word problem:

Step 1: Decide what you need to find.

Step 2: Draw pictures. Write down formulas.

Step 3: Use pictures and formulas to help write an equation.

Step 4: Solve the equation.

Step 5: Check if answer makes sense.

* Don't forget units in final answer.

Problem: Find the area of a 2-foot-wide path surrounding a rectangular garden that is 36 feet by 24 feet.

Step 1: Find the area of the path.

Step 2: Use pictures and formulas.

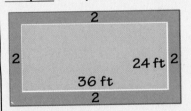

rectangle area = length X width

Step 3: Path area =
big rectangle – small rectangle

Step 4: Path area =
(36 + 2 + 2)(24 + 2 + 2) – (36)(24)
1120 – 864 = 256

Step 5: The path is 256 sq. ft.

Math

Keeping a Learning Log

A learning log allows you to write about what you are learning, think through new concepts, ask questions, and find answers.

Before you write . . .

- **Set up the log.** Use a notebook or a section of your three-ring binder.
- **Write the date** and topic at the beginning of each entry.
- **Leave wide margins** for writing questions and answers.

As you write . . .

- **Reflect on what you learn** by writing about what you understand and what is still confusing to you.
- **Summarize key concepts** and think about how they connect to your own experiences and to other ideas you have learned in math.

After you've written . . .

- **Review your log** before a test or to study a difficult topic.
- **Answer any questions** you've written in the margins.

Sample Learning Log

November 3, 2011 Pythagorean Theorem

A Greek mathematician named Pythagoras developed a formula to calculate the sides of a right triangle.

Right triangle: a triangle with right angle (90°)

leg   hypotenuse (across from the
                      right angle)
leg

Pythagorean Theorem Formula: $a^2 + b^2 = c^2$
c is always the side across from right angle (the hypotenuse).

Another way to state the formula:
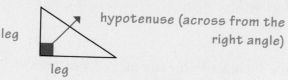
(length one leg)^2 + (length other leg)^2 =
(length of hypotenuse)^2

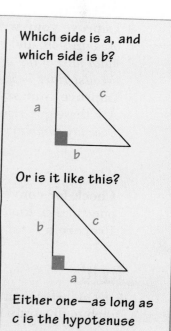

Which side is a, and which side is b?

Or is it like this?

Either one—as long as c is the hypotenuse

Writing Guidelines Article Summary

Many magazine articles, books, and news stories include statistics and mathematical concepts. Use the following guidelines to summarize a math-related article.

Prewriting

- **Find an article.** Choose a newspaper or magazine article that uses mathematics to support a story, a position, or an issue.
- **Read the article.** Read the selection first to get its overall message. Then reread it carefully, paying attention to details.
- **Find the focus.** Write down the main idea of the article.
- **Gather details.** Select only the most important details that support the main idea of the article.

Writing

- **Write your first draft.** Write your topic sentence, putting the main idea of the article in your own words. Supply supporting details. Close with a sentence that summarizes your thoughts.

Revising

- **Improve your writing.** Review your first draft for *ideas, organization,* and *voice.* Ask these questions: *Have I identified the main idea of the article? Have I included only the most important details? Have I explained the math concepts in clear language?*
- **Improve your style.** Check your *word choice* and *sentence fluency.* Ask these questions: *Have I used specific nouns and active verbs? Does my summary read smoothly?*

Editing

- **Check for conventions.** Proofread your summary for errors in punctuation, capitalization, spelling, and grammar.
- **Prepare a final copy.** Make a neat final copy of your summary.

Try It!

Find an article containing math data. Write a summary and create a graph to illustrate the data. Follow the tips above.

Math Article and Summary

A student read the following article in the newspaper and wrote a brief summary, including a graph to illustrate the statistics in the article.

Where Is All That Money Going?

Every parent of teenagers knows that they are spending quite a bit of money. A recent mall survey shows that suburban teenage boys are spending more than $70 per week on themselves and suburban teenage girls are spending more than $60 per week on themselves. The money is mainly coming from adults in the form of allowance, gifts, or just handouts. However, some teens are earning their own money by working part time.

Since the survey was conducted in a mall, it is not surprising that mall spending figured high for both genders. However, mall spending was nearly matched by online purchases and downloads. The respondents indicated that they engaged in "social" spending at the mall, but often bought "necessities" on the Internet.

So how are teens spending their money? The survey found that the biggest category for teen spending was fashion, which accounted for 41 percent of female spending and 34 percent of male spending. The next biggest category was electronics, including computer programs, video games and players, CD and MP3 players, and other gadgetry. In this category, young men spent 30 percent of their income, and young women spent 26 percent. As for the third biggest category—music—the genders spent nearly evenly, with males spending 21 percent and females spending 20 percent. Both genders tended to save about 10 percent of their income, and they also reported a few "other" purchases (females at 3 percent and males at 5 percent).

Should parents be worried about these spending habits? Some say these spending habits are a concern due to the rising number of bankruptcies filed by those 25 years and younger. Others say it makes sense that teenagers are spending more than saving in the years before they have more financial responsibility. Both groups, however, are asking for better financial lessons in school.

Sample Summary

Tracking Teen Spending

The article "Where Is All That Money Going?" tracks teen spending. Male suburban teens spend about $70 a week while females spend $60.

Although some work part time for the money, most of it comes from adults. Teens spend the most, at malls and online, for fashion, electronics, and music. Males spend slightly more on electronics and females slightly more on fashion. Music spending is nearly identical, and both genders save about 10 percent of their income. Some adults are concerned, and many feel that schools should do more to teach financial responsibility.

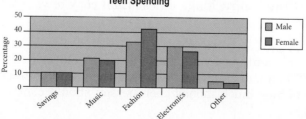

Writing Guidelines Written Estimate

Many workers, including builders, auto-repair persons, and engineers, write estimates for complex projects. An estimate includes these parts:

- **Assumptions** (statements believed to be true)
- **Evaluations** (step-by-step calculations and manipulations)
- **Explanations** (clarification of complex information)

Prewriting

- **Select a topic.** Think about projects or situations that require money.
- **Make assumptions.** Write down the givens as well as the variables of the situation and estimate the costs involved.
- **Plan the steps.** Find a way to arrive at a final cost.

Writing

- **Write your first draft.** First introduce the project and the assumptions involved, revealing the cost of the various items or services. Then lead the reader through the steps you took to arrive at a final cost. Clarify any difficult information and remind the reader that this is just an estimate.

Revising

- **Improve your writing.** Review your *ideas, organization,* and *voice.* Ask these questions: *Do I identify the project and explain the estimate process clearly? Do I sound knowledgeable?*
- **Improve your style.** Check your *word choice* and *sentence fluency.* Ask these questions: *Have I correctly used and defined any math terms? Do my sentences flow smoothly?*

Editing

- **Check for conventions.** Correct errors in spelling, punctuation, and grammar.
- **Prepare a final copy.** Make a neat final copy of your work.

Try It!

Ten friends are coming to your house to watch old monster movies. You will spend $25 on sub sandwiches to feed them and yourself. Write an estimate of how much money each person should contribute to reimburse you.

Written Estimate

The following estimate was written for a pizza party.

Sample Estimate

You and your friends want to watch the basketball game together next weekend. Your mother has agreed to allow you to invite five friends to your house, and she will pay $20 toward pizza to eat during the game. Write an estimate of the amount of money each person should contribute to provide pizza for everyone.

Assumptions:

The situation has two given quantities.

Given 1: Five friends and I will eat pizza—six people total.

Given 2: Mom will pay $20 toward pizza.

The situation has three variables that need to be defined.

Variable A: The average number of pieces each person will eat, estimated to be 4

Variable B: The number of pieces in a pizza, estimated to be 8

Variable C: The cost of each large pizza, with tax, delivery, and tip, estimated to be $14

Evaluations:

The total number of pieces = Variable A × Given 1

4 pieces × 6 people = 24 pieces of pizza needed

The total number of pizzas = 24 ÷ Variable B

24 pieces of pizza ÷ 8 pieces per pizza = 3 pizzas

The total cost of pizzas needed = 3 × Variable C

3 pizzas X $14 = $42

The total amount we need to pay = $42 − Given 2

$42 − $20 = $22

The amount each person needs to pay = $22 ÷ Given 1

$22 ÷ 6 = $3.66 per person

Explanations:

If my friends and I each eat 4 pieces of pizza, each of us should pay about $3.66. The cost could be higher if the pizzas have multiple toppings. The cost could be lower if we can use a coupon.

Given quantities and variables are provided.	
Each step of the calculation is shown.	
The estimate is explained and clarified.	

Writing Guidelines Statistical Argument

Mathematical statistics are often used—and abused—to prove a point. Writers ought to use statistics convincingly yet fairly.

Prewriting

- **Select a topic.** Think about statistics related to your school or community: graduation and dropout rates, SAT scores, crime rates, hours spent watching television, attendance rates, and so forth. Choose a topic that interests you.
- **Gather information.** Research the issue, gathering as many facts and figures as you can. Use reliable sources of information.
- **Form an opinion.** After reviewing the figures, form your opinion about the issue. Write a position statement.

Writing

- **Create a first draft.** Write a beginning that introduces the topic and leads to your position statement. Develop middle paragraphs that use statistics to support your position. Write an ending that restates your position.

Revising

- **Improve your argument.** Consider your *ideas, organization,* and *voice.* Ask these questions: *Is my thesis statement clear? Have I developed a convincing argument using statistics? Is my argument well organized? Does my voice sound assured?*
- **Improve your style.** Check your *word choice* and *sentence fluency.* Ask these questions: *Have I defined any unfamiliar terms? Do my sentences read smoothly?*

Editing

- **Check for conventions.** Correct any errors in punctuation, capitalization, spelling, and grammar.
- **Prepare a final copy.** Make a neat final copy of your argument and proofread it.

Try It!

Select a topic you care about, gather statistics, and form a position statement. Then write a statistical argument to make your point.

Statistical Argument

The following persuasive essay uses statistics about young voter turnout to argue a point of view about voter apathy.

Sample Statistical Argument

Statistics help build an argument.

The position statement is given (underlined).

The conclusion restates the position and offers some advice.

Caring About Apathy

In the 1960s, the armed services drafted thousands of 18-year-olds to fight in Vietnam, but none of these draftees had the right to vote. Many young people protested this situation, and as a result, the minimum voting age was lowered in 1972. That year, 52 percent of those 18 to 24 years of age voted, but over the next 30 years, voter turnout among young people slowly declined. By 2000, only 20 percent of young voters went to the polls—a year when their votes could have easily decided the election ("Youth"). <u>Voter apathy among young Americans has become a serious problem.</u>

The question is why. "The chief reason that young voters give for not voting is that they think nobody is listening to them," writes Jack Doppelt, author of *Nonvoters: America's No-Shows.* The young voter turnout in 1992 demonstrated this, when it spiked to 48 percent. Young people felt someone was listening. Bill Clinton was a young man who played saxophone on the *Tonight Show,* appeared on MTV, and answered questions about "guns or butter" and "boxers or briefs." After Clinton's election, however, the youth vote slid again.

Then, in 2004, an even bigger spike occurred. Youth turnout at the polls jumped 11 points to 47 percent. This time, the reason was not a charismatic candidate but the issues that young people cared about, specifically the war in Iraq. It seems that young voters once again had a cause to dispel their apathy.

The 2004 turnout showed that young voters come to the polls when they care about issues—and when they think someone will listen to them. There is still a long way to go, though. Even at 47 percent, turnout among voters aged 18 to 24 lagged far behind the 66 percent turnout of people over the age of 24. Candidates need to do more to woo the young vote, and young people need to do more to understand and help shape their government. The 2008 youth turnout of 49% suggests that this may finally be happening.

Writing Guidelines Response to a Math Prompt

A math prompt is a problem that is solved by writing as well as by mathematics. To answer a prompt, you need to analyze it, decide what you are supposed to do, and then respond to it, working one step at a time. Follow these guidelines.

Prewriting

- **Read the prompt.** Read carefully, paying attention to the directions. Watch for key words such as *find, solve, justify, demonstrate,* or *compare,* and perform the requested actions only. Also be aware that some prompts have more than one part.
- **Gather details and data.** Write down any values, assumptions, or variables provided in the prompt.

Writing

- **Build your solution.** Respond to each part of the prompt. Set up formulas or equations, and use diagrams if they will help solve the problem. Perform the necessary calculations to get an answer. Show all of your work.

Revising

- **Improve your response.** Reread the prompt after you do your calculations. If the problem has more than one part, be sure you have answered every part. Work the problem in another way to check that your solution is correct.

Editing

- **Check for conventions.** Check your solution for errors in punctuation, capitalization, spelling, and grammar.
- **Prepare a final copy.** Make a neat final copy of your solution.

Try It!

Find a math prompt and write a response. Choose a practice prompt from your textbook or one recommended by your teacher. Follow the tips above to write your solution.

Math

Response to a Math Prompt

The following math prompt contains three parts. The writer provides a solution using words, mathematics, and a diagram.

Sample Prompt and Response

1. Explain this formula: $(a + b)^2 = a^2 + 2ab + b^2$
  a. Using geometry
  b. Using algebra

2. Then show how your two explanations are related.

Trevor Hughes
Math 10, period 6

1a. <u>Geometry</u>
The area of the large square below is the length x the width.

The area = $(a + b)(a + b)$ or $(a + b)^2$
The area is also the sum of smaller boxes:
$(a)(a) + (a)(b) + (b)(a) + (b)(b) =$
$a^2 + ab + ab + b^2 = a^2 + 2ab + b^2$

The area is the same, so
$(a + b)^2 = a^2 + 2ab + b^2$

1b. <u>Algebra</u>
$(a + b)^2 = (a + b)(a + b) =$
$(a)(a) + (a)(b) + (b)(a) + (b)(b) = a^2 + 2ab + b^2$
So $(a + b)^2 = a^2 + 2ab + b^2$

2. <u>Relation</u>
The geometric solution comes from calculating area, while the algebraic solution comes from symbol manipulation. Even so, both solutions have the same middle stage: $(a)(a) + (a)(b) + (b)(a) + (b)(b)$. The underlying math is the same.

Other Forms of Writing in Math

Description
    Geometry—Describe a nature scene using geometry.

Definition
    Algebra—Write an expository paragraph on the definition of the word *algebra*.

Narrative
    Any Math—Write a narrative essay about a time when you used math in daily life.

Classification
    Geometry—Write an essay comparing and contrasting the different types of triangles.

Position
    Any Math—Read about new theories in math or economics that interest you. Choose one theory and write a position essay that supports the theory and defends it against opposing viewpoints.

Process
    Algebra—Write a process paragraph about the details needed to solve a linear equation.

Research
    Any Math—Write a report on a famous mathematician. In your report, include at least one interesting fact about the person's life, describe the time period in which she or he lived, and briefly explain the work or discoveries that made the person famous.

Writing in the Applied Sciences

Classes in the applied sciences provide hands-on learning. For example, in a textile arts class, you may learn about fabrics by sewing. In a machine shop, you may learn about internal combustion engines by taking one apart and putting it back together.

Writing is also important in the applied sciences. It can help you plan projects, remember procedures, reflect on successes and failures, and propose new projects for the future.

In this section, you will learn about taking notes, keeping a learning log, and writing essays in the applied sciences. You will discover how writing empowers hands-on learning.

- **Taking Notes**
- **Keeping a Learning Log**
- **Writing Guidelines: Descriptive Essay**
- **Writing Guidelines: Comparison-Contrast Essay**
- **Writing Guidelines: Essay of Analysis**
- **Other Forms of Practical Writing**

"Jump into the middle of things, get your hands dirty, fall flat on your face, and then reach for the stars."

—Ben Stein

Taking Notes

Note taking can help you keep your projects organized and on track.

Before you take notes . . .

- **Set up a three-ring binder** to hold your notes.
- **Draw a line down the middle of your page.** Put notes on the left and drawings or diagrams on the right.

As you take notes . . .

- **Date each entry** and keep the pages in order.
- **Jot down teacher instructions** as they are given in class.
- **Be brief.** Use phrases and lists to record ideas quickly.
- **Draw diagrams and use graphics** to organize details.

After you've taken notes . . .

- **Review your notes** and highlight main ideas.
- **Study your notes** before beginning a project or before a test.
- **Share your notes** with a partner or group.

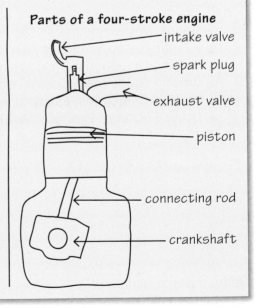

January 12, 2009

Four-Stroke Engines

The piston moves four times, and each stroke does something different.

Intake (Down): Intake valve opens and piston draws in air and fuel mixture.

Compression (Up): Valve closes, and piston compresses air/fuel mixture.

Combustion or Power (Down): Spark plug fires and explodes mixture.

Exhaust (Up): Exhaust valve opens and piston pushes out burned gases.

Parts of a four-stroke engine

- intake valve
- spark plug
- exhaust valve
- piston
- connecting rod
- crankshaft

Try It!

Prepare a binder and take notes in your next applied science class.

Keeping a Learning Log

A learning log is a journal for recording what you learn in a class. The log lets you reflect on ideas, make drawings, and comment on projects.

Before you write . . .

- **Use a separate section in your notes** or a separate notebook.
- **Leave space** for writing questions and answers later on.

As you write . . .

- **Date each entry** and keep the pages in order.
- **Write about what you experienced,** what you learned, what worked and what didn't, and your questions.
- **Consider your next steps.** Write about how the material connects with other things you have learned, and where it might lead.

After you've written . . .

- **Use your log as a supplement** to your notes to review for a test.
- **Write the answers to questions** you had during your project.

March 12, 2011—Consumer Sciences

    I didn't realize meal planning could be so complicated! We used the U.S. Dietary Reference Intake to try to balance our meals. When I charted my breakfast and lunch today, I found out I should eat just vegetables for supper. I joked that "that's what vitamins are for," but Mrs. Johnson said vitamins don't provide basic nutrition, like proteins, carbohydrates, and fats.

    Most foods sold in grocery stores have a label that gives nutrition information. You can use the nutrition facts to balance out the food groups, vitamins, and minerals you are getting, and to limit salt. All I can say is I'm way off what I'm supposed to eat. Potato chips aren't even a vegetable!

What makes a vitamin a vitamin?

A vitamin is an organic molecule that a person needs (in tiny amounts) to be healthy. People also need minerals, amino acids, and fatty acids.

Try It!

Set up a learning log in a notebook or in a section of your three-ring binder. Be sure to date each entry.

Writing Guidelines Descriptive Essay

A descriptive essay describes a person, place, or thing. The goal is to create a clear mental picture for the reader.

Prewriting

- **Select a topic.** If your teacher does not assign a specific topic, review your notes, journal, or textbook for ideas. For example, in Wood Shop, you might describe a tool and its parts and functions.
- **Gather details.** Freewrite everything you know about the topic. Use every sense that is appropriate—sight, sound, smell, taste, and touch. Also research the purpose and history of your topic.
- **Plan and organize.** Choose an organizational pattern. If you are describing something physical, consider using spatial organization: front to back, top to bottom, inside to outside, or the whole to the parts. If you are describing something that changes (for example, the movement of students through a cafeteria), consider using chronological organization.

Writing

- **Connect your ideas.** Write a beginning paragraph that introduces your topic and provides your thesis or focus. Then begin your description, using the organizational pattern you selected. Connect your ideas with transitions.

Revising

- **Improve your writing.** Review your first draft for *ideas, organization,* and *voice.* Ask these questions: *Is my thesis or focus clear? Have I included details that create a clear mental picture for the reader? Is my level of language appropriate to my audience and topic?* Ask someone else to read your essay and make comments.
- **Improve your style.** Check your *word choice* and *sentence fluency.* Ask these questions: *Have I used vivid descriptive words? Do my sentences naturally flow from one to the next?*

Editing

- **Check for conventions.** Look for errors in punctuation, spelling, and grammar.
- **Prepare a final copy.** Make a neat final copy of your essay.

Descriptive Essay

In her Home Living class, Andrea described her plan for furnishing a family room.

<table>
<tr>
<td>

The **beginning** introduces the topic and leads to a thesis statement (underlined).

</td>
<td>

Furnishing a Family Room

A family room should be comfortable and inviting—a place that brings the family together. Let's imagine a room 16 feet wide by 20 feet long, with a fireplace on one end and a large bay area on one side. <u>It's a nice space, but it won't be a family room until it is properly furnished.</u>

Creating a gathering spot near the fireplace is the initial focus. On either side of the fireplace should stand two armchairs, with a coffee table between them. Track lighting above the table lights up games and snacks.

</td>
</tr>
</table>

The **middle** presents each area and describes its arrangement.

Next, it's time to turn the bay area into a quiet place for study. A comfortable chair, a table, and a lamp create a reading nook on one side of the bay. On the other side, a small desk provides a good place for doing homework.

The rest of the room is perfect for larger gatherings. An entertainment center, a couch, and a chair are great for watching TV or listening to music.

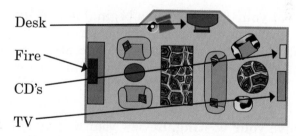

Desk
Fire
CD's
TV

The **ending** reflects on the arrangement of the room.

The family room is complete. The furnishings make the space comfortable and inviting for individuals, couples, and the whole family. Whether people want to play cards by the fire, read a book by the window, or watch the Bears in the playoffs, this room is waiting for them.

Try It!

Write a descriptive essay about a room or an area you know well. Use spacial organization and follow the guidelines on page **446**.

Writing Guidelines Comparison-Contrast Essay

A comparison-contrast essay examines the similarities and differences between two topics. When you write a comparison-contrast essay, be sure to focus on key points; otherwise, your essay will not hold the reader's interest. The goal of this type of writing is to share useful information.

Prewriting

- **Select topics.** Be sure the two topics you choose are in the same category and have enough qualities to compare and contrast. For example, in a computer science class you might compare and contrast two different operating systems or word processing programs. In a clothing class, you might examine the differences between a natural and a synthetic fabric.
- **Gather details.** List the qualities of each topic. Use a Venn diagram (see page **589**) to sort out similarities and differences.
- **Plan and organize.** Decide how to organize your essay. You could describe similarities first and then differences, discuss one topic first and then the other, or compare and contrast the two topics point by point.

Writing

- **Connect your ideas.** Write a beginning that introduces your topics and gives a thesis statement. Write middle paragraphs that provide the details of comparison and contrast, following your organizational plan. Then write an ending that sums up the topics.

Revising

- **Improve your writing.** Review your writing for *ideas, organization,* and *voice.* Ask these questions: *Have I showed equal points of comparison for both topics? Have I followed a clear pattern of organization? Do I sound knowledgeable?*
- **Improve your style.** Check your *word choice* and *sentence fluency* to be sure the information is clear and effective.

Editing

- **Check for conventions.** Look for errors in punctuation, spelling, and grammar.
- **Prepare a final copy.** Make a neat final copy of your essay.

Comparison-Contrast Essay

In an essay for Wood Shop, Paulo wrote about two types of wood.

The **beginning** introduces the topics and leads to a thesis statement (underlined).

The **middle** paragraphs provide the comparison and contrast, dealing with one topic and then the other.

The **ending** restates the thesis.

Which Wood Would You Use?

Selecting the right wood for a project can make the difference between beauty and a beast. Two popular woods are oak and pine. Each has its own distinctive beauty, but oak and pine have very different properties and uses.

All varieties of oak are hard and durable, and the most popular are white and red oak. Oak has a beautiful, tight grain that ranges from fine lines to burls and swirls. It is prized for its rich colors, from dusky red (red oak) to pale cream or gray (white oak). Oak is used for furniture, cabinets, and decorative woodwork. It also makes great hardwood flooring, resisting scratches and dents better than softer woods. Its solid composition makes oak tough to bend and shape and more difficult to work with hand tools. Because of its high cost, oak is not used for general building, though in Europe, some houses framed in oak have stood for a thousand years.

Pine has a number of popular varieties, such as white pine, red pine, and southern pine. The wood has a wide grain and ranges in color from white to yellow. It is excellent for woodworking since it is easily shaped and bent with hand tools. Because resin makes pine naturally resistant to insects, it is very good for outdoor furniture and for framing construction. However, since pine dents more easily than hardwoods, it is less resilient as flooring. Many prize pine for its casual, homey look and use it for doors or cabinetry. As one of the least expensive woods, pine is a preferred building material.

Oak and pine are both beautiful woods, though their colors, grains, hardness, uses, and cost are quite different. These differences mean that many homes are built of pine but furnished with oak.

Try It!

Write a comparison-contrast essay about two topics. Follow the guidelines on page **448**.

Writing Guidelines Essay of Analysis

An essay of analysis breaks down a topic into its parts and shows how they are related. Complex issues make the best topics for essays of analysis.

Prewriting

- **Select a topic.** If you are not given a topic, think about complex issues related to your class work. For example, in Family and Consumer Science, you could analyze the factors that affect the rising of yeast. In wood shop class, you could analyze the design and function of a piece of furniture.
- **Gather details.** Create a cluster diagram to break down your topic into different components, aspects, and reasons. Think of how each part of the topic connects to other parts.
- **Plan and organize.** Outline your essay. First write a thesis statement that names the topic and sums up the analysis. Then write a topic sentence about one part of the topic for each middle paragraph.

Writing

- **Connect your ideas.** Write a beginning that introduces your topic and leads to your thesis statement. Develop middle paragraphs by following your outline. Show how the different parts of the topic are related and use transitions to connect your ideas.

Revising

- **Improve your writing.** Review your analysis for *ideas, organization,* and *voice.* Ask these questions: *Is my thesis statement clear? Does each middle paragraph focus on one part of the topic? Do all the details in each paragraph support the main point of the paragraph? Do I show how the parts of the topic are connected?*
- **Improve your style.** Check your *word choice* and *sentence fluency* to make sure that everything is stated clearly and effectively. Ask these questions: *Have I defined terms associated with my topic? Do my sentences flow smoothly?*

Editing

- **Check for conventions.** Look for errors in punctuation, spelling, and grammar.
- **Prepare a final copy.** Make a neat final copy of your essay.

Essay of Analysis

In Consumer Economics, Nina wrote about the impact of severe weather on consumers.

The **beginning** presents the topic and provides the thesis statement (underlined).

The **middle** paragraphs analyze the main parts of the topic and show how they are related.

The **ending** restates the thesis and leaves the reader with a final thought.

Weathering High Prices

The Bureau of Labor Statistics reported that the Consumer Price Index rose 3.6 percent between August 2004 and August 2005. In part, this rise was due to the severe weather during that time. Damaging storms have shown the powerful economic impact of bad weather.

Severe weather directly affects food prices. A freeze in Florida, Texas, or California can reduce the citrus crops in these states. A severe drought in the Midwest can destroy whole fields of grain. As supplies drop, prices of these products rise, as do prices on derivative products such as cooking oil, cereals, and baked goods. A poor grain crop also raises the price of meat, leather, and soap, since high-cost grain makes it more expensive to feed livestock.

Severe weather patterns also can devastate industry. A brutal hurricane season in 2005 pummeled oil refineries and offshore drilling platforms in the Gulf of Mexico. As a result, gasoline prices nationwide skyrocketed. The storms also damaged many factories and deprived them of workers, who fled the area. The rebuilding that resulted drove up the prices of building supplies and services.

Storms can even prevent goods and services from reaching the market. Blizzards, tornadoes, and hurricanes ground airplanes, sink ships, and cause truck wrecks that spill cargo. Storms also can damage gas and electric lines, shutting down businesses and schools. Local and national agencies spend billions each year to reopen roads and repair utilities to get things running again.

Severe weather anywhere can spread its economic effects across the nation. When the weather is good, prices stay low, but when the weather is bad, everyone pays.

Try It!

Write an essay of analysis about a complex issue. Follow the guidelines on page **450**.

Other Forms of Practical Writing

Narrative Essay

Child Care—Write an account of your first babysitting experience. Include mistakes you made and techniques that worked best.

Process Essay

Drafting—Explain the steps to create an accurate floor plan of your classroom. Include each step in order, using imperative sentences.

Letter of Application

Career Explorations—Write a cover letter to accompany a résumé. Include an introductory paragraph, a brief background and experience paragraph, and a personal statement about why you want the job.

Classification Essay

Textile Arts—Define and explain the different types of stitches used in needlework. Tell what each is used for and the effect it can create.

Problem-Solution Essay

Machine Shop—Write a problem-solution essay about a motor that isn't working. Explain the cause of the problem and explore possible solutions. Indicate which solution is the best and why.

Proposal

Wood Shop—Design a piece of furniture meant for a specific place or function (for example, a bench along a garden path or a coatrack in a hallway). Write a proposal that explains your design and persuades your teacher to let you build it.

Compare-Contrast Essay

Cooking Class—Write a compare-contrast essay explaining the various leavening agents (yeast, baking powder, baking soda) and their effects on baked goods.

Writing in the Arts

Artists have special powers. A sculptor's chisel can turn rock into skin and cloth, a composer's pen can create landscapes out of sound, and a painter's brush can make a woman immortal. From ancient cave paintings to modern light shows, art empowers human beings to express thoughts and emotions that otherwise would go unspoken.

One way to capture the power of art is to write about it. When you translate paint and stone and notes into words, you understand art more deeply. This chapter will help you take notes, record learning log entries, and write essays and reports about the arts.

- Taking Classroom Notes
- Keeping a Learning Log
- Writing Guidelines: Response to an Art Prompt
- Writing Guidelines: Research Report
- Other Forms of Writing in the Arts

"I try to apply colors like words that shape poems, like notes that shape music."

—Joan Miro

Taking Classroom Notes

Even though most of your work in art and music classes is applied (you paint, you sing, you play an instrument), taking notes is also important.

Take notes when . . .

- **your teacher writes information on the board or an overhead.**
  This information is obviously important. Copying it into your notes helps make the information part of your own thinking. Be sure to write down new vocabulary words, as well as names, dates, and key phrases.
- **you have a demonstration in class.**
  Your class may view slides of art pieces or listen to recordings of various musical styles. Taking notes will help you keep track of the individual works.
- **you have a guest speaker/performer.**
  Professional artists may demonstrate or discuss their work. Your notes can help you participate during a question-and-answer session after the presentation.

Tip

- Date each entry and give it a heading so you can quickly find the topic.
- Copy new vocabulary words and leave space so that you can fill in definitions or examples later.
- Write down hints to help you remember a name, term, or concept.
- Draw sketches to help you recall individual works.
- Mark the spots in your notes where you get lost or confused so that you can ask about them later.
- Divide your page into two columns (one side wider than the other). Write classroom notes in the wider column and questions in the other.
- Find a "study buddy" who will compare notes, go over questions, or review for tests with you.

Try It!

Set up a notebook for your art or music class with a wide right column and a narrower left column (see page 455). Take notes during class.

Keeping a Learning Log

A learning log helps you think about things you are learning. Brent used the left side of his log for steps in a project and the right side for comments.

Sample Entry

Steps in Matting Artwork, Oct. 28

1. Choose a matting material and a color.	I chose a rag foam-core board for the backing and an acid-free, turquoise-colored mat for the border.
2. Measure the artwork and decide on the width of the mat frame, making sure it will fit inside the picture frame.	My photo is 8 x 10 inches, but with a quarter inch overlap, the image size is 7-1/2 x 9 1/2 inches. For the borders, I subtracted the image size from the frame size of 11 x 14 and then divided by two. I came up with 1 3/4 inches for the sides and 2 1/4 inches for the top and bottom.
3. Cut the backing material and the mat board.	I used a utility knife and steel ruler to cut the foam-core mounting board and the mat board to the size of the picture frame.
4. Attach the photo to the backing.	I centered the photo on the mounting board and positioned it with corner mounts.
5. Cut the window for the mat frame.	I drew pencil lines on the back of the turquoise mat so I could cut out a window for the image, starting at the corners.
6. Place the mat over the photo and put it into the frame.	This part was easy. I put the turquoise border behind the glass in the frame, added the mounted photo, and put on the back that came with the frame. Very pretty!

Try It!

Set up a learning log for your art or music class. Keep one side for notes or instructions and the other side for your own comments.

Writing Guidelines Response to an Art Prompt

Sometimes you will be asked to write a short essay in response to a prompt related to art or music. Responding to a prompt allows you to apply what you know about a specific work. Here are guidelines for planning and writing a response.

Prewriting

- **Understand the prompt.** Read through the prompt and focus on what it is asking you to do. Is the purpose of your response to explain, compare, describe, persuade?
- **Gather your details.** Go through your notes and any research materials you are allowed to use. Highlight or jot down the details you will use in your response. Be sure to record the sources of any quotations or facts you use.
- **Organize your details.** Check the prompt for clues about organizing your response. For example, if the prompt asks you to "describe Cezanne's painting *Girl at the Piano* and tell how the color choices affect the mood," you might begin with a general description of the painting, then zero in on the main figures, and end with a discussion of colors and mood.

Writing

- **Write freely.** Use your notes as a guide, and concentrate on getting all your ideas on paper. Don't worry too much about getting everything right. Most short-response essays are one paragraph long. However, if a prompt calls for several main points, write a separate paragraph for each.

Revising

- **Improve your writing.** Read your draft and cut any details that don't fit the prompt. Also add information that will clarify the ideas in your response. Be as complete as possible.
- **Improve your style.** Check your word choice and sentence fluency to make sure that your response reads smoothly.

Editing

- **Check for conventions.** Look for errors in spelling, punctuation, and grammar.
- **Prepare your final copy.** If necessary, and if time permits, copy your response onto a clean sheet of paper and proofread it a final time.

Response to an Art Prompt

Maria wrote this response to a prompt about architecture.

Prompt

> *Why is Frank Lloyd Wright's house Fallingwater so important to American architecture? Cite the design's special features and techniques and discuss the public's early response to it in a multiparagraph answer.*

Sample Response

The writer provides background and her main point.

Architect Frank Lloyd Wright designed Fallingwater in 1936 as a country retreat for a Pennsylvania family. In this house, Wright spotlighted his key principle of designing "organic" houses, letting people live in harmony with nature.

The writer supports her main point by citing special features and techniques of the house.

The house stands on top of a waterfall and seems like part of the rock formation. Its central core of stacked sandstone rises out of the rock, and terraces of reinforced concrete mimic the ledges over the waterfall. Glass walls on three sides open the house to the woods around it, and windows framed in a warm red offset the neutral sandstone.

Fallingwater was immediately famous, even appearing on the cover of <u>Time</u> magazine in 1938. The house's design renewed Frank Lloyd Wright's career and shifted the direction of modern architecture back toward natural materials. Critics and fans agree that Fallingwater is a revolutionary design.

The writer uses specific examples and details to demonstrate her understanding.

Many of the features of Fallingwater are still used in home building today. For example, Wright's idea of making walls of glass is popular in modern homes. The natural wood and stone in the home's interior are seen today in stone walls and fireplaces and in wood flooring, paneling, and trim. Wright's idea of making a home part of the natural setting also carries through in much of modern architecture.

Try It!

Respond to a short-essay prompt your teacher will supply about a topic you are studying. Write a multiparagraph answer.

Writing Guidelines Research Report

At some point, you may be asked to write a research report in an art or music class. Your topic may be a famous sculptor, painter, composer, or specific style of art or music. The following guidelines will help you with such an assignment.

Prewriting

- **Choose a subject.** If your teacher does not provide a general subject, create a cluster diagram of the people, artwork, and ideas that interest you most. Choose one subject.
- **List what you know.** Write down what you already know about the subject and jot down questions you have.
- **Conduct research.** Look for information in books, magazines, museum exhibits, and on Web sites.
- **Create a thesis statement.** Review your research and decide on a specific topic and focus for your paper. Write a thesis statement.
- **Plan and organize.** Outline your paper, placing details in the best order (chronological, spatial, order of importance, and so on).

Writing

- **Connect your ideas.** Write a beginning that introduces your topic and gives your thesis. Develop middle paragraphs that support the thesis with details, and write an ending that summarizes your ideas.

Revising

- **Improve your writing.** Check your *ideas, organization,* and *voice.* Ask these questions: *Have I created a clear thesis? Have I supported it with a variety of details? Are my details in the best order? Do I sound knowledgeable?*
- **Improve your style.** Check your *word choice* and *sentence fluency.* Ask these questions: *Have I explained any technical terms? Do my sentences flow smoothly?*

Editing

- **Check for conventions.** Watch for errors in punctuation, spelling, and grammar. Also be sure you have cited sources correctly.
- **Prepare a final copy.** Proofread it before handing it in.

Research Report

Sean wrote the following report about Tuvan throat singing. After listening to a CD, he had became curious about how this unusual music developed. He decided to research Tuva, its people, and its music.

Sample Report

The introduction presents the thesis statement for the report.

Tuvan Throat Singing: A Unique Vocal Art

The throat singers of Tuva, a remote area of Central Asia, bring a unique musical heritage into the twenty-first century. Throat singing is a vocal technique in which a single vocalist produces two or more distinct pitches simultaneously. One reviewer described the sound as a human bagpipe (Edmonds). This singing technique reflects the lifestyle and the surrounding natural world of the singers.

For many years, throat singing was not well known in the Western world. That's because this technique developed and flourished in places with little contact with the outside world. Tuva is a small Russian republic bordering Mongolia. The remote location and Soviet-era travel restrictions limited visitors but also allowed Tuvans to preserve their musical traditions (Leighton).

The body of the report explains what throat singing is and how and where it developed.

Throat singing developed among the seminomadic herders who make up much of the area's population. Tuvans herd their horses, sheep, and yaks across dry steppe lands and in the taiga, a cold, mountainous, forested area. Because throat singing produces a musical sound that carries over long distances, the music became a way for shepherds and horsemen to entertain each other and communicate. Variations of throat singing are also found in nearby areas of Mongolia, the Altai region, and other parts of Asia ("Types").

In Tuva, throat singers use their voices to include the sounds of the natural world—whistling birds, bubbling streams, and blowing wind—in their songs. Because the horse is such an important part of Tuvan culture, many traditional songs have a rhythm that sounds like a cantering horse.

Sources are cited in the report.

Khoomei, from the Mongolian word for throat singing, is the general name for Tuvan throat singing and also refers to a specific type of simple throat singing. Other styles of throat singing include *sygyt,* which features a whistling tone; *kargyraa,* which uses flaps (the so-called false vocal chords) in the throat to produce notes an octave below the sung note; and *ezengileer,* which incorporates a horseback-riding rhythm ("Types").

Throat singers perform alone or in groups, often accompanied by traditional Tuvan instruments. Common instruments include the igil, a two-stringed fiddle; the *dosh-poluur,* a guitarlike instrument; and the *xomus,* a type of mouth harp ("Types").

In recent years, scholars, musicians and even tourists have discovered Tuva and its music. An Academy-Award-nominated documentary, *Genghis Blues,* brought international attention to Tuva (Edmonds). Tuvan musicians now regularly tour in Europe and the United States as well as in Russia. Tuvan music is even online.

The essay concludes with information on recent developments.

Large music festivals and throat singing competitions each summer bring hundreds of international musicians and fans to Tuva. Tuvan organizations such as the Tuvan Institute for Humanities work with Tuvan musicians and scholars to preserve the country's unique musical form and encourage young singers to learn it (Leighton 55).

Works Cited

Turn to pages 381–384 for more on creating a "Works Cited" page.

Edmonds, Curtis. "Genghis Blues: The Best Movie You Haven't Seen." Rev. of *Genghis Blues*, dir. Roko Belic. *TXReviews.* N.p., 11 July 2006. Web. 16 Jan. 2011.

Leighton, Ralph. *Tuva or Bust: Richard Feynman's Last Journey.* New York: Norton, 2000. Print.

"Types of Throat Singing." *Khoomei.com.* Skysong Productions, 12 Dec. 2005. Web. 16 Jan. 2011.

Other Forms of Writing in the Arts

Descriptive Writing

- Describe the use of texture, composition, and color in Vincent van Gogh's *Starry Night*.
- Describe your response to Miles Davis's rendition of "Take Five."
- Describe the varied activity inside a theater from the time you enter until the curtain goes up on a play.

Expository Writing

- Develop a list of tips for making the most of practice time when you're learning a musical instrument.
- Explain how a computer program can turn a digital photo into a new piece of art.
- Explain how origami is created.

Narrative Writing

- Research and write the story of the self-taught quilters of Gee's Bend, Alabama.
- Write about the first time you played a musical instrument.
- Write about a time you viewed a piece of art that really moved you.

Persuasive Writing

- Write an editorial for the school newsletter explaining how dance, art, and music help students learn other subjects.
- Write a letter to the PTA to convince them to sponsor a fund-raiser for new uniforms for the marching band.
- Write a letter to the editor to convince readers that electronic music should be included in the music program.

Creative Writing

- Write a poem inspired by Beethoven's *Moonlight Sonata*.
- Create a short story based on one of the characters in the diner in Edward Hopper's painting *Nighthawks*.
- Write an imaginary letter from Antonin Dvorak to a friend in which he discusses what inspired him to write the *New World Symphony*.
- Pretend you are the girl in Andrew Wyeth's painting *Christina's World*. Write about what you are thinking as you sit in the field.

www.hmheducation.com/writesource

The Tools of Learning

Listening and Speaking   **463**
Taking Notes   **467**
Critical Reading   **473**
Summarizing and Paraphrasing   **483**
Understanding Writing Assignments **491**
Improving Your Vocabulary   **501**
Writing Business Letters   **513**
Taking Tests   **521**

Academic Vocabulary

Working with a classmate, read the definitions below and discuss possible answers to each question.

1. A guideline is a statement of standards or procedures that guide you.
   What behavior guidelines do you have to follow at school?

2. To demonstrate something is to show it or make it clear.
   In what ways can you demonstrate your knowledge about a topic?

3. To survey something can mean to examine it carefully.
   Why might you survey a text before you begin reading it?

4. When you predict, you use evidence and reasoning to guess what might happen.
   Is it ever possible to predict how a movie will end? Explain.

Listening and Speaking

In his book *The Poet at the Breakfast Table*, Oliver Wendell Holmes stated, "It is the province of knowledge to speak, and it is the privilege of wisdom to listen." This famous nineteenth-century poet understood the importance of strong speaking and listening skills. Effective speaking does, in fact, require that you plan what you say, and meaningful listening clearly requires concentration.

This chapter provides tips and strategies that will help you improve your speaking and listening skills. Mastering these skills will make you a better student, leader, coworker, and companion. But remember that true mastery will come only with effort and practice.

- **Listening in Class**
- **Speaking in Class**
- **A Closer Look at Listening and Speaking**

"There is only one rule for being a good talker: learn how to listen."

—Christopher Morley

Listening in Class

When you really listen, you concentrate. You do more than simply hear what is being said. The following tips will help you become a better listener.

- **Know why you're listening.** What is the speaker trying to tell you? Will there be a test? Are you being given an assignment?
- **Listen for the facts.** Listening for the 5 W and H questions— *Who? What? When? Where? Why?* and *How?*—will help you identify the most important information.
- **Take notes.** When you hear important information, write it down in your notebook. In the margins, write down any questions you may have. Review and complete your notes as soon after class as possible.
- **Put the speaker's ideas into your own words.** Paraphrase the speaker's key points as you take notes. Add your own comments.

Try It!

The next time you take notes in class, use your own words to record your teacher's ideas. Add comments in the margins.

The Marshall Plan (1947)	
known as the European Recovery Program (ERP) in effect from 1948-1951	The plan helped the economies of Europe and America.
designed by George C. Marshall – army chief of staff during WWII – secretary of state under President Truman	
gave economic aid to parts of Europe devastated by WWII – provided about $13 billion – Europe mostly used the money to buy goods from America. – During Korean War, some of the money helped rebuild the militaries of Western Europe.	Europe needed food, fuel, raw materials, and machines for rebuilding.

Speaking in Class

Speaking in class is a skill everyone should master. A good classroom discussion depends on cooperation. These basic strategies will help you and your classmates become better speakers.

Before you speak . . .

- **Listen** carefully and take notes.
- **Think** about what others are saying.
- **Wait** until it's your turn to speak.
- **Plan** how you can add something positive to the discussion.

As you speak . . .

- **Use a loud, clear voice.**
- **Stick to the topic.**
- **Avoid repeating** what's already been said.
- **Support your ideas** with examples, facts, or anecdotes.
- **Maintain eye contact** with others in the group or class.

Tip

- Focus your comments on ideas, not on personalities.
- Summarize what's been agreed upon in the discussion.
- Mention another person's comments and expand on them constructively.

Try It!

Play "Where will you be?" Warm up your impromptu speaking skills by interacting in the following activity.

1. Pair up with a classmate. Take turns interviewing each other about this topic: What do you plan to do after high school?
- As the interviewer, ask specific questions and get as much information as you can. Take notes as you go along.
- As the interviewee, answer the questions clearly and completely. Include important facts and interesting details.

2. Exchange roles after the first interview is complete.

3. In a mini-speech, present your partner's future plans to the class. Quickly organize your notes into a beginning, a middle, and an ending. Then follow the "As You Speak" strategies above.

A Closer Look at Listening and Speaking

Improving your listening and speaking skills will increase your confidence in and out of the classroom. Follow these basic guidelines to carry on productive conversations and discussions.

Good Listeners . . .	Good Speakers . . .
■ think about what the speaker is saying. ■ stay focused so that they are prepared to respond thoughtfully. ■ pay attention to the speaker's tone of voice, gestures, and facial expressions. ■ interrupt only when necessary to ask for clarification.	■ speak loudly and clearly. ■ maintain eye contact with their listeners. ■ emphasize their main ideas by changing the tone and volume of their voice. ■ respect their audience by explaining and clarifying information. ■ use gestures and body language effectively.

Try It!

Focus on speaking and listening skills with this activity.

1. Pick two classmates and number yourselves 1, 2, and 3.
2. Ask person 1 to take person 2 aside and read the paragraph below.
3. Then ask person 2 to take person 3 aside and try to repeat the paragraph from memory.
4. Finally, ask person 3 to repeat the paragraph from memory to the first two classmates.
5. Compare the original paragraph to what person 3 reports.

In the early 1920s, Roy Chapman Andrews, an explorer from Wisconsin, proposed studying geologic formations in Mongolia. Many fellow scientists felt that this trip would be a waste of time because the shifting sands of the desert would make such research difficult, if not impossible. Even Andrews began to wonder about the wisdom of his proposal, given the distance and the political uncertainties in Asia. Fortunately, he decided to go through with his plan. The scientific community was rewarded with the discovery of many unique fossils in the Gobi Desert of Mongolia. The most important find was a clutch of dinosaur eggs, the first ever discovered.

Taking Notes

John Steinbeck, one of the most famous American writers of the twentieth century, was sometimes overwhelmed with ideas. He said, "Ideas are like rabbits. You get a couple and learn how to handle them, and pretty soon you have a dozen." What should you do when you are faced with more ideas than your brain can process? Write them down.

How you record information is important. You need an organized and efficient system to process all of the new facts and details. That's where note-taking strategies can help. The art of note taking is a valuable study and learning tool. This chapter will help you take notes while listening to a lecture, reading a text, or attending a meeting.

- **Taking Classroom Notes**
- **Taking Reading Notes**
- **Taking Meeting Minutes**

"There is enormous power in stating something simply and well."

—Pat Conroy

Taking Classroom Notes

Your teacher may give a lecture to explain an important subject, introduce a new topic, or help the class review for a test. The following tips will help you take clear, organized lecture notes.

Guidelines for Class Notes

1. **Write the topic and date at the top of each page.** This will help you keep your notes organized and easy to use.

2. **Listen carefully.** This is the key to taking good notes. If you are too busy writing, you may miss important clues. For example, if a teacher says, "There are six steps in flying a hot-air balloon," listen for the six steps. Also listen for key words such as *first, second, next,* or *most importantly.*

3. **Use your own words.** You can't write down everything your teacher says. Instead, try to put the main points into your own words. You can fill in the details later.

4. **Begin taking notes right away** or you may miss something important. It's hard to catch up while taking notes.

5. **Write quickly, but be neat.** Your notes won't be helpful if you can't read them.

6. **Condense information.**
   - Use lists, phrases, and abbreviations (*p = page, ex = for example*).
   - Skip the small, unnecessary words, such as articles (*a, an, the*).
   - Shorten some words (*intro* for *introduction, chap* for *chapter*).
   - Use numbers and symbols (*1st, 2nd,* +, ↑, ↓,=).
   - Develop a personal shorthand (*w = with, w/o = without*).

7. **Draw sketches and diagrams** to explain something more quickly than you can in words.

8. **Copy important information** your teacher writes on the board.

9. **Ask your teacher** to explain something you don't understand, to repeat something, or to please slow down.

Try It!

Review some of your recent class notes in light of the guidelines above. How could you improve your note-taking skills? Explain.

Setting Up Your Notes

Keep your notes in a notebook, preferably one for each subject. You can also take notes on loose-leaf paper kept in a three-ring binder, which lets you add or remove pages as needed. Write only on one side of the paper. This makes it easier to read and find portions of your notes.

Record the topic and date.

Electricity   September 17

Electrical circuits
 Power source, a conductor, and load make up a simple circuit.
 A circuit can be in series or it can be parallel.
  1. In a series circuit, current follows one path. If a load is
   open, the circuit stops functioning.
  2. In a parallel circuit, current can follow other paths, so
   the circuit continues to function.

Skip a line between main ideas.

Four parts of a simple circuit
  1. battery (power source)
  2. conductor (wire)
  3. switch (shown open)
  4. load (in this case, a lamp)

Make sketches.

Important terms
 • volt—the force used to push electricity through a
  conductor
 • ohm—the amount of resistance in a conductor to the
  flow of the electric current
 • alternating current—electricity that flows back and
  forth through a conductor
 • direct current—electricity that flows in only
  one direction

Use bullets or numbered lists.

Reviewing Your Notes

As you read over your notes, follow these tips:

1. **Circle words that may be misspelled and underline words you don't understand.** After looking something up in a dictionary or glossary, write the correct spelling or meaning in the margin.

2. **Write any questions you have in the margin.** Then look for the answers on your own. If you can't find an answer, ask a teacher or classmate. Write the answer near the question.

3. **Use a highlighter** to mark the most important notes. You can use a different colored pen to circle or underline key ideas instead.

4. **Rewrite your notes.** Making a neat, organized copy of your notes gives you another chance to learn the material.

5. **Review your notes.** Look over your notes before the next class, especially if you are having a test or class discussion.

Electricity   September 17

Electrical circuits
    Power source, a conductor, and load make up a simple circuit.
    A circuit can be in series or it can be parallel.
        1. In a series circuit, current follows one path. If a load is
           open, the circuit stops functioning.
        2. In a parallel circuit, current can follow other paths, so
carbon, copper, the circuit continues to function.
or aluminum
        Four parts of a simple circuit
            1. battery (power source)
            2. conductor (wire)
    lamp,   3. switch (shown open)
    motor,   4. load (in this case, a lamp)
    heater
        Important terms
            • volt—the force used to push electricity through a
              conductor
            • ohm—the amount of resistance in a conductor . . .

Taking Reading Notes

Taking notes while you read an assignment is easier than taking notes during a lecture. You can stop to write at any time, which means you can write more neatly and thoughtfully. Here are some tips for taking reading notes.

Guidelines for Reading Notes

1. **Preview the assignment.** Look through your assignment to see what the reading is about. Look at the title, introduction, headings, and chapter summary. Also look at any pictures, maps, or graphics. (See pages **602–603**.)

2. **Quickly read the entire assignment** before you begin to take notes. This will give you an overview of the material and allow you to pick out the main ideas.

3. **Take notes while reading the material a second time.** Read carefully and stop at new ideas or words.
   - **Write down the important information.**
   - **Put notes in your own words.** Don't just copy entire passages from the book. You learn more when you rewrite ideas in your words. (See pages **483–490** for more information on how to summarize and paraphrase information.)
   - **Use headings and subtitles to organize your notes.** Write down the important information under each heading or subtitle as you read.
   - **Include notes about pictures, charts, and illustrations.** Make quick sketches of these visual elements.
   - **Use graphic organizers.** (See pages **588–589**.)
   - **List and define any new words.** As you read look up each unfamiliar word in the glossary or in a dictionary. Write down the appropriate meaning and include the page number where the word is located. This will help you to easily find it again.

4. **Learn more.** See "Critical Reading" on pages **473–482** for more information on taking reading notes.

Try It!

For your next reading assignment, take notes using the tips above.

Taking Meeting Minutes

Recording the minutes of a meeting is another form of note taking. Minutes must be well organized and should include complete information about who is present and what is discussed and decided. Always report minutes in an objective (impersonal) voice. Be sure to listen carefully and write down information accurately. Follow the tips below.

Guidelines for Taking Minutes

- Begin with the organization's name, the date, location, and topic of the meeting.

- Record what time the meeting begins.

- List those present (or absent). Indicate who leads the meeting and who records the minutes.

- Note "old business" (carried over from a previous meeting) that is discussed or resolved.

- Note "new business" initiated and discussed in the current meeting.

- Record any votes taken and their result.

- Record what time the meeting is adjourned.

King High School Homecoming Committee Minutes
   Date: September 16, 2011
   Location: Room 123 (Mr. Tesler, Faculty Advisor)
   Topic: Homecoming Parade

Attending
(Seniors) Todd Garrison, Tamy Singh (chair), Letisha Foreman, Sam Feldman, Gina Vance, Max Lang (Juniors) Alex Morgan, Jonelle Robinson, Sylvie Tenuta (Sophmores) Kate Lovanian (recording), Michele Block.

Absent
Marlette Santiago

Old Business
The City Council has agreed to shut off Main Street from 5:30 pm until 7:00 pm.

The Police Department has agreed to help with traffic and security during the parade.

Holy Angels Church will allow parade participants to use the church's parking lot starting at 5:00 p.m. The Homecoming Committee will be responsible for cleaning the parking lot after the parade. Max Lang and Alex Morgan will take care of clean-up.

New Business
Floats: Floats are almost done. How should we thank parents and businesses that provided places for float building? Bring ideas to the next meeting.

Marching Band: 26 alumni plan to march with the band. Mr. Greene would like them to be introduced at half time. Mr. Tesler will arrange this.

Dignitaries: Principal Stevens asked if we want to invite Mrs. Martha Davis to be our grand marshal. She is the oldest living former teacher from our school.

   • Vote 11-0 to invite Mrs. Davis. Todd Garrison will tell Principal Stevens.

Meeting Time: 2:45 pm–4:00 pm

Tip

Take meeting minutes to record the main points about what is discussed and decided upon by the group. It's not necessary to include all the details of a discussion. Be sure to accurately record any votes or official action taken.

Critical Reading

Publisher Charles Scribner, Jr., naturally did a great deal of reading, and he understood the value inherent in the reading experience. Scribner stated, "Reading is a means of thinking with another person's mind; it forces you to stretch your own." In other words, reading allows you to learn what other people have to say on different subjects, which, in turn, sharpens your own thinking. When you immerse yourself in reading material—carefully examining and questioning certain parts—you are reading critically.

Critical reading involves a number of steps, including *surveying* a reading assignment, *questioning* what the text is about, *taking notes* as you read, and giving the material a final *review*. In this chapter, you will learn how to use critical reading to gain a clearer understanding of your reading assignments. Following a proven reading plan will enable you to tackle even the most challenging reading assignments.

- **Critical Reading: SQ3R**
- **Before You Read**
- **As You Read**
- **After You Read**
- **Reading Fiction**
- **Reading Poetry**

"In truth, the reader should be as carefully and patiently trained as the writer."

—Sir Osbert Sitwell

Critical Reading: SQ3R

An effective reading technique for all types of nonfiction is the SQ3R method. SQ3R stands for the five steps in this reading process: *survey, question, read, recite,* and *review.* The steps in this technique are explained below.

Before you read . . .

- **Survey** Preview the reading assignment for its general content. Read titles, subtitles, headings, and subheadings to see what is being covered. Take note of illustrations and terms in bold or italic type. Also read the first and last paragraphs.
- **Question** Ask yourself what you already know about the topic of the reading. Then write down questions you still have about it. To get started, turn titles, subtitles, headings, and subheadings into questions. Asking questions keeps you actively involved while reading.

As you read . . .

- **Read** Take the time to read slowly and carefully. Look for the main idea in each paragraph, section, or chapter. Try to answer questions you have already identified. At different points, also ask these questions: *What does this mean? How does it connect with previous material? What will come next?* Take notes as you go along. Reread difficult parts as necessary.
- **Recite** Test your comprehension of the material by summarizing the main points out loud. Reciting is one of the most valuable parts of SQ3R. After you read a page, a section, or a chapter, try to answer the 5 W's and H (*Who? What? Where? When? Why?* and *How?*) about that part. Again, reread parts as needed.

After you read . . .

- **Review** Assess your knowledge by reviewing your notes. See how well you understand the entire reading assignment. Ask these questions: *Have all my questions been answered? Can I summarize each main section? Can I summarize or outline the whole assignment?* Consider outlining the material or using another type of graphic organizer to help you remember what you have read.

FYI

Critical reading means looking beyond surface details and thinking carefully about the information that is presented.

Before You Read

Try to get the big picture with each assignment.

Surveying the Reading

To begin, **survey** or preview the text. This will give you a general understanding of the main points. Use the following guidelines:

- **Scan** chapter titles, subtitles, headings, and boldfaced type.
- **Identify the purpose of the material:** to inform, to persuade, to entertain.
- **Read** the first and last paragraphs.
- **List** the topic and the main points you identify.

Below, Jeremy *surveys* the opening part of an article on global warming. He writes his notes on a copy of the article.

Sample Survey Notes

Greenhouse Gases

Many scientists report that the twentieth century was the hottest in centuries. The surface temperature of Earth increased 1 degree, and scientists predict it could rise between 2 and 10 degrees in this century. Industrial activities that emit greenhouse gases, they say, are the major cause of the warm-up. This evaluation resulted in a growing call for tougher industrial regulations, leading to a debate in the U.S. Senate.

Economic Impact

Not all senators agree with the scientists' assessment and prediction. Some argue that the information is overblown and, in part, inaccurate. They are concerned that imposing even stronger regulations on industries could significantly stall economic progress.

Purpose:
to inform
Topic:
global warming
Main points:
opposing
viewpoints
1. Stronger
   regulations
   on industry
   are needed.
2. Stronger
   regulations
   may stall
   economic
   progress.

Try It!

Survey a reading assignment from any of your classes. Identify its purpose, its topic, and the main points.

Questioning the Material

After you have surveyed the entire text, ask **questions** about the reading. Use the following guidelines:

- **Ask yourself what you already know** about the topic.
- **List questions** that you still have about the topic. Use the 5 W and H questions.
- **Turn headings and main points into questions.** For example, if the chapter title is "Scientific Discoveries of the Ancient World," you would ask, "What were the scientific discoveries of the ancient world?"

Below, Jeremy formed questions that he had about the topic. Next to his questions, he noted things he already knew about the topic.

Sample Question Notes

Global Warming: The Great Debate

1. Who are the scientists that did the research?
2. How did they predict that the temperature could rise between 2 and 10 degrees this century?
3. What will happen if the industrial regulations stay the same?
4. Why do some senators think that the scientists' information is inaccurate?
5. What kinds of tougher regulations would be put on industries?
6. What industries would be affected most?

Already know:

There's a debate about global warming. Some people want to put tougher regulations on industries. Others think regulations will stall the economy.

I think transportation industries will be affected most.

I worry about global warming, but I think we need a strong economy, too.

Try It!

Write down questions you have about the topic of the reading assignment you surveyed. Also note what you already know about the topic.

As You Read

Once you have surveyed the assignment and formed questions about it, you are ready to read carefully. Try to turn your reading into a conversation with the text. Respect what the writer has to say even as you question certain parts. And stay open to the unexpected.

Reading (and Taking Notes)

Always have a goal in mind when you read. Use the following guidelines to read the material and answer the questions you listed.

- **Read slowly** so that you don't miss anything.
- **Reread parts** that are challenging.
- **Write down boldfaced key concepts.**
- **Define key concepts** using context or a dictionary.
- **Record answers you find to your questions. Ask additional questions** you may have.
- **Keep these questions in mind** as you read: *What does this mean? How does it connect with what I already know about the topic? What will probably come next?*

Try It!

Read your assignment. Take careful notes using the guidelines above.

Reciting Out Loud

After you complete the entire reading, recite or repeat the information out loud to evaluate how well you understand it. Use the following guidelines:

- **Recite the main points** without looking at your notes.
- **Answer the 5 W and H** questions (*Who? What? Where? When? Why?* and *How?*) about the material.
- **Discuss (and answer) your other questions** about the topic.
- **Identify any new questions** that occur to you.

Try It!

Recite what you have learned from your reading assignment. Use the guidelines above to complete this step.

After You Read

Having completed the first four steps in the SQ3R method, it's time to review the reading. Reviewing will help you reinforce what you have learned.

Reviewing the Material

A final **review** of your reading assignment will make the information part of your own thinking. Use the following guidelines:

- **Go over your notes** one section at a time.
- **Keep searching** if you have any unanswered questions.
- **Ask for help** if you cannot figure out something on your own.
- **Add illustrations or graphic organizers** to your notes to make complex ideas clearer.
- **Summarize the reading** at the end of your notes.

In the example below, Jeremy summarized the article in a paragraph and added his own thoughts in the margin.

Sample Summary

"Global Warming"—Summary

This article shows both sides of the debate on global warming. Recent scientific studies find that the earth's temperature will continue to rise because of greenhouse gases discharged by industrial activity. This data caused some people to call for stronger regulations on industries that contribute to the greenhouse effect. This issue was debated in the U.S. Senate. Some senators support tougher regulations. Others think they aren't necessary and would stall economic development. These senators have asked for a reevaluation of the data.

I want to know how economic development would be stalled by imposing tougher regulations.

Global warming is a major problem. We have to do something about it!

Try It!

Review your reading assignment. Go over your notes and summarize the assignment. Be sure to include all the main ideas.

Reading Fiction

Fiction uses made-up characters and events to reveal what is real or true about life. This means fiction has something important for you to learn. Here are some tips for reading fiction.

Before you read . . .

- **Learn something about the author** and his or her other works.
- **React thoughtfully** to the title and opening pages.

As you read . . .

- **Identify** the following story elements: *setting, tone, main characters, central conflict,* and *theme.*
- **Predict** what will happen next.
- **Think** about the characters and what they do.
  - What motivates them?
  - Have you encountered people similar to these characters?
  - Have you faced situations similar to the ones faced by the main characters?
  - Would you have reacted in the same way?
- **Write** your reactions to the short story or novel in a reading journal as you go along.
- **Consider** how the author's life may have influenced the story.
- **Notice** the author's style and word choice. (See pages **298–299**.)
  - How effectively has the author used literary devices?
  - Why do you think the author used a particular word or phrase?
- **Discuss** the story with others who are reading it.

After you read . . .

- **Consider** how the main character changes during the course of the story. Often, this is the key to understanding a work of fiction.
- **Determine** the story's main message or theme; then decide how effectively this message is communicated.

Try It!

Use the information above as a guide to help you better understand and enjoy the next short story or novel you read.

Reacting to Fiction

The excerpt below is from George Eliot's famous novel *Silas Marner*. The margin notes reveal one student's reactions, which he wrote in his own paperback copy of the novel.

From *Silas Marner*
By George Eliot

It was fifteen years since Silas Marner had first come to Raveloe; he was then simply a pallid young man, with prominent short-sighted brown eyes, whose appearance would have had nothing strange for people of average culture and experience, but for the villagers near whom he had come to settle it had mysterious peculiarities which corresponded with the exceptional nature of his occupation, and his <u>advent</u> from an unknown region called "North'ard." So had his way of life:—he invited no comer to step across his door-sill, and he never strolled into the village to drink a pint at the Rainbow, or to gossip at the wheelwright's: he sought no man or woman, save for the purposes of his calling, or in order to supply himself with necessaries; and it was soon clear to the Raveloe lasses that he would never urge one of them to accept him against her will—quite as if he had heard them declare that they would never marry a dead man come to life again. This view of Marner's personality was not without another ground than his pale face and unexampled eyes; for Jem Rodney, the mole-catcher, <u>averred</u> that one evening as he was returning homeward, he saw Silas Marner leaning against a stile with a heavy bag on his back, instead of resting the bag on the stile as a man in his senses would have done; and that, on coming up to him, he saw that Marner's eyes were set like a dead man's, and he spoke to him, and shook him, and his limbs were stiff, and his hands clutched the bag as if they'd been made of iron; but just as he had made up his mind that the weaver was dead, he came all right again, like, as you might say, in the winking of an eye, and said "Good night," and walked off.

Margin notes:

"Advent" means "arrival."

Why did he keep so much to himself?

"Averred" means "to verify something as the truth."

I like this part. It gives me a spooky feeling. I can imagine how Jem felt.

What was in the bag?

"My opinion is that a poet should express the emotion of all the ages and the thought of his own."
—Thomas Hardy

Reading Poetry

You may not understand a poem completely in one reading, especially if it is lengthy or complex. In fact, each time you reread a poem, you will probably discover something new about it. Reacting to poetry in a reading journal will help you to appreciate it more. (See the next page.) Here are some strategies for reading poetry.

First Reading

- **Read the poem** at your normal reading speed to gain an overall first impression.
- **Jot down brief notes** about your immediate reaction to the poem.

Second Reading

- **Read the poem again**—out loud, if possible. Pay attention to the sound of the poem.
- **Note examples of sound devices** in the poem—alliteration, assonance, rhyme (see pages **340–341**). Finding a poem's phrasing and rhythm can help you discover its meaning.
- **Observe** the punctuation, spacing, and special treatment of words and lines.
- **Think** about what the poem is saying.

Third Reading

- **Identify** the type of poem you're reading. Does this poem follow the usual pattern of that particular type? If not, why not?
- **Determine** the literal sense or meaning of the poem. What is the poem about? What does it seem to say about its topic?
- **Look** for figurative language in the poem. How does this language—metaphors, similes, personification, symbols—support or add to the meaning of the poem? (See pages **340–341**.)

Try It!

Use the strategies above as a guide the next time you read a poem.

Reacting to Poetry

"The Apartment House" is a poem by Joyce Kilmer. The notes on the copy of the poem below show one student's reaction. She makes observations, asks questions, comments on word choice, and so forth. Whenever you read a challenging poem, try to react to it in several different ways.

"The Apartment House"
by Joyce Kilmer

In the first stanza, the poet creates a sad tone.

Severe against the pleasant arc of sky
The great stone box is cruelly displayed.
The street becomes more dreary from its shade,
And vagrant breezes touch its walls and die.
Here sullen convicts in their chains might lie,
Or slaves toil dumbly at some dreary trade.
How worse than folly is their labor made
Who cleft the rocks that this might rise on high!

The poem is a sonnet.

What are "vagrant breezes"?

What does "cleft" mean?

In the second stanza, despair turns to joy and hope.

Yet, as I look, I see a woman's face
Gleam from a window far above the street.
This is a house of homes, a sacred place,
By human passion made divinely sweet.
How all the building thrills with sudden grace
Beneath the magic of Love's golden feet!

Try It!

Write freely for 5 to 10 minutes when you finish reading a poem. Include any thoughts or feelings you have about the poem. Relate it to other poems you have read.

Summarizing and Paraphrasing

What is the best way to understand challenging reading material? One good way is to write about it. When you use writing to explore your thoughts and feelings about new information, you make that information part of your own thinking, which in turn helps you learn it. Summarizing and paraphrasing are two very similar and equally effective writing-to-learn activities. As you explore these activities, you will come to appreciate writing as a valuable learning tool.

When you summarize, you highlight the main points, reasons, and arguments, instead of writing down every detail. Paraphrasing is like summarizing, but it requires you to interpret the main points and put them into your own words. In this chapter, you will see examples of both kinds of writing and write your own summaries and paraphrases.

- **Sample Article and Summary**
- **Guidelines for Summarizing**
- **Summarize an Article**
- **Strategies for Paraphrasing**
- **Sample Paragraphs and Paraphrases**
- **Paraphrase a Paragraph**

"It is my ambition to say in ten sentences what others say in a whole book."

—Friedrich Nietzsche

"The discipline of real learning consists of The Self and The Others flowing into each other."

—Ken Macrorie

Sample Article

The following article is about the Global Positioning System, or GPS.

Where on Earth?

Global Positioning System, or GPS, is a worldwide radio navigation system developed by the United States Department of Defense. Its purpose is to pinpoint exact locations on Earth. The system consists of a "constellation" of satellites and ground-based receivers. The receivers can be placed almost anywhere: in motor vehicles, ships, planes, farm machinery, and so forth. The network of GPS satellites, in perpendicular orbit around the earth, transmits signals that can determine with great accuracy where the receivers are located.

The system works by triangulating a position using three coordinates, in this case, satellites, to identify a location. Each GPS satellite transmits data that indicates its position and the current time. The distance from the receiver to the satellites is determined by estimating the amount of time it takes for the satellite signals to reach the receiver. Data received collectively from three satellites calculates latitude and longitude. Data from a fourth satellite adds the dimension of altitude. The basic GPS signal is accurate to within approximately 328 feet lateral and 459 vertical everywhere on earth.

Initially, GPS was created to meet military needs, but today the use of GPS is expanding worldwide. Here are a few nonmilitary applications of GPS: Fire and rescue personnel use GPS to locate emergencies and plot the perimeter of forest fires. Pilots use GPS to find their way through the skies. Mapping, construction, and surveying companies rely on GPS to pinpoint locations. GPS is also used for roadside assistance, navigation of farm equipment, and location of lost pets.

Today, many people are purchasing GPS receivers. They are affordable, and sales have skyrocketed as consumers find more and more uses for the technology. With the Global Positioning System in place, there is a distinct address for every square yard on earth, and the future of GPS is as unlimited as the imagination.

Sample Summary

The following paragraph is a student summary of the preceding article. Pay special attention to the three main parts: the topic sentence, the body, and the closing sentence. (See the side notes.)

The **topic sentence** states the main idea.

Each sentence in the **body** summarizes part of the article.

The **closing sentence** adds a final thought.

Global Positioning System

GPS is a worldwide radio navigation system used to pinpoint locations on Earth. It consists of a network of satellites and ground-based receivers. Signals from the satellites can accurately determine the latitude, longitude, and altitude of any given receiver. GPS was initially created and used by the military, but today many businesses and consumers rely on the technology. The receivers are affordable and available to the public. **Since GPS provides an "address" for every square yard on Earth, the future of the system is unlimited.**

Respond to the reading. Answer the following questions.

Ideas (1) What is the main idea of the summary? (2) What details from the article are *not* included in the summary? Name two.

Organization (3) Does the summary paragraph follow the basic organization of the article? Explain.

Voice & Word Choice (4) How does the writer show that she or he has a clear understanding of the article? Identify two phrases or ideas from the summary in your explanation.

Tip

An effective summary includes only the necessary facts. Names, dates, times, places, and similar information are usually necessary, but examples and descriptive details are not.

Guidelines for Summarizing

Follow the guidelines below whenever you are asked to write a summary.

Prewriting

- **Select an article** on a topic that interests you or relates to a subject you are currently studying. Make a photocopy of the article if possible.
- **Read the article once, quickly.** Then read it again and underline passages (if working on a photocopy) or take notes on the key details.
- **Think about the article.** Identify and write down the main idea. For example, here is the main idea of the sample article: **GPS is a worldwide radio navigation system used for pinpointing locations on Earth.**

Writing

Write a summary paragraph.

- **Write a topic sentence** that states the main idea of the article.
- **Write body sentences** that communicate the most important ideas of the article.
- **Conclude** by reminding your reader of the main point of the article. (A summary should *not* contain your personal opinions.)

Revising **and** Editing

Read and revise your summary and make necessary changes. Also edit for conventions. Ask yourself the following questions:

Ideas *Do I correctly identify the article's main idea in my topic sentence? Do my body sentences contain only the most important details from the article?*

Organization *Does my paragraph arrange ideas in the same order used in the article?*

Voice *Does my voice sound informed and interested?*

Word Choice *Have I used my own words for the most part? Have I defined unfamiliar terms?*

Sentence Fluency *Have I varied sentence structures and lengths?*

Conventions *Have I eliminated all errors in punctuation, spelling, and grammar?*

Summarizing an Article

The following article is about the history of time.

It's About Time

Since the beginning of recorded history, in every culture, people have been obsessed with measuring calendar time. Ancient civilizations relied on the motion of celestial bodies—the sun, moon, planets, and stars—to measure seasons, days, months, and years. In ancient Europe, ice-age hunters scratched marks onto bones and sticks to count days between the phases of the moon. But the calendar, as we know it today, began evolving 5,000 years ago with the Sumerians.

Sumerians in the Tigris-Euphrates Valley measured time using lunar cycles. They divided their calendar into 12 lunar months and added a 13th month every several years to keep the calendar synchronized with the seasons. This crude system worked until the days of the Roman Empire when priests had the duty of maintaining the calendar. They did not pay close attention to coordinating it with the seasons, and by the time Julius Caesar was emperor, in 46 B.C.E., spring months were occurring in summer.

Caesar went about improving the lunar calendar by borrowing an idea from an Egyptian astronomer. The astronomer said that a year was closest to 365 days and that by adding a day every 4 years, the calendar and seasons would be in sync. Caesar decreed his new calendar the official measurement of time, and he gave the 12 lunar months new symbolic names. This calendar, the Julian calendar, proved better than the lunar one, but it was slightly short of accurate.

In 1582, Pope Gregory XIII adjusted the calendar again. He removed 10 days and declared that years divisible by 100 should not have leap days. This new calendar, the Gregorian calendar, was very similar to the one we use today. However, it took several hundred years for the calendar to become Earth's most widely used measurement of time.

Try It!

Summarize the article above. Write a summary paragraph about this article, using the guidelines provided on page **486**.

Strategies for Paraphrasing

A paraphrase is a type of summary that is very effective for clarifying or explaining the meaning of an important passage that you would like to use in your research. A summary is shorter than the original text and attempts to state its meaning. A paraphrase, on the other hand, is sometimes longer than the original material and tries to *interpret* its meaning. Use the following strategies as a guide when you paraphrase.

Follow a plan: In order to complete an effective paraphrase, you must follow a series of important steps. There are no shortcuts.

- **Review the entire passage.** This will help you identify the main point and purpose of the material.
- **Carefully read the passage.** If necessary, reread parts that seem especially important or challenging.
- **Write your paraphrase.** Be sure your interpretation is clear and complete. For the most part, use your own words. (See below.)
- **Check your paraphrase.** Make sure that you have captured the tone and meaning of the passage.

Use your own words: Avoid the original writer's words as much as possible. Exceptions include key words (*tribe, repertory theater*) or proper nouns (*Iroquois, Lake Erie, New York*).

- **Consult a dictionary.** Refer to a dictionary to help you think of new ways to express certain terms or ideas.
- **Refer to a thesaurus.** Find synonyms to use in place of words in the original text. For example, if the writer is describing an empire, a thesaurus will suggest synonyms such as *domain, realm,* and *kingdom.* Pick the synonym that fits the context of the passage.

Capture the original voice: In a paraphrase, you should try to communicate the original writer's opinions and feelings. Read the examples that follow.

Original News Report

> Police Chief Greg Hartman announced that he is frustrated by students loitering at the construction site.

- **Paraphrase lacking voice:** Chief Hartman mentioned that he disapproves of students spending time at the construction site.
- **Paraphrase with the proper voice:** Chief Hartman complained about groups of students lingering at the construction site.

Sample Paragraphs and Paraphrases

The following expository paragraph describes how ancient Greek coins were made.

> The ancient Greeks began minting their own coins around 600 B.C.E. These coins were mostly silver and imprinted with a mint mark—a picture or symbol identifying where the coin was made. The mint marks on the coins were different for each city. A coin was made by putting a small lump of silver onto an iron mold. The silver was struck with a hammer that was also fixed with a mold. In this way, the silver was compacted, and the mint mark was imprinted into both sides of the coin.

A student wrote the following paraphrase to demonstrate her understanding of the above paragraph.

> Ancient Greek coins were mostly silver. A mint mark identified in which city a coin was made. A lump of silver was put on an iron mold and hit with a hammer. The mold and the hammer were both stamped with a mint mark. So the mark was inscribed on both sides of a coin.

The following paragraph is a brief published review of a community theater production.

> Don't miss the local theater guild's production of "A Child's Christmas in Wales." Director Drew Gates does an outstanding job of bringing to life Dylan Thomas's holiday classic. Right away, you will find yourself carried into a lush tapestry of childhood memories and Welsh melodies. As usual, the talented cast does not disappoint. It is as if we are observing real people caught in the midst of life. This heartwarming production is the guild's best performance of the year!

A student wrote this paraphrase of the review taking care to reflect the writer's opinion in his paraphrase.

> Be sure to see the theater guild's production of "A Child's Christmas in Wales." Director Drew Gates does an outstanding job of bringing the story to life. The cast realistically presents childhood memories mixed with Welsh melodies. This is the theater's best show of the year.

Paraphrasing a Paragraph

Here are three sample paragraphs. Each has a main idea and a distinct author's voice.

> No one tendency in life in America today is more characteristic than the desire to take to the woods. Sometimes it disguises itself under the name of science; sometimes it is mingled with hunting and the desire to kill; often it is sentimentalized and leads strings of gaping "students" bird-hunting through the wood lot. Again, it perilously resembles a desire to escape from civilization and go "on the loose." Say your worst of it; still the fact remains that more Americans go back to nature annually than any civilized men before them.

> Avian influenza (bird flu) can be transmitted among birds worldwide. Specific species, most often water birds, act as hosts for the virus by carrying it in their intestines. They pass the virus via nasal secretions, saliva, and feces. Most often, the host birds do not become ill with the virus. Other susceptible birds, including domesticated chickens and ducks, get sick when they are exposed to contaminated surfaces and materials. Avian influenza can also occur in people. Most cases of human infection come from direct contact with an infected bird or a contaminated surface.

> Many portraits of George Washington exist, but until now, no one knew exactly what he looked like. Researchers at Arizona State University and the University of Pittsburgh have used data from sculptures, paintings, artifacts, and written records to create accurate three-dimensional computer models of the first president. The models show Washington at three different stages of life and include exact details, like eye color and skin texture. These models are being used to create life-sized replicas of Washington, which will be on display, beginning October 2006, at Mount Vernon.

◤ Try It!

Paraphrase a paragraph. Paraphrase one of the paragraphs above. Communicate all important details, including the author's point of view, in your own words. Use the strategies on page 488 to guide you.

Understanding Writing Assignments

Have you ever been asked to analyze a short story or summarize a key historical event? Easier said than done, right? Or how about evaluating a recent political decision? Not so simple. The truth is, analyzing, summarizing, and evaluating can be hard work, especially in some of your more challenging classes. Don't worry. There are strategies that will help you accomplish thinking and writing tasks like these.

This chapter explains six basic levels of thinking as they relate to writing assignments. These levels are *recalling, understanding, applying, analyzing, synthesizing,* and *evaluating.* As you work on an assignment, you will often use more than one type of thinking.

- **Types of Assignments**
- **Levels of Thinking**
- **Planning Your Writing Time**

"Imagination is a valuable asset . . . and she has a sister, understanding. . . . Together they make a splendid team."

—Alice Foote MacDougall

Types of Assignments

Throughout your school career, you will most often be assigned one of three basic types of writing assignments: specific, open-ended, or a combination of the two.

Types	Examples
Specific You are given a specific topic.	Explain the history of Veterans Day.
Open-ended You are given the chance to select your own topic.	Write a biographical essay about a person of significance who lived during the 1960s.
Combination You are given a subject area from which to choose a topic. This type of assignment is part specific and part open-ended.	Describe an important event that occurred in the United States during the women's suffrage movement.

Try It!

Label each assignment below as open-ended, specific, or a combination.

1. Explain the importance of the world's rain forests.

2. Share any anecdote about Abraham Lincoln that reveals an important trait of his personality.

3. Write a personal narrative about your early school years.

Understanding Your Task

Different types of writing assignments require you to use different levels of thinking, ranging from simply recalling information to understanding, applying, analyzing, synthesizing, or evaluating it. Because assignments can vary so widely, it's important that you clearly understand what you're being asked to do before you begin. Once you understand the assignment, you can confidently plan and carry out your writing.

Levels of Thinking

The chart on this page describes the levels of thinking required for different types of assignments; the next six pages give a closer look at each one.

When you are asked to . . .   **Be ready to . . .**

RECALL ──────────────────→ **Remember what you have learned.**

underline	circle
list	match
name	label
cluster	define

- collect information
- list details
- identify or define key terms
- remember main points

UNDERSTAND ──────────────→ **Explain what you have learned.**

explain	review
summarize	restate
describe	cite

- give examples
- restate important details
- tell how something works

APPLY ────────────────────→ **Use what you have learned.**

change	illustrate
do	model
demonstrate	show
locate	organize

- select the most important details
- organize information
- explain a process
- show how something works

ANALYZE ───────────────────→ **Break down information.**

break down	rank
examine	compare
contrast	classify
tell why	

- carefully examine a subject
- identify important parts
- make connections and comparisons

SYNTHESIZE ─────────────────→ **Shape information into a new form.**

combine	connect
speculate	design
compose	create
predict	develop
invent	imagine

- invent a better way to do something
- blend the old with the new
- predict or hypothesize (make an educated guess)

EVALUATE ──────────────────→ **Judge the worth of information.**

recommend	judge
criticize	argue
persuade	rate
convince	assess
weigh	

- point out a subject's strengths and weaknesses
- evaluate its clarity, accuracy, value, and so on
- convince others of its value/worth

Assignments

Recalling Information

The most basic type of thinking students use in school is **recalling**. You will use this type of thinking when you are asked to remember and repeat something you have learned.

You recall when you . . .

- supply details such as dates or other facts.
- identify or define key terms.
- remember main points.

Recalling

Most of your writing assignments will require that you do more than simply recall information. However, you may encounter multiple-choice, fill-in-the-blank, and short-answer test questions that ask you to do no more than recall what you have learned. For example, the test questions below ask students to remember key artistic concepts.

Directions: Underline the correct answer in each set of parentheses.

1. The French artist (Pierre-Auguste Renoir, <u>Claude Monet</u>, Eugéne Boudin) found inspiration for his paintings in his gardens.
2. Medieval manuscript illustration often used the color ultramarine. It was made from (<u>lapis lazuli</u>, copper, carbon).

Directions: Define each term by completing the sentence.

1. The term *contrast* means _____

   _____

2. Trompe *l'oeil* is _____

   _____

3. The *fresco* technique consists of _____

   _____

Try It!

Review your notes from a recent classroom lecture and underline key ideas. Set the notes aside and write down all of the details you can recall. Check your notes again to see how much you were able to remember.

Understanding Information

Understanding is a level of thinking that is more advanced than simply recalling facts and information. You show that you understand something when you can write about it in your own words.

You understand when you . . .

- explain how something works.
- provide reasons for something.
- summarize or rewrite information in your own words.

Understanding

You may be asked to show your understanding of a topic by writing an essay or a paragraph. Graphic organizers, charts, and maps can also be used to show understanding. The assignment below asks the writer to explain an art style.

Directions: Explain the surrealistic art style. Highlight two surrealistic artists in your explanation.

Surrealism is an art style that began in France in the 1920s. The subjects of surrealistic art were based on subconscious thought such as dreams. The style was greatly influenced by the work of the psychiatrists Sigmund Freud and Carl Gustav Jung. Surrealistic art shows unexpected objects in a fantasy or dreamlike setting. Two well-known artists from the surrealistic period are René Magritte and Salvador Dali. One of Magritte's most famous paintings is <u>Son of Man</u>, which shows a man dressed in a suit with a large, green apple blocking his face. Magritte said of this painting, "Everything we see hides another thing." Salvador Dali's most famous painting is <u>The Persistence of Memory</u>. It shows four pocket watches melting in the middle of a barren landscape. The painting is based on a vision that Dali had while eating a snack of soft cheese! Surrealism is not reality, as we experience it, but imagination tinted by reality that has been twisted by dreams.

Try It!

Write a paragraph that explains your understanding of a style of music, a method of cooking, or the features of an ethnic celebration.

Applying Information

When **applying** information, you use what you have learned to demonstrate or accomplish something. For example, using a manual to help you set up your computer requires that you understand the information and then apply what you have read to complete the process.

You apply when you . . .

- think about how you can use information.
- organize information so that it meets your specific needs.

Applying

Sometimes you will be asked to apply one type of information to another situation or idea. This assignment asks the writer to apply a specific invention, the camera, to the development of a style of art.

Assignment: Describe how the invention of the camera changed the impressionistic art style.

Impressionism is an art style based on realism. Subjects often include landscapes and real people doing everyday things. Impressionists paid close attention to detail, trying to capture a moment as accurately as possible. The invention of the camera had a great effect on impressionism because it allowed artists to capture a scene for later study. Impressionists were also intrigued by the odd, unbalanced images that a camera captured. As a result, the composition of the paintings took on a new form. Figures were cropped at a painting's edge to suggest motion, and the action was sometimes pushed to the corners leaving the center empty. The invention of motion picture cameras allowed impressionists to experiment even further with movement. For example, Monet discovered that slow shutter speeds created a blurred effect. He began to use this effect in his paintings. Because of the camera, the exact realism of impressionism gave way to a freer art style as artists incorporated their own ideas and feelings into their work.

Try It!

Write a paragraph explaining how a particular invention has significantly changed how you and your classmates do something.

Analyzing Information

When **analyzing** information, you are able to break it down into parts that you can further explain.

You analyze when you . . .

- show how things are similar or different.
- identify which things are most important.
- arrange things in groups or categories.
- carefully examine a subject.
- discuss causes and/or effects.

Analyzing

Assignments that ask you to analyze information may require you to compare and contrast, discuss causes and effects, and so on. In this assignment, the writer details the process of a special type of stone sculpting.

Assignment: Examine and discuss the process of Shona stone sculpting.

The Shona tribe, from Zimbabwe, Africa, is known for transforming rock into beautiful works of art. The sculpting process begins with a stockpile of stones that have been brought from excavation sites to the Shona village. From this pile of soapstones, serpentines, and opalines, the sculptor chooses a stone. Often, he "sees" an image inside. With this idea in mind, he uses a hammer and chisel to rough out the form. He continues working with finer chisels, adding layers of details. A rasp and a file are used to smooth and shape the sculpture. Then the artist uses various grades of wet and dry sandpaper to further smooth the stone and bring out its natural color. After the sanding, the work of art is placed near a fire and warmed. Once it is removed, a coat of beeswax or polish is applied. When the stone is cool, the sculptor buffs it to remove any excess polish. The result is a beautiful sculpture that shows the natural color, texture, and grain of the stone. Shona artists add human expression to natural formations producing highly prized, one-of-a-kind works of art.

Try It!

Write a detailed paragraph that carefully examines the process you use to create a piece of art, prepare a favorite food, or complete a simple household chore.

Synthesizing Information

When you employ reasoning to combine parts into a whole, you are **synthesizing**.

You synthesize when you . . .

- add new ideas to existing information.
- use information to create a story, a poem, or other creative work.
- predict what will happen based on information you have learned.

Synthesizing

The same thing that makes synthesizing a challenge also makes it fun: you get to use your imagination. This assignment asks the writer to use information about an art style to write a poem about a specific painting.

Assignment: Create a list poem about this painting, *Windy Day at Veneux* by Alfred Sisley. Describe the painting using ideas based on the characteristics of impressionism: visible brushstrokes, light colors, open composition, emphasis on light and its changing qualities, ordinary subject matter, and unusual visual angles.

Windy Day at Veneux

A landscape stretched beneath changing skies.
Pearly-gray clouds spilled from small strokes of a brush.
The great outdoors.
Small scraps of color, blended by the viewer's eyes.
Reflections of light in an overcast sky.
Trees bending in the wind. Free-flowing.
Created for delight.

Try It!

Write a list poem about a striking photograph that you find in a newspaper or a magazine. Attach a copy of the photograph to your poem.

Evaluating Information

When you are asked to express your opinion about an important issue or to discuss the good and the bad points of a subject, you are **evaluating**. Evaluating is an advanced form of thinking that requires a more thorough understanding and analysis of information.

You evaluate when you . . .

- give your opinion and support it.
- identify both the good and the bad points of a subject.

Evaluating

An effective evaluation begins with an overall opinion and then adds supporting details. This assignment asks the writer to evaluate the influence of a famous painting on the student's thoughts about Renaissance art.

Assignment: Assess how Michelangelo's painting on the ceiling of the Sistine Chapel has influenced your thinking about Renaissance art. What questions has it raised in your mind?

The ceiling of the Sistine Chapel presents a series of paintings showing scenes from the Bible's book of Genesis. Its greatest influence on my thinking is that it helped me to better understand the idea of Neoplationism. This is a Renaissance term that says that looking at and studying beautiful objects and sacred images leads the viewer closer to God. The images that Michelangelo painted on the ceiling are so detailed and beautiful that they make me curious to learn more about the stories that they represent. I also wonder about some things. Why did Michelangelo include characters from Greek mythology in his chapel paintings? Was the Church of Rome unhappy that he showed images of sibyls? Sibyls are female prophets who were inspired by Apollo and other Greek gods. Humanism was a popular idea of the time. Did that have an effect on Michelangelo's chapel paintings? Michelangelo's paintings challenge the viewer to ponder the connection between the human and the divine and what that connection means for everyday life.

Try It!

Write a paragraph discussing some of the positive or negative aspects of a topic you are studying in one of your classes.

Planning Your Writing Time

Be sure that you completely understand a writing assignment before you begin. Use the following guidelines.

1. **Read the directions** carefully.
2. **Focus on key words**—"describe," "evaluate," and so on—in order to understand the requirements of the assignment.
3. **Ask questions** if necessary.
4. **Plan your time** so that you can complete your work without rushing. (See the schedule below.)
5. **Review and revise** your writing.

The following schedule was created by a student who was asked to write a research report for a history class. The report was due in two weeks.

Sample Schedule

Week One

Day 1 PREWRITING
- Review the assignment.
- Search for a topic.

Day 2 PREWRITING
- Choose a topic.
- Start doing research.

Day 3 PREWRITING
- Gather and organize details.
- Find a focus for the report.

Day 4 WRITING
- Begin the first draft.

Day 5 WRITING
- Complete the first draft.

Week Two

Day 1 REVISING
- Revise the draft for ideas, organization, and voice.

Day 2 REVISING
- Ask a peer to review the draft.

Day 3 REVISING
- Check word choice and sentence fluency.

Day 4 EDITING
- Check the report for convention errors.
- Proofread the final copy.

Day 5 PUBLISHING
- Turn in the final copy.

Scheduling a Timed Writing

If you must complete a writing assignment in one sitting, such as during a single class period, it is especially important to use your time wisely. For example, you might use 5 to 10 minutes at the beginning of the period to plan your writing, 30 to 40 minutes to write your draft, and 5 to 10 minutes at the end to make any necessary changes.

Improving Your Vocabulary

Do you know that the average high school graduate has a vocabulary of more than 60,000 words? That is an incredible number of words. The more words you know, the better you can understand and respond to your class work. Vocabulary building is important because it helps shape your thinking and affects your day-to-day life. You can improve your vocabulary by studying new subjects, having new experiences, reading more, and listening carefully to other people.

In this chapter, you will find a detailed glossary of prefixes, suffixes, and roots. You can refer to these regularly to learn new words. By understanding word parts, you can decode the meaning of new and challenging words like *macrocosm* and *paleontology*. Think of this chapter as your special word-building resource.

- **Understanding Word Parts**
- **Prefixes**
- **Suffixes**
- **Roots**

"For me, words are a
 form of action, capable
 of influencing change."
—Ingrid Bengis

Understanding Word Parts

Some English words such as *ground, age,* and *clock* are called base words. They cannot be broken down into parts. However, many English words are made of prefixes, suffixes, and roots. Knowing the meaning of these parts can help you figure out the meanings of the words they form.

Transmission combines . . .

- the prefix *trans* (meaning *across*)
- the root *miss* (meaning *send*)
- the suffix *ion* (meaning *act of*)

Transmission is the act of sending something across a medium.

Benevolence combines . . .

- the prefix *bene* (meaning *good* or *well*)
- the root *vol* (meaning *will*)
- the suffix *ence* (meaning *action* or *state of*)

Benevolence is the state of good will.

Try It!

Look through the following pages of prefixes, suffixes, and roots. Then write down the parts, their meanings, and a final definition for each of the following words.

1. chronometric

2. prognostic

3. misanthropy

4. premonition

5. cardiology

Learning New Words

You already know and use many common prefixes, suffixes, and roots every day. To improve your speaking and writing vocabulary, study the meanings of prefixes, suffixes, and roots that are not familiar to you. The following pages contain nearly 500 word parts. Here is how to use these pages:

1. Scan the pages until you come to a word part that is new to you.

2. Learn its meaning and at least one of the sample words listed.

3. Apply your knowledge as you encounter new words in your course work.

Prefixes

Prefixes are those word parts that come *before* the root words (*pre* = before). Depending upon its meaning, a prefix changes the intent, or sense, of the base word. As a skilled reader, you will want to know the meanings of the most common prefixes in order to figure out the meanings of unfamiliar words.

a, an [not, without] amoral (without a sense of moral responsibility), atypical, atom (not cuttable), apathy (without feeling), anesthesia (without sensation)

ab, abs, a [from, away] abnormal, abduct, absent, avert (turn away)

acro [high] acropolis (high city), acrobat, acronym, acrophobia (fear of height)

ambi, amb [both, around] ambidextrous (skilled with both hands), ambiguous

amphi [both] amphibious (living on both land and water), amphitheater

ante [before] antedate, anteroom, antebellum, antecedent (happening before)

anti, ant [against] anticommunist, antidote, anticlimax, antacid

be [on, away] bedeck, belabor, bequest, bestow, beloved

bene, bon [good, well] benefit, benefactor, benevolent, benediction, bonanza, bonus

bi, bis, bin [both, double, twice] bicycle, biweekly, bilateral, biscuit, binoculars

by [side, close, near] bypass, bystander, by-product, bylaw, byline

cata [down, against] catalog, catapult, catastrophe, cataclysm

cerebro [brain] cerebral, cerebellum

circum, circ [around] circumference, circumnavigate, circumspect, circular

co, con, col, com [together, with] copilot, conspire, collect, compose

coni [dust] coniosis (disease that comes from inhaling dust)

contra, counter [against] controversy, contradict, counterpart

de [from, down] demote, depress, degrade, deject, deprive

deca [ten] decade, decathlon, decapod

di [two, twice] divide, dilemma, dilute, dioxide, dipole, ditto

dia [through, between] diameter, diagonal, diagram, dialogue (speech between people)

dis, dif [apart, away, reverse] dismiss, distort, distinguish, diffuse

dys [badly, ill] dyspepsia (digesting badly), dystrophy, dysentery

em, en [in, into] embrace, enslave

epi [upon] epidermis (upon the skin, outer layer of skin), epitaph, epithet

eu [well] eulogize (speak well of, praise), euphony, euphemism, euphoria

ex, e, ec, ef [out] expel (drive out), ex-mayor, exorcism, eject, eccentric (out of the center position), efflux, effluent

extra, extro [beyond, outside] extraordinary (beyond the ordinary), extrovert, extracurricular

for [away, off] forswear (to renounce an oath)

fore [before in time] forecast, foretell (to tell beforehand), foreshadow

hemi, demi, semi [half] hemisphere, demitasse, semicircle (half of a circle)

hex [six] hexameter, hexagon

homo [man] Homo sapiens, homicide (killing man)

hyper [over, above] hypersensitive (overly sensitive), hyperactive

hypo [under] hypodermic (under the skin), hypothesis

il, ir, in, im [not] illegal, irregular, incorrect, immoral

in, il, im [into] inject, inside, illuminate, illustrate, impose, implant, imprison

infra [beneath] infrared, infrasonic

inter [between] intercollegiate, interfere, intervene, interrupt (break between)

intra [within] intramural, intravenous (within the veins)

intro [into, inward] introduce, introvert (turn inward)

macro [large, excessive] macrodent (having large teeth), macrocosm

mal [badly, poorly] maladjusted, malady, malnutrition, malfunction

meta [beyond, after, with] metaphor, metamorphosis, metaphysical

mis [incorrect, bad] misuse, misprint

miso [hate] misanthrope, misogynist

mono [one] monoplane, monotone, monocle, monochrome

multi [many] multiply, multiform

neo [new] neopaganism, neoclassic, neophyte, neonatal

non [not] nontaxable (not taxed), nontoxic, nonexistent, nonsense

ob, of, op, oc [toward, against] obstruct, offend, oppose, occur

oct [eight] octagon, octameter, octave, octopus

paleo [ancient] paleoanthropology (pertaining to ancient humans), paleontology (study of ancient life-forms)

para [beside, almost] parasite (one who eats beside or at the table of another), paraphrase, paramedic, parallel, paradox

penta [five] pentagon (figure or building having five angles or sides), pentameter, pentathlon

per [throughout, completely] pervert (completely turn wrong, corrupt), perfect, perceive, permanent, persuade

peri [around] perimeter (measurement around an area), periphery, periscope, pericardium, period

poly [many] polygon (figure having many angles or sides), polygamy, polyglot, polychrome

post [after] postpone, postwar, postscript, posterity

pre [before] prewar, preview, precede, prevent, premonition

pro [forward, in favor of] project (throw forward), progress, promote, prohibition

pseudo [false] pseudonym (false or assumed name), pseudopodia

quad [four] quadruple (four times as much), quadriplegic, quadratic, quadrant

quint [five] quintuplet, quintuple, quintet, quintile

re [back, again] reclaim, revive, revoke, rejuvenate, retard, reject, return

retro [backward] retrospective (looking backward), retroactive, retrorocket

se [aside] seduce (lead aside), secede, secrete, segregate

self [by oneself] self-determination, selfish, self-employed, self-service,

sesqui [one and a half] sesquicentennial (one and one-half centuries)

sex, sest [six] sexagenarian (sixty years old), sexennial, sextant, sextuplet, sestet

sub [under] submerge (put under), submarine, substitute, subsoil

suf, sug, sup, sus [from under] sufficient, suffer, suggest, support, suspend

super, supr [above, over, more] supervise, superman, supernatural, supreme

syn, sym, sys, syl [with, together] system, synthesis, synchronize (time together), synonym, sympathy, symphony, syllable

trans, tra [across, beyond] transoceanic, transmit (send across), transfusion

tri [three] tricycle, triangle, tripod, tristate

ultra [beyond, exceedingly] ultramodern, ultraviolet, ultraconservative

un [not, release] unfair, unnatural, unknown

under [beneath] underground, underlying

uni [one] unicycle, uniform, unify, universe, unique (one of a kind)

vice [in place of] vice president, viceroy, vice admiral

Numerical Prefixes

Prefix	Symbol	Multiples and Submultiples	Equivalent	Prefix	Symbol	Multiples and Submultiples	Equivalent
tera	T	10^{12}	trillionfold	centi	c	10^{-2}	hundredth part
giga	G	10^{9}	billionfold	milli	m	10^{-3}	thousandth part
mega	M	10^{6}	millionfold	micro	u	10^{-6}	millionth part
kilo	k	10^{3}	thousandfold	nano	n	10^{-9}	billionth part
hecto	h	10^{2}	hundredfold	pico	p	10^{-12}	trillionth part
deka	da	10	tenfold	femto	f	10^{-15}	quadrillionth part
deci	d	10^{-1}	tenth part	atto	a	10^{-18}	quintillionth part

Suffixes

Suffixes come at the end of a word. Very often a suffix will tell you what kind of word it is part of (noun, adverb, adjective, and so on). For example, words ending in *-ly* are usually adverbs.

able, ible [able, can do] capable, agreeable, edible, visible (can be seen)

ade [result of action] blockade (the result of a blocking action), lemonade

age [act of, state of, collection of] salvage (act of saving), storage, forage

al [relating to] sensual, gradual, manual, natural (relating to nature)

algia [pain] neuralgia (nerve pain)

an, ian [native of, relating to] Canadian, African, Floridian

ance, ancy [action, process, state] assistance, allowance, defiance, truancy

ant [performing, agent] assistant, servant

ary, ery, ory [relating to, quality, place where] dictionary, bravery, dormitory

ate [cause, make] liquidate, segregate (cause a group to be set aside)

cian [having a certain skill or art] musician, beautician, magician, physician

cule, ling [very small] molecule, ridicule, duckling (very small duck), sapling

cy [action, function] hesitancy, prophecy, normalcy (function in a normal way)

dom [quality, realm, office] freedom, kingdom, wisdom (quality of being wise)

ee [one who receives the action] employee, nominee (one who is nominated), refugee

en [made of, make] silken, frozen, oaken (made of oak), wooden, lighten

ence, ency [action, state of, quality] urgency, difference, conference

er, or [one who, that which] baker, miller, teacher, racer, amplifier, doctor

escent [in the process of] adolescent (in the process of becoming an adult), obsolescent, convalescent

ese [a native of, the language of] Japanese, Vietnamese, Portuguese

esis, osis [action, process, condition] genesis, hypnosis, neurosis, osmosis

ess [female] actress, goddess, lioness

et, ette [a small one, group] midget, octet, baronet, majorette

fic [making, causing] scientific, specific

ful [full of] frightful, careful, helpful

fy [make] fortify (make strong), simplify, amplify

hood [order, condition, quality] manhood, womanhood, brotherhood

ic [nature of, like] metallic (of the nature of metal), heroic, poetic, acidic

ice [condition, state, quality] justice, malice

id, ide [a thing connected to or belonging to] fluid, fluoride

ile [relating to, suited for, capable of] missile, juvenile, senile (related to being old)

ine [nature of] feminine, genuine, medicine

ion, sion, tion [act of, state of, result of] contagion, aversion, infection (state of being infected)

ish [origin, nature, resembling] foolish, Irish, clownish (resembling a clown)

ism [system, manner, condition, characteristic] heroism, alcoholism, Communism

ist [one who, that which] artist, dentist

ite [nature of, quality of, mineral product] Israelite, dynamite, graphite, sulfite

ity, ty [state of, quality] captivity, clarity

ive [causing, making] abusive (causing abuse), exhaustive

ize [make] emphasize, publicize, idolize

less [without] baseless, careless (without care), artless, fearless, helpless

ly [like, manner of] carelessly, forcefully, quickly, lovingly

ment [act of, state of, result] contentment, amendment (state of amending)

ness [state of] carelessness, kindness

oid [resembling] asteroid, spheroid, tabloid, anthropoid

ology [study, science, theory] anthropology, biology, geology, neurology

ous [full of, having] gracious, nervous, spacious, vivacious (full of life)

ship [office, state, quality, skill] friendship, authorship, dictatorship

some [like, apt, tending to] lonesome, threesome, gruesome

tude [state of, condition of] gratitude, multitude (condition of being many), aptitude

ure [state of, act, process, rank] culture, literature, rupture (state of being broken)

ward [in the direction of] eastward, forward, backward

y [inclined to, tend to] cheery, crafty, faulty

Roots

A *root* is a base upon which other words are built. Knowing the root of a difficult word can take you a long way toward figuring out its meaning—even without a dictionary. For that reason, learning the following roots will be very valuable to you as you read.

acer, acid, acri [bitter, sour, sharp] acrid, acerbic, acidity (sourness), acrimony

acu [sharp] acute, acupuncture

ag, agi, ig, act [do, move, go] agent (doer), agenda (things to do), agitate, navigate (move by sea), ambiguous (going both ways), action

ali, allo, alter [other] alias (a person's other name), alibi, alien (from another place), alloy, alter (change to another form)

alt [high, deep] altimeter (a device for measuring heights), altitude

am, amor [love, liking] amiable, amorous, enamored

anni, annu, enni [year] anniversary, annually (yearly), centennial (occurring once in 100 years)

anthrop [man] anthropology (study of mankind), philanthropy (love of mankind), misanthrope (hater of mankind)

anti [old] antique, antiquated, antiquity

arch [chief, first, rule] archangel (chief angel), architect (chief worker), archaic (first, very early), monarchy (rule by one person), matriarchy (rule by the mother)

aster, astr [star] aster (star flower), asterisk, asteroid, astronomy (star law), astronaut (star traveler, space traveler)

aud, aus [hear, listen] audible (can be heard), auditorium, audio, audition, auditory, audience, ausculate

aug, auc [increase] augur, augment (add to; increase), auction

auto, aut [self] autograph (self-writing), automobile (self-moving vehicle), author, automatic (self-acting), autobiography

belli [war] rebellion, belligerent (warlike or hostile)

bibl [book] Bible, bibliography (list of books), bibliomania (craze for books), bibliophile (book lover)

bio [life] biology (study of life), biography, biopsy (cut living tissue for examination)

brev [short] abbreviate, brevity, brief

cad, cas [to fall] cadaver, cadence, caducous (falling off), cascade

calor [heat] calorie (a unit of heat), calorify (to make hot), caloric

cap, cip, cept [take] capable, capacity, capture, reciprocate, accept, except, concept

capit, capt [head] decapitate (to remove the head from), capital, captain, caption

carn [flesh] carnivorous (flesh eating), incarnate, reincarnation

caus, caut [burn, heat] caustic, cauterize (to make hot, to burn)

cause, cuse, cus [cause, motive] because, excuse (to attempt to remove the blame or cause), accusation

ced, ceed, cede, cess [move, yield, go, surrender] procedure, secede (move aside from), proceed (move forward), cede (yield), concede, intercede, precede, recede, success

centri [center] concentric, centrifugal, centripetal, eccentric (out of center)

chrom [color] chrome, chromosome (color body in genetics), chromosphere, monochrome (one color), polychrome

chron [time] chronological (in order of time), chronometer (time measured), chronicle (record of events in time), synchronize (make time with, set time together)

cide, cise [cut down, kill] suicide (killing of self), homicide (human killer), pesticide (pest killer), germicide (germ killer), precise (cut exactly right), incision, scissors

cit [to call, start] incite, citation, cite

civ [citizen] civic (relating to a citizen), civil, civilian, civilization

clam, claim [cry out] exclamation, clamor, proclamation, reclamation, acclaim

clud, clus, claus [shut] include (to take in), conclude, claustrophobia (abnormal fear of being shut up, confined), recluse (one who shuts himself away from others)

cognosc, gnosi [know] recognize (to know again), incognito (not known), prognosis (forward knowing), diagnosis

cord, cor, cardi [heart] cordial (hearty, heartfelt), concord, discord, courage, encourage (put heart into), discourage (take heart out of), core, coronary, cardiac

corp [body] corporation (a legal body), corpse, corpulent

cosm [universe, world] cosmic, cosmos (the universe), cosmopolitan (world citizen), cosmonaut, microcosm, macrocosm

crat, cracy [rule, strength] democratic, autocracy

crea [create] creature (anything created), recreation, creation, creator

cred [believe] creed (statement of beliefs), credo (a creed), credence (belief), credit (belief, trust), credulous (believing too readily, easily deceived), incredible

cresc, cret, crease, cru [rise, grow] accrue (to grow), crescendo (growing in loudness or intensity), concrete (grown together, solidified), increase, decrease

crit [separate, choose] critical, criterion (that which is used in choosing), hypocrite

cur, curs [run] concurrent, current (running or flowing), concur (run together, agree), incur (run into), recur, occur, precursor (forerunner), cursive

cura [care] curator, curative, manicure (caring for the hands)

cycl, cyclo [wheel, circular] Cyclops (a mythical giant with one eye in the middle of his forehead), unicycle, bicycle, cyclone (a wind blowing circularly, a tornado)

deca [ten] decade, decalogue, decathlon

dem [people] democracy (people-rule), demography (vital statistics of the people: deaths, births, and so on), epidemic (on or among the people)

dent, dont [tooth] dental (relating to teeth), denture, dentifrice, orthodontist

derm [skin] hypodermic (injected under the skin), dermatology (skin study), epidermis (outer layer of skin), taxidermy (arranging skin; mounting animals)

dict [say, speak] diction (how one speaks, what one says), dictionary, dictate, dictator, dictaphone, dictatorial, edict, predict, verdict, contradict, benediction

doc [teach] indoctrinate, document, doctrine

domin [master] dominate, predominant, dominion, domain

don [give] donate, condone

dorm [sleep] dormant, dormitory

dox [opinion, praise] doxy (belief, creed, or opinion), orthodox (having the correct, commonly accepted opinion), heterodox (differing opinion), paradox (contradictory)

drome [run, step] syndrome (run-together symptoms), hippodrome (a place where horses run)

duc, duct [lead] produce, induce (lead into, persuade), seduce (lead aside), reduce, aqueduct (water leader or channel), viaduct, conduct

dura [hard, lasting] durable, duration, endurance

dynam [power] dynamo (power producer), dynamic, dynamite, hydrodynamics

endo [within] endoral (within the mouth), endocardial (within the heart), endoskeletal

equi [equal] equinox, equilibrium

erg [work] energy, erg (unit of work), allergy, ergophobia (morbid fear of work), ergometer, ergonomic

fac, fact, fic, fect [do, make] factory (place where workers make goods of various kinds), fact (a thing done), manufacture, amplification, confection

fall, fals [deceive] fallacy, falsify

fer [bear, carry] ferry (carry by water), coniferous (bearing cones, as a pine tree), fertile (bearing richly), defer, infer, refer

fid, fide, feder [faith, trust] confidante, Fido, fidelity, confident, infidelity, infidel, federal, confederacy

fila, fili [thread] filament (a single thread or threadlike object), filibuster, filigree

fin [end, ended, finished] final, finite, finish, confine, fine, refine, define, finale

fix [attach] fix, fixation (the state of being attached), fixture, affix, prefix, suffix

flex, flect [bend] flex (bend), reflex (bending back), flexible, flexor (muscle for bending), inflexibility, reflect, deflect

flu, fluc, fluv [flowing] influence (to flow in), fluid, flue, flush, fluently, fluctuate (to wave in an unsteady motion)

form [form, shape] form, uniform, conform, deform, reform, perform, formative, formation, formal, formula

fort, forc [strong] fort, fortress (a strong place), fortify (make strong), forte (one's strong point), fortitude, enforce

fract, frag [break] fracture (a break), infraction, fragile (easy to break), fraction (result of breaking a whole into equal parts), refract (to break or bend)

gam [marriage] bigamy (two marriages), monogamy, polygamy (many spouses or marriages)

gastr(o) [stomach] gastric, gastronomic, gastritis (inflammation of the stomach)

gen [birth, race, produce] genesis (birth, beginning), genetics (study of heredity), eugenics (well born), genealogy (lineage by race, stock), generate, genetic

geo [earth] geometry (earth measurement), geography (earth writing), geocentric (earth centered), geology

germ [vital part] germination (to grow), germ (seed; living substance, as the germ of an idea), germane

gest [carry, bear] congest (bear together, clog), congestive (causing clogging), gestation

gloss, glot [tongue] glossary, polyglot (many tongues), epiglottis

glu, glo [lump, bond, glue] glue, agglutinate (make to hold in a bond), conglomerate (bond together)

grad, gress [step, go] grade (step, degree), gradual (step-by-step), graduate (make all the steps, finish a course), graduated (in steps or degrees), progress

graph, gram [write, written] graph, graphic (written, vivid), autograph (self-writing, signature), graphite (carbon used for writing), photography (light writing), phonograph (sound writing), diagram, bibliography, telegram

grat [pleasing] gratuity (mark of favor, a tip), congratulate (express pleasure over success), grateful, ingrate (not thankful)

grav [heavy, weighty] grave, aggravate, gravity, gravitate

greg [herd, group, crowd] congregation (a group functioning together), gregarian (belonging to a herd), segregate (tending to group aside or apart)

helio [sun] heliograph (an instrument for using the sun's rays to send signals), heliotrope (a plant that turns to the sun)

hema, hemo [blood] hemorrhage (an outpouring or flowing of blood), hemoglobin, hemophilia

here, hes [stick] adhere, cohere, cohesion

hetero [different] heterogeneous (different in birth), heterosexual (with interest in the opposite sex)

homo [same] homogeneous (of same birth or kind), homonym (word with same pronunciation as another), homogenize

hum, human [earth, ground, man] humus, exhume (to take out of the ground), humane (compassion for other humans)

hydr, hydra, hydro [water] dehydrate, hydrant, hydraulic, hydraulics, hydrogen, hydrophobia (fear of water)

hypn [sleep] hypnosis, Hypnos (god of sleep), hypnotherapy (treatment of disease by hypnosis)

ignis [fire] ignite, igneous, ignition

ject [throw] deject, inject, project (throw forward), eject, object

join, junct [join] adjoining, enjoin (to lay an order upon, to command), juncture, conjunction, injunction

juven [young] juvenile, rejuvenate (to make young again)

lau, lav, lot, lut [wash] launder, lavatory, lotion, ablution (a washing away), dilute (to make a liquid thinner and weaker)

leg [law] legal (lawful; according to law), legislate (to enact a law), legislature, legitimize (make legal)

levi [light] alleviate (lighten a load), levitate, levity (light conversation; humor)

liber, liver [free] liberty (freedom), liberal, liberalize (to make more free), deliverance

liter [letters] literary (concerned with books and writing), literature, literal, alliteration, obliterate

loc, loco [place] locality, locale, location, allocate (to assign, to place), relocate (to put back into place), locomotion (act of moving from place to place)

log, logo, ogue, ology [word, study, speech] catalog, prologue, dialogue, logogram (a symbol representing a word), zoology (animal study), psychology (mind study)

loqu, locut [talk, speak] eloquent (speaking well and forcefully), soliloquy, locution, loquacious (talkative), colloquial (talking together; conversational or informal)

luc, lum, lus, lun [light] translucent (letting light come through), lumen (a unit of light), luminary (a heavenly body; someone who shines in his or her profession), luster (sparkle, shine), Luna (the moon goddess)

magn [great] magnify (make great, enlarge), magnificent, magnanimous (great of mind or spirit), magnate, magnitude, magnum

man [hand] manual, manage, manufacture, manacle, manicure, manifest, maneuver, emancipate

mand [command] mandatory (commanded), remand (order back), mandate

mania [madness] mania (insanity, craze), monomania (mania on one idea), kleptomania, pyromania (insane tendency to set fires), maniac

mar, mari, mer [sea, pool] marine (a soldier serving on shipboard), marsh (wetland, swamp), maritime (relating to the sea and navigation), mermaid (fabled sea creature, half fish, half woman)

matri [mother] maternal (relating to the mother), matrimony, matriarchate (rulership of women), matron

medi [half, middle, between, halfway] mediate (come between, intervene), medieval (pertaining to the Middle Ages), Mediterranean (lying between lands), mediocre, medium

mega [great, million] megaphone (great sound), megalopolis (great city; an extensive urban area including a number of cities), megacycle (a million cycles), megaton

mem [remember] memo (a reminder), commemoration (the act of remembering by a memorial or ceremony), memento, memoir, memorable

meter [measure] meter (a metric measure), voltameter (instrument to measure volts), barometer, thermometer

micro [small] microscope, microfilm, microcard, microwave, micrometer (device for measuring small distances), omicron, micron (a millionth of a meter), microbe (small living thing)

migra [wander] migrate (to wander), emigrate (one who leaves a country), immigrate (to come into the land)

mit, miss [send] emit (send out, give off), remit (send back, as money due), submit, admit, commit, permit, transmit (send across), omit, intermittent (sending between, at intervals), mission, missile

mob, mot, mov [move] mobile (capable of moving), motionless (without motion), motor, emotional (moved strongly by feelings), motivate, promotion, demote, movement

mon [warn, remind] monument (a reminder or memorial of a person or an event), admonish (warn), monitor, premonition (forewarning)

mor, mort [mortal, death] mortal (causing death or destined for death), immortal (not subject to death), mortality (rate of death), mortician (one who prepares the dead for burial), mortuary (place for the dead, a morgue)

morph [form] amorphous (with no form, shapeless), metamorphosis (a change of form, as a caterpillar into a butterfly), morphology

multi [many, much] multifold (folded many times), multilinguist (one who speaks many languages), multiped (an organism with many feet), multiply

nat, nasc [to be born, to spring forth] innate (inborn), natal, native, nativity, renascence (a rebirth, a revival)

neur [nerve] neuritis (inflammation of a nerve), neurology (study of nervous systems), neurologist (one who practices neurology), neural, neurosis, neurotic

nom [law, order] autonomy (self-law, self-government), astronomy, gastronomy (art or science of good eating), economy

nomen, nomin [name] nomenclature, nominate (name someone for an office)

nov [new] novel (new, strange, not formerly known), renovate (to make like new again), novice, nova, innovate

nox, noc [night] nocturnal, equinox (equal nights), noctilucent (shining by night)

numer [number] numeral (a figure expressing a number), numeration (act of counting), enumerate (count out, one by one), innumerable

omni [all, every] omnipotent (all-powerful), omniscient (all-knowing), omnipresent (present everywhere), omnivorous

onym [name] anonymous (without name), synonym, pseudonym (false name), antonym (name of opposite meaning)

oper [work] operate (to labor, function), cooperate (work together)

ortho [straight, correct] orthodox (of the correct or accepted opinion), orthodontist (tooth straightener), orthopedic (originally pertaining to straightening a child), unorthodox

pac [peace] pacifist (one for peace only; opposed to war), pacify (make peace, quiet), Pacific Ocean (peaceful ocean)

pan [all] panacea (cure-all), pandemonium (place of all the demons, wild disorder), pantheon (place of all the gods in mythology)

pater, patr [father] paternity (fatherhood, responsibility), patriarch (head of the tribe, family), patriot, patron (a wealthy person who supports as would a father)

path, pathy [feeling, suffering] pathos (feeling of pity, sorrow), sympathy, antipathy (feeling against), apathy (without feeling), empathy (feeling or identifying with another), telepathy (far feeling; thought transference)

ped, pod [foot] pedal (lever for a foot), impede (get the feet in a trap, hinder), pedestal (foot or base of a statue), pedestrian (foot traveler), centipede, tripod (three-footed support), podiatry (care of the feet), antipodes (opposite feet)

pedo [child] orthopedic, pedagogue (child leader; teacher), pediatrics (medical care of children)

pel, puls [drive, urge] compel, dispel, expel, repel, propel, pulse, impulse, pulsate, compulsory, expulsion, repulsive

pend, pens, pond [hang, weigh] pendant pendulum, suspend, appendage, pensive (weighing thought), ponderous

phil [love] philosophy (love of wisdom), philanthropy, philharmonic, bibliophile, Philadelphia (city of brotherly love)

phobia [fear] claustrophobia (fear of closed spaces), acrophobia (fear of high places), hydrophobia (fear of water)

phon [sound] phonograph, phonetic (pertaining to sound), symphony (sounds with or together)

photo [light] photograph (light-writing), photoelectric, photogenic (artistically suitable for being photographed), photosynthesis (action of light on chlorophyll to make carbohydrates)

plac [please] placid (calm, peaceful), placebo, placate, complacent

plu, plur, plus [more] plural (more than one), pluralist (a person who holds more than one office), plus (indicating that something more is to be added)

pneuma, pneumon [breath] pneumatic (pertaining to air, wind, or other gases), pneumonia (disease of the lungs)

pod *(see ped)*

poli [city] metropolis (mother city), police, politics, Indianapolis, Acropolis (high city, upper part of Athens), megalopolis

pon, pos, pound [place, put] postpone (put afterward), component, opponent (one put against), proponent, expose, impose, deposit, posture (how one places oneself), position

pop [people] population, populous (full of people), popular

port [carry] porter (one who carries), portable, transport (carry across), report, export, import, support, transportation

portion [part, share] portion (a part; a share, as a portion of pie), proportion (the relation of one share to others)

prehend [seize] comprehend (seize with the mind), apprehend (seize a criminal), comprehensive (seizing much, extensive)

prim, prime [first] primacy (state of being first in rank), prima donna (the first lady of opera), primitive (from the earliest or first time), primary, primal, primeval

proto [first] prototype (the first model made), protocol, protagonist, protozoan

psych [mind, soul] psyche (soul, mind), psychiatry (healing of the mind), psychology, psychosis (serious mental disorder), psychotherapy (mind treatment), psychic

punct [point, dot] punctual (being exactly on time), punctuation, puncture, acupuncture

reg, recti [straighten] regiment, regular, regulate, rectify (make straight), correct, direction

ri, ridi, risi [laughter] deride (mock, jeer at), ridicule (laughter at the expense of another, mockery), ridiculous, derision

rog, roga [ask] prerogative (privilege; asking before), interrogation (questioning; the act of questioning), derogatory

rupt [break] rupture (break), interrupt (break into), abrupt (broken off), disrupt (break apart), erupt (break out), incorruptible (unable to be broken down)

sacr, sanc, secr [sacred] sacred, sanction, sacrosanct, consecrate, desecrate

salv, salu [safe, healthy] salvation (act of being saved), salvage, salutation

sat, satis [enough] satient (giving pleasure, satisfying), saturate, satisfy (to give pleasure to; to give as much as is needed)

sci [know] science (knowledge), conscious (knowing, aware), omniscient (knowing everything)

scope [see, watch] telescope, microscope, kaleidoscope (instrument for seeing beautiful forms), periscope, stethoscope

scrib, script [write] scribe (a writer), scribble, manuscript (written by hand), inscribe, describe, subscribe, prescribe

sed, sess, sid [sit] sediment (that which sits or settles out of a liquid), session (a sitting), obsession (an idea that sits stubbornly in the mind), possess, preside (sit before), president, reside, subside

sen [old] senior, senator, senile (old; showing the weakness of old age)

sent, sens [feel] sentiment (feeling), consent, resent, dissent, sentimental (having strong feeling or emotion), sense, sensation, sensitive, sensory, dissension

sequ, secu, sue [follow] sequence (following of one thing after another), consequence, sequel, subsequent, prosecute, consecutive (following in order), second (following "first"), ensue, pursue

serv [save, serve] servant, service, preserve, subservient, servitude, conserve, deserve, reservation, conservation

sign, signi [sign, mark, seal] signal (a gesture or sign to call attention), signature (the mark of a person written in his or her own handwriting), design, insignia (distinguishing marks)

simil, simul [like, resembling] similar (resembling in many respects), assimilate (to make similar to), simile, simulate (pretend; put on an act to make a certain impression)

sist, sta, stit [stand] persist (stand firmly; unyielding; continue), assist (to stand by with help), circumstance, stamina (power to withstand, to endure), status (standing), state, static, stable, stationary, substitute (to stand in for another)

solus [alone] soliloquy, solitaire, solitude, solo

solv, solu [loosen] solvent (a loosener, a dissolver), solve, absolve (loosen from, free from), resolve, soluble, solution, resolution, resolute, dissolute (loosened morally)

somnus [sleep] insomnia (not being able to sleep), somnambulist (a sleepwalker)

soph [wise] sophomore (wise fool), philosophy (love of wisdom), sophisticated

spec, spect, spic [look] specimen (an example to look at, study), specific, aspect, spectator (one who looks), spectacle, speculate, inspect, respect, prospect, retrospective (looking backward), introspective, expect, conspicuous

sphere [ball, sphere] stratosphere (the upper portion of the atmosphere), hemisphere (half of the earth), spheroid

spir [breath] spirit (breath), conspire (breathe together; plot), inspire (breathe into), aspire (breathe toward), expire (breathe out; die), perspire, respiration

string, strict [draw tight] stringent (drawn tight; rigid), strict, restrict, constrict (draw tightly together), boa constrictor (snake that constricts its prey)

stru, struct [build] construe (build in the mind, interpret), structure, construct, instruct, obstruct, destruction, destroy

sume, sump [take, use, waste] consume (to use up), assume (to take; to use), sump pump (a pump that takes up water), presumption (to take or use before knowing all the facts)

tact, tang, tag, tig, ting [touch] contact, tactile, intangible (not able to be touched), intact (untouched, uninjured), tangible, contingency, contagious (able to transmit disease by touching), contiguous

tele [far] telephone (far sound), telegraph (far writing), television (far seeing), telephoto (far photography), telecast

tempo [time] tempo (rate of speed), temporary, extemporaneously, contemporary (those who live at the same time), pro tem (for the time being)

ten, tin, tain [hold] tenacious (holding fast), tenant, tenure, untenable, detention, content, pertinent, continent, obstinate, abstain, pertain, detain

tend, tent, tens [stretch, strain] tendency (a stretching; leaning), extend, intend, contend, pretend, superintend, tender, extent, tension (a stretching, strain), pretense

terra [earth] terrain, terrarium, territory, terrestrial

test [to bear witness] testament (a will; bearing witness to someone's wishes), detest, attest (bear witness to), testimony

the, theo [God, a god] monotheism (belief in one god), polytheism (belief in many gods), atheism, theology

therm [heat] thermometer, therm (heat unit), thermal, thermostat, thermos, hypothermia (subnormal temperature)

thesis, thet [place, put] antithesis (place against), hypothesis (place under), synthesis (put together), epithet

tom [cut] atom (not cuttable; smallest particle of matter), appendectomy (cutting out an appendix), tonsillectomy, dichotomy (cutting in two; a division), anatomy (cutting, dissecting to study structure)

tort, tors [twist] torture (twisting to inflict pain), retort (twist back, reply sharply), extort (twist out), distort (twist out of shape), contort, torsion (act of twisting, as a torsion bar)

tox [poison] toxic (poisonous), intoxicate, antitoxin

tract, tra [draw, pull] tractor, attract, subtract, tractable (can be handled), abstract (to draw away), subtrahend (the number to be drawn away from another)

trib [pay, bestow] tribute (to pay honor to), contribute (to give money to a cause), attribute, retribution, tributary

turbo [disturb] turbulent, disturb, turbid, turmoil

typ [print] type, prototype (first print; model), typical, typography, typewriter, typology (study of types, symbols), typify

ultima [last] ultimate, ultimatum (the final or last offer that can be made)

uni [one] unicorn (a legendary creature with one horn), unify (make into one), university, unanimous, universal

vac [empty] vacate (to make empty), vacuum (a space entirely devoid of matter), evacuate (to remove troops or people), vacation, vacant

vale, vali, valu [strength, worth] valiant, equivalent (of equal worth), validity (truth; legal strength), evaluate (find out the value), value, valor (value; worth)

ven, vent [come] convene (come together, assemble), intervene (come between), venue, convenient, avenue, circumvent (come or go around), invent, prevent

ver, veri [true] very, aver (say to be true, affirm), verdict, verity (truth), verify (show to be true), verisimilitude

vert, vers [turn] avert (turn away), divert (turn aside, amuse), invert (turn over), introvert (turn inward), convertible, reverse (turn back), controversy (a turning against; a dispute), versatile (turning easily from one skill to another)

vic, vicis [change, substitute] vicarious, vicar, vicissitude

vict, vinc [conquer] victor (conqueror, winner), evict (conquer out, expel), convict (prove guilty), convince (conquer mentally, persuade), invincible (not conquerable)

vid, vis [see] video, television, evident, provide, providence, visible, revise, supervise (oversee), vista, visit, vision

viv, vita, vivi [alive, life] revive (make live again), survive (live beyond, outlive), vivid, vivacious (full of life), vitality

voc [call] vocation (a calling), avocation (occupation not one's calling), convocation (a calling together), invocation, vocal

vol [will] malevolent, benevolent (one of goodwill), volunteer, volition

volcan, vulcan [fire] volcano (a mountain erupting fiery lava), volcanize (to undergo volcanic heat), Vulcan (Roman god of fire)

volvo [turn about, roll] revolve, voluminous (winding), voluble (easily turned about or around), convolution (a twisting)

vor [eat greedily] voracious, carnivorous (flesh eating), herbivorous (plant eating), omnivorous (eating everything), devour

zo [animal] zoo (short for zoological garden), zoology (study of animal life), zodiac (circle of animal constellations), zoomorphism (being in the form of an animal), protozoa (one-celled animals)

The Human Body

capit	head	**gastro**	stomach	**osteo**	bone
cardi	heart	**gloss**	tongue	**ped**	foot
corp	body	**hema**	blood	**pneuma**	breathe
dent	tooth	**man**	hand	**psych**	mind
derm	skin	**neur**	nerve	**spir**	breath

Writing Business Letters

Memos, e-mail messages, and business letters are common forms of workplace writing. People in the workplace usually send memos and messages to people they know. These are brief and quickly composed forms of business writing. On the other hand, people sometimes send business letters to individuals they may not know very well. Business letters are formal in tone and carefully worded.

Effective business letters get the reader's attention and prompt some action—a meeting, an agreement, a contract, or a solution to a problem. You, too, can use the business letter to get things done—both in and out of school. For example, you can write a letter requesting information for a school project, or you can write a letter of application for a job.

This chapter will give you the basic information you need to write effective business letters that get results.

- **Writing a Business Letter**
- **Parts of a Business Letter**
- **Creating an E-Mail Message**
- **Sending a Letter**

"The word that is heard perishes, but the letter that is written remains."

—Proverb

Writing a Business Letter

If you need information, resources, or a recommendation from an individual or a group, a request letter is an effective way to accomplish this task. In the following example, Katie Mathews requests information about a summer music program. (See the writing tips on the next page.)

The letter follows the correct format. (See pages 516–517.)

617 Crabtree Lane
Belleview, Nebraska 67005
April 15, 2011

Mr. Alan DeRosa
Morgan Park Middle School
1123 South Pine Street
Belleview, Nebraska 67157

Dear Mr. DeRosa:

The beginning introduces the writer.

I am a sophomore at Hayes High School in Belleview. I play first trombone in the band and have been involved in the school music programs since I was 10. My goal is to become a band director someday, and I would like to teach and direct at the middle school level.

The middle identifies the request.

Ms. Simenek, our band director, mentioned that you are starting a junior marching band this summer. Would you be interested in hiring an intern? I would appreciate the opportunity to work with younger students.

The new band sounds very exciting, and I would like to know more about your plans. You can reach me at 555-1234 or at my family's e-mail address <tmathews@our.com>.

The ending expresses thanks.

Thank you for considering my request. If you could create an internship for me, I would be very grateful.

Sincerely,

Katie Mathews

Katie Mathews

"I consider it a good rule for letter writing to leave unmentioned what the recipient already knows, and instead tell him something new."

—Sigmund Freud

Tips for Writing Letters of Request

Before you write . . .

- **Determine your purpose.**
  Know exactly what you are requesting.
- **Gather information.**
  Collect information that supports your request, including specific dates, names, places, and so on. Also think about the best way to organize the information.
- **Consider your reader.**
  Decide what your reader must know to respond to your request.

As you write . . .

- **Keep it short.**
  Stay focused on the main idea and make your point quickly.
- **State your request.**
  Be specific about what you are asking the reader to do.
- **Be courteous.**
- **Focus on the outcome.**
  What do you want the reader to do, and when, and how?

After you've written a first draft . . .

- **Check for completeness.**
  Be sure that your main point is clear and that you have included all important information.
- **Check for appropriate voice.**
  Did you use a respectful, sincere tone?
- **Check for correctness.**
  Double-check the address and spelling of all names. Correct errors in punctuation, capitalization, spelling, and grammar.

Try It!

Write a request letter to a person or organization, politely asking for help or information. (Send the letter or simply treat it as a school assignment.)

Parts of a Business Letter

Every business letter is made up of the following six parts. Each part follows a specific form and has a specific function within the letter.

1. The **heading** includes the writer's complete address and the date. Write the heading at least one inch from the top of the page, at the left margin.

2. The **inside address** includes the recipient's name, company name, street address or post office box number, and the city, state, and ZIP code.
   - If the recipient has a short title, include it on the same line as the name, preceded by a comma.
   - If the title is long, write it on the next line.

3. The **salutation** is the greeting. For business letters, use a colon after the salutation, not a comma.
   - If you know the recipient's name, use it in your greeting.
     Dear Dr. Bauer:
   - If you don't know the name of the person who will read your letter, use a salutation such as one of these:
     Dear Veterinarian:
     Dear Sir or Madam:

4. The **body** is the main part of the letter. It is organized into three parts. The beginning states why you are writing, the middle provides the needed details, and the ending focuses on what should happen next. In a business letter, double-space between the paragraphs; do not indent.

5. The **complimentary closing** follows the body of the letter. Use *Sincerely* or *Yours truly* to close a business letter. Capitalize only the first word of the closing and place a comma at the end.

6. Your **signature** ends the letter. If you are typing, leave four blank lines under the closing; then type your name. Write your signature in the space between the closing and your typed name.

Tip

The word-processing program on your computer may have templates (built-in patterns) that will help you set up your business letters. Be sure the template you choose closely follows the format of the letter on the next page.

Business-Letter Format

1 3602 Wilmore Blvd.
Burlington, VT 05001
May 1, 2011

Four to Seven Spaces

2 Dr. Kenneth Bauer, Manager
Lakeside Veterinary Clinic
8753 Lakeside Drive
Burlington, VT 05001

Double Space

3 Dear Dr. Bauer:

Double Space

I saw your advertisement for a kennel assistant in the local newspaper. I called the number in the ad, and your receptionist said that I should send you a letter of application.

Double Space

4 I am a sophomore at Burlington High School. I would be able to work weekdays after school and full-time in the summer. I have had the opportunity to work with many animals since I volunteer every Saturday at the animal shelter. This experience has made me familiar with the duties of a kennel assistant. Last year, I had a part-time job cleaning cages and aquariums at Paws and Beaks Pet Shop. My boss, Mr. Rupinski, said that he could always count on me to keep the place looking great. My goal is to study veterinary medicine in college and eventually work with zoo animals.

Double Space

If you need more information, please call me at 555-6418 or contact me at my family's e-mail address <gholten@insight.com>. Thank you for considering me for the job. I look forward to hearing from you.

Double Space

5 Yours truly,

Four Spaces

6 Alex Holten

Business Letters

Creating an E-Mail Message

E-mail has become an important, quick communication tool for teachers, students, parents, and business people. However, in spite of e-mail's delivery speed, it still takes time to write a good message. In the following e-mail message, a student asks a reference librarian for help with a writing project.

The **heading** includes the recipient's address and the subject line.

The **beginning** greets the reader and tells the reason for the e-mail message.

The **middle** asks for advice.

The **ending** politely thanks the reader for her help.

New Message

To: mchavez@tristatelib.lib.il.us

Cc:

Subject: Reference question about Mark Twain

Dear Ms. Chavez:

I am a sophomore at Kennedy High School. In literature class we are studying Mark Twain, especially his literary humor. Our assignment is to write an essay about how his humor influenced the United States after the Civil War. I read that Mark Twain did a lot of public speaking and that he was a great storyteller.

Do you know if there is an audio recording of his actual voice? I found recordings of actors pretending to be Mark Twain, but I would like to know what he actually sounded like.

If you could answer this question for me, I would really appreciate it. My essay is due a week from today, so I would need a response within the next three or four days.

Sincerely,
Zachary Manka
zmanka@kennedyhigh.edu

Tips for Writing E-Mail Messages

Show respect for the recipients of your e-mail messages. Check your spelling, punctuation, and grammar, just as you would in a more formal business letter. Use a short, relevant subject line.

Before you write . . .

- **Jot down the main points you want to make.**
  List other necessary details.
- **Complete the e-mail heading.**
  Fill in the address line by typing in each character of the address or use your address book's automatic fill-in feature. Then write a subject line that briefly indicates the reason for the e-mail message.

As you write . . .

- **Greet the reader and give your reason for writing.**
  Start with a polite greeting and explain why you are e-mailing.
- **Use a conversational but proper tone.**
  Be sure your sentences are clear and complete. Even if you use an informal voice, your grammar should be correct.
- **Briefly state your main points.**
  Include only the most important information.
- **End politely.**
  Close with *Sincerely*, or another appropriate closing. Type your name below it and add your e-mail address and phone number if you wish.

After you've written . . .

- **Review your e-mail.**
  Be sure your message is clear and complete.
- **Check for attachments.**
  Don't forget to include any attachments you refer to in your message.
- **Check for correctness.**
  Correct any errors in punctuation, capitalization, spelling, and grammar.
- **Finally, press "send."**

Try It!

Think of a school-related situation that may require an e-mail message. Write a message about the matter to a teacher or a fellow student. You may send the e-mail or simply treat it as a class assignment.

Business Letters

Sending a Letter

Letters sent through the mail will get to their destinations faster if they are properly addressed and stamped. A typed envelope or one with printed address labels is preferred for a business letter. Always include a ZIP code.

Addressing the Envelope

Place the writer's name and address in the upper left corner of the envelope and the recipient's name and address in the center. Use correct postage.

ALEX HOLTEN
3602 WILMORE BLVD
BURLINGTON VT 05001

DR KENNETH BAUER
LAKESIDE VETERINARY CLINIC
8753 LAKESIDE DR
BURLINGTON VT 05001-1234

There are two acceptable forms for addressing an envelope: the older, traditional form, often written by hand, and the new form preferred by the postal service. This is usually typed.

Traditional Form
Mr. Alan DeRosa
Morgan Park Middle School
1123 South Pine Street
Belleview, NE 67157

Postal Service Form
MR ALAN DEROSA
MORGAN PARK MIDDLE SCHOOL
1123 S PINE ST
BELLEVIEW NE 67157

Following U.S. Postal Service Guidelines

1. Capitalize everything and leave out ALL punctuation.
2. Use the list of common address abbreviations on page **660**. Use numerals rather than words for numbered streets and avenues (9TH AVE NE, 3RD ST SW).
3. If you know the ZIP + 4 code, use it.

Taking Tests

Taking a test is like giving a speech: no matter how well you prepare, you always feel somewhat nervous about what lies ahead. And that's okay. A little tension can help you remain mentally alert. But being mentally alert will only get you so far. You also need to remain focused and organized, which means keeping up with all your class work and studying effectively. Then there will be no surprises when it's time to take the test.

An effective test-taking plan should include a process for arranging the test material, reviewing it, remembering it, and, finally, applying it on the test itself. Having a good plan gives you the best chance to succeed. Studying the guidelines and samples in this chapter will improve your test-taking skills.

- **Preparing for a Test**
- **Test-Taking Tips**
- **Taking Objective Tests**
- **Taking Essay Tests**
- **Taking Standardized Tests**
- **Tips for Standardized Tests**

"By failing to prepare, you are preparing to fail."

—Benjamin Franklin

Preparing for a Test

Good test-taking preparation includes laying the groundwork in advance. Most tests cover material you heard in class lectures and read in assignments. So good class notes and good reading notes will be valuable as you study for a test, as will previous tests and graded assignments. It is especially beneficial to review material that you've had difficulty remembering or understanding. In addition to reviewing your notes and assignments, follow the guidelines given in the test-prep cycle below.

Test-Prep Cycle

Practice learning every day . . .
Pay attention in class.
Take neat, organized notes.
Complete all assignments.

Talk to your teacher . . .
Ask what you can do to improve.
Ask what to expect on the test.
Record the date and the time of the test in a planner.

After the test . . .
Talk to your teacher or to a classmate about questions you missed.

Review and study for the test . . .
Get started early. Don't leave everything until the night before.
Look over your last test and graded assignments.
Review your classroom notes and reading notes every day until the test.
Quiz yourself and study with a partner.
Focus on areas where you know you're weak.

Test day . . .
Eat a healthy breakfast.
Follow the guidelines and tips in this chapter.
Stay calm and do your best.

The night before . . .
Get a good night's rest.
Set your alarm clock.

Try It!

Consider how you prepared for your last test. Did you leave out any of the steps above? Improve your next test score by following this test-prep cycle.

Test-Taking Tips

- **Listen carefully** as your teacher gives directions, makes any corrections, or provides other information. Don't try to get a head start on the test while your teacher is talking. You may miss important comments such as these:

"You have 30 minutes to finish the test."

"Make this change in number three."

"Write your answer to the final question on the back of the test sheet."

- **Put your name on the test right away.**
- **Take a quick look at the entire test.** This will help you decide how much time to spend on each section or question.
- **Read the instructions** before you begin to answer any questions. Do exactly what they tell you to do.
- **Read each question carefully.** Be sure you understand the question completely before you answer it.
- **Answer all of the questions you are sure of first.** Then go back to the other questions and do your best to answer each one. Keep track of the time as you work on the more difficult questions.
- **Check over your answers when you finish the test.** If you skipped any really hard questions, try to answer them now.

Try It!

Review these tips right before your next test and then put them into practice. After completing the test, determine how closely you followed this advice.

Taking Objective Tests

Tests often have four different types of objective questions: true/false, matching, multiple-choice, and fill-in-the-blanks.

True/False

In a true/false test, you decide if a statement is correct or incorrect. Most true/false questions focus on the details, so read each statement carefully.

- **Look for absolutes and qualifiers.** Statements with absolutes such as *always, never, all,* and *none* are often false. Statements that use qualifiers such as *often, rarely,* and *seldom* are more likely to be true.

  False 1. Until Waterloo, Napoleon Bonaparte was never defeated on the battlefield. *(Napoleon lost many battles.)*

  True 2. Napoleon Bonaparte was often described as a great military officer.

- **Test each part.** Even if only one word or phrase in a statement is false, the whole statement is false.

  False 3. Napoleon led his troops to victory in France, Italy, Egypt, and Russia. *(Russian troops repelled Napoleon's invasion of 1812.)*

- **Watch for negatives.** Words such as *don't, can't, doesn't,* and *wasn't* can be confusing, so be sure you know what the statement means.

  False 4. Napoleon wasn't Corsican; he was born in France. *(Napoleon was born in Corsica.)*

Matching

In matching tests, you are asked to match items from one column to those in another column.

- **Read both columns before answering any questions.** This helps you find the best match for each item.
- **Match the items you know first.** If each answer is used only once, cross out the letter or number after you've used it.
- **Find grammar clues.** For example, plural subjects need plural verbs.

  C 1. "O Captain! My Captain!"   A. written by Robert Frost

  A 2. "The Road Not Taken"   B. written by Emily Dickinson

  ___ 3. "I'm Nobody! Who Are You?"   C. written by Walt Whitman

Multiple-Choice

In multiple-choice questions, you will be asked to choose the right answer from several possibilities. Sometimes your choices will include "all of the above" or "none of the above" or both.

- **Read each question carefully** and choose the best answer.

    1. The primary way liquids and gases transmit heat is by the process of

       A. reflection   C. radiation   E. None of the above

       B. conduction   D. convection

- **Anticipate the answer.** Before reading the choices, try to answer the question or complete the sentence.

- **Read all the choices before you answer.** It's tempting to choose the first answer that seems close, but there may be another choice that is better.

- **Consider "all of the above" and "none of the above" answers carefully.** If there is even one statement that you know to be false, do not choose "all of the above." If there is one statement you know to be true, do not choose "none of the above."

- **Eliminate the wrong or unlikely choices first.**

    2. The Ming Dynasty began in:

       A. 46 C.E. *(too early)*   C. 1368 C.E.

       B. 1492 C.E. *(too late)*   D. 1620 C.E. *(too late)*

Fill-in-the-Blanks

Fill-in-the-blank questions require you to complete the missing parts of a statement.

- **Check the number of blanks.** Often, there is one for each word.

    1. In India and Pakistan, feelings of nationalism are intertwined with religious conflicts between ____Muslims____ and ____Hindus____.

- **Check for grammar clues.** If there is an *a* before the blank, the answer will begin with a consonant sound. If there is an *an* before the blank, the answer will begin with a vowel sound.

    2. Each complete cycle of phases of the moon is called a ____lunation____.

Try It!

Which types of objective questions are difficult for you? Which tips will you use to help you on your next test?

Taking Essay Tests

Many students feel that the essay test is the hardest type of test. Unlike objective questions, essay questions rarely contain clues to the right answer. Essay-test prompts require you to demonstrate your knowledge of a subject and to show how facts and supporting details are connected. The next few pages offer suggestions for taking essay tests.

Understanding and Restating the Prompt

- **Read the question carefully.**
- **Underline the key words** that explain what you are being asked to do. Here are some key words and their explanations.

Cause . . . . describe how one thing has affected another.

Compare . . . . tell how things are alike.

Contrast . . . . tell how things are different.

Define . . . . . . give a clear, specific meaning for a word or an idea.

Describe . . . . use sensory details to explain how something looks, sounds, and so on.

Evaluate . . . . . make a value judgment supported by facts or examples.

Explain . . . . . . use details and facts to tell what something means or how it works, or give reasons that tell why.

Identify . . . . . answer the question using one or more of the 5 W's.

Illustrate . . . . use examples to show how something works or why it's important.

Prove . . . . use facts and details to tell why something is true.

Review . . . . . . create an overall picture of the topic.

Summarize . . tell the main idea and key points about the topic.

- **Rephrase the prompt.** It often works well to drop the key word and then use the rest of the prompt to form your thesis statement.

Prompt: Explain how the Fourteenth Amendment affected slaves.

Thesis Statement: The Fourteenth Amendment provided former slaves with many new opportunities, including United States citizenship.

Try It!

Turn each essay-test prompt below into a thesis statement. (Refer to your textbook or a Web site to find more information on these topics.)

1. Explain how the Russian Revolution and the entry of the United States into the First World War affected the outcome of the Great War.
2. Describe how Earth's climate has changed over time.

Planning a One-Paragraph Response

Tests may include one or more prompts that call for a paragraph response rather than a full-length essay. The following guidelines will help you write an effective one-paragraph response to a prompt.

- **Read the prompt carefully.** Underline the key words and phrases.
- **Identify what the prompt is asking you to do** (explain, compare, prove, define).
- **Plan your response.**
  1. Turn the prompt into a topic sentence.
  2. Include at least three supporting details. Keep your topic sentence in mind when you select these details.

Tests

Prompt

> Briefly explain why NATO was formed.

Planning Notes

Topic sentence: The North Atlantic Treaty Organization, or NATO, was formed as a defense against Soviet aggression.

Supporting details:
1. Signed on April 4, 1949
2. Protects the freedom and security of member countries
3. Alliance of 12 countries: Canada, U.S., United . . .

Response

Formation of the North Atlantic Treaty Organization

The North Atlantic Treaty Organization, or NATO, was formed as a defense against Soviet aggression. On April 4, 1949, twelve countries joined in the alliance. They were Canada, the United States, the United Kingdom, Italy, Denmark, France, Iceland, the Netherlands, Norway, Portugal, Luxembourg, and Belgium. The United States was the most powerful military member. Western European countries were afraid of an attack by the Soviet Union. NATO members believed that the Soviet Union would not attack Western Europe if they thought it would trigger a war with the United States.

Planning an Essay Response

Some essay prompts require you to respond with a full-length essay. The following tips will help you write a clear, well-organized response essay.

- **Read the prompt** and restate it as a thesis statement.
- **Plan your response** by collecting and outlining details that support your thesis.
- **Write your essay answer.** Include your thesis statement in the opening paragraph. Use each main point of your outline to form the topic sentence for a body paragraph. In the final paragraph, write a meaningful conclusion that shows you truly understand the topic.

Prompt

Describe NATO's role in the fight against terrorism.

Planning Notes

Thesis statement: Since the September 11, 2001, terrorist attack, NATO has defended and supported the United States' fight against terrorism.

Outline:
I. Immediate reaction to 9-11-01
  A. Declared the attacks as an attack against all NATO members
  B. Condemned the attacks and offered support
  C. Provided NATO radar aircraft to patrol skies over the United States
  D. Provided naval units to patrol Mediterranean
II. Reaction after 9-11
  A. Agreed in part to help in Afghanistan and Iraq
  B. Debated what areas NATO should operate in

Try It!

Choose a topic you know something about. Use it to fill in the blank and respond to this prompt: "Explain how _____ is affecting your school or community."

Essay Response

The sample essay response below follows the outline on page **528**. The thesis statement appears at the end of the beginning paragraph. In the final paragraph, the writer restates the reasons that support her thesis.

Sample Essay Response

NATO's Role in the War on Terrorism

The North Atlantic Treaty Organization, or NATO, was formed more than 50 years ago. Most assumed that the treaty's Article Five, which declared an attack on one country was an attack on all member states, would one day force the United States to defend its European allies against Soviet attack. Instead, the first-ever use of Article Five brought European powers to the defense of the United States. Since the September 11, 2001, terrorist attack, NATO has defended and supported the United States' fight against terrorism.

Just hours after New York City and Washington, D.C., were hit, NATO declared that the assaults were an attack on all NATO countries, and member countries offered their support to the United States. NATO radar aircraft were deployed to patrol the skies over the U.S., and naval units were deployed to patrol the eastern Mediterranean.

In the months following the September 11 attacks, many NATO countries agreed to help the United States in Afghanistan by participating in "Operation Enduring Freedom." Some of them also participated in "Operation Iraqi Freedom," which started several months later. While allied with the U.S., NATO troops were not automatically part of the U.S.-led coalition. In fact, there was a debate concerning where and how NATO should be operating. NATO leaders met in Reykjavik, Iceland, in May 2002 and decided that NATO would fight wherever necessary to combat terrorism.

Later in 2002, at a NATO summit in Prague, the idea of a NATO response force team was accepted. Today, the NATO Response Force exists as a technologically advanced force of land, sea, air, and special forces. It can be deployed very quickly whenever needed.

NATO also provides and coordinates military and intelligence support for member states engaged against terrorists. Member nations provide each other with access to their ports and airfields to aid operations against terrorism. The treaty that helped keep Soviet Russia from overwhelming Europe is now an alliance against the new threat of global terrorism.

Taking Standardized Tests

At certain times throughout your school life, you will be required to take standardized tests. The guidelines below will help you take these tests.

Before the test . . .

- **Know what to expect.** Ask your teacher what subjects will be covered on the standardized test, what format will be used, and what day the test will be given.
- **Get a good night's rest.** As with other test days, be sure to eat breakfast that morning.
- **Be prepared.** Bring extra pens, pencils, and erasers. Be sure to have enough blank paper for notes, outlines, or numerical calculations.

During the test . . .

- **Listen to the instructions and carefully follow directions.** Standardized tests follow strict guidelines. You will be given exact instructions on how to fill in information and supply answers.
- **Pace yourself.** In general, don't spend more than one minute on an objective question; move on and come back to it later.
- **Keep your eyes on your own work.** Don't worry if others finish before you.
- **Match question numbers to answer numbers.** If you skip a question in the question booklet, be sure to skip the corresponding number on your answer sheet. Every few questions, double-check the question number against your answer sheet.
- **Answer every question.** As long as there is no penalty for incorrect answers, you should always answer every question. First eliminate all the choices that are obviously incorrect, and then use logic to make your best educated guess.
- **Review your answers.** If you have time left, be sure that you've answered all the questions and haven't made any accidental mistakes. In general, don't change an answer unless you are sure that it's wrong. If you need to change an answer, erase the original answer completely.

After the test . . .

- **Erase any unnecessary marks** before turning in your test. The machines used to grade some tests may pick up stray marks and record them as wrong answers.

Tips for Standardized Tests

Standardized tests in language arts assess your skills in areas such as vocabulary, word analysis, conventions, and reading comprehension.

Vocabulary and Word Analysis

These questions assess your vocabulary. They test your knowledge of a word's literal and figurative meanings, usage, concept, power, or origin.

1. Which of these words connotes the concept of rights and privileges?
   A. inhabitant
   B. visitor
   C. resident
   D. citizen

Conventions

These questions assess your command of the conventions of grammar, sentence structure, spelling, and punctuation.

2. Read this sentence.

   He went to the University of California and then to Harvard after he got well, where he earned a master's degree.

   What is the best way to rewrite the sentence to improve its clarity?
   A. After he got well, he went to the University of California and then to Harvard, where he earned a master's degree.
   B. He went to the University of California and then to Harvard, where he earned a master's degree after he got well.
   C. He went after he got well to the University of California and then to Harvard, where he earned a master's degree.
   D. To the University of California he went and then to Harvard, where he earned, after he got well, a master's degree

Reading Comprehension and Literary Responses

These tests give you a text passage to read and questions to answer about it. The questions measure your comprehension and your ability to draw conclusions. Use the guidelines below to help you answer these kinds of questions.

- **Skim the questions** before you read the passage.
- **Read the passage** quickly but carefully.
- **Read all the choices** before deciding which answer is best.

Basic Grammar and Writing

Writing Focus

Using Words Effectively   **533**

Understanding Sentence Style   **549**

Writing Strong Paragraphs   **561**

Academic Vocabulary

Working with a classmate, read the definitions below and discuss possible answers to each question.

1. A modifier is a word, a phrase, or a clause that changes or limits the meaning of other words.
   How can modifiers be overused?

2. To imply is to suggest something without directly saying it.
   What kinds of things might a writer imply rather than telling the reader outright? Why?

3. An anecdote is a short account of an interesting or humorous incident.
   How can an anecdote help engage your reader?

4. To vary is to change or give variety to.
   Why should you vary your word choice and sentence structure in a piece of writing?

Using Words Effectively

Just as atoms are the fundamental building blocks of matter, words are the building blocks of communication. And like atoms, words have power. Think about the word *yes*. That one little word can change your life forever—for better or for worse. So can the tiny word *no*. And what about the word *ridiculous*? Try shouting that word in just about any situation, and you'll see how powerful a word can be.

English has many types of words: nouns, pronouns, verbs, adjectives, adverbs, prepositions, and conjunctions. This chapter explores these parts of speech, helping you unlock the power each one has to offer.

- **Nouns**
- **Pronouns**
- **Verbs**
- **Adjectives**
- **Adverbs**
- **Prepositions**
- **Conjunctions**
- **Checking Your Word Choice**

"Give me the right word and the right accent, and I will move the world."

—Joseph Conrad

Nouns Using General and Specific Nouns

Since some nouns are general (*man, rock*) and some are specific (*Barnum Brown, sandstone*), they can affect the focus of your writing. As with a camera lens, you can start with general nouns and zoom in to specific nouns, or you can start with specific nouns and zoom out to general ones.

Zooming In (from general nouns to specific nouns)

In the wide *desert*, a *man* crouched under a blazing *sun* and dug. He spent most of his *time* kneeling in the *dirt* holding a small *tool*. Slowly he chipped *sandstone* away from what looked like a *vertebra*. *Stroke* by *stroke*, the *paleontologist Barnum Brown* was uncovering the *skeleton* of a *Tyrannosaurus rex*.

This paragraph starts with general nouns, which paint a broad picture and invite the reader to imagine the scene. Then it zooms in to specific nouns, which provide detailed information.

Zooming Out (from specific nouns to general nouns)

In early *July 1905, Barnum Brown* discovered the *skeleton* of a *Tyrannosaurus rex*. An avid *hunter* of dinosaur *bones*, *Barnum* had come to *Hell Creek, Montana*, in hopes of finding something special. However, he could not have suspected that his *discovery* would soon visit the *imaginations* of *children* everywhere.

This paragraph starts with specific nouns, providing exact information up front. Then it zooms out to general nouns to reflect on the importance of the discovery.

Try It!

Think of a topic that interests you. Then brainstorm a list of general and specific nouns about the topic. (See the sample chart below.) Afterward, write a paragraph, using the nouns to zoom in or zoom out.

Topic: Dinosaur Hunting			
General		**Specific**	
dinosaur	bones	Tyrannosaurus rex	vertebra
man	desert	paleontologist	Hell Creek, Montana

Creating Metaphors

A **metaphor** is a comparison of two unlike things in which no word of comparison (*as* or *like*) is used. A metaphor represents a high level of thinking and is a powerful writing technique.

Basic Metaphors

A basic metaphor can be a simple noun equation: Noun A = Noun B. In basic metaphors, the nouns are equated using a linking verb such as *is, am, are, was,* or *were*.

Janice **is a** human calculator.
(Janice = calculator)

Life **is a** banquet.
(life = banquet)

Advanced Metaphors

Some advanced metaphors *imply* the equation between the nouns. In this example, the highlighted nouns are equated without linking verbs

The gears **in Janice's** mind **grind through any math test.**
(The word *gears* implies that Janice's *mind* is a machine.)

Tip

Create an advanced metaphor by substituting Noun B for Noun A.

Her **lasers** scan problems while her **processor** builds solutions.

Noun A		Noun B
eyes	=	lasers
brain	=	processor

Extended Metaphors

Sometimes an author extends a metaphor, creating a series of pictures for the reader.

Bill's mind **is a** locker**, with his** letter jacket **hanging from a hook in the center,** pictures **of his girlfriend covering the inside of the door, and** textbooks **lying, forgotten, at the bottom.**

Try It!

Equate the name of a friend (Noun A) with another noun (Noun B). Then write one basic, one advanced, and one extended metaphor about this person.

Pronouns Engaging Your Reader

Most often, a pronoun should clearly refer to a specific noun (its *antecedent*). However, one special use of pronouns delays mentioning the antecedent, making the reader wonder who or what you are talking about. This technique can work on a sentence level or in a whole paragraph.

Sentence Hook

In the following examples, notice how the pronouns turn the sentences into riddles, causing the reader to wonder, "Who?"

When he did a screen test for Paramount, he was told, "[You] can't sing, can't act, but you can dance a little." Still, Fred Astaire was in more than 40 films.

Though she was fired from her first Broadway show after one night, and though Hollywood producers labeled her "box office poison," Katharine Hepburn became a leading lady of twentieth-century film.

Paragraph Hook

In this paragraph, the reader doesn't discover who *he* is until the end of the paragraph.

He was a short, unassuming comedian from New York, but he sat on a train bound for the Soviet Union in 1933. The tools of his trade were simple—a rumpled hat, a curly red wig, a worn-out coat, and a bicycle horn. The young pantomimist was traveling to the Soviet Union to open up a new market to American performers. Arriving in Moscow, he was greeted with suspicion, and when he performed, his audiences were afraid to laugh. In utter frustration, the young American was about to give up, but then the United States and the Soviet Union officially recognized each other. That changed everything. Suddenly, Soviet crowds went wild for Harpo Marx. He later wrote that he had never before played for an audience so desperate to laugh.

Try It!

Make a list of favorite performers—musicians, actors, comedians, dancers, or friends. Choose one, and think of (or learn) interesting anecdotes about his or her life and career. Write a paragraph about one of these anecdotes, using pronouns to withhold the person's identity until the end.

Persuading Your Reader

In persuasive writing, you can unite people, instruct them, or divide them, depending on the person of the pronouns you use.

Person of Pronouns		
First Person (Unite)	**Second Person** (Instruct)	**Third Person** (Divide)
we us our	**you your**	**they them their**

Selecting the Person of a Pronoun

Notice the effect that is created by changing the person of pronouns in the following sentence:

Word Style

These pronouns **unite** the writer and the reader: "We're all in this together."

> When we buy a car, van, truck, or SUV, we must consider how our consumption of gasoline will affect us in the future.

These pronouns **instruct** the reader.

> When you buy a car, van, truck, or SUV, you must consider how your consumption of gasoline will affect you in the future.

These pronouns **divide** the reader from those being written about.

> When they buy a car, van, truck, or SUV, they must consider how their consumption of gasoline will affect them in the future.

In persuasive writing, use pronouns carefully. Use first-person pronouns to create common ground with your reader. Use second-person pronouns (or the implied "you") to instruct the reader. Use third-person pronouns sparingly, perhaps to point an accusing finger.

Try It!

Check a newspaper opinion/editorial page to find an editorial that uses personal pronouns. Are they first-, second-, or third-person pronouns? Change the pronouns in one of the paragraphs, switching to another person. Then explain how the changes make the paragraph more or less persuasive.

Verbs Establishing Time

Verbs control time. For example, they tell whether an event happened in the past or is happening right now. These differences in time are expressed by the verb's tense.

Past Tense in Essays

Past-tense verbs work best for most of your writing, showing that events are completed. Past-tense verbs help you to express and analyze solid facts.

> **Throughout history, women have made major contributions to science. For example, in the fourth century C.E., Hypatia of Alexandria created an astrolabe, an instrument for tracking the position of stars and planets. It revolutionized astronomy and navigation.**

Present Tense in Narratives

Present-tense verbs work well for certain narratives. These verbs make action seem immediate, as if it were happening right now.

> **Lise Mitner glances down from the face of Albert Einstein and stares at the paper before her. On it, she has laid out the secrets of the atom. Always shy, Lise covers the equations with her hand. Einstein clucks, shaking his head. "Don't hide your work. You should trumpet it from the rooftops. Don't you know, my dear: You are the German Madame Curie."**

Present Tense in Process Essays

Present-tense verbs also work well for essays that describe action that happens routinely.

> **Every year, more young women decide to study mathematics and science; every year, more female researchers and doctors start their practices; every year, more women make the discoveries that advance human knowledge.**

Try It!

Pull out a recent expository essay or narrative you have written. What verb tense did you use? Choose a paragraph and replace the verbs in it with verbs of a different tense. How does the change affect the sense of time and action?

Creating Verbal Metaphors

Though most metaphors are based on nouns (Noun A = Noun B), some metaphors can be created using verbs.

Verbal Metaphors

My heart galloped in my chest.
(The heart is equated to a running horse.)

The letter ignited my mind.
(The letter is equated to a fire.)

Dad's junker staggered into the driveway, bled transmission fluid, and gasped its last breath.
(The junker car is equated to a dying animal.)

Note: In these examples, verbs that are usually used with one type of noun (the *horse* galloped) are used with nouns of a completely different type (my *heart* galloped).

Try It!

Study the bank of verbs below. Each is strongly associated with a specific noun. Select five verbs and write a sentence for each, creating metaphors by pairing the verb with a completely different type of noun.

Example: The gray sky frowned on our picnic plans.

anchored	eroded	hurdled	rotted
baked	flew	joked	sizzled
bucked	frowned	kindled	sprinted
burned	gargled	laughed	snored
catapulted	groomed	muttered	stomped
danced	hacked	punted	thundered
drummed	hollered	raced	tripped

FYI

When a metaphor implies that a nonhuman thing is performing a human action, the technique is called *personification*.

The day **snored** along, occasionally **muttering** empty promises of adventure before **rolling over** and **drowsing** again.

Adjectives Making a Precise Point

Some writers use adjectives like frosting, slathering their nouns as if the adjectives will make them tastier. You will do better to consider how adjectives subtract from a noun, rather than adding to it, by limiting its meaning and making it more precise.

> **DON'T Write**
> **I had a** big, beautiful **party.**
> (The adjectives do not make *party* more precise.)
>
> **DO Write**
> **I had a** sweet-sixteen birthday **party.**
> (The adjectives tell precisely what *kind* of party.)

Adjective Phrases and Clauses

Phrases and clauses that function as adjectives also need to be precise.

The house rocked like a dryer filled with shoes.
(The phrase *filled with shoes* tells precisely what kind of *dryer*.)

We played a game of truth or dare that resulted in a pillow fight.
(The phrase *of truth or dare* and the clause *that resulted in a pillow fight* tell exactly what kind of *game*.)

Try It!

Think of a special event that you have attended. Write down a list of nouns related to the event. Then write down one adjective and one adjective phrase or clause that would make the noun's meaning precise. (See the examples below.) Write a paragraph about the event, using some of the nouns and modifiers from your list.

Nouns	Adjectives	Adjective Phrases or Clauses
pool	above-ground	with a ten-foot-deep end
diving board	squeaky	which got a workout
dives	ridiculous	such as the "Spider"
belly flop	blistering	that nearly emptied the pool

Emphasizing the Quality of a Noun

One way to emphasize the quality of a given noun is to use a series of adjectives to describe it.

Series of Adjectives

The sentences below contain adjectives in a series. The first series is separated with commas and the word *and*. The second series is separated without commas, using only the word *and*. This provides special emphasis.

My friend Hanae is smart, quirky, funny, **and** driven.

She says I am kind **and** patient **and totally** infuriating.

Series of Phrases or Clauses

Phrases or clauses that function as adjectives can also be used in a series.

Sitting in her living room, propping her feet on the radiator, **and** balancing a notepad on her lap, **Hanae writes stories.** (Three participial phrases describe *Hanae*.)

Hanae writes stories about places that she has seen, that she wishes to see, **and** that she knows don't even exist. (Three relative clauses describe *places*.)

FYI

The quickest way to know whether a phrase or clause is functioning as an adjective is to decide whether it answers one of the adjective questions— *which? what kind of? how many?* or *how much?*

Try It!

Write down the name of a person. Beside the name, write two nouns you associate with that person. Under each noun, list descriptive words, phrases, or clauses. (See the sample chart below.) Then create a sentence that uses an adjective series.

Hanae	apartment	places
smart	on the eighth floor	that she has seen
funny	with a view of the alley	that she wishes to see
quirky	in the old downtown	that she knows don't even exist
driven	in Bloomington	

Word Style

Adverbs Writing Strong Beginnings

Adverbs make great sentence starters because they help create a context. Before the reader knows *what* happens in the sentence, the adverb can tell *how, when,* or *where* it happens. Single-word adverbs (as well as phrases and clauses that act as adverbs) answer these questions: *how? when? where? why? to what degree?* and *how often?*

Adverb Beginnings

Gradually, **the glowing twilight surrendered to spangled night.** *(How?)*

Afterward, **the Perseid meteor shower began.** *(When?)*

In the northern sky, **meteors were flashing overhead.** *(Where?)*

One by one, **shooting stars streaked across the sky.** *(To what degree?)*

Every few minutes, **a new fireball left its fleeting signature.** *(How often?)*

Because the earth was passing through the path of a comet, **there were hundreds of shooting stars.** *(Why?)*

Try It!

Rewrite each sentence below, moving the adverb (or adverbial phrase or clause) to the beginning of the sentence.

1. Dust particles often made slim dashes of light.
2. Marble-sized chunks of matter created bright shooting stars as they crossed the whole sky before burning out.
3. Fist-sized meteorites crossed the sky burning, spinning, and flaming.
4. Earth passes through this cloud of debris every August.

FYI

The regular subject-verb order may be reversed when an adverb starts a sentence.

At the top of the hill lay a clearing. *(A clearing lay at the top of the hill.)*

Overhead were the dancing stars. *(The dancing stars were overhead.)*

Try It!

Think about a natural phenomenon you've witnessed and write a paragraph about what you saw. Try starting a few sentences with adverbs.

Avoiding Adverb Props

Avoid propping up a weak verb with an adverb. Often, the two words can be replaced with a single verb that tells exactly what is happening.

Adverb Props

DON'T Write	DO Write
ran quickly	charged, darted, dashed, scurried, sprinted
walked heavily	marched, plodded, slogged, stomped, trudged
said angrily	growled, hissed, shouted, snarled

Avoiding Redundant Adverbs

A strong verb doesn't need an adverb. When you fix an adverb prop by replacing the weak verb with a stronger one, you can omit the unnecessary adverb.

Redundant Adverbs

DON'T Write	DO Write
dashed quickly (no one dashes slowly)	dashed
plodded heavily (no one plods lightly)	plodded
growled angrily (no one growls happily)	growled

Try It!

Read the passage below and identify the adverb props and redundant adverbs. Suggest how each adverb problem could be corrected.

Afghan refugees staggered unsteadily up the hill. Their world had been changed completely by the war, and now it was rocked deeply by an earthquake. "We are weary," an old man said quietly. Abdullah al Ibin had worked hard to survive the Taliban regime. He thought wishfully that things would become easier. They did not. He put up with robbers until he gave up and escaped away from his hometown. "Now, with this earthquake, even the mountains aren't safe," he murmured sadly.

Word Style

Prepositions Creating Similes

The preposition *like* allows you to compare two things, creating a simile. For a simile to be effective, it should point out an unexpected similarity.

> **DON'T Write**
>
> **Rain is** like water **that falls from the sky.**
>
> (Rain *is* water.)
>
> **DO Write**
>
> **Spring rain is** like a mother's voice **whispering to the world, "Wake up."**

Use similes as good cooks use spices—sparingly to enhance the flavor of the sentence. A simile pushed too far may become tiresome.

> **DON'T Write**
>
> **Spring rain is like a mother's voice whispering to the world, "Wake up," and the winds of March are like the rustle of covers drawn back from the slumbering planet.**

Try It!

For each of the terms listed below, write a one-sentence simile that shows a surprising similarity. Use the words *is like* or *are like*.

1. lightning **3.** a bird's song **5.** spring flowers
2. warm winds **4.** new leaves **6.** umbrellas

FYI

Many similes use the preposition *like* to introduce a prepositional phrase that functions as an adjective.

The winter sky was **like a woolen blanket.**
(The simile modifies the noun *sky*.)

Other similes use the subordinating conjunction *as* to introduce a subordinate clause that functions as an adverb.

Spring draws away the clouds **as a mother draws back a woolen blanket.**
(The simile modifies the verb *draws*.)

Using Prepositional Phrases as Adjectives

Prepositions can turn nouns into modifiers. By placing a preposition before a noun, you can create a phrase that acts as an adjective, answering the questions *which? what kind?* or *how many?*

The proposal with the blue cover **is mine.**
Which proposal?

Calculations for the construction costs **were inaccurate.**
What kind of calculations?

Letters from two hundred constituents **stopped the bill from passing.**
How many?

Prepositional phrases can be used to revise an awkward sentence that strings too many adjectives together.

The city budget debate's **end finally came.** (awkward)

The end of the debate over the city budget **finally came.**

Try It!

Rewrite each sentence below, turning at least one of the adjectives into a prepositional phrase. Be sure the new sentence makes sense.

1. The **mayor's hilltop** house needs painting.
2. The **busy street's anxious** residents spoke to the city council.
3. The **school board budget** referendum passed the vote.
4. An **environmental activist student** organization opposes the bypass.
5. The council passed the **2011 property tax reassessment** bill.

FYI

Prepositional phrases also can function as adverbs, answering the questions *how? when? where? why? to what degree?* and *how often?* However, these prepositional phrases can often be replaced by a single adverb—or by a stronger verb.

The mayor replied **with a firm voice** that the budget had been approved.

The mayor replied **firmly** that the budget had been approved.
(adverb)

The mayor **asserted** that the budget had been approved.
(strong verb)

Conjunctions Creating Tension

As a writer, you can create tension in a sentence by using certain subordinating conjunctions. The following conjunctions tell the reader that your train of thought will soon shift directions.

although	though	unless	while
even though	whereas	until	

Present a Contrast

In the following examples, ideas pull in opposite directions, building a powerful contrast.

Although the French Revolution was meant to provide "liberty, equality, and brotherhood" to all citizens, it actually resulted in repression, inequality, and war.

While royal oppression had been cruel, the mob's remedy for it—gauntlets and guillotines—proved crueler still.

Create Irony

In this example, the conjunction *even though* sets up a contrast that creates *irony*. Irony results when someone's actions lead to an effect that is opposite to what was intended.

Even though the French people thought they had escaped from King Louis XVI and his so-called "divine right" to rule France, they found themselves stuck with Emperor Napoleon, who felt he had the divine right to rule the world.

Try It!

Select four of the conjunctions listed at the top of the page and use each one at the start of a sentence. Work to create tension (and even irony) in your sentences.

FYI

Another way to create tension is to use correlative conjunctions.

not only . . . but also	neither . . . nor
either . . . or	both . . . and
if . . . then	whether . . . or

Creating Pivot Points

The coordinating conjunctions *but* and *yet* can provide pivot points in an essay. They allow the writer to present one line of thought and then create a reversal. In an expository essay, *but* or *yet* can show a shift from background information to the real issue. The technique also works in persuasive writing.

Expository Excerpt

This paragraph gives background and conventional wisdom.

But signals the shift to new information.

> Our climate should be a self-righting system. After all, the main greenhouse gas, carbon dioxide, is also the main food for plants. More carbon dioxide should cause more plant growth. More plants should mean less carbon dioxide and more oxygen. The levels of greenhouse gases should self-regulate.
>
> **But** experiments have shown otherwise. Increased levels of carbon dioxide increase plant growth, but not enough to reduce carbon-dioxide levels. In addition, with global warming, arctic tundras that once were "carbon sinks," absorbing more carbon dioxide than they lost, are becoming "carbon pumps"—accelerating the rise in greenhouse gases.

Persuasive Excerpt

The opposing position is presented.

Yet signals the shift to the writer's opinion.

> The politicians are right in this: The world economy is driven by oil, and capitalism is driven by consumption. To keep the economy and capitalism strong, the world needs a great deal of oil now—and an even greater amount in the future.
>
> **Yet** this argument breaks down. Yes, oil is needed now, but alternative energy sources will reduce the future demands. The standard argument fails to account for one great resource—human ingenuity.

Try It!

Think about an issue with two sides. Write a paragraph that explains one side of the issue. Then write a second paragraph, beginning with *but* or *yet,* to explain the other side of the issue.

Word Style

Word Choice Using a Checklist

After you finish a writing assignment, you can check your word choice by using the following checklist.

Word-Choice Checklist

_____ **1.** Have I used nouns to set my focus (zooming in or out)?

_____ **2.** Have I included any metaphors? List examples: The Calcutta massacre was a last gasp of the dying imperial beast.

_____ **3.** Have I used pronouns occasionally to create suspense? List examples: He was a small man of noble birth, but Mohandas Gandhi became a titan who fought for the common people.

_____ **4.** Have I used pronouns persuasively? List examples:

To unite: We wonder if the world holds more Gandhis.

To instruct: "Live as if you were to die tomorrow. Learn as if you were to live forever."

To divide: Though some may say passive resistance cannot stand up to armies and bombs, they have forgotten the lessons of Gandhi.

_____ **5.** Have I used verb tense to establish time?

_____ **6.** Have I used adjectives to make precise points?

_____ **7.** Have I used an adjective series?

_____ **8.** Have I started any sentences with adverbs?

_____ **9.** Have I used any similes? List examples: Gandhi's heart was like a magic box, larger on the inside than on the outside.

_____ **10.** Have I used prepositional phrases as adjectives?

_____ **11.** Have I used subordinating conjunctions to create contrast or irony where needed?

_____ **12.** Have I used *but* or *yet* to create pivot points in my writing?

Understanding Sentence Style

Close your eyes, and imagine a carefully handwoven scarf or shawl. Try to visualize how each stitch works with the next one to create a unique design. Now imagine that the sentences you write are like those stitches. As you weave them together, your design—your message—takes form, leaving a lasting impression on your reader.

Good writing holds sentences that are clear, creative, and effective. To become sentence-smart, look for well-crafted sentences as you read. Then write sentences of your own modeled after some of these published gems. If you read and write often, your writing style will continue to improve—one sentence at a time. The guidelines in this chapter will help.

- Sentence Patterns
- Sentence Length
- Sentence Variety
- Sentence Combining
- Sentence Problems
- Sentence Agreement
- Sentence Modeling

"The best advice on writing I've ever received is: 'Knock 'em dead with the lead sentence.'"
—Whitney Balliet

Sentence Patterns Understanding the Basics

In the English language, sentences follow basic patterns. Combining a variety of sentence patterns adds interest to your writing.

1. Subject + Action Verb

S   AV

Armin coughed. (Some action verbs, like *coughed*, are intransitive. They *do not need* a direct object to express a complete thought. See page **716.1**.)

2. Subject + Action Verb + Direct Object

S   AV   DO

Omaya directs the play. (Some action verbs, like *directs* in this sentence, are transitive. They *do need* a direct object to express a complete thought. See page **716.2**.)

3. Subject + Action Verb + Indirect Object + Direct Object

S   AV   IO   DO

The teacher read the students a description of the test. (The direct object *description* names who or what receives the action; the indirect object *students* names to whom or for whom the action is done. See **716.2**.)

4. Subject + Action Verb + Direct Object + Object Complement

S   AV   DO   OC

The class found the presentation entertaining. (The object complement *entertaining* describes the direct object.)

5. Subject + Linking Verb + Predicate Noun

S   LV   PN

Serafina is a dancer. (The predicate noun *dancer* renames the subject. See **702.3**.)

6. Subject + Linking Verb + Predicate Adjective

S   LV   PA

Our parents are interested in contributing to the fund. (The predicate adjective *interested* describes the subject. See **728.1**.)

Note: In the patterns below, the subject comes after the verb.

LV   S   PN

Is Dominic a sports fan? (A question)

LV   S

There were three limousines in the parking lot. (A sentence beginning with *there*)

"Whatever sentence will bear to be read twice,
we may be sure was thought twice."
—Henry David Thoreau

Sentence Length Varying Sentence Lengths

Using sentences of different lengths adds interest to your writing. If too many of your sentences have the same number of words, your writing may sound monotonous.

In this paragraph, all of the sentences have the same basic length.

> Being a veterinarian is hard work. Sometimes the veterinarian has to handle heavy animals. Some dogs can weigh more than 100 pounds. Rural veterinarians must care for large farm animals on-site. That means they must travel from farm to farm. Of course, there are also late-night emergencies. Still, there are many rewards. Veterinarians know the joy of helping animals. They have the satisfaction of relieving their pain.

The same paragraph has been improved below because the sentences now vary in length. The writer added and deleted words as needed.

> Being a veterinarian is hard work. A veterinarian must be able to handle heavy animals, including dogs that can weigh more than 100 pounds. In addition, rural veterinarians must care for large animals on-site, which means they must travel from farm to farm. Of course, there are also late-night emergencies to deal with. Still, there are many rewards, especially knowing the joy and satisfaction of helping animals and relieving their pain.

Try It!

Rewrite the following paragraph using a variety of sentence lengths.

> Thad is starting an internship as an audio/video technician. Technicians are part of the production crew for television shows. Thad will work on both live and taped television events. He is very excited about learning some new job skills. He will set up sound and video equipment. Thad's math and science skills will help him set up complicated productions. It is Thad's job to regulate and monitor audio levels. He is also responsible for setting up television video signals. Thad would like to work as an audio engineer.

Sentence Style

Sentence Variety Using Sentences for Effect

Short and long sentences can be used for special effect in your writing. Short sentences build tension and speed while longer ones add meaning in a paced way.

Using Short Sentences

- Short sentences grouped together build tension.
  The TV screen was lying. It couldn't be true. I blinked once, twice. The trail of puffy smoke remained. *The Challenger*, its crew, hope—were all gone.

- Short sentences pick up the pace of the action.
  The finish line lay just ahead. We ran close enough to smell each other's sweat. Four arms pumped hard. Four feet slapped the ground. We breathed only to win.

Using Long Sentences

- A long sentence builds layers of meaning.
  We hauled out the boxes of food and set up the camp stove, all the time battling the hot wind that would not stop, even when we screamed to the sky.

- Long sentences slow down the pace and facilitate reflection.
  Although I have no memory of the ordeals I faced during my first years of life, I shall always bear the orthopedic deformities that I was handed at birth. These deformities have been difficult to accept, but they have provided me with a unique life and greatly influenced the development of my character.

- A long sentence with a central idea forms a complex thought.
  "To those peoples in the huts and villages across the globe struggling to break the bonds of mass misery, we pledge our best efforts to help them help themselves, for whatever period is required—not because the Communists may be doing it, not because we seek their votes, but because it is right."
  —President John F. Kennedy

Try It!

Write a series of short sentences that build tension. Then write a long sentence that builds layers of meaning or slows down the pace.

"How can we combine the old words in new order so that they survive, so that they create beauty, so that they tell the truth?"

—Winston Weathers

Writing Loose Sentences

A loose sentence expresses the main idea near the beginning and adds details as needed. In loose sentences, the thoughts seem to be presented as they occur to the writer. When used effectively, this type of sentence can add a special style and rhythm to your writing. In the examples below, the main ideas are underlined. (See page **750**.)

Example Loose Sentences

<u>Sam was studying at the kitchen table</u>, memorizing a list of vocabulary words, completely focused, intent on acing tomorrow's Spanish quiz.

"<u>They are wonderfully built homes</u>, aluminum skin, double-walled, with insulation, and often paneled with walls of hardwood."

—John Steinbeck, *Travels with Charley*

"<u>Jeff couldn't see the musician clearly</u>, just a figure on a chair on the stage, holding what looked like a misshapen guitar."

—Cynthia Voight, *A Solitary Blue*

Tip

Remember these important points when writing loose sentences.

1. Structure the sentence carefully. If a sentence begins to ramble, the reader will lose track of the main idea.

2. Avoid using too many long, loose sentences. Remember that varying your sentence lengths will keep the reader interested.

Try It!

Write five loose sentences using these brief sentences as starting points.

1. Nayara gasped.
2. Storm clouds surged through the sky.
3. Ari wrote a free-verse poem.
4. Mr. Groves sauntered away.
5. Michael waited in line.

Sentence Style

Sentence Combining
Using Infinitive and Participial Phrases

Ideas from shorter sentences can be combined into one sentence using an infinitive phrase or a participial phrase.

Using an Infinitive Phrase

An infinitive phrase is a group of related words introduced by the word *to* plus a verb form—*to conquer* my fears. (See page **742**.)

- **Short Sentences:**
  Annetta searched the Internet. She needed information about the Serengeti Plain.
  I would really like to go to Africa. That's my dream vacation.

- **Combined Sentence:**
  Annetta searched the Internet to find information about the Serengeti Plain.
  To go to Africa is my dream vacation.

Using a Participial Phrase

A participial phrase is a group of related words introduced by a participle (a verb form ending in *–ing* or *–ed*)—*circling* the date. (See page **742**.)

- **Short Sentences:**
  Kyle walked barefoot in the garden. He stepped on a hornets' nest.
  Shannon covered her ears. She was annoyed by the sound of the air hammer.

- **Combined Sentence:**
  Kyle, walking barefoot in the garden, stepped on a hornets' nest.
  Annoyed by the sound of the air hammer, Shannon covered her ears.

Try It!

Combine these sentences using an infinitive or a participial phrase.

1. Marcus went to the ballet. He did it to please his mother.
2. The ring was locked in a safety deposit box. It was safe for many years.
3. A cold front swept through Michigan. It sent temperatures plummeting below zero.
4. The tornado swept through a small town. It left a trail of death and destruction.
5. McKenna studied the Web site. She wanted to learn more about Napoleon.

Creating Complex Sentences

Ideas from shorter sentences can also be combined into a complex sentence. A complex sentence is made up of two clauses that are not equal in importance. The more important idea should be included in the *independent clause,* which can stand alone as a single sentence. The less important idea should be included in the *dependent clause,* which cannot stand alone. (See pages **744** and **748**.)

The two clauses in a complex sentence can be connected with a subordinate conjunction (*after, although, because, before, even though, until, when,* and so on) or a relative pronoun (*who, whose, which,* or *that*).

- Even though Manu sprained his ankle, he sunk the winning free throw. [dependent clause, independent clause]

- It isn't funny when a practical joke continues until someone's feelings are hurt. [independent clause, two dependent clauses]

Using a Complex Sentence

- **Two Short Sentences:**
  Mt. McKinley rises 20,320 feet above sea level.
  It is the highest peak in the United States.

- **Combined Sentence:**
  Mt. McKinley, which rises 20,320 feet above sea level, is the highest peak in the United States.

Try It!

Combine each set of short sentences into a complex sentence using the subordinating conjunction or relative pronoun in parentheses.

1. Mrs. Lopez returned to work.
   School lunch tasted good again. (because)
2. We found a village called "Pity Me."
   The village is located in County Durham. (which)
3. I want my sister to proofread my report.
   I will give it to Ms. Belmont. (before)
4. My aunt loves to travel.
   She is planning a trip to France. (who)
5. We had to leave the golf course.
   The storm finally started. (when)

Sentence Style

Sentence Problems Avoiding Sentence Errors

Avoid sentence problems as you write—or correct them when you revise.

Correcting Run-On Sentences

Run-on sentences occur when two sentences are joined without punctuation or without a connecting word (*and, but, or, so*).

- **Run-on Sentence:** Lightweight cookware soon came on the market the idea of casseroles became popular.

- **Corrected as Two Sentences:** Lightweight cookware soon came on the market. The idea of casserole cooking became popular.

- **Corrected as a Compound Sentence:** Lightweight cookware soon came on the market, so the idea of casserole cooking became popular.

Eliminating Comma Splices

Comma splices occur when two independent clauses are connected with a comma and no conjunction.

- **Comma Splice:** Casseroles took little preparation time, women's magazines began promoting easy-to-prepare meals.

- **Corrected as Two Sentences:** Casseroles took little preparation time. Women's magazines began promoting easy-to-prepare meals.

- **Corrected as a Compound Sentence:** Casseroles took little preparation time, and women's magazines began promoting easy-to-prepare meals.

Try It!

On your own paper, rewrite the following paragraph, correcting the run-ons and comma splices.

(1) The word "soup" comes from the Old English word "sopp" it means a slice of bread over which roast drippings are poured. (2) Soup was eaten even in ancient times the first evidence of it dates back to around 6000 B.C.E. (3) The main ingredient of "ancient" soup may surprise you it was hippopotamus bones. (4) Soup is easily digested, so it is often prescribed as a nutritious meal for sick people. (5) Many families eat a lot of soup, most often it comes in cans and boxes and can be quickly heated.

Fixing Fragments

A fragment is not a sentence because it does not form a complete thought. In a sentence fragment, a subject, a predicate, or both are missing.

Fragment: **Was introduced in 4 B.C.E.** (The subject is missing.)

The mathematical decimal system **was introduced in 4 B.C.E.**

Fragment: **Roman emperors many lighthouses.** (A predicate is missing.)

Roman emperors built **many lighthouses.**

Fragment: **Including schools.** (A subject and predicate are missing.)

All public institutions, **including schools,** were closed.

Try It!

Rewrite each fragment as a complete sentence.

1. Under the Golden Gate Bridge.

2. About 200 feet deep.

3. Served in Iraq.

4. Steven Spielberg.

5. Is celebrated on November 11th.

6. John Philip Sousa his own band.

Rewriting Rambling Sentences

Rambling sentences seem to go on and on. Their parts are connected by coordinating conjunctions. While not grammatically incorrect, these sentences can be hard to read. As a rule, if a sentence links more than two complete ideas with *and, but,* or *so,* try to divide it into shorter sentences.

Rambling: I saw my band director, Mr. Balke, at the jazz concert, and I called to him but he didn't hear me and then he disappeared into the crowd.

Better: I saw my band director, Mr. Balke, at the jazz concert. I called to him, but he didn't hear me. Then he disappeared into the crowd.

Try It!

Rewrite this rambling sentence by eliminating one or more of the connecting words. Punctuate the new sentences correctly.

I wanted to be on the prom committee so I went to the first meeting and I knew I was on time and in the right place and I waited around for almost an hour but nobody showed up.

Correcting Double Subjects

Be careful not to use a pronoun immediately after the subject. The result is usually a double subject.

Double Subject: The Presidential election it is this Tuesday.

Corrected: The Presidential election is this Tuesday.

Double Subject: Alton he plays college football.

Corrected: Alton plays college football.

Correcting Double Negatives

Avoid sentences that contain double negatives. Double negatives occur when two negative words are used together in the same sentence (*not never, barely nothing, not no*, and so on). Double negatives also occur if you use contractions ending in *n't* with a negative word (*didn't never, can't not*).

Negative Words

| nothing | nowhere | neither | never | not | barely | hardly | nobody | none |

Double Negative: I could not go nowhere.

Corrected Sentence: I could not go anywhere.

Negative Contractions

| don't | can't | won't | shouldn't | wouldn't | couldn't | didn't | hadn't |

Double Negative: He didn't hear nothing unusual.

Corrected Sentence: He didn't hear anything unusual.

Try It!

Rewrite each sentence below, correcting the double-subject or double-negative errors.

1. King Richard he was known as "Richard the Lionhearted."
2. I didn't do nothing about the mistake on my application.
3. Why don't you never listen to hip-hop?
4. I hadn't never heard of The Hanging Gardens of Babylon. The gardens they are one of the Seven Wonders of the Ancient World.
5. We can't go nowhere without Steve's brother coming along.
6. Cho and I we went to the Usher concert.

Sentence Agreement
Making Subjects and Verbs Agree

A verb must agree in number (singular or plural) with its subject. The basic rules for subject-verb agreement are listed below.

- A **singular subject** needs a singular verb, and a plural subject needs a plural verb.

  Singular Subject and Verb: Los Angeles is the second-most populated city in the United States.

  Plural Subject and Verb: Most Los Angeles beaches provide plenty of sun.

- A **compound subject connected by the word *and*** usually needs a plural verb.

  Compound Subject and Verb: Ty and Janelle are going to Europe.

- A **compound subject connected by the word *or*** needs a verb that agrees in number with the subject nearest to the verb.

  Compound Subject and Verb: Either the pool managers or a Red Cross volunteer teaches the lifeguard class.

- **Indefinite pronouns** can be singular or plural when used as a subject. (See page **754.2**.)

  Singular Subject and Verb: Almost everyone in school likes the new coach.

  Plural Subject and Verb: Many of the parents appreciate his approach.

Try It!

Number your paper from 1 to 5. Write the correct verb choice for each of these sentences.

1. Some sodas or a juice container *(remains, remain)* in the refrigerator.

2. Kindra and Lawson *(is, are)* my friends from Mahone High School.

3. Vegetarians *(has, have)* some great recipe ideas.

4. Two coffee shops on our block *(sells, sell)* fair-trade coffee.

5. Each of the tourists *(has, have)* moved to another hotel.

Write a sentence using each of the subjects below. Remember to use verbs that agree in number with the subjects.

1. drivers
2. musician
3. Washington and Lincoln
4. the principal or counselors
5. everyone
6. all

Sentence Style

Sentence Modeling Writing Stylish Sentences

Many painters learn to paint by copying famous works of art. Student writers, too, can learn to write better by modeling sentence patterns used by professional writers.

Model: Eventually, all things merge into one, and a river runs through it.

—Norman Maclean, *A River Runs Through It*

New Sentence: Slowly, new players develop into a unit, and a team forms among them.

Try It!

Choose three of the sentences below and write your own sentences, modeling the sentence structure as closely as possible.

1. I neither marched up to the stage like a conquering Amazon, nor did I look in the audience for Bailey's nod of approval.

—Maya Angelou, *I Know Why the Caged Bird Sings*

2. A leftover smile of moon hides in the bottom branches of the sugar maple, teasing her to smile back.

—Barbara Kingsolver, *Pigs in Heaven*

3. Then from behind the black and wavy line of the forests a column of golden light shot up into the heavens and spread over the semicircle of the eastern horizon.

—Joseph Conrad, "The Lagoon"

4. I awoke that morning from a bizarre dream in which I had climbed down the stairs in our house, lifted the piano high above my head, then dropped it onto my right big toe.

—Joel Ben Izzy, *The Beggar King and the Secret of Happiness*

5. If General Jackson hadn't run the Creeks up the creek, Simon Finch would never have paddled up the Alabama, and where would we be if he hadn't?

—Harper Lee, *To Kill a Mockingbird*

6. I came, I saw, I conquered, as the first baby in the family always does.

—Helen Keller, *The Story of My Life*

Writing Strong Paragraphs

In the real world of literature, the paragraph is not considered a form of writing. You wouldn't, for example, head to the local bookstore to buy a book of paragraphs. Nor would you pursue a writing career because you wanted to write award-winning paragraphs.

But paragraphs are very important as building blocks for other kinds of writing. When you write an essay, for instance, you develop paragraphs to organize your thoughts into manageable units. The paragraphs work together to build a clear, convincing argument or explanation. Learning how to write effective paragraphs will give you control of all your academic writing—from essays to articles to research papers.

- **The Parts of a Paragraph**
- **Types of Paragraphs**
- **Writing Guidelines**
- **Types of Details**
- **Patterns of Organization**
- **Modeling Paragraphs**
- **Connecting Paragraphs in Essays**
- **Paragraph Traits Checklist**

"Excellence is doing ordinary things extraordinarily well."
—John W. Gardner

The Parts of a Paragraph

A typical paragraph consists of three main parts: a **topic sentence**, the **body sentences**, and a **closing sentence**. A paragraph can develop an explanation, an opinion, a description, or a narrative. Whatever form a paragraph takes, it must contain enough information to give the reader a complete picture of the topic. The following expository paragraph provides information about a remarkable ancient sculpture. Notice that each detail in the body supports the topic sentence.

Topic Sentence

Body

Closing Sentence

Power and Glory

The huge, leonine sculpture known as the Great Sphinx prompts feelings of awe and curiosity from visitors to Giza, Egypt. At 200 feet long and 65 feet high, the statue, depicting a lion's body with the head of a man, is the world's earliest known sculpture. The man was probably the pharaoh Kahfre, who also built the nearby pyramids around 2500 B.C.E. No records or building plans of the Great Sphinx have been found, and scientists are not sure what tools would have been used to create such a huge sculpture. Because the body consists of soft limestone, wind and sand have caused terrible erosion. Several attempts have been made to save it, including restoration work done by ancient Egyptians and, later, by Roman invaders. The 13-foot-wide head was sculpted from a harder rock, so it is in better shape, although it is missing its nose. Scientists also believe the head may have included a plume and a curled beard. Because of the blowing desert sand, the body of the Sphinx has been covered and dug out several times over the centuries, with the latest excavation occurring in 1905. The world seems to agree that this statue is just too magnificent and mysterious to hide beneath shifting sands.

 Respond to the reading. What main idea about the topic does this paragraph communicate? What specific details are included to support this idea? Name two or three of them.

A Closer Look at the Parts

Whether a paragraph stands alone or is part of an extended piece of writing, it contains three elements.

The Topic Sentence

A **topic sentence** tells the reader what your paragraph is about. The topic sentence should do two things: (1) name the specific topic of the paragraph and (2) identify a particular feeling or feature about the topic. Here is a simple formula for writing a topic sentence.

> a specific topic
> **+**   a particular feeling or feature about the topic
> **=** **an effective topic sentence**

> The huge, leonine sculpture known as the Great Sphinx
> **+**   prompts feelings of awe and curiosity from visitors
> **=** **The huge, leonine sculpture known as the Great Sphinx prompts feelings of awe and curiosity from visitors to Giza, Egypt.**

Tip

The topic sentence is *usually* the first sentence in a paragraph. However, it can also be located elsewhere. For example, you can present details that build up to an important summary topic sentence at the end of a paragraph.

The Body

The sentences in the **body** of the paragraph should all support the topic sentence. Each sentence should add new details about the topic.

■ Use specific details to make your paragraph interesting.
   At 200 feet long and 65 feet high, the statue, depicting a lion's body with the head of a man, is the world's earliest known sculpture.

■ Organize your sentences in the best possible order: time order, order of importance, classification, and so on. (See pages **571–574**.)

The Closing Sentence

The **closing sentence** comes after all the body details have been presented. This sentence can remind the reader of the topic, summarize the paragraph, or link the paragraph to the next one.

The world seems to agree that this sculpture is just too magnificent and mysterious to hide beneath shifting sands.

Types of Paragraphs

There are four basic types of paragraphs: *narrative, descriptive, expository,* and *persuasive.*

Narrative Paragraph

A **narrative paragraph** tells a story. It may draw from the writer's personal experience or from other sources of information. A narrative paragraph is almost always organized chronologically, or according to time.

Topic Sentence

Body

Closing Sentence

My First Driving Lesson

I began my first driving lesson thinking I would be a terrific driver. I got into the car and immediately turned the key. The instructor made a mark on his clipboard because in my excitement, I hadn't buckled my seat belt. After buckling up, I put the car into gear, which led to another mark. I hadn't checked my mirrors or looked to see if someone else was coming. After looking around, I stepped on the gas, and we sort of lunged to the practice area marked by orange highway cones. As I started through the practice course, I jerked the wheel to avoid one cone and knocked down two others. Then, in my panic, I hit the gas pedal instead of the brake! Two more cones went down before my instructor slammed on his master brake pedal. Unfortunately, the rest of my lesson didn't go any smoother. My instructor's pencil scratched noisily as he wrote on the clipboard. I figured I would never get my license. But when we finally stopped, he just handed me a copy of the checklist and said we would work on all my mistakes. I was relieved to know that they didn't expect perfection right away. Suddenly, I couldn't wait for my second lesson.

Respond to the reading. What transitional words or phrases does the writer use to indicate the passage of time? Find three. What tone does the writer use—serious, entertaining, or surprising? Explain.

Write a narrative paragraph. Share your first driving experience or some other "first" experience. (Follow the guidelines on page 568.)

Descriptive Paragraph

A **descriptive paragraph** provides a detailed picture of a person, a place, an object, or an event. This type of paragraph should contain a variety of sensory details—specific sights, sounds, smells, tastes, and textures.

Topic Sentence

Body

Closing Sentence

The Northside Youth Center

The Northside Youth Center is the perfect place to spend time after school and on weekends. When entering the multipurpose room, one's eyes are immediately drawn to the bank of six computers along the left wall. There, students play games or do homework on the softly humming machines, while nearby a teacher/supervisor sits at a desk, ready to help. Beneath the tall, narrow windows on the back wall is the art area, with glow-in-the-dark metal cabinets that contain art supplies. To the right of the cabinets are several vending machines, their flashy windows offering fruit, sandwiches, and juice. A table with a microwave oven sits next to the machines, and the inviting scent of a warming sandwich or popping popcorn often fills the air. A large door on the wall to the right is open, and echoing shouts mixed with a chorus of bouncing basketballs spill in from the gym. Games of a quieter nature are played at tables stacked with colorful board games along this wall. Next to the tables, an area dominated by a bookshelf sprawling behind comfortable chairs spreads out into the middle of the room. This is a favorite spot. Students usually occupy these chairs, reading, studying, or talking with a friend. The Northside Youth Center provides many positive opportunities for students, all in a safe, inviting environment.

Paragraphs

Respond to the reading. What senses are covered in this paragraph? Which two or three details seem especially descriptive?

Write a descriptive paragraph. Write a paragraph that describes someplace that is important to you. Use sensory details in your description. (Follow the guidelines on page 568.)

Expository Paragraph

An **expository paragraph** shares information about a specific topic. Expository writing presents facts, gives directions, defines terms, explains a process, and so forth. It should clearly inform the reader.

Topic Sentence

Body

Closing Sentence

Step, Toe, Heel

There are many types of dance shoes, but three of the most popular types are specially designed for ballet, jazz, and tap. Ballet shoes are soft, leather-soled slippers that have an adjustable tie to help them fit the foot. They often have ribbons sewn on to wrap around the leg for an elegant look. Some ballet slippers are designed especially for *pointe,* which is dancing on the tips of the toes. These have a more structured toe box that is heavily padded at the base to prevent damage to the toes. Jazz shoes, which lace on and look like street shoes, are generally made of leather with a rubber sole and heel. The sole might be whole or split to offer more flexibility. Jazz shoes may be boot height to give the dancer firmer ankle support. Tap shoes also vary in style and construction, but they usually include a layer of fiberboard glued and stapled to the leather sole. The extra layer provides a hard surface for the screws holding the metal taps. Men's tap shoes can be almost any style, while those for women generally have a stacked heel and a strap. A rubber pad is sometimes attached to the bottom of the sole to prevent slipping. Whether a dancer chooses to leap, glide, or tap, there is a shoe that will help get the "pointe" across.

Respond to the reading. What is the specific topic of this paragraph? What supporting facts or examples does the writer include? Name at least three of them.

Write an expository paragraph. Write a paragraph that shares information about a specific topic. Be sure to include plenty of supporting details. (Follow the guidelines on page 568.)

Persuasive Paragraph

A **persuasive paragraph** expresses an opinion and tries to convince the reader that the opinion is valid. To be persuasive, a writer must include effective supporting reasons and facts.

Topic Sentence

Body

Closing Sentence

Helping One Child Helps the World

The Midtown High School Spanish Club should sponsor a needy child in a Spanish-speaking country, working through the Save the Children Foundation. Such sponsorship would be extremely beneficial to all. Club members would be encouraged to communicate with the child. Sending and receiving letters in Spanish would enhance our Spanish reading and writing skills. In addition, we could ask questions and receive information about the child's city and country, further expanding our understanding of another culture. Finally, we would be doing something important. Offering humanitarian aid is one of the most selfless and beneficial things a person can do, and sponsoring a child could even prove to be life saving. Our sponsorship would help assure the child's nutritional and educational needs are met, giving that child a better life. Some members have said that our club could not afford to sponsor a child, but the cost of $18 a month could easily be covered for an entire year by our club's treasury. We could also do additional fund-raising to send extra materials and supplies to our adopted child. This shared sense of purpose would draw club members closer together, creating a family feeling. The Spanish Club sponsoring a needy child would benefit everyone and should begin as soon as possible.

Paragraphs

Respond to the reading. What is the writer's opinion in the paragraph? What reasons does the writer include to support the opinion? Name two.

Write a persuasive paragraph. Write a paragraph expressing your opinion about an event or an activity. Include at least two or three strong reasons that support your opinion. (Follow the guidelines on page 568.)

Writing Guidelines Developing a Paragraph

Before you begin your writing, make sure you understand the requirements of the assignment. Then follow the steps listed below.

Prewriting Selecting a Topic and Details

- Select a specific topic that meets the requirements of the assignment.
- Collect facts, examples, and other details about your topic.
- Write a topic sentence stating what your paragraph will be about. (See page 563.)
- Decide on the best way to organize the supporting details. (See pages 571–574.)

Writing Creating the First Draft

- Start your paragraph with the topic sentence.
- Follow with sentences that support your topic. Use your details and organizational plan as a general guide.
- Connect your ideas and sentences with transitions.
- Close with a sentence that restates your topic, gives a final thought, or, in the case of an essay, leads into the next paragraph.

Revising Improving Your Writing

- Add information if you need to say more about your topic.
- Move sentences that aren't in the best order.
- Delete sentences that don't support the topic.
- Rewrite any sentences that are unclear.

Editing Checking for Conventions

- Check the revised draft for punctuation, capitalization, grammar, and spelling errors.
- Write a neat final copy and proofread it one last time.

Tip

When you write a paragraph, remember that the reader wants to . . .

- learn something. *(Offer new and interesting information.)*
- hear the writer's voice. *(Let your personality come through in the writing.)*

Types of Details

There are many types of details you can include in paragraphs (and in longer forms of writing). The purpose of your writing determines which details you should use. The key types are explained below and on the following page.

Facts are *details* that can be proven.

> **The Great Chicago Fire began on October 8, 1871.**
>
> **Eating blueberries helps lower cholesterol and prevent urinary tract infections.**

Statistics present *numerical information* (numbers) about a specific topic.

> **From 1980 through 1995, 1,318 deaths in the United States were caused by lightning strikes, an average of 82 per year. (U.S. Centers for Disease Control and Prevention)**

Examples are *statements that illustrate a main point.*

> **A pancake may not always be called a pancake** *(main point).* **In Wales, pancakes are called Welshcakes and might be rolled into cigar shapes or served flat. France has its crepes, and Italy, its cannelloni. In the Middle East, you'll find a sweet wedding pancake called an ataif. In Russia or Poland, you can enjoy a delicious blini, but if you're hungry in Hungary, ask for a palascinta.**

Anecdotes are *brief stories* that help to make a point about a topic. They can be much more effective than a matter-of-fact list of details.

> **Members of the media might try to influence us, but they often find that they should not underestimate the American voter. Perhaps the best example of this occurred during the presidential election of 1948. Harry Truman was running for re-election against Thomas Dewey, the popular governor of New York. All the polls and commentators had predicted a landslide victory for Dewey, and even Truman's wife, Bess, felt her husband could not win.**
>
> **Truman refused to give up, and set off on a "whistle stop" campaign, traveling the country to talk to the people face-to-face. The night of the election, Truman went to bed early, convinced he would lose. Dewey's victory seemed such a sure thing, the *Chicago Tribune* even printed the next day's headline early: "Dewey Defeats Truman." But in the morning, the results showed that Truman had won. The American people had ignored the polls and had made the decision for themselves.**

Quotations are *people's statements* repeated word for word. Quotations can provide powerful supporting evidence.

> Hunger is a great motivator for change, as witnessed by the French Revolution and by the rise of Nazi Germany. Both governmental changes were precipitated by the poverty of the common people, who resorted to violence to improve their lives. As O. Henry wrote, "Love and business and family and religion and art and patriotism are nothing but shadows of words when a man's starving." People who are fed and comfortable will accept the status quo, while those who are in need often demand violent change.

Definitions give the *meaning* of unfamiliar terms. Definitions of technical terms are especially important for the reader. Defining such terms makes your writing clear.

> Chiaroscuro—the play of light and shade—to create mood was used effectively in films by Orson Welles and Alfred Hitchcock.

Reasons answer *why* and can explain or justify ideas.

> Carpeting the school would be an excellent idea. A good indoor-outdoor carpet would muffle noise in hallways and classes, creating an atmosphere conducive to learning. Carpeting creates a more formal feel, subtly encouraging better behavior and reducing litter. Carpeting is also easier to repair than hard flooring, as a damaged or stained area can simply be cut out and a new patch set in.

Comparisons address the *similarities* or *differences* between two things. It is especially helpful to compare something new or unknown to something your reader understands.

> Regular broadcast television and satellite television both depend on radio waves to deliver the signal to your TV. Broadcast television is limited because the waves transmitted follow a straight path, eventually heading into space. Satellite TV, however, uses a fixed-location space satellite to catch the waves and bounce them back, allowing for a greater number of signals and, consequently, a larger choice of TV stations.

Try It!

Find examples in this book's writing samples of any four types of details listed on the previous two pages. On your own paper, write the examples and the pages where you found them.

Patterns of Organization

On the following four pages, sample paragraphs show basic patterns of organization. Reviewing these samples can help you organize your own writing.

Chronological Order

Chronological (time) **order** is effective for explaining a process or sharing a story. The paragraph below explains how to change the oil and the oil filter in a car.

Graphic Organizer: Time Line

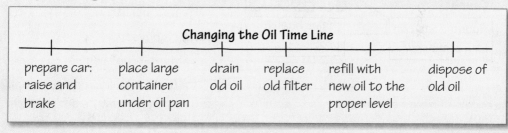

Changing the Oil Time Line

| prepare car: raise and brake | place large container under oil pan | drain old oil | replace old filter | refill with new oil to the proper level | dispose of old oil |

Topic Sentence

Body

Closing Sentence

Change Is Good

Changing the oil and oil filter in a car is easy. First, put several newspapers under the engine to catch any oil accidentally spilled while the oil is drained. Then place a large container under the oil pan to catch the old oil. Lie on some newspaper and use a wrench to loosen the plug. Wear rubber gloves and use your fingers to gently unscrew the plug and pull it quickly away, allowing the old oil to pour into the container beneath. When all the oil has drained, replace the plug, tightening it with the wrench. Next, loosen the old oil filter with a filter wrench. Finish removing the filter by hand and empty the contents into the used-oil container. Spread a small amount of oil around the new filter's gasket to create a good seal and hand-turn the new filter into place. Finally, remove the engine's oil cap and pour in the new oil to the proper level. Be sure to properly dispose of the old oil at a recycling center. With a little care and regular oil changes, an engine will continue to run smoothly for a long time.

Cause and Effect

Cause-effect paragraphs can take on a variety of forms: one cause with many effects (as in the sample below), many causes that create one final effect, and other variations. When writing about cause-and-effect relationships, you can use an organizer like the one below to arrange details.

Cause-Effect Organizer

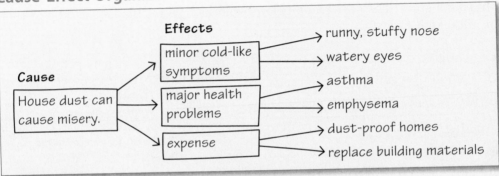

The Dust of the Earth

Topic Sentence

House dust, if considered at all, is usually dismissed as an unavoidable inconvenience; but for allergy sufferers, it can mean total misery. The allergic reaction to dust can include chronic year-round rhinitis, or runny nose. Other symptoms may include sneezing and a stuffy nose. The sufferer may have itchy, teary eyes, or even develop a rash or hives. Dust allergies can mimic major health problems such as asthma or emphysema, with wheezing or shortness of breath, accompanied by coughing. People who already have these diseases could find their conditions aggravated by dust. Many people who suffer from dust allergies may face significant expenses because they must dust-proof their homes with special air filters and substitute existing building materials with nonallergenic ones. A little dust doesn't seem so bad, but in extreme cases, it can lead to major health issues and heavy financial costs.

Body

Closing Sentence

 Respond to the reading. What are the three main effects of house dust on allergy sufferers? What could be another way that you could write about the topic of house dust? Explain.

Classification

Classification is a technique used to break down a topic into categories. The following paragraph classifies the different types of pyramids. The writer used a line diagram to plan her writing.

Line Diagram

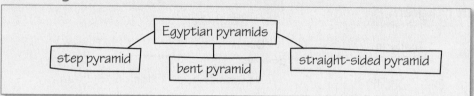

Topic Sentence

Body

Closing Sentence

Types of Pyramids

Three distinct styles of pyramids were created in ancient Egypt: the step pyramid, the bent pyramid, and the more commonly recognized straight-sided pyramid. The step pyramid actually evolved from the earliest burial chambers, the *mastabas,* which were low, flat structures built of mud brick. Around 2780 B.C.E., the architect Imhotep stacked six successively smaller mastabas, creating the first step pyramid as a burial chamber for King Djoser. This pyramid can be seen near Saqqara, south of Cairo. The next attempt at a pyramid came in Dashur, also south of Cairo, during the reign of Pharaoh Snefru. The limestone-faced sides were straight, but they changed angle and cut sharply inward about halfway up, creating a bent, squashed-looking top. Not satisfied with this design, Snefru ordered another pyramid to be built, this time with straight sides that met at a tip. The result was the first straight-sided pyramid, called the red pyramid because the sun gave it a reddish tint. Snefru's son, Khufru, also known as Cheops, perfected the pyramid, creating the magnificent Great Pyramid of Giza, today known as one of the Seven Wonders of the Ancient World. Whether step, bent, or straight-sided, the pyramids of Egypt are magnificent reminders of a great ancient nation.

 Respond to the reading. What facts or details did you learn about the straight-sided pyramid? Name three.

Comparison and Contrast

Organizing by **comparison** shows the similarities or differences between two subjects. To compare trolleys with modern buses, one student used a Venn diagram. After organizing her details, she found the two modes of transportation had key similarities, which became the focus of her paragraph.

Venn Diagram

Trolleys	Both	City Buses
needed a track	mass transit	ride on any roadway
nonpolluting	cost-effective	pollution emissions
closed or open	specific routes	windows, air conditioning
within city limits	reliable	city to city
	adaptable for comfort	

Topic Sentence

Body

Closing Sentence

Trolley Cars and Buses

Today's buses might seem like a huge improvement over the trolley cars of a century ago, but in some ways the old mode of transportation was very similar to its modern counterpart. Trolleys were an early form of mass transportation, and, like modern buses, they were able to move large numbers of people across cities in an efficient, cost-effective manner. Like buses, trolleys had established routes with specific schedules, making both modes of transportation convenient and reliable for commuters. Today's buses provide air-conditioned relief from hot weather and comfortable heat when the weather is cold. Similarly, trolleys also adapted for rider comfort, though they had to rely on removable wooden panels to let in cool summer breezes or to shut out cold winter winds. So while modern buses offer comfortable, efficient transportation, trolleys served well as a moving force of yesterday. The two really aren't that different after all, showing, perhaps, that the more things change, the more they stay the same.

Modeling Paragraphs

When you come across paragraphs that you really like, practice writing examples of your own that follow the author's pattern of writing. This process is called **modeling**. Follow these guidelines:

Guidelines for Modeling

- **Find a paragraph** you would like to model.
- **Think of a topic** for your practice writing.
- **Follow the pattern** of the paragraph.
- **Build your paragraph** one sentence or idea at a time.
- **Review your work** and change any parts that seem confusing.

Using an Anecdote

An anecdote is a brief story that can be used to illustrate a point. The following paragraph uses an anecdote in this way.

> I had always thought I lacked the genes for artistic expression. My artwork was chaotic and my sculptures misshapen. Even coloring inside the lines when I was little was an exercise in futility. Then I had an art class with Ms. Edelman. She laughed at my mistakes and encouraged me to try again. I learned to carefully follow her directions, but also to experiment with new ideas. Sometimes the results were awful, but Ms. Edelman said that failure is only a stepping-stone to success. She taught me to look at art not as a finished product, but as a creative process, and that I should value and have confidence in my efforts. Most important, I learned that everyone has the ability for creative expression, even if that expression is unconventional or unappreciated. Ms. Edelman taught me that a good, caring teacher can make a huge difference in a student's life.

 Respond to the reading. What is the topic of the above paragraph? In which sentence is the topic identified? Which main points provide the strongest support of the topic? Name two.

Try It!

Write your own paragraph modeled after the sample above. Refer to the guidelines near the top of the page to help you complete your writing.

Creating a List Paragraph

A creative way to develop a paragraph is to provide supporting sentences, one after another, almost in list form. In the following paragraph, the writer "lists" her friends like a lineup of television programs.

Lunchtime with my friends is like watching television—with a complete lineup of television programs. Drew supplies the news and commentary, advising us all of the latest school happenings, along with his sometimes sarcastic "editorials." Keisha provides us with our own private sitcom, as she hilariously describes her ups and downs of the morning, along with some dead-on impersonations of teachers and other students. Steve is our public service announcer, serenely reminding us of the importance of our music and drama departments, and trying to get us involved. Meanwhile, Yolanda rattles off sports anecdotes and updates for the current teams, including who is starting, injured, or benched because of grades. Squeezed in between all these formidable conversations, Leanne manages to give us a celebrity update, dropping in gossipy little tidbits about the social life of various CHS students. So what is my function while all this chatter is going on? I serve as the audience, appreciating the array of friends who offer me such varied programming.

 Respond to the reading. What is the topic of this paragraph? What do all of the sentences in the body have in common?

 ## Try It!

Write your own list paragraph modeled after the sample above. Refer to the guidelines for modeling on page 575 to help you complete your writing.

Connecting Paragraphs in Essays

To write strong essays, you must organize the ideas within each paragraph and then organize the paragraphs within the essay. The guidelines that follow will help you connect the paragraphs in your essay.

- **Be sure that your paragraphs are complete.** Each one should contain an effective topic sentence and supporting details.

- **Identify the topic and thesis (focus) of your essay** in the beginning paragraph. Start with some interesting details to get the reader's attention. Then share the focus of your writing.

- **Develop your ideas** in the middle paragraphs. Each middle paragraph should include information that explains and supports your focus. Often, the paragraph that contains the most important information comes right after the beginning paragraph or right before the final paragraph.

- **Review one or more of the main points in your essay** in the closing paragraph. The last sentence usually gives the reader a final interesting thought about the topic.

- **Use transition words or phrases** to connect the paragraphs. Transitions help the reader follow an essay from one paragraph to the next. In the sample below, the transitions are shown in red.

. . . Suddenly, sports enthusiasts discovered they did not need a boat to go sailing.

In addition to skateboard sailing, people started adding sails when they went skiing, snowboarding, or roller-skating. Using the principles of water sailing, they were able to increase their speed and skills, moving rapidly across the landscape. . . .

Because of several factors, wind sports have gained in popularity through the past decade. For one, wind power is free, and all the sailor needs is a sail and something to slide or glide on. Another reason for the popularity of wind sports is the availability of places to practice. Any snowy area, flat or hilly, works for winter sailing, while parking lots and quiet streets offer excellent summer conditions. . . .

Try It!

Turn to pages 592–593 to see examples of transition words and phrases. Find one or two writing samples that use some of these transitions.

Sample Essay

Read this sample essay about coffee production. Notice how the three parts—the beginning, the middle, and the ending—work together.

Java Crisis

The production of coffee beans is a huge, profitable business, but, unfortunately, full-sun production is taking over the industry and leaving destruction in its wake. The change in how coffee is grown endangers the very existence of certain animals and birds, and even alters the world's environmental equilibrium.

On a local level, the devastation of the forest required by full-sun fields affects the area's birds and animals. The forest canopy of shade trees provides a home for migratory birds and other species that depend on the trees' flowers and fruits. Full-sun coffee growers destroy this forest home. Many species have already become extinct due to deforestation, and many more are quickly dying out.

On a more global level, the destruction of the rain forest for full-sun coffee fields also threatens human life. Medical research often makes use of the forests' plant and animal life, and the destruction of such species could prevent researchers from finding cures for certain diseases. In addition, new coffee-growing techniques are contributing to toxic runoff that is poisoning the water locally—a poison that could eventually find its way into much of the world's groundwater.

Both locally and globally, the continued spread of full-sun coffee plantations could mean the ultimate destruction of the rain-forest ecology. The loss of shade trees is already causing a slight change in the world's climate, and studies show that the loss of oxygen-giving trees also contributes to air pollution and global warming. In addition, the new growing techniques are contributing to acidic soil conditions and erosion.

It is obvious that the way much coffee is grown affects many aspects of life, from the local environment to the global ecology. But consumers do have a choice. They can purchase shade-grown coffee whenever possible, although at a higher cost. The future health of the planet and its inhabitants is surely worth more than an inexpensive cup of coffee.

 Look at the transitions. What specific words does the author use to move from one paragraph to the next? Identify them.

Paragraph Traits Checklist

Use the checklist below as a basic guide when you review your paragraphs. If you answer "no" to any of the questions, continue to work with that part of your paragraph.

Revising Checklist

Ideas

_____ **1.** Have I selected a specific topic?

_____ **2.** Have I supported the topic with specific details?

Organization

_____ **3.** Is my topic sentence clear?

_____ **4.** Have I organized the details in an effective order?

Voice

_____ **5.** Do I sound interested in and knowledgeable about my topic?

_____ **6.** Does my voice fit the assignment and my audience?

Word Choice

_____ **7.** Do I use specific nouns, verbs, and modifiers?

_____ **8.** Do I define any unfamiliar terms?

Sentence Fluency

_____ **9.** Have I written clear and complete sentences?

_____ **10.** Do I vary my sentence beginnings and lengths?

Conventions

_____ **11.** Have I checked for punctuation, capitalization, and grammar errors?

_____ **12.** Have I checked for spelling errors?

Paragraphs

www.hmheducation.com/writesource

A Writer's Resource

Writing Focus

Getting Started   **582**
Finding the Right Form   **586**
Using Graphic Organizers   **588**
Connecting Sentences   **592**
Strengthening Your Essay   **594**
Learning the Vocabulary of Writing   **598**
Using Graphics   **602**
Marking Corrections to Writing   **603**

Academic Vocabulary

Working with a classmate, read the definitions below and discuss possible answers to each question.

1. A resource is something that can be used for help.
What resources do you rely upon when writing a paper?

2. An encounter is a meeting, especially an unplanned one.
Think of a surprising encounter you had with someone. Who was it and where did it take place?

3. Something that is appropriate is suitable for a given purpose.
What kind of language is appropriate in a research paper? What kind of language is appropriate in a short story?

4. To enhance is to improve or make greater.
What are some ways that you enhance your writing during the revision process?

A Writer's Resource

Personal narratives, persuasive essays, short stories, poetry, reports—writing assignments come in all shapes and sizes. Some assignments come together quite easily because you know a lot about the topic; others are more challenging because they require thoughtful planning and research. Whatever the situation, you should approach *all* writing assignments in the same way—with a commitment to do your best work.

This chapter contains tips and guidelines to help you complete any writing assignment creatively and effectively. Once you become familiar with this material, you'll find it easier to write essays, articles, research papers, and more.

- **Finding a Topic**
- **Knowing the Different Forms**
- **Collecting and Organizing Details**
- **Creating an Outline**
- **Using Transitions**
- **Writing Thesis Statements**
- **Writing Great Beginnings and Endings**
- **Integrating Quotations**
- **Learning Key Writing Terms**
- **Using Writing Techniques**
- **Adding Graphics to Your Writing**
- **Using Editing and Proofreading Marks**

"When everything seems to be going against you, remember the airplane takes off against the wind, not with it."

—Henry Ford

Finding a Topic

Searching for a topic can be a challenge even if the teacher provides a general writing subject. For example, you might be asked to write about the westward development of the United States in the 1800s. This subject is too broad to cover well in one paper. It would be necessary to narrow the focus to find a manageable topic. Here are some ideas to help you.

Using a Cluster Diagram

A cluster diagram can help you identify a topic. Place the general subject in the center and then break it down into categories. Break each category into yet smaller topics. Chose one that has enough information and is the most interesting to you.

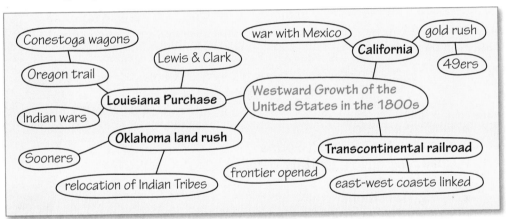

Trying Freewriting

Freewriting can help you identify a topic. Take a few minutes to write what you can remember about a general subject. Include questions that occur to you as you write. The freewriting below led one student to write about the relocation of Native American tribes.

The book Bury My Heart at Wounded Knee really made me think. I knew that people came from other countries to start a new life here and that the transcontinental railroad made it much easier to open the West to settlement. But why couldn't Native Americans and settlers share the land? The ownership of land seemed to make cooperation impossible. Were reservations the only answer? How long did it take to settle the West?

Reviewing a "Basics of Life" List

Most people find they need a few basic things in order to live a full life. The list below, a "Basics of Life" list, could help you focus on a topic. For example, choosing "trade/money" might lead you to explore and write about the gold rush to California.

family	warmth	food	shelter
friends	work	community	art/music
faith/religion	love	machines	natural resources
tools	education	clothing	health
hobbies	identity	trade/money	literature
water	rules/laws	freedom	government

Studying Visual Images

Paintings and visuals can give you topic ideas as well. The paintings and photographs of the Old West by nineteenth-century artists could prompt you to write about changes brought to the West by the transcontinental railroad.

Using Writing Prompts

Every day is full of experiences that make you think. You do things that you feel good about. You hear things that make you angry. You wonder how different things work. You are reminded of a past experience. These everyday thoughts can make excellent starting points for writing. As you write about one of these prompts, a number of specific topics will come to mind.

Best and Worst
My most memorable day in school
My best hour
My encounter with a bully

It could only happen to me!
A narrow escape from trouble
I was so shocked when . . .
My life began in this way.
My strangest phone conversation
If only I had done that differently
Whatever happened to my . . .

Quotations
"Someone who makes no mistakes does not usually make anything."
"When people are free to do as they please, they usually imitate each other."
"More is not always better."
"It is easier to forgive an enemy than a friend."
"Never give advice unless asked."
"Honesty is the best policy."
"Know thyself."
"Like mother, like daughter."
"Like father, like son."

I was thinking.
Everyone should know . . .
Where do I draw the line?
Is it better to laugh or cry?
Why do people like to go fast?
I don't understand why . . .

First and Last
My first game or performance
My last day of _____
My last visit with _____

School, Then and Now
The pressure of tryouts
Grades—are they the most important part of school?
Finally, a good assembly
What my school really needs is . . .
A teacher I respect
I'm in favor of more . . .

People and Places
Who knows me best? What does he or she know?
Getting along with my brother, sister, or friend
A person I admire
My grandparents' house
The emergency room
A guided tour of my neighborhood

Using Sample Topics

People, places, experiences, and information you encounter all offer springboards for writing. Here are some topic ideas for descriptive, narrative, expository, and persuasive writing.

Descriptive

People: friend, cousin, favorite uncle, minister, boss, cashier, waiter, parent, bus driver, librarian, professional athlete

Places: store, diner, river, amusement park, religious building, train station, airport, city center, zoo, cemetery

Things: video game, CD, bike, wrench, skateboard, basketball, warehouse, movie, shoes, spoon, book, bench, kiosk, postcard

Animals: elephant, walrus, pigeon, zebra, mouse, spider, moth, poodle, penguin, cat, lobster, rat, raccoon, squirrel

Narrative

Stories: entering an abandoned building, saving an injured bird, helping a lost child, attending the ballet, entering a contest, attending a concert, riding on the subway, visiting a museum

Expository

Comparison-Contrast: private school and public school, taxis and buses, apartments and condominiums, butterfly and moth, mopeds and motorcycles, two different city neighborhoods

Cause/Effect: thunder, street potholes, echo, sonic boom, earthquake, sunburn, erosion, capillary action, flooding

Classification: types of volcanoes, kinds of television shows, groups of invertebrates, types of birds, branches of the military, kinds of cameras

Persuasive

School: banning the use of cell phones in school, keeping cars out of the school bus loading area, eliminating all carbonated drinks

Home: Getting an electric guitar, negotiating rules about visitors when parents aren't around, sleeping in on Saturdays, taking the bus by yourself, getting a job, going downtown with friends

Community: relocating the stop sign by the library, creating a skateboard park, closing the city center to cars, setting up a teen advisory board for the city

Knowing the Different Forms

Finding the right form for your writing is just as important as finding the right topic. When you are selecting a form, be sure to ask yourself who you're writing for (your *audience*) and why you're writing (your *purpose*).

Anecdote	A brief story that helps to make a point
Autobiography	A writer's story of his or her own life
Biography	A writer's story of someone else's life
Book review	An essay offering an opinion about a book, not to be confused with *literary analysis*
Cause and effect	A paper examining an event, the forces leading up to that event, and the effects following the event
Character sketch	A brief description of a specific character showing some aspect of that character's personality
Descriptive writing	Writing that uses sensory details that allow the reader to clearly visualize a person, a place, a thing, or an idea
Editorial	A letter or an article offering an opinion, an idea, or a solution
Essay	A thoughtful piece of writing in which ideas are explained, analyzed, or evaluated
Expository writing	Writing that explains something by presenting its steps, causes, or kinds
Eyewitness account	A report giving specific details of an event or a person
Fable	A short story that teaches a lesson or moral, often using talking animals as the main characters
Fantasy	A story set in an imaginary world in which the characters usually have supernatural powers or abilities
Historical fiction	An invented story based on an actual historical event
Interview	Writing based on facts and details obtained through speaking with another person
Journal writing	Writing regularly to record personal observations, thoughts, and ideas

Literary analysis	A careful examination or interpretation of some aspect of a piece of literature
Myth	A traditional story intended to explain a mystery of nature, religion, or culture
Novel	A book-length story with several characters and a well-developed plot, usually with one or more subplots
Personal narrative	Writing that shares an event or experience from the writer's personal life
Persuasive writing	Writing intended to persuade the reader to follow the writer's way of thinking about something
Play	A form that uses dialogue to tell a story, usually meant to be performed in front of an audience
Poem	A creative expression that may use rhyme, rhythm, and imagery
Problem-solution	Writing that presents a problem followed by a proposed solution
Process paper	Writing that explains how a process works, or how to do or make something
Profile	An essay that reveals an individual or re-creates a time period
Proposal	Writing that includes specific information about an idea or a project that is being considered for approval
Research report	An essay that shares information about a topic that has been thoroughly researched
Response to literature	Writing that is a reaction to something the writer has read
Science fiction	Writing based on real or imaginary science and often set in the future
Short story	A short fictional piece with only a few characters and one conflict or problem
Summary	Writing that presents the most important ideas from a longer piece of writing
Tall tale	A humorous, exaggerated story about a character or an animal that does impossible things
Tragedy	Literature in which the hero fails or is destroyed because of a serious character flaw

Collecting and Organizing Details

Using Graphic Organizers

Graphic organizers can help you gather and organize your details for writing. Clustering is one method (see page 582). These two pages show other useful organizers.

Cause-Effect Organizer

Use to collect and organize details for cause-effect essays.

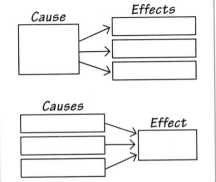

Problem-Solution Web

Use to map out problem-solution essays.

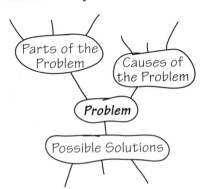

Time Line

Use for personal narratives to list actions or events in the order they occurred.

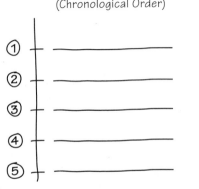

Evaluation Collection Grid

Use to collect supporting details for essays of evaluation.

Subject: _____

Points to Evaluate	Supporting Details
1.	
2.	
3.	
4.	

Venn Diagram

Use to collect details to compare and contrast two topics.

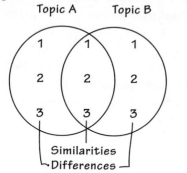

5 W's Chart

Use to collect the *Who? What? When? Where?* and *Why?* details for personal narratives and news stories.

Subject: _____

Who?	What?	When?	Where?	Why?

Line Diagram

Use to collect and organize details for academic essays.

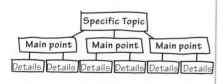

Process (Cycle) Diagram

Use to collect details for science-related writing, such as how a process or cycle works.

Topic: _____

(Chronological Order)

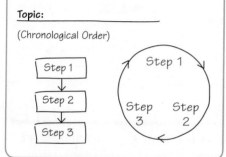

Definition Diagram

Use to gather information for extended definition essays.

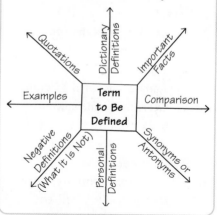

Sensory Chart

Use to collect details for descriptive essays and observation reports.

Subject: _____

Sights	Sounds	Smells	Tastes	Textures

Creating an Outline

An **outline** organizes a set of facts or ideas by listing main points and subpoints. An effective outline shows how topics or ideas fit together. A well-designed outline serves as a frame for an effective essay.

There are two types of outlines: *topic outlines* and *sentence outlines*. (See the samples below and on the next page.)

A Topic Outline

In a **topic outline**, main points and details appear as phrases rather than as complete sentences. Topic outlines are useful for short essays, including essay-test answers. The information after the Roman numerals (I., II., III., and so on) identifies the main points in the essay. The information after the capital letters (A., B., C., and so on) identifies the details that support the main points.

Sample Topic Outline

I. Effects of malnutrition on the body
   A. Extreme weight loss and stunted growth
   B. Frequent infections
   C. Lower resistance to life-threatening diseases
II. Marasmus—a form of malnutrition
   A. Extremely underweight
   B. Lack of body fat or defined muscles
   C. Puppet-like appearance
   D. Increased internal problems
III. Kwashiorkor—another form of malnutrition
   A. Badly swollen bellies
   B. Pale or red skin
   C. Thinning hair
IV. Effects of malnutrition on development
   A. Limited ability to walk and to talk
   B. Stunted intellectual development
   C. Ongoing effects into adulthood

Note: Information for the opening and closing paragraphs is not included in this outline for an essay on malnutrition.

Tip

In an outline, if you have a "I.," you must have at least a "II." If you have an "A.," you must have at least a "B.," and so on.

A Sentence Outline

A **sentence outline** is a detailed plan for writing. In this type of outline, the ideas are explained in complete sentences. This type of outline is useful for longer writing assignments like research reports and formal essays.

Sample Sentence Outline

I. Malnutrition limits the physical development of children.
   A. Malnutrition causes extreme weight loss and stunted growth.
   B. It can result in children suffering from frequent infections.
   C. It can lower children's resistance to diseases.
II. Marasmus is one form of malnutrition.
   A. Children with this condition lack body fat and muscle.
   B. They appear puppet-like.
   C. This condition causes the skin to sag and wrinkle.
   D. It also decreases the size of internal organs.
III. Kwashiorkor is another form of malnutrition.
   A. Children with this condition have swollen bellies.
   B. Kwashiorkor causes pale or red skin and thinning hair.
   C. This condition causes growth to stop.
IV. Malnutrition limits the mental development of children.
   A. It hinders toddlers' ability to walk and to talk.
   B. Iron and iodine deficiencies stunt intellectual development.
   C. Malnutrition in early childhood affects ongoing learning.

A Quick List

Use a **quick list** when there is no time for an outline. A quick list organizes ideas in the most basic way, but it will still help you organize or structure your writing.

Sample Quick List

Malnutrition
- effects on body (physical)
- marasmus
- kwashiorkor
- effects on development (mental)

Using Transitions

Transitions can be used to connect one sentence to another sentence within a paragraph, or to connect one paragraph to another within a longer essay or report. The lists below show a number of transitions and how they are used.

Each colored list below is a group of transitions that could work well together in a piece of writing.

Words used to show location

above	around	between	inside	outside
across	behind	by	into	over
against	below	down	near	throughout
along	beneath	in back of	next to	to the right
among	beside	in front of	on top of	under

Above	In front of	On top of
Below	Beside	Next to
To the left	In back of	Beneath
To the right		

Words used to show time

about	during	yesterday	until	finally
after	first	meanwhile	next	then
at	second	today	soon	as soon as
before	to begin	tomorrow	later	in the end

First	To begin	Now	First	Before
Second	To continue	Soon	Then	During
Third	To conclude	Eventually	Next	After
Finally			In the end	

Words used to compare things

likewise	as	in the same way	one way
like	also	similarly	both

In the same way	One way
Also	Another way
Similarly	Both

Words used to contrast (show differences)

but	still	although	on the other hand
however	yet	otherwise	even though

On the other hand	Although
Even though	Yet
Still	Nevertheless

Words used to emphasize a point

again	truly	especially	for this reason
to repeat	in fact	to emphasize	

For this reason	Truly	In fact
Especially	To emphasize	To repeat

Words used to conclude or summarize

finally	as a result	to sum it up	in conclusion
lastly	therefore	all in all	because

Because	As a result	To sum it up	Therefore
In conclusion	All in all	Because	Finally

Words used to add information

again	another	for instance	for example
also	and	moreover	additionally
as well	besides	along with	other
next	finally	in addition	

For example	For instance	Next	Another
Additionally	Besides	Moreover	Along with
Finally	Next	Also	As well

Words used to clarify

in other words	for instance	that is	for example

For instance	For example
In other words	Equally important

Resource

Writing Thesis Statements

An effective thesis statement tells the reader specifically what you plan to write about. In a longer essay or research report, your thesis statement generally comes at the end of the opening paragraph. It serves as a guide to keep you on track as you develop your writing.

The Process at Work

A thesis statement usually takes a stand or expresses a specific feeling about, or feature of, your topic. Write as many versions as it takes to hit upon the statement that sets the right tone for your writing. The following formula can be used to form your thesis statements.

A specific topic (*The Lincoln Memorial*)
+ **a particular stand, feeling, or feature** (*is being damaged by pollution.*)

= **an effective thesis statement.**

Sample Thesis Statements

Writing Assignment: Research report about aviation
Specific Topic: The DC-3 airplane
Thesis Statement: The DC-3 airplane established many structural standards for propeller aircraft.

Writing Assignment: Expository essay on cooking
Specific Topic: Gourmet meal
Thesis Statement: A gourmet meal results from careful preparation.

Writing Assignment: Analysis of a poem
Specific Topic: "Old Ironsides" by Oliver Wendell Holmes
Thesis Statement: Oliver Wendell Holmes wrote "Old Ironsides" to support the restoration of a historic warship.

Thesis Checklist

Be sure that your thesis statement . . .
_____ identifies a limited, specific topic,
_____ focuses on a particular feature or feeling about the topic,
_____ is stated in one or more clear sentences,
_____ can be supported with convincing facts and details, and
_____ meets the requirements of the assignment.

Writing Great Beginnings

As you write your opening paragraph, try one of these approaches to grab the reader's attention, introduce your topic, and present your thesis.

- **Start with an important or an interesting fact.**

  A catalytic converter is a key component in reducing automobile exhaust emissions.

- **Ask an interesting question.**

  How many people know that the internal temperature of a catalytic converter can reach 1,200 degrees Fahrenheit?

- **Start with a quotation.**

  George Wilson, a technician at Miller Motors, warned us, "A badly timed engine can raise catalytic temperatures to more than 1,200 degrees Fahrenheit!"

Trying a Beginning Strategy

If you have trouble coming up with a good opening paragraph, follow the step-by-step example below.

First sentence—**Grab the reader's attention.**
Write a sentence that will draw the reader into the topic. (See above.)

> How many people know that the internal temperature of a catalytic converter can reach 1,200 degrees Fahrenheit?

Second sentence—**Give some background information.**
Supporting information will add clarity and interest to your paper.

> A catalytic converter has no moving parts and is enclosed in stainless steel, so it should last the life of the car.

Third sentence—**Introduce the specific topic of the essay.**
Introduce the topic in a way that builds up to the thesis statement.

> Car companies have installed this device in automobiles to meet emission standards.

Fourth sentence—**Give the thesis statement.**
Clearly present the thesis statement. (See page **594**.)

> Fortunately, the installation of catalytic converters has greatly reduced exhaust emissions in cars.

Resource

Developing Great Endings

The closing paragraph of a paper should summarize your thesis and leave the reader with something to think about. When writing your closing paragraph, use two or more of the following ideas.

- Reflect on the topic.
- Restate your thesis.
- Review your main supporting points.
- Emphasize the special importance of one main point.
- Answer any questions the reader may still have.
- Draw a conclusion and put the information in perspective.
- Provide a final significant thought for the reader.

Trying an Ending Strategy

If you have trouble coming up with an effective closing paragraph, follow the step-by-step example below.

First sentence—**Reflect on the topic.**
Start by reflecting on the material presented previously about the topic.

> **Emission controls have greatly improved air quality in major cities.**

Second sentence—**Add another point.**
Include a significant point of interest that you didn't mention before.

> **Along with clearer skies, catalytic converters have also offered the bonus of greater fuel economy.**

Third sentence—**Emphasize the most important point.**
Stress the importance of one or more key points that support the thesis.

> **Continued improvements of the catalytic converter will mean longer equipment life and increased pollution control.**

Fourth sentence—**Wrap up the topic or draw a conclusion.**
Add one final thought about the topic or draw a conclusion from the points you've presented in the writing.

> **Although the cost of developing the catalytic converter may be substantial, there is no price too high to pay for cleaner, breathable air.**

Integrating Quotations

Always choose quotations that are clear and appropriate for your writing. Quotations should *support* your ideas, not replace them.

Trying Strategies for Using Quotations

Use the strategies below to get the most from quoted material in your writing.

- **Use quotations to support your own thoughts and ideas.**
  Effective quotations can back up your main points or support your arguments.

  > Doing what you know to be right will build your self-esteem. As Mark Twain noted, "A man cannot be comfortable without his own approval." That is why it is so important to let your conscience guide your actions.

- **Use quotations to lend authority to your writing.**
  Quoting an expert shows that you have researched your topic and understand its significance.

  > Albert Einstein observed the growth of nuclear power with concern, stating, "I know not with what weapons World War III will be fought, but World War IV will be fought with sticks and stones." His disturbing comment reminds people that a nuclear war would result in unthinkable destruction.

- **Use quotations that are succinct and powerful.**
  Any quotation that you use must add value to your writing.

  > Clearly, the education provided for today's students will determine the success of the future. As Benjamin Franklin put it, "An investment in knowledge always pays the best interest." A well-funded education system greatly benefits and enriches society.

Common Quotation Problems to Avoid

Keep these problems in mind when you consider using quotations.

- **Don't plagiarize.**
  Cite sources for all quotations (and paraphrases).
- **Don't use long quotations.**
  Keep quotations brief and to the point.
- **Don't overuse quotations.**
  Use a quotation only if you can't share the idea as powerfully or effectively in another way.

Learning Key Writing Terms

Here's a glossary of terms that describe aspects of the writing process.

Balance	Arranging words or phrases in a way to give them equal importance
Body	The main part of a piece of writing, containing details that support or develop the thesis statement
Brainstorming	Collecting ideas by thinking freely about all the possibilities; used most often with groups
Central idea	The main point of a piece of writing, often stated in a thesis statement or a topic sentence
Closing sentence	The summary or final part in a piece of writing
Coherence	The logical arranging of ideas so they are clear and easy to follow
Dialogue	Written conversation between two or more people
Emphasis	Giving great importance to a specific idea in a piece of writing
Exposition	Writing that explains and informs
Figurative language	Language that goes beyond the normal meaning of the words used, often called "figures of speech"
Focus (thesis)	The specific part of a topic that is written about in an essay
Generalization	A general statement that gives an overall view, rather than focusing on specific details
Grammar	The rules that govern the standard structure and features of a language
Idiom	A phrase or an expression that means something different from what the words actually say **That answer was really** out in left field. (This means the answer was not even close to being correct.) **Next year you'll** sing a different tune. (This means you'll think differently.)
Jargon	The special language of a certain group or occupation **The weaver pointed out the fabric's unique** warp **and** weft. Computer jargon: byte icon server virus
Limiting the subject	Narrowing a general subject to a more specific one

Literal	The actual dictionary meaning of a word; a language that means exactly what it appears to mean
Loaded words	Words slanted for or against the subject **The new tax bill** helps the rich **and** hurts the poor.
Logic	Correctly using facts, examples, and reasons to support a point
Modifiers	Words, phrases, or clauses that limit or describe another word or group of words
Objective	Writing that gives factual information without adding feelings or opinions (See *subjective*.)
Poetic license	A writer's freedom to bend the rules of writing to achieve a certain effect
Point of view	The position or angle from which a story is told (See page **322**.)
Prose	Writing in standard sentence form
Purpose	The specific goal of the writing
Style	The author's unique choice of words and sentences
Subjective	Writing that includes the writer's feelings, attitudes, and opinions (See *objective*.)
Supporting details	Facts or ideas used to sustain the main point
Syntax	The order and relationship of words in a sentence
Theme	The main point or unifying idea of a piece of writing
Thesis statement	A statement of the purpose, or main idea, of an essay
Tone	The writer's attitude toward the subject
Topic	The specific subject of a piece of writing
Topic sentence	The sentence that carries the main idea of a paragraph
Transitions	Words or phrases that connect or tie ideas together
Unity	A sense of oneness in writing in which each sentence helps to develop the main idea
Usage	The way in which people use language (*Standard* language follows the rules; *nonstandard* language does not.)
Voice	A writer's unique personal tone or feeling that comes across in a piece of writing

Resource

Using Writing Techniques

Experiment with some of these techniques in your own essays and stories.

Allusion | A reference to a familiar person, place, thing, or event
Mario threw me my mitt. "Hey, Babe Ruth, you forgot this!"

Analogy | A comparison of similar ideas or objects to help clarify one of them
"There is no frigate like a book, to take us lands away."
—Emily Dickinson

Anecdote | A brief story used to illustrate or make a point
It is said that the last words John Adams uttered were "Thomas Jefferson survives." Ironically, Jefferson had died just a few hours earlier. Both deaths occurred on July 4, 1826—the 50th anniversary of the Declaration of Independence shepherded by the two great men. (This ironic anecdote intensifies the importance of both men in our nation's history.)

Colloquialism | A common word or phrase suitable for everyday conversation but not for formal speech or writing
"Cool" and "rad" are colloquialisms suggesting approval.

Exaggeration | An overstatement or a stretching of the truth to emphasize a point (See *hyperbole* and *overstatement*.)
We opened up the boat's engine and sped along at a million miles an hour.

Flashback | A technique in which a writer interrupts a story to go back and relive an earlier time or event
I stopped at the gate, panting. Suddenly I was seven years old again, and my brother was there, calling me "chicken" from the edge of the stone well. Then I opened my eyes and heard only the crickets chirping. The years, the well, and my brother were gone. I turned back to the road, determined to get home before nightfall.

Foreshadowing | Hints about what will happen next in a story
As Mai explained why she had to break their date, she noticed Luke looking past her. Turning, she saw Meg smiling—at Luke.

Hyperbole | (hi-púr-bə-lē) Exaggeration used to emphasize a point
The music was loud enough to make your ears bleed.

Irony | An expression in which the author says one thing but means just the opposite
As we all know, there's nothing students love more than homework.

Juxtaposition	Putting two words or ideas close together to create a contrasting of ideas or an ironic meaning **Ah, the sweet smell of fuel emissions!**
Local color	The use of details that are common in a certain place
Metaphor	A figure of speech that compares two things without using the words *like* or *as* **The sheep were** dense, dancing clouds **scuttling across the road.**
Overstatement	An exaggeration or a stretching of the truth (See *exaggeration* and *hyperbole*.) **If I eat one more piece of turkey,** I will burst!
Oxymoron	Connecting two words with opposite meanings **small fortune, cruel kindness, original copy**
Paradox	A true statement that says two opposite things **As I crossed the finish line dead last, I felt a surge of triumph.**
Parallelism	Repeating similar grammatical structures (words, phrases, or sentences) to give writing rhythm We cannot undo, we will not forget, **and** we should not ignore **the pain of the past.**
Personification	A figure of speech in which a nonhuman thing is given human characteristics **The computer spit out my disk.**
Pun	A phrase that uses words that sound the same in a way that gives them a funny effect **I call my dog Trousers because he** pants **so much.**
Simile	A figure of speech that compares two things using *like* or *as* **Her silent anger was** like a rock wall, **hard and impenetrable.**
Slang	Informal words or phrases used by a particular group of people **cool it hang out shoot the curl**
Symbol	A concrete object used to represent an idea
Understatement	The opposite of exaggeration; using very calm language to call attention to an object or an idea **The car broke down, we were stranded for two days, and we missed the wedding. Other than that, we had a great trip.**

Resource

602

Adding Graphics to Your Writing

Graphics can enhance your writing by explaining your ideas in a visual manner. You can create graphics by hand or design them on a computer program and paste them into your document. Be sure to refer to the graphic in the text of your paper, either in the body of a paragraph or in a parenthetical reference. Here are some common types of graphics you can use.

Graphs

Graphs show information visually. Line graphs show change or trends across a period of time. Bar graphs compare data. Pie graphs show proportions and percentages of a whole. A graph should always include a clear title and labels for axes, sections, data points, and so forth.

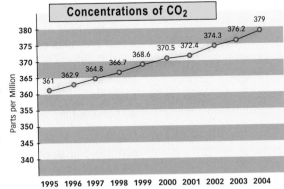

Concentrations of CO_2

Tables

Tables can organize information in a convenient manner. Most tables have rows (going across) and columns (going down). Rows contain one set of details, while columns contain another. At the left is a sample flight table, showing how far it is from one place to another. Check one place's column against the other's row.

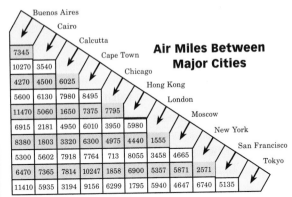

Air Miles Between Major Cities

Diagrams

Diagrams are drawings that show how something is constructed, how it works, or how its parts relate to each other. A diagram may leave out parts to show you only what you need to learn.

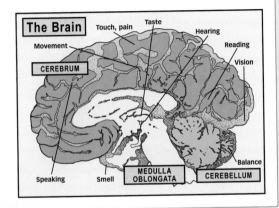

The Brain

Using Editing and Proofreading Marks

Use these symbols and letters to show where and how your writing needs to be changed. Your teachers may also use these symbols to point out errors in your writing. (This chart also appears inside the back cover of your book.)

Symbols	Meaning	Example	Corrected Example
≡	Capitalize a letter.	Willa Cather wrote *my Antonia.*	Willa Cather wrote *My Antonia.*
/	Make a capital letter lowercase.	Her novel tells the story of a Pioneer woman.	Her novel tells the story of a pioneer woman.
⊙	Insert (add) a period.	The story focuses on the right thing to do Antonia is . . .	The story focuses on the right thing to do. Antonia is . . .
◯ or sp.	Correct spelling.	Jim Burden narates the story.	Jim Burden narrates the story.
℮	Delete (take out) or replace.	Jim he tells about his relationship with Antonia.	Jim tells about his relationship with Antonia.
∧	Insert here.	Antonia represents Jim's childhood on the western frontier.	Antonia represents Jim's childhood on the western frontier.
∧ ∧ ∧	Insert a comma, a colon, or a semicolon.	Antonia's family, the Shimerdas came from Bohemia.	Antonia's family, the Shimerdas, came from Bohemia.
∨ ∨ ∨	Insert an apostrophe or quotation marks.	They are friends with Jims family on the frontier.	They are friends with Jim's family on the frontier.
? ! ∧ ∧	Insert a question mark or an exclamation point.	Why is Antonia condescending toward Jim?	Why is Antonia condescending toward Jim?
¶	Start a new paragraph.	¶Their friendship changes when . . .	Their friendship changes when . . .
∼	Switch words or letters.	Jim goes away to college attend.	Jim goes away to attend college.

Proofreader's Guide

Marking Punctuation   **605**

Checking Mechanics   **648**

Understanding Idioms   **672**

Using the Right Word   **678**

Parts of Speech   **700**

Understanding Sentences   **738**

Academic Vocabulary

Working with a classmate, read the definitions below and discuss possible answers to each question.

1. To Indicate can mean to show or signify.
   How do you indicate the correct answer on a multiple-choice test?

2. Function refers to the purpose or role of something.
   What is the function of a hospital emergency room?

3. To substitute means to put in place of another.
   When you are revising an essay, why might you substitute certain words for different ones?

4. Something that is abstract cannot be physically observed.
   Nouns can be described as either abstract or concrete. Which is *justice*? Explain.

Marking Punctuation

Period

605.1 At the End of a Sentence

Use a **period** at the end of a sentence that makes a statement, requests something, or gives a mild command.

(Statement) **The man who does not read good books has no advantage over the man who can't read them**.

—Mark Twain

(Request) **Please bring your folders and notebooks to class**.

(Mild command) **Listen carefully so that you understand these instructions**.

NOTE: It is not necessary to place a period after a statement that has parentheses around it and is part of another sentence.

My dog Bobot (I don't quite remember how he acquired this name) **is a Chesapeake Bay retriever—a hunting dog—who is afraid of loud noises**.

605.2 After an Initial or an Abbreviation

Place a period after an initial or an abbreviation (in American English).

Ms. **Sen**. **D**.**D**.**S**. **M**.**F**.**A**. **M**.**D**. **Jr**. **U**.**S**. **p**.**m**. **a**.**m**.
Edna St. **Vincent Millay** **Booker T**. **Washington** **D**. **H**. **Lawrence**

NOTE: When an abbreviation is the last word in a sentence, use only one period at the end of the sentence.

Jaleesa eyed each door until she found the name Fletcher B. Gale, M.D.

605.3 As a Decimal Point

A period is used as a decimal point.

New York City has a budget of $46.9 **billion to serve its** 8.1 **million people**.

Exclamation Point

605.4 To Express Strong Feeling

Use the **exclamation point** (sparingly) to express strong feeling. You may place it after a word, a phrase, or a sentence.

"That's not the point," said Wangero. "These are all pieces of dresses Grandma used to wear. She did all this stitching by hand. Imagine!**"**

—Alice Walker, "Everyday Use"

Question Mark

606.1 Direct Question

Place a **question mark** at the end of a direct question.

> Where do I go now? I wondered. Do I climb the stairs or take the elevator? Why is there no escalator in this building? Why should I be discouraged by the sound of ringing in my ears?

When a question ends with a quotation that is also a question, use only one question mark, and place it within the quotation marks.

> On road trips, do you remember driving your parents crazy by asking, "Are we there yet?"

NOTE: Do *not* use a question mark after an indirect question.

> While I was crossing through the park, I found a friendly looking woman and asked her where the nearest bus stop was.

606.2 To Show Uncertainty

Use a question mark within parentheses to show uncertainty.

> This summer marks the 20th season (?) of the American Players Theatre.

606.3 Short Question Within a Sentence

Use a question mark for a short question within parentheses.

> We crept so quietly (had they heard us?) past the kitchen door and back to our room.

Use a question mark for a short question within dashes.

> Maybe somewhere in the pasts of these humbled people, there were cases of bad mothering or absent fathering or emotional neglect—what family surviving the '50s was exempt?—but I couldn't believe these human errors brought the physical changes in Frank.
>
> —Mary Kay Blakely, *Wake Me When It's Over*

Grammar Practice

Periods and Question Marks

 Write a period where it is needed to end a sentence and after an abbreviation. Write a question mark where it is needed to end a sentence or for a short question within parentheses.

Example: Ms Henson is teaching a course in forensic science this year
        Ms.   year.

1. With the popularity of television shows featuring forensic science (isn't *CSI* one), many high schools have begun offering classes in the subject

2. What is forensic science

3. It's any area of science that could be used in a court of law

4. For instance, a forensic psychologist (Dr Sam Waters of *Profiler* is a TV example) studies a crime scene to determine clues to the criminal's personality

5. Have you heard of a *criminalist*

6. A criminalist, who uses chemical and microscopic techniques to examine physical evidence, can identify an individual through DNA analysis

7. A forensic pathologist is an MD and examines samples removed from the body to establish the time and cause of death

8. He or she might also be able to determine if a death was a homicide or a suicide

9. Ms Henson asked me if I'd like to be a forensic pathologist someday

Model

Model the following sentences to practice using the correct punctuation for direct and indirect questions.

Have you given any consideration to joining the military?

I asked him why he wants to join the armed forces.

Comma

608.1 Between Two Independent Clauses

Use a **comma** between two independent clauses that are joined by a coordinating conjunction (*and, but, or, nor, for, yet, so*).

> **I wanted to work in the garden, but it was raining too hard.**

NOTE: Do not confuse a sentence containing a compound verb for a compound sentence.

> **I decided to plant flower bulbs and then mow the yard.**

608.2 To Separate Adjectives

Use commas to separate two or more adjectives that *equally* modify the same noun. (Note: Do not use a comma between the last adjective and the noun.)

> **Bao's eyes met the hard, bright lights hanging directly above her.**
>
> —Julie Ament, student writer

A Closer Look

To determine whether adjectives modify equally—and should, therefore, be separated by commas—use these two tests:

1. Shift the order of the adjectives; if the sentence is clear, the adjectives modify equally. (In the example below, *hot* and *smelly* can be shifted and the sentence is still clear; *usual* and *morning* cannot.)

2. Insert *and* between the adjectives; if the sentence reads well, use a comma when the *and* is omitted. (The word *and* can be inserted between *hot* and *smelly*, but *and* does not make sense between *usual* and *morning*.)

> **Matty was tired of working in the hot, smelly kitchen and decided to take her usual morning walk.**

608.3 To Separate Contrasted Elements

Use commas to separate contrasted elements within a sentence. Often the word or phrase that is set off is preceded by *not*.

> **Since the book was about children and their antics, and not the problems that teenagers face, I was not that interested.**

Grammar Practice

Commas 1

■ To Separate Adjectives
■ To Separate Contrasted Elements

 Indicate where commas are needed in the following sentences by writing the commas along with the words that surround them.

Example: Marianna was very smart though not a genius.
smart, though

1. One of her favorite things was learning unfamiliar interesting words.

2. Marianna unlike many of her friends could solve tough word puzzles with little effort.

3. Putting together challenging complex word puzzles was her favorite pastime.

4. Marianna created her puzzles for personal satisfaction not for financial gain.

5. The puzzles she made had thought-provoking entertaining themes.

6. They included fascinating little-known facts about countries of the world.

7. Books of her puzzles were published overseas not in the United States.

8. She was pleasantly surprised when her hobby became a serious profitable business.

9. Now Marianna is a busy successful business owner.

Model

Model the following sentences to practice using commas to separate contrasted elements.

> Be a first-rate version of yourself, not a second-rate version of someone else.
>
> —Judy Garland

> Strive not to be a success, but rather to be of value.
>
> —Albert Einstein

Comma *(continued)*

610.1 To Set Off Appositives

A specific kind of explanatory word or phrase called an **appositive** identifies or renames a preceding noun or pronoun.

> **Benson**, our uninhibited and enthusiastic Yorkshire terrier, **joined our family on my sister's fifteenth birthday.**
>
> —Chad Hockerman, student writer

NOTE: Do not use commas with *restrictive appositives*. A restrictive appositive is essential to the basic meaning of the sentence.

> **Sixteen-year-old student** Ray Perez **was awarded an athletic scholarship.**

610.2 Between Items in a Series

Use commas to separate individual words, phrases, or clauses in a series. (A series contains at least three items.)

> **Dad likes** meat, vegetables, and a salad **for dinner.** (words)
>
> **I** took her for walks, read her stories, and made up games **for her to play.** (phrases)
>
> —Anne Moody, *Coming of Age in Mississippi*

NOTE: Do not use commas when all the words in a series are connected with *or*, *nor*, or *and*.

> **We washed the car** and **waxed the car** and **changed the oil.**

610.3 After Introductory Phrases and Clauses

Use a comma after an introductory participial phrase.

> Determined to finish the sweater by Friday, **my grandmother knit night and day.**

Use a comma after a long introductory prepositional phrase or after two or more short ones.

> In the oddest places and at the strangest times, **my grandmother can be found knitting madly away.**

NOTE: You may omit the comma if the introductory phrase is short.

> Before breakfast **my grandmother knits.**

Use a comma after an introductory adverb (subordinate) clause.

> After the practice was over, **Tina walked home.**

NOTE: A comma is not used if an adverb clause *follows* the main clause and is needed to complete the meaning of the sentence.

> **Tina practiced hard** because she feared losing.

However, a comma is used if the adverb clause following the main clause begins with *although, even though, while,* or another conjunction expressing a contrast.

> **Tina walked home**, even though it was raining very hard.

Grammar Practice

Commas 2

- ■ To Set Off Appositives
- ■ Between Items in a Series
- ■ After Introductory Clauses and Phrases

 Indicate where commas are needed in the following paragraph by writing the commas along with the words that surround them.

Example: Sharks probably the oldest predators in the sea live in every ocean in the world.

Sharks, probably   sea, live

1 Sharks belong to a family that includes dogfish skates and rays.

2 They are distinguished from other fish by their cartilaginous skeletons.

3 Besides this unusual feature the skin of a shark feels much like

4 sandpaper. Throughout the world's seas sharks search for something to

5 eat. Sharks bite off chunks of food and then swallow the pieces whole.

6 A tiny seven-inch-long shark the pygmy is dwarfed by the fifty-foot-long

7 variety the whale shark within this intriguing group. Though there are

8 more than 360 species most people have only heard of the great white

9 the tiger the hammerhead and the mako. Although it is foolish to ignore

10 them most sharks are not interested in eating every person who steps

11 into the sea.

 ## Model

Model the following sentences to practice using commas in a series, after an introductory phrase, and to set off an appositive.

> Only through experience of trial and suffering can the soul be strengthened, ambition inspired, and success achieved.
> —Helen Keller

> If you don't know where you are going, any road will take you there.
> —Lewis Carroll

> What we're all striving for is authenticity, a spirit-to-spirit connection.
> —Oprah Winfrey

Comma *(continued)*

612.1 To Enclose Parenthetical Elements

Use commas to separate parenthetical elements, such as an explanatory word or phrase, within a sentence.

The two children played together on the sand, away from the high, rough waves that were crashing onto the shore, **and they laughed as their sand castles grew higher and higher.**

Allison meandered into class, late as usual, **and sat down.**

612.2 To Set Off Nonrestrictive Phrases and Clauses

Use commas to set off **nonrestrictive** (unnecessary) clauses and participial phrases. A nonrestrictive clause or participial phrase adds information that is not necessary to the basic meaning of the sentence. For example, if the clause or phrase (in red) were left out in the two examples below, the meaning of the sentences would remain clear. Therefore, commas are used to set them off.

The Altena Fitness Center and Visker Gymnasium, which were built last year, **are busy every day.** (nonrestrictive clause)

Students and faculty, improving their health through exercise, **use both facilities throughout the week.** (nonrestrictive phrase)

Do not use commas to set off a **restrictive** (necessary) clause or participial phrase, which helps to define a noun or pronoun. It adds information that the reader needs to know in order to understand the sentence. For example, if the clause and phrase (in red) were dropped from the examples below, the meaning wouldn't be the same. Therefore, commas are *not* used.

The handball court that has a sign-up sheet by the door **must be reserved.**
The clause identifies which handball court must be reserved.
(restrictive clause)

Individuals wanting to use this court **must sign up a day in advance.**
(restrictive phrase)

A Closer Look: *That* and *Which*

Use *that* to introduce restrictive (necessary) clauses; use *which* to introduce nonrestrictive (unnecessary) clauses. When the two words are used in this way, the reader can quickly distinguish necessary and unnecessary information.

The treadmill that monitors heart rate is the one you must use.
(The reader needs the information to find the right treadmill.)

This treadmill, which we got last year, is required for your program.
(The main clause tells the reader which treadmill to use; the other clause gives additional, unnecessary information.)

Grammar Practice

Commas 3

■ To Enclose Parenthetical Elements
■ To Set Off Nonrestrictive Phrases and Clauses

 Indicate where commas are needed in the following sentences by writing the commas along with the words that surround them. If no commas are needed, write "none."

Example: Patrick who loves science tried to get me interested in astronomy.
Patrick, who loves science, tried

1. He has a Dobsonian telescope which he built from a kit.

2. Last July having time on my hands I stayed at his country home.

3. With Patrick's telescope we spotted the International Space Station which I was surprised to be able to see.

4. The "Dob" as my cousin affectionately calls it is popular among amateur astronomers.

5. When I got home, my dad helped me buy a telescope that is similar to the Dobsonian.

6. Patrick attempting to help me put it together accidentally broke one of the legs.

7. Dad's coworker whose experience with telescopes is amazing fixed it easily.

8. Next month armed with my new telescope I'll be searching the heavens for the space shuttle *Discovery*.

◀ Model

Model the following sentences to reinforce the difference between restrictive and nonrestrictive phrases and clauses and their correct punctuation.

> **Those who don't believe in magic will never find it.**
>
> —Roald Dahl

> **The hardest thing to explain is the glaringly evident, which everybody has decided not to see.**
>
> —Ayn Rand

Comma *(continued)*

614.1 To Set Off Dates

Use commas to set off items in a date.

On September 30, 1997, my little sister entered our lives.

He began working out on December 1, 2005, but quit by May 1, 2006.

However, when only the month and year are given, no commas are needed.

He began working out in December 2005 but quit by May 2006.

When a full date appears in the middle of a sentence, a comma follows the year.

On June 7, 1924, my great-grandfather met his future wife.

614.2 To Set Off Items in Addresses

Use commas to set off items in an address. (No comma is placed between the state and ZIP code.)

Mail the box to Friends of Wildlife, Box 402, Spokane, Washington 20077.

When a city and state (or country) appear in the middle of a sentence, a comma follows the last item in the address.

Several charitable organizations in Juneau, Alaska, pool their funds.

614.3 In Numbers

Use commas to separate numerals in large numbers in order to distinguish hundreds, thousands, millions, and so forth.

1,101   25,000   7,642,020

614.4 To Enclose Titles or Initials

Use commas to enclose a title or initials and names that follow a surname (a last name).

Letitia O'Reilly, M.D., is our family physician.

Hickok, J. B., and Cody, William F., are two popular Western heroes.

Grammar Practice

Commas 4

- ■ To Set Off Dates
- ■ To Set Off Items in Addresses
- ■ To Enclose Titles or Initials

 Indicate where commas are needed in the following sentences by writing the commas along with the words that surround them.

Example: Thomas Bonnicksen Ph.D. has written extensively about the forests that grew after the last ice age.

Bonnicksen, Ph.D., has

1. Professors in Columbus Ohio answered some questions about the role of carbon dioxide in warming the atmosphere.

2. Although many think the world is going to warm up considerably, Chronis Tzedakis Ph.D. believes we may be headed into a new ice age.

3. On April 30 2007 a science magazine reported the earth's climate has see-sawed over the last 9,000 years.

4. You can get information about glaciers and ice ages by writing to World Data Center for Glaciology University of Colorado Campus Box 449 Boulder Colorado 80309.

5. The coldest temperature on record for North America—81 degrees below zero Fahrenheit—occurred near the town of Beaver Creek Yukon Territory on February 3 1947.

6. John Margolies CPA counsels against buying investment property in the Yukon.

 ## Model

Model the following sentences to practice using commas to enclose titles or initials.

> **Richard Swenson, D.D.S., advises his patients to put their toothbrushes in the dishwasher.**

> **For his daughter's graduation gift, Mr. Blade had her office door painted with her new title: Miranda K. Blade, J.D.**

Comma *(continued)*

616.1 To Set Off Dialogue

Use commas to set off the speaker's exact words from the rest of the sentence. (It may be helpful to remember that the comma is always to the left of the quotation mark.)

"It's as if people no longer care about the problems of city life," **added Monica Torres, an urban studies student.**

616.2 To Set Off Interjections

Use a comma to separate an interjection or a weak exclamation from the rest of the sentence.

Hey, **how am I to know that a minute's passed?**
—Nathan Slaughter and Jim Schweitzer, *When Time Dies*

616.3 To Set Off Interruptions

Use commas to set off a word, a phrase, or a clause that interrupts the movement of a sentence. Such expressions usually can be identified through the following tests: (1) They may be omitted without changing the meaning of a sentence. (2) They may be placed nearly anywhere in the sentence without changing its meaning.

For most of the students, well, **it was just another normal day at school.**
The safest way to cross this street, as a general rule, **is with the light.**

616.4 In Direct Address

Use commas to separate a noun of direct address from the rest of the sentence. A *noun of direct address* is the noun that names the person(s) spoken to.

I don't think you understand, my friend, **how important it is for me to do well in school and create a successful life for myself.**

616.5 For Clarity or Emphasis

You may use a comma for clarity or for emphasis. There will be times when none of the traditional rules call for a comma, but one will be needed to prevent confusion or to emphasize an important idea.

Those who can see tomorrow, can **find the energy to continue.** (emphasis)
What the crew does, does **affect our voyage.** (clarity)

Grammar Practice

Commas 5

- ■ To Set Off Dialogue
- ■ To Set Off Interjections
- ■ In Direct Address

 Indicate where commas are needed in the following sentences by writing the commas along with the words that surround them.

Example: Hey do you have a hero?
    Hey, do

1. "My hero" said Jolene "is the science-fiction author Ray Bradbury."

2. In his introduction to *The Circus of Dr. Lao,* Bradbury stated "Science fiction balances you on the cliff. Fantasy shoves you off."

3. Writer Miriam Allen de Ford said "Science fiction deals with improbable possibilities."

4. Mr. Kelly says "Science fiction entertains and provides insights into sciences and society."

5. The main elements in science fiction may be real or imagined Jolene.

6. People often attribute the following words to the television show *Star Trek:* "Beam me up Scotty!"

7. Well did you know it was never said on the show?

8. Hey are you sure about that?

 ## Model

Model the following sentences to practice using commas to set off dialogue and interjections.

> **"I need to rake the leaves again," I inanely said to my old friend.**
> —Patricia Cornwell, *Black Notice*

> **Oh, life is a glorious cycle of song . . .**
> —Dorothy Parker

Semicolon

618.1 To Join Two Independent Clauses

Use a **semicolon** to join two or more closely related independent clauses that are not connected with a coordinating conjunction. (Independent clauses can stand alone as separate sentences.)

> A heart attack is a medical emergency; immediate care is required.

> Silence coated the room like a layer of tar; not even the breathing of the 11 Gehad made any sound.
>
> —Gann Bierner, "The Leap"

NOTE: When independent clauses are especially long or contain commas, a semicolon may punctuate the sentence, even though a coordinating conjunction connects the clauses.

> We waited all day in that wide line, tired travelers pressing in from all sides; and when we needed drinks or sandwiches, I would squeeze my way to the cafeteria and back.

618.2 With Conjunctive Adverbs

A semicolon is used *before* a conjunctive adverb (with a comma after it) when the word connects two independent clauses in a compound sentence. (Common conjunctive adverbs are *also, besides, finally, however, indeed, instead, meanwhile, moreover, nevertheless, next, still, then, therefore,* and *thus.*)

> I know that I need to finish the research for my essay; however, our Internet service is down and the library is closed on Sunday.

618.3 To Separate Groups That Contain Commas

A semicolon is used to separate groups of words that already contain commas.

> Every Saturday night my little brother gathers up his things—goggles, shower cap, and snorkel; bubble bath, soap, and shampoo; tapes, stereo, and rubber duck—and heads for the tub.

Grammar Practice

Semicolons

- ■ To Join Two Independent Clauses
- ■ To Separate Groups That Contain Commas

 Indicate where a semicolon is needed in the following sentences by writing the semicolon along with the words that surround it.

Example: "It's not what I can do it's what I *will* do." —Kyle Maynard
do; it's

1. Kyle Maynard has a rare disorder called "congenital amputation" he has been limbless since birth.

2. He wrestles, swims, and plays baseball competes in athletic contests and has written a book.

3. Kyle is a normal young man despite having no elbows or hands and no knees or legs below them, he has become an outstanding role model.

4. He stands only three feet tall and weighs 120 pounds those who know him hardly notice his unique proportions.

5. Kyle has traveled cross-country as a motivational speaker won an ESPN ESPY Award, a Courage Award, and wrestling awards and modeled for Vanity Fair and Abercrombie & Fitch.

6. What makes Kyle different isn't his body it's his heart.

7. His story goes way beyond athletics his story serves as an inspiration to anyone who must overcome huge odds.

8. Kyle's book is titled *No Excuses* it is a revealing autobiography.

 ## Model

Model the following sentence to practice using a semicolon to join two independent clauses.

His brows came together; his mouth became a thin line.
    —Harper Lee, *To Kill a Mockingbird*

Punctuation

Colon

620.1 After a Salutation

Use a **colon** after the salutation of a business letter.

Dear Judge Parker: **Dear Governor Whitman:**

620.2 Between Numerals Indicating Time

Use a colon between the hours, minutes, and seconds of a number indicating time.

8:30 p.m. **9:45 a.m.** **10:24:55**

620.3 For Emphasis

Use a colon to emphasize a word, a phrase, a clause, or a sentence that explains or adds impact to the main clause (also see **650.3**).

The newest candidates announced their platforms today: Lower taxes and more efficient services are the consistent themes.

620.4 To Introduce a Quotation

Use a colon to formally introduce a quotation, a sentence, or a question.

Directly a voice in the corner rang out wild and clear: "I've got him! I've got him!"
—Mark Twain, *Roughing It*

620.5 To Introduce a List

A colon is used to introduce a list.

I got all the proper equipment: scissors, a bucket of water to keep things clean, some cotton for the stuffing, and needle and thread to sew it up.
—Joan Baez, *Daybreak*

A Closer Look

Do not use a colon between a verb and its object or complement, or between a preposition and its object.

Incorrect: Min has: a snowmobile, an ATV, and a canoe.
Correct: Min has plenty of toys: a snowmobile, an ATV, and a canoe.
Incorrect: I watch a TV show about: cooking wild game.
Correct: I watch a TV show about a new subject: cooking wild game.

620.6 Between a Title and a Subtitle

Use a colon to distinguish between a title and a subtitle, volume and page, and chapter and verse in literature.

Encyclopedia Americana **IV: 211** **Psalm 23:1–6**

Grammar Practice

Colons

- Between Numerals Indicating Time
- For Emphasis
- To Introduce a Quotation

 Indicate where a colon is needed in the following sentences by writing the colon along with the words that surround it.

Example: The Orloj is a glorious old clock tower in Prague, unique for this reason It dates back to medieval times.
reason: It

1. The clock was built in 1410 by Mikulas of Kadan, royal clock maker under the reign of a familiar ruler King Wenceslas IV.

2. Whether it's 1200 midnight, 1200 noon, or any hour between, the Orloj will astound you with its moving statues.

3. After "The Walk of the Apostles," a rooster flaps and crows, and the clock chimes 900, 1000, 1100 . . .

4. Other moving figures include a Turk shaking his head, a miser watching his bag, and an individual admiring his reflection in a mirror Vanity himself.

5. The clock also has a calendar dial and an astronomical dial that displays the current state of the heavens sort of an ancient planetarium.

6. Otakar Zamecnik, a keeper of the Orloj, relates "The Orloj will soon be 600 years old, and I'm proud to be continuing the work of some 100 Orloj keepers before me."

 ## Model

Model the following sentence to practice using a colon for emphasis.

> Humanity's true moral test, its fundamental test, consists of its attitude toward those who are at its mercy: animals.
> —Milan Kundera, *The Unbearable Lightness of Being*

Test Prep!

Read the following paragraphs. Write the letter of the correct way to punctuate each underlined part from the choices given on the next page. If it is already correct, choose "D."

With all the natural disasters <u>happening recently one</u> might think
(1)
that <u>earthquakes, tsunamis and</u> hurricanes are the deadliest. Since 1900,
(2)
however, droughts, famines, floods, and epidemics have claimed the most
lives. Of these, one killed as many as 40 million <u>people: the Spanish flu</u>
(3)
epidemic that began <u>in September, 1918.</u>
(4)
Although it is thought to have <u>originated in China the</u> Spanish flu got
(5)
its name from the early cases and large number of deaths in Spain. Becoming
a <u>*pandemic* a worldwide epidemic,</u> the illness affected a fifth of the world's
(6)
population. It killed 25 million people in six months, as many as AIDS killed
<u>in 25 years.</u> Unlike other strains of <u>influenza which attack</u> mostly the very
(7) **(8)**
young, very old, and very weak, the Spanish flu infected seemingly healthy
individuals, ages 20 to 40. Symptoms overcame people quickly. Often, the viral
infection evolved into <u>pneumonia, which</u> could not be treated with antibiotics
(9)
at the time. Victims suffered <u>rapid, distressful deaths.</u>
(10)
The public health departments in the United States and Europe
developed ordinances to prevent the spread of <u>the flu those</u> who violated
(11)
them were fined. <u>People, who became ill,</u> were quarantined until they were
(12)
fever free for 48 hours. Medical staff and the general public wore gauze
masks. Public <u>institutions including schools,</u> <u>were closed Public gatherings</u>
(13) **(14)**
were banned. They even tried to regulate coughing and sneezing!

Just as the Spanish <u>flu disappeared, researchers</u> were beginning to
(15)
understand viruses. Today, people wonder if such an epidemic <u>could happen</u>
(16)

<u>again?</u> Scientists can create a vaccine, but its effectiveness depends on getting it to enough people in time to prevent a severe outbreak.

1
Ⓐ happening recently one,
Ⓑ happening, recently, one
Ⓒ happening recently, one
Ⓓ correct as is

2
Ⓐ earthquakes tsunamis and
Ⓑ earthquakes, tsunamis, and
Ⓒ earthquakes, tsunamis, and,
Ⓓ correct as is

3
Ⓐ people. The Spanish flu
Ⓑ people the Spanish flu
Ⓒ people; the Spanish flu
Ⓓ correct as is

4
Ⓐ in September 1918.
Ⓑ in September 1918
Ⓒ in September, 1918
Ⓓ correct as is

5
Ⓐ originated in China, the
Ⓑ originated, in China the
Ⓒ originated, in China, the
Ⓓ correct as is

6
Ⓐ pandemic: a worldwide
Ⓑ pandemic; a worldwide
Ⓒ pandemic, a worldwide
Ⓓ correct as is

7
Ⓐ in 25 years:
Ⓑ in 25 years;
Ⓒ in 25 years—
Ⓓ correct as is

8
Ⓐ influenza, which attack
Ⓑ influenza; which attack
Ⓒ influenza which, attack
Ⓓ correct as is

9
Ⓐ pneumonia which
Ⓑ pneumonia which,
Ⓒ pneumonia; which
Ⓓ correct as is

10
Ⓐ rapid distressful deaths
Ⓑ rapid, distressful, deaths
Ⓒ rapid distressful, deaths
Ⓓ correct as is

11
Ⓐ the flu; those,
Ⓑ the flu, those
Ⓒ the flu; those
Ⓓ correct as is

12
Ⓐ People who became ill
Ⓑ People, who became ill
Ⓒ People who became ill,
Ⓓ correct as is

13
Ⓐ institutions including schools
Ⓑ institutions, including schools,
Ⓒ institutions, including schools
Ⓓ correct as is

14
Ⓐ were closed; Public gatherings
Ⓑ were closed, Public gatherings
Ⓒ were closed. Public gatherings
Ⓓ correct as is

15
Ⓐ flu disappeared researchers
Ⓑ flu disappeared researchers,
Ⓒ flu disappeared; researchers
Ⓓ correct as is

16
Ⓐ could happen again.
Ⓑ could happen again
Ⓒ could happen again;
Ⓓ correct as is

Hyphen

624.1 In Compound Words

Use the **hyphen** to make some compound words.

great-great-grandfather   **maid-in-waiting**   **three-year-old**

624.2 To Create New Words

Use a hyphen to form new words beginning with the prefixes *self-, ex-, all-,* and *half-*. Also use a hyphen to join any prefix to a proper noun, a proper adjective, or the official name of an office. Use a hyphen before the suffix *-elect*.

self-**contained**   ex-**governor**   all-**inclusive**   **president**-elect
pre-**Cambrian**   mid-**December**   half-**painted**

Use a hyphen to join the prefix *great-* only to the names of relatives.

great-**aunt**, great-**grandfather** (correct)   **great-hall** (incorrect)

624.3 To Form an Adjective

Use a hyphen to join two or more words that serve as a single adjective (a single-thought adjective) before a noun.

When I am on the field, I see myself as a tall, well-built **quarterback armed with magic plays and an incredible ability to throw the ball.**

Use common sense to determine whether a compound adjective might be misread if it is not hyphenated. Generally, hyphenate a compound adjective that is composed of . . .

- a phrase   heat-and-serve **meal**   off-and-on **relationship**
- a noun + adjective   oven-safe **handles**   book-smart **student**
- a noun + participle (*ing* or *ed* form of a verb)   bone-chilling **story**

A Closer Look

When words forming the adjective come after the noun, do not hyphenate them.

In real life I am large and big boned.

When the first of these words is an adverb ending in *-ly,* do not use a hyphen.

delicately prepared **pastry**

Also, do not use a hyphen when a number or a letter is the final element in a single-thought adjective.

class B **movie**

624.4 To Join Letters and Words

Use a hyphen to join a capital letter or lowercase letter to a noun or participle. (Check your dictionary if you're not sure of the hyphenation.)

T-**shirt**   Y-**turn**   G-**rated**   x-**axis**

Grammar Practice

Quotation Marks 1

- ■ To Set Off Direct Quotations
- ■ Placement of Punctuation

 Write the following conversation, placing quotation marks correctly.

Example: Calvin, would you please get that? his mom asked.
"Calvin, would you please get that?" his mom asked.

The phone had already rung four times; Calvin picked it up.

Hello? he greeted the caller. He listened for a bit, and then said, Yes, I think so. What's the problem?

Calvin's mom came into the room and asked, Who is it?

Calvin gestured to his mom to wait a second and continued to speak into the phone. No, we'd prefer the black one. . . . Right. OK, hold on, please. He covered the mouthpiece and said to his mom, It's the repair shop. They can't fix our car by this weekend, but they have a rental car for us.

Calvin's mom said, Ask them when our car will be ready.

Calvin talked again to the mechanic. Did Calvin hear him right? Did he say, It won't be ready for at least a week?

We have to special order a part, the mechanic explained. I wish I had better news for you.

Exercise

Continue the phone conversation between Calvin and the mechanic. Use quotation marks correctly.

Quotation Marks *(continued)*

634.1 Quotation Marks Within Quotations

Use single quotation marks to punctuate a quotation within a quotation. Use double quotation marks in order to distinguish a quotation within a quotation within a quotation.

> **"For tomorrow," said Mr. Botts, "read 'Unlighted Lamps.'"**
> **Sue asked, "Did you hear Mr. Botts say, 'Read "Unlighted Lamps"'?"**

634.2 For Special Words

You may use quotation marks (1) to distinguish a word that is being discussed, (2) to indicate that a word is unfamiliar slang, or (3) to point out that a word is being used in a special way (such as ironically).

> **(1) If I had to choose a word to describe his attitude, it would be** "stoic."
> **(2) The next time I hear a New Zealander say** "ta," **I will know that I am being thanked.**
> **(3) Tom pushed the wheelchair across the street, showed the lady his** "honest" **smile . . . and stole her purse.**

NOTE: You may use italics (underlining) in place of quotation marks in each of these three situations. (See **636.3**.)

634.3 To Punctuate Titles

Use **quotation marks** to punctuate titles of songs, poems, short stories, one-act plays, lectures, episodes of radio or television programs, chapters of books, unpublished works, electronic files, and articles found in magazines, newspapers, encyclopedias, or online sources. (For punctuation of other titles, see **636.2**.)

> "Santa Lucia" (song)
> "The Chameleon" (short story)
> "Twentieth-Century Memories" (lecture)
> "Affordable Adventures" (magazine article)
> "Dire Prophecy of the Howling Dog" (chapter in a book)
> "Dancing with Debra" (television episode)
> "Miss Julie" (one-act play)

NOTE: Punctuate one title within another title as follows:

> **"Clarkson's 'Breakaway' Hits the Waves"**
> (title of a song in title of an article)

Grammar Practice

Quotation Marks 2

- Quotation Marks Within Quotations
- For Special Words
- To Punctuate Titles

 Write the word or words that should be enclosed in quotation marks in the following sentences.

Example: The players stood on the sidelines as Olivia sang the Star-Spangled Banner.
"Star-Spangled Banner."

1. Ms. Rupka said, "The exam will include Hills like White Elephants and other short stories by Hemingway."

2. He called himself benevolent, but everyone knew he was exaggerating his measly donations.

3. Hazim was featured in the *Trumpet* magazine article Flags to Riches.

4. No one answered correctly when asked to define the word pidgin.

5. I like Usher's new song Truth Hurts.

6. The coach shouted, "I called Ty, and he said, Madison West won 28–10!"

7. Merina asked, "Who sings Happy Ever After?"

8. My three-year-old nephew calls dogs oggies.

Model

Model the following sentence to practice using quotation marks within quotations.

> "'The Duke's Daughter' paid the butcher's bill, 'A Phantom Hand' put down a new carpet, and the 'Curse of the Coventrys' proved the blessing of the Marches in the way of groceries and gowns."
> —Louisa May Alcott, *Little Women*

Italics (Underlining)

636.1 Handwritten and Printed Material

Italics is a printer's term for a style of type that is slightly slanted. In this sentence, the word *happiness* is printed in italics. In material that is handwritten or typed on a machine that cannot print in italics, underline each word or letter that should be in italics.

> *My Ántonia* **is the story of a strong and determined pioneer woman.**
>
> (printed)
>
> **Willa Cather's** <u>My Ántonia</u> **describes pioneer life in America.**
>
> (typed or handwritten)

636.2 In Titles

Use italics to indicate the titles of magazines, newspapers, pamphlets, books, full-length plays, films, videos, radio and television programs, book-length poems, ballets, operas, paintings, lengthy musical compositions, sculptures, cassettes, CD's, legal cases, and the names of ships and aircraft. (For punctuation of other titles, see **634.3**.)

> *Newsweek* (magazine)   *Cold Sassy Tree* (book)
>
> *Shakespeare in Love* (film)   *Law & Order* (television program)
>
> *Caring for Your Kitten* (pamphlet)   *Hedda Gabler* (full-length play)
>
> *Chicago Tribune* (newspaper)   *The Thinker* (sculpture)

636.3 For Special Uses

Use italics for a number, letter, or word that is being discussed or used in a special way. (Sometimes quotation marks are used for this reason. See **634.2**.)

> **I hope that this letter** *I* **on my report card stands for** *incredible* **and not** *incomplete*.

636.4 For Foreign Words

Use italics for foreign words that have not been adopted into the English language; also use italics for scientific names.

> **The voyageurs—tough men with natural** *bonhomie*—**discovered the shy** *Castor canadensis,* **or North American beaver.**

Grammar Practice

Italics (Underlining)

■ In Titles
■ For Special Uses
■ For Foreign Words

 Write and underline the word or words that should be italicized in the following sentences.

Example: Kelly's embroidered jeans were très chic.
<u>très chic</u>

1. Jennifer Aniston was in last month's issue of People magazine.

2. We are studying Antigone, a Greek tragedy by Sophocles.

3. Sodium aluminum sulfate, also known as soda alum, is used in baking powder.

4. In the 1857 legal case Dred Scott v. Sandford, the Supreme Court claimed that African Americans were not considered United States citizens.

5. The first episode of The Real World aired on MTV in 1992.

6. When did the word props become slang?

7. My brother was stationed on the United States Navy ship the USS Richard Bonhomme.

8. The workshop featured an art technique called trompe l'oeil, which means "trick of the eye."

Model

Model the following sentence to practice using italics (underlining) for special uses.

I had no faith in pie charts or diagrams of humanity wherein the wicked were divided from the good and the *forever after* was in direct opposition to the *here and now*.

—Alice Hoffman, *The Ice Queen*

Parentheses

638.1 To Set Off Explanatory Material

You may use **parentheses** to set off explanatory or added material that interrupts the normal sentence structure.

> **Benson** (our dog) **sits in on our piano lessons** (on the piano bench), **much to the teacher's surprise and amusement.**
> —Chad Hockerman, student writer

NOTE: Place question marks and exclamation points within the parentheses when they mark the added material.

> **Ivan at once concluded** (the rascal!) **that I had a passion for dances, and . . . wanted to drag me off to a dancing class.**
> —Fyodor Dostoyevsky, "A Novel in Nine Letters"

638.2 With Full Sentences

When using a full sentence within another sentence, do not capitalize it or use a period inside the parentheses.

> **Since the judging has already begun** (the judges have narrowed their selection to the top six), **you'll have to wait until next year to enter your apple pie in the contest.**

When the parenthetical sentence comes after the period of the main sentence, capitalize and punctuate it the same way you would any other complete sentence.

> **Register for the event by completing this application.** (Use blue or black ink.)

NOTE: For unavoidable parentheses within parentheses (. . . [. . .] . . .), use brackets. Avoid overuse of parentheses by using commas instead.

Diagonal

638.3 To Show a Choice

Use a **diagonal** (also called a *slash* or forward *slash*) between two words, as in *and/or*, to indicate that either is acceptable.

> **Press the** load/eject **button.**
> **Don't worry; this is** indoor/outdoor **carpet.**

638.4 When Quoting Poetry

When quoting more than one line of poetry, use a diagonal to show where each line of poetry ends. (Insert a space on each side of the diagonal.)

> **In Venice behind,** / **Fall the leaves,** / **Brown,** / **And yellow streaked with brown.**
> —Amy Lowell, "The City of Falling Leaves"

Grammar Practice

Parentheses and Diagonals

 Write the word or words that should be enclosed in parentheses or divided by a diagonal. (Use the correct punctuation.)

Example: I tried tekka maki a kind of sushi at the restaurant.
(a kind of sushi)

1. Julia Alvarez she wrote *How the Garcia Girls Lost Their Accents* is my favorite author.

2. Push the up down button on the control panel to change the time.

3. Captain Chuck Yeager made famous as a test pilot was also a World War II flying ace.

4. Pizza and or lasagna will be served at the open house.

5. Raymond our Chihuahua likes to sleep in the bathroom sink.

6. Aunt Jo she's not really my aunt but a family friend is coming for a visit.

 Model

Model the following sentence to practice using parentheses with full sentences.

> One day he brought the teacher a dead chicken snake in a burlap sack, and a chicken was still in the snake's belly (or whatever snakes call bellies).
>
> —Willie Morris, *Good Old Boy*

Model

Write the lyrics to a favorite song to practice using diagonals when quoting poetry.

> Tell them at home I long to be there / While thro this wide world ever I roam; / Only to meet my darling so fair, / Only to see the dear folks at home.

Dash

640.1 To Indicate a Sudden Break

Use a **dash** to indicate a sudden break or change in the sentence.

Near the semester's end—and this is not always due to poor planning—**some students may find themselves in a real crunch.**

NOTE: Dashes are often used in place of commas. Use dashes when you want to give special emphasis; use commas when there is no need for emphasis.

640.2 To Set Off an Introductory Series

Use a dash to set off an introductory series from the clause that explains the series.

A good book, a cup of tea, a comfortable chair—**these things always saved my mother's sanity.**

640.3 To Set Off Parenthetical Material

You may use a dash to set off parenthetical material—material that explains or clarifies a word or a phrase.

A single incident—a tornado that came without warning—**changed the face of the small town forever.**

640.4 To Indicate Interrupted Speech

Use a dash to show interrupted or faltering speech in dialogue.

"Why—why are you doing this to me?"

640.5 For Emphasis

Use a dash to emphasize a word, a series, a phrase, or a clause.

After years of trial and error, Belther made history with his invention—the unicycle.

After several hours of hearing the high-pitched yipping, Petra finally realized what it was—coyote pups.

Grammar Practice

Dashes

- ◼ **To Indicate a Sudden Break**
- ◼ **To Set Off Parenthetical Material**
- ◼ **For Emphasis**

 A word, a phrase, or a clause follows each sentence below. Write the sentences to include those words, set off by one or two dashes.

Example: The ingredients he cooked with were strange and unfamiliar. (mustard oil and fenugreek seeds)

The ingredients he cooked with—mustard oil and fenugreek seeds—were strange and unfamiliar.

1. This machine was destined to change the world. (the computer)

2. Suddenly I realized exactly what he was telling me. (a lie)

3. The tsunami came without any warning. (caused by an underwater earthquake)

4. In the distance, a mournful cry echoed through the woods. (and this is not to say that it was miles away)

5. The *Greensboro Gazette* is doing a feature article on Blaine High School senior Todd Davis. (winner of the Langston Hughes Poetry Award)

6. Tears filled his eyes as he recognized the ring in the pawnshop window. (the emerald ring he had given Tamara)

 ### Model

Model the following sentence to practice using a dash to show emphasis.

The manager of the hotel switched us to a room with a beautiful view— its balcony overlooked the Pacific Ocean.

Ellipsis

642.1 To Show Omitted Words

Use an **ellipsis** (three periods with one space before and after each period) to show that one or more words have been omitted in a quotation.

(Original)

We the people of the United States, in order to form a more perfect Union, establish justice, insure domestic tranquility, provide for the common defense, promote the general welfare, and secure the blessings of liberty to ourselves and our posterity, do ordain and establish this Constitution for the United States of America.

—Preamble, *U.S. Constitution*

(Quotation)

"We the people . . . in order to form a more perfect Union . . . establish this Constitution for the United States of America."

642.2 At the End of a Sentence

If words from a quotation are omitted at the end of a sentence, place the ellipsis after the period that marks the conclusion of the sentence.

"Standing at the entrance were small groups of students. . . . As Will walked by, he could not help but overhear the murmurs of discontent as they continued to wait for the signal to return to class."

NOTE: If the quoted material is a complete sentence (even if it was not complete in the original), use a period, then an ellipsis.

(Original)

I am tired; my heart is sick and sad. From where the sun now stands I will fight no more forever.

—Chief Joseph of the Nez Percé

(Quotation)

"I am tired. . . . From where the sun now stands I will fight no more forever."

or

"I am tired. . . . I will fight no more. . . ."

642.3 To Show a Pause

Use an ellipsis to indicate a pause.

I brought my trembling hand to my focusing eyes. It was oozing, it was red, it was . . . it was . . . a tomato!

—Laura Baginski, student writer

Grammar Practice

Ellipses

- ■ To Show Omitted Words
- ■ At the End of a Sentence
- ■ To Show a Pause

 For each of the following paragraphs, select the least important information to replace with ellipses. Write the shortened paragraphs on your paper.

Example: Joseph Geissman, a local deputy sheriff who has been on the force for five years, was honored for his bravery during the recent flood.

Joseph Geissman, a local deputy sheriff . . . was honored for his bravery during the recent flood.

1. Plan now to land a part-time summer job. First, decide on what kind of job you want in terms of location, hours, and pay. Then think about what you have to offer—in particular, your skills and past experience. Next, write a résumé using one of the many online or printed guides. Then look for suitable jobs: Ask around, read newspaper job ads. Apply for any jobs that interest you. Finally, prepare for your interviews. Decide how you will make a great impression on potential employers.

2. Ancient Olympic events were different from modern games. For example, one of the most popular events was chariot racing. There were two-horse races and four-horse races. There were other types of races as well—with foals and mules, for example. The course was 9 miles long (12 laps around the track). Only rich people could afford the horses, equipment, and jockey. It was the owners, and not the winning jockey, who received the olive wreath of victory.

 ## Model

Model the following sentence to practice using an ellipsis to show a pause.

When the student is ready . . . the lesson appears.

—Gene Oliver

Brackets

644.1 To Set Off Clarifying Information

Use **brackets** before and after words that are added to clarify what another person has said or written.

> **"Those annoying pests** [the mosquitoes] **ruined our day fishing at the lake."**
> —Will Shepherd, student writer

NOTE: The brackets indicate that the words *the mosquitoes* are not part of the quotation but were added for clarification.

644.2 Around an Editorial Correction

Place brackets around an editorial correction inserted within quoted material.

> **"Brooklyn alone has 8 percent of lead poisoning** [victims] **nationwide," said Marjorie Moore.**
> —Donna Actie, student writer

NOTE: The brackets indicate that the word *victims* replaced the author's original word.

Place brackets around the letters *sic* (Latin for "as such"); the letters indicate that an error appearing in the material being quoted was made by the original speaker or writer.

> **"When I'm queen," mused Lucy, "I'll show these blockheads whose** [*sic*] **got beauty and brains."**

644.3 To Set Off Added Words

Place brackets around comments that have been added to a quotation.

> **"Congratulations to the astronomy club's softball team, which put in, shall we say, a 'stellar' performance."** [groans]

Punctuation Marks

´	Accent, acute	,	Comma	( )	Parentheses
`	Accent, grave	†	Dagger	.	Period
'	Apostrophe	—	Dash	?	Question mark
*	Asterisk	/	Diagonal/Slash	" "	Quotation marks
{ }	Brace	¨(ü)	Dieresis	§	Section
[ ]	Brackets	. . .	Ellipsis	;	Semicolon
^	Caret	!	Exclamation point	~	Tilde
(ç)	Cedilla	-	Hyphen	___	Underscore
^	Circumflex	...	Leaders		
:	Colon	¶	Paragraph		

Grammar Practice

Brackets

- ■ To Set Off Clarifying Information
- ■ Around an Editorial Correction
- ■ To Set Off Added Words

 Follow the directions for each activity below.

Example: In the following quotation, the speaker is talking about the English Industrial Revolution. Use words in brackets to clarify the quotation.

"The productive capacity of England was changed dramatically," Dr. Bates said. "Every class of people was touched by it."

. . . was touched by it [the English Industrial Revolution]."

1. In the following quotation, the speaker is talking about satellites. Use words in brackets to clarify the quotation.

"There has been some damage to them," the astrophysicist explained. "For the most part, it has been minor."

2. In the following quotation, replace the speaker's use of the word *repartee* with *witty reply*.

Mr. Daly reported, "She responded to my commentary with a repartee."

3. Quote the following statement and show that the error was made by the original writer, Joy Thayer.

James Monroe's secratary of state was John Quincy Adams.

4. Add the comment *sigh* to the following quotation.

"I'm so tired that I can't concentrate."

Model

Model the following sentence to practice using brackets to set off clarifying information.

Nobody thought that it [the airline strike] would last as long as it did.

Test Prep!

Read the following paragraphs. From the choices given on the next page, write the letter of the correct way to punctuate each underlined part. If it is already correct, choose "D."

Imagine seeing <u>The Taming of the Shrew,</u> a play by William
(1)
Shakespeare, in the early seventeenth century. Where would you be likely
to see such a performance? If you lived in London, perhaps you would be
lucky enough to see it at <u>Shakespeare's</u> own Globe Theater.
(2)

From the outside, the outdoor theater looked like <u>it's nickname—a</u> large
(3)
<u>"Wooden O".</u> However, it offered the most modern of theatrical experiences.
(4)
The stage was a high platform that jutted into a courtyard. A
trapdoor in its floor allowed for special effects, such as magical smoke
appearing or <u>actors' disappearing.</u> The <u>ceiling covering only the stage)</u> was
(5) **(6)**
supported by two pillars, and its mechanisms could lower and raise actors.

At the back of the stage was a large <u>"tiring house,"</u> a place for the
(7)
actors to change their attire. The wall of the tiring house served as the
background of the stage and included doors and curtains for entrances
and <u>exits. Above</u> the stage were balconies for love scenes, and above that,
(8)
a storage area called the hut. Topping it all was a tower with a flag used
to advertise the <u>days' play</u>: black for a tragedy, white for a comedy.
(9)
The theater had a capacity of 3,000. The audiences came from all
levels of life. The <u>"groundlings"</u> or common folk, stood in the courtyard
(10)
around the stage for the price of one <u>pence (penny.)</u> To sit on benches
(11)
in the second tier cost two pence, and top-tier seats cost three. Wealthy
people paid four to five pence to sit in <u>nicely-cushioned comfort</u> in the tier
(12)
above the back of the stage. There, although they had a poor view of the

<u>actors backs,</u> they could be seen by others.
     (13)
     Shakespeare himself <u>said, All the world's</u> a stage . . . " While
                         (14)
<u>todays' theaters</u> may be more elaborate than the Globe, they function in
     (15)
the same way and owe much to the Globe's <u>unique-for-its-time</u> design.
                                          (16)

1 Ⓐ "The Taming of the Shrew"
   Ⓑ *The Taming of the Shrew*
   Ⓒ 'The Taming of the Shrew'
   Ⓓ correct as is

2 Ⓐ Shakespeares
   Ⓑ Shakespeares's
   Ⓒ Shakespeares'
   Ⓓ correct as is

3 Ⓐ its nickname—a
   Ⓑ its nickname a
   Ⓒ it's nickname a
   Ⓓ correct as is

4 Ⓐ 'Wooden O'.
   Ⓑ Wooden O.
   Ⓒ "Wooden O."
   Ⓓ correct as is

5 Ⓐ actor's disappearing
   Ⓑ actors disappearing
   Ⓒ actors *disappearing*
   Ⓓ correct as is

6 Ⓐ ceiling covering only the stage
   Ⓑ ceiling (covering only
       the stage)
   Ⓒ (ceiling covering only
       the stage)
   Ⓓ correct as is

7 Ⓐ 'tiring house,'
   Ⓑ "tiring house",
   Ⓒ 'tiring house',
   Ⓓ correct as is

8 Ⓐ exits/Above
   Ⓑ exits—Above
   Ⓒ [exits]. Above
   Ⓓ correct as is

9 Ⓐ days play
   Ⓑ day's play
   Ⓒ days's play
   Ⓓ correct as is

10 Ⓐ "groundlings,"
    Ⓑ "groundlings",
    Ⓒ 'groundlings,'
    Ⓓ correct as is

11 Ⓐ pence [penny].
    Ⓑ pence (penny).
    Ⓒ pence-penny.
    Ⓓ correct as is

12 Ⓐ nicely-cushioned-comfort
    Ⓑ nicely cushioned comfort
    Ⓒ nicely cushioned-comfort
    Ⓓ correct as is

13 Ⓐ actor's backs
    Ⓑ actors' backs
    Ⓒ actors' back's
    Ⓓ correct as is

14 Ⓐ said "All the world's
    Ⓑ said, "All the world's
    Ⓒ said, 'All the world's
    Ⓓ correct as is

15 Ⓐ todays theaters
    Ⓑ today's theater's
    Ⓒ today's theaters
    Ⓓ correct as is

16 Ⓐ unique-for-it's-time
    Ⓑ unique-for-its time
    Ⓒ unique for-its-time
    Ⓓ correct as is

Checking Mechanics

Capitalization

648.1 Proper Nouns and Adjectives

Capitalize proper nouns and proper adjectives (those derived from proper nouns). The chart below provides a quick overview of capitalization rules. The pages following explain some specific rules of capitalization.

Capitalization at a Glance

Names of people	**Alice Walker, Matilda, Jim, Mr. Roker**
Days of the week, months	**Sunday, Tuesday, June, August**
Holidays, holy days	**Thanksgiving, Easter, Hanukkah**
Periods, events in history	**Middle Ages, the Battle of Bunker Hill**
Official documents	**Declaration of Independence**
Special events	**Elgin Community Spring Gala**
Languages, nationalities, religions	**French, Canadian, Islam**
Political parties	**Republican Party, Socialist Party**
Trade names	**Oscar Mayer hot dogs, Pontiac Sunbird**
Official titles used with names	**Mayor John Spitzer, Senator Feinstein**
Formal epithets	**Alexander the Great**
Geographical names	
Planets, heavenly bodies	**Earth, Jupiter, the Milky Way**
Continents	**Australia, South America**
Countries	**Ireland, Grenada, Sri Lanka**
States, provinces	**Ohio, Utah, Nova Scotia**
Cities, towns, villages	**El Paso, Burlington, Wonewoc**
Streets, roads, highways	**Park Avenue, Route 66, Interstate 90**
Landforms	**the Rocky Mountains, the Sahara Desert**
Bodies of water	**Yellowstone Lake, Pumpkin Creek**
Buildings, monuments	**Elkhorn High School, Gateway Arch**
Public areas	**Times Square, Sequoia National Park**

Grammar Practice

Capitalization 1

■ Proper Nouns and Adjectives

 For each sentence below, write the words that should be capitalized.

Example: On tuesday, mayor henke declared that all city offices would be closed on martin luther king day.

Tuesday, Mayor Henke, Martin Luther King Day

1. Edward the confessor ruled england from 1042 to 1066.

2. Admittance to the independence ball required a ticket from the presidential inaugural committee.

3. When sylvie attended carlton college, she learned to speak greek and latin.

4. The most popular car in italy is the fiat grande punto.

5. A severe earthquake hit san francisco on april 18, 1906.

6. The missouri river flows from its source in the rocky mountains to the mississippi river near st. louis.

7. Ancient greeks called mercury, venus, mars, jupiter, and saturn "wandering stars."

8. The teachings of the chinese philosopher confucius (551 to 479 B.C.E.) are called confucianism.

Model

Model the following sentences to practice capitalizing proper nouns and adjectives.

Though South Africa and Egypt were popular destinations, Carlos decided to travel to Chile, the country where his father was born.

While in Rome, Larissa saw the Colosseum, the Vatican, the Arch of Constantine, and the Roman Forum.

Mechanics

Capitalization *(continued)*

650.1 First Words

Capitalize the first word of every sentence, including the first word of a full-sentence direct quotation.

> **The crowd was quiet. A girl whispered, "I hope it's not Nancy," and the sound of her whisper reached the edges of the crowd.**
>
> —Shirley Jackson, "The Lottery"

650.2 Sentences in Parentheses

Capitalize the first word in a sentence enclosed in parentheses, but do not capitalize the first word if the parenthetical appears within another sentence.

> **In a bygone era, a fortunate New Orleans visitor could be entertained by a young Louis Armstrong playing the cornet. (A cornet is a kind of small trumpet with a mellower sound.)**
>
> **Damien's aunt (she's a wild woman) plays bingo every Saturday night.**

650.3 Sentences Following Colons

Capitalize the first word in a complete sentence that follows a colon when (1) you want to emphasize the sentence or (2) the sentence is a quotation.

> **When we quarreled and made horrible faces at one another, Mother knew what to say: "Your faces will stay that way, and no one will marry you."**

650.4 Sections of the Country

Capitalize words that indicate particular sections of the country; do not capitalize words that simply indicate direction.

> **Mr. Johnson is from the Southwest.** (section of the country)
>
> **After moving north to Montana, he had to buy winter clothes.** (direction)

650.5 Certain Religious Words

Capitalize nouns that refer to the Supreme Being, the word *Bible,* the books of the Bible, and the names for other holy books.

> **God   Jehovah   the Lord   the Savior   Allah   Bible   Genesis**

650.6 Titles

Capitalize the first word of a title, the last word, and every word in between except articles (*a, an, the*), short prepositions, and coordinating conjunctions. Follow this rule for titles of books, newspapers, magazines, poems, plays, songs, articles, films, works of art, photographs, and stories.

> ***Washington Post*   "The Diary of a Madman"   *Nights of Rain and Stars***

Grammar Practice

Capitalization 2

- Sentences Following Colons
- Certain Religious Words
- Titles

 For the paragraphs below, write the line number along with the words that should be capitalized.

Example: 2. What

1   When my grandfather was young, everyone asked the same

2 question: what would he be when he grew up? Hans was interested

3 in many things. He studied the bible and the torah. He considered

4 becoming a religious philosopher. When he read *a tale of two cities,*

5 *for whom the bell tolls,* and other great novels, he decided to be an

6 author. He also wanted to be an architect, an engineer, and even a

7 horse trainer! So what profession did my grandfather finally choose?

8 He became a typesetter!

9   Hans thought typesetting was a way to be a part of great events

10 in the world. He set type for some amazing headlines: "Pearl Harbor

11 attacked," "Yankees win the Series." He set articles about coronations and

12 the first astronauts' ventures into space. Yes, Hans was there for all the

13 great happenings. Shortly before he died, he summed it up this way: "if it

14 happened in the last 40 years, I was there—a mere shadow, perhaps, but

15 that was me."

 ## Model

Model the following sentences to practice capitalizing certain religious words, titles, and sentences following colons.

> Allah, Jehovah, Jah, and the Lord are different names for God.

> The class was stunned by the teacher's statement: "We'll be reading *Notes from the House of the Dead, Crime and Punishment,* and *The Idiot* this semester."

Mechanics

Capitalization *(continued)*

652.1 Words Used as Names

Capitalize words like *father, mother, uncle,* and *senator* when they are used as titles with a personal name or when they are substituted for proper nouns (especially in direct address).

> **We've missed you, Aunt Lucinda!** (*Aunt* is part of the name.)
> **I hope Mayor Bates arrives soon.** (*Mayor* is part of the name.)

A Closer Look

To test whether a word is being substituted for a proper noun, simply read the sentence with a proper noun in place of the word. If the proper noun fits in the sentence, the word being tested should be capitalized; otherwise, the word should not be capitalized.

> **Did Mom (Sue) say we could go?** (*Sue* works in this sentence.)
> **Did your mom (Sue) say you could go?** (*Sue* does not work here.)

NOTE: Usually the word is not capitalized if it follows a possessive —*my, his, your*—as it does in the second sentence above.

652.2 Letters

Capitalize the letters used to indicate form or shape.

> **U-turn   I-beam   S-curve   T-shirt   V-shaped**

652.3 Organizations

Capitalize the name of an organization, an association, or a team.

> **Lake Ontario Sailors   American Indian Movement   Democratic Party**

652.4 Abbreviations

Capitalize abbreviations of titles and organizations. (Some other abbreviations are also capitalized. See pages **660–662**.)

> **AAA   CEO   NAACP   M.D.   Ph.D.**

652.5 Titles of Courses

Capitalize words like *sociology* and *history* when they are used as titles of specific courses; do not capitalize these words when they name a field of study.

> **Who teaches History 202?** (title of a specific course)
> **It's the same professor who teaches my sociology course.** (a field of study)

NOTE: The words *freshman, sophomore, junior,* and *senior* are not capitalized unless they are part of an official title.

> **Rosa is a senior this year and is in charge of the Senior Class Banquet.**

Grammar Practice

Capitalization 3

■ Words Used as Names
■ Organizations
■ Letters

 For each of the following sentences, correctly write any word or word groups that are incorrectly capitalized or lowercased.

Example: The a-frame house, popularized by Architect Andrew Geller, was a popular style for vacation homes in the 1960s.
A-frame, architect

1. The American institute of architects has more than 74,000 members.

2. Last week, vice president Shannon Kraus from that Organization visited our school.

3. My Dad wanted to meet her; he was once a member of his high school's Future architects club.

4. That, of course, was before his stint on the School's lacrosse team, the Arlington eagles.

5. Back then, dad was so good that he was recruited by the Long island lizards.

6. He had to put his lacrosse career on hold, however, when he burned his hand while changing an o-ring on grandma's motorcycle.

7. Now he and mom own their own Cycle-repair Shop.

8. They also belong to the Canadian motorcycle association.

 ## Model

Model the following sentences to practice capitalizing organizations and words used as names.

We met Senator Blanche Lincoln at an American Heart Association fundraiser.

After the last election, Uncle Ray said he was going to vote for the Green Party next time.

Mechanics

Plurals

654.1 Most Nouns

Form the **plurals** of most nouns by adding *s* to the singular.

cheerleader — cheerleaders   wheel — wheels   crate — crates

654.2 Nouns Ending in *sh, ch, x, s,* and *z*

Form the plurals of nouns ending in *sh, ch, x, s,* and *z* by adding *es* to the singular.

lunch — lunches   dish — dishes   mess — messes   fox — foxes

Exception: When the final *ch* sounds like *k*, add an *s* (*monarchs*).

654.3 Nouns Ending in *y*

The plurals of common nouns that end in *y* (preceded by a consonant) are formed by changing the *y* to *i* and adding *es*.

fly — flies   jalopy — jalopies

Form the plurals of nouns that end in *y* (preceded by a vowel) by adding only an *s*.

donkey — donkeys   monkey — monkeys

NOTE: Form the plurals of all proper nouns ending in *y* by adding *s* (*Kathys*).

654.4 Nouns Ending in *o*

The plurals of nouns ending in *o* (preceded by a vowel) are formed by adding an *s*.

radio — radios   rodeo — rodeos   studio — studios   duo — duos

The plurals of most nouns ending in *o* (preceded by a consonant) are formed by adding *es*.

echo — echoes   hero — heroes   tomato — tomatoes

Exception: Musical terms always form plurals by adding *s*.

alto — altos   banjo — banjos   solo — solos   piano — pianos

654.5 Nouns Ending in *ful*

Form the plurals of nouns that end in *ful* by adding an *s* at the end of the word.

two tankfuls   three pailfuls   four mouthfuls

NOTE: Do not confuse these examples with *three pails full* (when you are referring to three separate pails full of something) or *two tanks full*.

654.6 Compound Nouns

Form the plurals of most compound nouns by adding *s* or *es* to the important word in the compound.

brothers-in-law   maids of honor   secretaries of state

Grammar Practice

Plurals 1

■ Regular Nouns
■ Nouns Ending in *sh, ch, x, s,* and *z*
■ Nouns Ending in *y, o,* and *ful*

 Write the correct plural of the underlined word in each sentence.

Example: The art <u>portfolioes</u> of seven students were on display.
  portfolios

1. The <u>keyes</u> for the table saw are in the industrial arts office.

2. Lila poured five <u>cansful</u> of water into the kettle and carefully stirred the soup.

3. We followed our guide across three mountain <u>pass's</u> to get to Blaine's Ridge.

4. The landscaping staff will plant lilac <u>bushs</u> along the walk to the main entrance.

5. The Wilmores looked at five different <u>patioes</u> before picking out a design they liked.

6. Harbor <u>authoritys</u> reported that ship traffic increased by 50 percent during the last quarter of 2005.

7. The home economics class used six different cake <u>mixs</u> to make one large cake.

8. A cow does not have four <u>stomaches</u>; it has one stomach with four parts.

9. No one can explain all the <u>mysterys</u> of the universe.

10. Use this paint to make 20 <u>dashs</u> across the wall.

11. Jayleen and Francine found five dust-covered <u>piccoloes</u> in the band's storage room.

 ## Exercise

Write a sentence for the plural of each of the following words.

ray, tress, glassful, territory

Mechanics

Plurals *(continued)*

656.1 Nouns Ending in *f* or *fe*

Form the plurals of nouns that end in *f* or *fe* in one of two ways: if the final *f* sound is still heard in the plural form of the word, simply add *s;* but if the final *f* sound becomes a *v* sound, change the *f* to *ve* and add *s.*

Plural ends with *f* sound: roof — roofs; chief — chiefs

Plural ends with *v* sound: wife — wives; loaf — loaves

NOTE: Several words are correct with either ending.

Plural ends with either sound: hoof — hooves/hoofs

656.2 Irregular Spelling

A number of words form a plural by taking on an irregular spelling.

crisis — crises	child — children	radius — radii
criterion — criteria	goose — geese	die — dice

NOTE: Some of these words are acceptable with the commonly used *s* or *es* ending.

index — indices/indexes   cactus — cacti/cactuses

Some nouns remain unchanged when used as plurals.

deer   moose   sheep   salmon   aircraft   series

656.3 Words Discussed as Words

The plurals of symbols, letters, numbers, and words being discussed as words are formed by adding an apostrophe and an *s.*

Dad yelled a lot of *wow's* and *yippee's* when he saw my A's and B's.

NOTE: You may omit the apostrophe if it does not cause any confusion.

the three R's or Rs   YMCA's or YMCAs

656.4 Collective Nouns

A collective noun may be singular or plural depending upon how it's used. A collective noun is singular when it refers to a group considered as one unit; it is plural when it refers to the individuals in the group.

The class was on its best behavior. (group as a unit)

The class are preparing for their final exams. (individuals in the group)

If it seems awkward to use a plural verb with a collective noun, add a clearly plural noun such as *members* to the sentence, or change the collective noun into a possessive followed by a plural noun that describes the individuals in the group.

The class members are preparing for their final exams.

The class's students are preparing for their final exams.

Grammar Practice

Plurals 2

- Irregular Spelling
- Words Discussed as Words
- Collective Nouns

 For each sentence below, write the plural form of the word in parentheses.

Example: How many (child) attend the Bayshore Science School?
children

1. When Diego opened the musty trunk, he was startled to see four (mouse) staring back at him.

2. It was disturbing to me to hear the president continue his incorrect pronunciation of all the *(nuclear)* in his speeches.

3. Isle Royale, an island in Lake Superior, supports a population of about 550 (moose).

4. Many of the university's (alumnus) donate money to help keep the school competitive both academically and athletically.

5. Mr. Lake pointed out that the writer had used six *(and)* in quite a rambling sentence.

6. Scientists count the number of protons and neutrons to distinguish between the (nucleus) of atoms.

7. Kev plans to ask the five (W) during the interview.

8. Najib and Sylvia were pleased with their catch of 15 (fish).

Model

Model the following sentences to practice using collective nouns correctly.

> **Make sure you have finished speaking before your audience has finished listening.**
>
> —Dorothy Sarnoff

> **After their honeymoon was interrupted by a hurricane, the couple were happy to be back home.**

Numbers

658.1 Numerals or Words

Numbers from one to nine are usually written as words; numbers 10 and over are usually written as numerals. However, numbers being compared or contrasted should be kept in the same style.

8 to 11 years old   eight to eleven years old

You may use a combination of numerals and words for very large numbers.

1.5 million   3 billion to 3.2 billion   6 trillion

If numbers are used infrequently in a piece of writing, you may spell out those that can be written in no more than two words.

ten   twenty-five   two hundred   fifty thousand

658.2 Numerals Only

Use numerals for the following forms: decimals, percentages, chapters, pages, addresses, phone numbers, identification numbers, and statistics.

26.2   8 percent   Highway 36   chapter 7
pages 287–89   July 6, 1945   44 B.C.E.   a vote of 23 to 4

Always use numerals with abbreviations and symbols.

8%   10 mm   3 cc   8 oz   90° C   24 mph   6' 3"

658.3 Words Only

Use words to express numbers that begin a sentence.

Fourteen students "forgot" their assignments.

NOTE: Change the sentence structure if this rule creates a clumsy construction.

Clumsy: *Six hundred thirty-nine* teachers were laid off this year.

Better: This year, 639 teachers were laid off.

Use words for numbers that come before a compound modifier if that modifier includes a numeral.

They made twelve 10-foot sub sandwiches for the picnic.

658.4 Time and Money

If time is expressed with an abbreviation, use numerals; if it is expressed in words, spell out the number.

4:00 A.M., 4:00 a.m., (or) four o'clock

If an amount of money is spelled out, so is the currency; use a numeral if a symbol is used.

twenty dollars (or) $20

Grammar Practice

Numbers

- ◼ **Numerals or Words**
- ◼ **Numerals Only**
- ◼ **Words Only**
- ◼ **Time and Money**

 For each sentence below, write the underlined numbers the correct way. If a number is already correctly presented, write "correct."

Example: In <u>1</u> year, an acre of trees produces enough oxygen for <u>eighteen</u> people.

one, 18

1. In that same year, those trees can absorb as much carbon as is produced by a car driven up to <u>8,700</u> miles.

2. A tree does not reach its most productive stage of carbon storage until it is <u>ten</u> years old.

3. Over its life, a <u>seventy</u>-year-old tree absorbs over three tons of carbon.

4. Trees that provide shade and shelter reduce yearly heating and cooling costs by <u>$2.1 billion dollars</u>.

5. A giant redwood in California, the world's tallest tree, measures <u>378</u> feet high.

6. The largest tree in the world, a sequoia in California, has a volume of <u>fourteen hundred eighty-seven</u> cubic meters.

7. Found in the White Mountains of California, bristlecone pines are the world's oldest trees at more than <u>four thousand, eight hundred</u> years old!

8. The *Apollo 14* mission of <u>January thirty-first, 1971</u>, had tree seeds among its cargo.

Exercise

Complete this sentence with your own numbers.

Please read chapter _____ in your science book. Remember, the test next week will count for _____ percent of your grade.

Abbreviations

660.1 Formal and Informal Abbreviations

An **abbreviation** is the shortened form of a word or phrase. Some abbreviations are always acceptable in both formal and informal writing:

Mr. Mrs. Jr. Ms. Dr. a.m. (A.M.) p.m. (P.M.)

NOTE: In most of your writing, you do not abbreviate the names of states, countries, months, days, or units of measure. However, you may use the abbreviation *U.S.* after it has been spelled out once. Do not abbreviate the words *street, company,* and similar words, especially when they are part of a proper name. Also, do not use signs or symbols (%, &, #, @) in place of words. The dollar sign, however, is appropriate with numerals ($325).

660.2 Correspondence Abbreviations

United States

	Standard	Postal
Alabama	Ala.	AL
Alaska	Alaska	AK
Arizona	Ariz.	AZ
Arkansas	Ark.	AR
California	Calif.	CA
Colorado	Colo.	CO
Connecticut	Conn.	CT
Delaware	Del.	DE
District of Columbia	D.C.	DC
Florida	Fla.	FL
Georgia	Ga.	GA
Guam	Guam	GU
Hawaii	Hawaii	HI
Idaho	Idaho	ID
Illinois	Ill.	IL
Indiana	Ind.	IN
Iowa	Iowa	IA
Kansas	Kan.	KS
Kentucky	Ky.	KY
Louisiana	La.	LA
Maine	Maine	ME
Maryland	Md.	MD
Massachusetts	Mass.	MA
Michigan	Mich.	MI
Minnesota	Minn.	MN
Mississippi	Miss.	MS
Missouri	Mo.	MO
Montana	Mont.	MT
Nebraska	Neb.	NE
Nevada	Nev.	NV
New Hampshire	N.H.	NH
New Jersey	N.J.	NJ
New Mexico	N.M.	NM
New York	N.Y.	NY
North Carolina	N.C.	NC
North Dakota	N.D.	ND
Ohio	Ohio	OH
Oklahoma	Okla.	OK
Oregon	Ore.	OR
Pennsylvania	Pa.	PA
Puerto Rico	P.R.	PR
Rhode Island	R.I.	RI
South Carolina	S.C.	SC
South Dakota	S.D.	SD
Tennessee	Tenn.	TN
Texas	Texas	TX
Utah	Utah	UT
Vermont	Vt.	VT
Virginia	Va.	VA
Virgin Islands	V.I.	VI
Washington	Wash.	WA
West Virginia	W.Va.	WV
Wisconsin	Wis.	WI
Wyoming	Wyo.	WY

Canadian Provinces

	Standard	Postal
Alberta	Alta.	AB
British Columbia	B.C.	BC
Labrador	Lab.	NL
Manitoba	Man.	MB
New Brunswick	N.B.	NB
Newfoundland	N.F.	NL
Northwest Territories	N.W.T.	NT
Nova Scotia	N.S.	NS
Nunavut		NU
Ontario	Ont.	ON
Prince Edward Island	P.E.I.	PE
Quebec	Que.	QC
Saskatchewan	Sask.	SK
Yukon Territory	Y.T.	YT

Addresses

	Standard	Postal
Apartment	Apt.	APT
Avenue	Ave.	AVE
Boulevard	Blvd.	BLVD
Circle	Cir.	CIR
Court	Ct.	CT
Drive	Dr.	DR
East	E.	E
Expressway	Expy.	EXPY
Freeway	Fwy.	FWY
Heights	Hts.	HTS
Highway	Hwy.	HWY
Hospital	Hosp.	HOSP
Junction	Junc.	JCT
Lake	L.	LK
Lakes	Ls.	LKS
Lane	Ln.	LN
Meadows	Mdws.	MDWS
North	N.	N
Palms	Palms	PLMS
Park	Pk.	PK
Parkway	Pky.	PKY
Place	Pl.	PL
Plaza	Plaza	PLZ
Post Office Box	P.O. Box	PO BOX
Ridge	Rdg.	RDG
River	R.	RV
Road	Rd.	RD
Room	Rm.	RM
Rural	R.	R
Rural Route	R.R.	RR
Shore	Sh.	SH
South	S.	S
Square	Sq.	SQ
Station	Sta.	STA
Street	St.	ST
Suite	Ste.	STE
Terrace	Ter.	TER
Turnpike	Tpke.	TPKE
Union	Un.	UN
View	View	VW
Village	Vil.	VLG
West	W.	W

661.1 Other Common Abbreviations

abr. abridged; abridgment
AC, ac alternating current
ack. acknowledge; acknowledgment
acv actual cash value
A.D. in the year of the Lord (Latin *anno Domini*)
AM amplitude modulation
A.M., a.m. before noon (Latin *ante meridiem*)
ASAP as soon as possible
avg., av. average
BBB Better Business Bureau
B.C. before Christ
B.C.E. before the Common Era
bibliog. bibliographer; bibliography
biog. biographer; biographical; biography
C 1. Celsius 2. centigrade 3. coulomb
c. 1. circa (about) 2. cup
cc 1. cubic centimeter 2. carbon copy
CDT, C.D.T. central daylight time
C.E. of the Common Era
chap. chapter
cm centimeter
c.o., c/o care of
COD, C.O.D. 1. cash on delivery 2. collect on delivery
co-op. cooperative
CST, C.S.T. central standard time
cu., c cubic
D.A. district attorney
d.b.a. doing business as
DC, dc direct current
dec. deceased
dept. department
DST, D.S.T. daylight saving time
dup. duplicate
DVD digital video disc
ea. each
ed. edition; editor
EDT, E.D.T. eastern daylight time
e.g. for example (Latin *exempli gratia*)
EST, E.S.T. eastern standard time
etc. and so forth (Latin *et cetera*)
ex. example
F Fahrenheit
FM frequency modulation
F.O.B., f.o.b. free on board
ft foot
g 1. gram 2. gravity
gal. gallon
gloss. glossary
GNP gross national product
hdqrs, HQ headquarters
HIV human immunodeficiency virus
Hon. Honorable (title)

hp horsepower
HTML hypertext markup language
Hz hertz
ibid. in the same place (Latin *ibidem*)
id. the same (Latin *idem*)
i.e. that is (Latin *id est*)
illus. illustration
inc. incorporated
IQ, I.Q. intelligence quotient
IRS Internal Revenue Service
ISBN International Standard Book Number
Jr., jr. junior
K 1. kelvin (temperature unit) 2. Kelvin (temperature scale)
kc kilocycle
kg kilogram
km kilometer
kn knot
kW kilowatt
l liter
lat. latitude
lb, lb. pound (Latin *libra*)
l.c. lowercase
lit. literary; literature
log logarithm
long. longitude
Ltd., ltd. limited
m meter
M.A. master of arts (Latin *Magister Artium*)
Mc, mc megacycle
M.C., m.c. master of ceremonies
M.D. doctor of medicine (Latin *medicinae doctor*)
mdse. merchandise
mfg. manufacturing
mg milligram
mi. 1. mile 2. mill (monetary unit)
misc. miscellaneous
ml milliliter
mm millimeter
mpg, m.p.g. miles per gallon
mph, m.p.h. miles per hour
MS 1. manuscript 2. Mississippi 3. multiple sclerosis
Ms., Ms title of courtesy for a woman
MST, M.S.T. mountain standard time
neg. negative
N.S.F., n.s.f. not sufficient funds
oz, oz. ounce
PA 1. public-address system 2. Pennsylvania
pct. percent
pd. paid
PDT, P.D.T. Pacific daylight time

PFC, Pfc. private first class
pg., p. page
P.M., p.m. after noon (Latin *post meridiem*)
P.O. 1. personnel officer 2. purchase order 3. postal order; post office 4. (also **p.o.**) petty officer
pop. population
POW, P.O.W. prisoner of war
pp. pages
ppd. 1. postpaid 2. prepaid
PR, P.R. 1. public relations 2. Puerto Rico
P.S. post script
psi, p.s.i. pounds per square inch
PST, P.S.T. Pacific standard time
PTA, P.T.A. Parent-Teacher Association
qt. quart
RF radio frequency
RN registered nurse
R.P.M., rpm revolutions per minute
R.S.V.P., r.s.v.p. please reply (French *répondez s'il vous plaît*)
SASE self-addressed stamped envelope
SCSI small computer system interface
SOS 1. international distress signal 2. any call for help
Sr. 1. senior (after surname) 2. sister (religious)
ST standard time
St. 1. saint 2. strait 3. street
std. standard
syn. synonymous; synonym
TBA to be announced
tbs, tbsp tablespoon
TM trademark
tsp teaspoon
UHF, uhf ultra high frequency
UPC universal product code
UV ultraviolet
V 1. *Physics:* velocity 2. *Electricity:* volt 3. volume
V.A., VA Veterans Administration
VHF, vhf very high frequency
VIP *Informal:* very important person
vol. 1. volume 2. volunteer
vs. versus
W 1. *Electricity:* watt 2. *Physics:* (also **w**) work 3. west
whse., whs. warehouse
wkly. weekly
w/o without
wt. weight
yd yard (measurement)

Acronyms and Initialisms

662.1 Acronyms

An **acronym** is a word formed from the first (or first few) letters of words in a phrase. Even though acronyms are abbreviations, they require no periods.

radar	radio detecting and ranging
CARE	Cooperative for American Relief Everywhere
NASA	National Aeronautics and Space Administration
VISTA	Volunteers in Service to America
LAN	local area network

662.2 Initialisms

An **initialism** is similar to an acronym except that the initials used to form this abbreviation are pronounced individually.

CIA	Central Intelligence Agency
FBI	Federal Bureau of Investigation
FHA	Federal Housing Administration

662.3 Common Acronyms and Initialisms

ADD	attention deficit disorder
AIDS	acquired immunodeficiency syndrome
AKA	also known as
ATM	automatic teller machine
BMI	body mass index
CD	compact disc
DMV	Department of Motor Vehicles
ETA	expected time of arrival
FAA	Federal Aviation Administration
FCC	Federal Communications Commission
FDA	Food and Drug Administration
FDIC	Federal Deposit Insurance Corporation
FEMA	Federal Emergency Management Agency
FTC	Federal Trade Commission
FYI	for your information
GPS	global positioning system
HDTV	high-definition television
IRS	Internal Revenue Service
IT	information technology
JPEG	Joint Photographic Experts Group
LCD	liquid crystal display
LLC	limited liability company
MADD	Mothers Against Drunk Driving
MRI	magnetic resonance imaging
NASA	National Aeronautics and Space Administration
NATO	North Atlantic Treaty Organization
OPEC	Organization of Petroleum-Exporting Countries
OSHA	Occupational Safety and Health Administration
PAC	political action committee
PDF	portable document format
PETA	People for the Ethical Treatment of Animals
PIN	personal identification number
PSA	public service announcement
ROTC	Reserve Officers' Training Corps
SADD	Students Against Destructive Decisions
SUV	sport utility vehicle
SWAT	special weapons and tactics
TDD	telecommunications device for the deaf
VA	Veterans Administration

Grammar Practice

Abbreviations, Acronyms, and Initialisms

 For each abbreviation, acronym, or initialism below, write out what it stands for. Then write whether it is an abbreviation, acronym, or initialism. (Do as many as you can before referring to the previous pages.)

Example: MI

Michigan, abbreviation

States/Provinces

1. NC
2. AK
3. QC
4. MA
5. MS
6. VI
7. IA
8. ON
9. PR

Addresses

10. PKY
11. CT
12. LK
13. HTS
14. RV

Miscellaneous

15. OPEC
16. B.C.E.
17. d.b.a.
18. PETA
19. DVD
20. i.e.
21. IRS
22. PIN
23. lb.
24. POW
25. pct.
26. UPC
27. avg.
28. SWAT

Model

Model the following acronyms and initialisms to come up with your own abbreviations. (Write at least one acronym and one initialism.)

HTML – hypertext markup language
HRH – Her Royal Highness
PERT – program evaluation review technique
MERCAD – measurement electronically recorded computer-aided design

Spelling Rules

664.1 Write *i* before *e*

Write *i* before *e* except after *c*, or when sounded like *a* as in *neighbor* and *weigh*.

relief   receive   perceive   reign   freight   beige

Exceptions: There are a number of exceptions to this rule, including these: *neither, leisure, seize, weird, species, science.*

664.2 Words with Consonant Endings

When a one-syllable word *(bat)* ends in a consonant *(t)* preceded by one vowel *(a)*, double the final consonant before adding a suffix that begins with a vowel *(batting)*.

sum — summary   god — goddess

NOTE: When a word with more than one syllable *(control)* ends in a consonant *(l)* preceded by one vowel *(o)*, the accent is on the last syllable *(con trol´)*, and the suffix begins with a vowel *(ing)*, the same rule holds true: double the final consonant *(controlling)*.

prefer — preferred   begin — beginning
forget — forgettable   admit — admittance

664.3 Words with a Silent *e*

If a word ends with a silent *e,* drop the *e* before adding a suffix that begins with a vowel. Do not drop the *e* when the suffix begins with a consonant.

state — stating — statement   like — liking — likeness
use — using — useful   nine — ninety — nineteen

Exceptions: *judgment, truly, argument, ninth*

664.4 Words Ending in *y*

When *y* is the last letter in a word and the *y* is preceded by a consonant, change the *y* to *i* before adding any suffix except those beginning with *i*.

fry — fries — frying   hurry — hurried — hurrying   lady — ladies
ply — pliable   happy — happiness   beauty — beautiful

When *y* is the last letter in a word and the *y* is preceded by a vowel, do not change the *y* to *i* before adding a suffix.

play — plays — playful   stay — stays — staying   employ — employed

Important reminder: Never trust your spelling even to the best spell-checker. Use a dictionary for words your spell-checker does not cover.

Grammar Practice

Spelling 1

 Find the 10 words that are misspelled in the following paragraph and write them correctly. (Each misspelled word is in the "Commonly Misspelled Words" list on pages 666–667.)

Example: 1. *wholly*

The Kyoto Protocol is an international agreement to avert climate change caused by greenhouse gases. Enforcement began in February 2005. More than 150 countries are wholey on board with this effort to aleviate global warming. Among those countries not joining are Australia and the United States. These two priviledged countries, with approxamitely 5 percent of the world's population, account for more than 20 percent of the world's fossil fuel emissions. Yet in niether of these two industreal nations do the leaders agree with the Protocol's approach. They claim that the effort would defenitely cost too much money and would hurt the economy. In addition, these polititions believe China and India should not be exempt from emission controls because China alone will soon become the largest emitter of greenhouse gases. Many other government leaders beleive the costs of the Kyoto Protocol are affordable, but no one really knows if the Protocol can acomplish its goals.

Model

Model the following sentences to practice using the "*i* before *e*" spelling rule. (Use the underlined words in your sentences, too.)

<u>Patience</u> serves as a protection against wrongs as clothes do against cold.

—Leonardo da Vinci

Art is <u>science</u> made clear.

—Jean Cocteau

Commonly Misspelled Words

A

abbreviate
abrupt
absence
absolute (ly)
absurd
abundance
academic
accelerate
accept (ance)
accessible
accessory
accidentally
accommodate
accompany
accomplish
accumulate
accurate
accustom (ed)
ache
achieve (ment)
acknowledge
acquaintance
acquired
across
address
adequate
adjustment
admissible
admittance
adolescent
advantageous
advertisement
advisable
aggravate
aggression
alcohol
alleviate
almost
alternative
although
aluminum
amateur
analysis
analyze
anarchy
ancient
anecdote
anesthetic
annihilate
announce
annual
anonymous
answer
anxious
apologize
apparatus
apparent (ly)
appearance
appetite
applies
appreciate
appropriate
approximately
architect
arctic
argument
arithmetic
arrangement
artificial
ascend
assistance
association
athlete
attendance
attire
attitude
audience
authority
available

B

balance
balloon
bargain
basically
beautiful
beginning
believe
benefit (ed)
biscuit
bought
boycott
brevity
brilliant
Britain
bureau
business

C

cafeteria
caffeine
calculator
calendar
campaign
canceled
candidate
catastrophe
category
caught
cavalry
celebration
cemetery
certificate
changeable
chief
chocolate
circuit
circumstance
civilization
colonel
colossal
column
commercial
commitment
committed
committee
comparative
comparison
competitively
conceivable
condemn
condescend
conference
conferred
confidential
congratulate
conscience
conscientious
conscious
consequence
consumer
contaminate
convenience
cooperate
correspondence
cough
coupon
courageous
courteous
creditor
criticism
criticize
curiosity
curious
cylinder

D

dealt
deceitful
deceive
decision
defense
deferred
definite (ly)
definition
delicious
descend
describe
description
despair
desperate
destruction
development
diameter
diaphragm
diarrhea
dictionary
dining
disagreeable
disappear
disappoint
disastrous
discipline
discrimination
discuss
dismissal
dissatisfied
dissect
distinctly
dormitory
doubt
drought
duplicate
dyeing
dying

E

earliest
efficiency
eighth
elaborate
eligible
eliminate
ellipse
embarrass
emphasize
employee
enclosure
encourage
endeavor
English
enormous
enough
enrichment
enthusiastic
entirely
entrance
environment
equipment
equipped
equivalent
especially
essential
eventually
exaggerate
examination
exceed
excellent
excessive
excite
executive
exercise
exhaust (ed)
exhibition
exhilaration
existence
expensive
experience
explanation
exquisite
extinguish
extraordinary
extremely

FG

facilities
familiar
fascinate
fashion
fatigue (d)
feature
February
fiery
financially
flourish
forcible
foreign
forfeit
fortunate
forty
fourth
freight
friend
fulfill
gauge
generally
generous
genuine
glimpse
gnarled
gnaw
government
gradual
grammar
gratitude
grievous
grocery
guard
guidance

H

happiness
harass
harmonize
height
hemorrhage
hereditary
hindrance
hoping
hopping
hospitable
humorous

Mechanics

hygiene
hymn
hypocrisy

IJ

ignorance
illiterate
illustrate
imaginary
immediately
immense
incidentally
inconvenience
incredible
indefinitely
independence
indispensable
industrial
industrious
inevitable
infinite
inflation
innocence
inoculation
inquiry
installation
instrumental
intelligence
interesting
interfere
interrupt
investigate
irregular
irresistible
issuing
itinerary
jealous (y)
jewelry
journal
judgment

KL

knowledge
laboratory
laugh
lawyer
league
legacy
legalize
legitimate
leisure

liaison
license
lightning
likable
liquid
literature
loneliness

MN

maintenance
maneuver
manufacture
marriage
mathematics
medieval
memento
menagerie
merchandise
merely
mileage
miniature
miscellaneous
mischievous
misspell
moat
mobile
mortgage
multiplied
muscle
musician
mustache
mutual
mysterious
naive
nauseous
necessary
neither
neurotic
nevertheless
ninety
nighttime
noticeable
nuclear
nuisance

OP

obstacle
obvious
occasion
occupant
occupation

occurred
occurrence
official
often
omitted
opinion
opponent
opportunity
opposite
optimism
ordinarily
organization
original
outrageous
pamphlet
parallel
paralyze
partial
particularly
pastime
patience
peculiar
pedestal
performance
permanent
permissible
perseverance
personal (ly)
personality
perspiration
persuade
petition
phenomenon
physical
physician
picnicking
planned
playwright
plead
pneumonia
politician
ponder
positively
possession
practically
precede
precious
preference
prejudice
preparation
presence
prevalent
primitive

privilege
probably
proceed
professional
professor
prominent
pronounce
pronunciation
protein
psychology
puny
purchase
pursuing

QR

qualified
quality
quantity
questionnaire
quiet
quite
quizzes
recede
receipt
receive
recipe
recognize
recommend
reference
referred
regard
regimen
religious
repel
repetition
residue
responsibility
restaurant
rheumatism
rhythm
ridiculous
robot
roommate

S

sacrifice
salary
sandwich
satisfactory
scarcely
scenic

schedule
scholar
science
secretary
seize
separate
sergeant
several
severely
sheriff
shrubbery
siege
signature
signify
silhouette
similar
simultaneous
sincerely
skiing
skunk
society
solar
sophomore
souvenir
spaghetti
specific
specimen
statue
stomach
stopped
strength
strictly
submission
substitute
subtle
succeed
success
sufficient
supersede
suppose
surprise
suspicious
symbolism
sympathy
synthetic

TU

tariff
technique
temperature
temporary
tendency

thermostat
thorough (ly)
though
throughout
tongue
tornado
tortoise
tragedy
transferred
tremendous
tried
trite
truly
unanimous
undoubtedly
unfortunately
unique
unnecessary
until
urgent
usable
usher
usually

V

vacuum
vague
valuable
variety
vengeance
versatile
vicinity
villain
visibility
visual

W

waif
Wednesday
weird
wholly
width
women
wrath
wreckage

Y

yesterday
yield
yolk

Steps to Becoming a Better Speller

1. **Be patient.**
   Becoming a good speller takes time.

2. **Check the correct pronunciation of each word you are attempting to spell.**
   Knowing the correct pronunciation of a word can help you remember its spelling.

3. **Note the meaning and history of each word as you are checking the dictionary for pronunciation.**
   Knowing the meaning and history of a word provides you with a better notion of how the word is properly used, and this can help you remember its spelling.

4. **Before you close the dictionary, practice spelling the word.**
   Look away from the page and try to "see" the word in your mind. Then write it on a piece of paper. Check your spelling in the dictionary; repeat the process until you are able to spell the word correctly.

5. **Learn some spelling rules.**
   For four of the most useful rules, see page **664**.

6. **Make a list of the words that you often misspell.**
   Select the first 10 and practice spelling them.

   STEP A: Read each word carefully; then write it on a piece of paper. Check to see that you've spelled it correctly. Repeat this step for the words that you misspelled.

   STEP B: When you have finished your first 10 words, ask someone to read them to you as you write them again. Then check for misspellings. If you find none, congratulations! (Repeat both steps with your next 10 words, and so on.)

7. **Write often.**

Grammar Practice

Spelling 2

Find the 10 words that are misspelled in the following paragraphs and write them correctly. (Each misspelled word is in the "Commonly Misspelled Words" list on pages 666–667.)

Example: 1. *scenic*

In the early part of the twentieth century—before air travel, before the interstate highway system, before cars—people took the train to travel long distances. Rail service provided passengers with a comfortable, seenic trip accross the country. Slowly, however, private railroads were dieing as ridership decreased.

In 1970, the goverment agreed to subsidize the passenger rail service that became Amtrak. A network of 23,000 miles of track connected 314 communities with 184 trains. The number of trains and cities served by them has grown since then, but skedules are always subject to change. Maintainance of the aging equippment has also become a problem. Allthough the railroad has always struggled finantially (it has never made a profit), it remains a prominint part of many Americans' transportation options.

Model

Model the following sentences to practice using the "words with a silent *e*" spelling rule. (Use the underlined words in your sentences, too.)

Behind every <u>argument</u> is someone's ignorance.

—Louis D. Brandeis

Journal <u>writing</u> is a voyage to the interior.

—Christina Baldwin

Test Prep!

Read the paragraphs below. For each underlined part, write the letter of the correct choice given on the next page. If it is already correct, choose "D."

Elizabeth Najeeb Halaby was an upper-class <u>young American. Her</u>
<u>Father</u> once headed the <u>Federal Aviation administration</u>. Born in
(2)
Washington, D.C., she attended <u>Private schools</u> there and in New York and
(3)
Massachusetts. She graduated from Princeton University in 1974. Her
degree in <u>architechture</u> and urban planning led her to Australia, to Iran,
(4)
and finally to Jordan, where she worked on an <u>airport design project</u>. There
(5)
she met <u>the King of that country</u>; two months later, they were married.
(6)

It was not easy for this strong-willed <u>Arab American to leave behind</u>
(7)
<u>her western</u> lifestyle. She converted from <u>christianity to Islam</u> and took
(8)
the name Queen Noor al-Hussein (meaning "light of Hussein"). She
adapted somewhat to a society in which women were subservient and
covered <u>themselfs with long veils</u>, but she also initiated projects to improve
(9)
educational and work <u>opportunityes for them</u>. Additionally, she stepped
(10)
away from her royal role to speak out against the use of land mines.

Queen Noor and King Hussein had <u>4 childs</u>. She became stepmother
(11)
to Hussein's <u>eight childs</u> from previous marriages. She learned to speak
(12)
<u>arabic besides English and french</u>. She gradually won the admiration and
(13)
loyalty of the Jordanian citizens through her dedication to them.

Since King Hussein's death in <u>1999, Ms Halaby</u> is still known as
(14)
Queen Noor, with her oldest son second in line to the throne. She keeps
homes in Jordan and in the United States and continues to <u>campain against</u>
(15)
<u>land mines</u>. The queen supports the U.N.'s efforts for women and children
and has written a book, <u>*Leap of Faith: Memoirs of an unexpected life*</u>.
(16)

1
  (A) young american. her father
  (B) young American. Her father
  (C) Young American. Her father
  (D) correct as is

2
  (A) Federal Aviation Administration
  (B) federal Aviation Administration
  (C) Federal aviation Administration
  (D) correct as is

3
  (A) private schooles
  (B) Private schooles
  (C) private schools
  (D) correct as is

4
  (A) Degree in architecture
  (B) Degree in Architecture
  (C) degree in architecture
  (D) correct as is

5
  (A) Airport Design Project
  (B) Airport Design project
  (C) Airport design project
  (D) correct as is

6
  (A) the King of that Country
  (B) the king of that Country
  (C) the king of that country
  (D) correct as is

7
  (A) Arab American to leave behind her Western
  (B) arab american to leave behind her western
  (C) arab American to leave behind her Western
  (D) correct as is

8
  (A) Christianity to Islam
  (B) Christianity to islam
  (C) christianity to islam
  (D) correct as is

9
  (A) themselves with long veiles
  (B) themselves with long veils
  (C) themselfs with long veiles
  (D) correct as is

10
  (A) opportunitys for them
  (B) opportunites for them
  (C) opportunities for them
  (D) correct as is

11
  (A) 4 children
  (B) four children
  (C) four childs
  (D) correct as is

12
  (A) 8 children
  (B) 8 childs
  (C) eight children
  (D) correct as is

13
  (A) Arabic besides English and French
  (B) Arabic besides English and french
  (C) arabic besides English and French
  (D) correct as is

14
  (A) 1999, Ms. Halaby
  (B) nineteen 99, Ms. Halaby
  (C) nineteen ninety-nine, Ms Halaby
  (D) correct as is

15
  (A) campain against land mins
  (B) campaign against land mins
  (C) campaign against land mines
  (D) correct as is

16
  (A) *Leap of Faith: Memoirs Of An Unexpected Life*
  (B) *Leap of Faith: Memoirs of an Unexpected Life*
  (C) *Leap Of Faith: memoirs of an unexpected life*
  (D) correct as is

Understanding Idioms

Idioms are phrases that are used in a special way. You can't understand an idiom just by knowing the meaning of each word in the phrase. You must learn it as a whole. For example, the idiom *bury the hatchet* means "to settle an argument," even though the individual words in the phrase mean something much different. This section will help you learn some of the common idioms in American English.

apple of his eye	Eagle Lake is the apple of his eye. (something he likes very much)
as plain as day	The mistake in the ad was as plain as day. (very clear)
as the crow flies	New London is 200 miles from here as the crow flies. (in a straight line)
at a snail's pace	My last hour at work passes at a snail's pace. (very, very slowly)
axe to grind	The manager has an axe to grind with that umpire. (disagreement to settle)
bad apple	There are no bad apples in this class. (a bad influence)
beat around the bush	Don't beat around the bush; answer the question. (avoid getting to the point)
benefit of the doubt	Everyone has been given the benefit of the doubt at least once. (another chance)
beyond the shadow of a doubt	Beyond the shadow of a doubt, this is my best science project. (for certain)
blew my top	When I saw the broken statue, I blew my top. (showed great anger)
bone to pick	Alison had a bone to pick with the student who copied her paper. (problem to settle)
brain drain	Brain drain is a serious problem in some states. (the best students moving elsewhere)
break the ice	The nervous ninth graders were afraid to break the ice. (start a conversation)
burn the midnight oil	Devon had to burn the midnight oil to finish his report. (work late into the night)

bury the hatchet	**My sisters were told to** bury the hatchet **immediately.** (settle an argument)
by the skin of her teeth	**Sumey avoided an accident** by the skin of her teeth. (just barely)
champing at the bit	**The skiers were** champing at the bit **to get on the slopes.** (eager, excited)
chicken feed	**The prize was** chicken feed **to some people.** (not worth much money)
chip off the old block	**Frank's just like his father. He's a** chip off the old block. (just like someone else)
clean as a whistle	**My boss told me to make sure the place was as** clean as a whistle **before I left.** (very clean)
cold shoulder	**I wanted to fit in with that group, but they gave me the** cold shoulder. (ignored me)
crack of dawn	**Ali delivers his papers at the** crack of dawn. (first light of day, early morning)
cry wolf	**If you** cry wolf **too often, no one will believe you.** (say you are in trouble when you aren't)
dead of night	**Hearing a loud noise in the** dead of night **frightened Bill.** (middle of the night)
dirt cheap	**A lot of clothes at that store are** dirt cheap. (inexpensive, costing very little money)
doesn't hold a candle to	**That award** doesn't hold a candle to **a gold medal.** (is not as good as)
drop in the bucket	**The contributions were a** drop in the bucket. (a small amount compared to what's needed)
everything from A to Z	**That catalog lists** everything from A to Z. (a lot of different things)
face the music	**Todd had to** face the music **when he broke the window.** (deal with the punishment)
fish out of water	**He felt like a** fish out of water **in the new math class.** (someone in an unfamiliar place)
fit for a king	**The food at the athletic banquet was** fit for a king. (very special)

Idioms

flew off the handle	**Bill** flew off the handle **when he saw a reckless driver near the school.** (became very angry)
floating on air	**Celine was** floating on air **at the prom.** (feeling very happy)
food for thought	**The boys' foolish and dangerous prank gave us** food for thought. (something to think about)
get down to business	**After sharing several jokes, Mr. Sell said we should** get down to business. (start working)
get the upper hand	**The wrestler moved quickly on his opponent in order to** get the upper hand. (gain the advantage)
give their all	**Student volunteers** give their all **to help others.** (work as hard as they can)
go fly a kite	**Charlene stared at her nosy brother and said, "**Go fly a kite.**"** (go away)
has a green thumb	**Talk to Mrs. Smith about your sick plant. She** has a green thumb. (is good at growing plants)
has a heart of gold	**Joe** has a heart of gold. (is very kind and generous)
hit a home run	**Rhonda** hit a home run **with her speech.** (succeeded, or did well)
hit the ceiling	**When my parents saw my grades, they** hit the ceiling. (were very angry)
hit the hay	**Exhausted from the hike, Jamal** hit the hay **without eating supper.** (went to bed)
in a nutshell	**Can you,** in a nutshell**, tell us your goals for this year?** (in summary)
in one ear and out the other	**Sharl, concerned about her pet, let the lecture go** in one ear and out the other. (without really listening)
in the black	**My aunt's gift shop is finally** in the black. (making money)
in the nick of time	**Janelle caught the falling vase** in the nick of time. (just in time)
in the red	**Many businesses start out** in the red. (in debt)
in the same boat	**The new tax bill meant everyone would be** in the same boat. (in a similar situation)

iron out	Joe will meet with the work crew to iron out their complaints. (solve, work out)
it goes without saying	It goes without saying **that saving money is a good idea.** (it is clear)
it stands to reason	It stands to reason **that your stamina will increase if you run every day.** (it makes sense)
keep a stiff upper lip	Keep a stiff upper lip **when you visit the doctor.** (be brave)
keep it under your hat	Keep it under your hat **about the pop quiz.** (don't tell anyone)
knock on wood	My uncle knocked on wood **after he said he had never had the flu.** (did something for good luck)
knuckle down	After wasting half the day, we were told to knuckle down. (work hard)
learn the ropes	It takes every new employee a few months to learn the ropes. (get to know how things are done)
leave no stone unturned	The police plan to leave no stone unturned **at the crime scene.** (check everything)
lend someone a hand	You will feel good if you lend someone a hand. (help someone)
let the cat out of the bag	Tom let the cat out of the bag **during lunch.** (told a secret)
let's face it	Let's face it. **You don't like rap.** (let's admit it)
look high and low	We looked high and low **for Jan's dog.** (looked everywhere)
lose face	In some cultures, it is very bad to lose face. (be embarrassed)
needle in a haystack	Trying to find a person in New York is like trying to find a needle in a haystack. (something impossible to find)
nose to the grindstone	With all of these assignments, I have to keep my nose to the grindstone. (work hard)
on cloud nine	After talking to my girlfriend, I was on cloud nine. (feeling very happy)
on pins and needles	Emiko was on pins and needles **during the championship game.** (feeling nervous)

out the window	**Once the rain started, our plans were** out the window. (ruined)
over and above	Over and above **the required work, Will cleaned up the lab.** (in addition to)
pain in the neck	**Franklin knew the report would be a** pain in the neck. (very annoying)
pull your leg	**Cary was only** pulling your leg. (telling you a little lie as a joke)
put his foot in his mouth	**Lane** put his foot in his mouth **when he answered the question.** (said something embarrassing)
put the cart before the horse	**Tonya** put the cart before the horse **when she sealed the envelope before inserting the letter.** (did something in the wrong order)
put your best foot forward	**When applying for a job, you should** put your best foot forward. (do the best that you can do)
red-letter day	**Sovann had a** red-letter day **because she did so well on her math test.** (very good day)
rock the boat	**I was told not to** rock the boat. (cause trouble)
rude awakening	**Jake will have a** rude awakening **when he sees the bill for his computer.** (sudden, unpleasant surprise)
save face	**His gift was clearly an attempt to** save face. (fix an embarrassing situation)
see eye to eye	**We** see eye to eye **about the need for a new school.** (are in agreement)
shake a leg	**I told Mako to** shake a leg **so that we wouldn't be late.** (hurry)
shift into high gear	**Greg had to** shift into high gear **to finish the test in time.** (speed up, hurry)
sight for sore eyes	**My grandmother's smiling face was a** sight for sore eyes. (good to see)
sight unseen	**Liz bought the coat** sight unseen. (without seeing it first)
sink or swim	**Whether you** sink or swim **in school depends on your study habits.** (fail or succeed)

spilled the beans	Suddenly, Kesia realized that she had spilled the beans. (revealed a secret)
spring chicken	Although Mr. Gordon isn't a spring chicken, he sure knows how to talk to kids. (young person)
stick to your guns	Know what you believe, and stick to your guns. (don't change your mind)
sweet tooth	Chocolate is often the candy of choice for those with a sweet tooth. (a love for sweets, like candy and cake)
take a dim view	My sister will take a dim view of that movie. (disapprove)
take it with a grain of salt	When you read that advertisement, take it with a grain of salt. (don't believe everything)
take the bull by the horns	It's time to take the bull by the horns so the project gets done on time. (take control)
through thick and thin	Those two girls have remained friends through thick and thin. (in good times and in bad times)
time flies	Time flies as you grow older. (time passes quickly)
time to kill	Grace had time to kill, so she read a book. (extra time)
to go overboard	The class was told not to go overboard. A $50.00 donation was fine. (to do too much)
toe the line	The new teacher made everyone toe the line. (follow the rules)
tongue-tied	He can talk easily with friends, but in class he is usually tongue-tied. (not knowing what to say)
turn over a new leaf	He decided to turn over a new leaf in school. (make a new start)
two peas in a pod	Ever since kindergarten, Lil and Eve have been like two peas in a pod. (very much alike)
under the weather	Guy was feeling under the weather this morning. (sick)
wallflower	Cho knew the other girls thought she was a wallflower. (a shy person)
word of mouth	Joseph learns a lot about his favorite team by word of mouth. (talking with other people)

Using the Right Word

a lot ■ *A lot* (always two words) is a vague descriptive phrase that should be used sparingly.

"You can observe a lot just by watching."

—Yogi Berra

accept, except ■ The verb *accept* means "to receive" or "to believe"; the preposition *except* means "other than."

The principal accepted the boy's story about the broken window, but she asked why no one except him saw the ball accidentally slip from his hand.

adapt, adopt ■ *Adapt* means "to adjust or change to fit"; *adopt* means "to choose and treat as your own" (a child, an idea).

After a lengthy period of study, Malcolm X adopted the Islamic faith and adapted to its lifestyle.

affect, effect ■ The verb *affect* means "to influence"; the verb *effect* means "to produce, accomplish, complete."

Ming's hard work effected an A on the test, which positively affected her semester grade.

The noun *effect* means the "result."

Good grades have a calming effect on parents.

aisle, isle ■ An *aisle* is a passage between seats; an *isle* is a small island.

Many airline passengers on their way to the Isle of Capri prefer an aisle seat.

all right ■ *All right* is always two words (not *alright*).

allusion, illusion ■ *Allusion* is an indirect reference to someone or something; *illusion* is a false picture or idea.

My little sister, under the illusion that she's movie-star material, makes frequent allusions to her future fans.

already, all ready ■ *Already* is an adverb meaning "before this time" or "by this time." *All ready* is an adjective meaning "fully prepared."

NOTE: Use *all ready* if you can substitute *ready* alone in the sentence.

Although I've already had some dessert, I am all ready for some ice cream from the street vendor.

Grammar Practice

Using the Right Word 1

accept, except; affect, effect; all right; allusion, illusion;
already, all ready

 Write the correct word if the underlined word is not used correctly. If it is,
then write "OK."

Example: 1. *already*

The small group of people staggering across the hot sand had **(1)** <u>all
ready</u> been without water for a day. One said, "I refuse to **(2)** <u>except</u> this
situation! We must find water!"

They forced themselves to continue—**(3)** <u>accept</u> for one man, who
was **(4)** <u>all ready</u> to give up. The other members of the group persuaded
the despairing man to keep up. If he stayed behind, surely his loss would
(5) <u>effect</u> the others negatively. A woman said, "This is not Gilligan's
Island, you know, where we could survive in huts." He didn't quite get
the **(6)** <u>illusion</u>, but he went along anyway.

Soon the lack of water would begin to have an adverse **(7)** <u>affect</u> on
them. Many times, of course, they would "see" water—only to realize that
it was just an **(8)** <u>illusion</u>. They knew that if they could only find water,
they'd be **(9)** <u>all right</u>.

◤ Model

Model the following sentences to practice using *allusion* and
illusion correctly.

I think we must quote whenever we feel that the allusion is interesting
or helpful or amusing.

—Clifton Fadiman

If power was an illusion, wasn't weakness necessarily one also?

—Lois McMaster Bujold, *A Civil Campaign*

altogether, all together ■ *Altogether* means "entirely." The phrase *all together* means "in a group" or "all at once."

> "There is altogether too much gridlock," complained the Democrats. All together, the Republicans yelled, "No way!"

among, between ■ *Among* is typically used when speaking of more than two persons or things. *Between* is used when speaking of only two.

> The three of us talked among ourselves to decide between going out or eating in.

amount, number ■ *Amount* is used for bulk measurement. *Number* is used to count separate units. (See also *fewer, less*.)

> A substantial amount of honey spilled all over a number of my CD's.

annual, biannual, semiannual, biennial, perennial ■ An *annual* event happens once every year. A *biannual* or *semiannual* event happens twice a year. A *biennial* event happens every two years. A *perennial* event is one that is persistent or constant.

> Dad's annual family reunion gets bigger every year.
> We're going shopping at the department store's semiannual white sale.
> Due to dwindling attendance, the county fair is now a biennial celebration.
> A perennial plant persists for several years.

anyway ■ Do not add an *s* to *anyway*.

ascent, assent ■ *Ascent* is the act of rising or climbing; *assent* is "to agree to something after some consideration" (or such an agreement).

> We completed our ascent of the butte with the assent of the landowner.

bad, badly ■ *Bad* is an adjective. *Badly* is an adverb.

> This apple is bad, but one bad apple doesn't always ruin the whole bushel.
> In today's game, Ross passed badly.

base, bass ■ *Base* is the foundation or the lower part of something. *Bass* (pronounced like *base*) is a deep sound. *Bass* (pronounced like *class*) is a fish.

beside, besides ■ *Beside* means "by the side of." *Besides* means "in addition to."

> Mother always grew roses beside the trash bin. Besides looking nice, they also gave off a sweet smell that masked odors.

Grammar Practice

Using the Right Word 2

among, between; amount, number; **anyway;** bad, badly; **base, bass;** beside, besides

 Write the correct choice from those given in parentheses.

Example: The team talked *(among, between)* themselves as they watched Lamar being carried off the field.
among

1. Lamar was hurt *(bad, badly)* when he was tackled during the game.

2. A cut near the *(base, bass)* of his skull caused concern.

3. *(Beside, Besides)* the cut, Lamar had also fractured his leg.

4. *(Anyway, Anyways),* he had to stay in the hospital for several days.

5. His classmates sent him a huge *(amount, number)* of get-well cards.

6. Lamar spotted a letter *(beside, besides)* his water pitcher.

7. It was from the player who tackled him—he felt *(bad, badly)* about the incident.

8. The player suggested that he and Lamar go *(base, bass)* fishing when Lamar felt better.

9. Now, *(beside, besides)* getting out of the hospital, Lamar had something else to look forward to.

10. *(Among, Between)* the medical treatment and the good *(number, amount)* of support from his friends, he knew he would be well soon.

Model

Model the following sentences to practice using the words *among* and *between*.

And in the midst of it, out sprang from among the trees and bushes the great white body of a man, who dashed into the stream and swam like a dolphin.
—Frances Hodgson Burnett, *His Grace of Osmonde*

The shortest distance between two points is under construction.
—Noelie Altito

Right Word

board, bored ■ *Board* is a piece of wood. *Board* is also an administrative group or council.

The school board approved the purchase of fifty 1- by 6-inch pine boards.

Bored is the past tense of the verb "bore," which may mean "to make a hole by drilling" or "to become weary out of dullness."

Watching television bored Joe, so he took his drill and bored a hole in the wall where he could hang his new clock.

brake, break ■ *Brake* is a device used to stop a vehicle. *Break* means "to separate or to destroy."

I hope the brakes on my car never break.

bring, take ■ *Bring* suggests the action is directed toward the speaker; *take* suggests the action is directed away from the speaker.

Bring home some garbage bags so I can take the trash outside.

can, may ■ *Can* suggests ability while *may* suggests permission.

"Can I go to the mall?" means "Am I physically able to go to the mall?"
"May I go to the mall?" asks permission to go.

capital, capitol ■ The noun *capital* refers to a city or to money. The adjective *capital* means "major or important." *Capitol* refers to a building.

The state capital is home to the capitol building for a capital reason. The state government contributed capital for its construction.

cent, sent, scent ■ *Cent* is a coin; *sent* is the past tense of the verb "send"; *scent* is an odor or a smell.

For forty-one cents, I sent my girlfriend a mushy love poem in a perfumed envelope. She adored the scent but hated the poem.

cereal, serial ■ *Cereal* is a grain, often made into breakfast food. *Serial* relates to something in a series.

Mohammed enjoys reading serial novels while he eats a bowl of cereal.

chord, cord ■ *Chord* may mean "an emotion" or "a combination of musical tones sounded at the same time." A *cord* is a string or a rope.

The guitar player strummed the opening chord to the group's hit song, which struck a responsive chord with the audience.

chose, choose ■ *Chose* (chōz) is the past tense of the verb *choose* (cho͞oz).

Last quarter I chose to read Chitra Divakaruni's *The Unknown Errors of Our Lives*—a fascinating book about Indian immigrants.

Grammar Practice

Using the Right Word 3

brake, break; bring, take; can, may; chord, cord; chose, choose

 Write the correct choice from those given in parentheses.

Example: The *(chord, cord)* on these blinds doesn't work right.
   cord

1. *(Can, May)* I get you something to drink?

2. Cheng wants to *(brake, break)* the old school record for consecutive free throws.

3. Make sure we *(bring, take)* some sunscreen with us when we go to the beach.

4. Wilson *(choose, chose)* a bright blue, sparkling sweater for his girlfriend's birthday present.

5. At the first *(chord, cord)*, the audience knew the song and went wild.

6. This printer *(can, may)* make two-sided copies.

7. I would not *(choose, chose)* a career as a septic-tank cleaner.

8. Tristan should *(bring, take)* his suit to the cleaners on his way to the concert.

9. Most often, a vehicle does not come to an immediate stop when the *(brake, break)* is applied.

10. You *(can, may)* leave the room when you are done with the test.

 ### Model

Model the following sentences to practice using *brake* and *break* correctly.

> Even though you may want to move forward in your life, you may have one foot on the brake. In order to be free, you must learn how to let go.
> —Mary Manin Morrissey

> A hole is nothing at all, but you can break your neck in it.
> —Austin O'Malley

Right Word

coarse, course ■ *Coarse* means "rough or crude"; *course* means "a path or direction taken." *Course* also means "a class or a series of studies."

Fletcher, known for using coarse language, was barred from the golf course until he took an etiquette course.

complement, compliment ■ *Complement* refers to that which completes or fulfills. *Compliment* is an expression of admiration or praise.

Kimberly smiled, thinking she had received a compliment when Carlos said that her new Chihuahua complemented her personality.

continual, continuous ■ *Continual* refers to something that happens again and again with some breaks or pauses; *continuous* refers to something that keeps happening, uninterrupted.

Sunlight hits Iowa on a continual basis; sunlight hits Earth continuously.

counsel, council ■ When used as a noun, *counsel* means "advice"; when used as a verb, it means "to advise." *Council* refers to a group that advises.

The student council counseled all freshmen to join a school club. That's good counsel.

desert, dessert ■ The noun *desert* (dĕz´ ərt) refers to barren wilderness. *Dessert* (dĭ zûrt´) is food served at the end of a meal.

The scorpion tiptoed through the moonlit desert, searching for dessert.

The verb *desert* (dĭ zûrt´) means "to abandon"; the noun *desert* (dĭ zûrt´) means "deserved reward or punishment."

The burglar's hiding place deserted him when the spotlight swung his way; his subsequent arrest was his just desert.

die, dye ■ *Die* (dying) means "to stop living." *Dye* (dyeing) is used to change the color of something.

different from, different than ■ Use *different from* in a comparison of two things. *Different than* should be used only when followed by a clause.

Yassine is quite different from his brother.
Life is different than it used to be.

farther, further ■ *Farther* refers to a physical distance; *further* refers to additional time, quantity, or degree.

Alaska extends farther north than Iceland does. Further information can be obtained in an atlas.

fewer, less ■ *Fewer* refers to the number of separate units; *less* refers to bulk quantity.

Because we have fewer orders for cakes, we'll buy less sugar and flour.

Grammar Practice

Using the Right Word 4

complement, compliment; counsel, council; desert, dessert; farther, further

 Write the correct choice from those given in parentheses.

Example: Saaid needs (*farther, further*) information for his essay.
further

1. Nadia's energy (*deserted, desserted*) her as she approached the end of the triathlon.

2. The student (*council, counsel*) sponsored this year's food drive.

3. Dylan (*complemented, complimented*) Renee on her new hairstyle.

4. Zach can punt the ball (*farther, further*) than any of his teammates.

5. Mr. Garcia (*counciled, counseled*) our class on the SAT tests.

6. Jorge's sly smile was a (*complement, compliment*) to his secretive disposition.

7. Mrs. Lang's (*deserts, desserts*) were always first to go at the church bake sale.

8. Soo got her just (*deserts, desserts*) when she missed the last bus.

9. To (*complement, compliment*) her costume, Yvette dyed her hair an outrageous purple.

10. My Midwest farm town looks like a (*desert, dessert*) compared to a Brazilian rain forest.

 ### Model

Model the following sentences to practice using the words *further* and *farther* correctly.

Gratitude is merely the secret hope of further favors.

—Francois de La Rochefoucauld

Men came from the east and built these American towns because they wished to go no farther, and the towns they built were shaped by the urge to go onward.

—Rose Wilder Lane, *Old Home Town*

flair, flare ■ *Flair* refers to style or natural talent; *flare* means "to light up quickly" or "burst out" (or an object that does so).

Ronni was thrilled with Jorge's flair for decorating—until one of his strategically placed candles flared, marring the wall.

good, well ■ *Good* is an adjective; *well* is nearly always an adverb. (When *well* is used to describe a state of health, it is an adjective: He was happy to be *well* again.)

The MP3 player works well.
Our team looks good this season.

heal, heel ■ *Heal* means "to mend or restore to health." A *heel* is the back part of a foot.

Achilles died because a poison arrow pierced his heel and caused a wound that would not heal.

healthful, healthy ■ *Healthful* means "causing or improving health"; *healthy* means "possessing health."

Healthful foods build healthy bodies.

hear, here ■ You *hear* with your ears. *Here* means "the area close by."

heard, herd ■ *Heard* is the past tense of the verb "hear"; *herd* is a large group of animals.

hole, whole ■ A *hole* is a cavity or hollow place. *Whole* means "complete."

idle, idol ■ *Idle* means "not working." An *idol* is someone or something that is worshipped.

The once-popular actress, who had been idle lately, wistfully recalled her days as an idol.

immigrate, emigrate ■ *Immigrate* means "to come into a new country or environment." *Emigrate* means "to go out of one country to live in another."

Martin Ulferts immigrated to this country in 1882. He was only three years old when he emigrated from Germany.

imply, infer ■ *Imply* means "to suggest or express indirectly"; *infer* means "to draw a conclusion from facts." (A writer or speaker implies; a reader or listener infers.)

Dad implied by his comment that I should drive more carefully, and I inferred that he was concerned for both me and his new car.

Grammar Practice

Using the Right Word 5

good, well; heard, herd; **idle, idol;** immigrate, emigrate; **imply, infer**

Choose the correct words from the list above to fill in the blanks.

Example: Let the engine _____ for a few minutes.
idle

1. Have you _____ the latest news?

2. My little sister's _____ is Blue of *Blue's Clues*.

3. Some people think the government should tighten restrictions on those wishing to _____ to the United States.

4. Everyone agrees that Dena has a _____ head on her shoulders.

5. If Yadira declined Al's invitation, she would _____ that she didn't want to spend time with him.

6. Victims of civil wars have every reason to _____ from their countries.

7. I had never seen a _____ of any kind of animal until we saw the buffalo in South Dakota's Custer State Park.

8. I _____ from your silence that you do not agree.

9. Granddad actually plays the violin quite _____, but he calls it "fiddling."

10. Dallas was suffering from the flu last week, but he is _____ again.

Model

Model the following sentences to practice using *imply* and *infer* correctly.

> The fact that some geniuses were laughed at does not imply that all who are laughed at are geniuses.
>
> —Carl Sagan

> That man is the noblest creature may also be inferred from the fact that no other creature has yet contested this claim.
>
> —G. C. Lichtenberg

Right Word

insure, ensure ■ *Insure* means "to secure from financial harm or loss." *Ensure* means "to make certain of something."

> To ensure that you can legally drive that new car, you'll have to insure it.

it's, its ■ *It's* is the contraction of "it is." *Its* is the possessive form of "it."

> It's hard to believe, but the movie Shrek still holds its appeal for many kids.

later, latter ■ *Later* means "after a period of time." *Latter* refers to the second of two things mentioned.

> Later that year we had our second baby and adopted a stray kitten. The latter was far more welcomed by our toddler.

lay, lie ■ *Lay* means "to place." *Lay* is a transitive verb. (See 716.1.)

> Lay your books on the big table.

Lie means "to recline," and *lay* is the past tense of *lie. Lie* is an intransitive verb. (See 716.1.)

> In this heat, the children must lie down for a nap. Yesterday they lay down without one complaint. Sometimes they have lain in the hammocks to rest.

lead, led ■ *Lead* (lēd) is the present tense of the verb meaning "to guide." The past tense of the verb is *led* (lĕd). The noun *lead* (lĕd) is a metal.

> We were led along the path that leads to an abandoned lead mine.

learn, teach ■ *Learn* means "to acquire information." *Teach* means "to give information."

> I learn better when people teach with real-world examples.

leave, let ■ *Leave* means "to allow something to remain behind." *Let* means "to permit."

> Would you let me leave my bike at your house?

lend, borrow ■ *Lend* means "to give for temporary use." *Borrow* means "to receive for temporary use."

> I told Mom I needed to borrow $18 for a CD, but she said she could only lend money for school supplies.

like, as ■ When *like* is used as a preposition meaning "similar to," it can be followed only by a noun, pronoun, or noun phrase; when *as* is used as a subordinating conjunction, it introduces a subordinate clause.

> You could become a gymnast like her, as you work and practice hard.

medal, meddle ■ *Medal* is an award. *Meddle* means "to interfere."

> Some parents meddle in the awards process to be sure that their kids get medals.

Grammar Practice

Using the Right Word 6

it's, its; lay, lie; **lead, led;** learn, teach; **leave, let;** like, as

 Write the correct choice from those given in parentheses.

Example: Let your mind wander *(like, as)* a bird searching for food.
like

1. In my opinion, an apple is a snack at *(it's, its)* best.

2. After dinner, Grandpa *(leaves, lets)* scraps on the porch for our cat.

3. The mountain guide *(lead, led)* the inexperienced campers down a winding path.

4. Mia wants Ms. Benke to *(learn, teach)* her how to play the flute.

5. Just as I *(lay, lie)* my head on the pillow, the smoke alarm went off.

6. Soccer is an aerobic activity because *(it's, its)* a running sport.

7. I wish I could fly on my own *(like, as)* the birds do.

8. The dogs enjoy being out this time of year; they *(lay, lie)* in the shade of the maple tree.

9. Children can *(learn, teach)* a foreign language more easily than adults can.

10. How can crystal be clear if it has *(lead, led)* in it?

11. The school board will not *(leave, let)* us use that fund-raiser.

12. My new digital camera looks *(like, as)* a credit card.

 ## Model

Model the following sentences to practice using *learn* and *teach* correctly.

The easiest way for your children to learn about money is for you not to have any.

—Katharine Whitehorn

We need to teach the next generation of children from Day One that they are responsible for their lives.

—Elizabeth Kubler-Ross

Right Word

metal, mettle ■ *Metal* is a chemical element like iron or gold. *Mettle* is "strength of spirit."

Grandad's mettle during battle left him with some metal in his shoulder.

miner, minor ■ A *miner* digs for valuable ore. A *minor* is a person who is not legally an adult. A *minor* problem is one of no great importance.

moral, morale ■ A *moral* is a lesson drawn from a story; as an adjective, it relates to the principles of right and wrong. *Morale* refers to someone's attitude.

Ms. Ladue considers it her moral obligation to go to church every day.
The students' morale sank after their defeat in the forensics competition.

passed, past ■ *Passed* is a verb. *Past* can be used as a noun, an adjective, or a preposition.

That old pickup truck passed my sports car! (verb)
Many senior citizens hold dearly to the past. (noun)
Tilly's past life as a circus worker must have been . . . interesting. (adjective)
Who can walk past a bakery without looking in the window? (preposition)

peace, piece ■ *Peace* means "tranquility or freedom from war." *Piece* is a part or fragment.

Grandma sits in the peace and quiet of the parlor, enjoying a piece of pie.

peak, peek, pique ■ A *peak* is a high point. *Peek* means "brief look" (or "look briefly"). *Pique*, as a verb, means "to excite by challenging"; as a noun, it is a feeling of resentment.

The peak of Dr. Fedder's professional life was his ability to pique children's interest in his work. "Peek at this slide," he said to the eager students.

pedal, peddle, petal ■ A *pedal* is a foot lever; as a verb, it means "to ride a bike." *Peddle* means "to go from place to place selling something." A *petal* is part of a flower.

Don Miller paints beautiful petals on his homemade birdhouses. Then he pedals through the flea market every weekend to peddle them.

personal, personnel ■ *Personal* means "private." *Personnel* are people working at a particular job.

plain, plane ■ *Plain* means "an area of land that is flat or level"; it also means "clearly seen or clearly understood."

It's plain to see why settlers of the Great Plains had trouble moving west.
Plane means "flat, level"; it is also a tool used to smooth the surface of wood.

I used a plane to make the board plane and smooth.

Grammar Practice

Using the Right Word 7

moral, morale; passed, past; peak, peek, pique; plain, plane

Write the correct word if the underlined word is not used correctly. If it is, then write "OK."

Example: 1. *passed*

The jet from Boston **(1)** <u>past</u> the mid-Atlantic states and crossed the Great **(2)** <u>Plains</u> on its way to Denver. After another short ride, we finally reached our **(3)** <u>plane</u> yet beautiful mountain lodge, greatly improving our **(4)** <u>morale</u>. An elderly gentleman spoke to some children gathered about him. "A ghost named Ahote lives on the mountain **(5)** <u>peek</u>," he said. I didn't catch much else of his speech, but it **(6)** <u>peaked</u> my curiosity, so I decided to do some research upon my return home.

I was not able to find much. An Internet search led me to a book about Native Americans of the **(7)** <u>passed</u> century. I found a copy at the city library and took a **(8)** <u>pique</u>. Yes, there was an Ahote—meaning "restless one"—from the area where we vacationed. He guided non-natives across the mountain. When he died, his grave was placed at the highest mountain pass. Pioneers knew they were headed in the right direction when they came upon it. I thought of this **(9)** <u>morale</u>: A guiding spirit can make its presence known in more ways than one.

Model

Model the following sentences to practice using *peak* and *peek* correctly.

Simplicity is the peak of civilization.

—Jessie Sampter

The only way for writers to meet is to share a quick peek over a common lamp-post.

—Cyril Connolly

poor, pour, pore ■ *Poor* means "needy or pitiable." *Pour* means "to cause to flow in a stream." A *pore* is an opening in the skin.

Tough exams on late spring days make my poor pores pour sweat.

principal, principle ■ As an adjective, *principal* means "primary." As a noun, it can mean "a school administrator" or "a sum of money." *Principle* means "idea or doctrine."

His principal concern is fitness. (adjective) The principal retired. (noun)
During the first year of a loan, you pay more interest than principal. (noun)
The principle of *caveat emptor* is "Let the buyer beware."

quiet, quit, quite ■ *Quiet* is the opposite of "noisy." *Quit* means "to stop." *Quite* means "completely or entirely."

quote, quotation ■ *Quote* is a verb; *quotation* is a noun.

The quotation I used was from Woody Allen. You may quote me on that.

real, really, very ■ Do not use *real* in place of the adverbs *very* or *really*.

Mother's cake is usually very (not *real*) tasty, but this one is really stale!

right, write, wright, rite ■ *Right* means "correct or proper"; it also refers to that which a person has a legal claim to, as in copyright. *Write* means "to inscribe or record." A *wright* is a person who makes or builds something. *Rite* refers to a ritual or ceremonial act.

Write this down: It is the right of the shipwright to perform the rite of christening—breaking a bottle of champagne on the stern of the ship.

ring, wring ■ *Ring* means "encircle" or "to sound by striking." *Wring* means "to squeeze or twist."

At the beach, Grandma would ring her head with a large scarf. Once, it blew into the sea, so she had me wring it out.

scene, seen ■ *Scene* refers to the setting or location where something happens; it also may mean "sight or spectacle." *Seen* is a form of the verb "see."

Serena had seen her boyfriend making a scene; she cringed.

seam, seem ■ *Seam* (noun) is a line formed by connecting two pieces. *Seem* (verb) means "to appear to exist."

The ragged seams in his old coat seem to match the creases in his face.

set, sit ■ *Set* means "to place." *Sit* means "to put the body in a seated position." *Set* is transitive; *sit* is intransitive. (See **716.1**.)

How can you just sit there and watch as I set all these chairs in place?

Grammar Practice

Using the Right Word 8

principal, principle; real, really, very; ring, wring; set, sit

 In each sentence, a word is misused. Write the correct word.

Example: My parents are trying to pay down the principle on their mortgage.

principal

1. I am real excited about my sister's engagement ring.

2. In this game, you must find something to set on when you hear a bell ring.

3. "That is a very interesting painting," remarked the principle to the art student.

4. Reina's hair is really long—she has to ring it out one section at a time when she washes it.

5. My ears are starting to wring; I think I'd better sit down.

6. Rosa Parks was a real hero who adhered to the principal of fairness.

7. Don't sit that candle on the wooden table . . . it could lead to a very bad situation.

8. The principle reason to recycle is really quite simple: it saves natural resources.

Model

Model the following sentences to practice using *real* and *really* correctly.

A man always has two reasons for doing anything—a good reason and the real reason.

—J. P. Morgan

All that is really necessary for survival of the fittest, it seems, is an interest in life—good, bad, or peculiar.

—Grace Paley

Right Word

sight, cite, site ■ *Sight* means "the act of seeing"; a *sight* is what is seen. *Cite* means "to quote" or "to summon," as before a court. *Site* means "location."

> In her report, the general contractor cited several problems at the downtown job site. For one, the loading area was a chaotic sight.

sole, soul ■ *Sole* means "single, only one"; *sole* also refers to the bottom surface of the foot. *Soul* refers to the spiritual part of a person.

> As the sole inhabitant of the island, he put his heart and soul into his farming.

stationary, stationery ■ *Stationary* means "not movable"; *stationery* refers to the paper and envelopes used to write letters.

steal, steel ■ *Steal* means "to take something without permission"; *steel* is a type of metal.

than, then ■ *Than* is used in a comparison; *then* tells when.

> Abigail shouted that her big brother was bigger than my big brother. Then she ran away.

their, there, they're ■ *Their* is a possessive personal pronoun. *There* is an adverb used to point out location. *They're* is the contraction for "they are."

> They're a well-dressed couple. Do you see them there, with their matching jackets?

threw, through ■ *Threw* is the past tense of "throw." *Through* means "from beginning to end."

> Through seven innings, Juma threw just seven strikes.

to, too, two ■ *To* is a preposition that can mean "in the direction of." *To* is also used to form an infinitive. (See **726.2**.) *Too* means "also" or "very." *Two* is a number.

vain, vane, vein ■ *Vain* means "valueless or fruitless"; it may also mean "holding a high regard for oneself." *Vane* is a flat piece of material set up to show which way the wind blows. *Vein* refers to a blood vessel or a mineral deposit.

> The vain prospector, boasting about the vein of silver he'd uncovered, paused to look up at the turning weather vane.

vary, very ■ *Vary* means "to change." *Very* means "to a high degree."

> Though the weather may vary from day to day, generally, it is very pleasant.

Grammar Practice

Using the Right Word 9

sole, soul; than, then; vain, vane, vein; vary, very

 Read the following paragraphs. If the underlined word is used incorrectly, write the correct word. If it's correct as is, write "OK."

How do credit cards work? Essentially, you (the card user) borrow money to buy something. The card issuer, a bank, agrees to the loan and **(1)** <u>than</u> deposits the money into the merchant's bank account.

If you cannot pay the full amount of the bill, the bank charges interest on the unpaid balance. Interest rates typically **(2)** <u>vary</u> from 11 to 23 percent. The next bill will be for the unpaid amount plus interest. The amount owed, even if you don't borrow a dollar more, keeps going up! It can be **(3)** <u>vary</u> difficult to pay off a balance. You may begin to think that you're making payments in **(4)** <u>vein</u>. You may even feel you owe your heart and **(5)** <u>sole</u> to the credit card company.

Banks also charge credit card users fees for cash advances and late payments. Anyone who uses credit cards should be aware of how easy it is to incur more debt **(6)** <u>then</u> he or she can comfortably repay. List your charges on some paper. **(7)** <u>Than</u> learn to use credit responsibly to build a positive credit record.

 ## Model

Model the following sentences to practice using the words *vain* and *vein* correctly.

> Liberty without learning is always in peril; learning without liberty is always in vain.
>
> —John F. Kennedy

> The work an unknown good man has done is like a vein of water flowing hidden underground, secretly making the ground green.
>
> —Thomas Carlyle

Right Word

vial, vile ■ A *vial* is a small container for liquid. *Vile* is an adjective meaning "foul, despicable."

It's a vile job, but someone has to clean these lab vials.

waist, waste ■ *Waist* is the part of the body just above the hips. The verb *waste* means "to spend or use carelessly" or "to wear away or decay"; the noun *waste* refers to material that is unused or useless.

Her waist is small because she wastes no opportunity to exercise.

wait, weight ■ *Wait* means "to stay somewhere expecting something." *Weight* refers to a degree or unit of heaviness.

ware, wear, where ■ *Ware* refers to a product that is sold; *wear* means "to have on or to carry on one's body"; *where* asks "in what place?" or "in what situation?"

The designer boasted, "Where can anybody wear my ware? Anywhere."

way, weigh ■ *Way* means "path or route." *Weigh* means "to measure weight" or "to have a certain heaviness."

My dogs weigh too much. The best way to reduce is a daily run in the park.

weather, whether ■ *Weather* refers to the condition of the atmosphere. *Whether* refers to a possibility.

Due to the weather, the coach wondered whether he should cancel the meet.

which, that ■ Use *which* to refer to objects or animals in a nonrestrictive clause (set off with commas). Use *that* to refer to objects or animals in a restrictive clause. (For more information about these types of clauses, see **612.2**.)

The birds, which stay in the area all winter, know where the feeders are located. The food that attracts the most birds is sunflower seed.

who, whom ■ Use *who* to refer to people. *Who* is used as the subject of a verb in an independent clause or in a relative clause. *Whom* is used as the object of a preposition or as a direct object.

To whom do we owe our thanks for these pizzas? And who ordered anchovies?

who's, whose ■ *Who's* is the contraction for "who is." *Whose* is a pronoun that can show possession or ownership.

Cody, whose car is new, will drive. Who's going to read the map?

your, you're ■ *Your* is a possessive pronoun. *You're* is the contraction for "you are."

Take your boots if you're going out in that snow.

Grammar Practice

Using the Right Word 10

vial, vile; ware, wear, where; **weather, whether;** which, that; **who, whom**

 In each numbered paragraph below, some words are used incorrectly. Write the correct word for each.

Example: This is my dad, Emerson Whitley, who you probably recognize from his work in commercials.

who—whom

1. Willis had been feeling a bit under the weather lately. He went to the doctor, whom ordered some tests. The doctor told him wear the blood lab was because Willis needed to provide a vile or two of blood to be tested.

2. "I don't know weather you're aware of this or not, but there is a vile odor coming from the science lab," Lupe informed Ms. Yiel.

"I'll have to talk to Dario, who I allowed to perform an experiment," Ms. Yiel said. "He must have used the sodium chloride instead of the potassium chloride, which I *did* warn him about!"

3. Aunt Yolanda's utensils are agate wear, that is not agate at all but enameled steel. Her plates are real china, and she uses the glasses which she got in Ireland. Mom thinks Aunt Yolanda's table settings are very beautiful, so she makes us where nice clothes whenever we eat there.

 ## Model

Model the following sentences to practice using *who* and *whom* correctly.

A jury consists of twelve persons chosen to decide who has the better lawyer.

—Robert Frost

We cannot really love anybody with whom we never laugh.

—Agnes Repplier, *Americans and Others*

Test Prep!

Write the letter of the line in which an underlined word is used incorrectly. If all the words are correct, choose "D."

1
(A) The school <u>principal</u> attended the pep rally.
(B) Dressed as the school mascot, she was attempting to raise <u>morale</u>.
(C) The team lost the game <u>anyways</u>.
(D) All are used correctly.

2
(A) Qiana wants to <u>teach</u> elementary school students when she is older.
(B) Her third-grade teacher, <u>who</u> she adored, inspired her.
(C) Some teachers have a big <u>effect</u> on their students.
(D) All are used correctly.

3
(A) Marvin spilled a <u>vile</u> of acid during science class.
(B) Fortunately, the glass container did not <u>break</u>.
(C) However, etching was visible <u>where</u> the acid contacted the countertop.
(D) All are used correctly.

4
(A) We had apple pie for <u>dessert</u> on Sunday.
(B) Reina and I split a large piece <u>among</u> ourselves.
(C) We had <u>already</u> eaten too much dinner!
(D) All are used correctly.

5
(A) Mr. Rochester ordered <u>stationery</u> for his new business.
(B) He <u>chose</u> a light blue stock speckled with fibers.
(C) He preferred it over the <u>plain</u> blue stock.
(D) All are used correctly.

6
(A) Jenise <u>may</u> make a fabulous steak sauce.
(B) It requires a good <u>amount</u> of tomato sauce and onion.
(C) She always gets <u>compliments</u> on it.
(D) All are used correctly.

7
(A) The <u>weather</u> forecast didn't call for precipitation.
(B) Yet the rain is <u>really</u> coming down!
(C) We will have to <u>ring</u> out all those wet towels on the line.
(D) All are used correctly.

8
(A) The Afghan hound came and sat <u>beside</u> me.
(B) He <u>peaked</u> through the long hair covering his eyes.
(C) I urged the big dog to <u>lay</u> his head on my lap.
(D) All are used correctly.

9 (A) I felt happier <u>then</u> I'd ever been.
(B) My driving test, <u>which</u> I'd been dreading, was over.
(C) I <u>passed</u> with flying colors!
(D) All are used correctly.

10 (A) We were passing the time with some <u>idle</u> chatter about cars.
(B) Shahzad made an <u>allusion</u> to the hot rods of the sixties.
(C) That <u>lead</u> to a plan to renovate his uncle's old GTO.
(D) All are used correctly.

11 (A) I admitted that I had behaved <u>badly</u>.
(B) She would not <u>except</u> my apology.
(C) From that, I <u>inferred</u> that the relationship was over.
(D) All are used correctly.

12 (A) Spring temperatures <u>vary</u> quite a bit in the Midwest.
(B) Often it still seems <u>like</u> winter.
(C) The usual <u>counsel</u> is to peel off layers as it warms up.
(D) All are used correctly.

13 (A) Please <u>set</u> the mail near the telephone.
(B) I hope Dorian's news is <u>well</u>.
(C) The poor <u>soul</u> has had a rough year.
(D) All are used correctly.

14 (A) Carmella remembers the time she caught a <u>bass</u>.
(B) The fish got the hook caught in <u>it's</u> throat.
(C) Carmella wanted to <u>take</u> the boat back to shore right away.
(D) All are used correctly.

15 (A) I <u>heard</u> an interesting piece of my family history recently.
(B) My great-grandmother <u>emigrated</u> from Ireland at age 12—by herself.
(C) Why did her parents <u>leave</u> her travel alone?
(D) All are used correctly.

16 (A) Wind blew the weather <u>vane</u> with a power not seen before.
(B) The metal pole holding it bent <u>further</u> toward the ground.
(C) A <u>real</u> bad storm was obviously coming.
(D) All are used correctly.

Right Word

Parts of Speech

Words in the English language are used in eight different ways. For this reason, there are eight parts of speech.

700.1 Noun

A word that names a person, a place, a thing, or an idea

Governor Smith-Jones   Oregon   hospital   religion

700.2 Pronoun

A word used in place of a noun

I   you   she   him   who   everyone   these   neither theirs   themselves   which

700.3 Verb

A word that expresses action or state of being

float   sniff   discover   seem   were   was

700.4 Adjective

A word that describes a noun or a pronoun

young   big   grim   Canadian   longer

700.5 Adverb

A word that describes a verb, an adjective, or another adverb

briefly   forward   regally   slowly   better

700.6 Preposition

The first word or words in a prepositional phrase (which functions as an adjective or an adverb)

away from   under   before   with   for   out of

700.7 Conjunction

A word that connects other words or groups of words

and   but   although   because   either, or   so

700.8 Interjection

A word that shows strong emotion or surprise

Oh no!   Yipes!   Good grief!   Well, . . .

Parts of Speech

Noun

A **noun** is a word that names something: a person, a place, a thing, or an idea.

    governor   Oregon   hospital   Buddhism   love

Classes of Nouns

The five classes of nouns are *proper, common, concrete, abstract,* and *collective.*

701.1 Proper Noun

A **proper noun** names a particular person, place, thing, or idea. Proper nouns are always capitalized.

Jackie Robinson	Brooklyn	World Series
Christianity	Ebbets Field	Hinduism

701.2 Common Noun

A **common noun** does not name a particular person, place, thing, or idea. Common nouns are not capitalized.

    person   woman   president   park   baseball   government

701.3 Concrete Noun

A **concrete noun** names a thing that is tangible (can be seen, touched, heard, smelled, or tasted). Concrete nouns are either proper or common.

    child   Grand Canyon   music   aroma   fireworks   Becky

701.4 Abstract Noun

An **abstract noun** names an idea, a condition, or a feeling—in other words, something that cannot be touched, smelled, tasted, seen, or heard.

    New Deal   greed   poverty   progress   freedom   awe

701.5 Collective Noun

A **collective noun** names a group or a unit.

    United States   Portland Cementers   team   crowd   community

Parts of Speech

Forms of Nouns

Nouns are grouped according to their *number, gender,* and *case.*

702.1 Number of a Noun

Number indicates whether the noun is singular or plural.

> A **singular noun** refers to one person, place, thing, or idea.
>
> actor   stadium   Canadian   bully   truth   child   person

> A **plural noun** refers to more than one person, place, thing, or idea.
>
> actors   stadiums   Canadians   bullies   truths   children   people

702.2 Gender of a Noun

Gender indicates whether a noun is masculine, feminine, neuter, or indefinite.

> **Masculine:** uncle   brother   men   bull   rooster   stallion
> **Feminine:** aunt   sister   women   cow   hen   filly
> **Neuter** (without gender): tree   cobweb   garage   closet
> **Indefinite** (masculine or feminine): president   plumber   doctor   parent

702.3 Case of a Noun

Case tells how nouns are related to other words used with them. There are three cases: *nominative, possessive,* and *objective.*

- A **nominative case** noun can be the subject of a clause.

   > Andrew's jacket was soaking wet. His new umbrella had broken in the wind and was useless in the pouring rain.

   A nominative noun can also be a predicate noun (or predicate nominative), which follows a "be" verb (*am, is, are, was, were, be, being, been*) and renames the subject. In the sentence below, *type* renames *Mr. Cattanzara.*

   > Mr. Cattanzara was a different type than those in the neighborhood.
   > —Bernard Malamud, "A Summer's Reading"

- A **possessive case** noun shows possession or ownership.

   > Unlike John's new baseball mitt, mine is old and dirty, but it still serves me well each time we take the field.

- An **objective case** noun can be a direct object, an indirect object, or an object of the preposition.

   > Keisha always gives Mylo science-fiction books for his birthday.

   (*Mylo* is the indirect object and *books* is the direct object of the verb "gives." *Birthday* is the object of the preposition "for.")

Grammar Practice

Nouns

- Classes of Nouns
- Number of a Noun
- Case of a Noun

 For each underlined noun, write its class (there will be at least two classes for each), number, and case.

Example: The <u>Bill of Rights</u> refers to the first ten amendments of the United States Constitution.
Class: proper, concrete; Number: singular;
Case: nominative

1. Checks and balances in the United States government allow <u>Congress</u> to override a presidential veto.

2. During the American Revolution, <u>George Washington</u> was commander of the Continental army.

3. The tax laws imposed on the <u>colonists</u> by the British government were viewed as unfair.

4. The Civil War began when the Confederate army captured <u>Fort Sumter</u>.

5. Frederick Douglass made the <u>argument</u> that African Americans should be allowed to serve in the army.

6. The Great Wall of China formed a <u>boundary</u> between China and Mongolia.

7. In feudal Japan, a shogun had more military <u>power</u> than an emperor.

8. A megalopolis is an urban area made up of adjoining cities and their <u>suburbs</u>.

 ## Model

Model the following sentence to practice using abstract nouns.

Beth could not reason upon or explain the faith that gave her courage and patience to give up life and cheerfully wait for death.
—Louisa May Alcott, *Little Women*

Pronoun

A **pronoun** is a word used in place of a noun.

> I, you, she, it, which, that, themselves, whoever, me, he, they, mine, ours

The three types of pronouns are *simple, compound,* and *phrasal.*

> Simple: I, you, he, she, it, we, they, who, what
> Compound: myself, someone, anybody, everything, itself, whoever
> Phrasal: one another, each other

All pronouns have **antecedents**. An antecedent is the noun that the pronoun refers to or replaces.

> Charlie is completely immersed in his family's decisions. His brothers seldom make a move without consulting him first, and he continually offers advice to his parents on a variety of topics.

> (*Charlie* is the antecedent of *his, him,* and *he.*)

NOTE: Each pronoun must agree with its antecedent. (See page **756**.)

704.1 Classes of Pronouns

The six classes of pronouns are *personal, reflexive and intensive, reciprocal, relative, indefinite, interrogative,* and *demonstrative.*

Personal

I, me, my, mine / we, us, our, ours
you, your, yours / they, them, their, theirs
he, him, his, she, her, hers, it, its

Reflexive and Intensive

myself, yourself, himself, herself, itself, ourselves, yourselves, themselves

Reciprocal

each other, one another

Relative

what, who, whose, whom, which, that

Indefinite

all	both	everything	nobody	several
another	each	few	none	some
any	each one	many	no one	somebody
anybody	either	most	nothing	someone
anyone	everybody	much	one	something
anything	everyone	neither	other	such

Interrogative

who, whose, whom, which, what

Demonstrative

this, that, these, those

Grammar Practice

Pronouns 1

■ **Antecedents**

For the following paragraphs, write the antecedent of each underlined pronoun.

Example: 1. Marian Anderson

In the early 1900s, nobody imagined that "Baby Contralto" would grow up to be the first African American to sing a leading role with the Metropolitan Opera. "Baby Contralto" is what the Baptist parishioners called Marian Anderson when **(1)** <u>she</u> began singing at **(2)** <u>their</u> church at age six.

Marian's family had a piano, but **(3)** <u>they</u> could not afford lessons, so Marian taught **(4)** <u>herself</u>. Soon she became a popular singer in her community. After graduating from high school, she applied to a local music school. **(5)** <u>It</u> coldly rejected Marian because of her color.

Prejudice did not stop her. She stalwartly pursued a successful singing career, and in 1930, **(6)** <u>she</u> became the first black female to perform at Carnegie Hall. Famed composer Jean Sibelius was so moved by her work that **(7)** <u>he</u> dedicated a song to her. Marian went on to perform all over the world. Audiences loved her, and **(8)** <u>they</u> demanded even more performances. In 1955, at the age of 58, she performed at the New York Metropolitan Opera as Ulrica in Guiseppe Verdi's *The Masked Ball*.

Model

Model the following sentence to practice using a pronoun and an antecedent in the same sentence.

> **There are many persons ready to do what is right because in their hearts, they know it is right.**
>
> —Marian Anderson

706.1 Personal Pronouns

A **personal pronoun** can take the place of any noun.

> Our coach made her point loud and clear when she raised her voice.

- A **reflexive pronoun** is formed by adding *-self* or *-selves* to a personal pronoun. A reflexive pronoun can be a direct object, an indirect object, an object of the preposition, or a predicate nominative.

> Miss Sally Sunshine loves herself. (direct object of *loves*)
>
> Tomisha does not seem herself today. (predicate nominative)

- An **intensive pronoun** is a reflexive pronoun that intensifies, or emphasizes, the noun or pronoun it refers to.

> Leo himself taught his children to invest their lives in others.

706.2 Relative Pronouns

A **relative pronoun** relates or connects an adjective clause to the noun or pronoun it modifies.

> Students who study regularly get the best grades. Surprise!
>
> The dance, which we had looked forward to for weeks, was canceled.

(The relative pronoun *who* relates the adjective clause to *students; which* relates the adjective clause to *dance*.)

706.3 Reciprocal Pronoun

An **reciprocal pronoun** refers to the individual members of a plural antecedent. It expresses mutual actions or relationships between those members.

> The playgoers enjoyed talking with one another about the amazing performance.

706.4 Indefinite Pronouns

An **indefinite pronoun** refers to unnamed or unknown people or things.

> I have never known anybody that well. (The antecedent of *anybody* is unknown.)

706.5 Interrogative Pronouns

An **interrogative pronoun** asks a question.

> Who is the oldest among you? What does he know that you would like to learn?

706.6 Demonstrative Pronouns

A **demonstrative pronoun** points out people, places, or things without naming them.

> This shouldn't be too hard. That looks about right.
>
> These are the best ones. Those ought to be thrown out.

NOTE: When one of these words precedes a noun, it functions as an adjective, not a pronoun. (See **728.1**.)

> That movie bothers me. (*That* is an adjective.)

Grammar Practice

Pronouns 2

■ Indefinite Pronouns
■ Interrogative Pronouns
■ Demonstrative Pronouns

 Identify each underlined pronoun as *indefinite, interrogative,* or *demonstrative*.

Example: <u>Whom</u> do you think is the funniest woman in America?
interrogative

1. <u>Many</u> of today's actresses have been cast in comedy roles.

2. <u>These</u> are a few well-known women comedians: Ellen DeGeneres, Rosie O'Donnell, Carol Burnett, and Lucille Ball.

3. <u>Which</u> of the above-named comedians was the voice of Dory in *Finding Nemo?*

4. <u>Who</u> would have guessed that *I Love Lucy* would still be on the air 50 years after it was made?

5. <u>This</u> is a famous quotation from comedian Gilda Radner: "I base most of my fashion taste on what doesn't itch."

6. <u>Those</u> are my favorite kind of clothes, too.

7. <u>None</u> of the women believed that they would grow up to be famous.

8. <u>All</u> of them became famous for their ability to make people laugh.

Model

Model the following sentence to practice using indefinite and interrogative pronouns.

Who is rich? He that is content. Who is that? Nobody.
—Benjamin Franklin

Forms of Personal Pronouns

The form of a personal pronoun indicates its *number* (singular or plural), its *person* (first, second, third), its *case* (nominative, possessive, or objective), and its *gender* (masculine, feminine, or neuter).

708.1 **Number of a Pronoun**

Personal pronouns are singular or plural. The singular personal pronouns include *my, him, he, she, it.* The plural personal pronouns include *we, you, them, our.* (*You* can be singular or plural.) Notice in the caption below that the first you is singular and the second you is plural.

"Larry, you need to keep all four tires on the road when turning. Are you still with us back there?"

708.2 **Person of a Pronoun**

The **person** of a pronoun indicates whether the person, place, thing, or idea represented by the pronoun is speaking, is spoken to, or is spoken about.

- **First person** is used in place of the name of the speaker or speakers.

    I went to the movies with some friends, but when we arrived at the theater, we realized the movie we wanted to see was not playing.

- **Second-person** pronouns name the person or persons spoken to.

    "If you hit your duck, you want me to go in after it?" Eugie said.

    —Gina Berriault, "The Stone Boy"

- **Third-person** pronouns name the person or thing spoken about.

    She had hardly realized the news, further than to understand that she had been brought . . . face to face with something unexpected and final. It did not even occur to her to ask for any explanation.

    —Joseph Conrad, "The Idiots"

Grammar Practice

Pronouns 3

■ Number of a Pronoun
■ Person of a Pronoun

 Identify the person and number of each underlined pronoun in the paragraphs below.

Example: 1. *second person, plural*

"Mom and Dad!" Greg yelled. "Are **(1)** <u>you</u> ready yet?" Greg, his sister, and **(2)** <u>their</u> folks were going to a football game; they were late. Greg was almost ready to say **(3)** <u>he</u> would leave without **(4)** <u>them</u>. The kickoff was less than an hour away, and Greg would be mad if he missed **(5)** <u>it</u>.

When they were finally on their way, Greg's dad said, "Uh-oh, I forgot **(6)** <u>our</u> tickets. We'll have to go back."

"**(7)** <u>I</u> can't believe it," Greg sighed, shaking his head.

"Why are **(8)** <u>you</u> so worried?" Greg's mom asked **(9)** <u>him</u>.

Before Greg could answer **(10)** <u>her</u>, his sister said, **(11)** "<u>We</u> don't have to turn around. I have the tickets."

Model

Model the following sentences to practice using first-, second-, and third-person pronouns.

Computers are useless; they can only give you answers.
—Pablo Picasso

We are so vain that we even care for the opinion of those we don't care for.
—Marie Ebner von Eschenbach

710.1 **Case of a Pronoun**

The **case** of each pronoun tells how it is related to the other words used with it. There are three cases: *nominative, possessive,* and *objective.*

■ A **nominative case** pronoun can be the subject of a clause. The following are nominative forms: *I, you, he, she, it, we, they.*

> I like life when things go well. You must live life in order to love life.

A nominative pronoun is a *predicate nominative* if it follows a "be" verb (*am, is, are, was, were, be, being, been*) or another linking verb (*appear, become, feel,* and etc.) and renames the subject.

> "Oh, it's only she who scared me just now," said Mama to Papa, glancing over her shoulder.
> "Yes, it is I," said Mai in a superior tone.

■ **Possessive case** pronouns show possession or ownership. Apostrophes, however, are not used with personal pronouns. (Pronouns in the possessive case can also be classified as adjectives.)

> But as I placed my hand upon his shoulder, there came a strong shudder over his whole person.
> —Edgar Allan Poe, "The Fall of the House of Usher"

■ An **objective case** pronoun can be a direct object, an indirect object, or an object of the preposition.

> The kids loved it! We lit a campfire for them and told them old ghost stories. (*It* is the direct object of the verb *loved. Them* is the object of the preposition *for* and the indirect object of the verb *told.*)

Number, Person, and Case of Personal Pronouns

	Nominative	Possessive	Objective
First Person Singular	I	my, mine	me
Second Person Singular	you	your, yours	you
Third Person Singular	he	his	him
	she	her, hers	her
	it	its	it
	Nominative	Possessive	Objective
First Person Plural	we	our, ours	us
Second Person Plural	you	your, yours	you
Third Person Plural	they	their, theirs	them

710.2 **Gender of a Pronoun**

Gender indicates whether a pronoun is masculine, feminine, or neuter.

Masculine: **he him his** Feminine: **she her hers**

Neuter (without gender): **it its**

Grammar Practice

Pronouns 4

■ Case of a Pronoun

Identify each underlined pronoun as *nominative, possessive,* or *objective*.

Example: 1. *possessive*

Mr. Lee, a neighbor, was taking out **(1)** <u>his</u> garbage. **(2)** <u>He</u> saw **(3)** <u>me</u> beginning to rake our yard and asked, "Do you need any help, Maria?"

Not one to turn down such an offer, **(4)** <u>I</u> accepted. The next thing I knew, he came from his garage with a new "toy." **(5)** <u>It</u> was a noisy, smelly leaf blower.

"Have **(6)** <u>you</u> ever seen one of these things?" he asked. He demonstrated **(7)** <u>its</u> powerful wind, aiming **(8)** <u>it</u> at a pile of leaves I had just raked.

"Well, I've seen people use them," I admitted, "but **(9)** <u>we</u> only have rakes at **(10)** <u>our</u> house. I guess we're a little old-fashioned that way."

Model

Model the following sentence to practice using both nominative and objective case pronouns in the same sentence.

> I will love the light for it shows me the way, yet I will endure the darkness because it shows me the stars.

—Og Mandino

Test Prep!

Read the following paragraphs. Write the letter of the correct description of each underlined word or words from the choices given on the next page.

One <u>reason</u> for people's fear of nuclear power plant accidents and
(1)
nuclear warfare is the resulting uncontrolled radiation. <u>Those</u> who escape
(2)
the effects of an initial explosion may still develop radiation sickness,

which causes effects that range from headache and nausea to cancer.

On the other hand, <u>radiation</u> in controlled amounts is actually used
(3)
medically to diagnose illness, cure cancer, and prevent death. In the late

1800s, <u>Wilhelm Roentgen</u> discovered how to use a form of radiation in
(4)
X-rays. <u>His</u> diagnostic tool became quite common and continues to be of
(5)
great value today. Modern X-ray machines, however, use much less

<u>radiation</u> than in the past because of its possible adverse effects.
(6)
For more than a century, scientists have known that a certain

amount of a radiated substance would damage <u>tissue</u>. The radiation
(7)
therapy that doctors currently use for cancer patients works on the same

principle: Radiation destroys the cells exposed to it. In the early 1900s,

<u>Marie Curie</u> (who made up the term "radioactivity") discovered radium.
(8)
<u>Her</u> work with the element made her famous, but <u>it</u> also ended up killing
(9)   **(10)**
<u>her</u> years later.
(11)
In the right hands, <u>something</u> harmful can become helpful. The
(12)
key is to learn as much as possible about <u>it</u>, as Roentgen and Curie did,
(13)
collecting a <u>wealth</u> of information. <u>Their</u> work paved the way for later
(14)   **(15)**
improvements in radiation therapies and diagnostic tools—a <u>fact</u> that
(16)
gratifies many cancer survivors.

1. (A) common concrete noun
   (B) common abstract noun
   (C) proper concrete noun
   (D) proper abstract noun

2. (A) demonstrative pronoun
   (B) interrogative pronoun
   (C) indefinite pronoun
   (D) relative pronoun

3. (A) common feminine noun
   (B) common indefinite noun
   (C) common masculine noun
   (D) common neuter noun

4. (A) common concrete noun
   (B) common abstract noun
   (C) proper concrete noun
   (D) proper abstract noun

5. (A) feminine possessive pronoun
   (B) masculine possessive pronoun
   (C) masculine objective pronoun
   (D) neuter possessive pronoun

6. (A) singular proper noun
   (B) plural indefinite pronoun
   (C) antecedent of "machines"
   (D) antecedent of "its"

7. (A) common objective noun
   (B) common nominative noun
   (C) common possessive noun
   (D) proper objective noun

8. (A) feminine possessive pronoun
   (B) feminine nominative noun
   (C) feminine objective noun
   (D) feminine possessive noun

9. (A) feminine possessive pronoun
   (B) feminine nominative pronoun
   (C) feminine objective pronoun
   (D) feminine possessive noun

10. (A) nominative pronoun
    (B) nominative noun
    (C) possessive pronoun
    (D) objective pronoun

11. (A) feminine possessive pronoun
    (B) feminine nominative noun
    (C) feminine objective pronoun
    (D) feminine possessive noun

12. (A) demonstrative pronoun
    (B) interrogative pronoun
    (C) reflexive pronoun
    (D) indefinite pronoun

13. (A) neuter nominative pronoun
    (B) neuter objective pronoun
    (C) feminine objective pronoun
    (D) neuter possessive pronoun

14. (A) abstract noun
    (B) concrete noun
    (C) collective noun
    (D) proper noun

15. (A) first-person plural pronoun
    (B) third-person singular pronoun
    (C) third-person plural pronoun
    (D) second-person singular pronoun

16. (A) singular abstract noun
    (B) singular concrete noun
    (C) plural abstract noun
    (D) plural concrete noun

Verb

A **verb** is a word that expresses action (*run, carried, declared*) or a state of being (*is, are, seemed*).

Classes of Verbs

714.1 Linking Verbs

A **linking verb** links the subject to a noun or an adjective in the predicate.

> In the outfield, the boy felt confident.
> He was the best fielder around.

Common Linking Verbs						
is	are	was	were	be	been	am

Additional Linking Verbs						
smell	seem	grow	become	appear	sound	
taste	feel	get	remain	stay	look	turn

714.2 Auxiliary Verbs

Auxiliary verbs, or helping verbs, are used to form some of the **tenses** (718.3), the **mood** (724.1), and the **voice** (722.2) of the main verb. (In the example below, the auxiliary verbs are in red; the main verbs are in blue.)

> The mud had flowed quickly down the mountain, covering everything in its path. By the time the rain had stopped, the rescue crews were faced with the daunting task of slogging through the mud to help those who had survived.

Common Auxiliary Verbs							
is	was	being	did	have	would	shall	might
am	were	been	does	had	could	can	must
are	be	do	has	should	will	may	

Grammar Practice

Verbs 1

■ Linking and Auxiliary Verbs

 Write whether each underlined word is a linking verb or an auxiliary verb.

Example: The earth's solid inner core <u>is</u> surrounded by a fluid outer core about 4,200 miles across.
auxiliary

1. Researchers <u>have</u> recently discovered that the core spins 1/4 to 1/2 of a degree faster than the rest of the planet.

2. Magnetic interaction <u>is</u> the most likely reason for the different spin rates.

3. The researchers <u>had</u> arrived at their discovery by studying the travel times of earthquake waves through the earth.

4. There <u>are</u> differences not only in the times but also in the shapes of the waves.

5. The researchers theorized there must <u>be</u> differences in the core as the waves pass through it.

6. The small difference in the rotation speed means that it <u>would</u> take 700 to 1,400 years for the core to get one full revolution ahead.

7. The rate, however, <u>could</u> vary from one decade to the next.

8. The inner core <u>appears</u> to spin slower than the outer core at other times.

 ## Model

Model the following sentences to practice using linking and auxiliary verbs.

> Thought is only a flash between two long nights, but this flash is everything.
>
> —Henri Poincare

> A loud voice cannot compete with a clear voice, even if it's a whisper.
>
> —Barry Neil Kaufman

716.1 Action Verbs: Transitive and Intransitive

An **intransitive verb** communicates an action that is complete in itself. It does not need an object to receive the action.

The boy flew **on his skateboard. He** jumped **and** flipped **and** twisted.

A **transitive verb** (red) is an action verb that needs an object (blue) to complete its meaning.

The city council passed **a strict noise** ordinance.

While some action verbs are only transitive *or* intransitive, some can be either, depending on how they are used.

He finally stopped **to rest. (intransitive)**

He finally stopped **the show. (transitive)**

716.2 Objects with Transitive Verbs

■ A **direct object** receives the action of a transitive verb directly from the subject. Without it, the transitive verb's meaning is incomplete.

The boy kicked **his** skateboard **forward.** (*Skateboard* is the direct object.)

Then he put **one** foot **on it and rode like a pro.**

■ An **indirect object** also receives the action of a transitive verb, but indirectly. An indirect object names the person *to whom or for whom* something is done. (An indirect object can also name the thing *to what or for what* something is done.)

Ms. Oakfield showed us **pictures of the solar system.**
(*Us* is the indirect object.)

She gave Tony **an A on his project.**

NOTE: When the word naming the indirect receiver of the action is in a prepositional phrase, it is no longer considered an indirect object.

Ms. Oakfield showed **pictures of the solar system to** us.

(*Us* is the object of the preposition *to*.)

Grammar Practice

Verbs 2

■ **Transitive and Intransitive Verbs**

 Write whether each underlined verb is transitive or intransitive. For a transitive verb, also write the direct object and, if present, the indirect object.

Example: The customer <u>provided</u> the cash.
  transitive — direct object: cash

1. Nasha <u>jogs</u> around the track every day after school.

2. My dad <u>found</u> the map under the front passenger seat.

3. <u>Look</u> at the sky!

4. Simone <u>guessed</u> correctly.

5. Simone <u>guessed</u> the answer exactly.

6. We <u>bought</u> my mom a new leather briefcase.

7. Kumar <u>allowed</u> me the use of his cell phone for one afternoon.

8. I'm not feeling well; I should <u>lie</u> down.

9. Jamal <u>opened</u> the jar of pickles quite easily after his sister couldn't.

10. Sergey <u>sent</u> his brother an autographed program from the game.

 ## Model

Model the following sentences to practice using transitive and intransitive verbs.

I don't like to write, but I love to have written.

—Michael Kanin

Life shrinks or expands in proportion to one's courage.

—Anaïs Nin

Forms of Verbs

A verb has different forms depending on its *number, person, tense, voice,* and *mood.*

718.1 Number of a Verb

Number indicates whether a verb is singular or plural. In a clause, the verb (in blue below) and its subject (in red) must both be singular or both be plural.

- **Singular**

  One large island floats off Italy's "toe."

  Italy's northern countryside includes the spectacular Alps.

- **Plural**

  Five small islands float inside Michigan's "thumb."

  The Porcupine Mountains rise above the shores of Lake Superior.

718.2 Person of a Verb

Person indicates whether the subject of the verb is first, second, or third person (is speaking, is spoken to, or is spoken about). The form of the verb usually changes only when a present-tense verb is used with a third-person singular pronoun.

	Singular	Plural
First Person	I sniff	we sniff
Second Person	you sniff	you sniff
Third Person	he/she/it sniffs	they sniff

718.3 Tense of a Verb

Tense indicates time. Each verb has three principal parts: the *present, past,* and *past participle.* All six tenses are formed from these principal parts. The past and past participle of regular verbs are formed by adding *ed* to the present form. For irregular verbs, the past and past participle are usually different words; however, a few have the same form in all three principal parts (see page **720.2**).

718.4 Simple Tenses

- **Present tense** expresses action that is happening at the present time, or action that happens continually, regularly.

  In September, sophomores smirk and joke about the "little freshies."

- **Past tense** expresses action that was completed at a particular time in the past.

  They forgot that just ninety days separated them from freshman status.

- **Future tense** expresses action that will take place in the future.

  They will recall this in three years when they will be freshmen again.

Grammar Practice

Verbs 3

- Person of a Verb
- Simple Tenses

 Write the verb or verbs in the sentences below. Then identify the person and tense of each.

Example: Every year sophomores plan a scuba diving trip.
plan: third person, present tense

1. Jacques-Yves Cousteau invented the Aqua-Lung® in 1942.

2. One day scientists will make artificial gills for divers.

3. Today, no one believes that is possible.

4. Scuba divers enjoy the freedom to dive without restraints.

5. If you dive deep into the ocean, make a series of timed stops on your way back to the surface.

6. Otherwise, nitrogen in your air mixture dissolves under pressure and enters your blood stream.

7. Rising directly to the surface will result in nitrogen narcosis.

8. Without special treatment in a decompression chamber, this dangerous condition will almost always lead to death.

9. A diver who follows proper diving protocol is in no danger.

10. Thousands of people safely dived last year with scuba gear and experienced the marvels of the undersea world.

Model

Model the following sentence to practice using past-tense verbs effectively.

In a sky of iron the points of the Dipper hung like icicles, and Orion flashed his cold fires.

—Edith Wharton, *Ethan Frome*

Forms of Verbs (continued)

720.1 Perfect Tenses

■ **Present perfect tense** expresses action that began in the past but continues in the present or is completed in the present.

Our boat has weathered **worse storms than this one.**

■ **Past perfect tense** expresses an action in the past that occurred before another past action.

They reported, wrongly, that the hurricane had missed **the island.**

■ **Future perfect tense** expresses action that will begin in the future and be completed by a specific time in the future.

By this time tomorrow, the hurricane will have smashed **into the coast.**

720.2 Irregular Verbs

Common Irregular Verbs and Their Principal Parts

Present Tense	Past Tense	Past Participle	Present Tense	Past Tense	Past Participle	Present Tense	Past Tense	Past Participle
am, be	was, were	been	go	went	gone	shrink	shrank	shrunk
begin	began	begun	grow	grew	grown	sing	sang, sung	sung
bite	bit	bitten	hang	hanged	hanged	sink	sank, sunk	sunk
blow	blew	blown	(execute)			sit	sat	sat
break	broke	broken	hang	hung	hung	slay	slew	slain
bring	brought	brought	(suspend)			speak	spoke	spoken
buy	bought	bought	hide	hid	hidden, hid	spring	sprang, sprung	sprung
catch	caught	caught	know	knew	known			
choose	chose	chosen	lay	laid	laid	steal	stole	stolen
come	came	come	lead	led	led	strive	strove	striven
dive	dove	dived	leave	left	left	swear	swore	sworn
do	did	done	lie	lay	lain	swim	swam	swum
draw	drew	drawn	(recline)			swing	swung	swung
drink	drank	drunk	lie	lied	lied	take	took	taken
drive	drove	driven	(deceive)			teach	taught	taught
eat	ate	eaten	lose	lost	lost	tear	tore	torn
fall	fell	fallen	make	made	made	throw	threw	thrown
fight	fought	fought	ride	rode	ridden	wake	waked, woke	waked, woken
flee	fled	fled	ring	rang	rung			
fly	flew	flown	rise	rose	risen	wear	wore	worn
forsake	forsook	forsaken	run	ran	run	weave	weaved, wove	weaved, woven
freeze	froze	frozen	see	saw	seen			
get	got	gotten	shake	shook	shaken	wring	wrung	wrung
give	gave	given	show	showed	shown	write	wrote	written

These verbs are the same in all principal parts: *burst, cost, cut, hurt, let, put, set,* and *spread.*

Grammar Practice

Verbs 4

■ Irregular Verbs

 Write the correct form (past tense or past participle) of the verb shown in parentheses to complete each sentence.

Example: Thirty-five students had _____ the bus to the wrestling match. *(ride)*

ridden

1. Salina _____ off her cold by getting lots of rest. *(fight)*

2. Nadia discovered that her backpack had been _____. *(steal)*

3. Owen _____ to get a perfect score on his algebra exam. *(strive)*

4. Rajan _____ to taste the egg roll, but it was too hot. *(begin)*

5. The fastest swimmers had _____ in the first heat. *(dive)*

6. Dontriece _____ at the assembly about the upcoming tournament. *(speak)*

7. My mom has a blanket that my great-great-grandmother _____ on a loom. *(weave)*

8. Virgil had _____ the book on the shelf and forgotten about it. *(lay)*

9. He knew he had _____ a good story by the look on his teacher's face. *(write)*

10. I liked the suit that my cousin _____ to my brother's wedding. *(wear)*

 ## Model

Model the following sentences to practice using irregular verbs.

I've grown to realize the joy that comes from little victories is preferable to the fun that comes from ease and the pursuit of pleasure.
—Lawana Blackwell, *The Courtship of the Vicar's Daughter*

Happy is the man who has broken the chains which hurt the mind and has given up worrying once and for all.

—Ovid

722.1 Continuous Tenses

- A **present continuous tense** verb expresses action that is not completed at the time of stating it. The present continuous tense is formed by adding *am, is,* or *are* to the *-ing* form of the main verb.

    Scientists are learning a great deal from their study of the sky.

- A **past continuous tense** verb expresses action that was happening at a certain time in the past. This tense is formed by adding *was* or *were* to the *-ing* form of the main verb.

    Astronomers were beginning their quest for knowledge hundreds of years ago.

- A **future continuous tense** verb expresses action that will take place at a certain time in the future. This tense is formed by adding *will be* to the *-ing* form of the main verb.

    Someday astronauts will be going to Mars.

  This tense can also be formed by adding a phrase noting the future *(are going to)* plus *be* to the *-ing* form of the main verb.

    They are going to be performing many experiments.

722.2 Voice of a Verb

Voice indicates whether the subject is acting or being acted upon.

- **Active voice** indicates that the subject of the verb is, has been, or will be doing something.

    For many years Lou Brock held the base-stealing record.

Active voice makes your writing more direct and lively.

- **Passive voice** indicates that the subject of the verb is being, has been, or will be acted upon.

    For many years the base-stealing record was held by Lou Brock.

NOTE: With a passive verb, the person or thing creating the action is not always stated.

    The ordinance was overturned. (Who did the overturning?)

| Tense | Active Voice | | Passive Voice | |
	Singular	Plural	Singular	Plural
Present	I see you see he/she/it sees	we see you see they see	I am seen you are seen he/she/it is seen	we are seen you are seen they are seen
Past	I/he saw you saw	we/they saw you saw	I/it was seen you were seen	we/they were seen you were seen
Future	I/you/he will see	we/you/they will see	I/you/it will be seen	we/you/they will be seen

Grammar Practice

Verbs 5

■ Active and Passive Voice

 If a sentence below is in the passive voice, rewrite it in the active voice. If it is already in the active voice, write "active."

Example: By then, the pizzas will have been eaten by my brothers.
By then, my brothers will have eaten the pizzas.

1. The announcement was heard by only half of the students.

2. My geometry textbook has been lost.

3. The student council is considering action on the proposal.

4. Most of the class is going to the afternoon assembly.

5. Winners' names will be published in the next issue of *The Bugle*.

6. The new menu was tested last week by the cooks.

7. A fossil of an unknown dinosaur was recently discovered by scientists in a remote area of New Mexico.

8. Stefan will perform his composition at the fall concert.

9. Since we hadn't missed any school all semester, we had been given movie passes by the attendance office.

10. You may use my computer today after school.

 ## Model

Model the following sentence to practice the effective use of passive voice.

> **More gold has been mined from the thoughts of men than has been taken from the earth.**
>
> —Napoleon Hill

724.1 Mood of a Verb

The **mood** of a verb indicates the tone or attitude with which a statement is made.

- **Indicative mood** is used to state a fact or to ask a question.

    Often, I face the challenge of another test by making a detailed study plan. I then work hard and stick to my plan so that I am ready for the test. How do you prepare?

- **Imperative mood** is used to give a command.

"Whatever you do, don't fly your kite during a storm."

—Mrs. Abiah Franklin

- **Subjunctive mood** is not as commonly used in English as it once was; however, careful writers may choose to use it to express the exact manner in which their statements are meant.

    Use the subjunctive *were* to express a condition that is contrary to fact.

    If I were finished with my report, I could go to the movie.

    Use the subjunctive *were* after *as though* or *as if* to express an unreal condition.

    Mrs. Young acted as if she were sixteen again.

    Use the subjunctive *be* in "that" clauses to express necessity, legal decisions, or parliamentary motions.

    "It is moved and supported that no more than 6 million quad be used to explore the planet Earth."

    "Ridiculous! Knowing earthlings is bound to help us understand ourselves! Therefore, I move that the sum be amended to 12 million quad."

    "Stupidity! I move that all missions be postponed until we have living proof of life on Earth."

Grammar Practice

Verbs 6

■ Mood of a Verb

Write whether each statement shows *indicative*, *imperative*, or *subjunctive* mood.

Example: Mr. Cerminera closes the windows, even on the nicest days.
    indicative

1. He moved as if he were a deer running from a hunter.

2. Don't forget to read chapters eight and nine before the test tomorrow.

3. What is wrong with Lamont's car?

4. The city councilwoman amended the proposal to include schools in our district.

5. Whatever happens, don't forget to call me tonight.

6. She acted as though the exam weren't important.

7. Everyone must attend the meeting.

8. Sarena arrived on time.

9. Where in Kansas is Cottonwood Falls?

10. Katrina would have gotten the part if she were a Redford or an Eastwood.

Model

Model the following sentence to practice using the subjunctive mood.

When there is no news, [newscasters] give it to you with the same emphasis as if there were.

—David Brinkley

Verbals

A **verbal** is a word that is derived from a verb but acts as another part of speech. There are three types of verbals: *gerunds, infinitives,* and *participles.* Each is often part of a verbal phrase.

726.1 Gerunds

A **gerund** is a verb form that ends in *ing* and is used as a noun.

Swimming **is my favorite pastime.** (subject)

I began swimming **at the age of six months.** (direct object)

Swimming in chlorinated pools **makes my eyes red.** (gerund phrase used as a subject)

726.2 Infinitives

An **infinitive** is a verb form that is usually introduced by *to*; the infinitive may be used as a noun, an adjective, or an adverb.

Most people find it easy to swim. (adverb modifying an adjective)

To swim the English Channel **must be a thrill.** (infinitive phrase as noun)

The urge to swim in tropical waters **is more common.** (infinitive phrase as adjective)

726.3 Participles

A **participle** is a verb form ending in *ing* or *ed* that acts as an adjective.

The workers raking leaves **are tired and hungry.** (participial phrase modifies *workers*)

The bags full of raked **leaves are evidence of their hard work.** (participle modifies *leaves*)

Grammar Practice

Verbals 7

- ■ Gerunds
- ■ Infinitives
- ■ Participles

 Write whether each underlined word or phrase is a *gerund*, a *participle*, or an *infinitive*.

Example: 1. *gerund*

(1) <u>Playing</u> the piano is an acquired skill. The piano is a popular instrument because it is relatively easy (2) <u>to learn</u>. Most people enjoy the piano's (3) <u>inviting</u> sound.

Many great pianists had excellent teachers. Franz Liszt, the famous pianist and composer, enjoyed (4) <u>teaching</u> young students. (5) <u>Studying</u> with Carl Czerny, an accomplished student of Beethoven, Liszt became a very capable teacher.

Usually, learning how (6) <u>to play</u> the piano involves (7) <u>taking</u> lessons from an (8) <u>experienced</u> professional. A good teacher knows how (9) <u>to make</u> practice fun. First, you will practice scales and chords and learn simple melodies. Before long, you will read music and learn (10) <u>to create</u> your own compositions.

◤ Model

Model the following sentences to practice using infinitives, gerunds, and participles.

The best way to live is by not knowing what will happen to you at the end of the day.

—Donald Barthelme

Good communication is just as stimulating as black coffee, and just as hard to sleep after.

—Anne Morrow Lindbergh

Adjective

An **adjective** describes or modifies a noun or a pronoun. The articles *a, an,* and *the* are also adjectives.

The young **driver peeked through** the big **steering wheel.**

(*The* and *young* modify *driver; the* and *big* modify *steering wheel.*)

728.1 Types of Adjectives

A **proper adjective** is created from a proper noun and is capitalized.

In Canada (proper noun), **you will find many cultures and climates.**

Canadian (proper adjective) **winters can be harsh.**

A **predicate adjective** follows a form of the "be" verb (or other linking verb) and describes the subject.

Late autumn seems grim **to those who love summer.** (*Grim* modifies *autumn.*)

NOTE: Some words can be either adjectives or pronouns (*that, these, all, each, both, many, some,* and so on). These words are adjectives when they come before the nouns they modify; they are pronouns when they stand alone.

Jiao made both **goals.** (*Both* modifies *goals;* it is an adjective.)

Both **were scored in the final period.** (*Both* stands alone; it is a pronoun.)

728.2 Forms of Adjectives

Adjectives have three forms: *positive, comparative,* and *superlative.*

■ The **positive form** describes a noun or a pronoun without comparing it to anyone or anything else.

The first game was long and tiresome.

■ The **comparative form** (*-er, more,* or *less*) compares two persons, places, things, or ideas.

The second game was longer **and** more tiresome **than the first.**

■ The **superlative form** (*-est, most,* or *least*) compares three or more persons, places, things, or ideas.

The third game was the longest **and** most tiresome **of all.**

NOTE: Use *more* and *most* (or *less* and *least*)—instead of adding a suffix—with many adjectives of two or more syllables.

Positive	Comparative	Superlative
big	**bigger**	**biggest**
helpful	**more helpful**	**most helpful**
painful	**less painful**	**least painful**

Grammar Practice

Adjectives

■ **Forms of Adjectives**

For each sentence below, write the adjective and its form (positive, comparative, or superlative). Some sentences contain more than one adjective. (For this activity, ignore any proper adjective.)

Example: Odysseus is one of the most famous characters in Greek mythology.
> most famous (superlative)

1. Also known as Ulysses, he was king of a smaller Greek island called Ithaca.

2. He was a suitor of Helen of Troy, the most beautiful woman on earth.

3. Some believe that he was more resourceful than other Greek warriors.

4. It was his idea to build a huge, hollow horse made of wood to sneak Greek soldiers into the city of Troy.

5. When the Trojans saw the big horse, they believed that it would bring them good luck.

6. The Trojan horse gave the Greeks an easier way to enter and destroy the city.

7. Odysseus is probably most renowned for his long journey back from Troy.

8. The trip was more difficult than Odysseus could ever have imagined.

9. Along the way, Odysseus encountered unusual places and creatures stranger than any he had ever seen.

Model

Model the following sentence to practice using forms of adjectives.

> One might have dreamed one's self in some forgotten Italian garden rather than a short two hours' trip away from the busiest and most congested city of the world.
>
> —Kathleen Norris, *Harriet and the Piper*

Adverb

An **adverb** describes or modifies a verb, an adjective, or another adverb.

She sneezed loudly. (*Loudly* modifies the verb *sneezed*.)

Her sneezes are really **dramatic.** (*Really* modifies the adjective *dramatic*.)

The sneeze exploded very noisily. (*Very* modifies the adverb *noisily*.)

An adverb usually tells *when, where, how,* or *how much.*

730.1 Types of Adverbs

Adverbs can be cataloged in four basic ways: *time, place, manner,* and *degree.*

Time (These adverbs tell *when, how often,* and *how long.*)

today, yesterday   daily, weekly   briefly, eternally

Place (These adverbs tell *where, to where,* and *from where.*)

here, there   nearby, beyond   backward, forward

Manner (These adverbs often end in *ly* and tell *how* something is done.)

precisely   effectively   regally   smoothly   well

Degree (These adverbs tell *how much* or *how little.*)

substantially   greatly   entirely   partly   too   much

NOTE: Some adverbs can be written with or without the *ly* ending. When in doubt, use the *ly* form.

slow, slowly   loud, loudly   fair, fairly   tight, tightly   quick, quickly

730.2 Forms of Adverbs

Adverbs of manner have three forms: *positive, comparative,* and *superlative.*

■ The **positive form** describes a verb, an adjective, or another adverb without comparing it to anyone or anything else.

Model X vacuum cleans well **and runs** quietly.

■ The **comparative form** (*-er, more,* or *less*) compares how two things are done.

Model Y vacuum cleans better **and runs** more quietly **than model X does.**

■ The **superlative form** (*-est, most,* or *least*) compares how three or more things are done.

Model Z vacuum cleans best **and runs** most quietly **of all.**

Irregular Forms		
Positive	Comparative	Superlative
well	better	best
fast	faster	fastest
remorsefully	more remorsefully	most remorsefully

Grammar Practice

Adverbs

■ **Types of Adverbs**

For each sentence below, write the adverb as well as its type (time, place, manner, degree). The number of adverbs in each sentence is given in parentheses.

Example: Today, all new cars are equipped with air bags. *(1)*

       today (time)

1. An air bag's inflation system is much like a solid rocket booster. *(1)*

2. The system has a device inside that tells the bag when to inflate. *(1)*

3. A solid propellant burns extremely rapidly to create a large amount of hot gas. *(2)*

4. It quickly inflates the bag, causing it to explode from its container at speeds up to 200 mph. *(1)*

5. The purpose of the air bag is to restrain the driver or passenger immediately with little or no damage to his or her body. *(1)*

6. They prevent a person from moving forward too fast in a collision. *(3)*

7. After the air bag is entirely inflated, the gas escapes through tiny holes. *(1)*

8. Used air bags should always be replaced by factory technicians. *(1)*

▶ Model

Model the sentence below to practice using types of adverbs.

> **He lay down low to the race, whining eagerly, his splendid body flashing forward, leap by leap, in the wan white moonlight.**
>
> —Jack London, *Call of the Wild*

Preposition

A **preposition** is the first word (or group of words) in a prepositional phrase. It shows the relationship between its object (a noun or a pronoun that follows the preposition) and another word in the sentence. The first noun or pronoun following a preposition is its object.

> **To make a mustache, Natasha placed the hairy caterpillar** under **her** nose.
> (*Under* shows the relationship between the verb, *placed*, and the object of the preposition, *nose*.)
> **The drowsy insect clung obediently** to **the girl's upper** lip.
> (The first noun following the preposition *to* is *lip; lip* is the object of the preposition.)

732.1 Prepositional Phrases

A **prepositional phrase** includes the preposition, the object of the preposition, and the modifiers of the object. A prepositional phrase functions as an adverb or as an adjective.

> **Some people** run **away** from caterpillars.
> (The phrase functions as an adverb and modifies the verb *run*.)
> **However, little** kids with inquisitive minds **enjoy their company.**
> (The phrase functions as an adjective and modifies the noun *kids*.)

NOTE: A preposition is always followed by an object; if there is no object, the word is an adverb, not a preposition.

> **Natasha never** played **with caterpillars** before. (The word *before* is not followed by an object; therefore, it functions as an adverb that modifies *played*, a verb.)

Common Prepositions

aboard	before	from	of	save
about	behind	from among	off	since
above	below	from between	on	subsequent to
according to	beneath	from under	on account of	through
across	beside	in	on behalf of	throughout
across from	besides	in addition to	onto	till
after	between	in back of	on top of	to
against	beyond	in behalf of	opposite	together with
along	by	in front of	out	toward
alongside	by means of	in place of	out of	under
along with	concerning	in regard to	outside of	underneath
amid	considering	inside	over	until
among	despite	inside of	over to	unto
apart from	down	in spite of	owing to	up
around	down from	instead of	past	upon
aside from	during	into	prior to	up to
at	except	like	regarding	with
away from	except for	near	round	within
because of	for	near to	round about	without

Grammar Practice

Prepositions

 Write the prepositional phrases from the sentences below.

Example: According to some people, the creature called Bigfoot lives in the forests of Washington and Oregon.

according to some people, in the forests, of Washington and Oregon

1. Since a 1959 magazine article, people have searched for solid evidence of this hairy humanoid creature's existence.

2. In 1967, Roger Patterson saw and filmed what he called a Sasquatch.

3. The animal moved over a riverbank and disappeared into the trees.

4. Many people around the world say they have seen a similar beast.

5. In Asia, this being, called a Yeti, is usually seen at 10,000 feet.

6. Presumably, a man standing beside a Bigfoot would look small.

7. Serious Bigfoot searchers say the animal remains elusive because it moves during the night.

8. Despite all the sightings, no solid proof of such a creature has ever been found.

Model

Model the following sentences to practice using prepositional phrases as adjectives.

Love is like an hourglass, with the heart filling up as the brain empties.

—Jules Renard

Life isn't a matter of milestones but of moments.

—Rose Fitzgerald Kennedy

Conjunction

A **conjunction** connects individual words or groups of words. There are three kinds of conjunctions: *coordinating, correlative,* and *subordinating*.

734.1 Coordinating Conjunctions

Coordinating conjunctions usually connect a word to a word, a phrase to a phrase, or a clause to a clause. The words, phrases, or clauses joined by a coordinating conjunction are equal in importance or are of the same type.

> I could see from the look on my sister's face that she was disappointed and wanted to come with me, but my parents said she had to stay home.

(*And* connects the two parts of a compound predicate; *but* connects two independent clauses that could stand on their own.)

734.2 Correlative Conjunctions

Correlative conjunctions are conjunctions used in pairs.

> They were not only exhausted by the day's journey but also sunburned.

734.3 Subordinating Conjunctions

Subordinating conjunctions connect two clauses that are *not* equally important, thereby showing the relationship between them. A subordinating conjunction connects a dependent clause to an independent clause in order to complete the meaning of the dependent clause.

> A brown trout will study the bait before he eats it. (The clause *before he eats it* is dependent. It depends on the rest of the sentence to complete its meaning.)

Kinds of Conjunctions

Coordinating: **and, but, or, nor, for, yet, so**

Correlative: **either, or; neither, nor; not only, but also; both, and; whether, or**

Subordinating: **after, although, as, as if, as long as, as though, because, before, if, in order that, provided that, since, so that, that, though, till, unless, until, when, where, whereas, while**

NOTE: Relative pronouns (pages **704.1** and **706.2**) and conjunctive adverbs (page **618.2**) can also connect clauses.

Interjection

An **interjection** communicates strong emotion or surprise. Punctuation—a comma or an exclamation point—sets off an interjection from the rest of the sentence.

> Oh no! The TV broke. Good grief! I have nothing to do! Yipes, I'll go mad!

Grammar Practice

Conjunctions

 Number your paper from 1 to 11. Write the conjunctions you find in the following paragraph and label them *coordinating, subordinating,* or *correlative.* (Write both correlative conjunctions as one answer.)

Example: 1. although; subordinating

The Afrikaans language is attributed to the Dutch, although many other languages influenced it over time. Words and phrases of shipwrecked sailors found their way into the language, and when slaves arrived from eastern regions, they contributed an Oriental dialect. Soon, the language was neither Dutch nor any other known language. It had become unique after the new accents, dialects, and words were added. Today, Afrikaans is the first language of almost 60 percent of South Africa's whites, but it is spoken by more than 90 percent of the mixed-race population. Afrikaans is spoken not only in South Africa but also in the Republic of Namibia and in Zimbabwe. Afrikaans is the only language in the world that has a monument dedicated to it (in Paarl, Western Cape Province, South Africa), yet it is not the only official language of South Africa—there are nine others!

 ## Model

Model the following sentences to practice using interjections effectively.

> With a disgusted look on her face, Lakendra exclaimed, "Ugh! I can't eat this!"

> Crikey, is that all?

> —Alan Grayson, *Mile End*

Test Prep!

Read the following paragraphs. Write the letter of the correct description for each underlined part from the choices given on the next page.

It's hard for teens to get any respect—especially when two or three
(1)
of them get caught cheating or stealing or vandalizing. The tendency is for

adults to generalize, labeling teens as "trouble." And once they're perceived

that way, it starts a maddening cycle of reaction and expectation.
(2)

How can a high school student change those perceptions? One of the
(3)

best ways is to become a volunteer. A teen volunteer not only helps to dispel
(4)

the "bad teenager" myth; he or she also effectively benefits the community.
(5)

And in many ways, volunteering benefits the volunteer, as well. A person's

self-esteem increases when others recognize that he or she has something
(6)

of value to offer. The recipients of the volunteer's time and effort aren't the

only ones who recognize that value. Parents, teachers, college admissions

officers, and employers do, too.
(7)

A student interested in volunteering has several avenues to pursue
(8)

in finding an opportunity that fits his or her personality. Youth Service
(9)

America, for example, matches volunteers with thousands of local, national,

and global organizations. AmeriCorps is a national service program for

volunteers age 17 and older; members get a small living allowance as

well as money for college or to repay student loans. Volunteers can also
(10)   (11)

get international experience. Amigos de las Americas trains and provides

opportunities for high school and college students to participate in service
(12)

projects in Latin America.

The teen years don't have to be a stereotype. Teens who volunteer <u>learn</u> and help others. They <u>get</u> a valid perspective on their own lives
(13)   **(14)**
by seeing how others live. <u>Soon</u>, teen volunteers become a source of real
(15)
change <u>where</u> it's needed.
(16)

1 (A) linking verb
    (B) infinitive
    (C) auxiliary verb
    (D) passive voice verb

2 (A) correlative conjunction
    (B) subordinating conjunction
    (C) coordinating conjunction
    (D) preposition

3 (A) direct object
    (B) indirect object
    (C) adjective
    (D) adverb

4 (A) action verb
    (B) linking verb
    (C) auxiliary verb
    (D) gerund

5 (A) adverb of time
    (B) adverb of place
    (C) adverb of manner
    (D) adverb of degree

6 (A) present tense verb
    (B) past tense verb
    (C) active voice verb
    (D) passive voice verb

7 (A) adverb of time
    (B) adverb of place
    (C) adverb of manner
    (D) adverb of degree

8 (A) infinitive
    (B) gerund
    (C) participle
    (D) past tense verb

9 (A) infinitive
    (B) gerund
    (C) participle
    (D) present tense verb

10 (A) preposition
    (B) conjunction
    (C) adjective
    (D) adverb

11 (A) action verb
    (B) linking verb
    (C) auxiliary verb
    (D) participle

12 (A) noun
    (B) adjective
    (C) adverb
    (D) participle

13 (A) intransitive verb
    (B) transitive verb
    (C) linking verb
    (D) gerund

14 (A) intransitive verb
    (B) transitive verb
    (C) linking verb
    (D) auxiliary verb

15 (A) adverb of time
    (B) adverb of place
    (C) adverb of manner
    (D) adverb of degree

16 (A) correlative conjunction
    (B) subordinating conjunction
    (C) coordinating conjunction
    (D) adverb of place

Understanding Sentences

Constructing Sentences

A **sentence** is made up of one or more words that express a complete thought. Sentences begin with a capital letter; they end with a period, a question mark, or an exclamation point.

What should we do this afternoon? We could have a picnic. No, I hate the ants!

Using Subjects and Predicates

A sentence usually has a subject and a predicate. The subject is the part of the sentence about which something is said. The predicate, which contains the verb, is the part of the sentence that says something about the subject.

We write **from aspiration and antagonism, as well as from experience.**

—Ralph Waldo Emerson

738.1 The Subject

The **subject** is the part of the sentence about which something is said. The subject is always a noun; a pronoun; or a word, clause, or phrase that functions as a noun (such as a gerund or a gerund phrase or an infinitive).

Wolves **howl.** (noun)

They **howl for a variety of reasons.** (pronoun)

To establish their turf **may be one reason.** (infinitive phrase)

Searching for "lost" pack members **may be another.** (gerund phrase)

That wolves and dogs are similar animals **seems obvious.** (noun clause)

■ A **simple subject** is the subject without its modifiers.

Most wildlife biologists **disapprove of crossbreeding wolves and dogs.**

■ A **complete subject** is the subject with all of its modifiers.

Most wildlife biologists **disapprove of crossbreeding wolves and dogs.**

■ A **compound subject** is composed of two or more simple subjects.

Wise breeders **and** owners **know that wolf-dog puppies can display unexpected, destructive behaviors.**

738.2 Delayed Subject

In sentences that begin with *There* or *It* followed by a form of the "be" verb, the subject comes after the verb. The subject is also delayed in questions.

There was nothing **in the refrigerator.** (The subject is *nothing*; the verb is *was.*)

Where is my sandwich**?** (The subject is *sandwich*; the verb is *is.*)

Grammar Practice

Constructing Sentences 1

■ Simple, Complete, and Compound Subjects
■ Delayed Subjects

 Write the complete subject of each sentence. Circle the simple subject or subjects.

Example: There is an art fair on the county grounds this weekend.
an art (*fair*)

1. Various artists are setting up their tents near the Picasso statue.

2. The Lakefront Art Fair is the best festival of the summer.

3. Colorful hot-air balloons float in the air, inviting people to the visit the event.

4. The bands and food tents are popular with the crowd.

5. There is a children's play area near the restrooms.

6. The fair, consisting of more than 100 vendors, attracts thousands of visitors each year.

7. The chamber of commerce spends a lot of time to put it together.

8. Pottery, paintings, and sculpture are featured items at the fair.

9. Is your sister-in-law looking for a special piece of art?

10. Most visitors come away with several purchases.

 Model

Model the following sentences to practice using delayed subjects.

There was such a glory over everything.
—Harriet Tubman

Hasn't the fine line between sanity and madness gotten finer?
—George Price

Sentences

740.1 Predicates

The **predicate** is the part of the sentence that shows action or says something about the subject.

> **Giant squid** do exist.

- A **simple predicate** is the verb without its modifiers.
  > **One giant squid** measured **nearly 60 feet long.**

- A **complete predicate** is the simple predicate with all its modifiers.
  > **One giant squid** measured nearly 60 feet long.
  > (*Measured* is the simple predicate; *nearly 60 feet long* modifies *measured*.)

- A **compound predicate** is composed of two or more simple predicates.
  > **A squid** grasps **its prey with tentacles and** bites **it with its beak.**

NOTE: A sentence can have a **compound subject** and a **compound predicate.**

> **Both** sperm whales **and** giant squid live **and occasionally** clash **in the deep waters off New Zealand's South Island.**

- A **direct object** is part of the predicate and receives the action of the verb. (See **716.2.**)
  > **Sperm whales sometimes eat** giant squid.
  > (The direct object *giant squid* receives the action of the verb *eat* by answering the question *whales eat what*?)

NOTE: The **direct object** may be compound.

> **In the past, whalers harvested** oil, spermaceti, **and** ambergris **from slain sperm whales.**

740.2 Understood Subjects and Predicates

Either the subject or the predicate may be "missing" from a sentence, but both must be clearly **understood.**

> Who is in the hot-air balloon?
> (*Who* is the subject; *is in the hot-air balloon* is the predicate.)

> **No one.**
> (*No one* is the subject; the predicate *is in the hot-air balloon* is understood.)

> Get out of the way!
> (The subject *you* is understood; *get out of the way* is the predicate.)

Grammar Practice

Constructing Sentences 2

■ Simple, Complete, and Compound Predicates

Write the complete predicate of each sentence. Circle the simple predicate or predicates.

Example: The flatness of the Great Plains allows dry, cold air to collide with warm, moist air.

(allows) *dry, cold air to collide with warm, moist air*

1. Most tornadoes form along the front between these air masses.

2. Meteorologists call this "Tornado Alley" and include in it parts of Texas, Oklahoma, Kansas, and Nebraska.

3. Many cities in Tornado Alley enforce stronger building codes.

4. States in Tornado Alley can experience millions of dollars in damage each year.

5. Who is responsible for paying for the damage?

6. The federal government often provides disaster aid.

7. Storm chasers travel throughout Tornado Alley and search for storms.

8. The chasers sometimes find themselves in dangerous situations.

9. Spotters used binoculars, barometers, and other simple forecasting methods to predict a tornado's proximity.

10. The sophisticated computer systems in current use accurately predict and pinpoint a storm.

Model

Model the following sentence to practice using a compound predicate.

> We learn and grow and are transformed not so much by what we do but by why and how we do it.
>
> —Sharon Salzberg, "The Power of Intention"

Sentences

Using Phrases

A **phrase** is a group of related words that function as a single part of speech. The sentence below contains a number of phrases.

Finishing the race will require running up some steep slopes.

finishing the race (This gerund phrase functions as a subject noun.)

will require (This phrase functions as a verb.)

running up some steep slopes (This gerund phrase acts as an object noun.)

742.1 Types of Phrases

■ An **appositive phrase,** which follows a noun or a pronoun and renames it, consists of a noun and its modifiers. An appositive adds new information about the noun or pronoun it follows.

> **The Trans-Siberian Railroad,** the world's longest railway, **stretches from Moscow to Vladivostok.** (The appositive phrase renames *Trans-Siberian Railroad* and provides new information.)

■ A **verbal phrase** is a phrase based on one of the three types of verbals: *gerund, infinitive,* or *participle.* (See **726.1, 726.2,** and **726.3.**)

■ A **gerund phrase** consists of a gerund and its modifiers. The whole phrase functions as a noun.

> Spotting the tiny mouse **was easy for the hawk.**
> (The gerund phrase is used as the subject of the sentence.)
> **Dinner escaped by** ducking under a rock.
> (The gerund phrase is the object of the preposition *by.*)

■ An **infinitive phrase** consists of an infinitive and its modifiers. The whole phrase functions either as a noun, an adjective, or an adverb.

> To shake every voter's hand **was the candidate's goal.**
> (The infinitive phrase functions as a noun used as the subject.)
> **Your efforts** to clean the chalkboard **are appreciated.**
> (The infinitive phrase is used as an adjective modifying *efforts.*)
> **Please watch carefully** to see the difference.
> (The infinitive phrase is used as an adverb modifying *watch.*)

■ A **participial phrase** consists of a past or present participle and its modifiers. The whole phrase functions as an adjective.

> Following his nose, **the beagle took off like a jackrabbit.**
> (The participial phrase modifies the noun *beagle.*)
> **The raccoons,** warned by the rustling, **took cover.**
> (The participial phrase modifies the noun *raccoons.*)

Grammar Practice

Constructing Sentences 3

- ■ Appositive Phrases
- ■ Verbal Phrases

 Identify each underlined phrase as an *appositive, gerund, infinitive,* or *participial phrase.*

Example: <u>Ice fishing on the lake</u> at this time of year is dangerous.
gerund phrase

1. Lucinda's goal of <u>becoming class president</u> was finally accomplished.

2. John Steinbeck, <u>the famous American author</u>, never graduated from college.

3. Dirk postponed <u>cleaning the garage</u> so he could go to the movies.

4. When he got his driver's license, Geoff wanted <u>to buy a used car</u>.

5. <u>Refusing to accept defeat</u>, Luis limped over the finish line.

6. The student <u>chosen to compete</u> will travel to Washington, D.C.

7. <u>To continue his education</u>, Reggie borrowed money from his uncle.

8. <u>Working hard</u> usually pays off.

9. Keleigh kept the secret to prevent anyone from <u>telling Mr. Bain</u>.

10. Arau*caria heterophylla,* <u>the Norfolk Island pine</u>, is a popular houseplant.

Model

Model the following sentence to practice using appositive phrases.

Everyone agreed that my father, my Baba, had built the most beautiful house in the Wazir Akbar Khan district, a new and affluent neighborhood in the northern part of Kabul.

—Khaled Hossein, *The Kite Runner*

Sentences

Using Phrases *(continued)*

- A **verb phrase** consists of a main verb preceded by one or more helping verbs.

  Snow has been falling **for days.** (*Has been falling* is a verb phrase.)

- A **prepositional phrase** is a group of words beginning with a preposition and ending with a noun or a pronoun. Prepositional phrases function mainly as adjectives and adverbs.

  Reach for that catnip ball behind the couch. (The prepositional phrase *behind the couch* is used as an adjective modifying *catnip ball.*)

  Zach won the wheelchair race in record time. (*In record time* is used as an adverb modifying the verb *won.*)

- An **absolute phrase** consists of a noun and a participle (plus the participle's object, if there is one, and any modifiers). An absolute phrase functions as a modifier that adds information to the entire sentence. Absolute phrases are always set off with commas.

  Its wheels clattering rhythmically over the rails, **the train rolled into town.** (The noun *wheels* is modified by the present participle *clattering.* The entire phrase modifies the rest of the sentence.)

Using Clauses

A **clause** is a group of related words that has both a subject and a predicate.

744.1 Independent and Dependent Clauses

An **independent clause** presents a complete thought and can stand alone as a sentence; a **dependent clause** (also called a *subordinate clause*) does not present a complete thought and cannot stand alone as a sentence.

Sparrows make nests in cattle barns (independent clause) so that they can stay warm during the winter (dependent clause).

744.2 Types of Dependent Clauses

There are three basic types of dependent clauses: *adverb, noun,* and *adjective.*

- An **adverb clause** is used like an adverb to modify a verb, an adjective, or an adverb. Adverb clauses begin with a subordinating conjunction. (See **734.3**.)

  If I study hard, **I will pass this test.** (The adverb clause modifies the verb *will pass.*)

- A **noun clause** is used in place of a noun.

  However, the teacher said that the essay questions are based only on the last two chapters. (The noun clause functions as a direct object.)

- An **adjective clause** modifies a noun or a pronoun.

  Tomorrow's test, which covers the entire book, **is half essay and half short answers.** (The adjective clause modifies the noun *test.*)

Grammar Practice

Constructing Sentences 4

- Verb Phrases
- Prepositional Phrases
- Absolute Phrases

 Identify the underlined part of each sentence as a *prepositional phrase*, an *absolute phrase*, or a *verb phrase*.

Example: <u>All things considered,</u> the Wildcats were headed for the finals.
absolute phrase

1. I could hear Min and Lissa whispering <u>in the next room</u>.

2. We <u>will meet</u> at Gerald's Diner at 4:30.

3. <u>The full moon lighting his way,</u> my brother followed the tracks through the field.

4. Once her speech was over, Heather <u>did feel</u> more relaxed.

5. <u>His heart pounding like a jackhammer,</u> Ty slam-dunked the ball.

6. Stuart reviewed his notes <u>before the test</u>.

7. <u>Her hands and feet stinging from the cold,</u> Danielle left the bleachers and went inside.

8. The baby clinging to the old woman <u>had been making</u> mewling noises for at least half an hour.

 ## Model

Model the following sentence to practice using prepositional phrases.

During the day I heard them tunneling through the walls of my bedroom, sounding like a radio tuned to static in the next room.
—Sue Monk Kidd, *The Secret Life of Bees*

Using Sentence Variety

A **sentence** may be classified according to the type of statement it makes, the way it is constructed, and its arrangement of words.

| **746.1** Kinds of Sentences |

Sentences can make five basic kinds of sentences: *declarative, interrogative, imperative, exclamatory,* or *conditional.*

- **Declarative sentences** make statements. They tell us something about a person, a place, a thing, or an idea.

   The Statue of Liberty stands in New York Harbor.

   For over a century, it has greeted immigrants and visitors to America.

- **Interrogative sentences** ask questions.

   Did you know that the Statue of Liberty is made of copper and stands more than 150 feet tall?

   Are we allowed to climb all the way to the top?

- **Imperative sentences** make commands. They often contain an understood subject *(you)* as in the examples below.

   Go see the Statue of Liberty.

   After a few weeks of physical conditioning, climb its 168 stairs.

- **Exclamatory sentences** communicate strong emotion or surprise.

   Climbing 168 stairs is not a dumb idea!

   Just muster some of that old pioneering spirit, that desire to try something new, that never-say-die attitude that made America great!

- **Conditional sentences** express wishes ("if . . . then" statements) or conditions contrary to fact.

   If I could design a country's flag, I would use six colors behind a sun, a star, and a moon.

   I would feel as if I were representing many cultures in my design.

Grammar Practice

Kinds of Sentences

■ Sentence Variety

 Write the kind of statement each sentence in the following paragraph makes: *declarative, interrogative, imperative, exclamatory,* or *conditional.*

Example: 1. *declarative*

(1) The earth's magnetic field has flipped many times in geologic history, and scientists think it is poised to flip again. (2) Think about what that means. (3) Compasses will point to the South Pole instead of to the North Pole. (4) What other effects would a flip have? (5) It most likely would confuse many types of migratory birds and sea creatures who use the earth's magnetic fields to find their way. (6) It would also leave the earth temporarily unprotected from some of the solar wind filtered out by the current magnetic field. (7) A solar flare could then disrupt communications and damage the ozone layer. (8) There is a trade-off, though. (9) If there were no magnetic field, people would be lucky enough to see auroras almost every night. (10) That would be cool!

Model

Model the following conditional sentences.

If you cannot convince them, confuse them.

—Harry S. Truman

If you aren't fired with enthusiasm, you will be fired with enthusiasm.

—Vince Lombardi

Sentences

748.1 Types of Sentence Constructions

A sentence may be *simple, compound, complex,* or *compound-complex.* It all depends on the relationship between independent and dependent clauses.

- A **simple sentence** can have a single subject or a compound subject. It can have a single predicate or a compound predicate. However, a simple sentence has only one independent clause, and it has no dependent clauses.

    My back aches.
    (single subject; single predicate)
    My teeth and my eyes hurt.
    (compound subject; single predicate)
    My throat and nose feel sore and look red.
    (compound subject; compound predicate)
    I must have caught the flu from the sick kids in class.
    (independent clause with two phrases: *from the sick kids* and *in class*)

- A **compound sentence** consists of two independent clauses. The clauses must be joined by a comma and a coordinating conjunction or by a semicolon.

    I usually don't mind missing school, but this is not fun.
    I feel too sick to watch TV; I feel too sick to eat.

NOTE: The comma can be omitted when the clauses are very short.

    I wept and I wept.

- A **complex sentence** contains one independent clause (in black) and one or more dependent clauses (in red).

    When I get back to school, I'm actually going to appreciate it.
    (dependent clause; independent clause)
    I won't even complain about math class, although I might be talking out of my head because I'm feverish.
    (independent clause; two dependent clauses)

- A **compound-complex sentence** contains two or more independent clauses (in black) and one or more dependent clauses (in red).

    Yes, I have a bad flu, and because I need to get well soon, I won't think about school just yet.
    (two independent clauses; one dependent clause)

Grammar Practice

Types of Sentence Constructions

■ Types of Sentences

 Identify each of the following sentences as a *simple, compound, complex,* or *compound-complex* sentence.

Example: 1. *simple*

(1) How do auroras form? (2) The solar wind contains charged particles that make the air glow when they blast into Earth's atmosphere. (3) The aurora borealis (or northern lights) and the aurora australis (southern lights) can take many different forms. (4) Sometimes simple lines appear across the sky, or pillars form at different points in the sky. (5) These lines or pillars can broaden into curtains of light, which wave back and forth overhead. (6) Lucky observers see more exotic forms. (7) Some aurora forms are petal shapes like giant blooming flowers, and others expand across the sky like slow-motion fireworks. (8) White aurora lights are most common, but when the solar wind is especially favorable, more vibrant colors such as purple, violet, green, and orange may appear. (9) Whatever colors they display or form they take, the lights of the aurora are always a sight to behold. (10) People who live in extreme north or south locales know this; they can see auroras almost 200 days a year!

Model

Model the following complex sentences.

When we blame ourselves, we feel that no one else has a right to blame us.

—Oscar Wilde, *The Picture of Dorian Gray*

Forgive me my nonsense as I also forgive the nonsense of those who think they talk sense.

—Robert Frost

Sentences

750.1 Arrangements of Sentences

Depending on the arrangement of the words and the placement of emphasis, a sentence may also be classified as *loose, balanced, periodic,* or *cumulative.*

- A **loose sentence** expresses the main thought near the beginning and adds explanatory material as needed.

  We hauled out the boxes of food and set up the camp stove, **all the time battling the hot wind that would not stop, even when we screamed into the sky.**

  Jet airplanes do the seemingly impossible—**moving us across countries and over oceans, transporting us to new continents, all within just a few hours.**

- A **balanced sentence** is constructed so that it emphasizes a similarity or a contrast between two or more of its parts (words, phrases, or clauses).

  The wind in our ears drove us crazy **and** pushed us on.
  (The similar wording emphasizes the main idea in this sentence.)

  Experience is not what happens to you; **it is what you do with** what happens to you.
  —Aldous Huxley

- A **periodic sentence** is one that postpones the crucial or most surprising idea until the end.

  Following my mother's repeated threats to ground me for life, I decided it was time to propose a compromise.

  There is only one way to achieve happiness on this terrestrial ball—and that is to have either a clear conscience or no conscience at all.
  —Ogden Nash, *I'm a Stranger Here Myself*

- A **cumulative sentence** places the general idea in the middle of the sentence with modifying clauses and phrases coming before and after.

  With careful thought and extra attention to detail, I wrote out my plan for being a model teenager, **a teen who cared about neatness and reliability.**

  With careful planning and diligence, students who finish high school and graduate from college will end up in high-paying, satisfying jobs, **an accomplishment we all admire and to which we all aspire.**

Grammar Practice

Arrangements of Sentences

■ Sentence Arrangements

Classify each of the following sentences as *loose, balanced, periodic,* or *cumulative.*

Example: From Chicago to Milwaukee it was cloudy, but north of Milwaukee it was clear.
balanced

1. The restaurant was nice, but the food was terrible.

2. The three of us climbed to the top of the hill and found the best spot, all the while darkness falling upon us, and then the fireworks began.

3. Suddenly, without a word and for no reason, Josh bolted out the open door.

4. The energetic horses ran hard, following each other through the tall grass, occasionally slowing to catch their breath and then hurrying on toward the horizon.

5. With grass in his hair, dirt between his fingers, and mud all over his face, Karif triumphantly held up the football.

6. After the ice storm, the woods looked hauntingly beautiful, as though diamonds had melted on the trees.

7. Although we were hungry, exhausted, and covered in mud, we continued to follow the moose tracks.

8. Some students study at home; others study at the public library.

9. Maria considered William a good friend—one who was trustworthy, honest, and reliable.

Model

Model the following balanced sentence.

We may brave human laws, but we cannot resist natural ones.
—Jules Verne, *20,000 Leagues Under the Sea*

Getting Sentence Parts to Agree

Agreement of Subject and Verb

A verb must agree in number (singular or plural) with its subject.

The student was proud of her quarter grades.

NOTE: Do not be confused by words that come between the subject and verb.

The manager, as well as the players, is required to display good sportsmanship. (*Manager*, not *players*, is the subject.)

752.1 Compound Subjects

Compound subjects joined by *or* or *nor* take a singular verb.

Neither Bev nor Kendra is going to the street dance.

NOTE: When one of the subjects joined by *or* or *nor* is singular and one is plural, the verb must agree with the subject nearer the verb.

Neither Yoshi nor his friends are singing in the band anymore. (The plural subject *friends* is nearer the verb, so the plural verb *are* is correct.)

Compound subjects connected with *and* require a plural verb.

Strength and balance are necessary for gymnastics.

752.2 Delayed Subjects

Delayed subjects occur when the verb comes before the subject in a sentence. In these inverted sentences, the delayed subject must agree with the verb.

There are many hardworking students in our schools.
There is present among many young people today a will to succeed.
(*Students* and *will* are the true subjects of these sentences, not *there*.)

752.3 "Be" Verbs

When a sentence contains a form of the "be" verb—and a noun comes before and after that verb—the verb must agree with the subject, not the *complement* (the noun coming after the verb).

The cause of his problem was the bad brakes.
The bad brakes were the cause of his problem.

752.4 Special Cases

Some nouns that are **plural in form but singular in meaning** take a singular verb: *mumps, measles, news, mathematics, economics, gallows, shambles.*

Measles is still considered a serious disease in many parts of the world.

Some nouns that are plural in form but singular in meaning take a plural verb: *scissors, trousers, tidings.*

The scissors are missing again.

Grammar Practice

Agreement of Subject and Verb 1

■ Subject-Verb Agreement

For each sentence, write the correct verb from the choice given in parentheses.

Example: The problem with both computers *(was, were)* their memory cards.

was

1. Mr. Malone *(are, is)* planning a quiz for this Friday.

2. There *(are, is)* rumors circulating that Rufus will be the starting quarterback on Friday.

3. *(Do, Does)* this skin cream really prevent acne?

4. The result of last week's drills *(was, were)* a seminar on fire safety.

5. Either Serena or Kim and Tyler Green *(take, takes)* the gerbils home over holiday breaks.

6. The news of his accident *(was, were)* not surprising.

7. There *(are, is)* remaining one medium-sized sweatshirt with the team logo.

8. Dale Earnhardt, Jr., and Kyle Bush *(are, is)* popular race-car drivers.

9. Neither DeWayne nor Kevin *(are, is)* going with us to the stadium.

10. *(Have, Has)* the fireworks started yet?

Model

Model the following sentences to practice subject-verb agreement with special-case nouns.

> **Your glasses need a good cleaning.**
>
> **The mathematics is not there until we put it there.**
>
> —Sir Arthur Eddington

Sentences

Agreement of Subject and Verb *(continued)*

754.1 Collective Nouns

Collective nouns *(faculty, committee, team, congress, species, crowd, army, pair, squad)* take a singular verb when they refer to a group as a unit; collective nouns take a plural verb when they refer to the individuals within the group.

> **The favored team is losing, and the crowd is getting ugly.** (Both *team* and *crowd* are considered units in this sentence, requiring the singular verb *is*.)
> **The pair were finally reunited after 20 years apart.**
> (Here, *pair* refers to two individuals, so the plural verb *were* is required.)

754.2 Indefinite Pronouns

Some **indefinite pronouns** are singular: *each, either, neither, one, everybody, another, anybody, everyone, nobody, everything, somebody,* and *someone.* They require a singular verb.

> **Everybody is invited to the cafeteria for refreshments.**

Some **indefinite pronouns** are plural: *both, few, many,* and *several.*

> **Several like chocolate cake. Many ask for ice cream, too.**

Some **indefinite pronouns** are singular or plural: *all, any, most, none,* and *some.*

NOTE: Do not be confused by words or phrases that come between the indefinite pronoun and the verb.

> **One of the participants is** (not *are*) **going to have to stay late to clean up.**

A Closer Look

Some **indefinite pronouns** can be either singular or plural: *all, any, most, none,* and *some.* These pronouns are singular if the number of the noun in the prepositional phrase is singular; they are plural if the noun is plural.

> **Most of the food complaints are coming from the seniors.**
> (*Complaints* is plural, so *most* is plural.)
> **Most of the tabletop is sticky with melted ice cream.**
> (*Tabletop* is singular, so *most* is singular.)

754.3 Relative Pronouns

When a **relative pronoun** *(who, which, that)* is used as the subject of a clause, the number of the verb is determined by the antecedent of the pronoun. (The antecedent is the word to which the pronoun refers.)

> **This is one of the books that are required for class.** (The relative pronoun *that* requires the plural verb *are* because its antecedent, *books,* is plural.)

NOTE: To test this type of sentence for agreement, read the "of" phrase first.

> **Of the books that are required for geography class, this is one.**

Grammar Practice

Agreement of Subject and Verb 2

■ Subject-Verb Agreement

 For each underlined verb, state the reason it does not agree with its subject.

Example: 1. _Were_ is plural, and its subject, _one_, is singular.

One of Edna Ferber's most popular works **(1)** <u>were</u> the novel *So Big*. (This is one book that **(2)** <u>are</u> required reading for literature class.) Some students **(3)** <u>wonders</u> about the author's reasons for writing the book. In one interview, Ferber answered: "I wrote my book because I wanted to write it more than anything in the world."

Many readers are aware that *So Big* won a Pulitzer Prize for literature. The main characters, Selina Peake DeJong and her son, Dirk "So Big" DeJong, **(4)** <u>makes</u> the story memorable. The pair **(5)** <u>faces</u> many challenges. Selina is a widow who **(6)** <u>are</u> forced to make her way in a male-dominated world. Dirk experiences many changes as he grows into a young man.

The novels *Showboat* and *Giant* **(7)** <u>is</u> other well-known works by Edna Ferber. Some of her fans **(8)** <u>believes</u> that she was the greatest novelist of her day.

◀ Model

Model the following sentence to practice subject-verb agreement.

He had preconceived ideas about everything, and his idea about Americans was that they should be engineers or mechanics.
—Willa Cather, *Alexander's Bridge*

Sentences

Agreement of Pronoun and Antecedent

A pronoun must agree in number, person, and gender with its *antecedent*. (The *antecedent* is the word to which the pronoun refers.)

> **Cal brought** his **gerbil to school.** (The antecedent of *his* is *Cal.* Both the pronoun and its antecedent are singular, third person, and masculine; therefore, the pronoun is said to "agree" with its antecedent.)

756.1 Agreement in Number

Use a **singular pronoun** to refer to such antecedents as *each, either, neither, one, anyone, anybody, everyone, everybody, somebody, another, nobody,* and *a person.*

> **Neither of the brothers likes** his **(not** their**) room.**

Two or more singular antecedents joined by *or* or *nor* are also referred to by a **singular pronoun.**

> **Either** Connie **or** Sue **left** her **headset in the library.**

If one of the antecedents joined by *or* or *nor* is singular and one is plural, the pronoun should agree with the nearer antecedent.

> **Neither the** manager **nor the** players **were crazy about** their **new uniforms.**

Use a **plural pronoun** to refer to plural antecedents as well as compound subjects joined by *and.*

> Jared **and** Carlos **are finishing** their **assignments.**

756.2 Agreement in Gender

Use a **masculine** or **feminine pronoun** depending upon the gender of the antecedent.

> **Is either** Connor **or** Grace **bringing** his **or** her **baseball glove?**

When *a person* or *everyone* is used to refer to both sexes or either sex, you will have to choose whether to offer optional pronouns or rewrite the sentence.

> **A person should be allowed to choose** her **or** his **own footwear.**
> (optional pronouns)
> **People should be allowed to choose** their **own footwear.**
> (rewritten in plural form)

Grammar Practice

Agreement of Pronoun and Antecedent

■ Pronoun-Antecedent Agreement

For each sentence below, first write the antecedent of the pronoun that appears later in the sentence. Then replace the incorrect pronoun with one that agrees with the antecedent. If the pronoun is correct as is, write "C."

Example: Should students always know the basics about how to maintain her computers?

students, their

1. Everyone should know how to delete files and save his documents to the network drive.

2. Tamyra and Stan know a lot about maintaining her computers.

3. Both of them keep his computers running smoothly.

4. The computer lab tech helps students with problems they can't fix.

5. Neither Tamyra nor Stan could help Arturo with their problem.

6. Arturo's computer was freezing up, and the lab tech fixed them.

7. The tech said that Arturo probably needs a new monitor for his computer.

8. Stan just got a new flat-screen monitor for their computer at home.

9. Most students at our school know how to fix his computers when something minor goes wrong.

Model

Model the following sentence to practice pronoun-antecedent agreement.

My parents gave up entirely their wandering life and fixed themselves in their native country.

—Mary Shelley, *Frankenstein*

Sentences

Test Prep!

Read the following paragraphs. From the choices given on the next page, write the letter of the best answer for each underlined part.

Marilyn vos Savant <u>writes a magazine column.</u> She attended a
(1)
<u>prestigious university in St. Louis but dropped out, and she currently lives</u>
(2)
<u>in New York City with her husband.</u> What's so unusual about Marilyn is

that <u>her IQ is over 200</u>, while a normal IQ ranges from 90 to 110.
(3)
"IQ" means "intelligence quotient." At first, tests <u>to determine</u>
(4)
<u>a person's IQ</u> were given only to children and <u>were used</u> to place
(5)
individuals <u>scoring below a certain point</u> in special education programs.
(6)
<u>The tests were meant to show a child's mental abilities relative to others</u>
(7)
<u>of the same age.</u>

<u>Modern intelligence testing</u> uses the same formula; <u>tests compare</u>
(8)   **(9)**
<u>one person's score with the scores of others of the same age.</u> A score of
(9)
100 is the arbitrary definition of "average" since half of the population

scores lower and half higher. <u>Approximately 2 percent of the population</u>
(10)
scores 132 or higher on a standard intelligence test.

Mensa, <u>a social organization for these people</u>, was formed in 1946. <u>In</u>
(11)   **(12)**
<u>Latin, "mensa" means "table"—symbolic of the group's "round-table" ethic,</u>
(12)
<u>which deems a member's sex, color, age, religion, or educational or social</u>

<u>background as unimportant.</u> According to Mensa's Web site, members

range from "preschoolers to high school dropouts to people with multiple

doctorates. There are welfare [recipients] and . . . millionaires . . . professors

and truck drivers, scientists and firefighters, computer programmers and

farmers, artists, military people, musicians, laborers. . . ."

Can IQ <u>tests</u> adequately measure and score a person's intelligence?
(13)

The fact is, there is no universally accepted definition of "intelligence."

Some professionals <u>assert</u> that intelligence does not apply just to the
(14)
intellect, but <u>to other areas</u> as well, such as emotion and creativity. <u>It's</u>
(15)
<u>clear that people choose to use their intelligence in different ways, and</u>
(16)
<u>no matter what a person's IQ is, he or she has something to offer.</u>

1
  (A) simple predicate
  (B) complete predicate
  (C) dependent clause
  (D) verb phrase

2
  (A) simple sentence
  (B) compound sentence
  (C) complex sentence
  (D) compound-complex sentence

3
  (A) independent clause
  (B) dependent clause
  (C) simple sentence
  (D) complete predicate

4
  (A) gerund phrase
  (B) infinitive phrase
  (C) participial phrase
  (D) verb phrase

5
  (A) complete predicate
  (B) verbal phrase
  (C) verb phrase
  (D) prepositional phrase

6
  (A) gerund phrase
  (B) infinitive phrase
  (C) participial phrase
  (D) verb phrase

7
  (A) simple sentence
  (B) compound sentence
  (C) complex sentence
  (D) compound-complex sentence

8
  (A) gerund phrase
  (B) infinitive phrase
  (C) participial phrase
  (D) verb phrase

9
  (A) independent clause
  (B) dependent clause
  (C) compound sentence
  (D) complete predicate

10
  (A) simple subject
  (B) complete subject
  (C) gerund phrase
  (D) appositive phrase

11
  (A) simple subject
  (B) complete subject
  (C) gerund phrase
  (D) appositive phrase

12
  (A) simple sentence
  (B) compound sentence
  (C) complex sentence
  (D) compound-complex sentence

13
  (A) simple subject
  (B) complete subject
  (C) gerund phrase
  (D) appositive phrase

14
  (A) simple predicate
  (B) complete predicate
  (C) dependent clause
  (D) verb phrase

15
  (A) gerund phrase
  (B) infinitive phrase
  (C) participial phrase
  (D) prepositional phrase

16
  (A) simple sentence
  (B) compound sentence
  (C) complex sentence
  (D) compound-complex sentence

Sentences

Diagramming Sentences

A **graphic diagram** of a sentence is a picture of how the words in that sentence are related and how they fit together to form a complete thought.

760.1 Simple Sentence with One Subject and One Verb

Chris fishes.

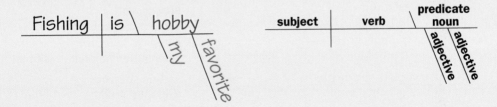

760.2 Simple Sentence with a Predicate Adjective

Fish are delicious.

760.3 Simple Sentence with a Predicate Noun and Adjectives

Fishing is my favorite hobby.

NOTE: When possessive pronouns (*my, his, their, etc.*) are used as adjectives, they are placed on a diagonal line under the word they modify.

760.4 Simple Sentence with an Indirect and Direct Object

My grandpa gave us a trout.

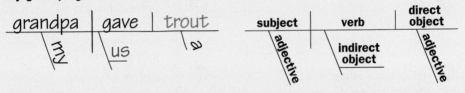

NOTE: Articles (*a, an, the*) are adjectives and are placed on a diagonal line under the word they modify.

Grammar Practice

Sentence Diagramming 1

■ Diagramming Sentences

 Diagram the following sentences.

Example: Wind is powerful.

Wind | is \ powerful

1. Wind turbines generate electricity.

2. This power is a clean energy source.

3. The turbine blades are huge.

4. My uncle made us a small wind turbine.

5. Our neighbors are glad.

6. We give them our excess power.

7. No wind means no power.

8. Wind is supplementary power.

Model

Model the following sentences to practice writing sentences with a direct object and with an indirect object.

Never give a party if you will be the most interesting person there.
—Mickey Friedman

Beauty is in the eye of the beholder, and it may be necessary from time to time to give a stupid or misinformed beholder a black eye.
—Miss Piggy

Sentences

Diagramming Sentences *(continued)*

762.1 Simple Sentence with a Prepositional Phrase

I like fishing by myself.

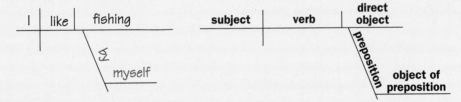

762.2 Simple Sentence with a Compound Subject and Verb

The team and fans clapped and cheered.

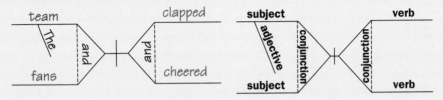

762.3 Compound Sentence

The team scored, and the crowd cheered wildly.

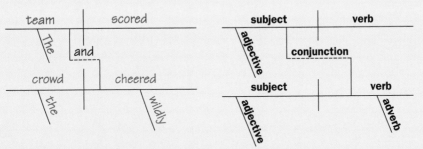

762.4 Complex Sentence with a Subordinate Clause

Before Erin scored, the crowd sat quietly.

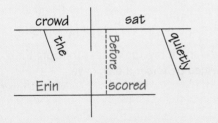

Grammar Practice

Sentence Diagramming 2

■ Diagramming Sentences

 Diagram the following sentences.

Example: The small boy on the swing emitted a squeal of delight.

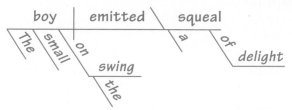

1. After the hawk landed, the rabbit ran across the field.

2. I put three new batteries in the silver flashlight.

3. Gene and Valeria planned and completed the school's mural.

4. My school won the state tournament, and my cousin's school captured third place.

5. The police and firefighters pushed and pulled the damaged crate.

6. All the students were gone, so the janitor locked the door.

7. Although the book was long, everyone wanted a copy.

8. The girl on the snowboard flew down the hill.

Model

Model the following sentences to practice writing compound and complex sentences.

Stay committed to your decisions, but stay flexible in your approach.
　　　　　　　　　　　　　　　　　　　　　—Tom Robbins

The whole world opened to me when I learned to read.
　　　　　　　　　　　　　　　　　　　—Mary McLeod Bethune

Sentences

Credits

Text:

p. 353: Copyright © 2010 by Houghton Mifflin Harcourt Publishing Company. Adapted and reproduced by permission from *The American Heritage College Dictionary,* Fourth Edition.

Photos:

pp. 334, 339 (t), **341** (t), **562, endsheet** ©Ablestock.com/Jupiter; **338** Don Couch/HRW Photo; **339** (b), **340** (b), **583** (t, r) ©Photodisc/Getty Images; **339** (c) ©tbkmedia.de/Alamy; **340** (t) ©Comstock/Getty Images; **341** (b) ©Corbis; **583** (l) ©Photos.com/Jupiter Images.

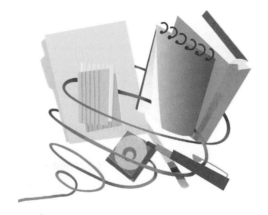

Index

The index will help you find specific information in this textbook. Entries in italics are from the "Using the Right Word" section. The colored boxes will contain information you will use often.

A lot, 678
Abbreviations
  acronyms, 662.1, 662.3
  capitalization of, 652.4
  common, 661
  in correspondence, 660
  initialisms, 662.2, 662.3
  punctuation of, 605.2
Abstract noun, 701.4
Academic vocabulary, 6, 88, 144, 200, 254, 312, 342, 404, 462, 532, 580, 604
Accent marks, 352–353
Accept/except, 678
Acronyms, 662.1, 662.3

Across the curriculum, writing
applied sciences, 443–452
arts, 453–461
math, 432–442
practical writing, 446–447, 450–452, 513–520
science, 405–416
social studies, 417–430

Action, in story development, 318–319
Action verbs, 538, 716.1
Active voice, 722.1
Adapt/adopt, 678
Address, direct, 616.4
Address (correspondence)
  abbreviations, 660
  envelope, 520
  punctuation of, 520, 614.4
Adjective clauses, 540
Adjective forms, 120
Adjective phrases, 540
Adjective series, 541
Adjectives
  articles, 728
  clauses, 540
  comparative, 728.2
  compound, 624.3
  equal, 608.2

forms of, 728.2
phrases, 540
positive, 728.2
predicate, 728.1, 760.2, 760.3
prepositional phrase used
  as, 545, 732.5
proper, 728.1
punctuation of
  compound, 624.3
punctuation of equal, 608.2
superlative, 728.2
types of, 728.1
Adverb props, 543
Adverbs
  answering questions
    with, 542
  beginnings, 542
  comparative, 730.2
  conjunctive, 618.2
  forms of, 730.2
  infinitive phrases as, 742
  -ly ending of, 730.1
  placement of, 542
  positive, 730.2
  prepositional phrases
    as, 545, 732.1, 744
  props, 543
  redundant, 543
  to show degree, 730.1
  to show manner, 730.1
  to show place, 730.1
  to show time, 730.1
  and strong beginning, 542
  superlative, 730.2
  types of, 730
  unnecessary, 543
Affect/effect, 678
Agreement
  "be" verbs, 752.3
  compound subjects, 752.1
  delayed subjects, 752.2
  indefinite pronouns, 754.2
  of pronoun and antecedent,
    756
  of sentence parts, 559, 752
  special cases of, 752
  of subject and verb, 752–754
  unusual word order, 752.2
Aisle/isle, 678

Algebra, writing in, 442
All right, 678
Alliteration, 340
Allusion, 600
Allusion/illusion, 678
Almanac, 351
Already/all ready, 678
Altogether/all together, 680
Among/between, 680
Amount/number, 680
Analogy, 600
Analysis, essay of, 450–451
Analysis, word, 531
Analysis (math problem),
  436–437
Analysis paragraph, 257
Analyzed prompts, 248
Analyzing information, 493,
  497
Analyzing a theme, 255–294
Anecdotes
  as detail, 569
  to illustrate a point, 575
  as writing technique, 600
*Annual/biannual/semiannual/
  biennial/perennial,* 680
Answering an objection, 210
Answers, essay test, 526–529
Antagonists, 322
Antecedents, 704, 756
Anthologies, citing, 381
Anyway/any way, 680
Apostrophes
  in contractions, 628.1
  to express time or amount,
    630.3
  to form certain plurals, 630.4
  to form plural
    possessive, 628.3
  to form singular
    possessive, 628.2
  to show possession in
    compound nouns, 630.2
  to show possession with
    indefinite pronouns, 630.1
  to show shared
    possession, 628.4

Appendix, 349
Applied sciences, writing in the
   comparison-contrast essay,
   448–449
  descriptive essay, 446–447
  essay of analysis, 450–451
  learning log, 445
  practical writing, 452
  problem-solution essay, 452
  process essay, 452
  taking notes, 444
Appositives
  phrases, 742.1
  punctuating, 610.1
Arguments,
  convincing, 209, 219
  pro and con, 249
  statistical, 438–439
Article summary
  math, 434–435
  sample, 484–487
  science, 414–415
Articles
  citing, 381
  finding magazine, 347, 351,
   354

Arts, writing in the
  learning log, 455
  other forms, 461
  prompts for, 456–457
  research report, 458–460
  taking notes, 454

As/like, 688
Ascent/assent, 680
Assessing final copy, 31

Assessment, rubric for
  expository essay, 180–183
  narrative essay, 124–127
  persuasive essay, 234–237
  response to literature,
   290–293
Assessment, self, 70–71
Assessment sheet, 68, 71
Assessment (test prep)
  marking punctuation,
   622–623, 646–647
  mechanics, 670–671
  understanding sentences,
   758–759
  using the parts of speech,
   712–713, 736–737
  using the right word, 698–699

Assignments, writing
  sample planning schedule, 500
  types of, 492
  understanding, 491–500
Assonance, 340
Asterisk (punctuation), 644
Atlas, 351
Audience, 46, 223
Author/responder roles, 56–57
Autobiography, 89–128, 586
Auxiliary verbs, 714.2

B

Bad/badly, 680
Balanced sentence, 51, 283, 750
Bar graphs, 602
Bartlett's Familiar Quotations,
  351
Base/bass, 680
"Basics of Life" list, 583
"Be" verbs
  agreement with subject, 752.3
  as helping verbs, 714.2
  as linking verbs, 714.1
Before-after chart, 139
Beginnings, writing
  cause-effect essay, 149, 159
  comparison-contrast essay,
   449
  essay of analysis, 451
  essay of definition, 186
  historical narrative, 134
  lab reports, 411
  phase autobiography, 102–103
  research reports, 375
  responding to expository
   prompts, 196
  responding to literature, 259,
   268–269
  responding to narrative
   prompts, 140
  responding to persuasive
   prompts, 250
  strategy for great, 595
Beside/besides, 680
Between/among, 680
*Biannual/annual/semiannual/
  biennial/perennial,* 680
Big picture
  in expository writing, 158
  in narrative writing, 102
  in persuasive writing, 212
  in response to literature, 268

Biography, 586
Biology, writing in, 416
Board/bored, 682
Body. *See also* Middle
  paragraphs
  of a business letter, 516
  definition of, 598
  of a paragraph, 563
Body language, 400
Body sentences, 257, 562–563
Book review, 586
Books
  capitalization of titles of,
   650.6
  citing, 381
  parts of, 349
  punctuation of titles of, 634.3,
   636.2
  reference, 347, 350–351
Borrow/lend, 688
Brace (punctuation), 644
Brackets (punctuation)
  around an editorial
   correction, 644.2
  to set off added words, 644.3
  to set off clarifying
   information, 644.1
Brainstorming, 598
Brake/break, 682
Bring/take, 682
Business letters
  addressing envelopes for, 520
  capitalizing parts of, 520
  parts of, 516–517
  tips for, 515

C

Call numbers, 348–349
Can/may, 682
Capital/capitol, 682
Capitalization
  abbreviations, 652.4
  certain religious words, 650.5
  first words, 650.1
  at a glance, 648
  individual letters, 652.2
  organizations, 652.3
  proper nouns and adjectives,
   648.1
  sections of the country, 650.4
  sentences following colons,
   650.3
  sentences in parentheses,
   650.2

titles, 650.6
titles of courses, 652.5
words used as names, 652.1
Career exploration class, writing in, 452
Caret (punctuation), 644
Caricature, 422
Cartoon, editorial, 422–423
Case, noun, 702.3
Cause-effect essays, 145–184
organizer, 155, 588
thesis statement, 155
Cent/sent/scent, 682
Central idea. *See* Themes
Cereal/serial, 682
Character chart, 264
Character sketch, 586
Characters, development of
in plays, 327, 328
in stories, 318
Charts
comparison, 589
details, 97
five W's, 589
ideas, 262
plot, 264
sensory details, 35, 589
T-bar, 35, 195, 249
time line, 35, 195
topics, 132, 152

Checklist, editing
analyzing a theme, 288
cause-effect essay, 178
editorial, 246
expository writing, 192
historical narrative, 136
narrative prompts, 142
phase autobiography, 122
problem-solution essay, 232
research reports, 391
writing plays, 331
Checklist, revising
analyzing a theme, 284
cause-effect essay, 174
creative writing, 320, 331
expository writing, 174, 191
historical narrative, 135
multimedia reports, 403
narrative writing, 135
paragraphs, 579
persuasive writing, 228, 245
phase autobiography, 118
plays, 331

research reports, 388
stories, 320
thesis statement, 594
writing about literature, 284

Chemistry, writing in, 416
Choice (story pattern), 321
Chord/cord, 682
Chose/choose, 682
Chronological order, 571
Cite/site/sight, 694
Citing sources (MLA)
documentation, 381–384
in text, 374
Clarification, words used to show, 593
Classification essay, 416, 452
Classification paragraphs, 573
Classroom skills
critical reading, 473–481
improving vocabulary, 501–512
listening, 463–466
paraphrasing, 483–490
summarizing, 483–490
taking notes, 406, 418, 432, 444, 454, 467–472
taking tests, 521–531
understanding assignments, 491–499
Clauses
adjective, 540, 744.2
adverb, 610.3, 744.2
dependent, 287, 555, 744.1, 744.2
independent, 287, 555, 744.1
introductory, 610.3
noun, 744.2
punctuation of, 608.1, 608.3, 618.1
restrictive, nonrestrictive, 612.2
subordinate, 610.3, 744.1
Cliches, 114
Climax
as part of plot, 314–315
technique for developing, 319
Closing sentences, 257, 562–563, 598
Cluster diagram, 139, 195, 249, 365, 582
Coarse/course, 684
Coherence, 277, 598
Collective nouns, 700.5, 754.1
Colloquialisms, 600

Colons
after a salutation, 620.1
for emphasis, 620.3
to introduce a list, 620.5
to introduce a quotation, 620.4
between numerals indicating time, 620.2
between title and subtitle, 620.6
Combining sentences, 173, 554–555
Comma splices, 556
Commands, 605.1
Commas
after introductory phrases, 610.3
in appositive phrases, 610.1
for clarity or emphasis, 616.5
in complex sentences, 610.1
in compound sentences, 608.1
with dates, 614.1
in direct address, 616.4
to enclose titles or initials, 614.4
with explanatory phrases, 612.1
between independent clauses, 608.1
with introductory word groups, 610.3
with items in a series, 610.2
in numbers, 614.3
with parenthetical elements, 612.1
to separate adjectives, 608.2
to separate contrasted elements, 608.3
to set off appositives, 610.1
to set off dialogue, 616.1
to set off interjections, 616.2
to set off interruptions, 616.3
to set off items in addresses, 614.2
to set off nonrestrictive phrases, 612.2
Common nouns, 701.2
Commonly confused words, 286
Comparative adjectives, 120, 728.2
Comparative adverbs, 730.2
Comparative suffixes, 728.2, 730.2
Comparison-contrast essay, 448–449
Comparison-contrast paragraphs, 574

Comparisons (as details), 570
Complement/compliment, 684
Complete predicates, 740.1
Complete subjects, 738.1
Complex sentences
creating, 555
punctuation of, 610.3, 748.1
and subordinate conjunctions,
555
Complimentary closings, in
business letter, 516
Compound adjectives, 624.3
Compound nouns, 630.2, 654.6
Compound predicates, 740,
762.2
Compound sentences
construction of, 748.1
diagram illustrating, 762.3
Compound subjects
definition of, 738.1
diagram illustrating, 762.2
Compound words
plurals, 654.6
using hyphens to create,
624.1
Comprehension, reading, 531
Computer catalog, 348
Computers
designing with, 76–78
writing with, 33–38
Concepts, abstract, 188
Conclusion, words to show, 593
Conclusions, 395
Concrete nouns, 701.3
Conflict
in plays, 327, 330
in stories, 318, 479
Conjunctions
coordinating, 734.1
correlative, 734.2
to create irony, 546
to create similes, 544
to create tension, 546
examples of, 734
subordinating, 546, 734.3
Conjunctive adverbs, 618.2
Connotation, 280
Consonance, 340
Constructive criticism, 56–57
Content areas
writing in the applied
sciences, 443–452
writing in the arts, 453–461
writing in math, 431–442
writing in science, 405–416

writing in social studies,
417–430
Continual/continuous, 684
Contractions, 558, 628.1
Contrast, words used to
show, 593

Conventions (trait)
expository writing, 136
on language arts tests, 531
multimedia presentation, 403
narrative writing, 120–122
paragraph, 579
persuasive writing, 230–232
plays, 331
research writing, 389–391
response to literature,
286–288
test tips for, 531
understanding, 52

Coordinating conjunctions,
608.1
Copies, tips for making, 28
Copyright page, 349
Correcting. *See* Editing;
Revising
Correction marks, 603
Correlative conjunctions, 734
Counsel/council, 684
Course/coarse, 684
Cover sheet, portfolio, 85, 86
Creative writing
plays, 323–332
poetry, 333–341
stories, 313–322
Crediting sources, 177
Critical reading
fiction, 479–480
nonfiction, 474–478
poetry, 481–482
SQ3R, 474–478
Criticism, constructive, 56–57

D

Dagger (punctuation), 644
Dash (punctuation)
for emphasis, 640.5
to indicate a sudden
break, 640.1
to indicate interrupted
speech, 640.4
to set off an introductory
series, 640.2

to set off parenthetical
material, 640.3
Data storage, 34
Dates, punctuation of, 614.1
Days of the week, capitalization
of, 648.1
Decimal points, 605.3
Declarative sentences, 746.1
Defining a concept, 185–192
Definition diagram, 589
Definition, essay of, 185–192
Definitions
dictionary, 352
as type of detail, 570
Delayed subjects, 738.2, 752.2
Delivering a presentation, 400
Demonstrative pronouns,
704.1, 706.6
Dependent clause, 287, 557
Descriptive essay, 446–447
Descriptive report, 420–421

Descriptive writing
essays, 446–447
lab report, 410–411
paragraph, 565, 572
report, 420–421
in science, 410–411
in social studies, 420–421

Desert/dessert, 684
Design, effective
example of, 77–78
guidelines for, 76
Web site, 80–81
Details
anecdotes, 569, 575, 600
before-after chart, 139
dialogue, 99
chart, 97, 195, 209, 243, 256,
264, 297, 299
cluster, 139, 195, 249
definitions, 570
facts, 43, 569
five W's chart, 139
graphic organizers, 139, 195,
249
list, 90, 188, 195, 249
outline, 305
plot chart for gathering, 264
quotations, 43, 202, 570
reasons, 209, 570
selecting appropriate, 90
sensory, 97, 109
statistics, 43, 569

taking notes, 132, 154, 189
T-bar, 249
time line, 133, 139, 195
topic chart, 132, 262
types of, 16, 43, 97, 569–570
Venn diagram, 195
Details, gathering and
     organizing, 16, 139
expository writing, 154, 189,
     195
narrative writing, 97,
     132–133, 139
persuasive writing, 243
writing about literature, 264
Details chart, 97, 195, 209, 243,
     256, 264, 297, 299
Dewey decimal system,
     347–349
Diagonal (punctuation)
to show a choice, 638.3
when quoting poetry, 638.4
Diagrams. *See also* Graphic
     organizers
definition, 589
graphic elements, 602
line, 589
process-cycle, 589
sentence, 760–763
Venn, 589
Dialogue
definition of, 598
in narrative writing, 99, 112
in a play, 324–326
punctuating, 120, 616.1
in radio script, 332
Dictionary
description of, 351
parts of, 352–353
used to paraphrase, 488
Die/dye, 684
*Different from/
     different than,* 684
Direct address, 616.4
Direct objects, 702, 710.1,
     716.2, 760.4
Direct questions, 606.1
Direct quotations
capitalization of, 650
for emphasis, 265
punctuation of, 632, 634.1
Directories, 351
Discovery (story pattern), 321
Documentation of MLA works-
     cited sources, 381–384
Document-based essays,
     424–430

Double negatives, 558
Double subjects, 231, 558
Draft, creating a first, 18, 134,
     190, 244
Drafting, writing in, 452
Dye/die, 684

E-mail messages
citing, 383
tips for, 518–519
Earth sciences, writing in, 416
Editing
analyzing a theme, 288
expository writing, 175–178,
     192, 198
multimedia presentations,
     403
narrative writing, 119
One Writer's Process, 26–27
persuasive writing, 229, 232
poetry, 337
research writing, 389
rubric for, 66–67, 120–121,
     176–177, 230–231, 286–287
stories, 320
Editing marks, 603
Editorial, 586
Editorial, writing an, 239–246
Editorial cartoons, responding
     to, 422–423
Electronic sources, citing,
     383–384
Elements of fiction, 322
Ellipsis (punctuation)
at the end of a sentence, 642.2
to show a pause, 642.3
to show omitted words, 642.1
Emigrate/immigrate, 686
Emphasis
creating, 541, 593
definition of, 598
using punctuation to show, 53
Encyclopedia, 350
End rhyme, 341
Endings, writing
cause-effect essay, 150
comparison-contrast essay,
     449
developing great, 596
essay of definition, 187
historical narratives, 131, 134
lab reports, 411

phase autobiography, 106
problem-solution essay, 206,
     216
research reports, 380
responding to expository
     prompts, 197
responding to literature, 260,
     268, 272
responding to narrative
     prompts, 141
responding to persuasive
     prompts, 251
Ensure/insure, 688
Enthusiasm in voice, 47
Entry words, on dictionary
     page, 352–353
Envelopes, addressing, 520
Essay of analysis, 450–451
Essay tests, 137–143, 193–199,
     247–253, 295–311

Essays
analysis of a problem,
     450–451
analyzing a theme, 258–294
cause-effect, 148–183
comparison-contrast,
     448–449
definition of, 586
descriptive, 420–421,
     446–447
document-based, 424–430
expository, 185–192
historical narrative, 129–136
narrative, 92–128, 129–136
organization of, 17
persuasive, 204–238,
     239–246
phase autobiography, 92–128
problem-solution, 204–237,
     412–413
response to literature, 258–
     291, 292–293, 300–301
structure, 102, 158, 212, 268

Estimates, written, 436–437
Etymology, 352–353
Evaluating information,
     493–499
Evaluating sources, 345
Evaluating writing, 126–127,
     182–183, 236–237, 292–293
Evaluation form, 87
Exaggeration, 600
Examples
definition of, 43
type of detail, 569

Except/accept, 678

Exclamation points, 605

Exclamatory sentences, 746.1

Expanding sentences, 173, 554

Experiences, writing about.
    See Narrative writing

Explanatory phrases, 612.1

Exposition
    definition of, 598
    as part of plot, 314
    techniques for developing, 319

Expository writing
    analyzing a theme, 255–294
    applied sciences, 446–449
    arts, 453–461
    assessment, writing for, 72
    cause-effect, 145–184, 574
    classification, 573
    comparison-contrast,
        448–449, 574
    defining a concept, 185–192
    e-mail messages, 518–519
    editing, 175–178, 192, 198
    essay, 148–184, 185–192,
        424–430
    math, 436–437
    oral presentations, 393–403
    paragraphs, 147, 566
    practical, 452
    presentations, 179
    prewriting, 151–156, 188,
        194–195
    problem-solution, 412–413
    prompts for, 193–199
    publishing, 179, 192
    revising, 163–174, 191, 198
    rubric for, 180–181
    sample topics, 152, 585
    science, 405–416
    social studies, 417–430
    structure of, 158
    summary, 414–415
    test taking, 193–199
    thesis statements, 155, 164,
        189
    topic sentences, 146, 147, 158
    topics, 152, 585
    traits, 258
    transitions, 214, 592, 593
    warm-up, 146
    writing, 157–162, 190,
        196–197

Extended metaphors, 49, 535

Eyewitness accounts, 586

F

Fables, 586

Facts, 43, 569

Facts About the Presidents, 351

Facts on File, 351

Falling action, 314–315

Fantasy, 586

Farther/further, 684

Favorites function, Web
    browser, 35

Fewer/less, 684

Fiction
    critical reading, 479
    elements of, 322
    reacting to, 479–480

Figurative language, 598

Figures of speech, 114, 340

Fill-in-the-blank tests, 525

First-person point of view,
    322

First-person pronouns, 708.2

First word, capitalizing, 650.1

Five W's and H
    chart, 139
    key to listening, 464
    part of SQ3R technique,
        474–477

Flair/flare, 686

Flashback, 600

Fluency, sentence. See
    Sentence fluency (trait)

Focus statement. *See* Thesis
    statements

Focus (thesis), definition of, 598

Focusing your topic, 42–43,
    164, 188

Foreign words, punctuation
    of, 636.4

Foreshadowing, 600

Foreword, 349

Format
    business letter, 517
    practical writing, 518–519

Forms of writing
    analysis of a problem,
        436–437
    analyzing a theme, 255–294
    in the applied sciences, 452
    in the arts, 461
    business letter, 513–517, 520
    cause-effect essay, 145–184

comparison-contrast essay,
    448–449
creative writing, 313–342
defining a concept, 185–192
definition of, 586–587
descriptive essay, 446–447
descriptive report, 420–421
document-based essay,
    424–430
e-mail, 518–519
editorial, 239–246
editorial cartoon, response to,
    422–423
essay of definition, 186–187
expository, 145–193
historical narrative, 129–136
lab report, 410–411
learning log, 408–409, 419,
    433, 445, 455
in math, 442
narrative, 89–137
oral presentation, 393–401
personal narrative, 89–128
persuasive, 201–254
plays, 323–332
poetry, 333–341
problem-solution essay,
    412–413
research report, 355–392,
    458–460
in science, 416
in social studies, 420, 422,
    424
statistical analysis, 438–439
stories, 313–322
summaries, 414–415,
    434–435, 484–487

Fractions, punctuation
    of, 626.1

Fragments, sentence, 557

Free verse, 334–337

Freewriting, 15, 35, 96, 153,
    582

Future perfect tense, 720.1

Future tense, 718.4

G

Gathering details. *See* Details

Gathering grid, 367

Gender
    agreement in, 756
    of nouns, 702.2
    of pronouns, 710.2, 756.2

General categories list, 152
General nouns, 534
Generalization, 598
Geographic names,
    capitalization of, 648.1
Geology, writing in, 416
Geometry, writing in, 442
Gerund phrases, 726.1, 742.1
Gerunds, 726.1
Giving credit, 363, 369, 370,
    374, 381–384
Goals
    previewing, 14
    understanding, 64–65, 92,
      148, 204, 258
Good/well, 686
Grammar, 598, *See also*
    Conventions
Grammar checker, 38
Graphic elements, 76–78, 602

Graphic organizers
    "Basics of Life" list, 583
    before-after chart, 139
    cause-effect, 155, 572, 588
    chronological order, 35, 571,
      588
    cluster diagram, 132, 139,
      195, 365, 582
    comparison-contrast, 195, 589
    definition diagram, 589
    details list, 97
    evaluation-collection grid,
      588
    for expository response, 195
    five W's, 139, 589
    gathering grid, 367
    ideas chart, 262
    line diagram, 299, 573, 589
    lists, 155, 189, 327, 328, 335
    for narrative response, 139
    outline, 156, 305, 356, 372
    picture diagram, 602
    plot chart, 264
    problem-solution web, 588
    process-cycle diagram, 589
    quick list, 195, 249
    reasons chart, 209
    for response to literature, 297
    for response to nonfiction
      prompt, 305
    sensory details, 35, 335, 589
    software table function used
      to create, 35
    specific details, 139

    time line, 35, 139, 195, 365,
      571, 588
    topic list, 188
    Venn diagram, 195, 574, 589

Graphs, 435, 602
Grid, gathering, 367
Group skills. *See* Peer response
Growth portfolios, 84
Guidelines
    business letters, 515
    connecting paragraphs in
      essays, 577
    note cards, 396
    note taking, 468
    peer responding, 56–57
    U.S. Postal Service, 520
    writing assignments, 568

H

Habits, good writing, 8
Heading
    business letter, 516
    e-mail messages, 518
Heal/heel, 686
Healthful/healthy, 686
Hear/here, 686
Heard/herd, 686
Helping verbs, 714.2, 752.3
Historical fiction, 586
Historical narrative, 129–136
Historical periods,
    capitalization of, 648.1
Hole/whole, 686
Holidays, capitalization of,
    648.1
Hooks, pronouns used as, 536
Hyperbole, 340, 600
Hyphens
    in compound words, 624.1
    to create new words, 624.2
    to divide a word, 626.5
    to form an adjective, 624.3
    to join letters and words,
      624.4
    to join numbers, 626.3
    between numbers and
      fractions, 626.1
    to prevent confusion, 626.4
    in special series, 626.2

I

Ideas (trait)
    definition of, 280, 598
    expository writing, 148, 152,
      164–165, 174, 180–181, 191
    focusing on, 20
    multimedia presentation, 403
    narrative writing, 92, 97,
      108–109, 118, 124–125,
      135
    paragraph, 579
    persuasive writing, 204, 208,
      218–219, 228, 234–235,
      242, 245
    plays, 331
    poetry, 337
    research writing, 388, 403
    response to literature,
      258, 263, 274–275, 284,
      290–291
    revising for, 164–165,
      218–219
    selecting effective, 34
    understanding, 42
    writing prompts, 584–585

Ideas chart, 262
Idioms, understanding,
    672–677
Idle/idol, 686
Illusion/allusion, 678
Illustrations, 352, 353
Immigrate/emigrate, 686
Imperative mood, 724.1
Imperative sentences, 746.1
Imply/infer, 686
Indefinite pronouns, 630.1,
    704.1, 706.4, 754.2
Independent clauses
    in compound and complex
      sentences, 555
    joining, 608.1, 618.1, 734.1
    punctuation of, 608.1, 618.1
Indicative mood, 724.1
Index, 349
Indirect objects, 702, 710.1,
    716.2, 760.4
Indirect questions, 606.1
Infer/imply, 686
Infinitive phrases, 554, 726.2,
    742.1
Information
    analyzing, 493, 497
    applying, 493, 496

evaluating, 345, 493, 499
giving credit for, 369
primary sources, 344
recalling, 493, 494
secondary sources, 344
synthesizing, 493, 498
understanding, 493–495
Input, data, 34
Initialisms, 662.2, 662.3
Initials, punctuation of, 614.4
Inside address, in business letter, 516
Insure/ensure, 688
Intensive pronouns, 704.1, 706.1
Interactive report. *See* Oral presentations
Interjections
definition of, 734
punctuation of, 605.4, 616.2
Internal rhyme, 341
Internet
citing sources on, 383
creating your own Web site, 80–81
publishing on, 79–81
using for research, 346
Interpreting a story, 258–294
Interrogative pronouns, 704.1, 706.4
Interrogative sentences, 746.1
Interruptions, punctuation of, 616.3, 640.4
Interview, 586
Intransitive verbs, 716.1
Introductions, 395
Introductory clauses, punctuation of, 121, 610.3
Introductory phrases, punctuation of, 121, 553, 610.3
Irony, 546, 600
Irregular verbs, 720.2
Italics (underlining)
for foreign words, 636.4
on handwritten and printed material, 636.1
for special uses, 636.3
in titles, 636.2
It's/its, 688

Jargon, 598

Journal writing, 4, 5, 35, 586
Juxtaposition, 601

Key words
in essay tests, 526
in expository prompts, 194
in literature prompts, 296, 302
in persuasive prompts, 248
for classroom notes, 468
for taking tests, 526
for understanding writing assignments, 493, 500
Keyboard, computer, 34
Knew/new, 688
Know/no, 688

Lab report, 410–411
Language arts tests, 531
Languages, capitalization of, 648.1
Later/latter, 688
Lay/lie, 688
Lead/led, 688
Leaders (punctuation), 644
Learn/teach, 688
Learning log
applied sciences, 445
the arts, 455
math, 433
science, 408–409
social studies, 419
Leave/let, 688
Lend/borrow, 688
Less/fewer, 684
Letters (correspondence)
business, 514
envelopes for, 520
parts of, 516, 517
Letters (in the alphabet)
capitalization of, 652.2
joined to a word, 624.4
punctuation of plural, 630.4, 656.3
Levels of thinking, 493–499
Library resources
call numbers, 349
computer catalog, 348
Readers' Guide, 351, 354

reference materials, 350–353
using, 347–354
Life list, basics of, 583
Like/as, 688
Limiting the subject, 599
Line breaks, in poetry, 336, 341
Line diagrams, 589
Line graphs, 602
Linking verbs, 714.2, 752.3
Linking words. *See* Transition words and phrases
List paragraphs, 576
Listener, role of the, 57
Listening skills, 464, 466
Lists
"Basics of Life," 583
concepts, 188
general categories, 152
punctuation of, 620.5
quick, 195, 243, 249
topics, 188
Literary analysis, 587
Literary response, test tips for, 531
Literary terms, 322
Literature
elements of fiction, 322
response to, 255–311
forms of, 586–587
Literature connections, 92, 131, 148, 187, 204, 241, 258, 317, 326, 334
Literature prompts, analyzing, 296
Loaded words, 599
Local color, 601
Logic, 599
Loose sentences, 553, 750.1
Lunes, 339

Magazines
citing, 382
in libraries, 347, 351, 354
Readers' Guide to Periodical Literature, 351
Main character
in plays, 327
in story development, 318
Main idea, finding, 486
Margins, page, 76–77, 357

Math, writing in
  article summary, 434–435
  learning log, 433
  other forms, 442
  problem analysis, 436–437
  prompts, 440–441
  statistical argument, 438–439
  taking notes, 432
  written estimate, 436–437

May/can, 682
Mechanics, checking, 648–677
Medal/meddle, 688
Meeting minutes, guidelines for, 472
Memory, computer, 34
Metal/mettle, 690
Metaphors, 340, 601
  advanced, 535
  extended, 49, 535
  verbal, 539
Middle paragraphs, writing
  cause-effect essay, 160–161
  comparison-contrast essay, 449
  editorial, 240, 244
  essay of definition, 186
  historical narrative, 130, 134
  lab report, 411
  phase autobiography, 104–105
  problem-solution essay, 205, 212–213
  research reports, 376–379
  responding to expository prompts, 197
  responding to literature, 259, 266, 268, 270–271
  responding to narrative prompts, 140
  responding to persuasive prompts, 250
Miner/minor, 690
MLA research report, 355–392
  works-cited source documentation, 381–384
Modeling paragraphs, 575
Modeling sentences, 560
Modes of writing. *See* Descriptive writing; Expository writing; Narrative writing; Persuasive writing
Money, numerals used for, 658.4
Monitor, computer, 34

Months, capitalization of, 648.1
Mood, of a verb, 724.1
Moral/morale, 690
Mouse, computer, 34
Multimedia report script, 402
Multiple-choice tests, 525
Myth, 586

Names, capitalization of, 648.1, 652.1
Narrative prompts, 137–143
Narrative suspense, 98

Narrative writing
  assessment, 137–143
  essay, 92–128, 129–136
  evaluating, 126–127
  historical narrative, 129–136
  paragraph, 91, 564
  personal narrative, 126–127
  phase autobiography, 89–128
  prompts, 143
  reflecting on, 148
  rubric for, 124–125
  short stories, 313–322
  structure of, 102
  for tests, 143
  topics for, 96, 585
  traits of, 92
  transitions in, 103, 592

Narrowing a subject, 146
Nationalities, capitalization of, 648.1
Necessary events, 108
Negative contractions, 558
Negative words, 558
Negatives, double, 558
New York Times Index, 351
Newspapers, citing, 382
Nominative case, 702.3
Nonrestrictive clause, 612.2
Nonrestrictive phrase, punctuation of, 612.2
Note cards
  avoiding plagiarism, 369
  guidelines, 396
  for oral presentations, 396–397
  organizing details, 154
  paraphrase, 16, 154

  recording questions and answers, 368
  recording quotations, 16, 154, 368–369
  for research report, 368–369
  sample, 154, 397
Notebook, writer's, 4–5
Notes, reviewing, 470
Notes, taking. *See also* Critical reading
  applied sciences, 444
  the arts, 454
  general classroom, 406, 418, 464, 466–469, 470
  general reading, 471, 477
  math, 432
  meeting minutes, 472
  reading, 407, 471
  research, 368–369
  science, 406, 407
  social studies, 418
  source, 370
Nouns
  abstract, 701.4
  cases of, 702.3
  classes of, 700
  collective, 656.4, 701.5, 754.1
  common, 701.2
  compound, 630.2, 654.6
  concrete, 701.3
  direct objects, 702.3
  forms of, 702
  gender of, 702.2
  general, 534, 700.1
  indirect objects, 702.3
  nominative case of, 702.3
  number of, 702.1
  object of a preposition, 732.1
  objective case of, 702.3
  phrase, 742.1
  plural forms with singular meanings, 752
  plurals of, 654, 656
  possessive case of, 702.3
  predicate, 702.3, 760.3
  proper, 701.1
  singular, 702.1
  specific, 115, 534
Novel, 587
Number
  of nouns, 702.1
  of pronouns, 708.1, 756.1
Number, agreement in
  pronoun-antecedent, 756
  subject-verb, 754
Number/amount, 680

Numbers
numerals only, 658.2
numerals or words, 658.1
punctuating, 605.3, 614.3, 626.1, 626.3
time and money, 658.4
words only, 658.3
Numerical prefixes, 504

O

Object of a preposition, 702.3, 710.1, 732.1, 762.1
Objections, identifying and countering, 210
Objective case, 702.3
Objective tests, 524–525
Objects, direct/indirect, 702, 710.1, 716.2, 760.4
One Writer's Process, 13–32
Online publishing, 79–81
Online services, 383
Onomatopoeia, 341
Open-ended assignments, 492
Opening paragraphs, 102
Opening sentences, 257
Opinion statements, 17, 224, 243
Opposing views essay, 416
Opposition, planning for, 249
Oral presentations
body language used in, 400
note cards for, 396–397
parts of, 396
planning, 394
practice tips, 399
reworking written report for, 395
visual aids used in, 398
voice, 400
Order, chronological, 571

Organization (trait)
expository writing, 166–167
narrative writing, 110–111
paragraphs, 571–574, 577
patterns of, 271, 571
persuasive writing, 220–221
research writing, 386–387
response to literature, 276–277
stories, 314, 319
understanding, 44–45

Organization, patterns of

cause and effect, 572
chronological, 571
classification, 573
comparison, 574
Organizations, capitalization of, 652.3
Organizers, graphic, 139, 588–591
Outlines
sentence, 156, 305, 356, 372, 591
topic, 17, 590
Output, data, 34
Overstatement, 601
Oxymoron, 601

P

Page design, 76–78
Paradox, 601
Paragraph symbol, 644.3
Paragraph traits checklist, 579
Paragraphs
body, 563
checklist for, 579
closing sentence, 563
coherence in, 598
connecting, 577
details in, 569–570
guidelines for, 568
modeling, 575
parts of, 562–563
summary, 485
topic sentence, 563
Paragraphs, types of
classification, 573
cause-effect, 572
comparison-contrast, 574
descriptive, 565, 572
expository, 147, 566
list, 576
narrative, 91, 564
persuasive, 203, 567
response to literature, 257
Parallelism, 601
Paraphrase
to avoid plagiarism, 369
strategies for, 488–490
Parentheses
with full sentences, 638.2
to set off explanatory material, 638.1
Participial phrases, 554, 726.3, 742.1

Participles, 726.3
Parts of a book, nonfiction, 349
Parts of speech, 700–735
adjectives, 700.4, 728
adverbs, 700.5, 730
conjunctions, 700.7, 734
interjections, 734
nouns, 700.1, 701–702
prepositions, 700.6, 732
pronouns, 700.2, 704–710
verbals, 726
verbs, 700.3, 714–724
Passed/past, 690
Passive voice, 722.2
Past participles, 720.2
Past perfect tense, 720.1, 720.2
Past tense, 718.4
Patterns, sentence, 550, 760, 762
Patterns, story, 321
Patterns of organization, 571–574
Peace/piece, 690
Peak/peek/pique, 690
Pedal/peddle/petal, 690
Peer response
author's role in, 56
for oral presentation, 401
responder's role in, 57
revising using, 23
sample sheet, 22, 60
traits, 58–59
Perennial/annual/biannual, 680
Perfect tenses, 720.1
Period, 605
Periodic sentences, 51
Periodicals
citing, 382
Readers' Guide to Periodical Literature, 351
as research sources, 347
Periodicals index, 351, 354
Person, 708.2
Personal/personnel, 690
Personal details, 97
Personal journals, 4–5
Personal narratives, 89–128
definition of, 586
details in, 97
Personal portfolios, 84
Personal pronouns, 704.1, 706.1
Personification, 340, 601
Persuasive prompts, 247–252

Persuasive writing
assessment writing, 247–253
beginnings, 213
editing, 230–232
endings, 216
essay, 213, 216
evaluating, 236–237
objections, handling, 210
paragraphs, 203, 567
presentation, 233
prewriting, 207–210
problem-solution, 201–238
process (cycle) diagram, 589
prompts, 247–252
publishing, 233
quotations used in, 202–203
reasons chart, 209
revising, 217–228
rubric for, 234–235
sample topics, 208, 585
structure, 212
traits of, 204
transitions, 220, 592–593
warm-up, 202

Phase autobiography, 89–128
Phrases
absolute, 744
adjective, 540
adverb, 742.1
appositive, 610.1, 742.1
combining with, 554, 555
explanatory, 612.1
gerund, 726, 742.1
infinitive, 554, 726.2, 742.1
introductory, 610.3
noun, 742
participial, 554, 726.3, 742.1
prepositional, 732.1, 744
punctuation of, 610.3
restrictive, nonrestrictive,
612.2
types of, 742.1
verb, 742, 744
verbal, 742.1
Physics, writing in, 416
Pie graphs, 602
Pivot points, 547
Plagiarism, avoiding, 202–203,
369, 381–384
Plain/plane, 690
Planning writing time, 500
Plays, 323–332, 586
Plot, 274, 314–315, 322
Plot chart, 264

Plot line, 98, 314
Plurals
collective nouns, 656.4
compound nouns, 654.6
irregular spelling, 656.2
most nouns, 654.1
musical terms, 654.4
nouns ending in *f* or *fe,* 656.1
nouns ending in *ful,* 654.5
nouns ending in *o,* 654.4
nouns ending in *sh, ch, x, s,*
and *z,* 654.2
nouns ending in *y,* 654.3
pronouns, 756.1
punctuation of, 630.4
subjects, 752, 754
verbs, 718.1, 722.1, 752, 754
words discussed as
words, 656.3
Poem, 586
Poetic license, 599
Poetic technique, 336, 340–341
Poetry
autobiographical 334–337
critical reading, 481
figures of speech, 340
free verse, 334–337
lunes, 339
quoting, 638.4
reacting to, 481–482
skeltonic verse, 338
sounds of, 340–341
special techniques, 340–341
Point of view, 278, 322, 537, 599
Poor/pour/pore, 692
Portfolios, 84–87
Position essay, 416
Positive adjectives, 120, 728.2
Positive adverbs, 730.2
Possessive nouns, 702.3
Possessive pronouns, 630.1,
710.1
Possessives, forming, 628.2,
630.2
Postal guidelines, 520, 660.2
Practical writing,
business letters, 513–517, 520
e-mail messages, 518, 519
forms of, 452
Predicate adjectives, 728.1,
760.2, 760.3
Predicate nouns, 702.3, 760.3
Predicate of a sentence
complete, 740.1
compound, 740.1

direct object as part of, 740.1
simple, 740.1
understood, 740.2
Preface, 349
Prefixes
basic, 503–504
hyphenated, 624.2
numerical, 504
Prepositions
to create similes, 544
examples of common, 732
followed by object, 732.1
object of, 702.3, 710.1,
732.1, 762.1
Prepositional phrases, 545,
732, 744
Present perfect tense, 720.1
Present tense, 718.4

Presentations
expository, 179
multimedia, 402–403
narrative, 123
oral, 393–401
persuasive, 246
research report, 392
response to literature, 289
tips for, 123

Prewriting
descriptive, 150
expository, 151–156, 188,
194–195
keys to effective, 95, 151, 207,
261, 364
narrative, 95–100, 132–133
paragraph, 568
persuasive, 207–210
poetry, 335–336
research writing, 364–372
response to literature,
261–266, 296–297
stories, 318
Primary sources, 344
Principal/principle, 692
Printer, computer, 34
Problem-solution essay,
201–238
organizer, 588
quotations in, 202–203
writing guidelines, 412–413
Process, understanding
the writing, 7–12
Process essay, 416, 589
Process paper, 587
Profile, 587

Programs, software, 34
Prompts
  analyzed, 248
  as thesis statement, 526–528
  as topic sentence, 527
  understanding, 526–528
  to select topics, 584–585
Prompts, responding to
  in the arts, 456–457
  essay response to, 528
  expository, 193–199
  literature, 295–311
  math, 440–441
  narrative, 137–143
  nonfiction, 304–305, 308
  persuasive, 247–252
  planning, 249
Pronoun-antecedent
  agreement, 230, 289
Pronouns
  agreement with antecedent,
    230, 287, 756
  case of, 710.1
  classes of, 704.1
  compound, 704
  demonstrative, 704, 706.6
  gender of, 710.2, 756.2
  indefinite, 630.1, 704, 706.4,
    754.2
  intensive, 704, 706.1
  interrogative, 704, 706.5
  number of, 708.1, 710, 756.1
  object, 710.1
  person of, 708.2, 710
  personal, 706.1, 708, 710
  in persuasive writing, 537
  phrasal, 704
  plural, 708.1, 756.1
  possessive, 630.1, 710.1
  reciprocal, 704, 706.3
  reflexive, 704
  relative, 704, 706.2, 754.3
  shifting person of, 537
  singular, 708.1, 756.1
  subject, 710.1
  types of, 704.1, 706
  used to hook readers, 536
Pronunciation, 352–353
Proofreader's guide, 605–763
  checking for mechanics,
    648–663
  improving spelling, 664–669
  marking punctuation, 605–647
  understanding idioms,
    672–677
  understanding sentences,
    738–757

  using the parts of speech,
    700–735
  using the right word, 678–697
Proofreading marks, 603
Proper adjectives, 728.1
Proper nouns, 534, 701.1
Proposals, 586
Props, adverb, 543
Prose, 599
Protagonist, 322
Publishing
  expository writing, 179, 192
  ideas, 75
  online, 79
  persuasive writing, 233
  places to publish, 82
  poetry, 337
  research writing, 392
  response to literature, 289
  tips, 74–75, 79
Pun, 601
Punctuation
  apostrophe, 628, 630
  bracket, 644
  colon, 620
  comma, 608, 610, 612, 614,
    616
  conventions, 605–647
  dash, 640
  diagonal, 638.3, 638.4
  ellipses, 642
  exclamation point, 605.4
  hyphen, 624, 626
  italics, 636
  parentheses, 638
  period, 605
  question mark, 606
  quotation marks, 632, 634
  semicolon, 618
  symbols, 644
  underlining, 636
Purpose, 221

Q

Quest (story pattern), 321
Question mark, 606
Questions, direct and indirect,
  606.1
Quick list, 195, 243, 249, 591
Quiet/quit/quite, 692
Quotation marks
  for long quotations, 632.3

  placement of punctuation
    when using, 632.2
  to punctuate titles, 634.3
  within quotations, 634.1
  to set off direct quotation,
    632.1
  for special words, 634.2
Quotations
  citing direct, 265, 286, 650
  definition of, 43
  direct, 265
  effective use of, 202–203, 265,
    274
  in persuasive writing, 244
  problems to avoid, 597
  punctuation of, 176, 632, 634.1
  in research reports, 369
  sample of, 16
  strategies for using, 597
  as type of detail, 570
  used to strengthen voice, 202
  as writing prompt, 584
Quote/quotation, 369, 692

R

Radio script, 332
Rambling sentences, 226, 557
Readers' *Guide to Periodical*
  Literature, 347, 351, 354
Reading comprehension, test
  tips for, 531
Reading strategies, 473–482
Real/really/very, 692
Reasons to write, 1–5
  to explain or justify, 570
  reasons chart, 209
Recalling information, 493, 494
Reciprocal pronouns, 704.1,
  706.3
Redundant adverbs, 543
Reference books, 350–353
Reference materials, citing,
  374
Reflecting on your writing, 32
Reflexive pronouns, 704.1,
  706.1
Relative pronouns, 704.1,
  706.2, 754.3
Religions, capitalization of,
  648.1
Repetition, in poetry, 341
Reports
  descriptive, 420–421
  lab, 410–411

MLA research, 355–392
multimedia, 402–403
oral, 393–401
research, 458–460, 587
Request, writing an e-mail,
518, 519

Research reports
in the arts, 458–459
beginning, 375
checklist for, 388, 391
definition of, 586
editing, 389–392
ending, 380
gathering grid used for, 367
library skills, 347–354
note cards, 368
outline, 356, 372
plagiarism, 369
presentation, 392
prewriting, 364–372
primary and secondary
sources, 344
publishing, 392
revising, 385–388
title page of, 356
topics for, 365
works cited in, 363
writing, 373–384
Research sources
citing, 374
documenting, 381–384
evaluating, 344–346

Resolution, 315
Respectful voice, 223
Responding, peer, 55–60
Response
essay, 529
one-paragraph, 528

Response to literature
analysis paragraph, 257
analyzing a theme, 255–294
assessment writing, 295–311
editing, 285–288
opening paragraph in, 269
planning, 297
plot chart, 264
prewriting, 256, 261–266
prompts, 296, 297, 298, 302,
304, 308
publishing, 289
reflecting on your writing, 294
response essay, 255–294
revising, 273–284

rubric for, 290–291
structure, 268
techniques for ending, 272
thesis statement, 266, 276
traits of, 258
warm up, 256
writing, 267–272

Restrictive phrases/clauses,
535, 612.2
Reversal (story pattern), 321
Review sheet, 166
Revising
checklists for, 118, 135, 174,
191, 245, 284, 320, 331,
388, 579
keys to effective, 107, 163,
217, 273, 385
multimedia
presentations, 403
paragraphs, 568, 579
peer response sheet, 22–23
poetry, 337
for repetition, 171
research writing, 385–388
responding to literature, 276
responding to prompts, 198
rubric for, 66–67, 108–118,
164–174, 218–228, 274, 284
stories, 320
using STRAP questions, 198
Revising for ideas (trait)
expository writing, 164–165
narrative writing, 108–109
persuasive writing, 218–219
response to literature,
274–275
Revising for organization
(trait)
expository writing, 166–167
narrative writing, 110–111
persuasive writing, 220–221
response to literature,
276–277
Revising for sentence
fluency (trait)
expository writing, 172–173
narrative writing, 116–117
persuasive writing, 226–227
response to literature,
282–283
Revising for voice (trait)
expository writing, 168–169
narrative writing, 112–113
persuasive writing, 222–223
response to literature,
278–279

Revising for word choice (trait)
expository writing, 170–171
narrative writing, 114–115
persuasive writing, 224–225
response to literature,
280–281
Rhyme, 341
Rhythm, 336, 341
Right/write/wright/rite, 692
Right word, using, 678–699
Ring/wring, 692
Rising action
as part of plot, 315
technique for developing, 319
Rite of passage (story
pattern), 321
Root words, 506–512
Rubrics
evaluating short stories, 322
expository writing, 180–181
narrative writing, 124–125
persuasive writing, 234–235
response to literature,
290–291
understanding, 62
using, 61–72
Run-on sentences, 556

Salutation (in business letter),
516
Sample topics, 585
Scene/seen, 692
Schedule, assignment, 500

Science, writing in
article summary, 414–415
lab report, 410–411
learning log, 408–409
other forms, 416
problem-solution essay,
412–413
taking notes, 406–407

Science fiction, 586
Script, radio, 332
Seam/seem, 692
Search engines, 346
Second-person point of view,
322
Second-person pronouns,
708.2
Secondary sources, 344

Section symbol
(punctuation), 644
Selecting a topic. *See*
Topics, selecting
Self-assessment
expository writing, 183
narrative writing, 126–127
persuasive writing, 236–237
response to literature,
293–294
sample, 31, 71
*Semiannual/annual/biannual/
biennial/perennial*, 680
Semicolon
with conjunctive
adverbs, 618.2
to join independent
clauses, 618.1
to separate groups that
contain commas, 618.3
Sensory chart, 35, 335
Sensory details, 97, 109, 565
Sentence agreement, 559
Sentence combining, 554
Sentence construction, 748.1
Sentence diagrams, 760–763
Sentence errors, 556–558

Sentence fluency (trait)
expository writing, 172–173
long/short sentences used
for, 117
persuasive writing, 226–227
research writing, 388
response to literature,
282–283
revising for, 172–173,
226–227, 282–283
understanding, 50–51
varied sentence types used
for, 226–227

Sentence fragments, 557
Sentence length, 117, 551–552
Sentence modeling, 560
Sentence outlines, 356, 372,
591
Sentence parts, 738, 740,
742, 744, 752
Sentence patterns, 550
Sentence problems, 556–558
Sentence starters, 15, 96, 242
Sentence style, 51, 549–560
Sentence variety, 50, 116–117,
227, 283, 746, 552–553
Sentences

arrangement of, 750.1
combining, 554
constructing, 738–744
expanding, 173, 554
punctuation of, 605–645
subject-verb agreement, 752,
754
Sentences, types of
balanced, 51, 283, 750.1
complete, 738
complex, 748.1, 762.4
compound, 748.1, 762.3
compound-complex, 748.1
conditional, 746.1
cumulative, 552, 750.1
declarative, 746.1
exclamatory, 746.1
imperative, 746.1
interrogative, 746.1
long, 117, 552
loose, 553, 750.1
periodic, 51, 750.1
problem, 556–558
rambling, 226, 557
run-on, 556
short, 117, 282, 551–552
simple, 748.1, 760–762
stylish, 560
topic, 146, 297, 563, 599
Series, adjective, 541
Series, punctuation of
commas, 610.2
hyphens, 626.2
semicolons, 618.3
Set/sit, 692
Setting in story development,
318
Short story, 313–322, 587
Showcase portfolios, 84
Sight/cite/site, 694
Signature, in letter, 516
Similes, 340, 544, 601
Simple predicate, 740.1
Simple sentence, 748.1, 760–762
Simple subject, 738.1
Singular nouns, 702.1
Singular pronouns, 708.1, 756.1
Singular subjects, 652.1, 652.4
Singular verbs, 722.1
Sit/set, 692
Site/sight/cite, 694
Skeltonic verse, 338
Slang, 601
Slash (punctuation), 644

Social studies, writing in
document-based essay,
424–430
editorial cartoon, 422–423
learning log, 419
taking notes, 418

Software, computer, 34, 36–38
Sole/soul, 694
Solutions, supporting, 209, 219
Sounds of poetry, 340
Sources
citing, 177, 363, 369, 374,
381–384
electronic, 346
evaluating, 345
library, 347
primary, 344
recording research, 370
secondary, 344
Spacing (design element), 76–77
Speaking and listening skills,
463–466
Specific assignments, 492
Specific details, 563
Specific nouns, 115, 534
Specific verbs, 538
Speech, figures of, 340,
598–601
Speech, interrupted, 640.4
Speech, parts of, 533–548,
700–737
Speech skills, 393–401
Spell-checker, 38
Spelling
commonly misspelled words,
666–667
dictionary, 352
irregular plurals, 656.2
rules, 664
Splice, comma, 556
SQ3R critical reading strategy,
474–478
Stage diagram, 329
State writing tests. *See* Tests
Statements
opinion, 17
sentence, 746
Stationary/stationery, 694
Statistical argument, 438–439
Statistics (details), 43, 218, 569
Steal/steel, 694
Step-by-step organization. *See*
Chronological order

Story patterns, 321
Story writing, 98, 313–322
STRAP questions
  expository writing, 194
  narrative writing, 138, 142
  persuasive writing, 248, 252
Strong verbs, 48
Structure, essay, 102, 158, 212, 268
Student response sheet. *See* Peer response

Study skills
  listening and speaking, 465, 466
  taking notes, 467–472
  taking tests, 521–531
  understanding assignments, 491–500
  vocabulary, 501–512

Style
  defined, 599
  focusing on, 24, 25
  sentence, 51, 549–560
Stylus, computer, 34
Subject, limiting the, 599
Subject of a sentence
  complete, 738.1
  compound, 738.1, 752.1
  delayed, 738.2, 752.2
  double, 231, 558
  plural, 752, 754
  simple, 738.1
  singular, 652.1, 652.4
  understood, 740.2
Subject noun, 702.3
Subject pronoun, 710.1
Subject-verb agreement, 718, 752, 754
Subject vs. theme, 256
Subjects, capitalization of school, 652.5
Subjunctive mood, 724.1
Subordinate clause, 610.3, 744.1
Subordinating conjunction, 546, 734.3
Suffixes, 505
Summarizing, guidelines for, 484–487
Summary
  defined, 586
  guidelines, 484–487
  math article, 434–435
  paragraph, 485

  sample, 485
  science article, 414–415
Superlative adjectives, 120, 321, 728.2
Superlative adverbs, 730.2
Supporting details. *See* Details
Surveys, 344
Suspense, narrative, 98
Syllable divisions, 352–353
Symbol (writing technique), 601
Symbols, editing and proofreading. *See* inside back cover
Syntax, 599
Synthesizing information, 493, 498

T

Table function, software, 35
Table of contents, 85, 349
Tables, 602
Take/bring, 682
Tall tale, 586
Teach/learn, 688
Technical writing. *See* Practical writing
Technique
  poetry, 340–341
  writing, 600–601
Tenses, verb, 538, 718.3–720.2, 718.4, 720.1
Tension, creating, 546
Terms, writing, 598–599

Test-prep cycle, 522
Test-taking skills, 521–531
Test tips
  essay, 526–529
  expository writing, 193–199
  general, 521–531
  language arts, 531
  narrative writing, 137–143
  persuasive writing, 247–253
Tests
  essay, 137–143, 193–199, 247–253, 295–311
  fill-in-the-blank, 525
  matching, 524
  multiple-choice, 525
  narrative writing, 137–143
  objective, 524–525

  persuasive writing, 247–253
  preparing for, 522
  responding to literature on, 295–311
  standardized, 530–531
  true/false, 524

Than/then, 694
That/which, 612, 696
Their/there/they're, 694
Themes
  analyzing, 255–293
  in critical reading, 479
  defined, 256, 322, 599
  identifying, 263
  subjects vs., 256
Thesaurus, 488
Thesis statements
  to analyze a theme, 266
  checklist for, 594
  defined, 599
  examples of, 164
  in expository writing, 155, 164, 189
  forming, 17, 594
  nonfiction prompt, 305
  in research reports, 371
  in response to literature, 266, 274, 299, 305
  in response to prompts, 299, 304–305
  to provide focus, 164
  structure of, 594
  as test prompt, 526–528
  writing, 594
Thinking, six basic levels of, 491, 493–499
Third-person point of view, 278, 322
Third-person pronouns, 708.2
Threw/through, 694
Tilde (punctuation), 644
Time, punctuation of, 620.2
Time line, 35, 133, 139, 195, 588
Time management, 139, 195, 249, 500, 523, 530
Time order, 571
Timed writing, 500
Tips, writing
  business letters, 515
  e-mail messages, 518–519
  taking notes, 467–472
  taking tests, 521–531
  writing poetry, 338

Title page, 349, 356
Titles (of people)
  capitalization of, 605.2
  punctuation of, 614.4
Titles (of works)
  adding, 122, 135, 178, 191,
    232, 245, 288, 392
  capitalization of, 650.6
To/too/two, 694
Tone, 599
Topic outline, 590
Topic sentence
  in cause-effect essay, 146
  defined, 599
  formula for building, 563
  in paragraph response, 527
  in response to literature, 297
Topics chart, 152
Topics list, 188, 208, 242, 262,
  335, 357
Topics, selecting, 15, 35, 132
  descriptive writing, 420, 585
  expository writing, 152,
    188, 585
  narrative writing, 96,
    132, 585
  paragraph, 568
  persuasive writing, 208,
    242, 585
  poetry, 335
  research writing, 365, 366
  response to literature, 262
  sample, 585
Tragedy, 587
Traits of writing. *See also*
    Conventions; Ideas;
    Organization; Sentence
    fluency; Voice; Word choice
  conventions, 52–53
  described, 12, 40
  ideas, 42–43, 208, 242, 263
  narrative writing, 92
  organization, 44–45, 209, 265
  poetry writing, 337
  sentence fluency, 50–51, 243
  special note about, 65
  understanding, 39–54
  voice, 46–47
  word choice, 48–49
Transition words and phrases,
  103, 111, 167, 214, 271,
  592–593
Transitive verbs, 716.1, 716.2
True/false test, 524
Two/to/too, 694
Typography, 76

U

Underlining (as italics), 636
Understanding assignments,
  491–500
Understanding rubrics, 62–63
Understanding the writing
  process, 7–32
Understatement, 601
Understood subject and
  predicate, 740.2
Union (story pattern), 321
Unity, 599
Unnecessary adverbs, 543
U.S. Postal Service
  guidelines, 520
Usage, 599
Using the right word, 678–696

V

Vain/vein/vane, 694
Vary/very, 694
Venn diagram, 195, 574, 589
Verb tenses
  future, 718.4
  past, 538, 718.4
  perfect, 720.1
  present, 538, 718.4
  simple, 718.4
Verbal metaphors, 539
Verbals
  gerunds, 726.1, 742.1
  infinitives, 726.2, 742.1
  participles, 726.3, 742.1
Verbs, 538–541, 714–727
  action, 716.1
  active, 225, 722.1
  agreement with subject, 752,
    754
  auxiliary, 714.2, 752.3
  "be," 714.1, 714.2
  classes of, 714–716
  dynamic, 538
  to establish time, 538
  forms of, 718
  helping, 714.2, 752.3
  intransitive, 716.1
  irregular, 720.2
  linking, 714.1
  mood of, 724.1
  number of, 718.1, 752.1
  objects with transitive, 716
  passive, 722

person, 718.2
phrase, 742, 744
plural, 718.1, 722.1, 752, 754
regular, 718.3
singular, 722.1
specific, 538
strong, 48
transitive, 716.1
voice of, 722.1
Vial/vile, 696
Videos, citing, 384
Viewpoint, 322
Viruses, avoiding computer, 78
Visual aids, 398
Visual images, used to select
  topic, 583
Vocabulary
  academic, 6, 88, 144, 200,
    254, 312, 342, 404, 462,
    532, 580, 604
  prefixes, suffixes, roots,
    501–512
  test tips for, 531
  using a dictionary, 352–353
  writing terms, 598–599
Voice
  active/passive, 722.1
  of verbs, 722.1
Voice, controlling your, 400

Voice (trait)
  appropriate, 112
  authoritative, 222
  characteristics of, 168–169,
    222–223
  confident, 169
  defined, 599
  engaging, 169, 279
  enthusiastic, 47
  expository writing, 148,
    168–169, 174, 180–181, 191
  interested, 113
  knowledgeable, 168, 222
  multimedia presentations,
    400, 403
  narrative writing, 92, 112–
    113, 118, 124–125, 135
  natural, 279
  in paragraph, 579
  in paraphrase, 488
  persuasive writing, 204,
    222–223, 228, 234–235,
    245
  research writing, 378, 388
  respectful, 223

response to literature, 258, 278–279, 284, 290–291
revising for, 112–113, 168–169, 222–223, 278–279
understanding, 46–47

Volume, appropriate speaking, 400

W

Waist/waste, 696
Wait/weight, 696
Ware/wear/where, 696
Warm-up
for expository writing, 146
finding themes, 256
for narrative writing, 90
for persuasive writing, 202
Way/weigh, 696
Weather/whether, 696
Web diagram. *See* Cluster diagram
Web sites
citing sources from, 383
creating your own, 80–81
Well/good, 686
Who/which/that, 696
Who/whom, 696
Whole/hole, 686
Who's/whose, 696
Why Write, 1–25
Word analysis, test tips for, 531

Word choice (trait)
connotation, 280
expository writing, 170–171
multimedia presentations, 403
narrative writing, 114–115
paragraph, 579
persuasive writing, 224–225
poetry, 337
research writing, 388
response to literature, 280–281
revising for, 114–115, 170–171, 224–225, 280
understanding, 48–49

Word pairs (homophones), 678–697
Word parts, understanding, 502–512

Words
base, 492
commonly confused, 286
compound, 624.1, 654.6
descriptive, 728, 730
division of, 626.5
negative, 558
order of, 752.2
parts of, 502–512
related to the human body, 512
root, 506–512
specific, 114
transition, 103, 592–593
using the right, 678–696
Workplace writing
business letters, 513–517, 520
e-mail messages, 518–519
Works cited, MLA, 363, 381–384, 391, 460
World Wide Web
creating a Web site, 80–81
publishing on the, 79
search engines, 346
sources, citing, 383
Writer's notebook, 4–5
Writer's Resource, 581–603

Writing. *See also* Essays; Forms of writing; Paragraphs
assessing, 31
assignments, 491–500
beginnings, 103, 134, 159, 190, 213, 244, 269, 375, 595
with computers, 33–38
contests, 82
creative 313–340
endings, 106, 111, 162, 166, 216, 272, 276, 380
guide for effective, 54
habits, 8
keys to effective, 101, 157, 211, 267, 373
middles, 104–105, 134, 160–161, 167, 190, 214, 221, 244, 266, 270, 376
plays, 323–332
poetry, 333–340
practical, 452
stories, 313–322
with style, 533–560
techniques, 600–601
terms, 598–599

topics, 3, 42, 584–585
vocabulary, 500–501

Writing, traits of
conventions, 14, 26–27, 40, 52–53
ideas, 14, 20, 40, 42–43
organization, 14, 20, 40, 44–45
sentence fluency, 14, 20, 40, 44–45
voice, 14, 20, 40, 46–47
word choice, 14, 20, 40, 48–49
Writing assignments
the arts, 461
keywords used in, 493
math, 442
practical writing, 452
science, 416
time management for, 500
types of, 492
Writing contests, 82

Writing guidelines
arts prompts, 456–457
cause-effect essays, 412–413
charts and graphs, 438–439
descriptive essay, 420–421
document-based essay, 424–430
editorial cartoon, 422–423
comparison-contrast essay, 448–449
lab reports, 410–411
math article, 434–435
math problem, 436–437
research reports, 458–459
science article summary, 414–415

Writing habits, 8
Writing in math, 431–442
Writing in science, 405–416
Writing in social studies, 417–430
Writing in the applied sciences, 443–452
Writing in the arts, 453–461
Writing modes. *See* Creative writing; Descriptive writing; Expository writing; Narrative writing; Persuasive writing
Writing plays, 323–332
Writing poetry, 333–340
Writing process, 1–88
editing 11, 26–27

prewriting, 10, 15–17
publishing, 11, 28–31
revising, 11, 20–25
understanding, 1–88
writing, 10, 18–19
Writing prompts
expository, 193–199
narrative, 137–143
persuasive, 247–253
response to literature, 295–311
used to select topic, 584
Writing stories, 313–322
Writing tests. *See* Tests
Writing the first draft, 10, 18–19
expository, 159–162, 190
narrative, 103–106, 134
paragraph, 568
persuasive, 213–216, 244
plays, 330
poetry, 336
research reports, 375–380
response to literature, 369–372
stories, 319
Written estimate, 436-437

Y

Your/you're, 696

Z

ZIP code, 520
Zooming in and out, 534